Theories of
Comparative Politics

Also of Interest

Worker Participation and the Crisis of Liberal Democracy, Sherri DeWitt

The Impasse of European Communism, Carl Boggs

Communism and Political Systems in Western Europe, edited by David E. Albright

Marxism in the Contemporary West, edited by Charles F. Elliott and Carl A. Linden

History of the International: World Socialism 1943–1968, Julius Braunthal

About the Book and Author

Theories of Comparative Politics:
The Search for a Paradigm
Ronald H. Chilcote

This critical examination and assessment of both orthodox and radical theories of comparative politics seeks to expose students to contrasting and challenging points of view. Professor Chilcote clarifies and synthesizes the major theoretical directions found in the literature of comparative politics and political science. His focus on system, culture, development, and class reflects the themes around which the literature tends to cluster.

This book also serves as a reference guide, incorporating the major literature in the field in discussions and providing an extensive annotated bibliography at the end of each chapter.

As a text for advanced undergraduate and graduate classes, and as a reference and guide for teachers, this book will prove to be (in the words of one review) "the definitive work on the contemporary study of comparative politics." It also may be useful as a supplementary text in introductory courses.

Ronald H. Chilcote is professor of political science at the University of California, Riverside. He is founder and managing editor of *Latin American Perspectives* and author and editor of numerous books and articles, including *Latin America: The Struggle with Dependency and Beyond* and *The Brazilian Communist Party: Conflict and Integration, 1922–1972.*

15.00

Theories of
Comparative Politics
The Search for a Paradigm

Ronald H. Chilcote

Westview Press • Boulder, Colorado

Copyright © 1981 by Westview Press, Inc.

Published in 1981 in the United States of America by
  Westview Press, Inc.
  5500 Central Avenue
  Boulder, Colorado 80301
  Frederick A. Praeger, Publisher

Library of Congress Cataloging in Publication Data
Chilcote, Ronald H
    Theories of comparative politics.
    Bibliography: p.
    Includes index.
    1. Comparative government. I. Title.
JF51.C44   320.3   80-19762
ISBN 0-89158-970-8
ISBN 0-89158-971-6 (pbk.)

Printed and bound in the United States of America

To the professional colleagues who search for alternatives and take the risk of attempting to implement them

To the students who shaped this book, its content, and direction, and from whom I have learned much

To my family who tolerated my struggle to prepare this book

Contents

PART 1
INTRODUCTION

PART 3
THEORETICAL DIRECTIONS

PART 4
CONCLUSION

Tables and Figures

Tables

Figures

Preface

The initial conception of this book was sparked by my dissatisfaction with the comparative politics literature and by my desire to provide a new overview. In the past and to some extent today the textual material for introductory courses in comparative politics generally addressed itself to patterns of government in four countries—England, France, Germany, and the Soviet Union. It was the task of students to compare institutions and processes, while absorbing details of history and culture. Concepts tended to be defined loosely, and theory was no more than a tangential concern. As interest broadened beyond the governments of the United States and Europe after the Second World War, the curricula of political science departments expanded to include courses focused on other geographical areas of the world; for example, Africa, Asia, Latin America, and the Middle East. At the graduate level, students confronted the seemingly impossible task of learning about governments everywhere. Furthermore, political science writing about other parts of the world tended to be detached, often generalized, sometimes uninformed, and not very interesting. Given these conditions that existed a decade ago, I set out to write a book. In the interim years between the conception and the realization of this book, my thoughts and writing evolved through three phases, each successive phase having been prompted by a reassessment of ideas and thought through dialogue with my students.

Initially, I was interested in putting together a comparative politics text based on careful conceptualization supported by examples drawn from the experience of the more developed (generally European) and the less developed (generally Third World) nations of the world. I wanted to move the study of comparative politics toward a theory of change and development. In addition, I favored an ordering of basic concepts within a general framework for inquiry. I proposed to trace the evolution of the field, first looking at traditional perspectives, then at attempts over the past two decades to innovate and reconstitute the field. I planned to identify criteria for assessment of political theory, then move toward a theory of comparative politics by focusing, first, on society as an inclusive framework and on system as an orienting concept; second, on some systemic variables such as decision making, policy, authority, and power; and third, on some reordering variables such as ideology, socialization, mobilization, and conflict. I also intended to look at political culture and construct a model for the study of nationalism and development.

The transitional phase in the writing of this book involved a reassessment of this ambitious proposal. Although students were at first receptive to many of the ideas, the initial proposal seemed to become entrapped in the very terminology and approach with which I wished to contend. It was not altogether clear to me and my students that new levels of understanding could be attained simply by clarifying and refining the old concepts and eclectically synthesizing them into theory. It was also apparent that the mainstream of ideas and concepts in the field was not allowing for a critical evaluation of many important problems in the real world. Development, for example, tended to be conceptualized within the Anglo-American capitalist experience rather than in the backwardness and underdevelopment of much of the rest of the world. Political culture was conceived within an ideal state of civic awareness and participation, yet such ideals tended to be mythologized rather than realized in many parts of the world.

The book began to take final shape about four years ago. As the reader will recognize, this book is committed to a clarification and an understanding of concepts and theory. The focus on system, culture, and development is retained, yet those terms are utilized less as central orienting concepts than as central thrusts around which the literature of the field tends to cluster. I have added the literature of elites and masses, with attention to theories of class and class struggle. As in its original conception, this volume strives toward an understanding of the whole rather than a microscopic examination of the parts. This holistic orientation relates to a desire that the comparative study of politics be integrated with a study of societal phenomena other than politics. I am especially interested in economic matters. Thus, this book builds upon theoretical foundations and attempts to relate the problems and actions of contemporary society. This enterprise adds a new dimension that is often neglected in the study of comparative politics: the early thought that shaped the study of nineteenth- and twentieth-century politics, which I examine in this book. And I assess the study of politics and science by noting two directions of scientific inquiry that emanate from the nineteenth century and continue today. The present book is molded around these two patterns of thought. A recognition of the differences in thought allows a student of politics to examine the inner convictions, values, and beliefs that appear in our investigations and analysis. It is therefore a major objective of this book to stimulate critical thinking and choice in the formulation and reinforcement of individual perspectives. It is hoped that each student will weigh arguments, find positions, and prepare to defend them in the difficult task of seeking comparative inquiry.

Some readers may complain that my presentation is too sketchy in places, but my intention is to impose upon the serious reader the obligation to delve into the subject matter. Thus, the present book purposely presents an outline of the major trends and theoretical directions in contemporary politics. As such it exposes issues, summarizes arguments and counterarguments, and beckons the reader to pursue study through related sources, identified in the text and listed in annotated form at the end of each chapter. This book should prove useful to the curious beginning student of politics. It is to be hoped that it will guide advanced undergraduate and graduate students in a comprehensive and critical overview of comparative politics, and it should also serve as a resource for teachers and as a reference work for scholars already familiar with the field. In addition, the attempt to draw paradigmatic distinctions between traditional mainstream and radical modes of thinking is intended to challenge the reader to seek a critical understanding and alternative explanations and analyses of societies examined in comparative perspective.

Ronald H. Chilcote

Acknowledgments

This book is dedicated to colleagues, students, and family, and I wish to express my appreciation to some of them who have been especially helpful in the book's preparation. First, there are the students in my graduate seminars who read and critiqued the various chapters. Those who offered extensive and helpful comments include Pamela Abrams, G. Bisharat, Robert Dash, Terrie Groth, James Mitchell, Jaime Regalado, Allen Westheimer, and Stanley Wiseman. Byong-Moo Hwang provided research assistance, and his wife, Chong Eui, typed many of the chapters. I am deeply grateful to Sheryl Lutjens who read, typed, and edited many of the chapters and whose index is an invaluable contribution. Among my colleagues at the University of California–Riverside, I thank Professor Howard Sherman for his critical reading of the entire manuscript and Francis Carney and John Stanley for comments on Chapter 3. I am grateful to Raúl Fernández of the University of California–Irvine for counsel on Chapter 9.

Professor Stephen Gorman of North Texas State University collaborated in the writing of Chapter 4. I especially appreciate the comments and encouragement of Professors Joel Edelstein of the University of Colorado–Denver and James Rosenau of the University of Southern California.

Because of my fervent desire to finish the book, Anne and Stan Price offered me their mountain cabin as a retreat from university and community pressures on my time. Finally, not enough appreciation can be expressed to my wife, Frances, and sons, Stephen and Edward, whose patience and understanding allowed me to complete the book. I should also like to acknowledge an intramural faculty research grant and assistance from my dean's office at the University of California, which facilitated library research, bibliographical searching, typing, and editing.

PART 1
Introduction

Comparative Inquiry

This initial chapter briefly examines comparative politics as a field in the study of politics and political science. I look at issues of theory in comparative inquiry, I describe the evolution of the field in four theoretical directions, and I identify the objectives of this book.

In addition, I have included two sections that relate to this chapter; one appears at the end of this chapter, and the other appears at the end of the book. The first attempts to clarify the terms employed in the mainstream of comparative politics, since the terminology of the field generally is used loosely and inconsistently in the literature. The other surveys the general literature of comparative politics and is followed by a selected bibliography.

Issues of Theory and Comparative Inquiry

The study of comparative politics has evoked much confusion for student and scholar alike. A variety of terms is used loosely and interchangeably in the comparative study of politics. *Comparative government*, for example, usually refers to the study of countries or nation-states in Europe, and the focus of study is on the institutions and functions of those countries, with attention to their executives, legislatures, and judiciaries, as well as such supplementary organizations as political parties and pressure groups. *Comparative politics*, in contrast, studies a broader range of political activity, including governments and their institutions as well as other forms of organizations not directly related to national government; for example, tribes, communities, associations, unions.

Political science and comparative politics relate both to theory and to method. *Theory* refers to sets of systematically related generalizations, and *method* is a procedure or process that involves the techniques and tools utilized in inquiry and for examining, testing, and evaluating theory. *Methodology* consists of methods, procedures, working concepts, rules, and the like used for testing theory and guiding inquiry, and the search for solutions to problems of the real world. Methodology is a particular way of viewing, organizing, and giving shape to inquiry.

Confusion arises over these terms because the comparative study of government often refers to the study of foreign governments, and comparative politics is utilized in the search for comparisons in the study of all forms of political activity—governmental as well as nongovernmental. Thus, the comparative politics specialist tends to view comparative politics as the study of everything political. Any lesser conception of comparative politics would obscure criteria for the selection and exclusion of what the field might study.

One might also explore the relationship of politics and comparative politics to other fields, as I do in Chapter 3. I note that both theory and method owe a great deal to the "classical" political philosophers Aristotle and Plato, Machiavelli and Montesquieu, and Hegel, Marx, and Mill. Comparative politics is also indebted to the early twentieth-century contributions of Woodrow Wilson, James Bryce, and Carl Friedrich, whose attention was directed toward the formal study of government and state. I also show that work in related fields has shaped comparative political inquiry, notably the work of A. R. Radcliffe-Brown and Bronislaw Malinowski in anthropology, Gaetano Mosca, Vilfredo Pareto, Max Weber, Emile Durkheim in sociology and political sociology, and John M. Keynes, Karl Marx, and V. I. Lenin in economics and political economy. Finally I suggest that attention should be directed toward political economy.

The movement toward the study of all political phenomena and the need to draw upon the theories and methods of other disciplines gave to comparative politics an all-encompassing orientation. The Second World War heightened interest among scholars in the study of foreign systems, especially systems in Europe and Asia. The decline of empires after the war and the turmoil of independence in the Third World influenced scholars to turn their attention from the established to the new nations. The consequences for comparative politics were substantial. According to Braibanti (1968), there was an acceleration of research on the new nations, prompted by research technology and the funding by and interests of foundations and government, which exacted from scholars the knowledge needed to guide programs in foreign aid. Additionally, a fragmentation of case materials was the result of problems related to method in the gathering of data, to research terminology that has not been standardized, and to the rapid proliferation of new nations in which research conditions are uncertain and the cumulation of knowledge is uneven. There was also an expansion of the sphere of politics so as to allow the examination of politics as a total system, on the one hand, and as an analysis of individual behavior, on the other. Finally, there was a tendency toward model building, including highly imperfect and transitory devices, and classificatory schemes easily divorced from reality and undermined by unreliable and tentative data.

Given these trends, still another problem faces the students of comparative politics, that of value-free investigation. For the study of political behavior, many political scientists emphasize attention to explicit assumptions and to systematic, quantitative, and cumulative investigation. Investigators assume the role of objective social scientists, separating themselves from the role of active citizens. Despite the pretensions of such political scientists, however, there is now a widespread understanding that values enter into all investigations of politics. Christian Bay (1965), for example, argued that work that pretends to be neutral is actually imbued with real value biases and indeed is both conservative and antipolitical. These concerns are supported in other assessments as well (McCoy and Playford 1967; Myrdal 1969). Searing (1970) delved deeply into the problem and concluded that value judgments enter six stages of research but do not necessarily bias consequences. In the first two stages, problem selection and concept formation, value decisions are significant but do not always bias research. The intrusion of value judgments into the stages of data selection, interpretation, and theory construction can result in bias. Searing admitted too that value choices represent a problem for the last stage, verification.

The above stages suggest a systematic method of procedure for social science investigation. That method may be construed as emulating the work of the natural scientists, who look for regularities in the abstractions that they select from the non-human world. Thus, social science might simply borrow the theories and rules of natural science to study the human world. But a stress on regularity will certainly obscure any recognition of irregularity. Values, beliefs, and personal interests might intrude upon the scientific enterprise, and in the end little understanding will be gained. Such has been the concern of many people interested in comparative politics.

All these problems relate to the search for theory and method in comparative politics. The reader may be interested in background reading and understanding in this search for theory and method, so I turn briefly to a summary of some of the major work that has influenced comparative politics.

Past and Present Literature

More than a century ago Edward A. Freeman (1873) optimistically manifested his belief that comparative politics offered promise for the discovery of universal laws through global investigation. Often it is maintained that we have established no basic universal laws or principles, although well into the past there were social scientists who were conscious of theoretical and methodological problems.

Two people who wrote about such problems were Max Weber in *The Methodology of the Social Sciences* (1949) and Emile Durkheim in *The Rules of Sociological Method* (1938). Weber focused on the meaning of value judgment and neutrality in sociology and economics, examined the implications of objectivity in social science, and examined the methodological views of scholars of his time. Durkheim attempted to describe and define the method used in the study of social facts; at the same time he acknowledged that among his predecessors, Herbert Spencer had devoted no attention to the problem of method, and John Stuart Mill had dealt with the question at great length, but only by synthesizing what Auguste Comte had set forth in his earlier work. Durkheim suggested rules for the observation of social facts, for classifying social types, for explaining social facts, and for establishing sociological proofs. Durkheim believed that his method separated social science and especially sociology from philosophy, as well as from positivistic, evolutionary, and idealistic orientations that had pervaded social science through successive periods.

Unlike Weber and Durkheim, Karl Marx did not prepare a manual on theory and method, but those concerns are apparent throughout his writings. Marx was a comparative analyst who focused on the monarchies of Europe but also extended his discussions elsewhere, most notably Asia. Marx would probably explain contemporary social science understandings of society in equilibrium as the consequence of actions of a ruling class. That class enforces rules and norms that legitimize the relations of production, which arise from particular means and forces of production. Those means and forces may become outmoded as change and equilibrium become dialectical parts of a single process. I shall elaborate later on the contributions of Marx and demonstrate that his theory and methodology tend to run counter to the dominant tendencies of the contemporary literature of comparative politics.

A number of recent attempts to deal with the theoretical and methodological problems of comparative politics can be mentioned. Maurice Duverger (1964) offered an introduction that is useful to the reader. First, he explored the idea of social science, tracing the historical development of the social sciences. Second, he described and discussed the techniques of observation, relating to written documents, and statistics as well as questionnaire methods and interviews. Third, he examined the use of theory and hypotheses as well as classifications and conceptualization in research. Supplementing Duverger but delving into the ramifications of inquiry is work by Frohock (1967) who examined the implications and issues of theory and the scientific method. Scientific method is assessed in terms of the search for paradigms, and the work of Max Weber is introduced as one basis for contemporary social science. Galtung (1967) also looked critically at theory and method.

Mayer (1972) and Meehan (1967) delved deeply into problems of theory and method. Mayer presented a defense of the "scientific" study of politics by first examining the empirical base of science, explanation and prediction in political science, laws and generalizations, and theory. Then he critically surveyed some of the contributions to the comparative method, citing examples from analyses of functionalism, political culture, and political psychology. Meehan pursued somewhat the same discussion of structure in political thought and methodology, followed by a critical assessment of some of the major contributions to political science. He attempted to determine what is "useful for political science in the methods of investigation and explanation employed in science."

Thus those writers have grappled with the major theoretical and methodological problems of the field. Other writers have concentrated on methods that are helpful in comparative inquiry. For example, Howard Scarrow (1969) offered a brief introduction to the methods of comparative analysis, and Holt and Turner (1970), Merritt (1969), and Przeworski and Teune (1970) explored more deeply the subject of political inquiry. MacKenzie (1971) reviewed the influences and directions in the politics and science of political science. Roberts (1972) focused on conceptualization, strategies, models, and theories of comparative politics, and Melanson and King (1971) assessed recent trends and analysis. Haas (1962) and Payne (1973) delved into similar concerns. Finally Merrill (1971) reviewed some of the above literature and related it to issues of comparative theory and method.

Outline of This Study

I have established the need for a new overview of comparative politics and have examined some general issues of theory and comparative inquiry. In some notes following this chapter are some definitions that facilitate a clarity and an understanding of the terminology of political science and comparative politics; also some prominent methods of and techniques for comparative political inquiry have been identified.

Since 1953 the major theoretical trends in the comparative field have tended to cluster into four general areas: systems theories, culture theories, developmental theories, and class theories. Although each of these areas is the focus of a chapter in the present book, it is instructive to identify briefly the major contributions that shaped each area and allowed each area to become a central thrust in the field of comparative politics.

SYSTEMS THEORIES

The impact of the systems literature on comparative politics first became evident during the early 1950s. Three writers are representative of trends in systems theory and all three utilized the system as a macro unit in comparative analysis. David Easton in *The Political System* and other works set forth the concept of the political system together with its inputs and outputs, demands and supports, and feedback. The basis of his conceptualization of system is contained in a well-known essay published in 1957. Gabriel Almond was influenced by the functionalist anthropologists Bronislaw Malinowski and A. R. Radcliffe-Brown as well as by the sociologists Max Weber and Talcott Parsons. Almond was also influenced by work on group theory, such as that of David Truman. Almond first offered a simplistic classification of political systems in *Journal of Politics* in 1956, which included political systems in non-Western and newly independent nations. Joining with other comparative specialists, he then set forth categories of structure and function, relating them to all systems in the introduction to *Politics of the Developing Areas*. Later he related his conception of system to culture and development. Finally, Karl Deutsch in *Nerves of Government* drew heavily upon the cybernetic theory of Norbert Wiener in postulating a systemic model of politics.

CULTURE THEORIES

The cultural thrust in comparative politics, conspicuously prominent during the 1960s, emanated from traditional work on culture in anthropology, socialization and small group studies in sociology, and personality studies in psychology. The concept of political culture was related to nations or national cultures. In this sense political culture represented a sort of recasting of the older notions of national character. Political culture related to systems as well. Political culture consisted of beliefs, symbols, and values that define situations in which political action occurs. Types of political culture characterized systems; for example, parochial, subject, and participant political cultures. These types of political cultures reflected the psychological and subjective orientations of people toward their national system. The pioneer comparative effort to construct a theory of political culture was Gabriel Almond and Sidney Verba's *Civic Culture*, which was based on a survey of the attitude of citizens toward their nation in the United States, Great Britain, Germany, France, Italy, and Mexico. Inherent in this study was the proposition, set forth earlier in the work of Almond, that the ideal political or civic culture could be found in an Anglo-American model of politics. Lucian Pye and Sidney Verba elaborated on the theory and brought together essays by prominent specialists in the field in *Political*

Culture and Political Development. Although there have been efforts to relate political culture to the politics of specific nations—such as Pye's *Politics, Personality, and Nation Building: Burma's Search for Identity*—generally the literature has been divided into two subareas: political socialization and communications. Edited volumes by James S. Coleman, *Education and Political Development*, and by Pye, *Communications and Political Development*, reflect the work in these areas.

DEVELOPMENTAL THEORIES

The third thrust in the comparative politics literature is related to theories of development. The concern with development was prompted by the emergence of many new states in the Third World. Almond and others in *Politics of the Developing Areas* directed attention to backward areas that promised to develop, and he found it necessary to tie his ideas about the nature of the political system and about political culture to development. The result was a journal article in *World Politics* in 1965 and a book with G. Bingham Powell, *Comparative Politics: A Developmental Approach*. In that work Almond more consciously began to work out a model of concepts and stages that would characterize development. The volumes commissioned by the Social Science Research Council's (SSRC's) Committee on Comparative Politics (1963 to present) also place an emphasis upon comparative developmental theory.

The literature on development actually falls into at least five categories. The first, represented by Almond and others, attempts to utilize traditional notions of democracy and political democracy and to recast them into more sophisticated, sometimes abstract, terminology. A stage theory of development is depicted in A.F.K. Organski's *The Stages of Political Development*, a work modeled after that of the economist Walt Rostow. These conceptions of political development, however, rest heavily upon the Anglo-American experiences in politics. Studies in the second category focus on conceptions of nation building. These studies attempt to combine old notions of nationalism, those of Hans Kohn for example, with new interpretations of development. Karl Deutsch's *Nationalism and Social Communication* is an excellent example of this combination, and Rupert Emerson's *From Empire to Nation* and Kalman Silvert's *Expectant Peoples: Nationalism and Development* are examples of works that apply to nationalism and development, respectively, to the areas of Africa and Latin America.

Modernization is the focus of a third category of studies on development. Examples of this type of literature include Marion J. Levy's *Modernization and the Structure of Societies*, an ambitious effort to apply structural-functionalism to a theory of modernization, and David Apter's *The Politics of Modernization*, a provocative attempt at model building. A fourth category comprises studies of change, a prominent example being Samuel P. Huntington's *Political Order in Changing Societies*. The fifth category includes works critical of ethnocentric theories of development, such as those mentioned above. Such criticism focuses on underdevelopment in backward nations as a condition brought about through the development of capitalism and industrialization in the advanced nations. André Gunder Frank's *Capitalism and Underdevelopment in Latin America* and Walter Rodney's *How Europe Underdeveloped Africa* exemplify this interpretation. Theorists attribute the condition of underdevelopment to the dependency of the less dominant nations upon dominant nations; a plethora of works exists on this theme.

CLASS THEORIES

Sometime during the mid-1960s, the SSRC's Committee on Comparative Politics decided to direct attention to studies of elites. During the 1950s Floyd Hunter and C. Wright Mills had concerned themselves with questions of power and who rules, but their work was attacked by Robert A. Dahl and others who relied on a pluralistic conception of politics. Weaknesses in a generation of community studies by political sociologists were exposed, and U.S. political scientists turned to the new field of urban politics. Comparative political scientists, however, tended not to be distracted altogether by the pluralist-elitist debates of the early 1960s. The rise of charismatic figures such as Fidel Castro and Kwame Nkrumah dramatized the need to study political leaders of the Third World. Then too, the failure of the parliamentary institutions to provide stability in the nations of Asia, Africa, and Latin America prompted the study of elites. Elite theory, however, moved in several directions, somewhat influenced by the earlier work of Marx, Mosca, and Pareto. In the tradition of C. Wright Mills and G. William Domhoff, some theorists focused on power structure alone, ignoring mass behavior. Other theorists pursued study along the lines of stratification analysis, outlined by sociologists, and Marxists turned to questions of class struggle and an analysis of a ruling bourgeois class and a proletariat.

The critical examination of these four areas of theory is a principal concern of this book. The curious reader, however, may wish to examine the more general references to the field. Thus the "Survey of the General Literature of Comparative Politics" classifies materials into general overviews, cross-national studies, comparative series, area and configurative studies, and institutional studies. The remainder of the volume delves more deeply into the field. Ideological tendencies are noted in an exposure of the contradictions in politics and the profession as well as the profession's ties to government and business. Chapter 3 focuses on the search for a paradigm in comparative analysis and probes into the historical roots and fundamental premises of positivist and historicist thought that have dominated the field.

Chapter 4 turns to the life, thought, and writing of both Karl Marx and Max Weber, two precursors of contemporary theorists whose influence has been substantial. Chapters 5, 6, 7, and 8 deal with the four theoretical areas noted above—systemic, cultural, developmental, and class theories. A critical synthesis of the trends in each of these areas is combined with an attempt to identify paradigmatic influences and conflicting understandings and explanations of politics.

Each of those four central chapters synthesizes the trends and assesses the literature of comparative politics, and each chapter carefully distinguishes paradigmatic influences. The chapters on systems and culture tend to emphasize orthodox theory, and the chapters on development and class stress radical theory. Chapter 5 identifies two major contributions to systems theory: the organic framework of David Easton and the structural-functional approach of Gabriel Almond. Juxtaposed to these two contributions are several radical perspectives, including a Marxist conception of the capitalist state. Chapter 6 presents a dichotomy of conceptions of political culture, showing the radical challenge to the orthodox conception of culture. In Chapter 7 orthodox concerns with political development, development and nationalism, and modernization are contrasted with radical perspectives of underdevelopment, dependency, and imperialism. In Chapter 8 various theories of class and state are identified, and the implications of a class analysis are discussed critically.

A concluding chapter argues for a reconstitution of comparative politics in the direction of comparative and international political economy. To aid the student, literature referred to in the text is listed, with annotation, at the end of each chapter, although a few sources are merely identified by author, book title, and date of publication.

References

Bay, Christian
  1965 "Politics and Pseudopolitics." *American Political Science Review* LIX (March), 39–51. Argues that political behavior work fails to make clear its real value biases, that it is not neutral, but that instead it is conservative and antipolitical.
Braibanti, Ralph
  1968 "Comparative Political Analytics Reconsidered." *Journal of Politics* XXX (February), 25–65. A review of trends in comparative politics up to 1966 with attention to four major problems: the relationship of configurative analysis to comparability; the relation between functional and institutional analysis; the relation of new political systems to established ones and the reliance upon scientific method; and the rapid and uneven expansion of comparative political analysis.

Durkheim, Emile
1938 *The Rules of Sociological Method.* Translated by Sarah A. Solovay and John H. Mueller and edited by George E. G. Catlin. Chicago: University of Chicago Press. An effort to move beyond such predecessors as Comte, Spencer, and Mill by setting forth a manual on method. The author distinguishes his methods from natural science as well as from philosophy.

Duverger, Maurice
1964 *An Introduction to the Social Sciences with Special Reference to Their Methods.* Translated by Malcolm Anderson. New York: Frederick A. Praeger. An introductory section on the nature of social science is followed by a section on techniques of observation and another section on systematic analysis, including discussion on the comparative method.

Freeman, Edward A.
1873 *Comparative Politics.* London: Macmillan. Offers the promise of discovering universal laws through global and longitudinal comparisons.

Frohock, Fred M.
1967 *The Nature of Political Inquiry.* Homewood, Illinois: Dorsey Press. Focuses on topics relating to theory, function, and causality in social science, science and social analysis, facts and values, and political inquiry.

Galtung, Johan
1967 *Theory and Methods of Social Research.* New York: Columbia University Press. Examination of strengths and weaknesses in social science methodology. Attempts to integrate "widely scattered approaches in data collection, data processing, data analysis, and theory formation."

Haas, Michael
1962 "Comparative Analysis." *Western Political Quarterly* XV (June), 294–303. Looks at "the methodology of the comparative method," in particular at source reliability, typologies, and sampling in the collection of comparable data; and at evidence and inference problems.

Holt, Robert T. and John E. Turner (eds.)
1970 *The Methodology of Comparative Research.* New York: Free Press. Essays on Methodology by Holt and Turner, Holt and Richardson, Riggs, La Palombara, Apter, Frey, and others.

McCoy, Charles A. and John Playford (eds.)
1967 *Apolitical Politics: A Critique of Behavioralism.* New York: Thomas Y. Crowell. Previously published essays are brought together to focus on the conservative implications and bias of behavioral studies, on the behavioralist perception that mass democracy and mass movements may be unmanageable and chaotic, and on the antipolitical orientation of the behavioralists. Included are essays by Bay, Kim, Schwartz, Petras, Gitlin, Bachrach, Baratz, and others.

MacKenzie, W.J.M.
1971 "The Political Science of Political Science."*Government and Opposition* VI (Summer), 277–302. Examines themes and controversies of research as related to three dimensions of political science: subject matter, purpose, and method.

Mayer, Lawrence C.
1972 *Comparative Political Inquiry: A Methodological Survey.* Homewood, Illinois:

Dorsey Press. Attempts a survey of the major substantive and analytical work in comparative politics as well as a restatement of the principles of scientific method. Divided into three parts: epistemology, approach, and selected application.

Meehan, Eugene J.
1967 *Contemporary Political Thought: A Critical Study*. Homewood, Illinois: Dorsey Press. Focus on methodology, explanations, and political evalution with critical discussion on the writings and ideas of major contributors to comparative politics and political science.

Melanson, Philip H. and Lauriston R. King
1971 "Theory in Comparative Politics: A Critical Appraisal." *Comparative Political Studies* IV (July), 205-231. A useful critical overview of problems of theory and methodology in comparative politics with reference to recent trends and analysis.

Merrill, Sally
1971 "On the Logic of Comparative Analysis." *Comparative Political Studies* III (January), 489-500. A critical review of Holt and Turner (1970), Przeworski and Teune (1970), and Scarrow (1969) and an assessment of issues related to comparative theory and method.

Merritt, Richard L.
1969 *Systematic Approaches to Comparative Politics*. Chicago: Rand McNally. A general behavioral approach to the methodology of comparative politics with attention to manipulation of data, statistical methods, content analysis, aggregate data in the cross-national research of elites, research design, and formulation of hypotheses.

Myrdal, Gunnar
1969 *Objectivity in Social Science*. New York: Pantheon Books. A critical look at values, beliefs, and opinions and a recognition that these are opportunistically injected into theory and research.

Payne, Geoff
1973 "Comparative Sociology: Some Problems of Theory and Method." *British Journal of Sociology* XXIV (March), 13-29. Discussion of theory and methodological problems in comparative analysis.

Przeworski, Adam and Henry Teune
1970 *The Logic of Comparative Social Inquiry*. New York: Wiley-Interscience. Concerned with the methodology of comparative inquiry, this volume is divided into two parts: theory and measurement. There are no case studies, only illustrative country citations. Topics include explanations in social science, research design, levels of system analysis, cross-national theory, conceptualization.

Roberts, Geoffrey K.
1972 "Comparative Politics Today." *Government and Opposition* VII (Winter), 38-55. Examines problems of conceptualization, strategies, models and theories, and methods of comparative politics.

Scarrow, Howard A.
1969 *Comparative Political Analysis: An Introduction*. New York: Harper and Row Publishers. Brief introduction to methodological aspects of comparative political analysis. Examines description through classification, typologies, rankings, and

surveys; sociological perspectives; problems of explanation; problems of evidence; explanatory modes; and descriptive focus and explanatory factors.

Searing, Donald D.

1970 "Values in Empirical Research: A Behavioralist Response." *Midwest Journal of Political Science* XIV (February), 71–104. Attempts to distinguish between value bias and value choices and their effect upon six stages of research, from problem selection to verification. Argues that value-free research is impossible but that rigorous attention to methodology can eliminate bias, even though the value choices may have significant consequences for research and application of research results to political life.

Weber, Max

1949 *The Methodology of the Social Sciences.* Translated and edited by Edward A. Shils and Henry A. Finch. New York: Free Press. Essays by Weber written between 1903 and 1917 that attempt to clarify problems of theory and methodology encountered in actual research.

Appendix 1.1:
NOTES ON
COMPARATIVE TERMINOLOGY

The following notes are intended as a guide, both for me and to the reader, so that this book can be read with some common understanding. It is not my intention, however, to delineate in an exhaustive manner the meaning of each term. Nor does the identification of the terms below imply that I necessarily employ them in my own teaching and research. They are mentioned frequently in political science and in social science in general, and they are often used indiscriminately and without definition. Thus I hope to provide the reader with a basis for understanding and, through the references, show how more precise definitions can be found for terms that abound in the mainstream of political science.

Theory and Inquiry

Many years ago Samuel Beer and Adam Ulam outlined the steps in comparative inquiry, and the steps involved description, classification, explanation, and confirmation. Roy Macridis has also proposed a procedure. First, the collection and description of facts are drawn from some classifactory scheme. Second, the uniformities and differences are identified and described. Third, tentative hypotheses about the interrelationships in the political process are formulated. Fourth, these tentative hypotheses are verified through rigorous empirical observation. Fifth, the acceptable findings are set forth.

A reformulation of the steps and procedures suggested by these specialists suggests, first, that comparative inquiry integrates with theory and, second, that theory relates to description, analysis, and synthesis. *Theory* involves viewing and thinking; theory generates insight. Loosely conceived theory comprises sets of systematically related generalizations. More specifically, theory is a coherent body of generalizations and principles associated with the practice of a field of inquiry. These generalizations and principles might be hypothetical and conceptual. *Description* is a statement about the parts or relations of something and may involve classification, identification, and specification. *Analysis* is the separation or breaking up of the whole into its fundamental parts and subjecting them to detailed qualitative or quantitative examination; analysis may involve clarification and explication. *Synthesis* is the combining of the parts into a whole, of diverse ideas and forces into a coherent or cohesive complex.

These are aspects of theory and inquiry generally understood by the investigator of comparative politics. However, there are divergent lines of thinking in the field. Those people who are influenced by Max Weber, for instance, tend to stress the notion of ideal types or situations. The ideal is projected as a possibility that might be realized through time. The ideal often is based on a particular example or experience that a society might emulate. For example, U.S. democracy often is recognized as an idealized political type that, given time, might be realized by a less developed society. Such a notion suggests a unilinear and an evolutionary pattern of change through which societies evolve, and when it is discovered that backward societies may not be permitted to advance, it is possible that the ideal becomes confused with reality.

In contrast, Marxists might relate theory not to ideal types, but to real situations, and they would combine theory with practice in a process called praxis. Marxists would see changes in society as the consequence of a dialectical and historical interplay of social forces in relation to production. Real historical changes would be explained theoretically in terms of synthesis as the dialectical outcome of thesis and antithesis.

Aspects of Theory

The example of divergent thinking just given justifies the need to elucidate further on theory. The literature tends to discuss theory in general terms, and definitions are likely to reflect the preferences of individual authors. Therefore, in order that the reader may reach an understanding of theory and its usefulness in inquiry, I turn now to a discussion of the following aspects of theory.

> Concepts
> Generalizations, Propositions, and Hypotheses
> Types and Levels
> Approaches
> Models and Paradigms

CONCEPTS

Comparative politics, indeed political science itself, suffers from ambiguity and imprecision of concepts. Conceptualization should be clear and well formulated, devoid of ambiguity and a multiplicity of different meanings, which may obfuscate connotation. Conceptualization must be realized prior to description and classification, prior to measurement and statistical application, and prior to testing of theory.

Concepts are ideas or thoughts expressed in differing ways. For example, Sartori (1970: 1044) suggested three levels of conceptualization: universal, general, and configurative. Universal conceptualizations are useful in cross-area comparisons and global theory. General conceptualizations are useful in intra-area comparisons and middle-range theory. Configurative conceptualizations are useful in country-by-country study and narrow-gauge theory. Another differentiation suggested by Dumont and Wilson (1967: 989) refers to abstract concepts that, on the one hand, are tied to implicit theory; implicit theory involves concepts in the form of intuitive or "prescientific" abstractions. On the other hand, concepts may be tied to explicit theory, which is "scientific" and recognized as legitimate and formal. Willer and Webster (1970) distinguished concepts along somewhat similar lines. Some concepts are observable within a real world situation in which details and complexities can be identified. Other concepts are general abstractions, less dependent on a particular case but related to people, places, and events.

Comparative politics makes use of basic concepts in theory building. Concepts may be worked into definitional schema, classificatory arrangements, or systematic orderings that accompany a particular theoretical approach. Measurement and evaluation procedures may come into play. The resulting data and information are then subject to either qualitative or quantitative analysis. Qualitative analysis relates to generality and sometimes imprecision, and quantitative analysis relates to specificity and exactness, criteria often exaggerated in an age of technological advances.

Comparative politics tends to combine qualitative and quantitative techniques of research. In research, concepts sometimes are called variables. Variables are concepts that have quantitative or qualitiative attributes. Numerical values, such as age or size, can be utilized with quantitative variables, whereas nonnumerical values are employed with qualitative variables. Variables also may be dependent or independent. Dependent variables depend on at least one other variable, and independent variables are completely autonomous from other variables. Although these definitions may assist the reader in understanding the terminology of comparative politics, a word of caution is in order. Sophisticated techniques are not an escape from questions of substantive theory. However precisely defined, conceptualization undoubtedly will suffer in comparative investigation. Differing language connotations from culture to culture may pose a problem. Differing attributes of a given concept may be limited in their interchangeability, as suggested by Chandler and Chandler (1974).

GENERALIZATIONS, PROPOSITIONS, AND HYPOTHESES

The terms generalizations, propositions, and hypotheses are often used interchangeably, although different connotations and nuances of language may be associated with each term. Certainly there is no widespread consensus as to meaning of many terms, but the discussion that follows attempts clarification. Qualitative analysts usually stress the term generalization, and quantitative analysts may employ the term hypotheses; propositions may be the concern of either type of analysis. A *generalization* is a general statement of uniformities and regularities. It is the simplest form of explanation. Knowledge of subject matter is essential to the capacity to generalize. Meehan (1965: 91–92) identified three forms of generalizations. The first is a universal generalization (all of one thing is the same as another); in some cases a universal generalization is a law, for it has withstood intensive testing. The second form is a probabilistic generalization (a percentage of one thing is equal to another); a probabilistic generalization frequently is referred to as a *proposition*. The third form is a tendency generalization (one thing tends to be another; a tendency generalization is expressed in tentative and conjectural terms and is thus a *hypothesis*, which may be true but not yet tested. Thus laws are universal, propositions are probabilistic, and hypotheses are tentative.

Generalizations, propositions, and hypotheses are especially useful in sciences such as chemistry and physics, which rely upon precise measurement and complex and detailed classifications. Classifications depend upon uniformities and similarities. However, political science finds its explanations of human behavior limited if only uniformities and similarities are noted. Human behavior is usually unpredictable. Thus diversity and dissimilar patterns of behavior become important in the study of politics. The demand for the study of patterns of dissimilarity as well as irregularity, echoed by Roy Macridis and other specialists in comparative politics over the past two decades, has caused skepticism about the application of science to politics.

TYPES AND LEVELS

Two types of explanatory reasoning are prominent in theory. *Induction* is the process of inferring a generalization from a pattern of specific observations, whereas *deduction* is the process of determining that if a universal generalization is true, then a lesser generalization can be true. In comparative politics, induced generalizations and propositions are suspect, because they may be viewed as deterministic or deemed to be correct and true when in fact conclusive evidence may be lacking or deviant cases to disprove them may exist. Since political science has few, if any, universal generalizations or laws, then deductive explanation is unlikely to have much impact on the discipline. Given this fact, Meehan assumed that probabilistic explanations will be utilized. That is, explanation is set forth that suggests it is probable that something will occur. Instead of reaching the certain conclusions anticipated in deductive reasoning, conclusions might be stated with uncertainty and in relative terms (for example, "usually" replaces " always").

These reservations are not held by social scientists who accept that the logic of deductive explanation in natural science is compatible with that in social science. Their defense of deductive explanation is widespread. Thus such terms as "scientific method" and "rules of science" pervade the most prestigious theoretical literature. For Meehan, deductive explanation has become "an albatross around the neck of the social scientists," a charge that is elaborated in an essay by John G. Gunnell (1969).

The debate over deductive and inductive explanation is not new to science. For centuries scientists and philosophers have exposed the misconceptions that have emanated from both forms of explanation. During the latter half of the nineteenth century, Frederick Engels, in his *Anti-Dühring* and *Dialectics of Nature*, decried the one-sided arguments in favor of deduction *or* induction and argued instead that they belong together, that they supplement each other.

Earlier in discussing concepts, three levels of theory were identified: *global*, *middle-range*, and *narrow-gauge* levels. Global or grand theory seeks universal conceptualizations; the efforts to establish such theory for comparative politics have been largely discredited because of generality, vagueness, and abstraction. Narrow-gauge theory has suffered from overemphasis with technique rather than substance; often sensitive issues of politics are obscured by limiting the scope of inquiry to small problems and to easily manageable data. This concern with scope allows for a dichotomization of theory into two broad categories. Among the social sciences global theory is known as *macro theory* and narrow-gauge theory may be called *micro theory*. In between these extremes is the middle-range theory preferred by most practitioners of comparative politics today.

APPROACHES

Three approaches to the study of politics are summarized by Apter and Andrain (1968). First, there is the *normative approach*, which in comparative politics usually implies the evolution of constitutional democracy as a central manifestation of modernization. Especially attractive to political scientists interested in the history of political ideas and the sociology of knowledge, the normative approach represents a traditional tendency, dating to times before philosophy was divorced from politics. This approach looks to the cultural values in society that are considered desirable. It also examines norms in the form of rules or rights and obligations that tell us how values are to be realized. Normative analysts attempt to transcend their crude empirical observations of events by seeking higher meaning as they relate their own values to those of the society they observe. Normative analysts use the whole society as their unit of analysis, and they sometimes assume that change in society is the consequence of a dialectical conflict between opposing values and ideas. Marxists, for example, might see such conflict among contending social classes in society. Many U.S. political scientists, in contrast, tend to assume that democracy and modernization are premised on shared rather than divisive values, and they look for compromise, bargaining, and consensus as the components of a democratic society.

Second, there is the *structural approach*. Apter and Andrain distinguish among five emphases: (1) legal and formal, usually administrative, institutions, which were the concern of specialists studying the nature of empires and colonies prior to the Second World War; (2) neo-institutional structures, such as a civil service and political parties, which are given attention along with legal structures and constitutions; (3) groups, including formal ones such as political parties, church, and army and informal ones such as trade unions, business groups, and farmers' groups; (4) structures and functions that constitute a system of related parts; and (5) structures in the form of groups and classes, which neo-Marxists analyze in terms of their economic interests. Structural analysts tend to examine issues of system maintenance and stability. Whole societies or nations, macro units, are studied, and assumptions about development range from an emphasis on separation of powers among the legal governmental institutions, on the one hand, to the struggle between dominant economic classes, on the other.

Third, there is the *behavioral approach*, influenced by psychology. Behavioralism focuses on a variety of problems related to the learning and socialization process, motivations, perceptions, and attitudes toward authority and other considerations. The unit of analysis is the individual and the small group. Apter and Andrain identified behavioral assumptions as those that relate to individual optimism that change is desirable and possible and that development is the consequence of peoples' needs for achievement.

The distinctions among these approaches help to identify the multiplicity of research tendencies employed in the study of comparative politics. The mainstream of comparative politics has tended to utilize the structural or structural-functional approach, labeling it middle range in theoretical orientation. More recently there has been a tendency to pursue narrow, micro orientations through the behavioral approach. Disillusionment with the failure of behavioralism to deal with the issues and problems of society and with the tendency of structuralism to deal with segments of systems without relating them to the whole society has led many professionals to emphasize the normative approach. On the one hand, there are those who continue to stress the values and norms of democratic society as evidenced by the Anglo-American experience. On the other, there are serious, more radical, attempts to criticize such interpretations as static and not very useful. The chapters in this book identify and distinguish between such radical and orthodox understandings of politics and attempt to transcend the three approaches suggested by Apter and Andrain.

MODELS AND PARADIGMS

I have already referred to the use of definitional schema, classificatory arrangements, and systematic orderings, which are useful in the search for theory. These terms might also be described as *taxonomies* or *frameworks*. *Typologies* divide and order information and facts along the lines of classifications, taxonomies, and frameworks, but they do so in somewhat precise, even subtle, ways so as to allow a utilization of quantitative techniques. The use of *models* in the study of comparative politics has broader implications. Models construct, bring disparate parts together, and demonstrate relationships. Models tend to simplify representations of the real world. They can facilitate understanding, but they do not explain. They help comparative specialists bring order to the mass of information available to students of comparative politics. Models, like typologies and classifications, are limited, however. They are mental constructions, not theories, although they are often distorted to signify theoretical advancement.

A *paradigm* is a scientific community's perspective of the world, its set of beliefs and commitments—conceptual, theoretical, methodologic, instrumental. A paradigm guides the scientific community's selection of problems, evaluation of data, and advocacy of theory. In Chapter 3 the existence of paradigms in comparative politics is elaborated on, and two principal paradigms that have influenced comparative politics during the past century are identified.

Methods and Inquiry

Methods involve techniques and are the procedures of inquiry. Methods may be qualitative or quantitative. Lijphart (1971: 683) suggested that the comparative method is basically simple: "a method of discovering empirical relationships among variables, not a method of measurement." The comparative method then, involves qualitative, not quantitative, analysis. The comparative method in this sense is a broad, general method, not a narrow, specialized technique.

This understanding of the comparative method recognizes that efforts to formulate solid theory and methods in the study of comparative politics have not always been successful. Lines of comparison have been drawn, but rigorous study has been limited by the complexities of comparative investigation. Ambitious comparative schemes have assimilated information from many nations, but the results have been largely descriptive. Data banks have gathered together statistics from throughout the world, but the data itself may not be reliable. These problems reflect the experience of most investigators of comparative politics. Warwick and Osherson (1973) outlined some of these problems in their treatment of the comparative research method and technique, and Ward and others (1964) set forth a manual of recommendations, which should be helpful to the study of politics abroad, especially in the Third World. More directly, the student might benefit from the critical examination of field experiences offered by Henry L. Bretton (1970) and William H. Form (1974). Howard A. Scarrow (1963) outlined six types of analysis that can be utilized in research across two or more political entities but not in research on a single entity. Sidney Verba (1967) looked at single-nation and global comparative studies and urged students to adopt a disciplined, narrow focus, but Merritt and Rokkan (1966) were more optimistic in their attempt to identify methods in use of quantitative data in cross-national research. Finally, Heinz Eulau (1962) argued that the narrow research of North American investigators might contribute to new understandings of comparative analysis and method.

Lijphart has argued persuasively for an identification of the comparative method, yet other methods are available and indeed are utilized by specialists of comparative politics. These other methods are the experimental, statistical, linguistic, and cause methods. A brief summary of the discussion of each method by Lijphart (1971) and Meehan (1965: 187–226) follows.

The experimental method utilizes an experimental group and a control group and studies the comparisons. Only the experimental group is exposed to a stimulus, and the other group is isolated. Meehan elaborated on one form of experimental technique, used in some branches of psychology. It involves the treatment of a single complex system within which behavior is observed in relation to various stimuli and the results are recorded and measured. The system is structured like a box in which stimuli serve as the inputs and behaviors represent the outputs and a feedback relationship exists between both elements. A psychiatrist might think of a human being as the box and accordingly study stimuli and behavior. As is noted in Chapter 5, this conception of system has been adapted to David Easton's study of politics. However, the experimental method is rarely used in political science research, largely because politics is difficult to control.

The statistical method is an "approximation" of the experimental method and is facilitated by the use of modern computers. According to Lijphart

(1971: 684), "It entails the conceptual (mathematical) manipulation of empirically observed data—which cannot be manipulated situationally as in experimental design—in order to discover controlled relationships among variables." Distinctions between the statistical method and the comparative method as conceived by Lijphart are unclear. Thus, a combination of the two methods might be appropriate, except where research focuses on national political systems and the number of cases is necessarily restricted, as in comparative politics.

The study of politics is muddled by fussy terminology, and a meticulous study of nomenclature and syntax is overdue. A clarification of meanings might eliminate ambiguous language and allow utilization of the linguistic method. The linguistic method employs procedures for identifying, recording, and measuring recurrent patterns in written and spoken communications. Recently the linguistic method has been combined with the statistical method and the use of computers.

The case study method is closely associated with the comparative method, and certainly it is useful to other methods as well. Lijphart (1971: 691–693) believed that the case study method can contribute to theory building in political science. He identified six types of case studies: (1) atheoretical traditional or single-country studies of no theoretical value; (2) interpretative studies that use theoretical generalizations but relate to a specific case and do not contribute to theory building; (3) hypothesis-generating studies of a number of cases; (4) theory-confirming and (5) theory-infirming studies of single cases within a framework of established generalizations; and (6) studies of single cases that deviate from established generalizations.

All of these methods employ a variety of sources of information. Among these sources are elite and voting data, mass opinion, aggregative figures, historical data, and content findings of documents and speeches. The comparative study of politics utilizes quantitative techniques in the analysis and synthesis of such information.

Conclusion

This discussion has emphasized the traditional terminology of comparative politics and social science. Many of these terms, however, are applicable both to the orthodox and the radical lines of thought that are delineated throughout the chapters in this book. In particular, the concluding chapter focuses on political economy and offers definitions of Marxist terminology. Major schools of political economy are identified, and Marxist theory, method, and concepts are described. An earlier chapter on Marx and Weber may also be helpful.

Michael Harrington in his *Twilight of Capitalism* observed that there are many Marxisms, believing that Marx interpreted things in different ways throughout an illustrative and prolific career of writing about the contradictions of capitalism. Thus the students of Marxism need not adhere to rigid formulations. The fact is, however, that the revision of some of Marx's theory has led to confusion, and the result is not unlike the indiscriminate use of terminology that pervades bourgeois social science. Frank Parkin in his "bourgeois critique" noted that contemporary Western Marxism "is wholly the creation of academic social theorists—more specifically, the creation of the professoriate that rose up on the wave of university expansion in the 1960s." He argued that "professorial" Marxism bears "the unmistakable imprint of bourgeois sociology—in particular that version of it associated with the writings of Max Weber" (1979: ix).

It is likely that the reader may desire to delve more deeply into the meaning of the terminology of Marxism. The intimidated yet curious reader might initially benefit from a brief look at the depiction by Rius, the Mexican cartoonist, in *Marx for Beginners* (1976), which includes a short dictionary of terms. Leo Huberman and Paul M. Sweezy in their *Introduction to Socialism* (1968) also provide access to an understanding of Marxism in the chapter on "The ABC of Socialism." In addition, Ralph Miliband's *Marxism and Politics* stresses a discussion of class and class conflict through strategies of reform and revolution. Ernest Mandel's *From Class Society to Communism: An Introduction to Marxism* (1977) is a comprehensive yet simply written work, which gives clear answers to basic questions and identifies the major theoretical issues. Mandel's work attempts to describe social inequality and social struggle throughout history, to examine the state and ruling classes, to trace development from petty commodity production to the capitalist mode of production, and to explain the impact of monopoly capitalism and the world imperialist system.

References to Appendix 1.1

Apter, David E., and Charles Andrain
    1968 "Comparative Government: Developing New Nations." In Marian D. Irish
    (ed.), *Political Science: Advance of the Discipline*, pp. 82–126. Englewood Cliffs, New
    Jersey: Prentice-Hall. Reprint from *Journal of Politics* XXX (May 1968). Identification of six trends in the study of new nations in relation to three approaches: normative, structural, and behavioral.
Bretton, Henry L.
    1970 "Political Science Field Research in Africa." *Comparative Politics* II (April),
    413–443. A critical examination of research problems for comparative analysis, including techniques of information gathering, use of sources, interviews, as well as testing of data and other matters.

Burrowes, Robert
  1970 "Multiple Time-Series Analysis of Nation-Level Data." *Comparative Political Studies* II (January), 419–442. Argues for the use of longitudinal techniques to test the strength of relationships among variables. Builds a case for longitudinal study of one or a small number of nations, long neglected by comparative political analysts.
Chandler, William M., and Marsha A. Chandler
  1974 "The Problem of Indicator Formation in Comparative Research." *Comparative Political Studies* VII (April), 26–46. Two or more indicators of a given concept are limited in their interchangeability; further, the theoretical bases of indicators may differ. Thus sophisticated techniques used in comparative empirical research are not an escape from questions of substantive theory.
Dumont, Richard G., and William J. Wilson
  1967 "Aspects of Concept Formation, Explication, and Theory Construction in Sociology." *American Sociological Review* XXXII (December), 985–995. Discussion of criteria for selection and use of theoretical concepts with attention to three types of concepts as related to "implicit theory," "theory sketch," and "explicit theory."
Eulau, Heinz
  1962 "Comparative Political Analysis: A Methodological Note." *Midwest Journal of Political Science* VI (November), 397–407. Argues that Americanists can contribute to an understanding of comparative analysis and method by relating their research to that of those working in comparative politics. Eulau supports his view by drawing upon experiences in research on state legislatures and offers methodological observations on comparative analysis.
Form, William H.
  1974 "The Politics of Distrust: Field Problems in Comparative Research." *Studies in Comparative International Development* IX (Spring), 20–48. Discussion of personal field experiences with informant distrust.
Gunnell, John G.
  1969 "Deduction, Explanation, and Social Scientific Inquiry." *American Political Science Review* LXIII (December), 1233–1246. A detailed critique of deductive explanation that has become the basis for most work in social science. Calls for a reexamination of the idea that "there is logical symmetry between explanations in the natural and social sciences" and urges an investigation into "the logical and epistemological foundations of these two enterprises."
Lijphart, Arend
  1971 "Comparative Politics and the Comparative Method." *American Political Science Review* LXV (September), 682–693. Differentiates the comparative method from the experimental, statistical, and case study methods. Comparative method is "a method of discovering empirical relationships among variables, not as a method of measurement." Comparative method is not a technique. The author examines strengths and weaknesses of the comparative method.
Meehan, Eugene J.
  1965 *The Theory and Method of Political Analysis.* Homewood, Illinois: Dorsey

Press. Examines major questions about science, explanation, epistemology, method and technique, and values with critical judgments that are especially useful for comparative politics.

Merritt, Richard L., and Stein Rokkan (eds.)
  1966 *Comparing Nations: The Use of Quantitative Data in Cross-National Research.* New Haven: Yale University Press. Critical discussion of recent efforts to quantify data across many nations.

Parkin, Frank
  1979 *Marxism and Class Theory: A Bourgeois Critique.* New York: Columbia University Press. Critical assessment of Marxist thinking on class analysis, class and state, and class and party. The critique is based largely on revision of Marx's original thinking.

Sartori, Giovanni
  1970 "Concept Misformation in Comparative Politics." *American Political Science Review* LXIV (December), 1033–1053. A plea for conceptualization and method. Criticizes most comparative research as being without comparative method and adequate logical skills.

Scarrow, Howard A.
  1963 "The Scope of Comparative Analysis." *Journal of Politics* XXV (August), 565–577. Discusses comparative analysis as a method for the discovery of attributes, trends, patterns for uniformity and regularity, broad-based hypotheses, causal variables, analytic schemes, and description.

Verba, Sidney
  1967 "Some Dilemmas in Comparative Research." *World Politics* XX (October), 111–127. Assessment of single-nation and global comparative studies in which the author urges students of macropolitics to focus on an intermediate goal of "a disciplined configurative approach."

Ward, Robert E. et al.
  1964 *Studying Politics Abroad: Field Research in the Developing Areas.* Boston: Little, Brown and Co. Essays on field research techniques, design, and setting especially relevant to the Third World.

Warwick, Donald P., and Samuel Osherson (eds.)
  1973 *Comparative Research Methods.* Englewood Cliffs, New Jersey: Prentice-Hall. Essays on problems of comparative research with attention to the random probe, linguistic comparability, unusual conditions, and participant observation, as well as sampling, measurement, and interviewing.

Willer, David, and Murray Webster, Jr.
  1970 "Theoretical Concepts and Observables." *American Sociological Review* XXXV (August), 748–757. Dichotomizes theoretical concepts into abstract (constructs) and real world (observables) categories.

PART 2
Ideology and Epistemology

Ideology and Issues of Comparative Politics

A new revolution is under way in American political science. . . . Its battle cries are relevance and action. Its objects of criticism are the disciplines, the professions, and the universities.

—David Easton, presidential address to the
Sixty-Fifth Annual Meeting of the American
Political Science Association, September 1969

It is not uncommon today for scholars and students of comparative politics to express their dissatisfaction with the field, the discipline, and the profession. One frequently hears or reads about the malaise that pervades political science and comparative politics. The discipline, it is argued, is notorious for its conservative stance and has been avoided by activists concerned with policy changes. Further, the flaws of the discipline are intimately related to the U.S. political system, which it seeks ethnocentrically to describe. In recent years the U.S. debacle in Vietnam and the Watergate crisis at home exposed flaws in that system. Some of the questions often asked revolve around the implications of the familiar situation in which the teacher-scholar assumes an advisory role to the government and contributes to the shaping of policy, to the propagation of that policy, to the decisions determining the allocation of research funds for studies that buttress that policy, and so forth. In the United States especially, students and scholars are examining the relationship of university research and other activities to government agencies, especially the Central Intelligence Agency (CIA), the

29

Federal Bureau of Investigation (FBI), the Pentagon, and the State Department. The significance of the industrial-military complex was made clear in the late 1950s. During the 1960s the universities and the private foundations were being implicated at a time when many comparative political scientists were professing the myth of a science neutral in its values.

The reality and some misconceptions of policies will be explored in the following discussion, along with a look at the profession in relation to the university and government. An assessment of the place of ideology in politics and science will also be attempted. It is my hope that this brief exposition of these issues will serve to confront the reader with and awaken the reader to the fact that all is not well with political science in the United States, that little can be taken for granted, and that there is room for activist scholars to rectify the situation.

Myth and Reality of Politics

Distinguishing between myth and reality is essential in the study of politics. Critical observers of politics frequently search for discrepancies and abuses of government or private power groups. Dissenting conclusions too often are manifested in clichés or unsubstantiated generalizations that lack historical perspective and understanding for effective action. A critical perspective, for example, might suggest that government is corrupt; the middle class is shallow, self-serving, and amoral; the upper class is conspiratorial; and the working class is compromised. This perspective may see the powerful oppressing the weak at every opportunity and racism as being ingrained in the heart of the United States. Although such a perspective may indeed reflect reality, it is necessary to uncover supporting evidence. Additionally, such evidence should be interpreted in the light of society as a whole. In general, interpretations of society and politics, especially those manifested in contemporary writings in political science and comparative politics, are rooted in a number of prevailing assumptions. Often these assumptions constitute political myth, at least in the sense suggested by Murray Edelman (1967: 121) who identified "magical associations permeating language [which] are important for political behavior because they lend authoritativeness to conventional perceptions and value premises and make it difficult or impossible to perceive alternative possibilities."

Both myth and reality permeate understandings of politics. In national politics some political scientists have stressed that traditional ideologies are no longer relevant to a contemporary technological and modernizing society; they see instead a harmonious society of varied and diverse political forces, which bargain and strive for consensus in their actions. Political scientists also tend to seek a boundary between the political and other activities of society. Such refinement of what is political frequently has been in response to the demand that a science must emerge from the study of politics. Thus, the behavioralists, with their methodology and quantitative techniques, contribute to the shaping of a modernizing society, technocratic and depersonalized in its thrust. In contrast, the interpretation of international affairs has been cast in the Cold War dichotomy of democratic and benevolent capitalist nations, on the one hand, and monolithic communist nations, on the other. During recent years this focus has shifted to a concern with three worlds of development, the consequence of a plethora of studies that no longer view Third World neutrals as naive and easily manipulated.

Thus it seems that interpretations of national and international politics are imbued with ideals, values, and biases. Or more simply stated, ideology tends to be all-pervasive, notwithstanding those people who advocate an "end of ideology" thesis, such as Daniel Bell (1962: especially 393–407) who argued that in advanced societies there has been an exhaustion of belief patterns, which support extremist political movements. Bell attributed the existence of ideology to revolutionary impulses of the past century and a half, manifested in particular by Hegel and Marx who sought the transference of ideas into action; but Bell believed that ideology, once it becomes a "road to action, has come to be a dead end."

The term *ideology* apparently originated among post-Enlightenment theorists and ideologues, who referred to it simply as a "science of ideas." For them, ideology was a means for discovering truth and dispelling illusions (Mullins 1972: 498–499). Marx, and later Karl Mannheim, gave the term a different meaning. The usage adopted by Marx, for example in *The German Ideology*, was concerned with false consciousness or any set of political illusions produced by the experiences of a social class. Only through the struggle of classes would true consciousness be achieved. Such struggle would involve a recognition of the misconceptions that relate to the failure of individuals to understand their alienated relationship to their surroundings. Thus, progressive advancement toward a classless society would eliminate all mythologies and superstitions and ensure a benevolent society, universal in scope and acceptance. This usage of ideology in Marx's early work is distinguishable, according to Mepham (1979), from a clearer theoretical position on the origin of ideology that appears in *Capital*. The notion of ideology as false consciousness, however, is sufficiently clear for our purpose. Mannheim (1936: 55–56), although not fundamentally altering Marx's definition, distinguished two meanings: the particular conception of ideology, "regarded as more or less conscious disguises of the real situation," and the more inclusive conception of "the ideology of an age or of a concrete historical-social group, e.g., of a class, when we are not concerned with the characteristics and composition of the total structure of the mind of this epoch or of this group." According to Mannheim (1936: 204), ideas exposed as distortions of a past or potential social order were ideological, and those realized in the social order were utopian.

These specific meanings of ideology have been distorted by contemporary social science. For instance, today ideology is used pejoratively to describe totalitarian regimes, lending credence to declarations that ideologies become exhausted in a modernizing world. Such a stance overlooks the fact that the wealthiest society the world has known is able to perpetuate inequalities, not by totalitarian force, but by subtle internal controls based on beliefs, values, and ideas to which most people willingly subscribe. For example, ideology, in the sense understood by Marx, is so deeply rooted in the consciousness of the U.S. people that they experience great difficulty in comprehending, indeed they tend to accept, the subtle forces that envelop their everyday actions. It is not even clear that the revelation of the U.S. policy failures in Vietnam or the Watergate scandals awakened people to the reality of their "false consciousness." Even though Vietnam and Watergate were exposed, the illusions of a democratic order are carried on.

Ideologies have evolved in a past and continuing association with the process of industrialization and the consequent economic and social problems that accompany that process. Ideologies tend to address themselves to utopian goals, to the resolution of the problems of human existence, and in the light of the contemporary world they tend to be defined in unrealistically optimistic terms, whether they profess a free market or a classless society. Modern ideologies flourished in the era of rapidly changing economic and political developments that accompanied industrialization, especially in Europe and the United States. With the growth of technology, it is often argued, conditions stabilized and a democratic consensus prevailed, resulting in the decline of universalistic, humanistic, and intellectually fashioned ideologies in the Western world. In contrast, it is sometimes believed that the mass ideologies of the Third World are parochial and created by political leaders seeking economic development and power. Those who argue that ideologies have reached an end in the modern world persist in the belief that the resulting political order in the nations of the Third World will lack democratic institutions and will be led by new elites in a totalitarian order.

Although the belief in the end of ideology undoubtedly has significantly influenced the comparative study of politics, so too have the critics of the school left their imprint on the field. Joseph LaPalombara (1966: 2) criticized many writers who did not seem to be concerned with ideology or *any* given set of values, beliefs, expectations, or prescriptions about society other than Marxism, or strongly held and dogmatically articulated ideas regarding class conflict. LaPalombara argued that aside from Marxism there are other ideologies worth examining. He questioned the beliefs that the so-called ideological decline is leading to a mild confluence around ideas that might be associated with pragmatism and that ideology is no longer necessary in the West. C. Wright Mills (1962: 11) confronted the issue by affirming that many social scientists are unaware that their methods and conceptions may actually be influenced by Marx and that "no one who does not come to grips with the idea of Marxism can be an adequate social scientist; no one who believes that Marxism contains the last word can be one either."

Other writers, such as David Apter (1964: 17), believed that "ideology is more important to study than ever before." The application of science to human affairs and the rational commitment to improve society are often associated with ideological conflict, for example. Although the ideological dispute over many old questions such as inequality and authoritarianism may be obscured by the rise of the welfare state, which institutionalizes the struggle toward equality, or by an emphasis on a politics of pluralism, in which power presumably is decentralized and shared by individuals in society, a close examination reveals that the old questions continue to be major concerns in contemporary politics.

In line with the argument that ideology is indeed a crucial concern in the comparative study of politics is the rebuttal that the study of politics is a science. This notion is rooted in the industrialization and technicalization of a society characterized by bureaucracy, specialization, and division of labor. These trends also have affected the university and education itself, because knowledge has been viewed by the new Left as a commodity, something detached from those who produced it and something that can be sold in the market. The consequence is alienation as the intellect becomes detached from the self and as fact is distinguished from value. The specialist in society and in the university ignores the whole process of learning, and "cumulative knowledge" becomes the assembly line of the modern university. The transformation of politics into a science was premised on the success of the natural sciences (Somit and Tanenhaus 1967: 110–117). Political science evolved as a "behavorial science," neutral in character and acceptable to both natural and social scientists seeking to find some unit of measurement, whether it be money for the economist or the vote for the political scientist.

A critical assessment of the ideology of political science most certainly must take into account the thesis, posited by Thomas Kuhn (1970), that scientists inevitably adopt a structure of beliefs, values, and myths about the objectivity of their work. Guiding the scientists' thought is a paradigm or a basic ordering notion about the fundamental character of reality.

In their search for a scientific paradigm, political scientists often skirt important substantive questions as they quantify and attempt to remove the personal biases of the observer, their scientific inquiry focuses upon the routine and repetitive processes of government, and their techniques and methodology reveal a tendency to manipulate reality for the sake of efficiency. That reality is based on the assumption that the nature of the U.S. society is correct and good, that an alternative arrangement is unrealistic. Such an assumption conditions the conceptualization of a "civic culture," seen in Anglo-American society, and of pluralism, represented by the U.S. democratic process. Such a conceptualization underlies any understanding of the prevailing ideology in U.S. political science.

Tentatively this ideology might be characterized as constituting the beliefs that the United States is good, that progress is inherent in the evolution of U.S. institutions, and that political relations with other nations are to protect and extend freedom and to ensure economic prosperity on a mutual basis. This progress is premised on the functioning of a free market in which firms compete for profits and workers compete for wages. The market is dominated by large, competing corporations, marginally regulated by government, which efficiently produce according to consumer demand the best-quality goods and services and the highest standard of living for the general population. The basis of individual freedom is the right to own private property, and civility is the basic standard of morality. Disrespect for authority threatens this order, and thus the United States must defend itself from the penetration of outside forces such as international communism, which has created a worldwide conflict between good and evil. At the same time, as the wealthiest and most powerful country on earth, the United States must manifest its civilizing traditions among the peoples of the world, especially those in the underdeveloped countries.

Although such an ideology probably is held by a majority of people in the United States today, its fundamental premises have been challenged on many fronts. Racial discrimination against blacks, Chicanos, Puerto Ricans, and other minority groups at home is now linked with war, imperialism, and exploitation abroad, and the focus that generated such a perspective was related to the U.S. involvement in Indochina. These realities exposed the student of comparative politics to the ideological mystique that pervades the relationship of political science to university professors, government officials, businessmen, and the military. At the same time, the realities of society have awakened some political scientists to an awareness of the mythological underpinnings of the U.S. ideology and to the ideological premises that buttress academia. Several examples illustrate this awakening.

First, Marvin Surkin (1969: 573), in a view representative of an emerging radical interpretation of politics, affirmed that we must "unmask the guise by which the most prevalent modes of thought, their institutional expression, and their ideologies keep us from grasping their real social meaning." He argued that social science in general and political science in particular are increasingly becoming ideological "in the service of the dominant institutions of American society." In other words, the end-of-ideology thesis is imbued with myth: "Knowledge and technology are free—neutral or non-ideological—to serve the interests and powers of the 'benevolent' American state and corporate elite both at home and abroad."

James Petras (1965) provided a second example in his reference to the ideological schools that dominate the thought of U.S. political scientists. Specifically he referred to the school that espouses stability and maintenance in the name of equilibrium and balance. Equilibrium and balance are conditioned on limited participation, limited commitment, limited interest, and elites who act. Cleavages thus remain marginal, and consensus pervades political action. Another ideological school is that of the group theorists who acknowledge cleavage and conflict in the group interactions of society but view politics as based on a balance of various forces contending for power and the making of decisions. A third school concerns itself with the role of the autonomous politician as a central figure in the configuration of political institutions. The politician is seen as a political broker or statesman in the resolution of issues. Yet another ideological school focuses on the infrastructure of political parties and their roles as directors, organizers, and decision makers. These parties make the political system accountable to the electorate and ensure popular participation. Thus the ideological thrust emanating from these schools stresses stability and maintenance, equilibrium and balance, consensus and pluralism, autonomy and participation.

Other radical perspectives abound among those critical of contemporary social science. Gitlin (1965) referred to "local pluralism" in characterizing the ideology of political science. Local pluralism implies that power is distributed among a variety of groups and institutions so that no one can dominate the others. The ideology of local pluralism has its historical roots in North America after the Second World War. Its premises suggest that there are no power elites, that power is widely distributed in communities, that power is observable and may be investigated in case studies of decisions by formal political bodies, and that the power system allows for change. Freiberg expressed concern about the "ideological production of knowledge" in social science, arguing that the social sciences "are not sciences but are instead purposively misnomered as part of the same ideological process which is in fact their essence, their project, and their meaning" (Freiberg 1973: 13). Aptheker summarized ideological tendencies in U.S. social science since 1945. He noted a preoccupation with "objectivity," "pure and exaggerated empiricism," an examination of phenomena "as static," elitist and conservative "bias," and a ridiculing of Marxism "as obsolete, irrelevant" (Aptheker 1966: 26–27). A useful Soviet synthesis of bourgeois conceptions of ideology is in L. N. Moskvichov (1974).

Given these ideological tendencies in U.S. political science, what about the relationship of the discipline to universities, government, and the corporate world? A number of provocative questions, relevant to comparative politics, come to mind. What are the implications, for instance, of the familiar situation in which the teacher-scholar also assumes an advisory role to government, contributes to the shaping of government policy, or participates in decisions determining research funds for studies that reinforce that policy? What about the relationship of political science to government and policymaking? What about the relationship of university research activities to government—especially the Pentagon and the CIA—and to the foundations?

Politics and the Profession

Noam Chomsky (1969) once referred to the failure of the social scientists to counterbalance government policies and actions with an emphasis on traditional values of democracy. Instead social scientists surrender their independent judgments, neglect teaching, and distort scholarship. The primary causes of this phenomenon are access to money and influence, an almost universally shared ideology, and professionalization. The social scientists have become a technical intelligentsia interested in stability and order. Not many years ago students and faculty in political science at the University of California, Berkeley, initiated a discussion about the discipline. They argued that political investigators have often tended to camouflage their partisan allegiances and contempt for human beings by professing themselves to be discoverers of truth, unchanging forces of history, or objective laws of science. "The political experimenter is part of the experimental system and his work is value-laden in terms of the system. If his methodology fails to take this into account his efforts may become irrelevant at best, or destructive at worst" (Berkeley Students and Faculty 1969?: 10). Such views were articulated in the professional associations, which confronted challenges from within their ranks during the late 1960s and early 1970s.

For example, political science had become a discipline that was conservative in stance and devoid of activists. Its professional organization, the American Political Science Association, sidestepped two resolutions at its annual meetings in 1967. One called for the dismissal of its executive director and its treasurer-counsel because of their involvement in a CIA-financed front organization. The other resolution called upon universities to withhold membership lists of campus groups from the House Un-American Activities Committee. The failure of the association to act on these two resolutions prompted the formation of a splinter group called the Caucus for a New Political Science. The association had never held a contested election for president, and the caucus challenged this traditional practice in the ensuing years. The causus also challenged a constitutional provision that disavowed organizational interest in the political issues of the day.

Alan Wolfe (1969), a caucus leader, delved into the structure, procedures, and cliques of the association. He found that few members attended the annual business meetings and that the nominating procedures tended to "take politics out of political science and place it into the hands of a gentlemanly club." He noted that nine of the ten-member nominating committee had received their doctorates from the top ten political science departments. He observed that the election process of the association resembled that of "either the state of Alabama or the Soviet Union, depending upon one's field of interest." He concluded that there was almost no way to become an established political scientist without accepting the association:

> Without the association, there is no career; with it, only an absence of intelligence or an excess of integrity stand in the way. This conclusion makes the question of who governs the association important. If little choice and democracy are present, then the rules of careerism and proper scholarship are established by a small, unrepresentative elite of political scientists, to which all others are responsive. Abstract principles like value neutrality and proper scholarship can then be seen not as eternal truths but as devices by which some try to maintain their position in the profession at the expense of others. [Wolfe 1969: 357]

Elsewhere Wolfe (1970) analyzed the professional mystique of political science. The demand for professional behavior, he argued, is a demand for conservative politics and for political conformity. The present practices of political science are defended in the name of professionalism. These practices include the acceptance of an unrepresentative elite, which militates against democracy within the profession; the preservation of only prevailing points of view, particularly political as well as methodological views; the affiliation of political scientists with institutions that support U.S. policy, namely, the State and Defense departments; and the systematic exclusion of research writing with a political bias in favor of "scientific" or "scholarly" writing.

The experiences of political science were not unlike those of other disciplines that were beset by dissident movements. In sociology, for example, a radical caucus emerged at the Boston convention of the American Sociological Association in 1968 and radical splinter groups such as the Sociology Liberation Movement and the Union of Radical Sociologists were formed at the San Francisco meeting in 1969 (Nicolaus 1969). The Union of Radical Sociologists soon launched a new journal, *Insurgent Sociologist*, as an alternative to the professional sociological journals. Then radical texts soon appeared (see Colfax and Roach 1971 and D. Horowitz 1971). Among the well-known sociologists who joined the movement, Alvin Gouldner (1970) has noted the growing importance of radical sociology and its exposure of the central contradictions of modern sociology, especially in the United States. He saw sociology as the "market researcher for the welfare state," and he acknowledged that academic "objectivity" fosters the sociologists' accommodation to the way things are. Gouldner demonstrated that the historical roots of sociology are found in the bourgeois reaction to the Enlightenment and the French Revolution. That reaction was evident in the sociological positivism of Saint-Simon and Comte, who viewed progress as slowly evolutionary and inevitable. Just as Comte understood positivism as a restraint upon the revolutionary spirit, so too did subsequent study of society call for a detached scientific method that sought apolitical alternatives to the political conflicts of society.

Social unrest in the 1960s also led to divisions in the field of economics. A young generation of radicals challenged the orthodox economists who, in defense of capitalism, guided the world's most advanced economy over traditional hurdles of inflation, unemployment, and uneven growth (Lifschultz 1974). As these problems persisted, public confidence in economists eroded. Divisions arose within the American Economic Association as a splinter group formed the Union of Radical Political Economics and launched a journal, *Review of Radical Political Economics*. Later they published a popular weekly, *Dollars and Sense*, and a group of radical economists in and around San Francisco combined with small collectives around the world in the irregular publication of a journal, *Kapitalistate*. Radical economics texts became popular in university courses (Mermelstein 1970 and Sherman 1972), and radical economists attacked orthodox economists for their defense of the capitalist system. They tended to adopt a Marxist alternative to the orthodox position, and their criticisms focused on the dominant characteristics of capitalism in the contemporary world. Specifically, they argued that the development of the advanced capitalist countries was based on the subjugation and exploitation of the backward countries. Trade, investment, and aid served as the foundation for relations between these two types of countries, resulting in development for one and underdevelopment for the other. The dependence of the backward nations upon the advanced nations was the inevitable consequence of the global capitalist system, and development could occur in the backward areas only if the existing pattern of relations was broken (Sweezy 1970).

Radical dissent in other disciplines was evident. In anthropology, Marvin Harris (1968) attempted to trace the rise of anthropological theory from the discipline's beginnings as a science of history in the nineteenth century to later ahistorical tendencies. The epistemological, philosophical, and methodological differences that have long divided anthropologists were brought forward into a struggle between radical and orthodox anthropologists in the late 1960s. Since about 1967 a radical caucus began to prod anthropologists to concern themselves with human problems rather than with the documenting of customs of "primitive" peoples for use by colonial powers. They challenged the manipulative procedures of the American Anthropological Association in an effort to establish democratic voting procedures. They established a Committee on Ethics to investigate the activities of social scientists in Thailand (Wolf and Jorgensen 1970), and they proposed resolutions opposing the participation of anthropologists in counterinsurgency research. Countertextbooks with a Marxist thrust were introduced to students in the classroom (Hymes 1969, for example).

The struggle to counter orthodox interpretations of society emerged in other disciplines as well. Divisions were clearly portrayed at the 1969 and 1970 conventions of the American Historical Association (Radosh 1970 and Weinstein 1970). Leftist concerns focused on the apolitical *American Historical Review* and on tensions between professionalism and social involvement in the problems of the day. In 1968 the annual meeting of the Modern Language Association of America was confronted with the demands of radical scholars (see Richard Ohmann 1969 for details). Noam Chomsky, the linguist and radical who had brought about a revolution in linguistics, began to tie his ideas on language to politics. The impact of his writing was to influence other scholarly fields, including psychology, philosophy, and biology (Sklar 1968). Attention by scholars like Chomsky to the war in Indochina and to the dominant influence of multinational firms on world affairs was to shake the foundations of the scientific community as well. Questions about the relevance of science and about the relationship of science and society were introduced to the meetings of the National Academy of Sciences in the late 1960s (Spiro 1969), and radical journals such as *Science for the People* were widely circulated to the scientific community.

These intrusions into the professional academic disciplines were extended into the associations of the area specialists. Black discontent, which surfaced at the Los Angeles meetings of the African Studies Association, exploded at the Montreal meetings a year later as black American and African scholars brought matters to a halt by insisting that there be racial parity on the association's board of directors. The Africa Research Group began to disseminate its findings on the ties of the profession to the U.S. intelligence community (Chilcote and Legassick 1971). From its inception the Latin American Studies Association has been wracked by the dissent of radicals concerned with the exploitation of Latin America. Political resolutions opposing U.S. imperialism and supporting developments in Cuba were approved in the association's business meetings, although the failure to implement those resolutions culminated in the founding of an alternative journal, *Latin American Perspectives* (Chilcote 1973). Publications of the North American Congress on Latin America provided useful information. The Committee for Concerned Asian Scholars directed attention against the U.S. military efforts in Asia, and the Pacific Studies Center was established to research and report on developments in that part of the world through a bimonthly publication, *Pacific Research and World Empire Telegram.*

Scholarship, Ethics, and the Establishment

> *Intellect has also become an instrument of national purpose, a component of the military-industrial complex.*
>
> —Clark Kerr, former president of the University of California, quoted in *Berkeley Students and Faculty* 1969?

The traditional idea that the university is neutral with respect to the major questions of society is mythical. It is usually assumed that the university is primarily devoted to teaching and research in the service of society. In an age of technology and science the university takes these patterns of society for granted, works within them, and serves to affirm them. At the same time the university depends on society for support, and it caters to those needs that society seeks to promote by providing university support. Given this mutual relationship between the university and society, knowledge becomes a commodity, something detached from those who produce it and something that can be sold in the marketplace—for instance, knowledge may be requisite for the holding of a particular job. Thus, the student learns to exercise intellect in a detached way rather than to use intellect in a dialogue between self and the outside world. This is similar to the way in which the social scientists tend to distinguish between fact and value, the assumption being that in a professional capacity one works without values and emotions. Reflecting the society around it, then, the university becomes a bureaucratic industry, oriented toward specialization and division of labor. The traditional ideal of the academic as learned first and specialized second has been turned upside down, and many of today's academics tend to be specialized and restricted to limited tasks. As such, the academic does not need to be concerned with the whole, nor with what the final product looks like. Indeed, as Clark Kerr suggested, intellectual endeavor has become a component of the modern military and industrial complex.

The relationship of the university to the society at large has been called into question by certain developments. The U.S. defeat in Indochina, the

Watergate scandals, and surveillance by intelligence agencies over the every-day affairs of thousands of U.S. citizens have prompted questions about the organization and purpose of society (Berman and Halperin 1975) and likewise about the organization and purpose of the university. Political science has been similarly affected, as mentioned above, because its profes-sional association was confronted with the revelation that its executive director and its treasurer-counsel had been officials of an active conduit foundation of the CIA.

This revelation led to the formation of a committee on professional stan-dards, responsibilities, and conduct. In its report to the association, this committee blandly concluded that ethical problems in the profession are peripheral and insignificant (American Political Science Association, Com-mittee 1968). The committee found that political scientists are "men of prop-erty"—affluent researchers who must balance conflicting institutional com-mitments between university and government. Further, scholars must be wary of research in foreign countries, especially research conducted under the auspices of other institutions. Also scholars may wittingly or unwittingly condition their findings on the assumed values of their financial sponsors, thereby sacrificing objectivity. Some people interpreted the report as invok-ing objectivity, detached scholarship, and methodological rigor in order to escape the commitments of action and responsibility. Students at Berkeley summed up their feelings, "We get the disquieting feeling that to become pro-fessional political scientists, we must strip ourselves of human feeling and abstain from political involvement. If that is so, it constitutes an ethical problem of the greatest magnitude. Yet most of our professors do not see it as a problem at all. And that is an ethical disaster" (Berkeley Students and Faculty 1969?: 21).

The magnitude of the ethical problems facing the political scientists, especially in comparative political inquiry, can be better understood by briefly summarizing some of the revelations of the 1970s, namely, those relating to a scholar's relationship, first, to government (including the military and intelligence agencies) and, second, to the corporate world (in-cluding private foundations).

Social Science and Government

Political scientists are concerned with policy, and their research may shape the formation of policy. Thus, the acceptance of funds from government agencies has ethical implications. Sponsoring public institutions do not always guarantee complete freedom to researchers to publish their findings without censorship or interference, and such restrictions or classification of information usually is imposed by defense and intelligence agencies. Perhaps the most blatant attempt to undertake clandestine research was Project Camelot (I. L. Horowitz 1967).

Project Camelot was conceived late in 1963 by U.S. army officers associated with the Army Research Office of the Department of Defense. They were concerned about insurgency movements around the world and desired to find ways of coping with such movements. Latin America was the first area selected for concentrated study, and under the aegis of the American University in Washington, D.C., a four-to-six-million-dollar contract over three to four years was arranged with the Social Operations Research Organization. Efforts to establish the project in Chile were exposed in 1965, in the Chilean leftist press and Congress, prompting opposition to the project by the U.S. Department of State and intervention by Pres. Lyndon B. Johnson to stop the project altogether. The repercussions for U.S. citizens undertaking research outside their own country were substantial. Such research was suspect, and many Third World countries attempted to establish guidelines and controls. The exposure and criticism of Project Camelot raised questions in the United States as well. The State Department viewed the Pentagon as intruding upon the State Department's authority in the area of foreign affairs, and congressional skeptics were fearful that foreign alliances might be shaken. Academic social scientists questioned the links between the Pentagon and U.S. universities. Not only did the unfavorable publicity leave a residue of distrust for U.S. social scientists all over Latin America, but the connections between U.S. universities and defense and national security projects constituted gross violations of the principle of nonintervention in the internal affairs of other countries.

Dissent over Project Camelot was a prelude to protests during the late 1960s by students and faculty members about Defense Department–sponsored foreign affairs research. Some of that research was carried out in federally contracted research centers at the University of Wisconsin, George Washington University, American University, Columbia University, Penn State, the University of Washington, Johns Hopkins University, and Massachusetts Institute of Technology (MIT); other research was conducted at military-sponsored institutions such as the Rand Corporation, the Institute for Defense Analysis, and the Hudson Institute. After complaints from social scientists in Japan and Sweden, it also became apparent that the Pentagon was sponsoring research in universities in those and other countries. Eighteen institutions in Japan, for example, held $170 million in U.S. defense contracts as of 1967, and $300 million was allocated to twenty-nine institutions in Sweden (U.S. Senate 1968, part 1: 20–24). In Latin America, the U.S. Army sponsored twenty-six projects in Argentina, Brazil, Chile, Peru, Uruguay, and Venezuela—all countries where the Pentagon maintained close ties with the domestic military. Given such disclosures, it was not out of order for one U.S. senator to question the usefulness of an $84,000 "Pax Americana" study by the Douglas Aircraft Corporation, which concluded that "While the United States is not an imperialistic nation, she exhibits many of the characteristics of past imperiums and in fact has acquired imperial responsibilities" (U.S. Senate 1968, part 2: 32).

Limited resources had resulted in many universities becoming dependent on the federal government for research funds. In return, the universities made available their "technical intellectual resources." In 1968 the Pentagon handed out some $40 million for nonmilitary studies in the social sciences alone. Some 250 colleges and universities were participating in such projects in that year, despite growing suspicions about government intrusions into the academic world. Under the Pentagon's Project Themis, 42 institutions in thirty-one states were provided with long-term financing to develop fifty new research centers in areas not then being supported; a total of 173 schools submitted 483 proposals for the minimum annual funding of $200,000 per project. Typical of the Pentagon-sponsored projects was Quantitative Political Science, which for $590,000 drew its information from the *New York Times Index* and the *International Yearbook*. According to the Pentagon this project related characteristics of nations to the occurrence of riots and revolutions and participation in external wars. Another project under the direction of a political scientist focused on "Comparative Research on Behavioral Change" and was funded at $4 million over five years (Rabb 1968).

The revelation of such projects prompted antiwar students and faculty to oppose contractual agreements between their universities and the Department of Defense. Their tactics shifted from teach-ins to strikes and occupations of administration buildings on the campuses. Because of the persistent disintegration of its university-based research system, the Pentagon offered to stop classified contracts for basic research, but the offer was of little avail. Princeton University and the University of Chicago severed some defense ties, and the University of California, Berkeley, MIT, and other institutions began reducing secret military research.

Ties between U.S. universities and the CIA were even more insidious. It was not uncommon, for instance, for university administrators to suggest that faculty on sabbatical leave in foreign countries cooperate with CIA agents. Military research carried out at the University of Michigan may have helped the CIA and the Pentagon, together with the Bolivian military, capture and assassinate Ché Guevara in Bolivia during 1967 (Sugarman 1968). Guevara, hero of the Cuban revolution, was apparently the victim of infrared photography, which can measure the human body temperature and was thereby able to trace Guevara's movements, speed, and campsites, and even able to identify the number of persons with him.

Especially shocking to the academic world was the revelation that the CIA had subsidized the National Students Association (NSA) with about $4 million from 1952 until 1967 and that about three-fourths of the NSA's top officers from 1956 to 1962 were recruited as CIA agents (*Los Angeles Times*, February 26, 1967). Millions of dollars of CIA funds were filtered into other youth organizations as well as into academic, research, journalistic, legal, and labor organizations in the Unites States and abroad. Among them were the Foreign Policy Research Institute of the University of Pennsylvania, the National Education Association, the Institute of Public Adminstration, the American Newspaper Guild, the International Confederation of Free Trade Unions, and the Operations and Policy Research. The last institution was headed by the executive directors of the American Political Science Association, as alluded to earlier (*New York Times*, February 19, 1967). Additionally, the CIA established conduit foundations through which money could be filtered to the academic community; for example, to the Pan American Foundation, connected with the University of Miami in Florida, the International Marketing Institute, which held seminars at the Harvard Business School, and the American Society of African Culture.

Finally, there were the CIA efforts to penetrate, even to direct the thinking of, various cultural organizations. (For a synthesis of CIA involvement in the cultural life of the United States, see Wills 1976.) The secret subsidization of *Encounter* magazine has been well publicized, and there were secret fundings of Henry Kissinger's journal, *Confluence*. In *Give Us This Day* Howard Hunt published an account of the Bay of Pigs operation, which he patronized with CIA money. William Buckley's semiautobiographical novel, *Saving the Queen*, reveals his CIA activities. CIA and other government agency subsidies through New York and Washington publishers permitted the publication of hundreds of other books favorable to U.S. policies and actions. Such subsidies did not reach Philip Agee, a former agent, who vividly described his day-to-day adventures in Ecuador, Mexico, and Uruguay in his best-selling *Inside the Company*, a book the CIA was successful in temporarily banning from publication in the United States. In addition to Agee's work, personal accounts by several former CIA agents have appeared, revealing the subversive activity of U.S. intelligence agencies in the internal affairs of other nations. These accounts include *The CIA and the Cult of Intelligence* by Victor Marchetti and John Marks, a revelation of secrets learned during fourteen years with the CIA; *Decent Interval* by Frank Snepp, an exposé of the period leading up to the fall of Saigon; and *In Search of Enemies* by John Stockwell, who unveils his role as director of CIA operations during the Angolan civil war of the mid-1970s. There is a review of these and other works critical of the U.S. intelligence establishment in Ransome (1980).

Obviously the CIA intrusion into academic and cultural life has affected political science. So too have the activities of the FBI. The recruitment by these agencies of student and faculty operatives to report on activities abroad and at home has undermined work in comparative politics, indeed it has jeopardized whatever integrity remains within the field. The linking of the intelligence activities abroad with those at home is evidenced by Howard Hunt's ability to move freely among counterrevolutionary Cuban exiles, Nixon's White House advisers, and the Watergate burglars and by the fact that FBI agents work hand in hand with Mexican customs officials to check on U.S. scholars flying to Cuba via Mexico City. The FBI also has harassed academics in the United States, one conspicuous case being that of Peter Bohmer, a radical economics professor who was run out of San Diego, a victim of FBI-promoted terrorism (Viorst 1976). One of Bohmer's chief antagonists was Howard Godfrey, a San Diego fireman and FBI agent who, with agency support, helped organize the Secret Army Organization (SAO) and served as its San Diego County coordinator. The SAO was a small vigilante group that terrorized persons who protested the Vietnam War, and it was organized partially to combat demonstrations at the 1972 Republican National Convention, once planned to be held in San Diego. Godfrey was known to have been in contact with Donald Segretti, the former White House employee of Watergate and "dirty tricks" fame (full details can be found in an eight-part series by Patrick Dillon, *San Diego Union*, January 11–18, 1976).

Such activities spurred Congress to investigate the consequences of intelligence activities at home and abroad. Two reports were published in 1976 (U.S. Senate 1976 and U.S. House 1976). The House investigation revealed that although in 1967 President Johnson had ordered that no federal agency provide any covert financial assistance or support to the nation's educational or private voluntary organizations, testimony in late 1975 revealed that the CIA still had ongoing contracts with some universities, some of which involved classified work. The Senate study reported that three-fourths of the CIA covert actions had never been approved or reviewed outside the agency. The agency also had sidestepped the presidential ban against CIA ties to universities by establishing direct links with individual academics, several hundred of whom were providing leads, arranging contracts, and producing books. Many of these academics were political scientists, and many were involved in research on foreign countries.

Social Science and the Multinationals

During the late 1960s radicals also directed attention to the corporations. They argued that academics work only for the administration and trustees of research and development corporations called universities. The decisions of these university corporations are made by their directors, who serve the nation's business corporations, banks, bureaucracy, and military. A public entity like the University of California is governed by members of the Hearst, Chandler, Simon, and other influential families, for example, while a private institution like Harvard University is run on a self-perpetuating basis (when a member of the governing board dies or resigns, his successor is chosen by seven members of that board). Harvard executives serve on the Council for Foreign Relations, and academics like Henry Kissinger shape foreign policy and promote links with the intelligence community (Africa Research Group 1970?).

It is further argued that the corporate ties of university to business serve the needs of the capitalist world and, in particular, U.S. capitalism at home and abroad. Universities and factories alike produce goods and services packaged to contain a U.S. view of the world. Thusly, according to Ivan Illich (1969), a basic need will be defined as owning a car while expensive remedies to relieve the traffic jams in our cities are being promoted, or as using the schools to get children out of their parents' hair or off the street, even though the children's schooling will seem endless and they will need incentives to endure the ordeal. Illich uses these examples to explain underdevelopment as "the surrender of social consciousness to pre-packaged solutions." Underdevelopment is the consequence of rising levels of aspirations brought about through the intensive marketing of "patent" products. Education really is "the awakening awareness of new levels of human potential and the use of one's creative powers to foster life" (Illich 1969: 22).

University research is also dependent on private foundations. The annual income of the Ford Foundation exceeds that of the world's largest bank, and the assets of the Ford Foundation exceed those of the Rockefeller Foundation fourfold. As nonprofit, charitable foundations they serve as "the base of the network of organizations through which the nerve centers of wealth impress their will on Washington" (D. Horowitz 1969 (1): 47). This network consists of research and policy organizations that are financed and staffed jointly by the foundations and the corporate community. Among these organizations is the Council on Foreign Relations and its prestigious quarterly, *Foreign Affairs*. The council has spawned such foreign affairs specialists as McGeorge Bundy and Henry Kissinger. The organizational complex also includes the Brookings Institution, the National Bureau of Economic Research, the Foreign Policy Association, and the Twentieth Century Fund—all of which finance academics and assimilate their findings into foreign policies and actions.

Foundation-sponsored research into foreign areas has, of course, been questioned by the host countries, as have the multinational corporations with which the foundations are allied. As a consequence the motives, objectives, and conduct of research by the comparative political analysts have come under heavy scrutiny. Particularly distasteful have been the corporation bribes to foreign officials. United Brands was implicated in such a scandal in Honduras, and Lockheed has been linked directly to bribes of government officials in Japan, the Netherlands, and Italy. A Venezuelan legislative committee accused Occidental Petroleum of "irregular and fraudulent" activities during the period 1967 through 1971. Gulf Oil was involved in a $3 million bribe in South Korea, and International Telephone and Telegraph (ITT) gave $270,000 to tax officials to help solve that corporation's tax problems in Italy. ITT also was implicated in attempts to overthrow the regime of Chilean President Salvador Allende. The Securities and Exchange Commission acknowledged that 110 corporations had admitted making questionable payments to maintain their foreign operations (*Los Angeles Times,* May 2, 1976).

Finally, the formation and activities of the Trilateral Commission make abundantly clear the connections among multinationals, government, and the academic world. Trilateralism was promoted by scholars and policymakers from Japan, North America, and Western Europe through a series of reports (see Trilateral Commission 1975–1978). Membership on the Trilateral Commission has included the banker David Rockefeller, Pres. Jimmy Carter, Vice-President Walter Mondale, presidential candidates George Bush and John Anderson, Secretaries of State Cyrus Vance and Henry Kissinger, and National Security Adviser Zbigniew Brzezinski.

Summary

The argument has been presented that ideology is relevant to politics. Ideological assumptions about industrialization and modernization, progress, stability, and order permeate the policies and actions of the university, government, and the corporate worlds. Indeed, ideology permeates political science and comparative politics. Political scientists tend to be ideological in that their values and beliefs are tied to property, money, and influence—a reflection of the capitalist world around them. In disguising their preferences, allegiances, and biases in professionalism and in scientific objectivity, they become apolitical and conservative.

The understanding of the ideologies of politics has provoked a reassessment of political science and comparative politics, however. Among the consequences of this reassessment are, first, a challenge to the ruling professional power structure (creating deep schisms within the professional associations) to promote a sense of ethics in scholarship and teaching and a movement toward radical understandings of society. Second, there is an awareness of the relationship of the universities to the modern military and industrial complex—exposed by investigations into foreign policy and surveillance by intelligence agencies. Third, there is a critical understanding of the government's penetration and control of much academic research and publication and the implications thereof for comparative political inquiry. Last, the network of notables who direct the universities, corporations, and foundations on behalf of U.S. capitalism has been identified.

References

Africa Research Group
> 1970? *How Harvard Rules.* Cambridge: Harvard University Press. A critique of Harvard University's ties to government and private enterprise, including documents and a chart depicting power structure.

American Political Science Association, Committee on Professional Standards and Responsibilities
> 1969 "Ethical Problems of Political Scientists." *PS* (Winter), 5–16. Report of the committee's findings to the American Political Science Association.

Apter, David E. (ed.)
> 1964 *Ideology and Discontent.* New York: Free Press of Glencoe. Essays on ideology by a variety of social scientists.

Aptheker, Herbert
> 1966 "Recent Ideological Developments in the United States." *World Marxist Review* IX (October 1966), 26–33. Relates Cold War and other characteristics of the post–Second World War period to the dominant bourgeois ideological tendencies of contemporary social science.

Bell, Daniel
> 1962 *The End of Ideology: On the Exhaustion of Political Ideas in the Fifties.* New York: Collier Books. Technology and modernization have brought about the exhaustion of the old ideologies, which have lost their truth and power to persuade, according to the author.

Berkeley Students and Faculty
> 1969? "An Invitation to a Discussion." Mimeographed. Argues that the malaise in U.S. political science is attributable to flaws in the discipline, flaws that are "intimately related to the American political system which it seeks to describe."

Berman, Jerry J., and Morton H. Halperin
> 1975 *The Abuses of the Intelligence Agencies.* Washington, D.C.: Center for National Security Studies. Analysis of the abuses of power committed by U.S. intelligence agencies against North Americans as well as covert actions against foreign governments.

Chilcote, Ronald H.
> 1973 "The Latin American Challenge to U.S. Scholarship in Latin America." *URLA Newsletter* III (April-May), 1–4. Also in *LASA Newsletter* V (June 1973), 30–34. Critical view of the professional activities of Latin Americanists in the United States and a call for the founding of a radical journal.

Chilcote, Ronald H., and Martin Legassick
1971 "The African Challenge to American Scholarship in Africa." *Africa Today* XVIII (January), 4-11. Radical critique of U.S. Africanist scholars and their professional activities.

Chomsky, Noam
1969 "The Menace of Liberal Scholarship." *New York Review of Books* XI (January 2), 29-38. Argues that liberal scholarship in the social sciences is undermined by the scholar's access to power, shared ideology, and professionalization.

Colfax, David, and Jack L. Roach (eds.)
1971 *Radical Sociology.* New York: Basic Books. Identifies what is radical sociology, what is the relationship between radical sociology and academic sociology, and how radical sociologists work in the United States.

Edelman, Murray
1967 *Symbolic Uses of Politics.* Urbana: University of Illinois Press. Important discussion of the use of language and distorted impressions of politics that preclude possibilities of change and alternatives.

Freiberg, J. W.
1973 "Sociology and the Ruling Class." *Insurgent Sociologist* III (Summer), 12-26. Argues that social science is not scientific but ideological.

Gitlin, Todd
1965 "Local Pluralism as Theory and Ideology." *Studies on the Left* V (Summer), 21-72. Critique of pluralist conceptions of power that pervade contemporary political science. Labels these conceptions as ideological rather than theoretical.

Gouldner, Alvin W.
1970 *The Coming Crisis in Western Sociology.* New York: Basic Books. Masterful treatment that traces the development of sociology from the evolutionary theory of Saint-Simon and Comte to detached scientific methods of studying society today. Radical perspective by an established sociologist.

Harris, Marvin
1968 *The Rise of Anthropological Theory: A History of Theories of Culture.* New York: Thomas Y. Crowell. A detailed examination of the epistemological and philosophical roots of anthropology and a critique of contemporary methods and theory.

Horowitz, David
1969 (1) "The Foundations of (Charity Begins at Home)," with David Kolodney; (2) "Billion Dollar Brains: How Wealth Puts Knowledge in Its Pocket"; and (3) "Sinews of Empire." *Ramparts* VII (April 1969), 39-48; (May 1969), 36-44; and VIII (October 1969), 33-42. Exposé of the network of foundations, corporations, and government agencies that operate on behalf of the capitalist establishment.

Horowitz, David (ed.)
1971 *Radical Sociology: An Introduction.* New York: Canfield Press. Skillfully designed text containing excerpts from leading nineteenth- and twentieth-century radical sociologists.

Horowitz, Irving Louis
1967 *The Rise and Fall of Project Camelot.* Cambridge, Massachusetts: M.I.T. Press. Essays on the controversial Pentagon-sponsored social science research project

that was halted after being condemned by members of the Chilean Congress.

Hymes, Dell (ed.)
1969 *Reinventing Anthropology.* New York: Pantheon and Vintage. Collection of radical perspectives on anthropology.

Illich, Ivan
1969 "Outwitting the 'Developed' Countries." *New York Review of Books* XIII (November 6), 20–23. Argues that the advanced industrial nations create underdevelopment in other countries through their intensive promotion of "patent" products.

Kuhn, Thomas S.
1970 *The Structure of Scientific Revolutions.* 2d ed. Chicago: University of Chicago Press. From II, 2 of *International Encyclopedia of Unified Science.* A scientist's historical perspectives about the struggle among scientists to formulate and work within dominant paradigms. Ideology becomes a part of each scientist's ordering notions about the character of reality.

LaPalombara, Joseph
1966 "Decline of Ideology: A Dissent and an Interpretation." *American Political Science Review* LX (March), 5–16. A critique of the behavioralist unquestioning belief in science and an effort to challenge advocates of the end-of-ideology thesis.

Lifshultz, Lawrence S.
1974 "Could Karl Marx Teach Economics in America?" *Ramparts* XII (April), 27–30 ff. An account of radical efforts to challenge the American Economic Association as well as neoclassical economics in U.S. universities.

Mannheim, Karl
1936 *Ideology and Utopia: An Introduction to the Sociology of Knowledge.* Tr. by Louis Wirth and Edward Shils. New York: Harcourt, Brace, and World. Significant effort to expand upon Marx's conception of ideology as false consciousness and to relate ideology to the problem of formulating a science of politics.

Mepham, John
1979 "The Theory of Ideology in *Capital.*" In John Mepham and David-Hillel Ruben (eds.), *Issues in Marxist Philosophy,* vol. 3: Epistemology, Science, Ideology, pp. 24–173. Sussex, England: Harvester Press. Argues that Marx's understanding of ideology was much clearer in *Capital* than in his earlier work. A rebuttal by Steve Butters and Kathryn Russell is offered.

Mermelstein, David
1970 *Economics and Mainstream Radical Critiques.* New York: Random House. Presents radical alternatives to traditional economics.

Mills, C. Wright
1962 *The Marxists.* New York: Dell Publishing. Argues that there can be no adequate social science without Marxism.

Moskvichov, L. N.
1974 *The End of Ideology Theory: Illusions and Reality: Critical Notes on a Bourgeois Conception.* Moscow: Progress Publishers. A useful overview of the origins and literature about the end-of-ideology theory, a look at the writing of Mannheim as the basis for liberal definitions of today, a critique of Weber and scientistic methodology.

Mullins, Willard A.
1972 "On the Concept of Ideology in Political Science." *American Political Science Review* LXVI (June), 498–510. Synthesis of various interpretations of ideology and an attempt to conceptualize ideology as well as to relate ideology to science.

Nicolaus, Martin
1969 "The Professional Organization of Sociology: A View from Below." *Antioch Review* XXIX (Fall), 375–387. Identifies the historical and contemporary foundations for conservative thinking in sociology, then relates these foundations to the workings of the American Sociological Association.

Ohmann, Richard
1969 "An Informal and Perhaps Unreliable Account of the Modern Language Association of America." *Antioch Review* XXIX (Fall), 329–347. Summary critique as well as discussion of the radical perspectives of the Modern Language Association of America.

Petras, James
1965 "Ideology and United States Political Scientists." *Science and Society* XXIX (Spring), 192–216. Identifies four ideological schools of political science as a basis for criticism of contemporary bourgeois studies of U.S. politics.

Rabb, Charles
1968 "Military 'Software.'" *Nation* CCVII (July 22), 46–48. Critical analysis of Pentagon-sponsored research in the social sciences.

Radosh, Ronald
1970 "The Bare-Knuckled Historian." *Nation* CCX (February 2), 108–110. An analysis of radical dissent within the American Historical Association.

Ransome, Harry Howe
1980 "Being Intelligent About Secret Intelligence Agencies." *American Political Science Review* LXXIV (March), 141–148. A review of twenty-four accounts of U.S. intelligence activities, including memoirs of former agents and government reports.

Sherman, Howard
1972 *Radical Political Economy: Capitalism and Socialism from a Marxist-Humanist Perspective.* New York: Basic Books. A radical synthesis of capitalism and socialism.

Sklar, Robert
1968 "Chomsky's Revolution in Linguistics." *Nation* CCVII (September 9), 213–217. Brief review of the life and works of Noam Chomsky. Relates Chomsky's revolution in linguistics to Thomas Kuhn's arguments on the structure of scientific revolutions.

Somit, Albert, and Joseph Tanenhaus
1967 *The Development of American Political Science.* Boston: Allyn and Bacon. Traces divergent tendencies in the field of political science from its origins in the late nineteenth century when the German university served as the model for contemporary efforts to formulate a science of politics.

Spiro, Thomas
1969 "Science and the Relevance of Relevance." *Antioch Review* XXIX (Fall), 387–403. Review of radical dissent within the community of scientists.

Sugerman, Albert G.
1968 "Michigan, Ché and the CIA." *New Republic* CLIX (November 9), 9–10. Analysis of how military research at the University of Michigan led to the capture and death of Ché Guevara in Bolivia.

Surkin, Marvin
1969 "Sense and Nonsense in Politics." *PS* II (Fall), 573–581. Critical examination of the ideological underpinnings of contemporary political science.

Sweezy, Paul M.
1970 "Toward a Critique of Economics." *Monthly Review* II (Spring), 1–8, and as Warner Modular Publication Reprint 43, 1973. Sharply distinguishes between marginalist and Marxist economics, while favoring the latter.

Trilateral Commission
1975–1978 *Task Force Reports, 1–7; The Crisis of Democracy* by Michel J. Crozier, Samuel P. Huntington, and Joji Watanuki; and *Task Force Reports, 9–14.* New York: New York University Press. The policy reports of scholars and policymakers from Japan, North America, and Western Europe.

U.S., Congress, House of Representatives
1976 *The Select Committee's Investigative Record.* Reprinted in *Village Voice* XXI (February 16), 70–92. Suppressed report of the Pike Committee on covert intelligence operations in the United States and abroad.

U.S., Congress, Senate
1968 *Defense Department Sponsored Foreign Affairs Research.* Washington, D.C.: Committee on Foreign Relations. Parts 1 and 2, May. Investigation into the dominance of Pentagon-sponsored research in North American and foreign universities.

1976 *Foreign and Military Intelligence.* Final Report of the Select Committee to Study Governmental Operations. Washington, D.C.

Viorst, Milton
1976 "FBI Mayhem." *New York Review of Books* XXIII (March 18), 21–28. Analysis of FBI repression of economics professor, Peter Bohmer, and support of right-wing terrorist activities in San Diego.

Weinstein, James
1970 "Can a Historian be a Socialist Revolutionary?" *Socialist Revolution* I (May–June), 97–106. Analysis of Marxist criticism within the discipline of history.

Wills, Garry
1976 "The CIA from Beginning to End." *New York Review of Books* XXII (January 22), 23–33. Overview and analysis of the CIA's intrusion upon the cultural life of the United States.

Wolf, Eric R., and Joseph G. Jorgensen
1970 "Anthropology on the Warpath in Thailand." *New York Review of Books* XV (November 19), 26 ff. A discussion of documents implicating U.S. social scientists in counterinsurgency activities in Thailand.

Wolfe, Alan
1969 "Practicing the Pluralism We Preach: Internal Processes in the American Political Science Association." *Antioch Review* XX (Fall), 352–373. Exposé of the

structure, procedures, and ruling clique of the American Political Science Association by a leader of the radical Caucus for a New Political Science.

1970 "The Professional Mystique." In Marvin Surkin and Alan Wolfe (eds.), *An End to Political Science*, pp. 288–309. New York: Basic Books. States that there is a bias in the methods and means by which professional social scientists seek understandings of reality and argues that without change in the rigidity with which academic professionals study politics, all other reforms will be meaningless.

Politics and the Science of Politics in Comparative Inquiry

Inquiry into the nature of politics seeks to incorporate methods of science. This is not simply a contemporary phenomenon, but one that dates well before the nineteenth century. In this chapter attention is focused on the search to formulate, and the struggle to maintain, a paradigm in the field of comparative politics. First three approaches that have dominated the field during the past century are examined: the traditional, behavioral, and postbehavioral approaches. Next, the historical roots and the fundamental premises of the paradigmatic search are looked at. On the one hand, positivist thought and the legacy of thinking and conceptualization that have shaped the movement to establish what is called the orthodox paradigm are examined. In this regard the early positivists, the early political sociologists, and the early behavioralists are identified and briefly discussed. On the other hand, historicist thought in the movement to establish a radical paradigm is examined, and the early historicists as well as the later historicist influences and trends are identified. Finally, the characteristics of these two dominant paradigms in comparative politics are contrasted and compared.

THE SEARCH FOR PARADIGMS (SYNTHESIZING THE FIELD OF COMPARATIVE ANALYSIS)

Contemporary students of politics generally distinguish among three approaches in their search for a science of politics. These are the traditional, behavioral, and postbehavioral approaches. All three approaches, which are discussed below, have been used in the study of comparative politics.

Three Approaches

The *traditional approach* historically interrelated fact and value in the study of comparative politics. During the early twentieth century, however, its orientation shifted to the study of the institutions of individual countries. As such, the traditional approach became noncomparative, descriptive, parochial, and static (Macridis 1955). The traditional approach focused analysis on the structure of the state, elections, and political parties. It tended to describe political institutions without attempting to compare them, other than to identify types, such as parliamentary in contrast to presidential institutions. Often traditional studies centered on the evolution of certain formal institutions, tracing, for example, the origin of the British parliamentary system to the Magna Carta. Then, too, there was concern with legal forms and prescriptions; the study of the various branches of government, for instance, referred to constitutional and legal provisions. Traditional studies usually limited their examination to Western European institutions, especially the so-called representative democracies of Great Britain, France, Germany, and Switzerland. This parochialism combined with attention to such questions as sovereignty and the nature of constitutions accounted for the essentially static character of the traditional approach.

The *behavioral approach* was a reaction to the speculation of theory that offered explication, inference, and judgments based on norms or authoritative rules and standards as well as to the Western ethnocentrism, formalism, and description characteristic of the contemporary traditional approach. A 1944 report of the American Political Science Association criticized the field of comparative politics as narrow in its descriptive analysis of foreign institutions and advocated a mixture of methods and designs to achieve a "total" science of social engineering. Another report a decade later called for systematic empirical research, including the elaboration of classificatory schemes, conceptualization at various levels of abstraction, hypothesizing, and testing of hypotheses by empirical data (Macridis and Cox 1953). These reports were to serve as the basis for the behavioral approach to the study of politics that accompanied most of the research in the rapidly expanding field of comparative politics during the 1950s and 1960s.

The goal of behavioral research, according to one of its chief advocates, is to explain "why people behave politically as they do, and why, as a result, political processes and systems function as they do" (Eulau 1963). The

TABLE 3.1
Three Approaches to Comparative Politics: Some Characteristics

Traditional Approach	Behavioral Approach	Postbehavioral Approach
Interrelates fact and value; speculative	Separates fact from value	Fact and value tied to action and relevancy
Prescriptive and normative	Nonprescriptive, objective, and empirical	Humanistically and problem-oriented; normative
Qualitative	Quantitative	Qualitative and quantitative
Concerned with irregularities and regularities	Concerned with uniformities and regularities	Concerned with regularities and irregularities
Configurative and non-comparative; focuses on individual countries	Comparative; focuses on several countries	Comparative, focuses on several countries
Ethnocentric; focuses especially on Western European "democracies"	Ethnocentric, especially concerned with Anglo-American model	Especially Third World oriented
Descriptive, parochial, and static	Abstract, ideologically conservative, and static	Theoretical, radical, and change-oriented
Focuses on formal (constitutional and governmental) structure	Focuses on formal and informal (group) structures and functions	Focuses on class and group relations and conflict
Historical or ahistorical	Ahistorical	Holistic

tendency of behavioral research in politics has been toward the construction of logically consistent models from which "truth" is deductively derived. Images of empirical reality undermine the pure theory of such formal models of politics, and behavioralists usually seek some mixture of experience and theory, while striving to mold the study of politics with a rigorously scientific discipline modeled on the methods of the natural sciences.

In an effort to differentiate between the behavioral and the traditional modes of inquiry, the major tenets of the "behavioral credo" have been identified. These tenets include (1) *regularities* or uniformities in political behavior, which can be expressed in generalizations or theory; (2) *verification* or the testing of the validity of such generalizations or theory; (3) *techniques* for seeking and interpreting data; (4) *quantification* and measurement in the recording of data; (5) *values* as distinguished between propositions relating to ethical evaluation and those relating to empirical explanation; (6) *systematization* of research; (7) *pure science*, or the seeking of understanding and explanation of behavior before utilization of knowledge for solution of societal problems; and (8) *integration* of political research with that of other social sciences (Easton 1965: 7).

In the challenge to the traditional approach, political scientists referred to their alternative as the behavioral revolution. During the 1960s, however, there was a great deal of dissatisfaction with research and teaching that was oriented toward making the study of politics into a more rigorously scientific discipline. This dissatisfaction evolved into what one major proponent of the behavioral revolution called the *postbehavioral revolution*. Future oriented toward "relevancy" and "action," the credo of postbehavioralism consisted of a number of tenets. First, substance precedes technique so that urgent problems of society become more important than the tools of investigation. Second, behavioralism itself is ideologically conservative and limited to abstraction rather than to the reality of the times in crisis. Third, science cannot be evaluatively neutral, fact cannot be separated from value, and value premises must be related to knowledge. Fourth, intellectuals must bear the responsibility of their society, defend human values of civilization, and not become mere technicians isolated and protected from the issues and problems that envelop their work. Fifth, the intellectual must put knowledge to work and engage in reshaping society, and sixth, the intellectual must enter the struggles of the day and participate in the politicalization of the professions and academic institutions (Easton 1969; see Melanson 1973 for an elaboration of a post-behavioral view, Kirn 1977 for distinctions between postbehavioralism and behavioralism, and Stretton 1969 for an overview).

The confrontation and shifting emphases of the above approaches, as well as the "revolutionary" replacement of one approach by another as political science has evolved through time, make clear the struggle of social science to seek a paradigm. Thomas Kuhn's use of paradigm has recently interested political scientists. His notion of paradigm relates to "research firmly based upon one or more past scientific achievements, achievements that some particular scientific community acknowledges for a time as supplying the foundation for its further practice" (Kuhn 1970: 10). Those achievements become paradigmatic—examples of actual scientific practice. These examples "include law, theory, application, and instrumentation together—[providing] models from which spring particular coherent traditions of scientific research."

Newton conceived the first accepted paradigm for physical optics. His predecessors, who advocated one or another variant of Epicurean, Aristotelian, or Platonic theory, for example, tended to build their respective fields anew. Each lacked a set of standards or methods, and thus they all tended to direct much of their attention to the explanations of other schools. A true science of physical optics evolved once an identifiable paradigm had emerged. Thus, a paradigm is a scientific community's perspective of the world, its set of beliefs and commitments—conceptual, theoretical, methodological, instrumental. The paradigm guides a scientific community's selection of problems, evaluation of data, and advocacy of theory.

Upon first appearance a paradigm's impact may well be limited. A paradigm gains in status as it becomes more successful than a competing paradigm in solving problems recognized as important. Let us briefly review the writings of some social scientists who have debated the existence or nonexistence of paradigms in political science.

Identification of Paradigms

In discerning the nature of a paradigm, Kuhn acknowledged the difficulty of discovering rules that guide scientific traditions. The concepts, laws, and theories of science are found historically in prior experience, not in the abstract, and they become the basis of scientific learning and initiation into one's profession. They thus shape and condition one's orientations. The paradigm to which one subscribes, however, guides research by direct modeling and abstracted rules. Paradigms establish the limits of what is possible, the boundaries of acceptable inquiry. A successful paradigm then enables a scientific community to maintain criteria for the selection of problems to be used for finding solutions. Scientists working with a successful paradigm, however, might be unable to perceive possibilities beyond their own assumptions. The consequence of their parochialism may be a failure to keep adherents from shifting their attention to competing modes of scientific activity. A new scientific revolution may ensue.

The literature on politics is confused because of varying interpretations of paradigms. This confusion is partly clarified by distilling from Kuhn a number of phases through which science tends to pass (see Effrat 1972).

First, there is the *preparadigmatic phase* in which no single theoretical approach or school predominates in the scientific community, although a number of such approaches or schools are in competition with each other. Second, there is the *paradigmatic phase*, in which the scientific community adheres to a dominant paradigm. Third, there is the *crisis phase*. The dominant paradigm is subject to challenge and revision, and new paradigms may evolve and old ones may be revived, giving rise to debate and competition among a variety of perspectives. Fourth, there is the *phase of scientific revolution*, which occurs when the scientific community shifts to significantly different paradigms.

The traditional, behavioral, and postbehavioral approaches described earlier do not precisely fit Kuhn's definition and discussion of paradigms, and they will continue to be identified simply as varying approaches to comparative politics. Within these approaches, however, the struggle to find a dominant paradigm is evident. Since Kuhn's work on the use of paradigms, the behavioralists have alluded to themselves as "normal scientists," in recognition of the fact that they accept and work with a dominant theory approved by the scientific community. But, argued Wolin (1968 and 1969), no such scientific revolution has occurred, and no new and dominant theory such as the one described by Kuhn has been erected. In fact, Wolin insisted, no dominant theoretical paradigm of normal political scientists yet exists. He acknowledged, however, that even though there is no extraordinary theory such as the one Newton produced, there is a framework of guiding assumptions—"the ideological paradigm reflective of the same political community"—that applies to political science (Wolin 1969: 1064; see Sigler 1962; Ricci 1977; and Heyl 1975 for a similar and updated perspective; see Ball 1976 for an attempt to transcend paradigms).

Beardsley (1974) essentially agreed with Wolin that neither in the past nor in the present has a paradigm along the lines identified by Kuhn been established for political science, although Beardsley believed that political science can and should establish one in the future. He disagreed with David Truman's (1965) assumption that since the 1880s political science has evinced something similar to a paradigm. And he described as ambiguous Gabriel Almond's (1966) identification of an unscientific paradigm that established itself in the eighteenth and nineteenth centuries. Both Truman and Almond saw political science acquiring a new paradigm, however. Truman's paradigm is associated with a renewal of interest in the political system, in political theory, and in science. Almond's "scientific" paradigm is tied to a statistical approach, "the differentiation and specification of variables and the assumptions of probability and reflexivity in their relations" (Almond, in Beardsley 1974: 54), and the system.

Comparative political scientists, however, tend to search for paradigms in the past and present experience of the discipline. Samuel P. Huntington (1974), for example, noted three directions in U.S. politics. One direction, based on "progressive theory," stressed conflict and emphasized economic interests and differences between elites and masses. In opposition to the ideas of these progressive historians, political scientists developed their notions of pluralism. Influenced by early efforts to analyze the role of groups in the shaping of public life, these political scientists stressed the multiplicity of groups in U.S. politics. This dichotomy between the progressive historians and the pluralist political scientists prevailed until the Second World War. Thereafter, the "consensus" interpretation of U.S. politics was elaborated.

Holt and Richardson (1970) identified the competing paradigmatic tendencies in comparative politics. They are structural-functional analysis (the work of Gabriel Almond is especially representative); systems analysis, which usually incorporated functional elements (such as David Easton's input-output model and Karl Deutsch's efforts to emulate Norbert Wiener's theory of cybernetics through the formulation of a "nerves of government" system); psychological analysis (Harold Lasswell and Lucian Pye); and analysis of rational behavior to justify the existence of a *positive* science of politics (Anthony Downs's work). Most of these tendencies, they argued, are heuristic schema—interesting ways of looking at political phenomena. They sought a deductively powerful and conceptually rich paradigm, along with solutions for basic technical and methodological problems that hamper cross-cultural comparative research.

Four scientific revolutions in the study of politics are identified by Rogowski (1978). During the 1930s and 1940s the formal-legal assumptions of the past century were replaced by attention to studies of psychology and coercion; during the 1950s behavioralism was in effect; during the 1960s the Parsonian social model, with its related theory of political culture and system, dominated; and in the 1970s there was a shift, in the Kuhnian sense, toward theories of rational choice in such areas as conflict and strategy, coalitions, participation and influence, institutions, collective choice, and constitutional choice and legitimacy.

According to Eugene Meehan (1968), the search by social scientists for deductive explanations has been largely an unsuccessful enterprise. Deductive analysis subsumes particular cases under universal laws of explanation. Analysis moves from the general to the particular, and deduction implies that the inference of a particular fact is to be explained from a generalization. Thus, an event can be explained only in relation to an established general law or empirical generalization. Such laws or generalizations are deduced from higher sets of generalizations or theories, and all are logically held together. Meehan argued that both social scientists and philosophers of science usually base their explanations on deductive explanation. Thus, most efforts to systematize social inquiry are based on the deductive paradigm of explanation. Although some traditionalists in social science reject such efforts, indeed they reject the search for explanation altogether, the deductive paradigm itself has rarely been attacked by social scientists or philosophers of science. They have accepted this paradigm uncritically, while failing to recognize its limited usefulness, primarily because social science cannot emulate the successful deductive inquiry of the natural sciences.

The broad debate on the use of paradigms provoked Albert Hirschman (1970) to attack the search for paradigms and the accompanying impatience for theoretical formulation. He believed that the consequence is a hindrance to understanding and he argued that paradigms guide explanation and analysis. Through an examination of two books on Latin America, one laced with deductively contrived paradigmatic explanation and the other based on a feeling for and an intimacy with the subject matter as well as conclusions drawn with diffidence and circumspection, Hirschman (1970: 339) concluded that "large-scale social change typically occurs as a result of a unique constellation of highly disparate events and is therefore amenable to paradigmatic thinking only in a very special sense."

HISTORICAL ROOTS AND FUNDAMENTAL PREMISES
OF THE PARADIGMATIC SEARCH

Two styles of thought provide the foundation of comparative political analysis. One, historicism, grew out of German academic debate late in the nineteenth century (Adorno et al. 1976). It was embraced by Hegel, Marx, and others. Sometimes referred to as perspectivism, subjectivism, relativism, and instrumentalism, historicism dealt with history. The German sociologist, Karl Mannheim, considered historicism as an extraordinary intellectual force that epitomized "world views" and permeated everyday thinking. Eugene Miller (1972: 792) characterized the philosopher Karl Popper's understanding of historicism as "the view that the main task of the social scientist is to discover the laws by which whole societies develop and, on the basis of these laws of historical development, to make predictions about the future," while the German historian, Friedrich Meinecke, used the term in reference to the singular or unique character of all social phenomena, an emphasis that originated with some eighteenth-century writers. A second style of thought, positivism, served as a reaction to historicism. David Hume was the chief precursor of positivism, which grew out of classical British empiricism and apparently was the basis of positivism in contemporary political science. Partially influenced by Henri Saint-Simon who stressed science, knowledge, and technology (Manuel 1962), Auguste Comte elaborated some principles of positivism, despite having been molded in the historicist tradition. These and other thinkers provided some of the principles of positivism, which today emphasize empirical science—with concepts, laws, and theories that reflect occurrences in the real world. Knowledge is based on objectivity and on observations of real experience. Let me now identify some of the assumptions underlying these two styles of thought. Each style relates to a dominant paradigm in comparative politics (see Figure 3.1).

Positivist Thought: The Legacy of Thinkers and Concepts
in the Movement to Establish an Orthodox Paradigm

A reconstruction of positivist thought suggests the following tendencies. First, scientific principles are based on sensory experience and thus are independent of time, place, and even circumstance, although they may be

FIGURE 3.1
Theoretical and Conceptual Roots of Dominant Paradigms in Comparative Politics

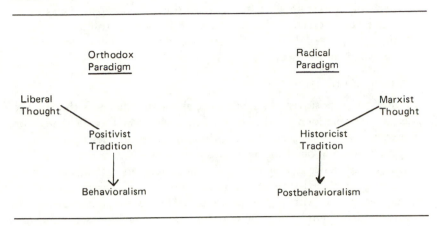

revised according to subsequent experience. Such principles are the foundation of the empirical sciences, which stress laws, concepts, and theories that differ from metaphysical accounts of the world as well as from nonempirical endeavors in logic and pure mathematics. Second, generalizations about the external world are meaningful only if they are constructed from or tested by the raw material of experience. Knowledge based on experience is objective. One cannot know what one cannot see, touch, or hear.

Positivists (including some early positivists who had been historicists) criticize the early historicists for theorizing about broadly conceived questions, for utilizing data to illustrate rather than to test their theories, and for failing to tie theory to data. The historicists, it is argued, postulated overly ambitious theories of history rather than engaging in any meticulous empirical testing of hypotheses and formulations of concepts. Historicism thus was vulnerable because of its emphasis on universal history, in particular because of its predictions of an imminent universality of democracy. Historicism often stressed evolutionary theory, unilinear and deterministic in scope. (See Popper 1957, for an elaboration of the antihistorical view and Himka 1975, for a refutation of Popper.)

The positivist reaction to historicism, especially that which emanated from German academia and influenced U.S. political scientists at the turn of this century, moved the study of politics toward abstract, formal legal and configurative studies and toward evolutionary theory (Eckstein 1963: 9–16). At the same time a school of political sociologists, broadly ranged in their theory and dedicated to formulating a science of politics, emerged from their

European experience. These early political sociologists in turn influenced contemporary social science thinkers to use the behavioral approach in comparative inquiry. The theoretical and conceptual contributions of these three schools constitute what we shall call the orthodox paradigm in comparative politics today. Let us examine each school of thinkers and then identify the legacy of the liberal and positivist concepts upon which the orthodox paradigm is based.

THE EARLY POSITIVISTS

The roots of positivist thought, especially as it influences the study of politics today, are found in the works of three thinkers. David Hume is considered to be the precursor to positivist thought and its conception of science. Hume reasoned in his *Treatise of Human Nature* that knowledge based on experience is objective and that statements are factually meaningful only if verified through empirical observation. These notions later became associated with logical positivism. Hume's thought provided the epistemological foundations for contemporary behavioral science (Miller 1971 although Conniff 1976 takes exception to this generally accepted view). Writing about obedience and authority, Hume believed that usually it is best to accept the authority of those who actually govern, as long as the existing rulers are not oppressive. Government should be stable, power depends on obedience, and social order based on inequality may be useful and acceptable.

Auguste Comte, who together with Saint-Simon was a founder of sociology, was concerned with establishing a new science of society, and Comte conceived of a system based on three stages of philosophical thought: theological, metaphysical, and positive. In the third stage one could observe and understand facts with empirical certainty. Sociology, he believed, was the most advanced and complicated of the many sciences. In his *Cours de philosophie positive* he stressed that progress is dependent on the consolidation of authoritarian *order*, and that progress emanates from stages of evolution.

Herbert Spencer, a philosopher of evolutionism, was influenced by the Darwinian theory of natural selection (Perrin 1976). In his works, *Social Statics* and *The Man Versus the State*, he differed with Comte's notion of authoritarianism by advocating that the state should play a minimum role in society, and the state should not be allowed to intervene in private enterprise. Through evolution, he believed, *equilibrium* would result in a perfect society.

These three thinkers and their ideas stimulated a reaction to historicism. Whereas historicist studies tended to combine thought with data, the emphasis on abstract political analysis resulted in a separation of content and form from political thought. This accounted for the frequent isolation of political thought from the study of political institutions in the curriculum of political science, a development mentioned in the initial chapter that profoundly influenced the study of comparative political institutions — constitutions and structure of government. A stress on the hard facts found in formal legal documents and an adherence to a purported neutral empiricism often led to superficial and mechanistic interpretations of politics. Political analysis also tended to become configurative (focused on a particular country) and not comparative. This trend was not only a consequence of the formal legal attention to government but was also a response to the influence of and attention to nationalism, as well as a reaction to broad speculative theory. Evolutionism in politics also was a reaction to historicism. Evolutionary theory focused in a detailed fashion on the rise of the state in its primitive form and on its evolution through stages to more complex forms.

THE EARLY POLITICAL SOCIOLOGISTS

A number of thinkers were deeply interested in constructing a science of political and social life, thinkers who were influenced by positivism (Giddens 1974) but were not limited to the study of formal distinctions among types of governments. Instead they contructed broad theories of politics and incorporated a wide range of data into their analyses. They were interested in questions of power and rule, and their contributions were especially significant for sociology and comparative politics.

Gaetano Mosca, a Sicilian political theorist and practitioner, was one of the first to distinguish between elites and masses and to build a science of politics based on that formulation. Specifically, Mosca was concerned with the political or ruling class, defined as the people who directly participate in government or influence it. His conception of the ruling class, elaborated in *Elementi di scienza política*, is narrower than that of Marx, who was concerned with an economic class of property owners and employers who ruled politically. Thus, Mosca's ruling class is a *political class* that represents the interests of important and influential *groups*, especially in parliamentary democracies. Mosca's detailed examination of this political class reveals its divisions as well as the lower strata of civil servants, managers, and intellectuals. Participation is dependent on *competition* among the segments of the political class. The political class, however, undergoes changes in composition through the recruitment of members from the lower strata and through the incorporation of new social groups. This phenomenon is known as the *circulation of elites*.

Vilfredo Pareto, an Italian aristocrat and liberal, also elaborated on the circulation of elites in *Cours d'économie politique* and other works, but Pareto distinguished more sharply and systematically than did Mosca between the rulers and the ruled in every society. He referred to governing elites and nongoverning elites, arguing that correlations could be found in the degree of political and social influence and position in the hierarchy of wealth of any and all societies. Pareto conceived of society as a system of interdependent forces moving together in *equilibrium*.

Roberto Michels, a German sociologist and a naturalized Italian, was influenced by the ideas of both Mosca and Pareto. Although he criticized classical theory, which viewed governments as divided among democracy, aristocracy, and tyranny, Michels argued that in fact governments are always led by the few. Democracy and a large bureaucracy engendered by the complexity of an advancing society are incompatible, a thesis he attempted to demonstrate in *Political Parties*. In this regard Michels differed with his predecessors over the assumption that competitive struggle within the political class would allow access to political power. He demonstrated the impossibility, in his view, of ending the division between the rulers and the ruled within complex society. He agreed with the Marxist interpretation of history, that history consists of a series of class struggles, tying that conception to his own doctrine that class struggle would culminate in the creation of new oligarchies.

Max Weber, a German liberal and political sociologist, wrote prolifically on many methodological and theoretical subjects. He was concerned with whether the German bourgeoisie could assume the leadership of the nation. In *The Protestant Ethic and the Spirit of Capitalism* he examined implications of motivation and drives of the entrepreneurial individual in capitalist economies. In his work on economic and social history he analyzed the evolution of Western civilization in terms of a developing rationality brought about through the impact of capitalism and technology and science, as well as the gradual specialization of the bureaucracy. Weber also referred to ideal types or conceptual formulations, which describe and classify phenomena that approximate empirical probability. His attention to the question of authority was premised on ideal types—traditional, charismatic, and legal authority. An unequal distribution of powers and therefore opportunity, he believed, became a basis for class, but he also focused on groups and status. In summary, his concern with the stages of development and the rationalization of social activity, his focus on the groups that compete for power, and his perception of the ideal types of authority served as one of the intellectual foundations of contemporary social science and contributed substantially to the orthodox paradigm of contemporary politics.

During the early twentieth century comparative politics at first reacted against the broad sweep of propositions inherent in the work of the early sociologists. The ideas of Mosca, Pareto, and Weber in particular were common to the mainstream of comparative political inquiry, and were incorporated into political science theory. At the same time, the early sociologists influenced the study of parties and pressure groups. This attention to informal rather than formal legal political institutions was tied to conceptions of pluralism, especially as related to beliefs about political competition and distribution of power among semiautonomous groups and interests in society. This tendency was carried on later in the writings of Arthur F. Bentley and David Truman.

Then too there was an effort, as demonstrated in James Bryce's *Modern Democracies* or Carl Friedrich's *Constitutional Government and Democracy*, to combine theory and data through a synthesis of configurative studies in comparative works. Such works tended, at least implicitly, to envisage a comparison of political systems and to analyze data within structural and functional categories. Friedrich referred frequently to Mosca, Pareto, Michels, and Weber, and his work is an early example of the systemic and structural-functional analysis that explicitly came to dominate comparative inquiry toward the middle of the century (see Eckstein 1963: 18–23 for a discussion of Bryce's and Friedrich's contributions).

In summary, then, the early sociologists were interested in formulating a science of politics. They constructed broad theories and sought data through empirical inquiry. They were inclined to examine informal institutions and processes and not become entrapped by legal-formal and configurative studies. They were influenced by evolutionary theory and viewed societies as progressing through successive stages of development. They also emphasized the division of labor and specificity of institutions as societies reached advanced stages. They were particularly concerned with refuting a Marxist conception of the ruling class by showing a continual circulation of elites, which in turn precluded the existence in most societies of a stable and closed ruling class. They attempted to demonstrate that classlessness was impossible given the hierarchical structure of most societies.

THE EARLY BEHAVIORALISTS

After the Second World War, comparative politics rapidly expanded to the study of the non-Western world as old empires collapsed and new nations were created. There was also a gradual awareness that comparative political inquiry no longer adhered to the assumption of an inevitable representative democracy in the development of nations. Totalitarianism in Germany and Italy, authoritarianism in most of the socialist nations, and a highly differentiated Third World shattered the traditional conception of representative democracy. The enlargement of the field into areas and aspects of politics previously little studied was accompanied by a recognition that the study of politics should become more scientific. Consequently, new concepts, methods, and rigorous testing procedures became commonplace in the attempt to systematize the study of political behavior into a science.

The evolution of political science as a behavioral science was related to the discipline's incorporation of quantitative procedures for the testing of theory. Comparative politics was especially influenced by sociology and cultural anthropology. In comparative politics there was a movement toward two levels of analysis. The first level consisted of the introduction of broad frameworks of analysis, somewhat in the tradition of the early political sociologists. Talcott Parsons, for example, in the *Social System* (1951) attempted to build a systematic theory of action. Explicitly acknowledging the influence of Pareto and Weber upon his work, Parsons elaborated on his structural-functional level of analysis, and alluded to the functional prerequisites of social systems. Later, he identified five sets of pattern variables: affectivity versus affective neutrality; self-orientation versus collective orientation; universalism versus particularism; achievement versus ascription; and specificity versus diffuseness. Finally, he described the characteristics of systems of human action: they are profoundly influenced by physical, chemical, and biological properties; they are boundary-maintaining systems; and they are related to culture and shared symbolic patterns. Parsons was thus attempting to introduce a broad framework, showing the interrelationship of all social phenomena. At the same time, he was setting forth new categories that permitted analysis at a second, narrower level, where political phenomena would be subject to rigorous qualitative analysis.

Parsons's work contributed substantially to the growth of behavioralism in comparative political analysis. His attention to systems stimulated David Easton to formulate a systemic theory of politics based on stability and equilibrium. Parsons's elaboration of structural-functional categories influenced not only fellow sociologists, such as Marion Levy and Robert Merton, but also Gabriel Almond, one of the major figures in comparative politics. Parsons's identification of pattern variables moved Almond and later Sidney Verba to the study of political culture, and Parsons's concern with a theory of action and his concern for change in society provoked Almond and others to relate their concerns with system and culture to the study of development. Broad frameworks for the study of political behavior on a narrower categorical level, however, did not stimulate interest in the study of elites and in questions of power and class. These concerns of the early sociologists were often obscured by the early behavioral writings. Instead the study of elites became the endeavor of those political scientists and sociologists who focused on power in the local community. Floyd Hunter and C. Wright Mills were prominent in such study, and Robert Dahl attacked their work. Not until the mid-1960s, was there a reversal of interest on the part of those studying comparative politics in the study of elites. These four central concerns—system, culture, development, and elites—are examined in considerable detail in Chapters 5 to 8.

Historicist Thought: Past and Present
in the Movement to Establish a Radical Paradigm

Historicists take exception to positivist thought by arguing that data based on sensations are not acquired in unbiased situations. The mind is active, not passive, and it selects and shapes experience according to prior awareness. One cannot determine if the source of experience corresponds to the perspective of the objective world. Furthermore, historicists argue that there are a variety of views, not a single view, of the objective world. Distinctive perspectives of the world are found from one epoch or culture to another. Truth is relative to the world view characteristic of the epoch or culture to which one belongs. Thus, world views are temporal and relative, not absolute. Writing in the historicist tradition, Hegel and Marx dealt with this problem by showing that a succession of historical epochs would lead to the creation of a final epoch, which would represent the historical process as a whole (summary of arguments from Miller 1972: 800–801).

With these premises of historicism in mind, we turn to an assessment of the impact of historicism on social science and the study of politics. Historicism questioned the positivistic belief in the progressive character of scientific development. Science, it is argued, must be understood in terms of history. Thomas Kuhn, to whom reference was made earlier, exemplifies the antipositivist position of contemporary historians of science. He argued that the scientific community is governed by a prevailing paradigm and that the paradigm represents the historical perspectives of the scientific community. The paradigm guides and determines the selection of problems, data, and theory—until another paradigm takes its place. This process represents what Kuhn called the "scientific revolution." Within this context the positivist and historicist movements have been involved in the search for a paradigm, and behavioralism and postbehavioralism are the latest manifestations of this hundred-year-old struggle. Liberalism and positivism clearly have reigned in the study of politics, but the antipositivist historicist tradition and the effort to establish a radical paradigm remain ever challenging. In a penetrating review and an analysis of these two conflicting paradigms, Eugene Miller (1972: 797–798) affirmed that "historicism is a far more potent and pervasive force today than a half century ago . . . yet surprisingly, it tends to be less visible or manifest now, perhaps because of its very pervasiveness."

We turn now to a brief look at some of the early historicists, then to the political sociologists who carried on in the historicist tradition, and finally to those contemporary writers who contribute to postbehavioralism.

THE EARLY HISTORICISTS

The roots of historicist thought, especially as it influences the radical study of politics today, are found in the works of several German thinkers. Georg Hegel, a German philosopher and nationalist, was concerned with a conception of the authoritarian state. His approach in *History of Philosophy* and *The Science of Logic* was a historicist approach as he searched for reality and for truth. His thought embraced the experience of many generations and civilizations, both past and present, and his search for truth involved a process of stages. As described by one of his critics, "What Hegel has in mind is that each stage in the forward movement of the mind negates the preceding stage, yet could not exist without its having that preceding stage to reject; it is built upon its antecedent. That which vanishes in the process must itself be looked upon as essential, yet not as something fixed which is cut off from what is true, as something outside. Nor is the true to be looked upon as something similarly static, dead, and only positive" (Friedrich 1954: xxviii-xxix). From this process emanates Hegel's conception of dialectics and his triad of thesis, antithesis, and synthesis. New levels of understanding are reached in synthesis.

Hegel distinguished three powers within the state and tried to fit them into his dialectical scheme. One power was to determine the universal will (legislative power), another to settle particular matters in conformity with the universal will (executive power), and a third to will with ultimate decision (sovereign power). Sovereign power symbolizes the unity of the state, and it relates to the other two powers as synthesis relates to thesis and antithesis. Here his conception of state is unclear and different from that of Marx, who characterized Hegel's thought as idealist and as a defense of the Prussian state. So too is Hegel's conception of social classes. He saw society as divided into three classes: the agricultural class, those who work or derive income from the land; the business class, all who work in commerce or industry; and the universal class of magistrates and civil servants. Unlike Marx, Hegel failed to distinguish landowners from peasants or employers from the employed; nor did he distinguish merchants from industrialists, or owners of property from workers who have nothing other than their labor to sell.

Karl Marx and Frederick Engels were German thinkers who took a special interest in the distinct roles of different classes in the process of production and in their relations to the state. From previous philosophy Marx and Engels retained a materialist conception of the world and dialectic thought, and they fused the two into a world outlook that posed a struggle for emancipation of the working class and a transformation of society. In the preface to his *Contribution to the Critique of Political Economy*, Marx stated that "relations of production correspond to a definite stage of the development of the material forces of production. The totality of these relations of production constitutes the economic structure of society—the real foundation on which legal and political superstructures arise and to which definite forms of social consciousness correspond." Relations and forces of production are tied to class and class conflict. One's class depends on ownership of property and the type of property owned. The proletarian owns his or her labor, which can be sold to others. The slave does not own his or her labor, and the serf is obliged to work for the lord at some periods. The capitalist, in contrast, owns the means of production, which allows the appropriation of a large portion of other people's work. Thus, these classes are unequal and an exploitation of class by class is evident. Therefore, the history of all societies has witnessed class struggle. Society divided by class requires a state or an organized hierarchy to govern. This state serves the interests of or can become an instrument of class rule. Thus, if a society becomes classless, the state will disappear. Since these ideas are discussed in a subsequent chapter, let us now focus briefly on some trends that carry the historicist tradition to the postbehavioralism of today.

LATER HISTORICIST INFLUENCES AND TRENDS

Another German thinker, the sociologist Karl Mannheim, was deeply committed to historicism. He believed that all thought is socially determined and historically variable, as is evident in his *Ideology and Utopia* and in his conceptions of "particular" and "total" ideologies. All thinking, including scientific inquiry, relates to a particular perspective and to each thinker's epoch and culture. This perspective provides an individual with beliefs and values as well as with concepts for the interpretation of experience. Ideology evolves from perspective. Ideology comprises beliefs and assumptions about the world that are accepted but not fully verified. Additionally, one's outlook is bound by inherited knowledge and beliefs as well as by social position.

Mannheim's approach differed considerably from the efforts of positivist sociologists to seek models in the natural sciences, to formulate empirical generalization into systems, and to place an overriding concern on rigor, quantifications, statistics, and so on. Exceptions to the domination of positivism in sociology, according to one critic (House 1976), are the classical sociology of some of the major social thinkers of the nineteenth century, the so-called Chicago school of sociology in the early part of the present century, and contemporary critical sociology, which since the crises of the 1960s has redefined the task of understanding social structure and process.

The competing efforts of the positivists and historicists in sociology were similar to those that emerged in political science, especially in the study of U.S. politics. In this regard Samuel Huntington (1974) identified three competing models of U.S. politics, but he distorted this use of models by calling them paradigms. The first, related to progressive theory, stressed class conflict and the significance of economic interests in history. This model was reflected in the works of Charles Beard, Frederick Jackson Turner, and others at the turn of this century. The reaction to this historical approach was set in motion by an emphasis on a pluralist model in connection with the emergence of the new discipline of political science in the late nineteenth century. Political scientists at that time were influenced by the systematic study of politics and government in German universities. The pluralist character of U.S. politics was seen in the role of multiple groups and interests in the shaping of public life.

The progressive model, advocated by historians, and the pluralist model, held in esteem by political scientists, were dominant until the Second World War. Thereafter, a consensus interpretation of U.S. politics, with Tocqueville as prophet, established itself in the writings of Louis Hartz, Daniel Bell, Seymour Martin Lipset, and others. The consensus interpretation influenced many historians who abandoned the progressive interpretation, in which sociologists promoted an "end to ideology" and models of equilibrium. Political scientists related the earlier pluralist analysis, evident first in Arthur Bentley and later in David Truman and Robert Dahl, to the consensus interpretation. The pluralist and consensus interpretation fits neatly into positivist notions about science, behavioralism, and empirical inquiry.

The postbehavioral attempt to link the past historicist and progressive interpretations to an antipositivist view of U.S. politics is evident in the writings of several political scientists. The revolt against positivism relied on the position of Kuhn and attacked the deductive explanation of the positivist conception of science and social science. John Gunnell (1969), for example, has stated that although a significant intellectual gap exists today between political science and the philosophy of science, political science derives its conception of science and empirical inquiry from a restricted segment of the literature dealing with the philosophy of science, namely that of logical empiricism.

Logical empiricism assumes a tie between the meaning and the verification of a statement; statements that cannot be verified are meaningless. Political scientists have derived from logical empiricism a basis of explanation known as the deductive model. According to this model the logic of social science must be compatible with the logic of natural science. However, faith in the unity of science is offset by the absence of an argument supporting the logical equivalence of the social and natural sciences. Notwithstanding references to the "scientific method," "scientific rules," and "scientific credo" in the prestigious theoretical literature of political science, political scientists seldom interpret the meaning of science beyond formal and empty statements relating to "generalization" or "proposition" or the like. Gunnell thus challenged the advocates of behavioralism who believe that within the philosophy of science there is a consensus favoring a positivist conception of scientific inquiry. Thorson (1970) joined the antipositivist revolt with a detailed examination of the links between science and social science, essentially revealing the misconceptions that pervade the political science literature. Wolin (1968 and 1969) attacked positivist behavioralism of political science; so too did Nun (1966), who moved his arguments toward a position of critical Marxism. Hollis (1977) drew a distinction by outlining two models of man.

SUMMARY COMPARISON OF DOMINANT PARADIGMS IN COMPARATIVE POLITICS

The movement toward the formulation of an orthodox paradigm has been traced from its positivist tradition, especially the logical empiricism that captivated many positivist thinkers of the late nineteenth century and the behavioralists of the mid–twentieth century. In part, the orthodox paradigm evolved as a reaction to the noncomparative, descriptive, parochial, and static character of the traditional approach, which focused on formal and legal aspects of government. The orthodox paradigm also incorporates a critique of traditional political thought, including Marxism, that interrelates fact and value in comparative analysis. Finally, the orthodox paradigm, despite the nonideological nature of inquiry which it advocates, in fact assimilates some liberal premises; for example, the separation of religion from government. Secularism in politics was accompanied by the liberal notion, in the tradition of John Locke and later of John Stuart Mill, that every person has the right to hold and profess an opinion, as long as the opinion is not seditious. A positive belief in the liberty of conscience was seen as a law of nature. These premises were to reinforce the pluralist and consensus interpretation of U.S. politics in the present century. (For background on the liberal and pluralist positions, see Ford 1970, Fox 1975, Garson 1974, and Smith 1964.)

The movement toward the formulation of a radical paradigm has been traced from its historicist origins and antipositivist reactions to the postbehavioralism of the mid–twentieth century. Historicism takes the position that science can only be understood in terms of history, and the radical paradigm draws its historicist assumptions from Marxist thought. Although

TABLE 3.2
Comparison of Dominant Paradigms in Comparative Politics

Characteristics	Orthodox Paradigm	Radical Paradigm
Thrust	Ahistorical Micro or macro Compartmentalized Disciplinary boundaries	Holistic Macro Unified Interdisciplinary
Unit of analysis	System, in equilibrium, stable	State, in conflict
Structure	Groups, interaction and civic culture	Classes, struggle between bourgeoisie and proletariat
Authority	Order decentralized with authority narrowly based within specialized units	Order centralized with scope of authority broad and general
Rulers	Diffused, dispersed among many centers, pluralist competition in decision making	Concentrated and unified in a dominant position of authority and decision making
Development	Evolutionary, unilinear, materialistic, progressive	Revolutionary, multilinear, materialistic, and humanistic in attention to needs of all people

Michael Harrington in his *Twilight of Capitalism* argues that a Marxist paradigm is firmly established today (especially in the socialist world), it is clear that in comparative politics and political science in general such a paradigm has not embedded itself. Instead, radicals and Marxists continue to challenge the dominant ideas of the discipline in their search for a new paradigm.

A comparison of the characteristics of the orthodox and radical paradigms is given in Table 3.2. Six general characteristics distinguish these paradigms in their interpretation of the most advanced, especially the capitalist, societies. First, the orthodox paradigm tends to be ahistorical in interpretation and analysis, a consequence of its micro orientation, its compartmentalized view of society, its rationalist orientation, and its focus on problems delimited by disciplinary boundaries. In contrast, the radical paradigm is holistic in interpretation and analysis. Its macro perspective views society as unified and nonrationalist in behavior, and its analysis is interdisciplinary. Second, whereas the orthodox paradigm focuses on stable systems whose elements are in equilibrium, the radical paradigm relates politics to a conception of the state in concert with a hierarchy of constituencies in conflict with the masses of society. Third, the orthodox paradigm envisages an ideal civic culture of participation and interaction among diverse groups that compete for power and influence in decision making. In contrast, the radical paradigm offers a class analysis of society. Classes and the conflict between them are defined by their relationship to the mode and forces of production.

Fourth, both paradigms relate to authority, with the orthodox stressing decentralized order in an increasingly specialized society and the radical emphasizing centralized authority with a broad and general base. Fifth, the orthodox paradigm views rulers as diffused and rationally dispersed among many centers of power or as representative of broad segments of population, and the radical paradigm sees rulers as dominant, concentrated socially, and unified in political and economic interests. Finally, the orthodox paradigm defines development as evolutionary, generally unilinear, materialistic, and progressive. In contrast, the radical paradigm understands development to be revolutionary and multilinear, and attentive to the basic needs of all people. Subsequent chapters will delineate and elaborate on these general characteristics. The reader may be interested too in examining some efforts that have been made to differentiate between paradigms in the field of comparative politics. In this regard, the studies by Bodenheimer (1971) and Hildebrand (1974) are interesting attempts to identify paradigmatic influences in the study, respectively, of Latin America and Africa.

References

Adorno, Theodor W. et al.
   1976 *The Positivist Dispute in German Sociology*. Translated by Glyn Adey and David Frisby. London: Heinemann. Essays stemming from a conference and debate in Germany during 1961. Contributors include Adorno, Karl R. Popper, and Jürgen Habermas.
Almond, Gabriel A.
   1966 "Political Theory and Political Science." *American Political Science Review* LX (December), 869–879. Presidential address to the American Political Science Association—identifies traditional and new scientific paradigms in political science. Places stress on "system."
Ball, Terence
   1976 "From Paradigms to Research Programs: Toward a Post-Kuhnian Political Science." *American Journal of Political Science* XX (February), 151–177. Examination of three stages of thinking relating to the work of T. S. Kuhn—two stages that uncritically accept his thought and one that rejects him.
Beardsley, Philip
   1974 "Political Science: The Case of the Missing Paradigm." *Political Theory* II (February), 46–61. Argues that it is doubtful that political science has had a paradigm in past and present, but believes it possible that political science can ac-

quire a paradigm and desirable that it do so.

Bodenheimer, Susanne

1971 *The Ideology of Developmentalism: The American Paradigm Surrogate for Latin American Studies.* Beverly Hills, California: Sage Publications. Comparative Politics Series (01-015). Reprinted from *Berkeley Journal of Sociology* (1969). Paradigmatic differences are analyzed in Latin American studies.

Conniff, James

1976 "Hume's Political Methodology: A Reconsideration of 'That Politics May be Reduced to a Science.'" *Review of Politics* XXXVIII (January), 88-108. Argues that Hume's later works on politics and history are consistent with his earlier works, which are believed to be based on empirical science. Concludes that Hume's approach is historical and concrete, not deductive or rationalistic nor insisting of precision.

Easton, David

1965 *A Framework for Political Analysis.* Englewood Cliffs, New Jersey: Prentice-Hall. Includes an elaboration of the "behavioral credo" and a framework for comparative analysis of political systems.

1969 "The New Revolution in Political Science." *American Political Science Review* LXIII (December), 1051-1061. Presidential address to the American Political Science Association; focuses on approaches to the field with attention to the "post-behavioral revolution."

Eckstein, Harry

1963 "A Perspective on Comparative Politics, Past and Present." In Eckstein and David Apter (eds.), *Comparative Politics, A Reader,* pp. 3-32. New York: Free Press of Glencoe. Comprehensive, yet concise overview of the field.

Effrat, Andrew

1972 "Power to the Paradigms: An Editorial Introduction." *Sociological Inquiry* XLII (3-4), 3-33. Identification of phases through which paradigms evolve; offers a typology of paradigms.

Eulau, Heinz

1963 *The Behavioral Persuasion in Politics.* New York: Random House. A classic statement of the behavioral approach to politics.

Ford, Trowbridge H.

1970 "Bagehot and Mill as Theorists of Comparative Politics." *Comparative Politics* II (January), 309-324. Exposes Walter Bagehot as a "derivative thinker" whose literary source was John Stuart Mill. This essay looks at some of the liberal influences that emanate from the writings of both thinkers; it shows the impact of these thinkers upon contemporary comparative politics; and it criticizes Bagehot's contrived use of Darwinism in an effort to bring science to the study of politics.

Fox, William T. R.

1975 "Pluralism, the Science of Politics, and the World System." *World Politics* XXVII (July), 597-611. Examines ideas in Charles Merriam to demonstrate the influence of pluralism on the study of world politics.

Friedrich, Carl J. (ed.)

1954 "Introduction." In *The Philosophy of Hegel,* pp. 13-64. New York: Modern Library. A critical overview and synthesis of Hegel's thought.

Garson, G. David
1974 "On the Origins of the Interest-Group Theory: A Critique of a Process." *American Political Science Review* LXVIII (December), 1505–1519. Survey of articles and books reviewed in the APSR since its inception in 1906 in an effort to examine the origins and evolution of group theory and to demonstrate that the shortcomings of the past recur in the present.

Giddens, Anthony (ed.)
1974 *Positivism and Sociology.* London: Heinemann Educational Books. The introduction by Giddens deals with past and current interpretations of positivism. The essays that follow concern various aspects of positivism, including an essay by Max Weber.

Gunnell, John G.
1969 "Deduction, Explanation, and Social Scientific Inquiry." *American Political Science Review* LXIII (December), 1233–1246. Antipositivist critique of the deductive model that serves behavioral research.

Heyl, John D.
1975 "Paradigms in Social Science." *Society* XII (July-August), 61–67. Reviews the impact of Kuhn's ideas upon social science, especially in economics, sociology, and political science. Argues that Kuhn gave interdisciplinary studies a language, method, and target.

Hildebrand, Stanley J.
1974 "A New Paradigm in African Studies." *UFAHAMU* V (Fall), 3–19. An attempt to distinguish between the orthodox and radical paradigms in African studies.

Himka, John-Paul
1975 "The Limits of Historical Poverty: the Philosophical Basis of Social Science." *Science and Society* XXXIX (Summer), 215–218. Utilizing Popper's (1957) own rules of logic, Himka refutes his arguments against historicism.

Hirschman, Albert O.
1970 "The Search for Paradigms as a Hindrance to Understanding." *World Politics* XXII (April), 329–343. Critical assessment of the "compulsive and mindless theorizing" in the social sciences.

Hollis, Martin
1977 *Models of Man: Philosophical Thoughts on Social Action.* Cambridge: Cambridge University Press. Draws two models of man, one plastic and the other autonomous, in a critical examination of past and contemporary theory.

Holt, Robert T., and John M. Richardson, Jr.
1970 "Competing Paradigms in Political Science." In Robert T. Holt and John E. Turner (eds.), *The Methodology of Comparative Research,* pp. 21–71. New York: Free Press. The authors identify competing paradigmatic tendencies in comparative politics.

House, J. D.
1976 "A Note on Positivism." *Insurgent Sociologist* VI (Winter), 94–103. Critique of positivist influences in sociology and discussion of antipositivist tendencies.

Huntington, Samuel P.
1974 "Paradigms of American Politics: Beyond the One, the Two, and the Many."

Political Science Quarterly LXXXIX (March), 1–26. Focuses on three tendencies in U.S. politics: progressive theory, pluralism, and consensus.

Kirn, Michael E.

1977 "Behavioralism, Post-Behavioralism, and the Philosophy of Science: Two Houses, One Plague." *Review of Politics* XXIX (January), 82–102. Looks at the dispute between behavioralism and postbehavioralism and shows that both schools emphasize the scientific study of politics and the influence of natural science. Shows differences between the postbehavioralists and Thomas Kuhn whom they rely upon.

Kuhn, Thomas S.

1970 *The Structure of Scientific Revolutions.* 2d ed. Chicago: University of Chicago Press. From II, 2 of *International Encyclopedia of Unified Science.* Argues that the theory and practice of science are found historically in prior experience and become established as paradigms.

Macridis, Roy C.

1955 *The Study of Comparative Government.* Studies in Political Science (21). New York: Random House. A critique of the traditional approach to comparative government and an outline of a new scheme for comparative analysis, based on deliberations by political scientists during 1953–1954.

Macridis, Roy C., and Richard Cox

1953 "Research in Comparative Politics." *American Political Science Review* XLVII (September), 641–675. A report embodying the deliberations and findings of the Social Science Research Council Interuniversity Research Seminar on Comparative Politics.

Manuel, Frank E.

1962 *The Prophets of Paris: Turgot, Condorcet, Saint-Simon, Fourier, and Comte.* New York: Harper and Row. A review of each thinker's life and ideas.

Mayer, Lawrence C.

1972 *Comparative Political Inquiry: A Methodological Survey.* Homewood, Illinois: Dorsey Press. Critical examination of theory in comparative politics.

Meehan, Eugene J.

1968 *Explanation in Social Science: A System Paradigm.* Homewood, Illinois: Dorsey Press. Rejects the deductive paradigm of explanation, argues for an alternative system paradigm.

Melanson, Philip H.

1973 "The Dominant Normative Paradigm and Political Science." *Political Science* XXV (July), 49–57. A critique of the normative paradigm that "employs a comparison of the normative deficiencies of extant reality to visions of reforms or Utopia."

Miller, Eugene F.

1971 "Hume's Contribution to Behavioral Science." *Journal of the History of the Behavioral Sciences* VII (April), 154–168. Discussion of Hume's contribution to positivist approaches to the study of behavior in contemporary society.

1972 "Positivism, Historicism, and Political Inquiry." *American Political Science Review* LXVI (September), 796–817. Important discussion of two modes of thought that influence inquiry in political science.

Nun, José
1966 "Los paradigmas de la ciencia política: un intento de conceptualización." *Revista Latinoamericana de Sociología* II (March), 67–97. Examines the "crisis of scientific legitimacy" faced by contemporary political science and analyzes four models: formal-legalism; sociologism based on the liberal democracy and theories of authority and bureaucracy of Max Weber; dogmatic Marxism, influenced by Stalinism; and critical Marxism, which the author prefers.

Parsons, Talcott
1951 *The Social System.* Glencoe, Illinois: Free Press of Glencoe. The classic work by this renowned sociologist, who influenced systemic study in comparative politics.

Perrin, Robert
1976 "Herbert Spencer's Four Theories of Social Evolution." *American Journal of Sociology* LXXXI (May), 1339–1359. Argues that Spencer applied the term "social evolution" to four different theories and attempts to document what Spencer understood by the term. Social progress in Spencer's thought is identified as progress toward an ideal "social state"; as differentation of social aggregates into functional subsystems; as advancing division of labor (equilibrium theory); and as the origin of species of societies.

Popper, Karl R.
1957 *The Poverty of Historicism.* London: Routledge and Kegan Paul. A positivist argument against historicism, both Marxist and non-Marxist. Offers first a synthesis of the anti- and pro-naturalistic doctrines of historicism, then criticizes both doctrines. Himka (1975) refutes Popper's arguments.

Ricci, David
1977 "Reading Thomas Kuhn in the Post-Behavioral Era." *Western Political Quarterly* XXX (March), 7–34. Elaborate discussion of the relevance for contemporary political science of Kuhn's notion of paradigm and scientific revolution. Shows the relevance of Popper's understanding of science to behavioralism.

Rogowski, Ronald
1978 "Rationalist Theories of Politics: A Midterm Report." *World Politics* XXX (January), 296–322. A review of four major books on theories of rational choice, which leads the author to the conclusion that a "fourth great scientific revolution" is under way in the study of politics.

Sigler, Jay A.
1962 "Politics and the Philosophy of Science." *Western Political Quarterly* XV (June), 314–327. A review of philosophical traditions in the study of politics, with some emphasis on logical positivism and its impact. Concludes that the effort to establish a scientific and empirical theory of politics has not yet been successful.

Smith, David G.
1964 "Pragmatism and the Group Theory of Politics." *American Political Science Review* LVII (September), 600–610. An examination of the common philosophical suppositions of pragmatism and its offshoot, group theory. Assessment of the contributions of Follett, Mayo, and Homans on one side, and Bentley, Dewey, and Truman on the other; also an attempt to clarify confusions in the literature.

Stretton, Hugh
    1969 *The Political Sciences.* New York: Basic Books. Argues that all explanation is
    selective and based on values and thus there cannot be value-free inquiry. This
    synthesis reviews the work of major positivists and historicists, among others.
Thorson, Thomas Landon
    1970 *Biopolitics.* New York: Holt, Rinehart, and Winston. Critique of assump-
    tions that tie political science to science.
Truman, David B.
    1965 "Disillusion and Regeneration: The Quest for a Discipline." *American
    Political Science Review* LIX (December), 865–873. Presidential address to the
    American Political Science Association; identifies traditional and emerging
    paradigms in political science.
Wolin, Sheldon S.
    1968 "Paradigms and Political Theories." In P. King and B. C. Parekh (eds.),
    Politics and Experience: Essays Presented to Michael Oakeshott, pp. 125–152. Cam-
    bridge: Cambridge University Press.

    1969 "Political Theory as a Vocation." *American Political Science Review* LXIII
    (December), 1062–1082. Although acknowledging that a framework of assump-
    tions dominates contemporary political science, Wolin argues that no dominant
    theoretical paradigm of normal political scientists yet exists.

Marx and Weber as Precursors

Karl Marx and Max Weber are two of the early major thinkers whose ideas have substantially influenced the orthodox and the radical paradigms. The work of Max Weber seems to have enjoyed the widest influence among North American students of comparative politics. Weber made little attempt to synthesize his ideas into a tight and comprehensive theory, but as a whole his writings reveal a line of thought that has been fully assimilated into the contemporary social sciences. Talcott Parsons has been largely responsible for this assimilation of Weberian theory into contemporary thought, and Parsons has successfully refined many of Weber's general propositions into a set of statements that have been employed in a wide range of comparative investigations.

The work of Karl Marx also represents a body of propositions that facilitates comparative analysis. Unlike Weber, Marx worked progressively toward a comprehensive work grounded in the accumulated insights of his previous writings and empirical investigation. Engels was responsible for much elucidation and refinement of Marxist theory. There are obvious differences between Weber and Marx, especially in their theoretical assumptions and the direction of their investigations. Marx, especially in his later work, consciously worked toward an all-inclusive explanation of human history and social transformation. Weber, in contrast, worked consciously

Professor Stephen M. Gorman of North Texas State University, a doctoral recipient at the University of California, Riverside, collaborated in writing the early parts of this chapter, in particular the biographical sketches of Marx and Weber.

at a critique and refutation of Marxism.

Whether Marx or Weber intended that their works should serve as the starting point for future investigations need not concern us here. Whether it does justice to their intentions or not, their works have come to serve the paradigms of thought and inquiry of comparative analysis.

This chapter begins with a summary of the life and works of Marx and Weber. Then these two thinkers are examined in comparative perspective, and finally, their influence upon comparative politics is traced and their thought and ideas are looked at in relation to theories of system, culture, development, and class.

Karl Marx

The philosophical foundations of Karl Marx's thought are rooted in the traditional German preoccupation with idealism and history. In the second decade of the nineteenth century these two dominant trends came together in the philosophical system of Georg Hegel. Hegel's conception of cyclical historical change allowed Marx, in his own way, to elaborate a revolutionary theory of society.

In 1818, Hegel presented an inaugural lecture in philosophy at the University of Berlin. Deeply troubled by the recurrent violence of European history, Hegel undertook to construct a philosophical system that would at once explain the source of the social upheaval that attends human development and reveal the future of civilization. The device by which he advanced his interpretation of civilization and its history was the dialectic, which traces its origin to the ancient Greeks, but to which Hegel added a new twist.

In Hegel's system, mind and spirit are declared the moving forces of history, and civilization is carried continually to a higher attainment through their interaction. The dialectic consists of three elements: thesis, antithesis, and synthesis. For Hegel, each stage of history is characterized by a dominant viewpoint or idea, which represents the thesis. Through its elaboration, the thesis produces its own contradictions or oppositions, which formulate themselves into a contrary viewpoint or idea, the antithesis. The antithesis represents the negation, or the contradiction, of the existing viewpoint or thesis. The violent clash of thesis and antithesis yields a synthesis or a new viewpoint for civilization. The synthesis is not a combination of the better elements of the thesis and the antithesis, but an entirely new phenomenon of human thought. Once extant, the synthesis itself becomes the thesis in a new stage of history and the dialectic is set in motion again (Hook 1968: 61–64; Beer 1942: 11–17). The clash between thesis and antithesis manifests itself in history as war or rebellion, from which it follows that the progress of man is accompanied by inescapable, but ultimately beneficial, violence. For Hegel, the dialectic was an eternal movement toward the perfection of mind and spirit, whose culminating point he perceived to be the modern state. His system, therefore, logically settled upon the Prussian autocracy as the highest achievement of the German spirit and mind.

Hegel's philosophy of history found an immediate acceptance among German intellectuals, who responded from the standpoint of traditional mysticism and frustrated nationalism. (At that time in history, Germany did not exist as a nation-state but was divided into numerous independent kingdoms and municipalities. German liberals had anticipated German unification at the close of the Napoleonic wars, but the Congress of Vienna failed to bring the unification about in 1815). The Hegelian admiration of the Prussian state, it should be noted, ignored completely the reactionary police tyranny upon which it reposed (Beer 1942: 25–26; Howard 1972: 7–23).

In the same year that Hegel presented his first lecture at Berlin, Karl Marx was born in Trier, in the Rhine province of Prussian Germany. His father, a prosperous and highly educated lawyer, desired his son to pursue a career in law, and accordingly Marx began the study of jurisprudence at the University of Bonn in 1835. He continued his legal studies in 1836 at the University of Berlin, where Hegel had been a professor until his death in 1831. As a youth, Marx valued art and poetry over other endeavors, but between 1836 and 1838 he replaced his idealistic romanticism, first with intense investigations of philosophy generally and then with a complete immersion in the Hegelian system. During this period, Marx became an atheist and concluded that the Hegelian system would itself do better without the notion of God (Garaudy 1967: 89–91). Under the influence of a new circle of intellectual companions, Marx substituted a specialization in philosophy for jurisprudence and began preparation to assume a lectureship at the University of Bonn upon completion of his doctorate from the University of Jena. (These and other biographical details are in Riazanov, 1973.)

The atmosphere at the University of Berlin during this period was neo-Hegelian. Various intellectual factions competed for control of the Hegelian philosophical patrimony, and Marx aligned himself with the left-wing Young Hegelians (Cornu 1957: 55–72). Prominent within this group were Arnold Ruge, Bruno Bauer, and Ludwig Feuerbach. The Young Hegelian outlook maintained that the Prussian state did not represent a satisfactory embodiment of spirit and mind, so that the dialectic of history must be helped to produce yet another advance in German civilization. The Young Hegelians believed that a higher stage of civilization could be achieved in Germany. To bring it about simply required the historical negation of the present state of affairs. Their role was that of assisting in the appearance of an antithesis, which would take the form of a direct contradiction of the existing German society. The means for achieving this acceleration of the historical dialectic were ruthless journalistic criticism and political opposition (Berlin 1952: 63–64). All dogmatisms and utopias that aimed at outlining the configuration of the new order that would flow out of the dialectic were radically proscribed, since the negation of the present thesis would of itself produce a superior embodiment of mind and spirit. The Young Hegelians conceived of themselves as the catalyst of change, not as its architects.

In 1841 Marx received his doctorate in philosophy, but both he and Bauer were refused the appointments they anticipated at the University of Bonn as a consequence of their radical views. As the Young Hegelians' perspective was in vogue in journalistic circles, Marx turned to that field when it became evident that he would not be permitted an academic career. By 1843, however, Prussian censorship caused Marx to emigrate to Paris, where he assumed the position of coeditor of the political journal, *Jahrbücher*. In Paris, Marx became acquainted with French socialism (whose leading figure was Pierre Joseph Proudhon) and English political economy (to which he was introduced by an article submitted to his journal by Frederick Engels). During this stay in Paris, Marx wrote the *Economic and Philosophical Manuscripts of 1844* (Fromm 1961), which were not discovered until after his death and were first published in 1927. In that work, Marx developed his thesis on alienation in capitalist society. More important for the development of his thought, Marx formed what became a lifelong friendship with Engels about this time.

In 1845 the Prussian government pressured French authorities to curtail the journalisitic activities of Marx, who was directing a political critique against the German monarchy from the safety of exile. The French acquiesced and Marx was forced to move to Brussels. At this point, Marx began to distinguish his ideas from those of his contemporaries. His first effort in this direction was the *Theses on Feuerbach* (1845), published posthumously, in which Marx sought to disassociate his notion of materialism from that of the young Hegelian Feuerbach. Feuerbach maintained that the material world was composed of static objects, which in turn served as the subjects of human contemplation. Despite Feuerbach's attempts to elaborate a system of materialism, however, his emphasis on the primacy of contemplation meant that he remained well within the Hegelian tradition of metaphysics and mysticism. Marx, on the contrary, argued that men directly interact with their material reality and thus create their own history in conformity with the possibilities of that material reality. Marx moved from the conceptualization of static materialism to the position that materialism consists of processes in which men participate.

In his first year in Brussels, Marx also joined with Engels to publish the *Holy Family* (1845), which attacked the Young Hegelians' inability to break with the notion that mind and spirit are independently preeminent in the course of history. Marx called upon Bauer to realize that only those ideas in history that find a parallel in the interests of the classes ascending to power have succeeded in provoking dialectical change. Bauer, for his part, insisted that once ideas are seized upon by the masses, they become adulterated and lose their efficacy in the dialectic. Subsequently, in *The German Ideology* (1846), which was refused for publication, Marx and Engels asserted that even the most recent and divergent developments in the German school of philosophy remained well within the mysticism of Hegel's system, were built on abstractions of mind and spirit, and were therefore sterile.

In *The Poverty of Philosophy* (1847), Marx systematically attacked utopianism within the existing forms of socialism. The main body of socialism in mid-nineteenth-century Europe was typified by escapist solutions such as Owenism. Robert Owen, a member of the English capitalist class, invested considerable time and effort in the founding of socialistic communes in the western frontier of North America. His scheme relied on an artificial simplification of community life and the organization of production. The approach was not well suited to the realities of industrial society.

Marx also attacked the French socialist and anarchist Pierre Joseph Proudhon, author of *Philosophy of Poverty* to which *The Poverty of Philosophy* was intended as a rebuttal. Proudhon had attempted to make an advance on the Owenist orientation by drawing upon German philosophy and English works on political economy (Dupré 1966: 77–78). But Marx revealed that Proudhon had misunderstood the Hegelian dialectic. Proudhon mistakenly thought that the synthesis represented the better elements of the thesis and the antithesis. More damaging was Proudhon's incomplete grasp of the way that wealth accumulates in the hands of the bourgeoisie in industrial society. He held that exploitation occurred in the market place where the workers bought goods for more than it cost the entrepreneur to produce them. He proposed, then, that the problem could be solved by a decentralized system of exchange in which workers traded among themselves in equivalent values. Marx correctly demonstrated that the source of accumulation in industrial society exists in the very act of production, wherein a portion of the worker's labor is alienated from him. This perspective rendered Proudhon's solution utopian and laid the groundwork for Marx's later elaboration of exploitation in capitalist production.

Between 1846 and 1849 Marx was involved consecutively in organizing German workers in Brussels, stimulating the League of Justice in London to reorganize as the League of Communists, writing the *Communist Manifesto* for the league, and editing a prorevolutionary journal in Prussia during the revolutions of 1849. Having already established a unique system of thought, during these years Marx acquired his practical political experience, which he subsequently drew upon in organizational activities in England. About 1850, with the failure of the Revolution of 1848 in France a historical fact, Marx retired to London where he resided for the remainder of his life.

The thrust of Marx's works during the London period reflects a more mature analysis and a concern with producing a synthesis of his life's work. For example, as an application of scientific socialist analysis, the *Eighteenth Brumaire of Louis Bonaparte* (1851–1852) was Marx's most serious attempt to explain a specific historical event in terms of material forces and class conflict. The notable product of Marx's last years was *Capital*, the first volume of which was published in 1867, with the remaining volumes published under the editorship of Engels from notes and drafts after Marx's death in 1883. In this work, Marx undertook to empirically validate the system of thought embodied in the *Communist Manifesto* and other writings of the late 1840s.

Two other works from this period are notable. As a concise statement on communist programmatic orientations, the "Critique of the Gotha Program" (1875) was an important statement by Marx on political practice. Finally, *Grundrisse*, consisting of seven notebooks drafted during 1857 and 1858, was intended by Marx to represent his first scientific and theoretical elaboration of communism. *Grundrisse* was not published in the German original until 1953 and not in English until 1973. According to its English translator, this work stands as an outline of Marx's full project.

> The manuscripts display the key element in Marx's development and overthrow of the Hegelian philosophy. They cast a fresh light on the inner logic of *Capital*, and are a source book of inestimable value for the study of Marx's method of inquiry. The *Grundrisse* challenges and puts to the test every serious interpretation of Marx yet conceived. [Nicolaus 1973: 7].

After Marx took up residence in London, there were few if any changes in his thinking. His efforts were directed toward elaborating and documenting his system and making it the dominant mode of thought within working-class organizations. In this latter sphere, the efforts of Engels count as much as those of Marx. Aside from the important works of this period, both Marx and Engels engaged in violent polemics against leaders of the European labor movements who did not subscribe to a Marxist line. The concern of Marx and Engels was to prevent the proletarian movement from falling into the hands of ideologically suspect opportunists. In reviewing the body of literature that dates from this time, it is necessary to separate the expedient polemics from the seriously theoretical.

In summarizing this discussion of Marx, let us first outline the major periods and works of his life and thought and then focus on some of his principal ideas. The following outline draws upon Louis Althusser (1970), Lucio Colletti (1972), and Martin Nicolaus (1973).

EARLY WORKS: 1840–1845

This is Marx's "ideological" period, including his doctoral dissertation, *Economic and Philosophical Manuscripts of 1844*, and *The Holy Family*. In this period Marx broke with Kant, contended with Hegel's idealism, and modified Feuerbach's materialism.

WORKS OF THE BREAK: 1845 AND 1846

As representative works of this period, *The German Ideology* and *Theses on Feuerbach* signify Marx's break with "ideological philosophy" as well as his development of a "new theoretical consciousness" embracing conceptualization of dialectical and historical materialism. Marx himself located his break in *The German Ideology*. Althusser (1970: 33) described it as an "epistemological break." "By founding the theory of history (historical materialism), Marx simultaneously broke with his erstwhile ideological philosophy and established a new philosophy (dialectical materialism)."

TRANSITIONAL WORKS: 1846–1857

The transition from "ideological" to "scientific" works was represented by such works as the *Communist Manifesto*, *Eighteenth Brumaire*, and *The Poverty of Philosophy*.

MATURE WORKS: 1857–1883

These include in particular *Capital* but also *Grundrisse*.

The outline relies especially upon the periods suggested by the French Marxist scholar Althusser (1970: 31–39), who marked the break in Marx's works at 1845. He was concerned with Marx's critique of Hegel and Feuerbach, while the Italian Marxist scholar Colletti (1972) identified the break at 1843. Nicolaus demonstrated the significance and the scientific nature of Marx's mature works, while at the same time making clear the continuity in thought that pervades the early as well as the later writings.

The concept of *alienation* is of considerable significance in Marx's writings. The Young Hegelians gave an idealistic conception to Hegel's metaphysical use of the term. Influenced especially by Feuerbach's humanism, Marx turned against idealism and gave a concrete meaning to the term by rooting it in the labor process and thereby establishing a basis for a humanistic critique of capitalist society. According to Marx, labor and its product assume an existence separate from the individual once private property and the division of labor develop. This separation results in alienation for the worker. Marx's elaboration of this idea in the 1844 manuscripts was followed shortly by his criticism of Feuerbach, set down in eleven theses.

The manuscripts provide an initial framework for a critique of capitalism. It is argued by some that they are an early draft of *Capital*, that the explicit discussion of alienation that appears in Marx's early works is implicitly rooted in his later works; a point argued, for example, by Giddens (1971: 8–10). Erich Fromm also asserted the continuity in thought between the young and the mature Marx. Fromm's argument demonstrates the importance of alienation as a concept in Marx's late as well as his early writings (Fromm 1961: 76–79). Fromm's position also opposes the view and analysis of Althusser, who carefully distinguished between Marx's early and late writings and noted "the false transparency of his youthful ideological conceptions" (1970: 37) in contrast to his mature "scientific" work.

Some early themes, such as alienation, are not dealt with directly in *Capital* but appear in *Grundrisse* where they are clarified (Nicolaus 1973: 50–51). Writers such as David McLellan (1973) placed the *Grundrisse* at the center of Marx's thought, and they stressed the linkage with the alienation theory of 1844 to show the humanistic aspects of Marxist theory and to project a utopian vision of the individual and society. Such a vision deviates from the interpretation of Engels and other early writers, who argued that Marx gave socialism its scientific foundation while eliminating its utopianism. Clearly Marx was concerned in his mature writings with the discovery of economic laws. Thus the *Grundrisse*, indeed the full range of Marx's work, brings humanistic aspects and a vision of society beyond capitalism together with a scientific theory that exposes the workings of a capitalist political economy.

Also deserving of elaboration is Marx's theory of history or *historical materialism*. In setting forth his theory Marx repudiated the metaphysical and ideological abstractions of the German philosophers. His conception of historical materialism is alluded to in the 1844 manuscripts and elaborated in *The German Ideology*. Marx understood alienation as a historical and social phenomenon related to the emergence of private property and the division of labor. He attacked the philosophy but retained the *dialectic* of Hegel's writings. He criticized Feuerbach's philosophical materialism as ahistorical and passive. He argued that human consciousness is conditioned by the dialectical interplay between the subject, or the individual in society, and the object, or the material world in which one lives. Thus history is a process of continuous creation, satisfaction, and re-creation of human needs. A summary of Marx's perspective of history, drawn from *The German Ideology* (Marx and Engels 1973: 48–57), follows.

The initial premise of history is that people must be able to live in order to shape history. This involves the production of means, such as tools, land,

and machinery, to satisfy the basic needs of food, shelter, clothing, and the like. Satisfaction of these primary needs leads to new needs. By the procreation of life, families develop both natural and social relationships. Social relationships involve the cooperation of several individuals. It follows that a certain *mode of cooperation* or relation is always combined with a certain *mode of production*. The mode of production is the totality of the relations of production and the *productive forces* of the members of society. The forces of production comprise the productive capacity of a society and the machinery, level of technology, and size and skill of the working population. In these primary historical relationships people possess a *consciousness* of sensuous environment and of relationships with other persons and things. Consciousness comes into contradiction with the forces of production, which results in a *division of labor*. The division of labor provokes an unequal distribution of labor and its products in the form of property, so that wife and children may become slaves of the husband in the family, or the family may become the slave of some alien entity, which takes the form of the state. The division of labor determines social classes of rulers and masses.

The struggles of history in illusory form are those among democracy, aristocracy, and monarchy, but in real form they are the struggles of the different classes. And these struggles extend from individual and family, to community and nation, and ultimately to the whole world. Under capitalism, one class lives by owning, and the other class lives by working. The interests of those who own the means of production and of those who work for them are opposed. The owners defend their property; the workers defend humanity. Thus conflict exists between the two classes. Class struggle disappears with the abolition of private property and the implementation of a communistic regulation of production, which in turn destroys the alien relation between people and what they produce—this results in exchanges and production under their own control.

This summary and the preceding discussion have been concerned with concepts such as alienation, historical materialism, dialectic, mode of production, productive forces, relations of production, consciousness, division of labor, and class structure and struggle. As will be demonstrated in ensuing chapters, these concepts are essential in understanding the efforts of Marxist and other scholars to establish a radical paradigm in comparative politics.

Max Weber

In 1864 Marx finished the first volume of *Capital* and participated in the founding of the First International. That was also the year Max Weber was born in Frankfurt in western Germany. The son of a civil servant and an erstwhile politician, Weber grew up under the influence of the narrow intellectual circle in which his father moved. Historians held sway in the group, and art and literature were neglected. The outcome was that Weber remained something of a philistine throughout his life.

Weber entered the University of Heidelberg in 1882, electing to study economics, philosophy, and Roman law. In 1883, the year Marx died in London, Weber served briefly in the military on the eastern marches of the new Prussian Empire, returning to his studies later at the University of Berlin. Unlike the impact it had on the young Marx nearly a half century earlier, Weber's study at Berlin does not seem to have had any special influence on the development of his thought. His intellectual crises came later in life. By 1885 Weber had moved to the University of Göttingen where, in 1889, he completed his doctoral dissertation on medieval trading companies.

From 1889 to 1891 Weber served in a minor legal post in Berlin, while composing a thesis in order to qualify for university teaching. He subsequently received an appointment in 1892 to the University of Berlin law school, where he lectured until receiving a full professorship in economics at the University of Freiburg im Breisgau in 1894. In 1896 Weber was elected to a chair in economics at the University of Heidelberg, thus having attained the status of full professor in the space of four teaching years. The distinction he received as a scholar, however, did not prove sufficient compensation for his failure to achieve success in active politics. Weber openly detested the responsibilities of university lecturing. During these early years he pursued a separate career alongside his university post, serving as a consultant to several public and private organizations. In connection with these duties, he examined a wide range of subjects, including the German stock exchange and the East Prussian agrarian question. The results of these studies, along with his university lectures, reveal the formative phase of his thinking, and are a prelude to the subjects and techniques that distinguish his later works.

The topics that recur in Weber's works may be traced to his membership in the Social-Political Union, to which he belonged from 1888 until his death. The union was a learned society founded in 1872, and at its founding, and under the later leadership of Gustav Schmoller, it rejected the abstract and generalistic systems of scholarship prominent at the time in favor of a direct treatment of pressing social problems. Donald MacRae (1974: 25), in his intellectual biography of Weber, observes that Weber enthusiastically embraced this purview, and consequently he trained his intellectual powers upon an analysis of the great socioeconomic questions of his day. This brought him to question the very foundations of German society as it was constituted under the Prussian monarchy that had unified the nation in 1871. The dominant figure of the era, however, was not so much the Hohenzollern monarch, but his first chancellor, Otto von Bismarck. Bismarck was for Weber both an inspiration and a dilemma. The paradox was that Bismarck wielded power successfully and completely dominated the political life of the nation, but at the same time he failed miserably in the exercise of that power to mold the future as he intended. Weber saw in this paradox a modern parable, whose moral was that even the most deliberate and intentional actions of men can result in unintentional consequences.

The theoretical approach that Weber devised to accommodate these subjects may be termed historical, but he did not relate his thought to the historicism of many nineteenth-century thinkers. We will not attempt to attach a label to Weber's historical approach, since that would only add to the general confusion of the terminology employed to distinguish systems of thought during this period in Europe. It is enough to say that Weber's historiography differed from the English discipline as influenced by David Hume, from German historiography as handed down from Hegel, and from French positivism as formulated by Auguste Comte. We will leave the comparison of Weber and Marx on this point for later.

In 1897 Weber suffered a nervous breakdown, and eventually he found it necessary to suspend his university duties. Between 1899 and 1904 he found a partial remedy to his illness in traveling, and during that time he toured much of Europe. By 1903 he was sufficiently recovered to join Werner Sombart and Edgar Jaffe as a coeditor of the *Archiv für Sozialwissenschaft und Sozialpolitik*. This facilitated his reaffiliation with the academic community and the beginning of a new period of productivity. About this time, he was offered a new university appointment, but in the end he felt compelled to decline for reasons of health. In reality, a family inheritance allowed him to live the life of a private scholar, thus sparing him the "drudgery" of university life. The significance of Weber's nervous breakdown for his intellectual orientation has been treated by MacRae (1974: 24–32), and the nature and origin of Weber's mental illness are discussed by Arthur Mitzman (1970: 148–157).

In 1904, after a short visit to the United States, Weber undertook to write his most widely known work, *The Protestant Ethic and the Spirit of Capitalism*. In this study Weber sought to demonstrate that the tenets of Protestantism concerning the notion of predestination transformed themselves over time into a class pathos of the bourgeoisie (Weber 1958b: 160–176). His intention was to prove that the Reformation of the sixteenth century was necessary (along with a number of other social and economic considerations) for the subsequent development of modern capitalism. In this vein, he attempted to explain the special behavior of the entrepreneur by referring to the possibilities of the socioeconomic environment and to the motivating influence of the Protestant ethic as infused into the secular sphere of life.

During this same period, Weber published an essay on methodology in which he outlined the use of "ideal types." The ideal type is an artificial construct the social scientist can use to conceptualize analytical categories with utility for historical understanding (Weber 1962: 32–33). Weber's most famous ideal types are those that pertain to authority: Traditional Authority, Charismatic Authority, and Legal-Rational Authority. These are not presumed to exist in history in the "pure form" portrayed in the ideal type, Weber asserted, but they provide typical features of different systems of authority visible in history. The scholar can, therefore, assess the relative proximity or divergence of a system of authority found in history to the three types and, on the basis of the theoretical propositions implicit for each ideal type, assess the impact of that system of authority upon the subject civilization (Lachmann 1970: 26–28).

In the following years Weber worked on a comparative study of the great world religions in an effort to substantiate his contention in *The Protestant Ethic* that religion is crucial in one's explanation of the alternative paths along which the major civilizations have developed. During this study, Weber became certain that the division between church and state that developed gradually within European civilization was central to the explanation of modern rationalism. It was in the course of these investigations that Weber declared himself preeminently a "sociologist," and he set for himself for the remainder of his life the task of developing this nascent discipline. Oddly enough, however, he remained largely ignorant of the findings of his greatest contemporary, the French sociologist Emile Durkheim.

In the later years of his life and in accord with his increasingly pessimistic evaluation of the era he lived in, Weber was strongly influenced by the work of Nietzsche. Weber became concerned that the rationalization of behavior that made European society great would also be its undoing. Rational authority worked largely through the institution of bureaucracy, and it involved the rationalization of *means* in pursuit of culturally defined goals. In this instance, rationalization was a positive influence, since it imposed a deliberative and contemplative quality on behavior by which men became aware of the possible side effects of their actions. What Weber feared, however, was that modern rationalism would eventually result in a rationalization of *means and ends*. This would imply that there are goals that can be rationally upheld as preferable to others: a proposition antithetical to Weber's belief that values are historically relative. In the final analysis, an overrationalization of life would spell the end to democratic freedom, despite Weber's contention that bureaucracy in the first instance increases the likelihood of democracy. The solution that Weber visualized called for political leaders with charismatic qualities who could offset the power of the rationalizing bureaucracies and lead people in defense of freely selected cultural goals.

Weber never succeeded in political life on the scale he set for himself. In his later years, nevertheless, he served as a hospital administrator during the First World War, served as a member of the Armistice Committee, and participated in the drafting of the Weimar Constitution that governed Germany in the postwar years. He maintained hope that he would be called upon by the new democratic government of Germany to serve in public office, but this never came about. Although in theory, Weber understood that politics was the art of compromise and accommodation, a large part of his own failure in securing a political career stemmed from his own inflexibility in dealing with others. In the end, he preferred the integrity of his principles to the horse trading of politics.

In 1918 Weber returned to academia in a specially created chair of sociology at the University of Vienna. In 1919 he was appointed professor of sociology at Munich and began the writing of a comparative study of sociology that was to serve as the core of the new discipline and the starting point for later elaborations of the field. Weber died in 1920 with only a portion of that work completed. It was published in German two years later. Only fragments of the final attempt at a synthesis of his thought have been translated into English. Weber was only 56 when he died of influenza, and had he lived longer he might have succeeded in pulling the diverse strands of his writings into a coherent whole. But since this did not happen, the modern student of Weber's sociology is confronted with a vast body of literature that contains contradictions and ambiguities.

In summary, we identify the major periods and works of Weber's life, then turn to a brief discussion of some of his principal ideas. The summary draws especially on Bendix (1960) and Giddens (1971: pt. 3, 119–184).

EARLY WORKS: 1889–1897

During this period Weber wrote a doctoral dissertation, "A Contribution to the History of Medieval Business Organizations," a technical work dealing with legal aspects of the medieval trading enterprise. His second work (1889), "Roman Agrarian History and Its Significance for Public and Private Law," presented a detailed analysis of Roman land tenure. From 1894 to 1897 he published articles on the operation of the stock exchange and its relationship to capital financing; he argued that the stock exchange did not operate solely for speculation but also facilitated planning for the businessman. These early writings reflect the thrust of Weber's later work, notably the concern with an analysis of European capitalism. Giddens acknowledged that this concern brought Weber "into direct relation with the areas in which Marxist thought was concentrated" (1971: 124) but stated that his views were developed not only in the context of a confrontation with Marxism but within the intellectual milieu of his time.

WORKS ON RELIGION AND SECULARITY: 1903–1920

Weber was not productive during the years of his illness from 1897 until about 1903 when he became a journal editor. Two long articles published in 1904 and 1905 constituted his *Protestant Ethic and the Spirit of Capitalism*. In this examination of the relationship of Protestant beliefs and disciplines to modern capitalism, Weber contended with Engels's premise that Protestantism is an ideological reflection of the changes that accompanied the early development of capitalism. In subsequent works Weber also delved into the comparative study of religion in other parts of the world, including China, India, and ancient Palestine. His attention to religious beliefs led him to focus on the degree of rationalism in many forms of economic activity. At the same time he advocated the rejection of a materialist as well as an idealistic interpretation of history.

WORKS ON POLITICAL SOCIOLOGY AND METHODOLOGY

English translations of Weber's original writings in German have tended to draw from portions rather than the complete works. For example most of his relevant work on the social sciences has been extracted from *Wirtschaft und Gesellschaft*, a series of incomplete studies that was edited and published posthumously. Bendix (1960: xi–xiv) provided a guide that clarifies the relationship between the original and the translated versions of Weber's work.

Portions of *Wirtschaft und Gesellschaft* are found in a number of modern editions of Weber's work (especially Weber 1947, 1958a, and 1967). In addition, the reader should examine Weber's *Basic Concepts in Sociology* (1962), a fragmentary effort at conceptualization, and *The Methodology of the Social Sciences* (1949), which comprises Weber's most important essays on the topic.

Weber came to his *view of history* by way of Heinrich Rickert and Theodor Mommsen, who influenced him both personally and academically, and in response to the intellectual atmosphere of his childhood. From the historian, Rickert, he accepted the proposition that the "sensible" world with which social science contends is infinite, and hence no knowledge of it can be complete. In contradistinction to the natural sciences, then, social science cannot proceed systematically to the discovery of universal axioms. History cannot, in this view, supply social science with general laws. But where positivistic naturalism would conclude from this that such a perspective precludes history as a science (because it permits of no laws), Weber held firmly to the position that history was the science of development.

Since the sensible world is infinite, the historian must select a number of topics for investigation with the understanding that those subjects will yield insights in not only a portion of reality. The means by which Rickert suggested that the historian select his particular subjects was on the basis of "interest." Weber accepted this means as well, and maintained that the selection of topics on the basis of interest is as valid as any other criterion. What Weber rejected in Rickert's position was the assumption that there is a universal element of truth that runs throughout the variations in value systems observable in history. Through abstraction from present values, then, the historian can hit upon this underlying truth and thereby render all of history explicable in terms of comparison to the present. By this technique, Rickert asserted that history could be reduced to an objective endeavor. Weber, for his part, took a Kantian stance, which presumed that "truth" per se was beyond the purview of science. Weber was never convinced that an objectively value-neutral history is possible (J. Mayer 1956: 38–39; Aron 1964: 70–73).

From Mommsen's history of Rome, Weber extracted the basis of his historical technique. Mommsen employed the terminology of the nineteenth-century partisan political struggle to construct a narrative of Roman history that would be at once comprehensible to his contemporaries (while recognizing that the concepts denoted orientations not in existence for the time period under study). Given Weber's notion of the relativity of values in history, he approved of Mommsen's approach and used it as the jumping-off point for his own treatment of history. Drawing upon conceptualizations grounded in his own age, Weber built a matrix of analytical categories by means of which a comparative analysis of history could be undertaken (Freund 1968: 15–17). This approach aims at understanding history through the process of comparing the past to the present. The assumption is that the historian can never succeed in taking on the perceptual framework of the civilization he studies because he has only an indirect knowledge of it. Besides, the historian can never completely extricate himself from his own culture. The best that can be done is to set up a system of classification that provides for a similar ordering of data from the various periods of history. Although this set of categories is an artificial construct (in the sense that it is derived from values that are historically relative), Weber dismissed the possible criticisms in line with his epistemological outlook (based on Rickert).

Congruent with the specializations of his education, Weber began refining his comparative historical perspective by concentrating upon political and economic phenomena. By this selection, he arrived at a preoccupation with capitalist behavior, rational systems of social authority, and the manipulation of power through the institution of bureaucracy. In adopting these topics as guidelines for the study of history, he did not aim at revealing them to be teleological outgrowths of antecedents to be found in earlier civilizations. For Weber, history was valuable for its heuristic properties: history reveals the principles of cause and effect for the particular subjects under study, but history is incapable of producing laws of causation. Moreover, the principles of causation that history can teach us are complex, and composed of the counterconditioning of a multiplicity of variables.

Weber believed that one cannot deduce from history what is not there and that history contains no universal laws, much less single-factor laws such as the economic explanation of development (Aron 1964: 70–79). What the study of history does permit is the identification of probabilities. From this standpoint, the researcher searches for variables that militate in this or that direction; variables that increase the likelihood that history will unfold in a given direction. Weber's historical methodology seeks for the "necessary" conditions of a given path of historical development, and it abandons the notion that the "sufficient" conditions can be pinpointed. When applied to an extended period of time, this methodological outlook attempts to demonstrate that at each successive stage of a civilization, an array of variables will combine to render a particular future course of development more or less likely. With this treatment of history, the scholar can affirm the hypothesis that a certain variable (say, religion) was critical in the subsequent course of events, by conceiving the civilization without that variable and constructing a hypothetical alternative history based on logical deduction. If the alternative that is most probable in history leads to developments markedly different from those that in fact occurred, the scholar is justified in theorizing about the importance of the variable that has been isolated for the society in question. Such is the methodological basis for Weber's causal imputations.

Weber was not directly enmeshed in the tradition of positivism that had influenced his French contemporary, Emile Durkheim, that is, to build his ideas on Comte and those before him. Weber rejected the Comtian notion that the sciences are ordered into some logical hierarchy. However, he frequently has been identified with positivist and liberal social science (Roth 1965). Indeed there are aspects of Weberian thought that provoke some critics to associate him with contemporary positivist social science, upon which he has exerted a considerable influence. On the one hand, Weber was readily assimilated into structural functionalism. On the other, pieces of his work have been torn out of context and adapted to the narrow ahistorical forms of many social scientists in the United States.

One area of criticism relates to Weber's attention to objectivity and empirical science, to values in inquiry, to ideal type constructs, and to rationalization, which has come to dominate economic life in the Western world. Weber's use of sociology was oriented to a separation of empirical and normative tendencies and an acknowledgment of sociology as an empirical science; to a distinction between sociology and history; and to an empirical investigation that would use qualitative tools to find facts and information about contemporary phenomena (Roth 1969: 196–200).

Weber argued, for example, that *objectivity* must not be sacrificed in social science inquiry, that intuition must not be substituted for causal analysis. Although value judgments may intrude upon scientific discussion, they cannot be validated through scientific inquiry. Weber was not apolitical in everyday life, however. He held a highly articulate view of politics, and he took positions on political issues of his day (Bendix and Roth 1971: chap. 3; Scaff 1973; Leiserson 1975: 182; and for Weber's conception of politics and that of his successors, see Frohock 1974).

Weber's understanding of objectivity and values led him to compare ideal types and facts. He did so by the construction of an *ideal type* in a heuristic way. The ideal type construction was the means for explicitly relating a historical event to its real causes. He even went so far as to argue that all specifically Marxian laws and developmental constructs—insofar as they are theoretically sound—are ideal types. Clearly Weber was not a Marxist, and he held doubts about the prospects for democratic socialism in Germany, but he also hesitated to reject many of Marx's ideas out of hand. For example, he was very much concerned with the dialectical view, and thus there was an ambivalence in his desire to be as scientific as possible. Schneider (1971) has elaborated on this ambivalence in his work. The curious reader might also wish to examine Cahnman's (1965) discussion of Weber's use of ideal types and its extension as found in the writings of others.

Weber's obsession with science became wrapped up in his ideas of *rationality*. Essentially his essays on Protestantism and the rise of capitalism in the West challenged Marxist interpretations of history. Efficiency, professionalization, and bureaucratization were all characteristics that Weber saw in the rationalization process (Ritzer 1975 and Swidler 1973). Here again, it is argued, critics have distorted Weber's interpretation. "The critics concentrate on the problem of the causal significance of the Protestant ethic for the rise of capitalism, while Weber himself stated explicitly that his purpose had *not* been to explain the origin or the expansion of capitalism" (Bendix 1960: 50 n. 2).

Influenced by Weber, some contemporary social scientists have unwittingly confused their interpretations of Weber's work. One example is Talcott Parsons, whose early writing focused on Weber. In their critique Cohen, Hazelrigg, and Pope (1975) stated, for example, that it is assumed that Parsons has offered a faithful interpretation. Yet Parsons, by building on the strengths of Weber and enhancing his views by allusions to the heritage of Weberian ideas, has confused readers as the direction of his own theoretical perspectives has changed from a voluntaristic theory of action in his early writings to structural functionalism and evolutionism in his later works. This confusion is a consequence of Parsons's emphasis on some aspects of Weber's theory in a manner different than that of Weber; his assertion of interpretations rejected by Weber; his equation of concepts, resulting in distortion of Weber's meaning; and his generalization of aspects of Weber's work in contradiction of a particular characterization.

Marx and Weber in Perspective

In many respects, the writings of Karl Marx are a logical outgrowth of the period in which he lived. The course of European thought during his lifetime was subject to a variety of currents, and it was from this very diversity that Marx was able to build his own system. What he approved of in the works of his predecessors and contemporaries, he incorporated; what he dissapproved of, he rejected. From German philosophy he adopted the dialectic, but he stigmatized the metaphysical formulations in which Hegel had first cast it. From France Marx first learned about socialism, but after doing so he destroyed its previous proponents polemically for their utopian and escapist mentalities. From the English political economists Marx gleaned a composite picture of the abuses inherent in the capitalist mode of accumulation and production, and he rejected any notion that mere reforms might ameliorate the abuses. But Marx passed beyond simply abstracting facts from others; he brought a new insight to bear on the pressing questions of his age.

Marx sought to impose a coherence on knowledge by forcing it into the confines of a single, all-inclusive theory of history. In the development of this theory, Marx may be observed to pass moral judgement on his own civilization, which can be paraphrased as follows. Capitalist society, with its abuses and exploitation, has played out its hand in history and contributed to the progress of man by elevating human productivity to a new plane. The very success of the capitalists has now rendered them superfluous, and the workers themselves will overthrow the state and take over the management of production for the benefit of society as a whole and not for the benefit of a select few.

The political implication of this prophecy was that the class conflict is inevitable and, in the final analysis, beneficial. Marx's emphasis on action stemmed from his rejection of the romanticism of his youth. At the same time, European thought in the mid-nineteenth century was, for all the advances of the Enlightenment, still heavily romanticized. Consequently, Marx was seldom at a loss for a strain of thought to criticize for its fanciful reasoning or utopian undertones. Against such intellectualism, Marx distinguished his theories by a rigorous system and produced historical materialism as the basis of "scientific socialism." The political unrest of the late 1840s and the intellectual ferment that preceded it for a generation confronted Marx with a course of events that seemed to substantiate his insights. And the capitalism of his day was not inaccurately revealed in its excess and exploitation in the writings of Marx, as even his critics will attest. It can be seen, therefore, that the socioeconomic milieu in which Marx lived was extremely conducive to his genius developing in the directions it did.

But by the time Max Weber was a young man, the Europe of Marx no longer existed. The entire array of political, technological, and economic conditions of the Continent were changed. From the Franco-Prussian War of 1870 until the outbreak of the First World War, the major European states were at peace internally and externally (exclusive of colonial struggles). The internal setting of the more developed European states seemed to present a refutation to the Marxist prophecy of revolutionary change. In this content, Weber, as the student par excellence of the unfolding rationalism of capitalist society, appears to many as a counterpoint to Marx (Bendix and Roth 1971: 13–22).

It must be remembered, however, that a number of Marxist writings were not published until after Weber's death, nor was it Marx himself who was controversial so much as the political activists who claimed to be Marxists. It was against the Social Democratic Party (SPD) of the German Empire, then, that Weber took most direct exception. Espousing a "Marxist ideology," the SPD pursued a progam of participation in the parliament as the representative of enfranchised workers. But Weber held the leadership of the SPD to be politically unskilled and unable to wield power effectively should they chance to acquire it. On the more theoretical side of the issue, Weber took the Marxist notion of class consciousness (upon which the SPD attempted to build its electoral strength) to be a gross error, and he stigmatized the explanation of history found in dialectial materialism as simplistic and unscientific. Throughout all of this his references to Marx are never direct, and the depth of his investigation into the other aspects of Marxism is not notable.

A fundamental difference between the orientations of Marx and Weber that helps reveal the nature of their thought is that Marx concerned himself with discovering the patterns of uniformities that underlie every period of history. Weber, for his part, viewed European capitalism as the culmination of European history considered as a single civilization. In this sense, every period in European history is important for its uniqueness (which in turn provides insight into the uniqueness of capitalist civilization) rather than for its regularity (which causes difficulty when trying to explain the difference of other civilizations, e.g., Chinese culture). Both systems of historical conceptualization, however, have gained utility in the comparative study of government and politics.

On behalf of the curious reader we now delve into some of the critical literature that compares and contrasts the thought of Marx and Weber.

First, we attempt to establish the setting of contemporary social science into which their ideas have been cast. Then we summarize some major distinctions between their thinkings.

Many lines of thinking that divide contemporary social scientists, especially sociologists, are myths, according to Anthony Giddens (1976), and he urged a rethinking of the foundations of contemporary thought. The 1890 to 1920 generation of thinkers, led by Durkheim and Weber, substantially influenced today's social science, but criticism of them by partisans of socialism and conservativism obscured the contributions of the early generation of nineteenth-century thinkers, especially Comte and Spencer as well as Marx. Comte gave social science its positivist origins, and Weber adapted positivist notions to his liberal social theory. Such connections of thought as well as schisms must be held in perspective by critics of positivism and contemporary social science.

The interpretations of Comte and Saint-Simon provided the French intellectual tradition, upon which Durkheim based much of his work. Durkheim's early works were also concerned with the ideas of contemporary German thinkers, especially those who were influenced by Darwin's theory of biological evolution and who directed attention to organic analogies through comparisons of organs of the body to parts of society. In this sense, Durkheim set forth the foundations of systemic theory, which has influenced contemporary social science and especially sociology. The Brazilian social scientist Fernando Henrique Cardoso (1971: 10–19) included Durkheim among three legacies of "classical" thought that have influenced contemporary political science. Durkheim, he believed, "codified" Montesquieu's systemic approach to politics along functional and structural lines. He also referred to the legacies of thought established by Weber and Marx. This trilogy of thinkers—Durkheim, Weber, and Marx—absorbed the attention of Giddens (1971) in his synthesis of their thought. Although we agree that an understanding of Durkheim as a precursor is useful in a critical assessment of the mainstream of today's social science, our attention will primarily be devoted to Marx and Weber and their influence upon the struggle to establish a dominant paradigm.

With its positivist roots intact, the orthodox paradigm continues to prevail in U.S. social science, and its pervasive impact already has been identified in an earlier chapter. Although the thought of Comte and probably of Saint-Simon, among others, serves as a basis for this paradigm, Weber's work, especially as it has been assimilated by Parsons into U.S. sociology and political science, reinforces and preserves the positivist thrust. In contrast, the historicist influences upon the radical paradigm, notably the idea of dialectics in the thought of Hegel and Marx, have resulted in an alternative way of thinking about the contemporary world. Apparently this tradition of dialectical social science remains embedded today in German thought. In fact, although U.S. social science hardly recognizes any alternative paradigm, debate in Germany today centers around distinctions between positivist and dialectical considerations.

Gerhard Hofmann (1972) sets forth several distinguishing categories. First, dialectical social science does not separate knowledge from the observer, and instead it examines the total world. In contrast, positivist social science looks at bits and pieces, and variables are isolated as parts of a system. Second, positivist social science allows for only controlled observation of behavior under conditions that can be replicated, whereas dialectical social science claims that a reliance on such limited experience interferes with a theory of society. Third, positivist social science assumes a duality of facts and values, and theory can only be constructed on reality or what is known to exist. Dialectical social science makes no claim that hypotheses and concepts can be verified or falsified on the basis of empirical evidence alone.

It has been argued (Tiryakian 1975) that the thought of Weber rather than that of Marx most appropriately relates to an interpretation of U.S. society. This is so because Weber visited and knew more about the United States. Further, his Protestant background and his insights into Puritan culture and the Protestant ethic facilitate the "fit" of his thinking with a conception of U.S. society (for an elaboration of Weber's Protestant ethic thesis, see Berger 1971). Weber's view of liberalism often is associated with his impact on U.S. social science. Richard Ashcraft argues that Marx and Weber have profoundly influenced divergent tendencies. "Their common agreement on the characterization of liberalism as bourgeois ideology concealed differences of historical interpretation, conflicting conceptions of methodology, and opposing views of the social structure" (1972: 131). Some of the differences he cited relate to views on economic causes, ideology, and class.

The significance of comparing the thought of Marx and Weber has been emphasized by Carl Mayer, who stated that prior to Weber's illness at the turn of the century he was not much influenced by Marx nor did he attempt any critical analysis of Marx until the later years of his life. Mayer noted substantial differences between their understanding of system and ideology, social action, dialectic, evolution, and science, and he concluded that in the thought of Marx and Weber "there is agreement in many essential details, but there is a fundamental difference in regard to the decisive methodological positions with which we are confronted in the social sciences (C. Mayer 1975: 714–715). He attributed these differences ultimately to his belief that Marx methodologically was a Hegelian and Weber, a Kantian. Curiously, such a dichotomy of philosophy continues to permeate German academic life today.

Günther Roth believed that the thought of Marx and Weber is not as incompatible as many critics suggest. For example, Irving Zeitlin (1968: chap. 11) focused on Weberian thought as an elaboration of Marxism, and George Lichtheim supported the view that "the whole of Weber's sociology of religion fits *without difficulty* into the Marxian scheme" (1961: 385). No doubt the German academic milieu was profoundly influenced by Marx at the turn of the century, and often it is assumed that Weber too was so influenced. One of Weber's contemporaries, Ernst Troeltsch, who had compared the holistic and dynamic character of the dialectic with the piecemeal and static character of positivism, interpreted Weber's work as profoundly Marxian and argued that it may even have transcended the Marxian dialectic: "Marx, in particular, seems to have made a deep and lasting impression" (Troeltsch, quoted in Bendix and Roth 1971: 230). Early in his career Talcott Parsons wrote that Weber's *Protestant Ethic* was a "refutation of the Marxist thesis" (1929: 40), and Roth documented that Weber opposed Marxism, but he examined alleged Marxist influences upon Weber's early work and concluded that "Weber never had a Marxist phase." Even though Weber accepted the heuristic usefulness of historical materialism, he considered it unscientific, assumed it not to be linked to socialism, and condemned determinism in Marxism (Bendix and Roth 1971: 240).

Giddens (1971: 190–195) and Atkinson (1972) outlined the major differences between Marx and Weber. Weber, for example, argued that revolution need not be necessary for the advancement of the working class; indeed the interests of the bourgeoisie, within capitalism, might involve an improvement in the political and economic conditions of the working class. Weber also acknowledged the importance of class conflicts in history but placed emphasis on the conflict among status groups and within other interests, such as those of political parties. Further, Weber, unlike Marx, separated factual from normative statements: "It is Weber's conviction that historical development cannot be interpreted in terms of a rational scheme which expresses what is normatively valid" (Giddens 1971: 195).

Colletti critiqued Weber's use of the ideal type as "a purely abstract and *conventional* 'model.'" Weber's scientific concept became "a utopia," he argued, and theoretical generalization could not contend with reality. An understanding of the present meant the exclusion of the past, for Weber "failed to see that the differences *between* past and present also divide the past from *today*" (Colletti 1972: 42–43). Marx, in contrast, offered a history of economic thought, examining in particular the historical dynamics of the mode of production of bourgeois society. Colletti attempted to awaken the reader to some misinterpretations of Marx's work. First, there is the orthodox view of some Marxists that Marxism is a science, not an ideology, and it makes only objective and impartial judgments of fact. Colletti argued that such a "view clearly allows no room for a link between *science* and *class* consciousness, between science and ideology" (1972: 230). Another distortion is the view of some Marxists that political economy is essential. But, argued Colletti, all of Marx's major works focus on political economy: "For Marx, political economy is born with the extension and generalization of commodity production. It is born with capitalism and dies with it" (232).

Many differences and some similarities in the thought of Marx and Weber have been identified. Table 4.1 summarizes in a schematic way some of the major ideas that flow through their works.

Paradigmatic Influences on Comparative Politics

Advances in knowledge are facilitated by the existence of a base of ideas upon which new theory can be built. Marx and Weber presented the study of politics with two such bases, each with its set of assumptions and understandings. Contemporary students of comparative politics might benefit by a close examination of their theories and insights, for the extent of the influence of past thinkers is not always fully understood. Our purpose is to focus on the thought of Marx and Weber in an effort to search for the roots of a paradigm of comparative politics. The reader should be cognizant, however, that exclusive attention to Marx and Weber ignores a wide range of other thinkers whose ideas might be helpful in the paradigmatic search.

The influence of Marx and Weber on each of the subfields of comparative politics is not uniform, nor are the subfields themselves free from spillover. In examining the influence of Marxian and Weberian thought upon each subfield, we do not mean to imply a degree of categorical distinctiveness that in practice may be illusory. The subfields of system, culture, development, and class cluster around theories and do indeed overlap, but we shall discuss each separately. Table 4.2 may also help the reader identify the essential concepts in the thought of Marx and Weber that are distinguishable among the four subfields.

SYSTEMS THEORY

Contemporary politics has been considerably influenced by theories of system. The contributions of the anthropologists A. R. Radcliffe-Brown and Bronislaw Malinowski stimulated inquiry about system, especially its functional and structural characteristics. The sociologist Talcott Parsons drew upon their work as well as that of Weber in a formulation of system. In political science David Easton abstracted a theory of political system, with its inputs of demands and supports and outputs of decisions and policies. Influenced by Easton as well as by Parsons and Weber, Gabriel Almond combined their various approaches so that the applicability of systems theory to comparative politics might become more apparent. Almond explicitly

TABLE 4.1
Synthesis of the Thought of Marx and Weber: An Inventory of Ideas

Concept Idea	Marx	Weber
View of history	Holistic, historical, and materialistic. Based on mode of production.	Fragmentary and ahistorical. No knowledge of the world can be complete.
Reality	Reality is the objective of science.	Reality is unattainable because investigator and scope of inquiry are limited.
Theory (praxis)	Theory and practice combined in thought and action.	Theory is the foundation of inquiry. Application of knowledge to inquiry is marginal.
Social science knowledge	Liberated from ideology, social scientific knowledge exposes exploitation of one class over another.	Social science explains through empirical findings.
Politics	Social scientist is political, and should mix investigation with political activity.	Social scientist is apolitical and objective.
Values	Values mixed with knowledge and facts. Values have material bases.	Values separated from facts that are a basis for inquiry. Empirical science cannot provide binding norms.
Laws	History predicated on common laws related to differing modes of production, productive forces, and relations of production and economic development.	History has no common laws. History cannot generate general laws for social science.
Capitalism	Promotes exploitation of worker, resulting in alienation. Capitalism is wasteful, inefficient, and irrational.	Promotes development through rationalization, efficiency, and stability.
Dialectic	Contradictions of capitalism bring about its demise.	Capitalism transcends its contradictions through rational planning.
Society	Ultimately socialist, then communist, as means of production pass from private control to public control and to hands of workers committee for managing affairs of bourgeoisie.	Ultimately secular and rationally bureaucratic in industrial capitalism. Competition. The highest good viewed in a nationalist context.
State	Disappears with emergence of classless society.	Strengthens with industrial capitalism, imperialist expansions, and rationalization of bureaucratic order.

TABLE 4.1 (cont.)

Concept Idea	Marx	Weber
Action	Reflection of objective material conditions determined by production of individuals.	Actors reflect on subjective meaning of what they do or refrain from doing.
Industrial freedom	Possible under socialism, but limited under capitalism where choices are determined by class position. Freedom with elimination of alienation.	Possible under capitalism, as long as people can choose among alternative life styles.
Heuristic device (construct or categories)	Mode of production as material basis of society.	Ideal types in comparison with real situations.
Method	Dialectic.	Ideal typification.
Power	Dominating interests.	Competing and diffused interests.
Authority	Illegitimate through state or ruling class.	Legitimate domination through traditional, charismatic, and rational forms.
Imperialism	Historical phenomenon necessitated by capitalism and later characterized by Lenin as the highest stage of capitalism.	Expansive foreign policies of governments.

substituted a conception of system for the more elusive term, *state*. Neither Marx nor Weber directed attention explicitly to system, but both concerned themselves with the state, especially under capitalism. Thus, we turn to a discussion of their respective conceptions of the state.

Marx offered an important conception of the state and its ruling class. All history, he believed, was the struggle of classes. Through time and struggle, society has become increasingly more simplified as antagonisms divide people into two hostile classes, the bourgeoisie and the proletariat. The first elements of the bourgeoisie sprang from the merchant class in towns that had been established in feudal times. Manufacturing quickly replaced the earlier form of production of the closed guilds, and as manufacturing was stimulated by the demands of new markets, a manufacturing bourgeoisie pushed aside the guild masters. With the further expansion of the markets and the invention of machinery, modern industry began to take the place of early manufacturing. A modern bourgeoisie emerged along with the estab-

TABLE 4.2
Essential Concepts in the Thought of Marx and Weber That Are Applicable to Four
Subfields of Comparative Politics

Theoretical Thrust	Marx	Weber
System	Monolithic capitalist state and ruling class (the economic class that rules politically through the state). Superstructure (Ideology) and structural base (Reality). Changes in the substructure of material forces, relations of production, and modes of production result in conflict and transformation of the superstructure.	Pluralist state of physical force and legitimized domination that promotes competition and distribution of power. Rationality, functional differentiation, and specialization, resulting in order, harmony, and efficiency.
Culture	Dominant authority is hierarchical and related to state and ruling class. Beliefs and symbols of culture conceived as part of the superstructure of ideology and false consciousness. Exploitation and illegitimate authority are parameters of ruling class dominance.	Dominant authority based on beliefs and symbols in relation to ideal types: traditional, charismatic, and rational. Routinization of rational authority reflects increasing socialization. Individualism plus voluntarism (obedience) and legitimate control are parameters of liberty.
Development	Historical materialism and the dialectic method. Theory grounded in the facts of historical reality, not in idealist and illusory conceptions. Development relates to human needs and human consciousness is based on the dialectical interplay of human beings with the material world: its productive forces and modes of production. Focus on capitalist development.	Rationalization and ideal typology method. Theory grounded in clarification. Systematization of ideas and their impact on society. Emphasis on requisites of development. Focus on capitalist development.
Class	Bourgeoisie and proletariat as opposing classes under capitalism. Industrial capitalists and landowners conflict with wage laborers but fragmentation found in each of these big classes. Power concentrated in the dominant classes that control means of production.	Class and status groups seen as ideal types that affect dispersion of power and interests in the community. Mobility of individuals within status groups and status groups within classes based on initiative, achievement, and talent. Class fragmentation rather than solidarity viewed as consequence of religious beliefs, ethnic loyalties, and nationalism.

lishment of modern industry and world markets, and it became essential that this bourgeoisie assure not only its economic dominance but also its political control over the modern state. As a consequence, "The executive of the modern state is but a committee for managing the common affairs of the whole bourgeoisie" (Marx 1974a: 69).

In his understanding of state Marx was influenced by Hegel, but their conceptions differed nevertheless (the reader might benefit from the recognition of their respective positions presented in Boulder Kapitalistate Collective and Fay 1976). The state was essential in Hegel's philosophy. He considered the state to be separate from civil society, that is, a society with government and laws, yet the state moderates and resolves the conflicts that emerge within civil society. After Hegel's death, his followers diverged in their interpretations of the state. The left or Young Hegelians criticized his idea of state, and Marx took a radical position as early as 1843, arguing that the state is a creation of the civil society; the state perpetuates a hierarchical class structure and thus protects the interests of the ruling class. Although the interests of the ruling class may promote clashes with the state from time to time, the relationship between the ruling class and the state must not be obscured by such conflict; ultimately both the state and the ruling class should be abolished.

In Marx's view the class that rules economically, that is, owns and controls the means of production, also rules politically. Under capitalism the state is the agency that maintains the property relations of the wealthy minority, and the consequence is the oppression of one class by another. Thus the state does not represent all the people, rich and poor. The state does not stand above class as long as classes exist; it is always on the side of the rulers.

In drawing the relationship of the state to the ruling class Marx offered a perspective of society. Differentiation exists within society between its superstructure and its structural base, sometimes referred to as the substructure or infrastructure. The base comprises productive forces and the social relations of production built upon them; that is, productive forces and the control and ownership of the means of production determine the divisions of labor that separate some members of society from other members. The legal and political superstructure consists of low or high levels of conceptions that the people have about the world. Such conceptions are dependent upon the base. They also are ideologies, resulting in false consciousness. The role of science, said Marx, is to expose those ideologies that are preserved in the interest of the dominant class. Only a revolution against those classes can rid the system of such ideologies. In the preface to his *Contribution to the Critique of Political Economy* Marx summarized the following position as the essence of his thought.

In the social production of their existence, men inevitably enter into definite relations, which are independent of their will, namely relations of production appropriate to a given stage in the development of their material forces of production. The totality of these relations of production constitutes the economic structure of society, the real foundation, on which arises a legal and political superstructure and to which correspond definite forms of social consciousness. The mode of production of material life conditions the general process of social, political, and intellectual life. It is not the consciousness of men that determines their existence, but their social existence that determines their consciousness. At a certain stage of development, the material productive forces of society come into conflict with the existing relations of production. . . . From forms of development of the productive forces these relations turn into their fetters. Then begins an era of social revolution. The changes in the economic foundation lead sooner or later to the transformation of the whole immense superstructure. In studying such transformations it is always necessary to distinguish between the material transformation of the economic conditions of production, which can be determined with the precision of natural science, and the legal, political, religious, artistic or philosophic—in short, ideological forms in which men become conscious of this conflict and fight it out. . . . No social order is ever destroyed before all the productive forces for which it is sufficient have been developed, and new superior relations of production never replace older ones before the material conditions for their existence have matured within the framework of the old society. . . . In broad outline, the Asiatic, ancient, feudal, and modern bourgeois modes of production may be designated as epochs marking progress in the economic development of society. [Marx 1975: 425–426]

In summary, the essential elements of Marx's thinking that may be relevant to a critical discussion of system theory are state and ruling class, superstructure and structural base, reality and ideology, material forces and relations of production, as well as modes of production that have characterized epochs of history. The state exists alongside the ruling class and manages its affairs. The structural base is found in the material forces and relations of production—the mode of production or the real foundation that determines division in labor and class. The superstructure consists of the legal and political conceptions or theories that envision society as it should be, not as it is; they are ideals, abstracted from concrete historical phenomena, but such ideals perpetuate the false ideologies about the world in which people live.

Weber certainly was familiar with the Marxian use of superstructure and structural base as well as with the connotation of ideology. Weber, however, did "not accept Marx's assertion that social existence determines consciousness" (C. Mayer 1975: 706). Instead he examined the differences between the ideal and the real, an approach Mayer called "dualist." This willingness to focus on the ideal as well as on the real undoubtedly inspired Parsons and and many other systems theorists to suggest abstractions and schemes that today pervade much of the comparative politics literature.

Weber was interested in general theory of society, and his use of the "ideal" type proved useful in such theory. He believed that the investigator could place himself subjectively into an actor's place and thereby interpret actions and motives. Weber also was concerned with the "interests" of individuals as linked with what Parsons has referred to as "systems of meanings" (Parsons, in Weber 1968: xxiii). It is not clear, though, that Weber stood as a systems theorist: "He explicitly repudiated the desire to set up a 'system' of scientific theory, and never completed a systematic work" (Parsons, in Weber 1947: 3). But Parsons insisted that there are important systematic elements in Weber's thought. For example, Weber believed that capitalism was essential to the modern world. Further, he identified Protestantism as an ingredient in the capitalist world-wide enterprise of market, money, property, and profit. Protestantism characterizes what Parsons inferred was Weber's modern Western system. Two aspects of the Protestant orientation help us understand Weber's conception of system. One is rationality; the drive of Protestantism is "for rational mastery over the world." The other is "functional differentiation and specialization of roles," a Protestant orientation promoted by valuing individualism in the "process of active mastery over the world" (Parsons, in Weber 1947: 80–81).

Weber also referred to the "ideal and material interests" in which all people are engaged. His observation implied a multiplicity of interests and many competing forces, and authority was based on "legitimate order" (Bendix 1960: 477). All these terms are incorporated into Weber's conception of the state.

Weber defined the state as "a human community that (successfully) claims *the monopoly of legitimate use of physical force* within a given territory" (Weber 1958a: 78). Weber ascribed to the state the sole right to use physical force or violence, and it is within this context that he offered an understanding of politics as the "striving to share power or striving to influence the distribution of power, either among states or among groups within a state . . . the state is a relation of men dominating men, a relation supported by means of legitimate . . . violence" (Weber 1958a: 78). Through its right to use violence the state presides over a situation in which the dominance of some prevails over others. But dominance is the consequence of the competition among groups to gain power, all this within an order of legitimacy. Weber identified three legitimations of domination: traditional domination by the patriarch or patrimonial prince; charismatic domination by the prophet, warlord, demagogue, or party leader; and legal domination by the bureaucrat or state servant. Weber called these "pure" or ideal types. He preferred legal domina-tion, for it implies routinization, harmony, efficiency, and order in the bureaucratic organization of the state.

What are the characteristics of this idealized bureaucracy? A high degree of specialization prevails because of the clear division of labor in the distribu-tion of organizational tasks. Positions are structured hierarchically into a pyramid of authority, formal rules and regulations guide decisions and ac-tions, lines of communication are clearly established among administrative levels, and impersonal detachment and relations ensure the rational carry-ing out of duties. Those are the rational and efficient characteristics of Weber's typical bureaucracy. Blau mentioned criticisms of that idealized con-ception. As an implicitly functional scheme, it does not specify dysfunctions and thus overlooks the conflicts that arise among the elements of the system. "Weber's one-sided concern with the functions of bureaucratic in-stitutions blinds him to some of the most fundamental problems bureaucratization creates." In addition, Weber's preoccupation with formal aspects of the bureaucracy precludes an examination of the informal rela-tions and patterns in formal organization (Blau, in Wrong 1970: 141–145).

In summary, the aspects of Weber's thinking that relate to contemporary formulations of systems theory are rationality, functional differentiation, and specialization of roles within the framework of the state. Within the state and its physical force, there are competing forces and a plurality of in-terests that share in the power and influence the distribution of power. This competition takes place with an order of legitimized domination. Weber's idealized conception envisions routinization, harmony, and efficiency. Marx would condemn it as an aberration of false consciousness that distorts an understanding of the modern capitalist world.

The systemic conceptions of Marx and Weber are sharply different. Although both thinkers focused on the political ramifications of the state in the society at large Marx interpreted the structure of the state as monolithic and tied to the interests of the ruling class, whereas Weber saw that structure as sanctioning a plurality of interests. Both concerned themselves with dominance: Marx viewed all forms of dominance under the capitalist state as illegitimate, and Weber looked to the legitimate forms of dominance. Marx advocated the abolition of the state and its classes; Weber envisioned the enhancement of the state through the legitimation of its activities. Marx understood changes in the state and the ruling class as reflections of historical materialism and the conflictual interplay of social relations and forces of production that have characterized various epochs. Weber, in con-trast, concerned himself with the resolution of conflict through the ra-tionalization of the bureaucratic order, for he saw European capitalism as promoting a highly rationalized and therefore stable form of society and felt that its maintenance was tantamount to preserving order. Both Marx and Weber examined how states use physical force or violence. Weber's explanation combined state force and violence with legitimacy, but Marx offered a broader definition in which the state can be nothing but a subtle instrument of coercion to suppress the lower strata.

CULTURE THEORY

The politics of culture constitutes another major thrust in the literature of comparative politics. In its contemporary usage, political culture has a variety of meanings. In general it refers to beliefs, symbols, and values. For Gabriel Almond all political systems are embedded in a pattern of orientations to political action. Samuel Beer and Adam Ulam argued that the pattern consists of ideas and traditions about authority. Sidney Verba referred to political culture as the orientations of all the members of a political system. These patterns may be cognitive, involving feelings about politics, or evaluative, involving judgments about politics. They are transmitted from generation to generation by varied institutions of communication and socialization such as the family, school, and work place. These contemporary meanings of political culture suggest a concern with general patterns, such as cultural traditions relating to authority, on the one hand, and with particular patterns such as individual preferences about politics, on the other hand. Both Marx and Weber were interested in these two levels.

The contemporary use of political culture usually encompasses the subjective or psychological milieu for politics. Marx would relate this idea of culture to his general treatment of the superstructure, which pervades society at large. At a particular level he viewed culture in the context of human alienation. In contrast, Weber related culture on a general level to authority and legitimacy; this was apparent in his examination of religion. Weber's particular treatment of culture incorporated a belief in individualism and voluntarism. At bottom, Marx defined culture in materialistic terms, while Weber defined culture in idealistic terms. We turn now to their different conceptions.

Marx perceived materialism as the basis of all history, and therefore of culture, and he conceived of materialism as including the means and modes by which people reproduce their existence through production. Culture, with its beliefs and symbols, forms part of the superstructure of a capitalist society. As such, culture is static, for it serves to legitimize the materialist base, thus protecting the interests of the privileged ruling class. Culture manifests, promotes, and perpetuates ideology as false consciousness, and culture tends to persist through time. Transformations in the mode and in the relations and means of production have characterized periods of history. The contrast between the static culture and the dynamic materialist base reveals inherent contradictions and makes apparent the increasingly irrelevant culture in relation to the actual material practices of society. Thus, Marx identified periods of history as characterized by new cultural formulations upon which the state rested and within which the dominant class—be it composed of feudal lords, merchants, or industrial capitalists—legitimized its role of exploitation.

The contradictions of the base and the culture are evident at the individual level. In the *Economic and Philosophical Manuscripts* Marx expounded on the concept of alienated labor. He saw capitalism tending toward the impoverishment of the worker, while enriching the capitalist and allowing concentration of capital. "Labor is external to the worker . . . he therefore does not confirm himself in his work, but denies himself, feels miserable and not happy, does not develop free mental and physical energy, but mortifies his flesh and ruins his mind" (Marx 1975: 326). In *The German Ideology* Marx discussed how division of labor and private property results in cleavage. "As long as a cleavage exists between the particular and the common interest, as long, therefore, as the activity is not voluntary, but naturally divided, man's own deed becomes an alien power opposed to him, which enslaves him instead of being controlled by him." Marx described the relationship between the individual and the community as undermined once the interest of the community takes the "form of the state, divorced from the real interests of individual and community" (Marx and Engels 1973: 53). In the *Grundrisse* Marx distinguished between the private individual, meaning the owner of the means of production and labor power, and the social individual, meaning the new human being or "the universally developed individual" of a classless society (Marx 1973: 161–162).

"Weber's thinking was dominated by the concept of the ideal type, which he applied to both cultural content and individual motives." In this statement Talcott Parsons (Weber 1968: lxiii) implied that Weber's attention to culture was directed to the general as well as to the particular level of thinking. The essence of Weber's concern with culture, as has been true of many of his successors who have dealt with culture and personality theory, was the use of ideal types of legitimate authority.

Weber identified three ideal types of legitimate authority that affect culture (Weber 1947: pt. 3): traditional, charismatic, and rational authority. The legitimacy of traditional authority is based on rules handed down from the past, and personal status and authority rest with an individual or chief who has been chosen on a traditional basis. The legitimacy of this traditional system of authority is questioned only when new and unmanageable crises arise, for which solutions prove impotent. When the traditional authority crumbles, the society may come under the control of a charismatic authority, resting on loyalty to the exceptional heroism or the exemplary character of an individual, who stimulates faith among his followers.

The legitimacy of charismatic authority depends upon success in coping with the crisis that toppled the traditional order. The culture propagated by this style of authority is that of the prophet leading a people to a new future. Submission to faith in charismatic authority is in contrast to the submission to the religion or mysticism of traditional authority. Charismatic authority is opposed to the routine control of action, which characterizes both traditional and rational authority. With the fall of a charismatic leader, there are alternative ways for the followers to legitimize their new social standing. They may choose to construct a new traditionalism on the basis of the teachings of the charismatic leader. In this event a return to traditional authority comes about. They may decide instead to routinize authority, rationalizing it along several lines. This latter direction necessitates a secularization or separation of religious and governmental practices, which involves a proliferation of administrative regulatory functions, the introduction of impersonal discipline and rules of procedure, and an expansion of economic activity and taxation to finance the emerging bureaucracy.

These developments promote legal rational authority as the consequence of some religious impact, for example, the Reformation, and of the capital accumulation that brought deep changes to Europe, whose history Weber believed to be of one coherent civilization. Thus those in the comparative field who model their cultural analysis after Weber must take caution not to generalize about the directions underdeveloped nations might follow, given changes in their culture, by referring to the European experience.

Weber identified examples of authority types in the collective cultural experiences of nations, groups, and even tribes, but he also noted particular orientations toward culture. Weber condemned the Prussian Junkers, for example, for their exploitation of the farm workers, yet he emphasized their positive contributions to the evolving German state. He did not see their motives and actions as a product of economic interests, as the Marxists maintain; instead he emphasized their individualism and determination in the face of a harsh environment. He also noted the individualism and basic drive of the farm workers who opposed the Junker ruling class: "We want to cultivate and support what appears to us as valuable in man: his personal responsibility, his basic drive toward higher things, toward the spiritual and moral values of mankind, even where this drive confronts us in its most primitive form" (Weber, quoted in Bendix 1960: 44). Weber's concern with the autonomy of the individual was clearly a reflection of the liberal legacy of the nineteenth century. It also became a basis upon which liberal scholars tended to examine individual orientations toward culture in the twentieth century.

For Weber, then, culture was an important determinant of social action and, therefore, of the historical development of civilization. Beliefs and symbols are distinctive features of his notion of authority. Authority rests on two levels, the general and the particular. Peter M. Blau related Weber's conception of authority to "two basic types of power, the domination of others that rests on the ability to influence their interests, and the domination that rests on authority, that is, the power to command and the duty to obey" (in Wrong 1970: 147–148). Ignored in this conception is coercive power, and assumed to exist is a belief system that legitimizes control as well as a voluntary obedience and compliance of subordinates to accept the will of their superiors. Blau called attention to the paradox between voluntarism and authoritarian control. Weber, he argued, assumed the existence of a legitimate authority without relating it to the structural conditions from which it emanates. Finally, Blau described the ideal type as "an abstraction that combines several analytical elements which appear in reality not in pure form but in various admixtures" (in Wrong 1970: 153). Blau cited the criticism of Alexander von Schelting, who argued that implicit in Weber's approach are two basic constructs: the individualizing ideal type, exemplified only once in history by Western capitalism, and the generalizing type, which includes many examples. The former type "is doomed to failure," and the latter led Weber to introduce value judgments into his analysis (153–155).

In summary, the Marxist conception explains culture by referring to the political, social, and economic settings of society, whereas the Weberian conception explains the political, social, and economic settings by referring to the culture. Marx understood dominant authority as hierarchically vested in the capitalist state in concert with the ruling class. Exploitation characterized this class's dominance and illegitimate authority. Its so-called legitimacy was simply disguised within the ideology of beliefs and symbols that pervaded the culture and ideological superstructure. Weber considered that the beliefs and symbols of the culture reinforced and legitimized the various ideal types of dominant authority. Marx emphasized that the alienation of the individual in a materialist society was the consequence of a dominant authority and the exploitation of capitalism. Weber stressed the drive of the individual within a context of voluntary obedience and legitimate controls—the parameters of a liberal society in which rationalized bureaucratic order thrives. Thus, significant differences are apparent in the Marxist and Weberian interpretations of culture. Clearly each conception yields different categories and consequently, different assumptions and explanations that affect the outcome of study in comparative politics.

DEVELOPMENT THEORY

Theories of development cluster around a variety of themes in the comparative politics literature. Democracy is a topic found in the traditional literature of political science. Democracy usually referred to the experience of Europe and the United States, but when comparativists turned to the many new nations, especially in the Third World, there was a reassessment. Scholars such as Lucian Pye tended to replace democracy with the term political development. Stage theories of development also were common. Walt W. Rostow set forth a number of stages through which capitalist development progresses, and A.F.K. Organski modeled an approach to political development somewhat along the lines of Rostow. Literature on nation building, nationalism, and development was widely recognized after the Second World War; it is perhaps best represented by the contributions of Karl Deutsch and Rupert Emerson. Finally, there were interpretations based on modernization, usually in the form of industrialization and other advances of the capitalist nations; the works of David Apter and Samuel Huntington exemplify this tendency. All these theories of development reflect the prevailing orthodox paradigm of comparative politics. It is also clear that the ideas and thought of Max Weber have influenced the formulation of these theories.

A counterthrust emerged to oppose these mainstream theories of development in comparative politics. The new thrust examined underdevelopment, especially in the nations of Latin America, Africa, and Asia. Although the mainstream literature understood development to be the consequence of the diffusion of capital and technology from the advanced to the backward areas, critics of this interpretation saw the consequence of such diffusion to be underdevelopment itself. Attempts of the industrialized nations to apply their models of democracy and civic culture to backward areas were also futile, resulting in increased repression and exploitation.

Writers such as André Gunder Frank focused on the development of underdevelopment, arguing that capitalism on a world scale produces developing metropoles and underdeveloping satellites. Theotonio dos Santos referred to the era of "New Dependency" in characterizing monopoly capitalism and the activities of the multinational corporations throughout the world. Fernando Henrique Cardoso argued that dependent capitalist development was evident in the underdeveloped world. Cardoso and others also began to link their theories of dependency to Lenin's theory of imperialism. Many interpretations and applications of dependency were soon adopted by social scientists of many persuasions. The confusion that ensued was partially because of the failure of many writers to root their theory in the writings of Marx.

Marx's materialistic view focused on the developmental process. Marx saw most theories, except his own, as bourgeois and ideological. His attack on Hegel "was a materialist view of an idealist argument" (Sprinzak 1975: 401). In his *Theses on Feuerbach*, Marx rejected speculative and philosophical views of reality and indicted both idealists and materialists. The eleventh thesis states, for example, "The philosophers have only *interpreted* the world, in various ways; the point is to *change* it" (Marx and Engels 1973: 123). Marx urged the scientific study of reality, of "the actual life process," and consequently he focused most of his attention on a critique of bourgeois capitalist society rather than on speculation about the future of society. Thus Marx sought a clear and direct view, a materialist view, of the world and, in particular, its developmental process through historical periods. His perspective of development was tied to his understanding of dialectical and historical materialism.

Marx intended his understanding to be scientific in the sense of avoiding materialist or idealist abstractions in favor of "human science." With Engels in *The German Ideology*, he wrote, "Where speculation ends, in real life, there positive science begins: the depiction of the practical activity, of the practical process of development, of men" (quoted in Thomas 1976: 7). The use of science here was not positivistic in the Comtian sense. "Marx uses the word throughout his writings in such a way that it is always quite incompatible with a crude, positivistic usage, although not all of Engels' formulations are incompatible with positivism in anything like the same way" (Thomas 1976: 7).

Marx's concepts of development are not definable in positivist terms. "Neither the 'relations of production' nor the 'mode of production' is definable in terms of physical objects; and even the 'forces of production,' which seem at first glance to be more empirical, are seen not as a concatenation of things but as a development, as something in transition, a development that takes place whenever the underlying social circumstances permit" (Thomas 1976: 9).

Marx believed that economic change can transform the superstructure of ideology, because human actions are dependent on changes in economic structure, in transformations affecting the dominant mode of production. Change for Marx is a reflection of a dialectical contradiction in the diverse social forces emerging from conflict. Carl Mayer described Marx's notion of dialectic as follows: "First, the conflict is only latently and potentially present and hidden by a relative harmony of interests. Then it becomes actual. It continues to rise, finally reaching a point where it puts the existence of the society in question" (C. Mayer 1975: 710).

Marx intended but never did write a full explanation of the dialectic, but its use is evident throughout his work. Marx of course gave a materialist interpretation to Hegel's idealist conception of the dialectic, and he turned Hegel's conception on its head by stripping it of mysticism and rigid schema. Howard Sherman called Marx's dialectic "a non-dogmatic method of approach to problems of science or politics of everyday life." He outlined five rules of the dialectic method along with questions for inquiry. First, *interconnection*: how does a problem relate to all of society? Second, *change*: how did the problem evolve and where is it headed? Third, unity of *opposites*: what are the opposing forces, where is the conflict? Fourth, *quantity and quality*: if a quantitative change is noted, what of qualitative change? Fifth, *negation of negation*: if one aspect eliminates another, can it in turn be eliminated? (Sherman 1976: 58–62). The method thus generates questions, it does not provide answers, but it does allow for a look at dynamic, not static, and at real, not ideal, aspects of society.

One example, drawn from Marx's *Introduction to a Critique of Political Economy*, demonstrates the dialectic method. Marx refuted the perspective of those economists who tended to treat four economic activities (production, distribution, exchange, and consumption) in isolation from each other. He began by demonstrating that production and consumption are one and the same and that each provides a means of bringing the other about.

> Production is thus at the same time consumption, and consumption is at the same time production. Each is simultaneously its opposite. But an intermediary movement takes place between the two at the same time. Production leads to consumption, for which it provides the material; consumption without production would have no object. But consumption also leads to production by providing for its products the subject for whom they are products. [Marx and Engels 1973: 131]

The dialectic method stimulates a continuous reassessment of theories according to new facts. It also promotes the search for new facts and their interpretation according to new theories.

Marx's materialism emphasized the grounding of theory on the facts of historical reality, and historical materialism provided Marx with a perspective of development.

> History is nothing but the succession of the separate generations, each of which exploits the materials, the capital funds, the productive forces handed down to it by all preceding generations. . . . This conception of history depends on our ability to expound the real process of production, starting out from the material production of life itself, and to comprehend the form of intercourse connected with this and created by this mode of production . . . as the basis of all history. [Marx and Engels 1973: 57–58]

Marx carefully separated this material base of successive generations in history from all idealistic views of history. The materialist view "remains constantly on the real ground of history," while the idealistic view looks for a category in every period; the materialist view "explains the formation of ideas from material practice," whereas the idealistic view explains "practice from the idea" (Marx and Engels 1973: 58). Marx believed that in history human consciousness is conditioned on the dialectical interplay between human beings and the material world. Accordingly, history is a continuous process of creating and satisfying human needs. Once needs are satisfied, new needs are created:

> there is found a material result: a sum of productive forces, an historically created relation of individuals to nature and to one another, which is handed down to each generation from its predecessor; a mass of productive forces, capital funds and conditions, which, on the one hand, is indeed modified by the new generation, but also on the other prescribes for it its conditions of life and gives it a definite development, a special character. [Marx and Engels 1973: 59]

Marx analyzed various types of society, including those manifesting Asiatic, ancient, and feudal modes of production, but his principal interest lay with an interpretation of the bourgeois mode of production in a capitalist society. His theory of capitalist development is found in *Capital*: "The wealth of those societies in which the capitalist mode of production prevails, presents itself as 'an immense accumulation of commodities,' its unit being a single commodity" (Marx 1967, 1: 35). A commodity he said, is "an object outside us" that "satisfies human wants of some sort." Every commodity has a "use-value" or utility as well as "exchange-value" or the value of a product offered in exchange for other products. Marx relates both of these values to labor in the production of a commodity. Labor itself is viewed as a commodity and is exchanged on the market. The worker produces enough to cover his cost of subsistence, but whatever he produces over and beyond is surplus value. Surplus value is a source of profit and capital accumulation. In simplified form these are the concepts used in Marx's theory of capitalist development, which are elaborated in *Capital*.

Weber's ideal types of dominant and legitimate authority have already been noted. Weber clearly considered the development of legal rationality to be a major consideration in Western civilization, upon which he focused most of his attention. Bendix suggests that "Weber was not interested in developmental theories" (1960: 326). He tended to move abruptly from one type of domination to another, somewhat in piecemeal fashion. He was not interested in explanation that traced the evolution of the European state from its feudal foundations, but he was willing to identify the distinctive characteristics of the modern bourgeois state. Although there were many types of capitalism—for example, political, imperialist, colonial, adventure, fiscal, and modern industrial capitalism (Weber 1958a: 66–68)—capitalism was the highest formal rationalization in Western civilzation. Weber isolated aspects that typified rational bourgeois capitalism: secularity was one such aspect, maximization of effency was another. Alongside bureaucratization, professionalization also was essential in the rationalization of society (Ritzer 1975).

Ann Swidler characterized rationalization in Weber's thought as a process by which ideas are systematized to influence action, provide for change, and promote stability and autonomy.

> First, rationalization is the key process which gives ideas the capacity to influence social action. Secondly, rationalization provides an internal dynamic of change for systems of ideas. It is one of the major sources of change in ideas *as ideas*. Thirdly, it is through rationalization that systems of ideas gain stability and autonomy in relation to the social world. [Swidler 1973: 36]

Rationalization clarifies, systematizes, and integrates ideas, thus providing societies with ideal frameworks within which action, change, and stability are achieved; for example, as ideas become consistent and integrated within a society at large, they tend to create new problems that demand resolution. Rationality also may promote irrationality; capitalism, for instance, might be based on the accumulation of wealth but not on the enjoyment of life for a majority of individuals. Carl Mayer (1975: 710–711) accordingly characterized Weber as a theorist of conflict, not of harmony as many critics have claimed. Weber assumed that a society may continue to exist in spite of conflict or that conflict may be resolved. Tradition becomes decisive in Weber's perspective of a changing society. Mayer also believed that Weber rejected the necessity of developmental stages as well as the notion that modern societies should be more highly valued than, say, ancient civilizations.

This view contrasts with Talcott Parsons's assertion that Weber contributed "a generally evolutionary view of the development of human society" (Parsons, in Weber 1968: lx). Daniel Rossides took exception to Parsons's position by arguing that most social scientists of modern times have engaged in "a metaphysical quest," the exception to this practice being Weber. He acknowledged, however, that the "diffusion of Weber's thought to the United States . . . has been highly selective . . . I would not be too wide of the mark to say that Weber's ideas . . . are the stock-in-trade of almost every practicing sociologist" (Rossides 1972: 184).

The nuances in Weber's thought no doubt deserve careful study, for the manner by which he described the rationalization of European capitalism at the turn of the century has come to constitute a model of development of considerable influence for comparative politics today. The rationalization of bureaucracy, the separation of church and state that leads to secularization, and the gradual institutionalization of parliamentarianism all form integral elements of that model. Characteristics of the model include administrative efficiency made possible by an insistence on professional skill for advancement; impersonal discipline that elevates the office over the occupant in a clearly deniable hierarchy of authority, elaboration of unambiguous written rules of operation, and specialization of functions in response to expanding social activity. Such a model institutes in society a stabilization of the socioeconomic order to a degree sufficient for the calculated risk that is capitalist investment. At the same time Weber argued that the bureaucratization of life brings in its wake an increasing probability of democratic practice. The requisites of democratic practice are tolerance, precise legality, and representative government. Within this context, a highly efficient order extracts social resources and utilizes them in realizing socially determined goals while, at the same time, mediating the competing demands of the citizenry.

Herbert Marcuse (1968) exposed some problems in Weber's conception of development. He examined the connections among capitalism, rationality, and domination in Weber's work. Western rationality, argued Marcuse, promotes a system of material and intellectual culture that develops in industrial capitalism and tends toward bureaucratic domination. This capitalist rationality evolves through private enterprise; thus the satisfaction of human needs is dependent on the profit possibilities of capitalist enterprise and the labor at its disposal. Marcuse insisted that such a conception is outmoded today by experience in the capitalist world—industrial capitalism has become irrational, not rational, because "the struggle for existence and the exploitation of labor must be intensified more and more if increased accumulation is to be possible"; development becomes irrational because "higher productivity, domination of nature, and social wealth become destructive forces " (Marcuse 1968: 207).

Weber did not anticipate such development, according to Marcuse, even though Weber envisioned "capitalist industrialization wholly as a form of power politics, that is imperialism" (208). Large-scale industry could guarantee national independence through the international competitive struggle of imperialist power politics and the expansion of colonialism and militarism. Ultimately, domination was based on the rationality of industrial capitalism, which in modern form became inseparable from bureaucratic control. The intensification of an efficient industrial organization extends to society as a whole and to control through bureaucratic administration.

In summary, Marx offered a dynamic conception of development premised on the interaction of people with the material world of productive forces and modes of production. Weber posited a static conception of development based on the identification of distinctive rational characteristics of the bureaucratic order of industrial states. Both Marx and Weber focused on bourgeois capitalism. Some critics would characterize Marx's perspective as revolutionary and realist, Weber's perspective as evolutionary and idealist. Marx used dialectics as his method; Weber employed ideal typologies. Marx looked for transformation in the structural base and grounded his theory on the facts of historical reality. Weber gave attention to the requisites of development, emphasizing routinization, efficiency, professionalization, secularity, differentiation, and specialization; and Weber grounded his theory on ideas and their impact on society.

CLASS THEORY

Studies of ruler and ruled have marked the comparative literature of politics from ancient times until the present. The theoretical contributions of Marx and Weber on this subject have provoked controversy and deep polemical and intellectual divisions within the social sciences. A generation of community studies revealed fundamental differences related to questions of who rules in a society. A dichotomy of positions has evolved in the theory emanating from these studies.

One position, resting upon a prevailing assumption in U.S. politics called pluralism, holds that multiple diverse interests and, therefore, a wide dispersion of power characterize the democratic order. Sometimes pluralism envisions society as made up of conflicting power groups, each group using power to further its own interests. For U.S. politics this view is found in the work of Robert Dahl, V. O. Key, and a host of other political scientists. Its origins are often traced to James Madison's *Federalist Papers* and to group theorists David Truman and Arthur Bentley. Pluralist assumptions are also indebted to the formulations of Gaetano Mosca and Vilfredo Pareto, who recognized the distinctions between a class that rules and a class that is ruled and tended to identify divisions within the ruling class, especially in democratic societies. They emphasized rule according to interests, not simply by force, and they referred to a circulation of elites or changes in elite membership over time. It is also evident that advocates of pluralism have been influenced by Weber's thinking.

The pluralist elite theory of Mosca, Pareto, and Weber attempted to refute Marx's conception of the ruling class. In recent times Dahl, Nelson Polsby, and others have continued this critique. Marx's thought has influenced a counterposition, commonly known as the ruling elite theory, although many of its advocates do not relate directly to a Marxist framework. This position is identifiable in Floyd Hunter's study of power structure in Atlanta and in C. Wright Mills's examination of the U.S. power elite. More recently G. William Domhoff has carried on the tradition. Their interpretations have challenged assumptions of democratic pluralism in the United States.

The debate between the plural elitists and the ruling elitists deflected attention from Marx's essential concern with a class analysis. Unlike Weber, who used class as a category for describing capitalist society at a particular point in time, Marx linked class to the material base in order to examine the source of changes in capitalist society. Thus under capitalism two classes stand in dialectical opposition to each other. In the *Communist Manifesto* these classes are the bourgeoisie, "the class of modern capitalists, owners of the means of the social production and employers of wage-labour," and the proletariat, "the class of modern wage-labourers who, having no means of production of their own, are reduced to selling their labour power in order to live" (Engels, in Marx 1974a: 67 n. 12). A Marxist understanding of capitalism necessitates an examination of the conflict between the two opposing class interests. Thus the ruling-elite analysis of Hunter and Mills does not relate to a Marxist framework, for their focus on a single class is static and exclusive of masses, nor does the stratification analysis of the political sociologists who emphasize position according to income, status, and other criteria. Whereas Marx looked for opposite attributes, stratificationists examine individual and group positions in relation to similar attributes.

Marx did not fully elaborate a conception of class, but class analysis is a central concern of his work. In the *Communist Manifesto*, Marx briefly traced the history of class antagonisms: patricians, knights, plebeians, and slaves in ancient Rome; feudal lords, vassals, guild masters, journeymen, apprentices, and serfs in the Middle Ages; and bourgeoisie and proletariat under modern bourgeois capitalism. Historically the bourgeoisie fulfilled a historical role; they put an end to feudal relations.

> The bourgeoisie cannot exist without constantly revolutionizing the instruments of production, and thereby the relations of production, and with them the whole relations of society. Conservation of the old modes of production in unaltered form, was, on the contrary, the first condition of existence for all earlier industrial classes. Constant revolutionizing of production, uninterrupted disturbance of all social conditions, everlasting uncertainty and agitation distinguish the bourgeois epoch from all earlier ones. . . . The need of a constantly expanding market for its products chases the bourgeoisie over the whole surface of the globe. It must nestle everywhere, settle everywhere, establish connections everywhere. [Marx 1974a: 70–71]

In contrast, the proletariat, the working class "who live only so long as they find work, and who find work only so long as their labor increases capital," are subservient to the bourgeois class. The proletariat assimilates

> the lower strata of the middle class—the small tradespeople, shopkeepers, and *rentiers*, the handicraftsmen and peasants—all these sink gradually into the pro-

letariat, partly because their diminutive capital does not suffice for the scale on which modern industry is carried on, and is swamped in the competition with the large capitalist, partly because their specialized skill is rendered worthless by new methods of production. Thus the proletariat is recruited from all classes of the population. [Marx 1974a: 75]

In *The German Ideology* Marx described the ruling class as a force that rules materially over production and intellectually over ideas.

The ideas of the ruling class are in every epoch the ruling ideas, i.e. the class which is the ruling *material* force of society, is at the same time its ruling *intellectual* force. The class which has the means of material production at its disposal, has control at the same time over the means of mental production, so that thereby, generally speaking, the ideas of those who lack the means of mental production are subject to it. The ruling ideas are nothing more than the ideal expression of the dominant material relationships, the dominant material relationships grasped as ideas; hence of the relationships which make the one class the ruling one, therefore, the ideas of its dominance. [Marx and Engels 1973: 64]

In *The Class Struggles in France, 1848–1850* and *The Eighteenth Brumaire of Louis Bonaparte*, Marx directly applied his conception of class to the revolutionary events of the mid-nineteenth century. His analysis focused on such class terms as the finance aristocracy, industrial bourgeoisie, petty bourgeoisie, peasantry, lumpenproletariat, industrial proletariat, bourgeois monarchy, and big bourgeoisie. An excerpt from his journalistic account of the complex struggle reveals his use of class analysis.

In France the petty bourgeois does what the industrial bourgeois would normally have to do; the worker does what would normally be the task of the petty bourgeoisie. Who then does the task of the worker? Nobody. It is not accomplished in France; it is only proclaimed. And it will not be accomplished within any national walls. The class war within French society will be transformed into a world war in which nation confronts nation. The worker's task will begin to be accomplished only when the world war carries the proletariat to the fore in the nation that dominates the world market, i.e. England. [Marx 1974b: 111–112]

Finally, in a brief last chapter of the third volume of *Capital*, Marx attempted to set forth a conception of classes: "Wage-labourers, capitalists and landowners constitute the three big classes of modern society based upon the capitalist mode of production." He urged caution in the stratification of classes, for in highly developed England, "Middle and intermediate strata even here obliterate lines of demarcation everywhere" (Marx 1967: 3: 885). Marx acknowledged the existence of less important classes – physicians and bureaucrats are two separate classes. Likewise, "the infinite fragmentation of interest and rank into which the division of social labour splits labourers as well as capitalists and landlords—the latter, e.g. into owners of vineyards, farm owners, owners of forests, mine owners and owners of fisheries" (Marx 1967: 3: 886).

This cursory review of Marx's writings on class is not meant to be definitive or even an attempt at a reconstruction of Marx's theory of classes and class struggle. Such a discussion is found elsewhere, for example, in Friedman (1974), Andrew (1975), Ollman (1968), Bendix and Lipset (1966), and Hodges (1959). What is clear, however, is that Marx's theory and analysis of class are neither doctrinaire nor deterministic and that he applied his criteria more prudently than did many of his followers. In a letter to Weydermeyer, Marx explained that he had proved

> (1) that the *existence of classes* is only bound up with particular historical phases in the development of production; (2) that the class struggle necessarily leads to the dictatorship of *the proletariat*; (3) that this dictatorship itself constituted the transition to the abolition of all classes and to a classless socity. [Quoted in Sprinzak 1975: 399]

In *Wirtschaft und Gesellschaft* Weber delineated a conception of class, and in a discussion on the distribution of power within a community, he focused first on class.

> We may speak of a "class" when (1) a number of people have in common a specific causal component of their life chances, in so far as (2) this component is represented exclusively by economic interests in the possession of goods and opportunities for income, and (3) is represented under the conditions of the commodity or labor markets. [Weber 1958a: 181]

His reference to life chances relates to "the way in which the disposition over material property is distributed among a plurality of people, meeting competitively in the market for the purpose of exchange" (Weber 1958a: 181). Possession of goods and opportunities for income implies ownership or lack of ownership of property. For Marx, property and the lack of property signified the class relations of the material productive base of society. For Weber, they were simply "basic categories of all class situations" (182). Ultimately, Weber said, a class situation is a market situation.

Concerned that class is an economically determined concept, Weber proposed that status groups also affect the distribution of power in a community, but his definition distinguishes between class and status group.

> In contrast to the purely economically determined "class situation" we wish to designate as "status situation" every typical component of the life fate of men

that is determined by a specific, positive or negative, social estimation of *honor*. This honor may be connected with any quality shared by a plurality, and, of course, it can be knit to a class situation: class distinctions are linked in the most varied ways with status distinctions. . . . But status honor need not necessarily be linked with a "class situation." [Weber 1958a: 187]

All status groups exist within the confines of what, according to Weber, can be defined as economic classes. These larger classes are not precisely circumscribed, nor do they reflect a high degree of commonality in the interests, dispositions, and loyalties of their members. Each class is composed of many status groups, so that it is possible to speak of a stratification of status groups within a class, hierarchically ranked in accord with relative market advantage. As the market demands change, the relationship of the status groups within a class may be constantly rearranged. Some of the market changes might elevate one status group from a lower to a higher class. Similarly, some status groups might slip in ranking. This argument suggests that persons are more interested in the fortunes of their status group than in the overall fortunes of the class to which they nominally belong. This leads Weber to a rejection of the Marxist notion of class consciousness since, in his view, there is insufficient shared interest among a group of individuals constituting the descriptive category of one or another class.

Not only is the mobility of status groups in flux, so too are the varying fortunes of individuals within status groups. Important is the ethic of individualism and achievement inherent in, according to Weber, modern capitalist democracy. By force of talent and initiative, an individual can move to membership in a higher status group through training, profession, and change in life style.

Reinhard Bendix (1974) synthesized and interpreted these propositions by contrasting Weber's stance to Marx's position. Weber, he said, accepted Marx's assertion that property ownership and division of labor are bases for the formation of classes, but Weber's approach differed from Marx's analysis in three ways. First, whereas Marx understood class as a consequence of productive forces and relations, Weber treated class as an ideal type. Second, Marx identified three large classes (landowners, capitalists, and workers) under capitalism and noted a tendency toward the formulation of two opposing classes of bourgeoisie and proletariat, but Weber anticipated a greater variety of class situations. Third, Marx optimistically believed that class consciousness would solidify the working class into a revolutionary force, but Weber argued that nationalism, religious beliefs, and ethnic loyalties would prove stronger than class consciousness and would promote class fragmentation.

Other distinctions are discernible in the class perspectives of Marx and Weber. Ashcraft mentioned that a large segment of U.S. political sociologists have adopted the Weberian view that income is a criterion of class, a position Marx clearly rejected. Further, Weber refused to consider class as anything other than an economic grouping; thus his sharp distinction between the economic and the social orders. The Weberian position influenced Weber's successors: "in removing from 'class' the social relationships Marx had included in his definition, Weber opened the door for a sociology based conceptually on the 'infinite dissipation of interests,' which, of course, liberalism had every ideological reason to embrace" (Ashcraft 1972: 147).

Ultimately one must decide if the configuration of classes leads research in useful directions, in which case Marx has provided a helpful formulation of class analysis. If, however, we see attention to classes as distractive, since it diverts inquiry from the situational and institutional nature of power in society as Weber suggested, then class analysis might be discarded. For the most part, it is Weber's model that prevails in comparative politics. Researchers look not to class divisions but to personal and institutional categories that distinguish power characteristics among countries.

In this chapter we briefly reviewed the life and thought of two precursors whose theoretical contributions have influenced contemporary comparative politics. We have identified their major works and ideas, and we have attempted to demonstrate the relationship of their thinking to the four subfields around which the comparative politics literature tends to cluster. The remaining chapters examine in some depth the origins and paradigmatic directions of those subfields.

References

Abel, Theodore
    1965 *Systematic Sociology in Germany: A Critical Analysis of Some Attempts to Establish Sociology as an Independent Science*. New York: Octagon Books. A critical but sympathetic examination of the sociological contributions of Georg Simmel, Alfred Vierkandt, Leopold von Wiese, and Max Weber. Originally published in 1929.
Althusser, Louis
    1970 *For Marx*. Translated by Ben Brewster. New York: Vintage Books. Essays published originally in French during the early 1960s. The author stresses the scientific nature of Marx's mature works in contrast to the ideological orientation of the earlier works.
Andrew, Edward
    1975 "Marx's Theory of Classes: Science and Ideology." *Canadian Journal of Political Science* VIII (September), 454–466. A review of attempts by numerous writers to define Marx's theory of classes and an attempt to offer a summary of Marx's position.

Aron, Raymond
1964 *German Sociology*. Translated by Thomas Bottomore. New York: Free Press of Glencoe. A comparison and contrast of the systematic, historical, and interpretive schools of German sociology, with emphasis on the works of Openheimer and Weber.

Ashcraft, Richard
1972 "Marx and Weber on Liberalism as Bourgeois Ideology." *Comparative Studies in Society and History* XIV (March), 130–168. Contrasts the theories of Marx and Weber and states that "their common agreement on the characterization of liberalism as bourgeois ideology concealed differences of historical interpretation, conflicting conceptions of methodology and opposing views of the social structure."

Atkinson, Dick
1972 *Orthodox Consensus and Radical Alternative: A Study in Sociological Theory*. New York: Basic Books. An interpretative and critical examination of the ideas and concepts in Parsons, Marx, and Weber, as well as their influence on modern sociologists. Seeks flexible but radical alternative.

Beer, M.
1942 *The Life and Teachings of Karl Marx*. London: George Allen and Unwin. A reprint of a 1924 work representing one of the first attempts to synthesize the personal influences in Marx's work and to present an overview of Marxist theory and its significance.

Bendix, Reinhard
1960 *Max Weber: An Intellectual Portrait*. Garden City, New York: Doubleday and Company. A detailed analysis of the sociopolitical problems and intellectual dispositions that guide Weber in his work. Emphasis is placed on the pragmatic identification of critical social problems in the development of Weber's writing.

1974 "Inequality and Social Structure: A Comparison of Marx and Weber." *American Sociological Review* XLIV (April), 149–161. Contrasts the Marxian argument on class in the organization of production with the Weberian emphasis on status differences and organized collective action.

Bendix, Reinhard, and Seymour Martin Lipset
1966 "Karl Marx's Theory of Social Classes." In Bendix and Lipset, *Class, Status and Power: A Reader in Social Stratification*, pp. 6–11. New York: Free Press. Interpretative synthesis of Marx's theory of classes. Critical and unsympathetic.

Bendix, Reinhard, and Guenther Roth
1971 *Scholarship and Partisanship: Essays on Max Weber*. Berkeley: University of California Press. Revisions of previously published essays that criticize Weber's substantive and methodological contributions as well as the place of his life in intellectual and political history. The first part examines his scholarship and partisanship, the second looks at authority and legitimacy, and the third deals with the intellectual influences, including that of Marx, on his thought.

Berger, Stephen
1971 "The Sects and the Breakthrough into the Modern World: On the Centrality of the Sects in Weber's Protestant Ethic Thesis." *Sociological Quarterly* XII

(Autumn), 486–499. A look at Weber's analysis of religious sects and an appraisal of their revolutionary potential in comparison to that of the proletariat as defined by Marx.

Berlin, Isaiah
1952 *Karl Marx: His Life and Environment*. London: Oxford University Press. A study of personal and cultural influences, as well as intellectual forces, that shaped Marx's thought.

Boulder Kapitalistate Collective and Margaret Fay
1976 "Hegel and the State." *Kapitalistate* 4–5 (Summer), 158–185. Influenced by Shlomo Avineri's *Hegel's Theory of the Modern State*, the authors argue that Hegel's ideas about the state are useful to contemporary Marxists. Familiarity with Hegel's ideas "deepen our comprehension of Marx's own political thought," and his theory illustrates the use of the dialectic method.

Cahnman, Werner J.
1965 "Ideal Type Theory: Max Weber's Concept and Some of Its Derivations." *Sociological Quarterly* VI (Summer), 268–280. The author departs from the premise that "Max Weber's concept of the ideal type rests on the generalized concept of rational social action, but it tends to beome a historical totality concept when applied to research problems." Interpretations and extensions of Weber's ideal-type constructions are reviewed and critiqued.

Cardoso, Fernando Henrique
1971 "Ideologias e estructuras de poder na ciência política." In *Política e desenvolvimento em sociendades dependentes: Ideologias do empresariado industrial argentino e brasileiro*, pp. 9–56. Rio de Janeiro: Zahar Editores. Distinguishes between the ideas of Marx and Weber and traces their respective influences upon contemporary social science.

Cohen, Jere, Lawrence E. Hazelrigg, and Whitney Pope
1975 "De-Parsonizing Weber; A Critique of Parsons' Interpretation of Weber's Sociology." *American Sociological Review* XL (April), 229–241. Critique of Talcott Parsons's interpretation of the work of Weber, demonstrating that his interpretation is erroneous and misleading.

Colletti, Lucio
1972 *From Rousseau to Lenin: Studies in Ideology and Society*. New York: Monthly Review Press. Essays translated by John Merrington and Judith White. The most useful for this study of Marx are "Marxism as a Sociology," 3–44, and "Marxism: Science or Revolution?" 229–236.

Cornu, August
1957 *The Origins of Marxist Thought*. Springfield, Illinios: Charles Thomas. An analysis of the precursors of Marxist theory and their incorporation into his work.

Dupré, Louis
1966 *The Philosophical Foundations of Marxism*. New York: Harcourt, Brace and World. A summary intended to introduce students to the major original works of Hegel and Marx. Examines how Marx derived his theory from Hegel's social philosophy and then focuses discussion on the humanistic and materialistic components of the Marxian system.

Freund, Julien
1968 *The Sociology of Max Weber*. New York: Pantheon Books. Advances a non-critical overview of Weber's world vision and methodology. Examines the special systems of sociology developed by Weber in the areas of economics, religion, politics, and law.

Friedman, Daniel J.
1974 "Marx's Perspective on the Objective Class Structure." *Polity* VI (Spring), 318–344. Attempts to clarify and define Marx's view of class structure. Identifies Marx's criteria as ownership versus nonownership of the means of production; degree of control over the products of labor; and productive versus unproductive work. Examines inconsistencies in Marx's application of these criteria.

Frohock, Fred M.
1974 "Notes on the Concept of Politics: Weber, Easton, Strauss." *Journal of Politics* XXXVI (May), 379–408. Examines conceptions of politics in the writings of these three thinkers. Concludes that Weber and Easton in the empirical tradition violate their own premises of neutrality and that Leo Strauss in his normative tradition does not account for "the full range of political experience. Thus, we do not yet have an accurate statement reflecting the relationship between evaluative and descriptive components in the concept of politics."

Fromm, Erich
1961 *Marx's Concept of Man*. New York: Frederick Ungar Publishing. Includes a translation from Marx's *Economic and Philosophical Manuscripts* by T. B. Bottomore and an introductory essay by Fromm, which demonstrates the unity of thought in Marx's early and later works.

Garaudy, Roger
1967 *Karl Marx: The Evolution of His Thought*. New York: International Publishers. A critical analysis of the evolution of Marx's thought, which identifies both its continuity and contradictions.

Giddens, Anthony
1971 *Capitalism and Modern Social Theory: An Analysis of the Writings of Marx, Durkheim, and Max Weber*. Cambridge: Cambridge University Press. A reconsideration of the works of Marx, Durkheim, and Weber in the light of modern sociology. Affirms the intellectual contribution of Marx and the relationship of his early and later writings, then shows irremediable divergences between Marxist thought and Weber's "radical neo-Kantianism."

1976 "Classical Social Theory and the Origins of Modern Sociology." *American Journal of Sociology* LXXXI (January), 703–729. Reassessment of interpretations on the origins of sociology, with particular attention to Durkheim and Weber as well as Marx.

Gouldner, Alvin W.
1970 *The Coming Crisis in Western Sociology*. New York: Basic Books. Critique of the orthodox paradigm in contemporary sociology. Traces sociology through periods, from the sociological positivism of Saint-Simon and August Comte; to Marxism; to the classical sociology of Weber, Durkheim, and Pareto; to Parsonian structural functionalism (Chapter 4: 88–163).

Hodges, Donald Clark
1959 "The Role of Classes in Historical Materialism." *Science and Society* XXIII (Winter), 16–26. Systematically attempts to examine Marx's writings on class and to relate his thinking to a theory of classes.

Hofmann, Gerhard
1972 "A Comparison of Some Aspects of German and American Sociology." *Journal of International and Comparative Studies* V (Winter), 1–17. Argues that contrasting research paradigms have developed in U.S. and German sociology. The influences of Hegel and Weber are touched upon.

Hook, Sidney
1968 *From Hegel to Marx*. Ann Arbor: University of Michigan Press. An examination of the relationships between the Hegelian dialectic and philosophical system and Marxist theory.

Howard, Dick
1972 *The Development of the Marxian Dialectic*. Carbondale: Southern Illinois University Press. A critical examination of the properties of the Marxian dialectic and its relation to other important aspects of Marx's work.

Lachmann, L. M.
1970 *The Legacy of Max Weber*. London: Heinemann. A study of the method of social interpretation developed by Weber, with discussion of specific methodological techniques. Also looks at Weber's study of institutions.

Leiserson, Avery
1975 "Charles Merriam, Max Weber, and the Search for Synthesis in Political Science." *American Political Science Review* LXIX (March), 175–185. Presidential address to the American Political Science Association in which Merriam and Weber are compared as to their view of science and their participation in politics.

Levine, Norman
1973 "Anthropology in the Thought of Marx and Engels." *Comparative Communism* 1 and 2 (Spring and Summer), 7–25. Argues that there are fundamental differences in the interpretations by Marx and Engels; that Marxism and Engelism constitute two schools of historical and sociological thought; and that different understandings of anthropology are evident.

Lichtheim, George
1961 *Marxism, An Historical and Critical Study*. New York: Frederick A. Praeger. Views Weber's framework as compatible with Marxism.

McLellan, David
1973 *Karl Marx: His Life and Thought*. New York: Harper and Row. The *Grundrisse* is viewed as central to Marx's thought and linked with his alienation theory of 1844.

MacRae, Donald G.
1974 *Weber*. London: William Collins Sons. A semibiographical overview of the major themes in Max Weber's works with emphasis on the inherent ambiguities and unresolved issues in his sociology.

Marcuse, Herbert
1968 *Negations: Essays in Critical Theory*. Boston: Beacon Press. A Marxist critique

of Weber's analysis of industrialization, capitalism, and self-preservation; the connection among these phenomena "motivates Max Weber's passionate and . . . spiteful fight against the socialist efforts of 1918." Marcuse's discussion is in Chapter 6, "Industrialization and Capitalism in the Work of Max Weber," pp. 201–226.

Marx, Karl
1967 *Capital: A Critique of Political Economy*. Edited by Frederick Engels. New York: International Publishers. 3 vols.

1973 *Grundrisse: Foundations of the Critique of Political Economy*. Translated with an introduction by Martin Nicolaus. New York: Vintage Books.

1974a *The Revolutions of 1848*. Edited with an introduction by David Fernbach. New York: Vintage Books.

1974b *Surveys from Exile*. Edited with an introduction by David Fernbach. New York: Vintage Books.

1975 *Early Writings*. Introduction by Lucio Colletti; translated by Rodney Livingstone and Gregor Benton. New York: Vintage Books. Collection of Marx's writings of 1843 and 1844, including the *Economic and Philosophical Manuscripts*.

Marx, Karl, and Frederick Engels
1958 *Selected Works*. Moscow: Foreign Languages Publishing House. 2 vols. Originally published in Russian.

1973 *The German Ideology, Part One*. Edited with introduction by C. J. Arthur. New York: International Publishers. Written in 1845–1846. Marx and Engels set forth a synthetic world outlook later called historical materialism. Nature and ideal are examined in dialectical relationship in an understanding of man and labor in society.

Mayer, Carl
1975 "Max Weber's Interpretation of Karl Marx." *Social Research* XLII (Winter), 701–719. An examination of differences in the work of Weber and Marx as manifested in German criticism.

Mayer, Jacob P.
1956 *Max Weber and German Politics: A Study in Political Sociology*. London: Faber and Faber. A semihistorical analysis of Weber's early influences, his shift in emphasis from economics to sociology, and the Weberian bifurcation of politics and science with respect to social values.

Mitzman, Arthur
1970 *The Iron Cage: An Historical Interpretation of Max Weber*. New York: Alfred A. Knopf. A study of the impact of Weber's thought on modern science by reference to the interrelation of his ideas and the crisis in European culture at the turn of the century. Focuses on Weber as a prognosticator of the ills of twentieth-century civilization.

Nicolaus, Martin
1973 "Foreword." In Karl Marx, *Grundrisse: Foundations of the Critique of Political*

Economy, pp. 7–63. New York: Vintage Books. Nicolaus, the translator, describes and analyzes this work's significance in understanding the full sweep of Marxist thought.

Ollman, Bertell

1968 "Marx's Use of 'Class.'" *American Journal of Sociology* LXXIII (March), 573–580. Systematically identifies the many uses of class in Marx's writings.

1973 "Marxism and Political Science: Prolegomenon to a Debate on Marx's Method." *Politics and Society* III (Summer), 491–510. Identifies reasons for the failure of a school of Marxist political science to emerge and summarizes Marx's theory of state and capitalism in order to stress the importance of the Marxist method.

Parsons, Talcott

1929 "'Capitalism' in Recent German Literature: Sombart and Weber." *Journal of Political Economy* XXXVII (February-December), 31–57. Parsons affirms Weber's refutation of Marxism.

Riazanov, David

1973 *Karl Marx and Friedrich Engels: An Introduction to Their Lives and Work.* Translated by Joshua Kunitz with an introduction by Dirk J. Struik. New York: Monthly Review Press. Reprint of work originally published by Riazanov, a Ukrainian, in 1927. In a foreword, Paul Sweezy recommends this work not only for "the main facts about the lives and works of the founders of Marxism, but also, by way of example, something of the Marxist approach to the study and writing of history."

Ritzer, George

1975 "Professionalization, Bureaucratization, and Rationalization: The Views of Max Weber." *Social Forces* LIII (June), 627–634. An examination of Weber's perspectives on the relationship of professionalization, bureaucratization, and rationalization.

Rossides, Daniel W.

1972 "The Legacy of Max Weber: A Non-Metaphysical Politics." *Sociological Inquiry* XLII (3–4), 183–210. Attempts to demonstrate Weber's separation of reason, fact, and value as oriented to removing social science from the metaphysical tradition and concludes that Weber's approach is much more useful than that of Marx.

Roth, Günther

1965 "Political Critiques of Max Weber: Some Implications for Political Sociology." *American Sociological Review* XXX (April), 213–223. Review of political critiques of Weber from the perspectives of Marxism, fascism, and natural law.

1969 "Max Weber's Empirical Sociology in Germany and the United States: Tensions Between Partisanship and Scholarship." *Central European History* II (September), 196–215. An assessment of the impact of Weber and his ideas on sociology in Germany and the United States.

1971 "Max Weber's Generational Rebellion and Maturation." *Sociological Quarterly* XII (Autumn), 441–461. A look at the ideological conflicts in Weber's life and thinking, at Weber's role as spokesman of a new political generation, and at his attitudes toward youth and women.

Sánchez Azcona, Jorge

1973 "Marx y Weber, un estudio comparativo en la metodología de las ciencias." *Revista Mexicana de Ciencia Política* XIX (July-September), 75–87. Looks at Marx's concept of ideology, Weber's theory and scientific method, and distinguishes differences between the two authors.

Scaff, Lawrence A.

1973 "Max Weber's Politics and Political Education." *American Political Science Review* LXVII (March), 128–141. Critically examines Weber's political writings to demonstrate his role as a political educator as well as social scientist. Affirms that "with Marx and Durkheim, Weber rightly deserves recognition as a major founder of modern social science."

Schneider, Louis

1971 "Max Weber: Wisdom and Science in Sociology." *Sociological Quarterly* XII (Autumn), 462–472. Examines Weber's use of the dialectic even though he was neither Hegelian nor Marxist. Also looks at Weber's orientation to scientific social science and concludes that Weber probably was inclined to move away from a positivistic paradigm.

Sherman, Howard

1976 "Dialectics as a Method." *Insurgent Sociologist* VI (Summer), 57–66. Explanation of dialectics and its usefulness in the practice of social science. "Attempts to rescue the dialectic from the clutches of vulgar Marxists and refutes critics who see dialectics as "a useless piece of unscientific baggage."

Sprinzak, Ehud

1975 "Marx's Historical Conception of Ideology and Science." *Politics and Society* V (4), 395–416. Attempts to clarify Marx's use of ideology and science. Argues that Marx rejected abstract empiricism and ideological uses of philosophy but believed that a unifying philosophy of history must be based on scientific research and knowledge.

Swidler, Ann

1973 "The Concept of Rationality in the Work of Max Weber." *Sociological Inquiry* XLIII (1), 35–42. Examines the concept of rationality in Weber's sociology of religion with a look at rationalism, rationalization, and rationality.

Thomas, Paul

1976 "Marx and Science." *Political Studies* XXIV (March), 1–23. Argues that not Marx but his successors, beginning with Engels, popularized the term "scientific socialism" and that Marx should not be included among those who "advocated extension of the methods of natural science to history and to society."

Tiryakian, Edward A.

1975 "Neither Marx nor Durkheim . . . Perhaps Weber." *American Journal of Sociology* LXXXI (July), 1–33. Assessment of the applicability of the perspectives on modern society of Marx, Durkheim, and Weber, with attention to the United States. Concludes that Weber is "of greatest heuristic worth in interpreting American society."

Wagner, Helmut R.
   1975 "Marx and Weber as Seen by Carl Mayer." *Social Research* XLII (Winter),
   720–728. An elaboration of Mayer's lecture on Marx and Weber (1975).
Weber, Max
   1927 *General Economic History.* Translated by Frank H. Knight. Glencoe, Illinois:
   Free Press. An economic analysis of historical periods from ancient to modern
   times.

   1947 *The Theory of Social and Economic Organization.* Edited with an introduction
   by Talcott Parsons. New York: Oxford University Press. Reprinted by Free Press
   of Glencoe, 1964. Translation of Weber's *Wirtschaft und Gesellschaft,* which deals
   with concepts of sociology, sociological categories of economic action, and types of
   authority.

   1949 *The Methodology of the Social Sciences.* Translated and edited by Edward A.
   Shils and Henry A. Finch. New York: Free Press. Three of Weber's most important essays on methodology: the meaning of "ethical neutrality" in sociology and
   economics; objectivity in social science and social policy; and critical studies in the
   logic of cultural science.

   1958a *From Max Weber: Essays in Sociology.* Translated and edited with an introduction by H. H. Gerth and C. Wright Mills. New York: Oxford University
   Press. Essays on science and politics, power, religion, and social structures as well
   as an introduction by the translators on the life and thought of Weber.

   1958b *The Protestant Ethic and the Spirit of Capitalism.* Translated by Talcott Parsons with a foreword by R. H. Tawney. New York: Charles Scribner's Sons. A
   historical and sociological interpretation of the relations between Protestantism
   and capitalism.

   1962 *Basic Concepts in Sociology.* Translated with an introduction by H. P. Secher.
   New York: Citadel Press. A later work and a fragmentary effort at systematization
   of concepts, which serves as a useful, although incomplete, introduction to
   Weber's thinking.

   1965 *Politics as a Vocation.* Translation by H. H. Gerth and C. Wright Mills.
   Philadelphia: Fortress Press. Weber's major work that advances the distinction
   between the "ethics of ultimate ends" and the "ethics of responsibility." Defines the
   proper limits of political leadership.

   1967 *Max Weber on Law in Economy and Society.* Edited with introduction and an-
   notations by Max Rheinstein; translated by Edward Shils. New York: Clarion
   Book, Simon and Schuster.

   1968 *The Sociology of Religion.* Translated by Ephraim Fischoff. Boston: Beacon
   Press. Contains Weber's later work on religion as well as a useful analytical introduction by Talcott Parsons.
Wrong, Dennis (ed.)
   1970 *Max Weber.* Englewood Cliffs, New Jersey: Prentice-Hall. The editor's in-

troductory notes are followed by a series of essays on Max Weber by Raymond Aron, Talcott Parsons, Peter M. Blau, Reinhard Bendix, and others.

Zeitlin, Irving
    1968 *Ideology and the Development of Sociological Theory.* Englewood Cliffs, New Jersey: Prentice-Hall. Attempts to demonstrate, especially in Chapter 10, the proximity in the thinking of Marx and Weber.

PART 3
Theoretical Directions

Theories of
System and State

Philosophers and social scientists long have related some conception of system to their understandings of politics. Weber looked for the qualities of stability and order in a modern productive society. He saw historical change as gradualist and noted that evolutionary progress depended on the fundamental conditions of each society. He classified societies into systems of authority: traditional, charismatic, and rational-legal. For Marx, order and stability were undermined by the contradictions of each society. He classified societies into economic systems based on mode of production and relations of production manifested through social classes: feudal, bourgeois, and proletarian. Changes in the economic base, the intensification of contradictions, and the subsequent struggle among the classes would dialectically bring about changes in society.

Classical conceptions divided societies into monarchies, aristocracies, and democracies. Among recent classifications, Gabriel Almond has provided comparative politics with a breakdown of Anglo-American, continental European, totalitarian, and preindustrial systems. F. X. Sutton broke societies into agricultural and industrial systems. James S. Coleman wrote of competitive, semicompetitive, and authoritarian systems, and David Apter divided the world into dictatorial, oligarchical, indirectly representational, and directly representational systems. Fred W. Riggs analyzed fused, prismatic, and refracted systems. S. N. Eisenstadt has offered a comprehensive classification of primitive systems, patrimonial empires, nomad or conquest empires, city states, feudal systems, centralized bureaucratic empires, and modern systems; the last he divided into democratic, autocratic, totalitarian, and underdeveloped categories. Leonard Binder differentiated among three types: traditional, conventional, and rational systems. Edward Shils has referred to political democracies, tutelary democracies, modernizing oligarchies, totalitarian oligarchies, and traditional oligarchies. An extensive summary discussion of these classifications can be found elsewhere (Wiseman 1966: 47–96), and Lijphart (1968) might be consulted for an elaboration of the typologies that relate specifically to democratic systems.

System for these and other writers might represent an entity such as a legislature, political party, or labor union, but usually the term connotes nation or state (Klausner 1967). Classifications of system reveal a variety of viewpoints and interpretations, as implied above. The emergence of many new nations in the contemporary world, the amassing of information and data, and the development of many technological advances have brought increased complexity to the world. Scientists and social scientists alike have attempted to bring order to this complexity by utilizing system as a common basis for analysis and synthesis.

With the national political system as the focus, Gabriel Almond and G. Bingham Powell, Jr. (1966: 217) outlined an eclectic scheme. Drawing from the earlier classifications of Aristotle, Weber, Eisenstadt, Shils, Coleman, Apter, and others, the new scheme offers a typology of systems according to primitive, traditional, and modern categories. Primitiveness is associated with a minimal structural differentiation and a parochial culture, while modernity is reflected by a substantial differentiation and a high degree of secularity. A variety of examples illustrate the many different national systems through history since classical times.

There is no doubt that the idea of system has implanted itself firmly in social science theory, and this chapter examines in some depth the strengths and weaknesses of systems theory. After offering some general definitions of systems terminology and identifying the origins and orientations of systems theory, three major trends in the literature are analyzed. Early influences upon each trend are related to contemporary writings in comparative politics, and a critical assessment is offered. Finally, some perspectives on systems theory and its usefulness for comparative study are presented.

Understanding the Systems Terminology

Society is usually viewed as the most inclusive entity within which systems may be evaluated. *Systems* thus are abstractions of the real society. Any phenomena of society may be viewed as a system or systems. In reality all societal phenomena are interrelated, although *boundaries* may be employed to delineate different systems, for example, political, economic, social, and cultural-psychological systems. The investigator thus abstracts from the whole society some *elements* that seem to cohere more closely than others and views those elements as a system. Usually those elements exist in conceptually measurable amounts, and as such they are termed *variables*. Elements that are constant rather than variable, because they are insulated from change in society, are called *parameters*.

When we speak of a political system, an economic system, a social system, or a cultural-psychological system, we mean all those variables associated with political life, economic life, social life, or cultural-psychological life. The variables of any system may include *structures, functions, actors, values, norms, goals, inputs, outputs, response,* and *feedback*. The meaning of each of these terms will become evident in the discussion below.

Origins and Orientations of Systems Theory

The social scientists' obsession with systems theory can be attributed in large measure to compulsion to predict correctly and thereby to be able to change things for the better. Social scientists tend to emulate classical Newtonian physics in the search for general laws that have universal application. Contemporary social scientists attempt to transcend the logical positivism of Saint-Simon, Comte, and others who attempted to apply science to the study of social life. Today, however, the origins of systems theory emanate from many different sciences. Lilienfeld (1975) has referred to the fields of biology, cybernetics, and operations research. Systems theory in political science also is indebted to contributions from economics, sociology, and other social sciences. History, too, has exerted some influence (Berkhofer 1969). Briefly these fields are examined in order to identify some influences and ideas that have shaped systems theory and its implementation in contemporary comparative politics. First, we summarize Lilienfeld's discussion, and then we turn to the contributions of social science.

Biology. The literature of systems theory frequently refers to the contributions of Ludwig von Bertalanffy (1968) and others, who combined scientific and philosophical views to formulate a conception of system they called general systems theory. They founded the Society for General Systems Research and a journal, *Behavioral Science,* as well as a yearbook. Their basic conception differentiated the physical sciences (which deal with closed systems isolated from their environment) from biology (which concerns itself with open systems of living organisms or cells). By open system is implied the exchange of matter and energy in the environment. These writers sought to apply the conception of open system to society and to explain the nature of human history by seeking laws that apply to all systems, including that of the living organism or society. The fundamental aim of general systems theory is the integration of "the various sciences, natural and social," the development of "unifying principles" through the individual sciences, and the establishment of "exact theory in the nonphysical fields of science" (Bertalanffy 1968: 38). Ervin Laszlo (1972) has elaborated extensively on general systems theory.

Cybernetics. Cybernetics is the systematic study of communication and control in all kinds of organization. Developments in communications engineering led scientists to make social applications. Norbert Wiener (1961), for example, determined that the performance of machines may be corrected and guided by information in a sort of feedback process similar to the functioning of living individuals. Wiener believed that "While human and social communications are extremely complicated in comparison to the existing patterns of machine communication, they are subject to the same grammar; and this grammar has received its highest technical development when applied to the simpler content of the machine" (quoted in Deutsch 1963: 77). Wiener not only drew an analogy between the nervous system and the automatic machine, both of whose performances are governed by means of communicating information, but he also concluded that the network of communications extends itself everywhere so that the world society can integrate into an organic whole (Wiener 1954). He considered his concept of cybernetic control through feedback to be a model for legitimizing government operations.

W. Ross Ashby's (1956) work assimilated communications and information theory in an effort to demonstrate that animals, machines, people, and even societies operate along cybernetic lines. The past behavior of an animal, machine, or person can be represented by a set of variables making up a system or "black box."

Operations Research and Systems Analysis. Operations research was an outgrowth of attempts to apply a systems approach to the use of radar installations during the Second World War. It was utilized to predict military outcomes on the basis of the design of weapons and the implementation of tactics and strategy. Operations research sought a system of minimal wastage of resources. The statistical and quantitative techniques of wartime became useful later in industries such as petroleum, chemicals, and electronics. The founding of a new profession was signified by the establishment in 1957 of the International Federation of Operations Research Societies. Soon thereafter operations research was applied to solutions of social problems, especially in education, urban areas, and health services. With the shift from military to civic applications, operations research eventually became known as systems analysis.

The Social Sciences. Among the social sciences, economics made early contributions to systems theory. Although economic problem solving today is still dominated by piecemeal and incrementalist schemes, econometric techniques have long been used to determine linear cause-and-effect relationships. These techniques, however, tend to be restricted to mechanistic systems, which do not account for the processes of change and lose touch with social reality.

In recent years computer simulation has begun to supplant many of the econometric techniques. Computers must be used, for example, in an input-output analysis such as that developed by Wassily Leontief, who sought to analyze the relations among all segments of an economic system. Such analysis has been utilized in the Soviet Union for planning at the national level. Input-output analysis usually is static in nature and thus limited to short time periods. Input-output analysis in political science generally has been limited to qualitative rather than to quantitative applications.

Game theory has generated mathematical explanations of strategies, especially for marketing and advertising in business firms. Game theory has had an impact on economics, and it has been widely used in political science analyses of international confrontations and electoral strategies. In fact, game theory has been used extensively by political scientists in the testing and implementation of rational choice theory, which assumes that the structural constraints of society do not necessarily determine the actions of individuals and that individuals tend to choose actions that bring them the best results. Cooperative and competitive relations in one's bargaining with allies and opponents are emphasized by the political scientist in a fashion modeled after the economist's attention to exchange, especially through competitive market systems.

In focusing on systemic forecasting Jantsch identified a number of tendencies in the other social sciences. For sociology, he alluded to "ways of guiding human thinking in systematic fashion," and he mentioned scenario writing, gaming, historical analogy, and other techniques. For the policy sciences he referred to the "outcome-oriented framework for strategic planning," known as the Planning-Programming-Budgeting System, which is used by the U.S. government and other countries as well. For urban and regional planning, he stressed the computer models of "exploratory man-technique interaction" as well as environmental modeling (Jantsch 1972: 482–484).

We have seen that systems theory in comparative politics has its origins in physical, biological, and social schemes. We have reviewed the trends in biology, cybernetics, and operations research and systems analysis. We have identified the influences of the social sciences. J. David Singer (1971) would synthesize these trends and influences into a dichotomy of social science orientations consisting of systems analysis and general systems. Systems analysis, he argued, suffers from abstraction and lacks a developmental and historical point of view. He preferred the use of general systems and the study of regularities in various systems. Pablo González Casanova (1973), the Mexican political scientist, suggested a somewhat similar dichotomy. He referred to two types of systemic study. The first type has its roots in nineteenth-century positivist explanations and today can be called functionalism (its major theoretician is Talcott Parsons). The second type is known as systems analysis, which emphasizes the problems of decision making, and since the Second World War this type has benefited from operations research and mathematical applications. Under certain conditions both types are self-limiting and self-defeating. Thus, González Casanova studied the history of change in contemporary systems. His stress on history allowed him to introduce a radical reinterpretation of functionalism and systems analysis.

The identification of these dichotomies may be helpful in discerning the principal tendencies in the literature of systems theory, yet further discussion is necessary. Our synthesis of the literature on systems theory seeks clarity and understanding; specifically, three trends are emphasized in this chapter.

One trend, sometimes called grand theory and ahistorical in orientation, emanates from the natural and physical sciences and culminates in the contributions of David Easton in political science. The impact of Easton can be traced to several influences in comparative and international politics. In particular, these influences are exemplified by Karl Deutsch, Morton Kaplan, and Herbert Spiro.

A second trend, known as structural functionalism, strives to be holistic but tends toward ahistorical and middle-range analysis. Its roots are strongly embedded in two academic traditions. In the first academic tradition, there is the work of the anthropologists Malinowski and Radcliffe-Brown, as well as the contributions of the sociologist Parsons. In the second tradition falls the work of the political scientists Arthur Bentley and David Truman. Both traditions converge in the important writings of Gabriel Almond, which have had a significant impact upon comparative politics.

A third trend in the literature of systems theory is that of the radical and Marxist understandings of systems theory. These understandings reach toward global theory and a historical and holistic synthesis. The discussion that follows examines the radical interpretations of orthodox theory as well as orthodox Marxist and independent radical and Marxist orientations in the literature of systems. In addition, the radical interpretation recasts system in terms of state and looks to theories of the capitalist state.

SYSTEMS AS ORGANIC OR PHYSIOLOGICAL:
DAVID EASTON AND GENERAL SYSTEMS THEORY

More than a generation ago sociologist Karl Mannheim (1957) addressed himself to "systematic sociology" in offering his readers an introduction to the study of society. Soon thereafter political scientist Charles E. Merriam (1966) wrote about "systematic politics." Merriam drew heavily from a variety of disciplines, for he searched into the action patterns of institutions by reaching into biology, sociology, anthropology, economics, philosophy, and other areas. Guided by "reason, reflection, experiment," he sought to utilize "both the naturalistic and the rationalistic approach." Intrigued by "the evolutionary quality of political effort and achievement," he viewed the whole life process, including government and politics, as part "of creative evolution in which the type and values of the species continually rise in the scale" (Merriam 1966: ix).

This traditional search for a systematic interpretation of society was carried on by David Easton in his application of general systems theory to politics. The following discussion of Easton's contributions includes, first, a synthesis of his fundamental ideas; second, a look at the origins of thought and the influences which shaped those ideas; third, a review of several subsequent efforts to apply Easton's ideas; and fourth, a critique of Easton's interpretation.

Easton's Framework

David Easton's efforts to build an empirically oriented political theory have evolved through three phases, each represented by the publication of a major work. The first of these works, *The Political System* (1953), presented a case for general theory in political science. The second, *A Framework for Political Analysis* (1965a), set forth the major concepts for the development of such a general theory. The third, *A Systems Analysis of Political Life* (1965b), attempted to elaborate those concepts in the hope that they might become empirically applicable; in fact, Easton attempted later to move his theory toward an empirical situation with a study of how and when children's support for political authority arises in the U.S. political system. A brief outline of Easton's major contributions to political theory through a synthesis of the major ideas in each of these three phases follows.

PHASE I

Easton initially set forth some assumptions. First, the empirical search for reliable knowledge "requires ultimately the construction of systematic theory, the name for the highest order of generalization" (Easton 1953: 4). Scientific knowledge is theoretical and based on facts, but facts alone do not explain events and must be ordered in some way. Political science has become a fact-gathering discipline and also has contributed to the reform of society through the application of knowledge. Yet these concerns reflect a neglect of "the general framework within which these facts could acquire meaning to transcend any particular time and place . . . political science has impeded its own movement towards a fundamental understanding of political life" (1953: 89).

Second, students of political life must view the political system as a whole rather than concentrate on solutions for particular problems. Theory must combine with reliable knowledge and empirical data. "Theory without facts may be a well-piloted ship with an unsound keel. But when preoccupation with fact-gathering siphons away energy from seeing the facts in their theoretical significance, then the ultimate value of factual research itself may well be lost" (1953: 78).

Third, research on the political system draws from two kinds of data (1953: 194–195). *Psychological* data relates to personalities and motivations of participants, and *situational* data refers to activity shaped by environmental influences. These influences emanate from the physical environment (topography, geographical dispersion of nations); the nonhuman organic environment (flora, fauna); and the social environment (people, their actions and reactions).

Fourth, political life may be described as in disequilibrium. Disequilibrium suggests not only change or conflict but a countertendency to equilibrium, which is a "condition that never materializes, a kind of normal situation which is a pure abstraction." Equilibrium then is a concept in the mind of the social worker—"a heuristic, simplifying device to help understand the empirical world" (Easton 1956: 282). That is, the mind envisions a normal outcome of what might be. This outcome is contrasted with what actually takes place, and the differences can be explained.

Thus, Easton's quest for theory involved the formulation of a general framework, a focus on the whole system rather than merely on its parts, an awareness of environmental influences upon the system, and a recognition of the differences between political life in equilibrium and in disequilibrium. Easton rejected the concept of the state by referring to the confusion and variety of meanings (1953: 107); system for him permits clear conceptualization. Likewise, power is understood as only one of many significant concepts useful in the study of political life. Power, however, relates to the shaping and carrying out of authoritative politics in a society. Power rests on the ability to influence actions of others, and control of the way others make and carry out decisions determines policy. A policy, thus, "consists of a web of decisions and actions that allocates values" (1953: 130). The concepts of power, decision making, authority, and policy are essential in Easton's idea of political life as the authoritative allocation of values for a society.

Having established the need for systemic theory, Easton later (1957) identified some attributes of political systems in an attempt to move in the direction of a general political theory. These attributes were (1) properties of identification in the form of units and boundaries, (2) inputs and outputs, (3) differentiation within a system, and (4) integration within a system. Each attribute was described and illustrated through a "primitive" diagram, which is now familiar to most students of political science and is reproduced in Figure 5.1.

The diagram suggests that for analytical purposes the use of system allows the separation of political life from the rest of society, which Easton called the environment. This separation is demarcated by a boundary. The case of a political system, for example, is defined by action related to "binding decisions" of a society. The units of the political system are "political actions." Inputs in the form of demands and supports feed the political system. Demands arise either in the environment or within the system itself. Whether externally or internally stimulated, demands become issues

FIGURE 5.1
Easton's Diagram of a Political System

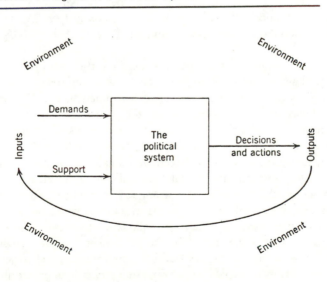

Reprinted from David Easton, *A Framework for Political Analysis* (1965, p. 112) by permission of the University of Chicago Press.

"members of a political system are prepared to deal with as a significant item for discussion through the recognized channels in the system" (1957: 389). Supports are "actions or orientations prompting and resisting a political system" (1957: 390). Outputs emanate from the political system in the form of decisions and policy actions. These feed back into the environment by satisfying the demands of some members of the system, and thus they generate support for the system. There may be negative consequences too, resulting in new demands on the system.

PHASE 2

In his second work Easton set forth "a logically integrated set of categories, with strong empirical relevance, that will make possible the analysis of political life as a system of behavior" (1965a: x). Essentially the second work is an elaboration of Easton's earlier scheme, and it reiterates some assumptions related to system, environment, response, and feedback (1965a: 24). Society "incorporates all other social systems and therefore refers to the overarching, inclusive, suprasystem in which a group of biological persons participates" (1965a: 38). Society as suprasystem is the most inclusive social system. The political system then is "a set of interactions abstracted from the totality of social behavior, through which values are authoritatively allocated for a society" (1965a: 57). Easton referred to closed and open systems. Political life, he argued, forms an open system, open to influences from its environment. Boundaries distinguish political systems from other systems, and boundaries serve to delimit what is included or excluded in inquiry.

All these concepts allowed Easton to examine the relationships between the political system and the environment, and he illustrated the relationships with a scheme, as in Figure 5.2. Environment is divided into an intrasocietal part and an extrasocietal part. The intrasocietal part is "that part of the social and physical environment that lies *outside* the boundaries of a political system and yet *within* the same society" (1965a: 71). Ecological (physical, nonhuman), biological (genetic makeup of human beings), personality (psychological), and social (cultural, social structural, economic, and demographic) systems are important to the political system as part of the intrasocietal part of the environment. The extrasocietal environment lies "outside the society of which the political system itself is a social subsystem; yet it may have important consequences for the persistence or change of a political system" (1965a: 73). The international society or environment is an example of a system in the extrasocietal environment, according to Easton, and it comprises international ecological systems, international social systems, and international political systems. Subsystems of the international political systems include national political systems, the

FIGURE 5.2
Easton's Flow Model of a Political System

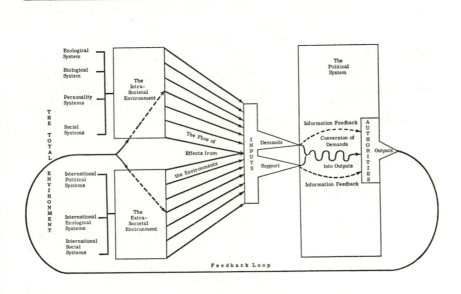

Reprinted from David Easton, *A Framework for Political Analysis* (1965, p. 110) by permission of the University of Chicago Press.

United Nations, and the North Atlantic Treaty Organization.

Finally, Easton turned to the persistence and dynamics of systems. He asserted that political systems persist in times of change and that these systems are not defenseless in the face of pressure. Stress to change the system may come from two directions, one internal from the intrasocietal environment and the other external from the extrasocietal environment. Thus the political system is influenced by what is happening in the environments. Easton then could suggest a dynamic response model of a political system, as is shown in Figure 5.2.

PHASE 3

Having argued the case for a general theory and having set forth concepts and diagrams, Easton next attempted to move his discussion toward the construction of a general theory (1965b). He continued to view political life as an open system subject to stress from a variety of surrounding environments. Threatened by stress, the political system, Easton argued, tends to persist, and he delved into explanations as to why systems persist in the face of frequent or constant crises. His task was to provide some generalizations in the process of theory building, but he admitted that his outcome was not yet a fully elaborated theory. That must come later. Thus, in this third phase Easton began with his broad conceptual framework and succeeded generally in the elaboration of that framework. His hope was to provide a foundation for empirical investigation.

Easton in his third phase reviewed his basic categories of analysis, looked exhaustively at demand inputs, turned to support inputs, identified responses to the stress placed on support for the system, and discussed outputs as regulators of specific support. His diagrams were more complicated, but the fundamental thrust remained intact.

Origins of Thought and Influences
That Shaped Easton's Interpretation

Easton sought generalization in his efforts to formulate sytematic theory, and it was his desire to relate his ideas to all the social sciences. Mackenzie argued, however, that Easton's work emanated primarily from political science itself. "He was (it is clear) caught up in a movement which he did not originate, and there is no 'Eastonian theory' as there is no 'Parsonian theory'! Rather he now interprets and adapts for political scientists a stream of thought which has been growing in strength for some forty years" (Mackenzie 1967: 96–97). Easton himself acknowledged that both a technical and a theoretical revolution in political science stimulated his work, and he cited the work of Charles Merriam and George Catlin, Harold Lasswell, and others as examples (Easton 1965b: 19–22). Easton focused his attention on political theory. First, he believed that past attention to legal and formal institutions was outmoded and that political science should theorize about the political system and its processes rather than about the state and its institutions. Second, he sought a grand theory that would relate to the whole system and transcend the limitations of middle-range efforts to study parties and pressure groups.

It is clear, however, that Easton was indebted to sources outside political science. Although he disclaimed any direct influence on his work, Easton acknowledged the importance of several alternative analyses. First, he looked to Talcott Parsons, who had derived from Max Weber an action frame of reference applicable to macro theory in the social sciences. Parsons formulated generalizations about the social system, yet he questioned the validity of political theory "as a fundamental element of the theory of social systems" (quoted in Easton 1953: 60). This is only one of several differences between Easton and Parsons, and it probably accounts for the minimal attribution of Easton to the ideas and writings of Parsons.

A specific comparison of Parsons and Easton is offered by Lewis (1974), who noted a number of similarities (for example, the work of both men is laden with value implications) but placed emphasis on one major distinction between the two. Classical liberalism, argued Lewis, employs the concepts of equality and consent. These concepts are inherent in the classic formulation of the state set forth in the work of Thomas Hobbes and John Locke. Whereas Parsons's notions of capacity and generalized support are "consistent" with the concepts of equality and consent found in classical liberalism, Easton's "statements about the level of diffuse support and system persistence do not fall within the liberal perspective" (Lewis 1974: 683). Nor should Easton's allocation of values be confused with the liberal perspective.

Easton also referred to function, derived from anthropology and used prevalently in sociology, as a "unit, somewhat slippery to handle, to be sure, but nevertheless a unit that could be utilized in many of the disciplines" (Easton 1965a: 15). There is an occasional reference in Easton's work to the anthropologists Radcliffe-Brown and Malinowski as well as to the sociologists Merton and Levy, but Easton affirmed that "structural analysis, so called, is not a theory but a concept intrinsic to all scientific research. Indeed, it is fundamentally devoid of theoretical content" (Easton 1965b: 13 n. 12). At the outset, Easton's 1953 work was perceived to relate essentially to the middle-range analysis of parties, interest groups, and the like, but he refused to integrate such "partial study" into his generalized conception of the political system, and in his later writings (1956) he extensively criticized the equilibrium theory upon which middle-range analysis rests.

Another alternative direction for analysis, according to Easton, is found among the works of those people who have been influenced by social psychology and have placed an emphasis on decision or choice. Decision making, of course, is an element in the Eastonian framework for political analysis.

Easton's framework seems to have been influenced by macroeconomic conceptions. William Mitchell astutely observed that Easton's notion of allocation resembled "theories of income distribution and the allocation of resources in economics, and particularly neoclassical theory since there, too, the emphasis is upon the economy as a distributive process or system" (Mitchell 1961: 79). The similarity to the classical economic model of Adam Smith is the focus of analysis elsewhere, for "the Eastonian model and the traditional economic approach share not only the notions of system and input-output but those of scarcity, allocation, competition, maximization, homeostatic equilibrium, functional interdependence, self-regulation, goal-seeking, and feedback" (Sorzano 1975: 91).

Easton's conception of system quite naturally derived from the physical and life sciences. "Just as we may have a general theory of motion in physics or of life in biology, we require a general theory of the vital processes in politics" (Easton 1965b: 14). At one point he contrasted the interactions in physical, biological, and social systems. The simplest of the physical systems would be a boulder, whose density separates it from the surrounding air. An apple is a simple organic system, with its skin separating it and its internal growing processes from the external environment. The body is another organic or biological system. A political system consists of social interactions diffused throughout a society. Thus Easton's conception reflects ties to other sciences in two ways: firstly, that "behavior in political systems may be governed by analogous, if not homologous processes, as in the natural sciences; and, secondly, a search for 'stable units of analysis' which might possibly play the role in social research that the particles of matter do in the physical sciences" (Campbell 1971: 26). Astin (1972) has analyzed the organic or physiological assumptions of Easton's conception.

Easton acknowledged that his principal debt was to colleagues at the University of Chicago, where the Committee on Behavioral Sciences stimulated some of his formative thinking. This committee included specialists in psychology, history, neurophysiology, internal medicine, economics, physics, mathematical biology, biology, and anthropology. Formed in 1951 the committee devoted itself to "a prolonged and intensive discussion of common problems in a systems approach as viewed from all the sciences, physical, biological, and social" (Easton 1965a: xii).

In particular, Easton's work seems to have paralleled that of James G. Miller, a psychologist who initiated the interdisciplinary discussions at Chicago, but who was not particularly concerned with politics. Miller set forth the basic assumptions of general systems theory, drawing upon Bertalanffy's meaning of system as "a set of units with relationships among them." He contrasted concrete systems and abstract systems, and he preferred concrete systems, while expressing skepticism for the abstract systems formulated by Parsons. Further, he referred to open and closed systems; to equilibrium as stable, unstable, or neutral; to living systems as open; to structure as "a static arrangement of a system's parts" whereas process is a "dynamic change . . . of that system over time"; and to systems and subsystems. All these themes are elaborated in the work of Easton (J. Miller 1969 and summarized in Mackenzie 1967: 99–102).

Whatever the influences upon his work, Easton clearly placed himself in the mainstream of general systems theory, which he adapted to political science. The influence of the functionalists in anthropology and sociology may be remote, and there are certainly fundamental differences between Easton and Parsons. A similarity to neoclassical economic theory is apparent. Ties with the physical and life sciences are explicit, and the organic and physiological assumptions of the Eastonian system are easily identifiable. Thus, Easton joined the interdisciplinary tradition of seeking an understanding of the "whole" system. The physical sciences may provide a foundation for this understanding, and metaphysics must be transcended through the development of a science of systems that incorporates biology, psychology, and the other social sciences. The parallel developments in cybernetics, control engineering, and computer work all may contribute to a framework of general systems theory. In combination, the work in these various fields constitutes a new paradigm in the sense used by Thomas Kuhn. Ervin Laszlo synthesized across the various disciplines and set forth the notion of systems philosophy as the paradigm of general theory in contemporary thought.

> The most consistent as well as most general paradigm available today to the inquiring, ordering mind is the systems paradigm. Explicated as a *general theory of systems*; both "physical" and "mental," and applied to the analysis of human experience and its problems, it constitutes *systems philosophy* . . . the systems philosophical paradigm takes man as one species of concrete and actual system, embedded in encompassing natural hierarchies of likewise concrete and actual physical, biological, and social systems. [E. Laszlo 1972: 298]

Three Applications of Systems Analysis

Attempts to apply systems analysis have taken various forms. On the one hand, there are efforts to set forth concepts and generalizations for immediate application. For example, C. A. Laszlo, Levine, and Milsum (1974) have expressed concern about solving problems in the evolution toward the postindustrial society, and they aimed "to plan for and to control the system so as to perform in a socially good way" (1974: 79). McLeod (1974) explored the use of systems theory and simulation in the belief that simulation is one of the best techniques to use to explore the future, understand the impacts of proposed action, and allow man to intervene in the many problems now facing humanity. On the other hand, there have been attempts to analze national political systems through the measurement of empirical data (see, for example, Abramson and Inglehart 1970; Farace and Donohew 1965; Gregg and Banks 1965; and Teune and Ostrowski 1973).

Now we turn to three other uses of systems analysis. The three, represented, respectively, by the works of Herbert Spiro (1962), Karl Deutsch (1963), and Morton Kaplan (1957), either relate to the Eastonian framework or run parallel to it. Spiro's work pertains directly to comparative politics, and Kaplan's has become a central thrust in international politics; that of Deutsch is useful to both fields.

Spiro's Comprehensive Scheme

Herbert J. Spiro (1962), departing from Easton's early formulation of the political system, offered a comprehensive scheme for comparative politics. Spiro defined a political system as a community that processes issues. Issues relate to problems, needs, and goals about which consensus or dissension may exist. Issues are generated and dealt with through the "flow of policy" through four phases, as is evident in the diagram in Figure 5.3. *Formulation* occurs once a problem is recognized as an issue and goals are set for its solution, *deliberation* relates to the examination of the alternative solutions to the problem, *resolution* involves the narrowing of these alternatives into one policy, and *solution* is the achievement of the goals set at the beginning. Spiro understood that this policy process is related to problems in constitutional, economic, power, and cultural areas and the success or failure of the

FIGURE 5.3
Spiro's Comprehensive Scheme for Comparative Politics

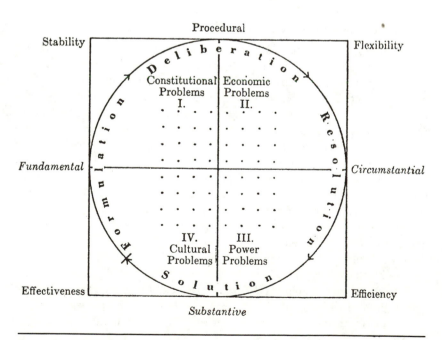

Source: Spiro (1962:580).

process is dependent on the stability, flexibility, efficiency, and effectiveness of the system, which are the goals of the system in dynamic equilibrium.

Spiro offered the following advantages of his scheme. First, he insisted that the same aspects of any two or more political systems may be compared. Second, superficial distinctions need not be made of the political, economic, or cultural aspects of a system. Third, the compartmentalization of functions can be avoided. Fourth, the scheme can be applied to any political system, large or small, developed or developing.

Among the disadvantages, Spiro mentioned the intentional neglect of formal institutions like presidents and cabinets. He also did not incorporate the role of groups in politics, but he did feel he had facilitated the explanation of differences through systematic comparison.

Other than making some reference to the historical experience of some nations, Spiro did not attempt to apply his scheme systematically to empirical data, and there probably is no published effort that does so. Thus, the scheme serves as an attempt to abstract political concepts into whole systems. In this sense, it may be helpful to students as a model for building their own schemes.

DEUTSCH AND SYSTEMS OF COMMUNICATIONS AND CONTROL

Karl Deutsch in a synthesis (1963) of past and present communications theory attempted to provide the basis for comparing the complex communications channels of modern society to the nervous system of the body. Deutsch first surveyed classical political theory. He then turned to the classical idea of mechanism as applied to gravitational astronomy and other disciplines and found that notions of growth, evolution, and innovation are completely excluded. Mechanism was challenged by the classic conception of organism, but this too was restrictive until refinements by modern biologists allowed for the identification of points of decision, feedback, and flow paths, which would be useful to general systems theory and models of communication. Deutsch also acknowledged another conception, that which emerged from the dialogue and struggle of historical experience and was elaborated by Hegel and Marx in the nineteenth century and Toynbee in the present century. Second, Deutsch discussed the implications of recent models in the social sciences. He looked at the contributions of Max Weber, then turned to structural-functional analysis, and finally reviewed the assumptions of game theory.

Deutsch focused attention, however, on cybernetics as new models of communication and control, especially as they are related to systems of political decision. A simple cybernetics model is elaborated, and concepts are introduced such as self-controlling system, memory and recognition, feedback, and equilibrium. Deutsch viewed politics as "the steering or manipulation of human behavior" (1963: 243). It is thereby possible for politics to be shaped by the major facilities of communication and memory and other means.

Deutsch did not fully elaborate a conception of system, but he clearly saw parallel developments in biology and social science. The relationship of system to environment is crucial to an understanding of change. He noted four types of political systems: self-destroying systems, which usually break down in their environment; nonviable systems, which have difficulty surviving in their environment; viable systems, which probably can survive the conditions of their environments; and self-developing systems, which have the greatest probability of surviving and overcoming the conditions of their environments (1963: 249).

Finally, Deutsch's grand synthesis emerges in the form of a crude functional diagram of information flow applied in foreign policy decisions. Although this diagram probably has little applicability to empirical investigation, the student may wish to examine it (1963: 258-261).

KAPLAN AND INTERNATIONAL POLITICS

Undoubtedly the seminal work on the application of systems theory to international politics is Morton Kaplan's *System and Process in International Politics* (1957). His basic concept, the system of action, is similar to Easton's formulation. This system is "a set of variables so related, in contradistinction to its environment, that describable behavioral regularities characterize the internal relationships of the variables to each other and the external relationships of the set of individual variables to combinations of external variables" (1957: 4). As summarized in Weltman (1972), Kaplan referred to stability and instability in discussing the transformations of systems, he assumed that all systems are in equilibrium, and he delineated the political order as a body of rules. Six types of international system were identified: balance of power, loose bipolar, tight bipolar, universal, hierarchical, and unit-veto systems.

A number of critics have identified the origins of systemic theory in international politics (Weltman 1972; Tierney 1972; and Stephens 1972). They found that the notion of system is borrowed from the physical sciences and that the foundations of systems theory emanated from biology, especially the work of Bertalanffy. They also related contemporary systems theory to the epistemology and positivist philosophy of Comte and the empiricism of Hume. More recently, they have attributed Kaplan's formulation to the early writings of David Easton.

Easton's own claim that his systems framework is applicable to international systems has been refuted by Nicholson and Reynolds (1967). Tierney distinguished between systems theory and systems analysis, suggesting that analysis relates to planning, programming, and budgeting as decision-making techniques for the efficient management of government. In contrast, systems theory is represented by an abstraction of reality and delineated by boundaries, subsystems, and other terminology used by Easton and others. A systems theorist, then, looks for "law or behavior regularities . . . seeks prediction" (Tierney 1972: 312). Although this distinction is obvious and helpful, Easton clearly worked in the direction of theory without fully establishing theory. Instead he interpreted general systems theory of the study of politics, and he anticipated that analysis would ensue.

Essentially, though, contemporary systems theory in the field of international politics, like comparative politics, moves in two directions. One lies within general systems theory. Stephens (1969) identified the work of Charles McLelland and Robert C. North as being in this tradition, and we have already included Kaplan. The other direction incorporates functional analysis as it is tied to system needs or requisites and structure. Since Kaplan introduced rules into his systems formulation, argued Stephens, and rules are system requisites or needs, then there is a similarity between Kaplan's conception and the structural functionalism of Parsons and others. The affinity of Kaplan's theory both to general systems theory and to structural functionalism thus makes difficult a clear identification of his theory's origins. But the resulting confusion has not precluded criticism of the theory itself.

Some Criticisms of the Eastonian Framework

Through his systems framework David Easton attempted to awaken political scientists to ways of analyzing the complex interrelationships of political life. His framework represents an effort to organize political data within an integrated system of concepts, and it places emphasis on the study and interpretation of the whole political system rather than on its elements. In stressing unity rather than diversity, Easton shared some of the characteristics of many thinkers of the behavioral movement.

Richard Wilson (1961: 750–751) identified four such characteristics. One was the rejection of those traditional concepts of political science, such as state and power, that are considered to be ambiguous and value laden. A second was the use of new concepts such as inputs and outputs and feedback that are given precise meaning as elements in the building of a system. A third characteristic was the setting forth of comprehensive conceptions such as the authoritative allocation of values, which may be used in explanations of total political knowledge, and the fourth was the emphasis on interdisciplinary endeavor in theory construction. The Eastonian framework is not without its critics, however. We turn therefore to a review of the criticisms, which tend to concentrate in three areas: conceptual prospects, operational possibilities, and ideological orientations.

CONCEPTUAL PROSPECTS

Easton devoted much attention to clarifying and simplifying concepts. Yet many critics have attacked his work on the grounds of inadequate conceptualization. Their concerns have related to an excessive preoccupation with stability and persistence in the face of the conflict and change of everyday political life, to the central orienting conception of the allocation of values, and to the use of boundary.

Easton's concern with stability is evident in his extensive discussion of systems persistence. Thorson (1970: 62) argued that "the persistence of the system is central not only to Easton's theory but to his exposition as well. Everything hinges on the system persisting." Easton's idea of persistence is derived from biology; in the organic system persistence relates to life or death. The parts of an organic system function so that the system may function. Likewise, Easton referred to the "life processes" of the political system; if they fail to function, the system cannot persist. By life processes Easton meant the "authoritative allocation of values" for society, which in turn constitutes his definition of politics. Thus a political system fails to persist when there is no politics, but Easton's definition of politics is meant to apply to any and all cases.

Thorson reflected on this dilemma with examples from the European experience and demonstrated the difficulties in applying Easton's notion of persistence to real situations. He also noted that although Easton did not want to use persistence to mean stability, maintenance, or equilibrium—all static concepts—he was unable to deal with particular changes. "We can in no sense then regard Easton's theory as a theory of political change—as a theory which answers questions concerning why any particular political change occurred" (Thorson 1970: 67). Eugene F. Miller (1971: 233) argued in a similar fashion that Easton's abstractions lead to misperceptions about real situations and people. Reid R. Reading (1972) also found unsatisfactory Easton's later efforts to apply systems persistence to comparative empirical data drawn from a field study of political socialization. Peter Leslie (1972) also criticized the concept of persistence.

The notion of politics as the allocation of values was taken to task by William C. Mitchell (1961). That idea can lead to some "misleading assumptions on which to construct an adequate theory of politics" (1961: 82). For example, the focus on problems of allocation may result in the view that the political system has but a single function, that of allocation. Also, the polity does not allocate all values of a society; the economy distributes resources and income. Further, the question of power may be obscured by inordinate attention to the demands of interest groups upon government, when in fact the demands of government and ruling classes upon people may be more important.

These criticisms allowed Mitchell to reformulate later the notion of political system as a theory of rational choice. "As economic systems produce 'solutions' to . . . problems so, too, polities provide solutions or make choices through time." With this emphasis on political economy, Mitchell suggested an exchange model with attention to "a complex circular flow of exchanges including resources, demands, support, benefits (income, status, opportunities), controls, and actual public goods and services" (Mitchell 1969: 103, 106). Rational choice models and theories were offered as alternative explanations to functionalist or structural-functionalist theory (in which the institutions of a given society are understood in terms of their social functions or contributions to the maintenance of the system as a whole) as well as to conformist theory (which assumes that uniformities of individual behavior in a given society are understood in terms of commonly accepted social values). In a classic statement advocating a theory of rational choice, Harsanyi (1969) joined other critics in their attack on structural-functional theory because of its overemphasis on consensus and its static and conservative bias. These criticisms are elaborated later in the discussion on systems formulated in terms of structures and functions.

Easton's attention to boundary has provoked concern. How do we distinguish the political system from the economic system, the cultural system, and the social system? How do we explain political outcomes and avoid any reference to relevant economic, cultural, or social phenomena? J. David Singer suggested that "we must cross back and forth over the misty boundaries between and among these systems and must therefore try to cope with several overlapping and elusive systems of action at the same time. It has yet to be done successfully" (1971: 10). There is the problem, too, that some systems analysts stress the importance of one system over the others. Talcott Parsons, for instance, assumed that the social system is all-encompassing, and Herbert Spiro placed emphasis on the political system. The separation of system from subsystem is difficult in other than abstract terms, as is the differentiation of a system from its environment. Evans concluded that "Easton has not defined the political, and has therefore made no distinction between the political and the non-political. . . . The repercussion on his solution to the 'boundary problem' seems clear" (Evans 1970: 129).

At the heart of all the above problems is Easton's avoidance of the human element. Singer placed Easton along with Almond, Kaplan, Parsons, and others into the "system of action school" in contrast to the "system of entity school" into which Singer placed himself, James G. Miller, Thomas Kuhn, and Bertalanffy. This distinction is blurred by inconsistencies in meaning among these writers, but Singer suggested that the "entity school" relates to individuals and aggregations of people while the "action school" focuses on action, interaction, and behavior but devotes little attention to people (1971: 8). This point was emphasized by Thorson. "Easton, because of his need for uniformity and generality, specifically excludes people as biological entities from the political system. The system is emphatically not a group of people, it is a system of behavior, the set of relevant interactions" (1970: 63).

OPERATIONAL POSSIBILITIES

It has already noted that Easton's framework, by his own admission, is not yet a theory. He has posited some generalizations, but his framework has yielded few, if any, testable hypotheses. His framework and ideas have had an impact upon the study of politics, but there has been little empirical consequence for comparative politics.

One of the problems was clearly analyzed by Astin (1972) who identified in Easton's framework the incorporation of two incompatible approaches. One is mechanistic and derived from Newton. It employs mathematics in computation and other purposes; it is "analytical and reductionist and assumes the validity of mechanical cause-and-effect explanation" (1972: 726). The other is organicist or vitalist and draws upon a view once prevalent in biology but now abandoned by most contemporary biologists, with the exception of those who follow Bertalanffy — "who revived the organicist outlook in biology in the 1920s and generalized it into a cosmology in 1949" (1972: 726). Thorson saw Easton's system as approximating that of physiology, which broke the organism into a respiratory system, a reproductive system, and other systems. "Both as a matter of history and as a matter of logic this notion of system is biology's version of Newton's mechanics. It is, in short, a sort of machine that is alive" (Thorson 1970: 59).

The incompatibility of these approaches was demonstrated rather exhaustively by Astin, who described Easton as "a floating object caught up in the orbit of mechanism so long that one felt confident that, despite the vitalistic origins of his thought, he adhered to the vocabulary of cause and effect which he employed" (1972: 735). Thorson even more convincingly cast aside any illusions that the Eastonian framework offers operational possibilities.

> He painstakingly creates the *reductio ad absurdum* for the idea of an absolutely general, any-time-any-place, theory of politics. By showing us that a political system construed in an absolutely general way fails to persist only in those cases where it fails to persist, Easton convinces us of what no mere critic — because he would lack the necessary persuasive and psychological

leverage—of the idea of a general theory of politics could possibly convince us of, namely, that the enterprise is futile. [Thorson 1970: 70–71]

Finally, Kress referred to Easton's "empty vision of politics" in his critical summary of "the theory's lack of substance, the artificial nature of system and member" (1966: 11).

IDEOLOGICAL ORIENTATIONS

Eugene Miller (1971) delved into the ideological underpinnings of the Eastonian framework. He noted the evolution of Easton's thought, beginning with the elaboration of a comprehensive view of politics. Early in his writings (1950, for example) Easton was concerned with an intellectual crisis and the imminent waning of democratic liberalism. He relegated political science to the position of an applied science or reforming discipline, and at the same time he also blamed historicism for the impoverishment of political theory. He referred to the value theory of historicism while attacking Weber's ideal of a value-free social science. At the same time he recognized the importance of scientific or causal theory; he considered value theory and causal theory to be inseparable. In his 1953 work he emphasized science and causal theory, however, and thereafter he became optimistic about the prospects for a true science of politics. The influence of behavioralism seemed to reinforce this position, and value theory diminished in importance in his thought.

The separation of theory from practice accompanied what Miller called the constructionist stage of Easton's thought, in which he designated and described the elements of his systems framework. Easton distinguished systems analysis from functional analysis. The latter implied stable conditions, cohesion, and equilibrium, and the former assumed that a system persists while adapting and transforming itself creatively to the stress upon it.

Miller identified a reassessment of thinking in Easton's 1969 presidential address to the American Political Science Association, in which he placed a renewed emphasis on applied research and attention to the value assumptions of research. In that renewed emphasis Easton returned somewhat to his earlier stance. At issue was the debate over values in scientific inquiry between historicism and positivistic social science, but, argued Miller, Easton failed "to meet the epistemological objections which historicism has raised against projects such as his own" (E. Miller 1971: 210). Easton's methodological position is ambiguous. He "makes concessions to historicism" yet "appears to agree with the positivist tradition that social scientists can establish theoretical knowledge that is generally reliable and objectively valid if they test their speculations against the facts of experience" (1971: 220–221). Miller concluded that Easton has failed to identify "the object of political inquiry," he has failed to offer an adequate definition of society, and he has failed to deal with political change in other than abstract terms, which leads him to "an inhumane conclusion" (1971: 233). Finally, Miller questioned "if systems analysis, as a kind of political biology, is concerned with questions that are, properly speaking, political in nature." He argued that we must distinguish between "the biological problem of how life is sustained and the ethical problem of the way of life that men should choose," and he concluded that "political things must be understood by analogy with ethics rather than biology" (1971: 234).

SYSTEMS AS STRUCTURE AND FUNCTION: GABRIEL ALMOND AND HIS PRECURSORS

Influenced by the work of systems analysts in the natural sciences and the social sciences, David Easton was successful in firmly implanting a formulation of system in political science. In 1956, three years after Easton published his first book on the political system, Gabriel Almond applied a simple typology to national political systems. Together with other comparative political scientists, Almond set forth a new formulation, utilizing the political system as a base and turning to a set of concepts related to structure and function. Almond's formulation movement was spawned by some of the same influences that had affected Easton, but it turned away from grand theory and directed attention to middle-range concerns. It thus paralleled the Eastonian movement, although ultimately it was to exert substantially more impact upon comparative politics.

In this section the assumptions of Almond's formulation are examined, and the use of system in Almond's work is traced. Next the origins of influence upon his ideas are identified, and finally, the major criticisms of structural functionalism are summarized in an effort to assess its significance for comparative politics.

Almond's Formulation

Almond's conception of the political system evolved through a number of phases. We now turn to a discussion of each of these phases.

PHASE I

Almond's early typology of the political system, elaborated in his 1956 article, is notable in several aspects. First, he drew the notion of system from Easton; system is an "inclusive concept which covers all of the patterned actions relevant to the making of political decisions" (1956: 393). For Almond, system was more useful than process: system implied "totality," interactions among units within the totality, and stability in those interactions, which he described as "changing equilibrium."

Second, Almond relied heavily upon Max Weber and Talcott Parsons in his consideration of political systems of action. His emphasis on action, he argued, allows the political observer to avoid describing the system merely as a formal or a legal entity. Instead of relying on such concepts as institution, organization, or group, Almond turned to role and structure. Roles are the interacting units of the political system, and structures are the patterns of interaction. The use of these terms allows for the study of formal as well as informal offices (for example, families) in investigation.

Finally, Almond introduced the concept of political culture, which is not the same as the general culture nor does it coincide with a given system or society. Political cultures relate to political systems, however, since every political culture is embedded in a particular pattern of orientations to political action, and these patterns usually extend beyond the boundaries of the political system.

PHASE 2

During meetings at Princeton University in 1958 and 1959 Almond and collaboraters focused on the politics of the developing areas. They elaborated on a theory of structures and functions in a conscious effort to avoid the examination of constitutions and formal government institutions in areas where changes are widespread. The result was a book under the editorship of Almond and James S. Coleman in which Almond (1960) introduced a number of assumptions.

At the outset Almond made clear his intention to renovate the concepts of comparative politics. Thus, political system is used instead of the state and the legal and institutional apparatus that have caught the attention of traditional political scientists. Function replaces power, which Almond also considered to be legalistic in connotation. Role takes the place of office, and structure substitutes for institution.

Almond essentially set forth the thesis that political systems have universal characteristics and that for the purposes of theory and analysis these characteristics can be conceptualized into a schematic approach to the comparative study of politics. Four characteristics stand out (1960: 11).

1. All political systems have political structures.
2. The same functions are performed in all political systems.
3. All political structure . . . is multi-functional.
4. All political systems are mixed in the cultural sense.

These characteristics provide the basis for the comparative study of advanced and backward nations. Almond argued that similar structures are found everywhere, but to locate them, the correct functional questions must be addressed. Only in this way "are we led to an accurate representation of a dynamic process" (1960: 13).

Almond was partially influenced by Easton's framework of inputs, outputs, and feedback, which he felt moves toward "systemic functional theory." This framework is limited, however: "It is still too close to the generic model of a system, with its interdependence, its boundaries, and its inputs and outputs, to be particularly discriminating in the political field" (1960: 15). Almond then outlined his own functional categories, separating them according to inputs and outputs:

Input Functions
  Political socialization and recruitment
  Interest articulation
  Interest aggregation
  Political communication
Output Functions
  Rule making
  Rule application
  Rule adjudication

The outputs are government functions and correspond to the traditional use of three separate powers within government. Thus rule making replaces legislation, rule application implies administration, and rule adjudication relates to the judicial process. These categories bias Almond's scheme, for his output functions clearly reflect a U.S. and European conception of Western government, indeed the traditional orientation of comparative politics.

Almond argued that the input or political functions, not the output or government functions, are crucial in characterizing the political systems of the developing areas. These functions represent the ingredients of the system: that is, who recognizes problems; identifies, deliberates, and resolves issues; and presents solutions; and how are those actions carried out. Spiro called this a process of "policy flow," and Easton characterized it as consisting of demands and supports for action. For Almond, political socialization induces people to participate in the political culture of a society; socialization takes place through the family, school, job, religious group, voluntary association, political party, and even government institutions. Political socialization involves the recruitment of people from classes, ethnic groupings, and the like into the political system of parties, bureaucracy, and so on. Interest articulation is the expression of political interests and demands for action. Interest aggregation is the coalescing of those interests and demands that are articulated by political parties, interest groups, and other political entities. Political communication serves all of these political functions. Political socialization, recruitment, articulation, and aggregation occur through communication.

Almond viewed political culture as dualistic rather than monistic. Thus political systems may be characterized as modern and premodern, developed and underdeveloped, industrial and agrarian. Essentially he saw political systems as evolving through stages of development. Structures tend to become more differentiated and specialized as political systems reach higher stages of development. In particular, Almond referred to primitive, traditional, transitional, and modern systems. The less developed systems are characterized by the "traditional" styles of diffuseness, particularism, ascriptiveness, and affectivity, and the more developed systems are characterized by the "rational" styles of specificity, universalism, achievement, and affective neutrality (1960: 63). Rational styles penetrate primitive and traditional systems, yet traditionality is never completely eliminated in the modern system. The modern system tends to regulate and control traditionality.

Almond believed that his scheme allows political scientists to move toward a "probabilistic" theory of the polity. His designation of functions and structure suggests "that political systems may be compared in terms of the probabilities of performance of the specified functions by the specified structures" (1960: 59). He even speculated that his theory of the political system might lend itself to mathematical and statistical applications. Further, he expressed the hope that a theory of modernization and its application to the problems of the world might be posited.

PHASE 3

Almond's earlier scheme was refined in a journal article (1965) and elaborated in a book (Almond and Powell 1966), which has been widely used by specialists of comparative politics. The refinement of his functional approach to comparative politics resulted in a sixfold classification, including the original three government or output functions as well as interest articulation, interest aggregation, and communication. These functions become conversion processes, which allow for the transformation of the demands and supports that flow into the political system. Out of that system flows extraction, regulation, and distribution into society or the international environment. In this sense, the approach is similar to that of Easton.

Almond's reformulation attempted to account for criticism of his earlier work. First, he argued that his conception of political system deals with "interdependence" but not "harmony." He admitted that systems theorists "have been too much under the influence of mechanical and biological analogies" (1966: 12). His stress on "interdependence" was an effort to confront the criticism that his approach implied a static or conservative bias, because of its emphasis on equilibrium or harmony of parts. Second, he considered his new formulation of systems theory to be dynamic rather than static and conservative because it permits the examination of "developmental patterns" (1966: 13). In effect, Almond was recognizing the significance of the substantial literature on political development published in the early 1960s. This effort to tie systems theory to developmental theory, however, was pervaded by ethnocentric considerations, which will be examined later. Third, Almond seemed to be seeking a holistic rather than a partial theory: "We need to look at political systems as whole entities and being shaped by their environments" (1966: 13–14). In this sense, he followed in the path of Easton, but Almond gave substance to the theory by referring to actual experiences of a variety of nations and to actual situations.

Figure 5.4 illustrates the elements of Almond's political system. Almond introduced many terms into his conception of the political system, and these are defined and discussed in considerable detail in his work, but the figure may assist the reader in understanding the relationships among the terms and functional levels. The figure serves only as an abstraction of what is more fully delineated in his writing, however.

Almond's political system comprises many interdependent parts. These parts include government institutions as well as "all structures in their political aspects" (1966: 18). A boundary exists between the system and its environment. Inputs and outputs affect the system, and feedback exists between the system and its environment. Almond identified four examples of demands and four examples of supports, which serve the system as inputs. He also described four types of transactions that relate to the output side of the process. Figure 5.4 includes these aspects of an essentially Eastonian framework, but it also incorporates the three levels of functions that Almond incorporated into his own formulation. One level consists of six *conversion* functions: interest articulation, interest aggregation, political communication, rule making, rule application, and rule adjudication; these functions relate to input demands and supports and to output decisions and actions as internalized within the political system. Demands are formulated through interest articulation and are combined into alternative courses of action through interest aggregation. Rules are drawn up through rule making, they are implemented and enforced through rule application, and sometimes they are assessed through rule adjudication. Communication affects all of these activities.

A second level of activities comprises *capability* functions: regulation, extraction, distribution, and symbolic response; these functions relate to the performance of the system within its environment. Almond applied these functions to totalitarian and democratic societies. He felt that in democratic

FIGURE 5.4
Diagram of Almond's Political System and Levels of Functions

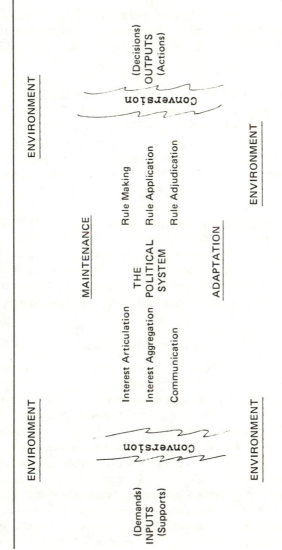

Source: Adapted from Almond and Powell (1966:16–41).

societies "outputs of regulation, extraction, and distribution are more affected by inputs of demands from groups" and that these societies therefore have "a higher responsive capability" (1966: 28–29). Totalitarian societies in contrast are less responsive to demands, regulate behavior through coercion, and extract maximum resources from their people. Symbolic capability relates to the symbol flow from the political system into the international environment.

Maintenence and adaptation functions include political socialization and recruitment and represent a third level of activities. According to Almond, a theory of the political system can be based on understanding the relations among these three levels and the relations of the functions at each level.

REASSESSMENT

Easton in his 1969 address to the American Political Science Association offered a reassessment of his early work. About the same time Almond also reviewed his own work (1969–1970). Despairing the mood of "disillusionment" that was sweeping the field of comparative politics, he lauded the impressive accomplishments of the previous two decades and asserted his faith in a systems approach to politics. In an effort to deal with the "counter productive polemic" of the late 1960s, he proposed a research design "intended to draw us a little closer to a systematic exploitation of historical experience using a causal scheme which combines system-functional analysis, aggregate quantitative analysis and rational choice analysis at appropriate points in the explanation of developmental episodes" (1969–1970: 28). Essentially, this effort was an attempt by Almond to retain his structural-functional formulation and to combine it with other approaches so as to deal empirically with specific historical cases and to give relevance to his own theory.

Origins of Thought and Influences on Almond

There are many assumed advantages of structural functionalism as an approach to the study of politics. Running through the literature is the viewpoint that structural functionalism has served to recast attention on the concept of system at a time when social scientists had become concerned with the analysis of individual behavior. Additionally, it is sometimes believed that structural functionalism allows for objective analysis, by emphasizing an organic social system or what Radcliffe-Brown once called the "natural science of society" (1957). Finally, structural functionalism attempts to relate all social phenomena into one system of thought.

Such positive perspectives emanate essentially from the work of the anthropologists Radcliffe-Brown and Malinowski and the sociologist Parsons and his followers Levy and Merton. They clearly have influenced contemporary political science, for example, William C. Mitchell's *The American Polity* (see his theoretical views in 1958), but most notably in the writings of Gabriel Almond and a host of comparative political scientists who have followed in his path. Herein we note one pattern of thought that influenced Almond. Because of its concern with the whole system, it might be called a pattern of macro-structural functionalism. Another pattern of thought that influenced Almond relates to the traditions of pluralism and liberalism, which sprang from the *Federalist Papers* and were incorporated into contemporary political science through the seminal works of Arthur Bentley, David Truman, and Robert Dahl. Because attention is directed to a plurality of interests within the system, it might be labeled a pattern of micro-structural functionalism. Although "middle range" in orientation, this micro pattern allows comparative political scientists to study group and individual behavior in an empirical rather than an abstract theoretical manner. Both patterns, as we shall discuss below, relate to the thought of Max Weber.

The division into macro and micro patterns of structural functionalism simply allows for distinction according to the size of the political unit studied. A macro unit might comprise a national political system either in an abstract or a real sense. Actual comparative investigation of such units has tended to be abstract and theoretical rather than empirical and theoretical. A micro unit might consist of a political party or a special interest group. Comparative investigation of such units has tended to be empirical and theoretical rather than abstract and theoretical. This basic division according to the size of unit is adapted from Martindale's (1965: 128) dichotomy of functionalism in contemporary sociology.

MACRO-STRUCTURAL FUNCTIONALISM OR GRAND THEORY

We have already noted that Almond's early work on the political system (1956) acknowledged a debt to Easton's original conception (1953). By "system" Almond (Almond and Powell 1966: 16–21) referred to interdependence of parts, input and outputs, boundary, and environment—all aspects of Easton's systems framework. By "political" he cited Easton's definitions of "authoritative allocation of values," but he emphasized Weber's idea that "legitimate force is the thread that runs through the actions of the political system, giving it its special quality and importance, and its coherence as a system" (Almond and Powell 1966: 17–18). In defense of his conception, Almond later referred to a traditional usage of system and its "proud, essentially Enlightenment origin in which British science—particularly Newtonian mechanics, and British political theory of the 17th and 18th centuries—played a role" (Almond 1969–1970: 22).

To these roots of Eastonian, Weberian, and Newtonian thought, Almond fused the terms structure and function. Structures are "observable activities that make up the political system" (Almond and Powell 1966: 21). These structures are characterized by regularity and, according to the level of systemic development, by structural differentiation. Functionalism for Almond was "an old theme in political theory." Presumably he referred to the establishment of functionalism in biology during the 1920s, its use in studies of the personality in primitive society, and its penetration into all the social sciences thereafter.

Almond (1968) considered that the concept of system came to Easton by way of the work of Parsons but that his own formulation diverged somewhat from both theorists. Whereas they have moved toward a theoretical formalization, drawing on systems theory and cybernetics, Almond believed that he plowed "a muddier course attempting to draw the notions of system and function closer to the main currents of empirical research in political science" (1968: 277). Almond stuffed Easton's simplified black box with "functional and structural categories" while updating the classic system-functional theory of a separation of power doctrine. He called his systems formulation "probabilistic functionalism" (1968: 278). The reader who desires to examine a simplified synthesis of the writings of Almond and Easton on systems might consult Scott (1972).

Despite Easton's insistence that his framework differed from functional formulations and Almond's emphasis on the divergence of his ideas from those of general systems theory, there are some important similarities as indicated by Stephens (1969). For one thing, the idea of persistence runs through both tendencies. For another, there is Easton's reference to the "fundamental functions" of political systems; these are allocation and acceptance of values and have the same status as functional requisites.

Specifically, Almond attributed his use of functionalism to its chief contemporary theorists Malinowski and Radcliffe-Brown in anthropology and Parsons, Levy, and Merton in sociology: "They have said that the ability to explain and predict in the social sciences is enhanced when we think of social structures and institutions as performing functions in systems" (Almond and Powell 1966: 28). Briefly, then, we turn to a discussion of these functionalists and attempt to identify aspects of their thinking that are incorporated into Almond's thought.

1. Malinowski and Radcliffe-Brown. These anthropologists were more concerned with descriptive inquiry than their counterparts in sociology who directed attention to theoretical generalization. Both tendencies, however, drew from organicism, much in the tradition of Spencer who introduced the concept of functionalism to social science from physiology (Eister 1964).

A. R. Radcliffe-Brown admitted the influence of organicism upon his thought: "The concept of function applied to human societies is based on an analogy between social life and organic life" (Radcliffe-Brown 1952: 178). He defined function as "the contribution which a partial activity makes to the total activity of which it is a part. . . . the contribution it makes to the total social life as the functioning of the total social system" (1935: 397). The analogy between social life and organic life and the relationship of parts and wholes are perhaps clarified in Table 5.1. The analogy as outlined in the table is self-explanatory and is presented to allow the reader to comprehend more vividly the organicist influence upon the functionalists. Structure, continuity of structure, life process, and function are understood as parallel phenomena in social as well as organic life. In drawing this analogy, Radcliffe-Brown stressed that what is good for an institution is good for the society as a whole. The criterion of the good is the maintenance of society in a stable equilibrium. Institutions function to deal with disruptive tendencies and to ensure stability and equilibrium.

Bronislaw Malinowski set forth his ideas on functionalism as a contem-

TABLE 5.1
Analogy of Social and Organic Life

	Social Life (Community of People)	Organic Life (Animal Organism)
Structure of units	Individual human beings connected by social relations to an integrated whole.	Agglomeration of cells or molecules and fluids arranged as an integrated whole.
Continuity of structure	Individuals may die or be born but these changes do not disrupt the maintenance of society, which is dependent on the process of social life that consists of activities and interactions of human beings and of organized social groups into which they are united.	Constituent units (molecules or cells) may be lost or changed through excretion or respiration (for example), but structural arrangement of units is continued through maintenance of the organism's life.
Life process	Defined as the functioning of the social structure of the community—comprised of the activities of the constituent units or people.	Consists of activities and interactions of the constituent units (cells or molecules) of the organism, the cells, and the organs with which the cells are united.
Function	Activity of people, such as punishment of a crime or funeral ceremony. These activities relate to social needs of society.	Activity of a part (e.g., an organ such as the stomach). These activities relate to physiological needs of the organism.

Source: Adapted from Radcliffe-Brown (1935:394–396).

porary of Radcliffe-Brown, although both men spent considerable time discounting the mutual influence upon their simultaneous writings. Radcliffe-Brown referred occasionally to functionalism and needs, as is evident in Table 5.1. However, Malinowski emphasized functionalism in terms of needs, indeed he defined functionalism as such. Needs serve the maintenance of the system. An institution, he believed, functions to meet the immediate needs of individuals or groups in society. He tied this notion of need to a "functional theory of culture." Human beings have to be nourished; they have to conform to elementary conditions in order to survive. Thus they live by physiological drives, but those drives are shaped by the conditions of culture. "Culture appears as a vast conditioning apparatus which, through training, the imparting of skills, the teaching of norms, and the development of tastes, amalgamates nurture with nature and produces beings whose behavior cannot be determined by the study of anatomy and physiology alone" (Malinowski 1945: 43).

Whatever the conceptual differences between Malinowski and Radcliffe-Brown, the functionalist would do well to combine their two definitions rather than force a choice. The empirical work of Malinowski and Radcliffe-Brown focused on "primitive system," and their findings and generalizations were helpful to Almond in his own systemic classifications. Although there is no direct acknowledgment of the influence of these two anthropologists, their work most certainly can be utilized in an assessment of other studies in comparative politics. Two examples perhaps will suffice. S. N. Eisenstadt (1959) defined primitive political systems in terms of structure and function and concerned himself with maintenance and solidarity in the face of disruptive behavior. He offered a detailed typology and some hypotheses about primitive political systems. At yet another level, Roger D. Masters (1964) compared primitive and international political systems and found that their structures and functions are similar.

2. *Parsons and his followers.* Sociologists refer less to cultural patterns than to processes, actions, and other phenomena. They tend to deal in theoretical generalization, and their theory derives from organicism. Their functionalism commonly relates to whole systems, identifies specific functions as requisites for the maintenance of systems, and demonstrates the functional interdependence of diverse structures within the whole system. Parsons, Merton, and Levy have contributed most ambitiously to a functionalism that has influenced political science. Almond explicitly acknowledged his debt to these writers (Almond and Powell 1966: 27–28). Let us turn to the ideas that most decisively influenced Almond and other political comparativists.

Although Almond drastically restated Parsonian functionalism, two aspects of Parson's scheme appear to have influenced Almond's own formulation. These are the theories of action and social system. The following summary is based essentially on Parson's *Social System* (1951) and Mitchell's critical synthesis of Parsonian theory (1967). The reader might also find useful the critical essays on Parsons in Max Black (1961) and the careful attempt by Harold Kaplan (1968) to analyze the criticism of Parsons, especially as it is related to political science. Parsons considered his theory of action as his large conceptual scheme within which may be found a theory of social systems, a theory of personality, and a theory of culture (Parsons 1951: 537). Personality and culture were topics of interest to Almond, but a discussion of them shall be confined to the next chapter. Now we turn to the theories of action and system.

Parsons's theories owe much to the theories of his precursors. As an undergraduate at Amherst College in the early 1920s, he majored in biology, and he has acknowledged (1951: vii) the influence of L. J. Henderson, a biochemist with sociological interests, who at the time insisted that the concept system be employed by the social scientists (Mitchell 1967: 2, 7). Parsons also came into contact with Malinowski during a year of study in England during 1924 and 1925, and a year later at Heidelberg Parsons was influenced by the late Max Weber, whose ideas were the subject of his doctoral dissertation. Weber's stress on ideal types as approximations of general theory seems to have moved Parsons to posit a perfectly integrated society so as to generate hypotheses about the gaps between real systems and the ideal type (H. Kaplan 1968: 892–893).

In his early work on a theory of action Parsons based his thinking on that of Weber as well as on the thinking of other great theorists, namely, Alfred Marshall, Emile Durkheim, and Vilfredo Pareto. Each contributed to Parsons's theory since Parsons, through a secondary analysis of their work, synthesized "two quite different traditions, the positivist (Pareto and Durkheim) and the idealist (Weber), into the now well-known voluntaristic conception" (Mitchell 1967: 23–24). In addition, Parsons treated such topics as authority, based on Weber, norms, on Durkheim, and elites, power, and ideologies, on Pareto. Indeed Pareto seems to have inspired Parsons to elaborate on structural functionalism; Parsons's *Social System* "is an attempt to carry out Pareto's intention, using an approach, the 'structural-functional' level of analysis, which is quite different from that of Pareto" (Parsons 1951: vii). Parsons's concern with harmony and order in society, which he recognized as not inherently peaceful, prompted him to deal with ways of controlling and regulating conflict, and in this regard he seems to have been influenced by Thomas Hobbes and John Locke (Mitchell 1967: 10).

In building a general theory of action, Parsons attempted to embrace all actions, from particular individual acts to collective events. This general theory evolved through two phases separated by the Second World War.

The first dealt with the individual; the second, with social systems.

The first formulation comprised action as relating to an action, a goal or goals, an alternative means, a situation in which there is only partial control, and values, norms, and beliefs. Later he acknowledged the limitations of this formulation: "The structure of social systems cannot be derived directly from the actor-situation frame of reference. It requires functional analysis of the complications introduced by the interaction of a plurality of actors" (Parsons, quoted in Mitchell 1967: 25). The second formulation was worked out under Parsons's leadership in collaboration with other social scientists who turned to large systems and set forth in detail categories of an action theory. Three volumes, one by Parsons (1951) and two with others (Parsons and Shils 1951 and Parsons, Bales, and Shils 1953), elaborated this theory, and, according to Mitchell (1967: 26), "they are offered as paradigms for social science." The vocabulary of this theory was jargonistic, the orientation was positivistic, and social science was equated to other sciences. Mitchell confirmed these tendencies. "Four generalized conditions of the equilibrium of action are produced as analogues to certain principles of classical mechanics: The principles of inertia, action and reaction, effort, and integration are so offered" (1967: 27). In this new formulation Parsons stressed interaction, not of the individual actor, but of *personalities, social systems,* and *cultures.*

Parsons developed five pairs of "pattern variables" as a means of describing each of these units of the action theory: orientations for personalities, roles for social systems, and values for cultures. Each pattern variable offered dichotomous choices in any situation (Parsons 1951: 67).

1. Affectivity versus Affective Neutrality (choice of expressing *or* controlling feelings and emotions)
2. Self-Orientation versus Collectivity Orientation (choice of being selfish and private *or* selfless and collective)
3. Universalism versus Particularism (choice of value orientation in use of universal *or* particular norms)
4. Achievement versus Ascription (choice of evaluation based on performance *or* qualities or attributes independent of performance)
5. Specificity versus Diffuseness (choice of specific obligations and properties *or* more diffused ones)

These pattern variables were utilized in Almond's efforts to relate political culture to political systems, which is examined in the ensuing chapter. In any event, they are the essence of Parsons's macro theory of *social* systems and of his structural functionalism.

Parsons is well known for his elaboration of a theory of the social system.

A society is the largest type of social system, and it is capable of maintaining itself in equilibrium over long periods of time. The polity is a subsystem of the larger society. Systems analysis implies order and predictability. Parsons agreed with general systems theorists like Easton that a system comprises interrelated units and is definable in terms of boundaries and interaction with an environment. Both have agreed that a system has internal structure and processes, but Parsons's emphasis on functionalism and in particular on biological influences differentiates his work from general systems specialists, who are more influenced by engineering and physics (Mitchell 1967: 51). Parsons stressed role as the "conceptual unit of the social system," and this allows for analysis by the pattern variables.

Parsons was particularly concerned wtih functional problems, prerequisites that face all social systems: maintenance, adaptation, goal attainment, and integration (Parsons, Bales, and Shils 1953: 177–181). Maintenance refers to satisfying the manual needs of much of the population and managing or controlling tension within the system. Adaptation is the provision of facilities and resources for the use of the system. Goal attainment relates to mobilization of people and resources to achieve collective ends. Integration is the coordination of interrelationships among the members of a system.

Parsons also was concerned with structure. By structure he meant "a set of interrelated roles, collectivities, norms and values, institutions which prescribe, proscribe, encourage, discourage, and permit certain courses of action" (Mitchell 1967: 70). Parsons was interested in a comparative and evolutionary formulation. Thus, social structures are differentiated along functional lines. According to Parsons (1966: 106) goal attainment relates to the polity and political structures, while maintenance is performed in the culture by religious groups, families, schools, and a variety of other structures; integration is evident in the legal order and social control; and adaptation is found in the economy and economic structures. Advancing societies are explained in terms of increasing specialization and differentiation. These Parsonian aspects—the functional prerequisites, structural differentiation, and specialization—were incorporated in modified form into the Almond formulation. Parsons also was interested in the cultural secularization of developing social systems, and that, too, was assimilated by Almond.

A word on the Parsonian use of input and output categories is in order. Mitchell compared these categories as used in Almond, Easton, and Parsons, and Table 5.2 illustrates them. Parsons's categories are more complex, varied, and numerous, but they seem to include those of Almond and Easton. Mitchell (1967: 84) made it clear, however, that the Parsonian categories are simply listings deserving of operationalization, measurement, and explanation.

TABLE 5.2
Categories of Inputs and Outputs: Comparison of Almond, Easton, and Parsons

	Almond		*Easton*	*Parsons*
Inputs	Demands Supports		Demands Supports	Interests-Demands Supports Control of productivity Legitimation of authority Legality of powers of offices
Outputs	Decisions Actions	⎧Regulations ⎨Extractions ⎪Distributions ⎩Responses	Decisions Actions	Policies Allocations of resources Effectiveness Responsibilities ⎧Leadership ⎨Operation ⎩Moral

Source: Adapted from Mitchell (1967:83). For an elaboration of Parsons's formulation of political system, see his essay (1966:105–112).

The major followers of Parsons are Robert K. Merton and Marion J. Levy, Jr. Influenced by Malinowski and Radcliffe-Brown as well as by Max Weber, Merton (1949) formulated a conception of functionalism in a lucid and detailed manner. He examined manifest and latent functions, and he elucidated on the concept of dysfunction as well. Because his formulation is clear and precise and because his theoretical statements suggest empirical utility, Merton has influenced many political scientists who have turned to functionalism (for a summary of his theory, see Lehman 1966). Levy (1952) offered a synthesis of Parsons and Merton. His discussion tends to be formalistic and often superficial, although he carefully defined each of his terms. In his early work he elaborated on the meaning of structural and functional requisites and prerequisites, and in at least one article (Levy 1958) he discussed the relevance of his analysis to political science.

MICRO-STRUCTURAL FUNCTIONALISM
AND PARTIAL OR MIDDLE-RANGE THEORY

Although the macro or grand theory of the anthropologists and sociologists dealt with whole societies and systems, a growing number of social scientists have turned their attention to the study of the parts rather than the whole of society. Gestalt psychology adopted the concept of system in its explanation of learning, and sociologists such as Kurt Lewin utilized individuals or groups in explanations that included sociocultural as well as psychological perspectives. Ian Whitaker (in Martindale 1965: 137–138) identified these tendencies as microfunctionalist. In contrast to the exaggeration of theorizing by the macrofunctionalists, he found that the microfunctionalists place too much stress on trivial data. Merton (1949) once proposed bridging this gap with "theories of the middle range," or partial theory.

The stress on the study of groups has long been of interest to political scientists. In comparative politics the structural categories established by Almond (1960) influenced many scholars to investigate basic units or subsystems. Almond and others stimulated specialized studies on political parties, bureaucracies, labor unions, and special interest groups in countries throughout the world. Such studies allowed stress on empirical data at a time of growing and widespread discontent with abstract general theory. These political scientists thus found refuge in the "middle range," that is, they could escape both abstract theory as well as narrow empirical studies of behavioralism. Although utilizing smaller units in their analyses, the concepts of political system as well as structural functionalism remained relevant to their investigations.

Almond referred to such study as growing out of classical political theory. Theories of the separation of powers were functionalist in orientation. In the seventeenth and eighteenth centuries political systems were understood in terms of administrative, legislative, and judicial powers or functions. "The political theory of the *Federalist Papers* is pre-eminently a functional theory. . . . The authors of the *Federalist Papers* were systems theorists as well, for they dealt with the interaction and equilibrium of the other social systems with the political system, and with the interaction of the subsystems of the polity one with the other" (Almond and Powell 1966: 10–11).

This idea of interaction and equilibrium, inherent today in middle-range theory of structural functionalism, indeed is not new to political science. In his critique of such theory, David Easton (1953: 269–274; 1956) noted its origins in the study of political process, in which a variety of elements—interest groups, parties, legislatures, and the like—interact to shape the policies of a political system. This idea of process, he affirmed, "can be traced back in political thought to the growth of pluralism." The association of a pluralistic process and equilibrium was introduced early in Arthur F. Bentley's *Process of Government*, published at the turn of the century, and later was reinforced in David Truman's monumental study of group pressures, *The Governmental Process* (1951).

Truman inquired into the role of political groups in the governing process. He was interested in formal and informal groupings and his conception of the political process sought to account for the *functioning* of political groups. All groups are interest groups, he claimed, and interest group refers "to any group, that on the basis of one or more shared attitudes, makes certain claims upon other groups in the society for the establishment, maintenance, or enhancement of forms of behavior that are implied by the shared attitudes" (Truman 1951: 33). Interestingly, Truman attributed the recognition of group pressures in the United States to James Madison's classic statement about the impact of diverse groups upon government. According to Madison,

> A landed interest, a manufacturing interest, a mercantile interest, a moneyed interest, with many lesser interests, grow up of necessity in civilized nations, and divide them into different classes, actuated by different sentiments and views. The regulation of these various and interferring interests forms the principal task of modern legislation, and involves the spirit of party and faction in the necessary and ordinary operations of the government. [Madison, Essay 10 in the *Federalist Papers*, quoted in Truman 1951: 5]

This is not the place to explore critically the origins of interest group or middle-range theory. Those origins have been traced and critiqued exhaustively by G. David Garson (1974), who synthesized all articles and book reviews on the subject that have appeared in the *American Political Science Review* since its inception in 1906. William T. Bluhm (1965) linked the interest group theory in the United States, in particular that of Bentley, to the naturalistic political science of the seventeenth-century English theorist, James Harrington.

What is clear, however, is that Almond assimilated "pluralist theory into an explicitly functionalist framework, supposedly confirming thereby the universal applicability always claimed for the theory" (Baskin 1970: 71). Darryl Baskin's work is helpful in identifying some of the underlying ideological and conservative assumptions of U.S. group theory and pluralism. "In the resulting unity of theory and practice, pluralist theory is reduced to the status of partisan apologetics at worst and ideology at best" (1970: 94–95). This observation is a critical perspective of pluralist theory itself as well as of Almond's major contribution to middle-range theory so commonly accepted in comparative politics. Many years ago Roy Macridis exposed the essential problems of the focus on interest groups: "The study of interest groups and of their manner of action is no substitute for theory" (1961: 26). He doubted that even a simple taxonomy of groups could be useful for comparative analysis.

Criticisms of Almond and Structural Functionalism

Functionalism and structuralism in political science derive essentially from anthropology, economics, and sociology. Critics of those approaches have found their mark, however. Functionalism frequently is identified as deterministic or ideological, conservative or restrictive, or simply false. Anthropologist I. C. Jarvie argued that functionalism is limited by "its lack of

explanatory power, its unsatisfactoriness as explanation, and the constrict-
ing effect of its assumptions about the nature and working of social systems."
Economist Sherman Roy Krupp warned of problems in stressing the
equilibrium character of functional systems: there is a tendency to exag-
gerate the cohesiveness of such systems; highly integrated systems may
obscure goals, resulting in vague description and lack of analysis; and ideal
situations are often confused with the observed situations of systems.
Sociologist Don Martindale noted four drawbacks to functionalism: the
conservative ideological bias and preference for status quo; a lack of
methodological clarity; an overemphasis on the role of closed systems in
social life; and a failure to deal with social change (Martindale 1965:
156–160; above references to Jarvie in Martindale 1965: 18; and to Krupp, in
Martindale 1965: 78–82). The charge that functionalism does not account
for processes of change was backed up by Barber (1956), and Buckley (1966)
stressed a predisposition for functionalism to assume consensus. Hempel
(1959) argued that functionalism is illogical. Terry N. Clark concerned
himself with the structural-functional overemphasis of institutionalized
behavior (1972: 277–279), and David Apter (1971) discussed a number of
weaknesses in functionalism in a critical look at developments in comparative politics.

All these problems are relevant to a critique of structural functionalism
and Almond's formulation of the political system. Groth (1970), for example, referred to the difficulties of defining a system and its boundaries and to
the political biases that result in perceptions of "equilibrium, stability, and
survival as implicit values and goals of the system" (1970: 486). His own concerns with the work of Almond and Powell were threefold: ambiguity in terminology, difficulties in determining political relationships, and confusion in
the use of facts and values. Melanson and King (1971) discussed
epistemological problems in Almond and Powell and specifically turned to
the ambiguity of terms, the obsession with empirical detail as detached from
theory, and the implicit preferences for Western so-called democratic
systems. We now turn to three problems: first, the conservative ideological
bias in structural functionalism; second, conceptual obfuscation; and third,
limited applicability.

Conservative Ideological Bias

Functionalism blossomed in an era of consolidation and conservativism
following the Second World War. C. Wright Mills attacked the conservative
bias in the writings of the proponents of functionalism and especially
castigated Parsons, claiming that his functionalism was grand theory that
neither related to facts nor reached a level of theory (Mills 1959: 25–49). Barrington Moore, Jr. (1955), Ralf Dahrendorf (1958), and Andrew Hacker

(1961) joined the polemic against Parsons and the functionalists.

Almond's early work was strongly criticized as ethnocentric (Spiro 1966), and Lijphart (1968) considered its emphasis on stability in the light of Anglo-American norms and political tradition. Acknowledging some of these difficulties, Almond combined his structural functionalism with a theory of development. Objections to his later work were not mitigated, however. Jonathan A. Sanford (1971), for example, expressed concern for the ideological undercurrents of the structural functionalism of Almond and Powell and identified their "most serious defect, their liberal bias" (1971: 4). Sanford accused them of weaving liberal premises into their work; drawing from Bentham and Mill they injected the philosophy that "increased individual freedom liberates the natural forces which benefit human existence, while any interference with the marketplace leads to inefficiency and limits on the system's natural benefits, reducing the aggregates of human satisfactions" (1971: 4). Almond and Powell traced development from a primitive stage to a fully developed plural democracy: "Their theory is implicitly designed to convert the reader to a belief in liberal democracy and liberal pluralism" (1971: 5).

Other critics reinforced these objections. Campbell referred to Almond's expressed desire to avoid undue attention to organistic or mechanistic formulations, but concluded that "his faith in technology and 'rational' procedures belies an organistic stance skewed in the direction of modernization" (1971: 29). Campbell accused Almond of not taking into account an alienation of the members of a political system or the fact that modernization does not necessarily assure human fulfillment. At the root of this problem is Almond's "secular bias" and political science's "misplaced emphasis on the diffusion of rational means" (1971: 29).

Charles A. Powell explained these problems as a reflection of "American cultural mythology" and in particular cited interest group theory and its "'classless' view of a society stratified by religious and ethnic distinctions. In this view, the state withers away to a nonpartisan referee within a context of political norms that constrain activity into a framework of functionalist conflict resolution" (Powell 1971: 58). Such a perspective, he believed, can lead to a purposeful misreading of reality in other cultures. In other words, it is culture bound. He concluded that Almond's structural functionalism is "establishmentarian, non-operational, formally inadequate. . . . As a vehicle for research it goes nowhere, and as a language of discourse it leads to obfuscation. . . . the pluralistic neutralism of structural-functionalism . . . renders it useless as theory" (1971: 63).

CONCEPTUAL OBFUSCATION

Powell was especially upset by the widespread use of contemporary jargon.

In a celebrated presidential address to the American Sociological Association, Kingsley Davis (1959) examined the myth of functional analysis as method. William Mackenzie wondered if anything is gained by restating the old story in new terminology. Structural functionalism is a reformulation of old topics: "Topics are structural and can be rephrased in the old jargon of constitutional practice and constitutional law. . . . Almond's terms are in one sense no better than the old terms, because they offer no better definitions" (Mackenzie 1967: 319–320).

S. E. Finer summed up these criticisms in a close look at the nomenclature of Almond's political system. "What Almond has to say could have been said without using this systems approach and it would have been said more clearly." Finer disdained the use of "modish" concepts, concluding that Almond's conception of "political" was misconceived and that his notion of system, with its inputs and outputs, was "otiose and confusing" (Finer 1969–1970: 4). Finer's detailed discussion of the terminology utilized by Almond was related as well to Max Weber and David Easton who preceded and influenced Almond. The reader interested in deciphering the jargon of comparative politics would do well to look at Finer's treatment.

OPERATIONAL IMPLICATIONS

William Flanigan and Edwin Fogelman argued that "structural functionalists have not taken the enormously difficult step of refining, operationalizing, and testing hypotheses" (in Martindale 1965: 123). They attributed these failings to the limitations of scholars, the early stage in the development of theory, and the deficiencies of functionalism. In this regard, Holt and Turner examined Almond's analysis of the modern political system. Almond viewed the modern political system as structurally differentiated and secular, but Holt and Turner found limitations with this formulation. "It is difficult to apply on a broad basis to include both historical and contemporary cases. The formulation also tends in effect to equate the modern political system with the modern Anglo-American democratic system . . . its definitions employ too many dimensions, and it neglects the problem of variation in the *societal functions* of government" (Holt and Turner 1966: 12–13). They illustrated these limitations with an example. According to Almond, there is no modern political system in the Soviet Union. Its system is not highly differentiated because it is totalitarian and its structures lack autonomy. Thus it is traditional, not modern. Holt and Turner refuted this description by referring to the variety of interests that were manifested after the death of Stalin. Almond's categories become too rigid, and specific cases do not necessarily relate to his scheme. However, Abrahamson (1973), although accepting as valid most of the problems of structural functionalism, presented an analysis of the assumptions that would be necessary to test empirically hypotheses from functional theory. His findings suggest that functional theory might yield empirically testable hypotheses.

RADICAL PERSPECTIVES OF SYSTEM

U.S. conceptions of pluralist politics generally stress consensus, but some attention recently has been devoted to conflict as well. Easton recognized the limitations of systems in equilibrium. Almond, in the image of Parsons, combined his formulation of systems with perspectives on action. These efforts, however, really do not satisfy radical critics of systems theory. Lilienfeld, for example, labeled systems theory as an "ideological movement" with a "central doctrine and a syncretistic or ecumenical way of thinking" (1975: 646). The systems literature contains little relevance to the real world. Even the application of systems analysis has exerted little impact on U.S. politics, he claimed, and he cited a number of cases of system "fiascoes" and wasted expenditure. His review of recent literature illustrating the failure of a practical application of systems analysis is well worth the reader's attention.

Almond, absorbed in the ideal Anglo-American model of politics, paid scant attention to Marx who also was concerned with the idea of system, which he conceived as a political economy whose changes were the consequences of class conflict according to material forces of production. Parsons also devoted little attention to Marx, but at one point Parsons acknowledged that "Marx is one of the symbolic 'grandfathers' of the theory of action" (Black 1961: 361). Easton, in his early work, was more generous. Marx and Comte, he affirmed, were preoccupied with a premature building of systems: "The complete immersion of these thinkers in something called the scientific approach distinguishes and links them." Easton summarized what he understood was the Marxist approach. Marx, he claimed,

> thought that appropriately mastered tools of inquiry, historical and dialectical materialism, which he developed from Hegel, would reveal the nature of inexorable laws and goals towards the realization of which those laws tended. . . . Marx sought to prove that it [society] evolved basically from primitive communism to feudalism to capitalism and must eventuate in socialism. [Easton 1953: 12]

Although recognizing political science criticisms of Marx, Thorson, who is not a Marxist, asserted that "Marx was correct in his basic perspective" (1970: 85). Furthermore, he contrasted "the Newtonian universal-generalization paradigm of understanding with the Darwinian evolutionary-development paradigm of understanding" (209). The Newtonian paradigm he associated with Hobbes and Locke, Harrington and Madison, and

Easton, while he related the Darwinian paradigm to Hegel and Marx. Marx gave political science and political philosophy "essentially a time-oriented theory of change," which differed sharply with "the static, enduring processing machine" of the Newtonian paradigm (210).

Given this latter distinction, we now discuss two orientations of a Marxist conception of system. The first orientation examines functionalism within a materialist perspective. We look at Frederick Engels's explication of a dialectical materialist explanation of the natural sciences, and then we turn to Al Szymanski's application of functionalism to Marxist dialectics. We note Marvin Harris's rejection of dialectics but his acceptance of materialism in scientific analysis. We review the efforts of Jonathan A. Sanford and others to revise a liberal perspective of structural functionalism into a radical framework. The second orientation of a Marxist conception of system examines system conceptualized as the state, beginning with a Hegelian view and the Marxist critique of Hegel's understanding of state and concluding with a summary of the contemporary approaches to an analysis of the state. Finally, we study an attempt to apply systems theory to centralized planning in the German Democratic Republic.

System in a Dialectical Materialist Perspective

A radical view of system, like its orthodox counterpart, roots itself in science. Science long has stressed generalization and broadly ranged theory in opposition to the partial, subjective, and irrational perspectives that pervade the orthodox underpinnings of contemporary politics. During the eighteenth century, writers moved from the Newtonian model to a deterministic view of history. Montesquieu in *The Spirit of Laws* discovered order in the histories of all nations, noted interconnected laws, and attributed changes to material causes. Marquis de Condorcet's *Outline of the Intellectual Progress of Mankind* attempted to apply the uniform and natural laws of the universe to society. He also identified ten epochs or stages in the history of civilization, a sort of incremental approach to development steeped in idealism, which nevertheless set the basis for an interpretation of evolution in the work of nineteenth-century thinkers, including Comte, Spencer, and Darwin.

Herbert Spencer focused on the themes of progress and race, laissez-faire individualism, and economic and political liberalism, and he opposed socialism and communism. Charles Darwin offered a materialist explanation of the origin of the species and emphasized progress through struggle. According to Marvin Harris (1968), who has concisely summarized and interpreted all these intellectual currents, Darwin's position was confused by prevailing, yet contrasting, views related to inherited and learned traits.

Nevertheless, it was Spencer and other conservatives who applied the term Social Darwinism to an interpretation of the nature and functioning of society. Harris blamed Spencer, not Darwin, for "the onus of having crippled the explanatory power of cultural evolutionary theory by merging and mixing it with racial determinism." "The conversion of biological theory to evolutionism was an outgrowth of the social scientists' interest in progress and perfectability, while the concept of natural selection itself arose from an interest in racial, national, and class forms of war and conflict" (Harris 1968: 129). Harris also admonished us to beware of the "myth of unilinear evolutionism," which usually characterizes classical evolutionary theory, and he argued that society and culture may skip steps in a sequence or evolve divergently (171).

Darwinism and evolutionary ideas influenced Frederick Engels who, in *Dialectics of Nature* (1934), examined the achievements of the natural sciences during the nineteenth century. In particular, Engels was interested in the discovery of the organic cell as the basic structural unit of the human organism; he critiqued metaphysical and idealist conceptions in natural science, prevalent in his time as well as in ours, and drawing upon Marx's use of Hegelian dialectics, he offered a dialectical materialist explanation of natural science. His perspective focused on the development of the capitalist mode of production and advances in technology and their impact on the natural sciences.

Unlike static general systems theory, Engels combined inorganic physical science with organic life sciences into a dialectical materialist classification of the natural sciences (1934: 248–249). Emphasizing "the general evolutionary connection in nature," he interrelated all matter, organic and inorganic. Engels attacked the piecemeal arrangement of science proposed by Comte and Saint-Simon, "where one science is always exhausted before another is even broached" (250). Engels's critique, of course, counters the attempt by general systems theorists to distinguish closed (inorganic) systems from open (organic) ones. It also counters efforts by Bertalanffy, Laszlo, and others to combine scientific with philosophical views, for Engels struggled against the metaphysics, idealism, mechanism, and vulgar materialism of his contemporaries. Extracting the mysticism from Hegelianism, Engels called on scientists to apply the laws of materialistic dialectics, thereby giving a dynamic method to natural science.

Engels traced the patterns of scientific revolution through historical periods (1934: 23–28 ff.), similar to the later treatment of Thomas Kuhn. Man, he argued, "reacts on nature, changing it and creating new conditions for himself" (213). Causality thus relates directly to the actions of the individual upon nature rather than to deterministic causality based on laws in nature itself.

Engels exposed as pseudoscience the "natural-philosophical systems" of the German socialist Eugen Dühring and others who wrote "in ignorance" about all ideas and put forward their thought as adhering to scientific method. Engels acknowledged the need for classifying knowledge into fields for systematic investigation, but he insisted on making clear the connections of one field to another—empiricism becomes suspect, theory necessary at this point. "Natural science enters the field of theory and here the methods of empiricism will not work, here only theoretical thinking can be of assistance" (1934: 42). Engels understood theory as "a historical product, which at different times assumes different forms and, therewith, very different contents." The science of thought is "the science of the historical development of human thought," but the laws of thought do not signify "eternal truth." Thus dialectics, following in the tradition of Aristotle and Hegel, "constitutes the most important form of thinking for present-day natural science, for it alone offers the analogue for, and thereby the method of explaining, the evolutionary processes occurring in nature, interconnections in general, and transitions from one field of investigation to another" (43).

A holistic, not segmented, view of system is essential, according to Engels, because nothing takes place in isolation. Everything affects and is affected by every other thing. An individual makes the environment serve his or her purposes and thus brings about devastating social consequences. Engels analyzed these consequences in terms of production and labor. "All hitherto existing modes of production have aimed merely at achieving the most immediately and directly useful effort of labour. . . . All higher forms of production, however, led to the division of the population into different classes and thereby to the antagonisms of ruling and oppressed classes" (1934: 182).

Al Szymanski (1972) argued that Marx was a functionalist and functionalism should be employed in radical analysis when interpreted dialectically. Acknowledging the inherently conservative nature of prevailing functional theory, Szymanski believed that functionalism can be "a fundamental part of Marxist methodology, and a very powerful tool for the advance of social science" (1972: 35).

Szymanski examined the functionalism of Malinowski who saw society as culturally responding to seven basic biological needs, a formulation especially relevant for understanding classless, primitive societies. Malinowski's functionalism is not useful in the study of class societies in which needs other than biological needs develop, for example, the need to preserve and advance the interests of the class system. "When the imperatives of biology conflict with those of the preservation of class society, more likely than not, the imperatives of biology give way. Thus people go hungry so that business might make a profit" (Szymanski 1972: 38). If Malinowski's emphasis on biological needs could be combined with the historical needs of a given society, then his functionalism might become compatible with Marxist analysis, for Marx grounded his functionalism on an explanation of the contributions major institutions make to the social system of capitalism. Marx related each institution's relationship to profit maximization: religion is the opium of the people, the state is the managing force of the bourgeoisie, and the family is the replica of the greater society.

Szymanski also critiqued Parsons and Merton. Parsons's functional requisites distort reality, his schema of historical interpretation is inadequate and internally inconsistent, and his notion of culture is determinist. Further, he has no understanding of the fundamental contradictions of society. "Parsons simply fails to provide an adequate systematic theory of change that is both integrated with his abstract scheme *and* which can explain with any accuracy historical evolution" (1972: 39). In contrast, Merton is more sensitive to the problems of functionalism in his use of function and dysfunction, which moves toward an understanding of the contradictory nature of society, but Merton also has stripped functionalism of the concept of system and its holistic implications.

Finally, Szymanski introduced dialectics to functionalism, drawing upon Marx and Engels. Dialectics, he believed, is a method for understanding the physical and social world. Dialectics implies a moving back and forth between abstractness and concreteness, between theory and reality. Three principles prevail and can be related to functionalism; Szymanski called them principles of dialectical functionalism. First, things tend to be interrelated with one another, to form systems, and they must be understood as parts of a greater whole. Societies must be understood in historical context. Presently they relate to the satisfaction of biological needs and to the maintenance of the capitalist system. Second, although things are interdependent, they also have internal contradictions. In contemporary society dialectical functionalism both contributes to as well as undermines the existing system. Capitalism may result in an accumulation of real goods in society but also result in an expanded proletariat, which may struggle against those who control the means of production. Third, things tend to change as a consequence of contradictions in the system. Change emanates from the opposing forces within a given system, and change is the essential aspect of dialectical functionalism. For example, in maximizing profits through monopoly capital, the capitalist system tends to undermine its early practice of free competition.

These are the principles of Marx and contemporary Marxists who analyze racism, education, family, military, the state, and the like in functional terms; each is explained in terms of the economic requirements of monopoly capitalism. Not only are the contributions of each recognized, but the undermining and transformation of the system are also emphasized.

Marvin Harris (1968) leaned toward a materialist stance but also critically assessed the contributions of Marx and Engels to theory. He noted that they "depended upon a 'functional' model of sociocultural life," sharing with Comte and Spencer an interest in functionalism, which was compatible and subordinate to a primary interest in change. Yet all these nineteenth-century thinkers contrast sharply with the twentieth-century functionalists who are capable only of eclectic and piecemeal investigation. As to the functionalism of Marx and Engels, "As a causal, as well as diachronic and synchronic model, the economic-structural-ideological concatenation provides the basis for stipulating the more or less durable and influential parts of the system" (Harris 1968: 235). Harris noted that Marxist functionalism explicitly denies "that all the features of a sociocultural system contribute equally to its maintenance. . . . dysfunctional ingredients are not only accommodated, but assigned a central role as system-changing variables" (235). Conflict, he believed, is taken care of through a model that is evolutionary, not dialectical. Thus he indicted the "vague dialectical excursions" of Marx and Engels. "As a mode of analysis, which arose at the juncture of romanticism and industrialization, it is ill suited for the general history of mankind. It is a romanticized, mysticized, partisan materialism, appropriate to men who wish to foment a revolution based on mid-nineteenth-century European class structure and ideology" (230). Harris insisted that we turn to Marx's materialism and his distinction between economic base and superstructure.

Jonathan Friedman sketched a Marxist "model" of analytical categories that are interrelated hierarchically into "a set of functional distinctions" (1974: 445), as in Figure 5.5. Friedman took exception to Harris's "vulgar materialism," which he interpreted as the "new mechanical materialism developed out of a quite understandable reaction to the almost exclusive concern for ideology and semantics which has come to dominate much of anthropology" (444). Harris, Friedman believed, embedded himself "in a tradition of empiricist-functionalist ideology" (465). Like Szymanski, Friedman introduced the dialectic into his formulation, but he also attempted to elaborate a structural-Marxist model.

If Marx and Engels were functionalists, as Friedman, Harris, and Szymanski have affirmed, then how do their conceptions relate to orthodox conceptions of system? Sanford partially attempted to answer this question by returning to the structural functionalism of Almond and Powell, and he offered a revision of their formulation by breathing into it "a radical and existential ideological bias" (Sanford 1971: 27). Using similar procedures, he sharply differentiated conclusions from the liberal pluralist findings of Almond and Powell. In his discussion Sanford referred to Marx and Engels as "the two most famous structural-functional analysts" whose emphasis on the

FIGURE 5.5
Friedman's Functions of Marxism

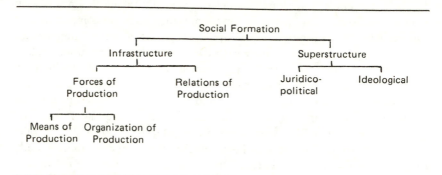

Source: Adapted from Friedman (1974:445).

role of socioeconomic forces in promoting political change is echoed by Almond and Powell (Sanford 1971: 7). Sanford also drew from the "systematic" discussions by the Russian Marxist Nikolai Bukharin, and he cited from the works of U.S. Marxists Paul Baran and Paul Sweezy. Sanford's critique and formulation attempted to transcend the limitations of the liberal pluralism of Almond and Powell, but he essentially retained their categories. His contribution is a useful example of an interpretation that moves toward the radical paradigm of comparative politics, however.

Those who espouse the radical paradigm, incorporating a Marxist perspective, would argue that Almond and Powell failed to see cleavages, tensions, and conflict in their analysis of systems; failed to differentiate among social classes; and failed to relate national systems to an international order, thereby offering no explanation for underdevelopment, which afflicts most countries. The pluralist assumptions in their model suggested that competing groups and interests would be dominated by ruling classes, thus isolating the masses of people. The ruling or dominant classes would perpetuate development for their own purposes, while promoting underdevelopment for the powerless and isolated lower classes. The state and its ruling classes would break through groups and organization, isolate individuals, and undermine the autonomy of the subsystems.

The radicals understand system as a whole and its holistic perspective as historical in orientation. González Casanova, for example, interpreted historical perspectives of system as dealing with process, struggle, organization, spontaneity, and other tendencies. He envisioned combinations of classical Marxism with new perspectives of social science, so that the contradictions of general systems theory, cybernetics, and even a discredited structural functionalism might be incorporated into a theory based on dialectics. Essentially, however, history is struggle.

> History as struggle emphasizes human, political categories with dialectical relations, with reciprocal actions, which are not simple relations of cause and effect, since in the midst of historical regularities a series of novelties or surprises are generated both in the structure and sequence of historical development. [González Casanova, 1973: 234]

In his effort to set forth a systematic conception of society, Mannheim also delineated a Marxist theory of social change, based on the material forces of production. "The basic organization of society is expressed in its economic structure which to a large extent determines the legal and political organization, and even the form of social consciousness . . . the kind of thought and ideas people hold in any particular age" (Mannheim 1957: 136). Mannheim reminded his readers that according to Marx social change comes about as the material forces of production are subject to change, and this occurs through technical inventions. Changes in the forces of production affect class relations and result in class conflict.

System as State: Toward a Marxist Critique

A radical understanding of state draws upon the thought of Hegel, Marx, Engels, and Lenin. It also focuses on recent study that expands upon the conceptions of Marx and others in order to interpret and analyze the role of the state in the contemporary world. We turn now to a review of the radical literature on the state.

Through a critique of Hegel's notions of the state, Marx elaborated some initial assumptions that are useful to theory. Painstakingly Marx worked from within Hegel's dialectical framework to expose its contradictions and inconsistencies. Hegel distinguished between the state and civil society: the state comprises an ideal relationship of the elements of society and it aggregates the communal concerns of humanity; in contrast, civil society comprises the private world of individual interests and activities. Hegel envisioned that unity between the state and civil society would evolve through several institutions. Using Prussia as his example, these institutions included the hereditary sovereign, who was considered independent of political groupings; the bureaucracy, whose interests coincided with those of the state; and an assembly of estates, which represented a consensus of the divergent interests of civil society.

In his *Critique of Hegel's Doctrine of the State*, Marx agreed with Hegel that a fundamental contradiction existed between the state and the civil society of citizens. Marx, however, separated forms of the state from an ideal or abstract conception and rooted them in "the material conditions of life." Marx stated that in ancient Greece the state and community were combined into the *polis*; there was a sense of unity between the people and the state, between private and public interests. In medieval times there was less separation between the state and civil society, "because civil society was political society; because the organic principle of civil society was the principle of the State" (Marx 1975: 137). Under capitalism, however, the state separates from civil society, and there is an estrangement between public and private life; in addition, there is an estrangement of individuals from each other as the civil society or the society fragments into private interests competing against each other. Under such conditions the state legitimizes the right of individuals to pursue particular interests through the possession of private property. Private property promotes inequality, enhances disunity among people, and undermines the equality and general intent of the community at large. Private property dominates contemporary society.

One solution to this dilemma is the return to democracy, but not to bourgeois democracy, which stresses parliamentary government, division of powers, and equality under the law of the state. Lucio Colletti, an Italian Marxist, was fascinated with this aspect of Marx's work.

> At this point in his evolution, what strikes us most forcibly is that while Marx has not yet outlined his later materialist conception of history he already possesses a very mature theory of politics and the state. The *Critique*, after all, contains a clear statement of the dependence of the state upon society, a critical analysis of parliamentarism accompanied by a counter-theory of popular delegation, and a perspective showing the need for ultimate suppression of the state itself. Politically speaking, mature Marxism would have relatively little to add to this. [Colletti, in Marx 1975: 45–46]

Colletti compared Marx's position with that of Lenin and Engels, who also were concerned with a conception of the state, based on Marx's elaboration. Colletti argued that Engels and Lenin tended to generalize their conception, overlooking the essential distinction, drawn by Marx, in which the state becomes separated from society under emerging capitalism. In turn, this led Engels and Lenin to "their marked subjectivism and volunteerism, based on their conception of the state as a 'machine' knowingly, consciously formed by the ruling class in deliberate pursuit of its own interest" (Colletti, in Marx 1975: 45–46). This distinction between Marx and Engels, in particular, was not recognized by Hal Draper (1977), who synthesized Marx's conception of the state. Draper argued that Marx and Engels collaborated in much of their work and that any scholarly emphasis of the differences between them is of little significance.

We turn now to a summary of Draper's discussion (1977: bk 1, 237–162), which begins with the *Critique* and evolves through *The German Ideology* and other works by Marx and Engels in an effort to clarify their conception of the state.

Stateless societies existed before the ancient city-state of Greek times as tribal and primitive communities lacking state institutions. Such communities maintained themselves without any special means of enforcement. Their integration rested on the premise that each individual, although acting in his or her own interests, is conscious of the responsibility to maintain all society. In a stateless society specialized roles and social networks are not tolerated, and "neither economic nor political ends can be exclusively pursued by anyone to the detriment of society, because these ends are intertwined with each other" (A. Southall, quoted in Draper 1977: 238).

Coercion may be found in stateless or state societies. Nature, for example, might coerce a tribe to fish or hunt in order to avoid starvation. In primitive stateless communities coercion is based on a collective judgment and is applied by the whole society; punishment is not relegated to a particular institution, separate from the collectivity. Once a society divides into opposing social classes, the interests of the whole society become fragmented, and the power for the enforcement of coercion separates from the collectivity, thereby ushering the state into existence. Engels described this historical process in his *Origin of the Family, Private Property, and the State.*

> The state . . . is rather a product of society at a certain stage of development; it is the admission that this society has become entangled in an insoluble contradiction with itself, that it is cleft into irreconcilable antagonisms which it is powerless to dispel. In order that these antagonisms, these classes with conflicting economic interests, may not annihilate each other and society in sterile struggle, a power, apparently standing above society, became necessary for the purpose of moderating the conflict and keeping it within the bounds of "order"; and this power, arising out of society, but placing itself over it, and increasingly alienating itself from it, is the state. [Engels (n.d.): 140]

Marx and Engels focused on the impact of coercion in the process of production and in economic relations. They noted that once coercion is sifted from the economic base of society, it tends to concentrate in the state or the political superstructure, a term they identify in *The German Ideology* as, "The social organization, evolving directly out of production and commerce, . . . in all ages forms the basis of the state and of the rest of the ideological superstructure" (quoted in Draper 1977: 252).

Drawing upon Marx and Engels, Draper elaborated the characteristics of the state in modern history as distinguished from tribal communities. First, the state exercises power over a territory (usually with some urban concentration) rather than over a kinship group. Second, it wields power through institutions or instruments of coercion, which separate it from the collective society. Third, it is financed through taxes imposed upon the citizens. Fourth, it maintains its power through the establishment of a bureaucracy, which stands apart from and above the population as a whole. In the *Communist Manifesto* Marx and Engels referred to the "executive" of the state as a committee for managing the affairs of the bourgeoisie. More concretely the state serves the economically dominant class

> Because the state arose from the need to hold class antagonisms in check, but because it arose, at the same time, in the midst of the conflict of these classes, it is, as rule, the state of the most powerful, economically dominant class, which, through the medium of the state, becomes also the politically dominant class, and thus acquires new means of holding down and exploiting the oppressed class. [Engels, quoted in Draper 1977: 257]

One of the state's major tasks is to mediate the differences and conflicts that are found within the dominant or ruling class. This class is not necessarily monolithic, especially in a competitive capitalist society, and may comprise conflicting and antagonistic individual and group interests. The state thus exists to ensure the domination of the ruling class over all society. The state acts in the interests of the ruling class, and all other interests of society are subordinated to the interests of the ruling class.

> The needs of society . . . cannot be met without passing through the political (and other) institutions set up by a class-conditioned society; and it is in the course of being processed through these channels that they are shaped, sifted, skewed, molded, modeled, and modulated to fit within the framework established by the ruling interests and ideas. This is how the class nature of the state and the society asserts itself, even without malevolent purposes or sinister plots. [Draper 1977: 262]

In *State and Revolution* Lenin succinctly summarized the theory of state elaborated by Marx and Engels. At the same time he rebutted "bourgeois" distortions of the theory. First, he insisted that the state does not reconcile class conflict but ensures the oppression of one class by another. "The state is the product and the manifestation of the *irreconcilability* of class antagonisms. The state arises when, where, and to the extent that the class antagonisms *cannot* be objectively reconciled. And, conversely, the existence of the state proves that the class antagonisms *are* irreconcilable (Lenin 1932: 8). Second, he argued that state power must be destroyed through violent revolution, that compromise and reformist solutions will not resolve class antagonisms.

> If the state is the product of the irreconcilable character of class antagonisms, if it is a force standing *above* society and "increasingly separating itself from it," then it is clear that the liberation of the oppressed class is impossible not only without a violent revolution, *but also without the destruction* of the apparatus of state power, which was created by the ruling class and in which this "separation" is embodied. [Lenin 1932: 9–10]

The chief instruments of the force or power are a standing army and police rather than an armed power organized among all the people. The struggle against the state and its instruments of power will be carried on by the proletariat. As the development of production reaches a high stage, the existence of classes will no longer be necessary: "They will disappear as inevitably as they arose at an earlier stage. Along with them, the state will inevitably disappear" (15). The proletariat will seize power and transform the means of production from private to state property. The transition from capitalism to communism will inevitably lead to rule by the proletariat and the dictatorship of the proletariat (31). Bourgeois democracy will become proletarian democracy. The majority will suppress the oppressive minority, and the functions of state power will devolve upon the people until there is no need for such power and the state disappears altogether (37).

Drawing upon Marx's polemical writing such as the *Communist Manifesto* and *The Critique of the Gotha Programme*, Lenin outlined a theory in which communism evolves from capitalism. This is not a utopian but a scientific conception: "Marx treated the question of Communism in the same way as a naturalist would treat the question of the evolution of, say, a new biological species, if he knew that such and such was its origin, and such and such the direction in which it changed" (1932: 70). Several phases are evident in this evolution. First, a bourgeois society, capitalistically developed, emerges. Second, there is a "political transition" from a capitalist to a communist society, during which period "the state can be no other than the revolutionary dictatorship of the proletariat" (Marx, in Lenin 1932: 71). Third, in an early phase of communism, generally known as socialism, the means of production are no longer the private property of individuals but belong to the whole society, but the inequalities of bourgeois society are not eliminated altogether. Fourth, in a higher phase of "full" communism, in which bourgeois inequalities are eliminated, the state has been replaced by the rule of all society, and people work voluntarily according to their abilities and are recipients according to their needs (78–81).

There has been a resurgence of interest in the theory of the state, and the thought of Marx, Engels, and Lenin has served as a foundation for a variety of directions. Alan Wolfe (1974) suggested two trends: one embraces pluralism, the other turns to Marxism with attention to the capitalist state.

Within Marxism two schools are evident. One school is influenced by Marx's early writings and the critique of Hegel and emphasizes an understanding of the human condition. The other school concentrates on Marx's later writings and stresses a "scientific" rather than a "critical" perspective. Within this latter school there are two approaches, Leninist and Althusserian. Lenin emphasized the proletariat's taking control of the state. Thus the theory of Marx and Engels serves practice, that is, the implementation of revolutionary action. Louis Althusser attempted to give coherence to a theory of the state by identifying structural characteristics that ensure the stability and cohesion of the state and the dominant classes under capitalism.

Wolfe critiqued both approaches. Although the Leninist perspective "too often results in a mechanistic determinism, a confusion between form and content, and a tendency to view the state as all powerful and unchangeable" (Wolfe 1974: 136), the Althusserian view suffers from "dogmatism" and "scholasticism" as well as from an obsession with "this century's preoccupations with positivism and scientific rationality" (142). Wolfe related the capitalist state to alienation; although the state "arises out of alienated politics, it continues to exist by perpetuating alienated politics" (149). This observation leads to his suggestion that we should develop a theory of alienated politics, not a Marxist theory of the state (155). Concern with an elaboration of a theory of the capitalist state, however, has moved many Marxists to a reassessment. In Germany contemporary debate traces its origins to the past century (Holloway and Picciotto 1978), and in the United States much work has evolved around the journal *Kapitalistate: Working Papers on the Capitalist State*. Gold, Lo, and Wright (1975) have synthesized this work into three traditions that have attracted the attention of Marxist scholars: the instrumentalist, structuralist, and Hegelian-Marxist perspectives. Esping-Andersen, Friedland, and Wright (1976) have suggested four perspectives: pluralist, instrumentalist, structuralist, and political class struggle. We now turn briefly to a discussion of each of the perspectives.

PLURALIST PERSPECTIVE

The state is a political marketplace through which filter the demands and interests of competing groups and individuals. Two views prevail. On the one hand, neutral state agencies mediate conflict that emanates from party and group competition. On the other, agencies of the state function as the bases of political power; competition among the agencies for funding determines their relationship to parties and interest groups. These views reflect the liberal, non-Marxist tradition of U.S. social science although such thinking is found elsewhere, for example among many leftist Portuguese intellectuals and political leaders during the aftermath of the Portuguese revolutionary coup of 1974, when "socialist pluralism" was a central concern.

HEGELIAN-MARXIST PERSPECTIVE

This perspective stems from the ideas of Hegel, Marx, and Engels (elaborated above) and has been promoted in recent times by Herbert Marcuse and others representative of the Frankfurt school. Their "critical theory" exposes the mystification of the state, with an emphasis on ideology and false consciousness. Criticism of this perspective concerns the lack of analysis "of specific state actions or concrete politics . . . so it is difficult to connect these ideas with empirical reality" (Gold, Lo, and Wright 1975: 40).

INSTRUMENTALIST PERSPECTIVE

Lenin once referred to the standing army and police as instruments of state power. Marx and Engels alluded to the executive of the state as a committee. Paul Sweezy viewed the state as "an instrument in the hands of the ruling classes" (1942: 234). Ralph Miliband argued that the ruling class of a capitalist society uses "the state as its instrument for the domination of society" (1969: 23). A theory of corporate liberal instrumentalism focused on progressive segments of corporate capital, which determine the extent of societal reform, is attributed to G. William Domhoff (1976), his protest notwithstanding. All of these views are tied to the idea that the state is the "instrument" of the ruling or dominant class. The instrumentalist perspective thus focuses on the class that rules and on the ties and mechanisms that link ruling class instruments and state policies. Instrumentalism has been criticized for its failure to transcend the framework of the pluralists: "The emphasis . . . has been on social and political groupings rather than classes defined by their relationship to the means of production" (Gold, Lo, and Wright 1975: 34–35).

STRUCTURALIST PERSPECTIVE

"The fundamental thesis of the structuralist perspective is that the functions of the state are broadly determined by the structures of the society rather than by the people who occupy positions of state power" (Gold, Lo, and Wright 1975: 36). Opposed to instrumentalism, those who advocate the structural perspective examine the constraints and contradictions of capitalism within the structure in which the state is embedded. This structure, rather than a struggle by individuals, classes, and the like, is of central concern. Althusser provided a foundation and Nicos Poulantzas (1973) elaborated a political side of this structuralism. He argued that the bourgeoisie is unable as a class to dominate the state, that the state itself organizes and unifies the interest of this class. The economic side of a structuralist approach is exemplified by the work of Paul Baran and Paul Sweezy; they stressed the activity of the state in resolving economic contradictions and averting crises related to monopoly capitalism. Critics of the structural perspective argue that it cannot explain class action that arises from class consciousness (Best and Connolly 1979).

In fact both the structuralist and the instrumentalist perspectives are criticized in terms of systemic inputs and outputs. Instrumentalists tend to relate analysis to contemporary class activity rather than to historically known constraints of the system. Structuralists tend to downplay class activity.

> The instrumentalist view of the state stresses the *political input* into the state and the importance of the unequal class distribution of power. The structuralist view of the state stresses the *political output* of state activity by which capitalist domination is reproduced and the cohesion of the social formation assured. Neither approach contains a theory of the mechanisms that link political inputs and systemic constraints to the outputs of state activity. Neither approach can analytically distinguish the extent to which class action mediates between constraints and state structures, generates those constraints and structures, or at times is irrelevant to the relationship of economic constraints to the state. [Esping-Andersen, Friedland, and Wright 1976: 189–190]

POLITICAL CLASS STRUGGLE PERSPECTIVE

Given the criticisms of all these perspectives, Gold, Lo, and Wright have suggested that the works of Wolfe, O'Connor, and Offe are helpful. Wolfe (1974) sought to relate the abstractions of the Hegelian-Marxist perspective to concrete reality. James O'Connor (1973) looked at the fiscal crisis of the state and analyzed crises of corporate profitability and state bankruptcy "to deal both with the relationship of internal structures of the state to contradictions in the accumulation process and with the relationship of class struggle to those state structures." He also analyzed "the ways in which class struggle limits the state's ability to rationalize capitalism and the ways in which state structures have been reorganized to make them more impermeable to working class challenge" (Esping-Andersen, Friedland, and Wright 1976: 191). Claus Offe (1972) found fault with the instrumentalists and structuralists who ignore the mechanisms of the state that reflect its class character, structure, ideology, process, and repression.

Esping-Andersen, Friedland, and Wright suggested a focus on political class struggle as an alternative perspective. "A political class struggle perspective on the state tries to locate the state within the dialectical relationship between class dominance and systemic constraints" (1976: 190). They focused on the internal structures of the state and the relationship of those structures to systemic contradictions; they also were concerned with how those structures shape the class struggle and state policies, examining the organization and content of class struggle as well as the structures and policies of the state. The empirical and theoretical ramifications of this class struggle perspective are examined in Chapter 8.

Marx and Engels distinguished between state and society in order to clarify the interrelationship of political and economic life. They envisioned the prospect of a stateless society in modern times, a notion deemed unattainable by most political scientists. For that reason, among others, the contemporary political scientist downgrades the concept of state, replacing it with "system," perhaps to obscure the conditions of enforcement and constraint that society holds over individuals in a capitalist world today. However, we need not be deluded by such distractions. One of the proponents of the systems approach, David Easton, had reminded us of the origins of our discipline and acknowledged our debt to Marx: "In part, political science could emerge as a discipline separate from the other social sciences because of the impetus Marx had given to the idea of the difference between state and society, an idea virtually unheard of before his time" (quoted in Draper 1977: 237).

The present generation of political scientists has also wrestled with the question of what is political and what is political science. Marx and Engels defined politics in terms of the power of the state, the superstructure that represents a bourgeois society and reflects the economic needs of the class controlling production. Marx and Engels established a relationship between the state and the class structure of society. Draper summed up their conception: "The state is the institution, or complex of institutions, which bases itself on the availability of forcible coercion by special agencies of society in order to maintain the dominance of a ruling class, perserve existing property relations from basic change, and keep all other classes in subjection" (1977: 251). Although some political sociologists and other social scientists have utilized this conception in their work, most tend to steer clear of the onus of Marxism, preferring instead to distinguish politics from economics and to avoid questions of power and coercion, class and class struggle.

Systems Analysis in a Socialist Society

Marxists might call the orthodox systems theory simply a mystification of technocrats seeking power. In an age of widespread technology, it is argued, the new technician of the United States defends the interests of a new class oriented to planning and administration and appropriates "American values based on progress through scientific rationality" (Lilienfeld 1975: 658–659). This indictment probably is acceptable to many specialists of comparative politics.

Systems theory has been utilized in the Soviet Union (Blauberg, Sadovsky, and Yudin 1977) and in Eastern Europe. For the latter, Peter C. Ludz (1975) assessed its significance and utility in the German Democratic Republic; his findings are now reviewed, and an attempt is made to deter-

mine if the radical indictment of systems theory in the United States is relevant to one of the most advanced socialist societies.

Ludz argued that the language of Marxism-Leninism has provided empty
formulas, even though it has become the major communication pattern.
Given this condition, technological concepts of the West were easily
assimilated into Marxism-Leninism, in particular functionalism and
cybernetic systems theory. In 1961 a Society of Cybernetics was founded,
and philosopher George Klaus became the major proponent of the application of systems theory to Marxist theory. Borrowing from Ashby, Wiener,
and others, Klaus envisaged a cybernetics theory of dynamic and self-
regulating systems characterized by connections with the environment. This
conception is formulated in terms of the biological organism, and it assumes
maintenance and stability as well as control. Klaus considered information
to be the link between cybernetics and dialectical materialism, and information is tied to organization. Cybernetics systems theory thus defines
categories of historical and dialectical materialism precisely; serves to rationalize automation; assists economic planning and increases labor productivity; and facilitates autonomous control within organizations. Klaus also
established connections between cybernetics and dialectical logic. The terminology of Western systems theory—function and structure, inputs and
outputs, and feedback—was employed in the East German formulation.
Eventually control of society by the state is to be replaced by the feedback
system of a socialist society. Mass participation and consciousness will
replace the central regulating institutions of a socialist society.

Ludz believed that systems theory threatened to undermine central control in the German Democratic Republic. Further, he noted contradictions
between capitalist and socialist applications of systems theory. He admitted
that "cybernetic systems theory in itself has developed characteristics which
resemble the empty formulas of Marxism Leninism" (1975: 671). In any
event, a ten-year experiment in the application of systems theory in a
socialist country was ended in 1971, probably, he believed, because of the
ideological and political implications of systems theory. He argued that "the
ideas of technical rationality and economic efficiency" (1975: 674) inherent
in the theory, are still in effect, however. It is not clear that systems theory
served to mystify and defend the interests of the new German technocratic
bureaucracy.

Directions for a Radical or Marxist Understanding of Systems Theory

Two significant themes are suggested in radical criticisms of systems
theory: inquiry must take into account the human condition, and theory

must orient to a world system. Doris and Francis Bartlett (1971) decried the social implications of the biological determinism that has crept into social science literature. They criticized flaws in analogies of animal and human behaviors, and they condemned the "bio-social syndrome" of explanation as simply "an ideology of despair. . . . Despair is the ultimate product of this application of 'science' to human affairs" (1971: 219). Baskin (1970) more emphatically denounced the absence of the human element in the pluralism upon which systems theory is often premised: "A more human politics would organize public life as an adventurous avenue for self-discovery and community-building so that men might transcend that which divides them as rivals and through citizenship in a community might experience instead that which unites them as brothers" (1970: 95).

Marx and Lenin and their followers conceived of system in international terms. This theme is carried on by several ambitious works (Wuthnow 1979), and two examples are mentioned. Immanuel Wallerstein in his *Modern World System* (1974) examined capitalist agriculture and the origins of the European world economy in the sixteenth century. In his introduction he recounted the difficulties in his past theoretical perspective. He abandoned a focus on the sovereign state or the national society, stating that "neither one was a social system. . . . one could only speak of social change in social systems. The only social system in this scheme was the world system" (1974: 7). He attempted to transcend the boundaries of disciplines as he utilized a "unidisciplinary" approach—he combined all the social sciences into a historical and holistic perspective. Samir Amin in his *Accumulation on a World Scale* (1974) pursued a similar approach, utilizing an explicit Marxist framework and building a radical paradigm of understanding. He too was historical and holistic as he transcended national capitalist and socialist systems to posit the thesis, "There are not two world markets, one capitalist and the other socialist, but only one, the capitalist world market" (1974: 4). His theory of accumulation on a world scale is a theory of capitalist formations between the center and the periphery of a world system.

SUMMARY CONCLUSION

From ancient and medieval thought Western man derived the habit of visualizing the organic world in terms of the smallest possible units to which it could be reduced (Martindale 1965: 144).

Don Martindale distinguished the above approaches, calling them, respectively, *holism* and *elementarism*. Holism views interrelated wholes as superior to individuals and their acts. Elementarism views social reality as consisting of individuals and their actions. In this chapter the Eastonian framework and general systems theory, the macro-structural functionalism of Almond and Parsons, and some radical orientations have been cast into a holistic context. The striving for the middle range of inquiry by many specialists of comparative politics has been cast as micro-structural functionalism and to some extent implied elementarism. Martindale's own synthesis is helpful in that it distinguishes a variety of currents linked to the positivist and historicist traditions from which emanate the orthodox and radical paradigms of contemporary comparative politics. Combining some of his ideas with the discussions in earlier chapters, some assumptions about systems theory can be set forth and then related to the orthodox and radical paradigms.

First, some assumptions:

1. The ancient and medieval thinkers distinguished between mind and matter in the construction of systems. The mind, which yields intuition and reason, for example, relates to the spiritual world and to the humanities, and matter relates to the material world and the sciences.

2. The social scientists have attempted to reconcile the intellectual distinctions between the humanities and the sciences. Auguste Comte set forth positivism as a means of transmitting the method of the physical sciences to the humanities. John Stuart Mill proposed that social science rest on physiology and physical science method. Applications of physical science continue today as the basis of positivistic social science.

3. Antipositivism emerged in the form of historicism, which objects to the intrusion of the physical science method into the social, political, and cultural disciplines. The historicists have found fault with the ahistorical interpretations of the positivists and condemned their narrow scope of inquiry.

4. Both the positivist and antipositivist positions relate to the study of whole systems or parts of systems. Orthodox holistic theory generally is organicist, and sometimes mechanistic, and dependent upon harmonious systems usually in equilibrium. Radical holistic theory focuses on systems in disequilibrium and seeks explanations that usually are not tied to organicistic or mechanistic frameworks. Orthodox narrow- and middle-range theories are concerned with parts of systems, structural functionalism being a prominent example, and radical theory attempts to relate to some parts only in the context of the whole system.

Table 5.3 illustrates these relationships and serves to summarize the discussion of the present chapter. Positivist and ahistorical perspectives, which characterize the orthodox paradigm, pervade both partial and holistic theories of system. The partial theories are liberal and pluralist in orientation and are represented by Bentley, Truman, and Almond in the tradition

TABLE 5.3
Systems Theory and Paradigms: Types, Scope, Orientations, and
Representative Thinkers

Types	Scope of System	Orientations of Theory	Representative Thinkers
Orthodox (Positivist and Ahistorical)	Partial (individual group)	Liberal Pluralist	Hume, Locke, Bentley, Truman, and Almond
	Holistic	Conservative Organicist	Comte, Mill, Spencer, Easton, Almond, Parsons, Merton, and Levy
Radical (Anti-Positivist and Historical)	Partial (individual)	Orthodox Marxist Existentialist Marxist	Sartre and Schaff
	Holistic	Collectivist Reformist Marxist	C. Wright Mills, Marx, and Engels

of Hume and Locke. The holistic theory is generally conservative in orientation and is represented by Parsons and his followers in sociology and Easton
and Almond in political science in the tradition of Comte, Mill, and
Spencer. Both Parsons and Easton would consider themselves to be part of
the antipositivist tradition, and their early work reflects this concern; but
the ahistorical abstraction and lack of concern for detail in the real world,
which mark the bulk of their work, suggest the appropriateness of including
them in the positivist tradition.

Partial and holistic theories of system also characterize the radical
paradigm. The French philosopher Jean-Paul Sartre and the Polish philosopher Adam Schaff are representative of partial theory in that their concerns run counter to the technocratic and scientific movement of capitalist
systems, in which the individual must survive, and of socialist systems, in
which individuality and collectivity must be compatible. The collectivist and
Marxist orientations of holistic theory are found, respectively, in Mills and
Marx.

Such a summary is indeed simplistic, but it is to be hoped that it orients
the reader to recognize and distinguish among the many tendencies of
systems theory.

References

Abrahamson, Mark

1973 "Functionalism and the Functional Theory of Stratification: An Empirical Assessment." *American Journal of Sociology* LXXVIII (March), 1236–1246. Examines common criticisms of functional theory and analyzes assumptions necessary to empirically test hypotheses from these theories. Concludes that "functional theories may provide a fruitful source of empirically testable hypotheses."

Abramson, Paul R., and Ronald Inglehart

1970 "The Development of Systemic Support in Four Western Democracies." *Comparative Political Studies* II (January), 419–442. Examines "the development of systematic support" in the Netherlands, France, United States, and Great Britain. Three variables of willing obedience are analyzed: conditioning, structural commitment, and transfer of affect.

Almond, Gabriel A.

1956 "Comparative Political Systems." *Journal of Politics* XVIII (August), 391–409. An early attempt to offer a typology of political systems.

1960 "Introduction: A Functional Approach to Comparative Politics." In Almond and James S. Coleman (eds.), *The Politics of Developing Areas*, pp. 3–64. Princeton: Princeton University Press. Refinement and elaboration of the author's 1956 formulation. Influenced by the earlier work of Weber and Parsons, Almond sets forth a "probabilistic theory of the polity" formulated around a scheme of structures and functions.

1965 "A Developmental Approach to Political Systems." *World Politics* XVII (January), 183–214. Almond recognizes the need to combine his functional theory with developmental theory in the study of comparative politics. This essay is a refinement of his 1960 contribution.

1968 "Political Development: Analytical and Normative Perspectives." Boston: Benedict Lectures on Political Philosophy, Boston University, March. Reprinted in Almond, *Political Development: Essays in Heuristic Theory*, pp. 273–303. Boston: Little, Brown and Co., 1970. Useful for the author's discussion of the influences of other social scientists upon his work.

1969–1970 "Determinacy-Choice, Stability-Change: Some Thoughts on a Contemporary Polemic in Political Theory." *Government and Opposition* V (Winter), 22–40. Acknowledging disillusionment in the field of comparative politics, Almond sets out to defend his previous work by incorporating its approach into a new strategy for research. He proposes a "systematic exploitation of historical experience using a causal scheme which combines system-functional analysis, aggregate quantitative analysis and rational choice analysis at appropriate points in the explanation of developmental episodes."

Almond, Gabriel, and G. Bingham Powell, Jr.

1966 *Comparative Politics: A Developmental Approach.* Boston: Little, Brown and Co. Drawing from equilibrium theory and the influence of Newtonian mechanics, the authors set forth a functional approach to comparative politics.

Amin, Samir
1974 *Accumulation on a World Scale: A Critique of the Theory of Underdevelopment.* New York: Monthly Review Press. A comprehensive synthesis of the world political economy viewed in terms of a Marxist perspective.

Apter, David E.
1971 "Comparative Studies: A Review with Some Projections." In Ivan Vallier (ed.), *Methods in Sociology,* pp. 3–15. Berkeley: University of California Press. Critical review of pluralist tendencies in the field of comparative politics; discussion of weaknesses in functionalism; and a look at recent developments in comparative study.

Ashby, W. Ross
1956 *An Introduction to Cybernetics.* New York: John Wiley. Systems are explained in terms of cybernetics and self-regulation of machines, animals, and people.

Astin, John D.
1972 "Easton I and Easton II." *Western Political Quarterly* XXV (December), 726–737. Suggests that there are two approaches in Easton's work: the mechanist or Easton I and the vitalist or Easton II. Although these approaches are incompatible they are combined in Easton's work.

Barber, Bernard
1956 "Structural-Functional Analysis: Some Problems and Misunderstandings." *American Sociological Review* XXI (April), 129–135. Argues that functionalism and functional theories do not account for processes of change, that these theories tend to be abstract and tend to deal with static, closed systems.

Bartlett, Doris, and Francis Bartlett
1971 "Social Implications of Biological Determinism." *Science and Society* XXXV (Summer), 209–219. Discusses the implications of interpretations that relate biology to human problems. Understands that technology has come to dominate man and that there are no options.

Baskin, Darryl
1970 "American Pluralism: Theory, Practice, and Ideology." *Journal of Politics* XXXII (February), 71–95. Detailed critique of pluralism, which confirms prevailing indictments of this theory.

Berkhofer, Robert F., Jr.
1969 *A Behavioral Approach to Historical Analysis.* New York: Free Press. An historian's sensitivity to the problems of behavioral analysis leads to a critical look at models and systems as well as systems analysis, respectively in chapters 8 and 9.

Bertalanffy, Ludwig von
1969 *General Systems Theory: Foundations, Development, Applications.* New York: G. Braziller. Open (biological) systems are contrasted with closed (mechanical) systems in an effort to set forth a general systems theory. This movement combined philosophy with science to seek laws that would apply to all systems.

Best, Michael H., and William E. Connolly
1979 "Politics and Subjects: The Limits of Structural Marxism." *Socialist Review* IX (November-December), 75–99. A critical assessment of structuralist theory.

Black, Max (ed.)
1961 *The Social Theories of Talcott Parsons.* Englewood Cliffs, New Jersey: Prentice-

Hall. Useful in-depth critiques of the work of Parsons.

Blauberg, I. V., V. N. Sadovsky, and E. G. Yudin

1977 *Systems Theory: Philosophical and Methodological Problems.* Moscow: Progress Publishers. A surprisingly objective review of the trends and literature on systems, including scientific advances in the Soviet Union.

Bluhm, William T.

1965 *Theories of the Political System: Classics of Political Thought and Modern Political Analysis.* Englewood Cliffs, New Jersey: Prentice-Hall. Comparative analysis of classic and contemporary political theory. Especially relevant are essays on the liberal ideological premises of political science and interest group theory in Chapter 10.

Buckley, Walter

1966 "Structural-Functional Analysis in Modern Sociology." In Howard Becker and Alvin Boskoff (eds.), *Modern Sociological Theory in Continuity and Change*, pp. 236–259. New York: Holt, Rinehart and Winston. Criticizes functionalists for their predisposition to assume consensus.

Campbell, Colin

1971 "Current Models of the Political System: An Intellective-Purposive View." *Comparative Political Studies* IV (April), 21–40. Discusses the problem of selecting models and identifies the types available to comparative politics. Critically examines models of Easton, Deutsch, Almond, and Lasswell. Then introduces a model of human problem solving.

Clark, Terry

1972 "Structural-Functionalism, Exchange Theory, and the New Political Economy: Institutionalization as a Theoretical Linkage." *Sociological Inquiry* XLII (3–4), 275–298. Criticizes a number of prevailing theories, including structural-functionalism, and argues for a closer look at the process of institutionalization. In particular, raises questions about Parsons's work. An exchange of comments between Clark and Parsons follows the article.

Dahrendorf, Ralf

1958 "Out of Utopia: Toward a Reorientation of Sociological Analysis." *American Journal of Sociology* LXIV (September), 115–127. Critique of Parsons as a utopian in his functionalist theory.

Davis, Kingsley

1959 "The Myths of Functional Analysis as a Special Method in Sociology and Anthropology." *American Sociological Review* XXIV (December), 757–772. Address to the American Sociological Association in which the author argues that the claims and problems of functionalism are those of sociology and that functionalism cannot call itself a "school nor claim it is the sole holistic approach in sociology."

Deutsch, Karl W.

1963 *The Nerves of Government: Models of Political Communication and Control.* New York: Free Press of Glencoe. Argues that "it might be profitable to look upon government somewhat less as a problem of power and somewhat more as a problem of steering . . . that steering is decisively a matter of communication." Drawing upon classic political theory of communications and control, theory of games and decisions, and theory on international communications, Deutsch seeks "a theory of politics, both national and international."

Domhoff, G. William

1976 "I Am Not an 'Instrumentalist': A Reply to 'Modes of Class Struggle and the Capitalist State' and Other *Kapitalistate* Critics." *Kapitalistate* 4-5 (Summer), 221-224. A rebuttal to Esping-Andersen, Friedland, and Wright (1976) and a refutation of the allegation that the author is an instrumentalist.

Draper, Hal

1977 *Karl Marx's Theory of Revolution; Book I: State and Bureaucracy.* New York: Monthly Review Press. This first of three volumes generally covers the earlier works of Marx, focusing on politics. This volume, notable for its clarity of exposition and summary synthesis of Marx's ideas, is divided into two parts: the first deals with the young Marx and his political development from about 1842; the second deals with the Bonapartist state and the period 1848-1851.

Easton, David

1950 "Harold Lasswell: Policy Scientist for a Democratic Society." *Journal of Politics* XII (August), 450-477. In this, one of his early writings, Easton searches for values of democratic politics and scientific inquiry in the social sciences. He finds in Lasswell's work the "lesson" that "each social science ought to re-examine the value premises upon which its empirical research rests."

1953 *The Political System: An Inquiry into the State of Political Science.* New York: Alfred A. Knopf. The first of Easton's works on the political theory of systems, this work presents a case for general theory in political science.

1956 "Limits of the Equilibrium Model in Social Research." *Behavioral Science* I (April), 96-104. Views the equilibrium model as "an inarticulate theoretical framework" for political science as well as for other disciplines. Equilibrium analysis canot be useful without more quantifiable data.

1957 "An Approach to the Analysis of Political Systems." *World Politics* IX (April), 383-400. Following his first effort to outline the need for a theory of political systems, Easton here sets forth some concepts and a general model for an analysis of the political system.

1965a *A Framework for Political Analysis.* Englewood Cliffs, New Jersey: Prentice-Hall. The second of the author's work on political systems, this work sets forth the major categories and concepts for the formulation of theory.

1965b *A Systems Analysis of Political Life.* New York: John Wiley and Sons. This is the author's third work on systems theory; it elaborates on concepts set forth earlier in an effort to make them applicable to empirical situations.

Eisenstadt, S. N.

1959 "Primitive Political Systems: A Preliminary Comparative Analysis." *American Anthropologist* LXI (April), 200-218. Surveys the available material on the comparative analysis of primitive political systems, which the author considers inadequate. Sets forth a typology for the analysis of primitive political systems: segmentary tribes and centralized chiefdoms.

Eister, Allan W.

1964 "Function." In Julius Gould and William L. Kolb, *Dictionary of the Social Sciences*, pp. 277–279. New York: Free Press of Glencoe. Synthesis of various definitions and conceptualizations of functions.

Engels, Frederick

[N. d.] *Origin of the Family, Private Property, and the State: In the Light of the Researches of Lewis H. Morgan*. New York: International Publishers. A critical review of theories and histories of the family and the emergence of the state from ancient to modern times.

1934 *Dialectics of Nature*. Moscow: Progress Publishers. "It gives a dialectical materialist generalisation of the principal achievements of the natural sciences in the mid-nineteenth century, develops materialist dialectics, and criticises metaphysical and idealist conceptions in natural science."

Esping-Andersen, Gosta, Roger Friedland, and Erik Olin Wright

1976 "Modes of Class Struggle and the Capitalist State." *Kapitalistate* 4–5 (Summer), 186–220. A review of approaches to the study of the capitalist state and an elaboration of a new approach emphasizing political class struggle.

Evans, Michael

1970 "Notes on David Easton's Model of the Political System." *Journal of Commonwealth Political Studies* VIII (July), 117–133. A critical summary of Easton's work on systems and an assessment of conceptual, interpretive, and internal difficulties.

Farace, Vincent, and Lewis Donohew

1965 "Mass Communication in National Social Systems: A Study of 43 Variables in 115 Countries." *Journalism Quarterly* XLII (Spring), 253–261. Examination and analysis of many variables common to most countries of the world.

Finer, S. E.

1969–1970 "Almond's Concept of 'The Political System' A Textual Critique." *Government and Opposition* V (Winter), 3–21. A detailed critique of nomenclature in Almond's writings on political system. Quarrels with his use of "political" and "system" and argues for a return to traditional language.

Friedman, Jonathan

1974 "Marxism, Structuralism, and Vulgar Marxism." *Man* IX (September), 444–469. A critique of vulgar materialism, for example, that of Harris (1968), an identification of "functional distinctions" in the Marxist "model," and an attempt to relate structuralism to Marxism.

Garson, G. David

1974 "On the Origins of Interest-Group Theory: A Critique of a Process." *American Political Science Review* LXVIII (December), 1505–1519. Historical review and synthesis of past and present trends in interest group theory. Useful in understanding origins of Almond's functionalism.

Gold, David A., Clarence Y. H. Lo, and Erik Olin Wright

1975 "Recent Developments in Marxist Theories of the Capitalist State." *Monthly Review* XXVII (October), 29–43, and (November), 36–51. A review of traditional approaches to the study of the capitalist state and of new theoretical directions.

González Casanova, Pablo
1973 "Historical Systems and Social Systems." *Studies in Comparative International Development* VIII (Fall), 227–246. Identifies two thrusts in the literature of systems theory: functionalism and systems analysis. Describes orthodox interpretations of these thrusts and their weaknesses and then attempts a radical reinterpretation by stressing history as process, as struggle, as bureaucracy, as social reorganization, and as spontaneity.

Gregg, Phillip M., and Arthur S. Banks
1965 "Dimensions of Political Systems: Factor Analysis of a Cross-Polity Survey." *American Political Science Review* LIX (September), 602–614. Influenced by Easton's early work, the authors utilize data from a cross-polity survey to identify and compare variables common to all political systems.

Groth, Alexander J.
1970 "Structural Functionalism and Political Development: Three Problems." *Western Political Quarterly* XXIII (September), 485–499. Focuses on three problems of structural functionalism: "terminological ambiguity; interminacy of relationships among 'things political'; and confusions of facts with values."

Hacker, Andrew
1961 "Sociology and Ideology." In Max Black (ed.), *The Social Theories of Talcott Parsons*, pp. 289–310. Englewood Cliffs, New Jersey: Prentice-Hall. Criticizes the theories of Talcott Parsons as "ideological."

Harris, Marvin
1968 *The Rise of Anthropological Theory: A History of Theories of Culture.* New York: Thomas Y. Crowell Co. An interpretative overview of the principal thinkers and ideas relating to culture. Harris assumes a materialist position, sympathetic to Marx but critical of the dialectical method.

Harsanyi, John C.
1969 "Rational-Choice Models of Political Behavior vs. Functionalist and Conformist Theories." *World Politics* XXI (July), 513–538. As an alternative to functionalist and conformist theories, the author sets forth the rational-choice model of political behavior.

Hempel, Carl G.
1959 "The Logic of Functional Analysis." In Llewellyn Gross (ed.), *Symposium in Sociological Theory*, pp. 271–307. New York: Harper and Row. Argues that structural functionalism is illogical.

Holloway, John, and Sol Picciotto (eds.)
1978 *State and Capital: A Marxist Debate.* Austin: University of Texas Press, 1978. Essays from Germany about differing theoretical perspectives. The introduction reviews and summarizes the history of the debate on the state.

Holt, Robert T., and John E. Turner
1966 *The Political Basis of Economic Development: An Exploration in Comparative Political Analysis.* Princeton, New Jersey: D. Van Nostrand. Especially relevant is the criticism of Almond's work in the first chapter. Among its limitations are difficulties in applying his theory to historical and contemporary cases, the equation of the modern political system to the modern Anglo-American democratic system, the use of too many dimensions, and the neglect of variation in the societal

functions of government.

Jantsch, Erich

1972 "Forecasting and the Systems Approach: A Critical Survey." *Policy Sciences* III (December), 475–498. Begins with a typology of internal self-organizing systems—mechanistic, adaptive, and inventive; then turns to external self-organizing systems, which are discussed in terms of planning—normative or policy planning, strategic planning, and operational or tactical planning. Approaches useful in systems analysis and forecasting are identified—in economics, sociology, policy science, urban and regional planning, and other areas.

Kaplan, Harold

1968 "The Parsonian Image of Social Structure and Its Relevance for Political Science." *Journal of Politics* XXX (November), 885–909. Identifies some of the major criticism of Parsons and concludes that Parsons's lack of clarity or inconsistency should not diminish the possibilities of applying his work to political science.

Kaplan, Morton A.

1957 *System and Process in International Politics.* New York: John Wiley and Sons. A pioneering effort to apply systems theory to the study of international politics.

Klausner, Samuel Z. (ed.)

1967 *The Study of Total Societies.* Garden City, New York: Doubleday Anchor Books. Essays on methodology, conceptual issues, and research strategies in the study of total societies or nation-states. Contributions by James S. Coleman, Kenneth E. Boulding, Marion J. Levy, Jr., and others.

Kress, Paul F.

1966 "Self, System, and Significance: Reflections on Professor Easton's Political Science." *Ethics* LXXVII (October), 1–13. Critical of Easton's work and theory. The author assumes Easton has proposed a paradigm in Kuhn's sense of the term.

Laszlo, C. A., M. D. Levine, and J. H. Milsum

1974 "A General Systems Framework for Social Systems." *Behavioral Science* XIX (March), 79–92. The authors, two engineers and a medical doctor, desire to plan and control the system so that it can "perform in a socially good way." They relate general systems theory to social systems.

Laszlo, Ervin

1972 *Introduction to Systems Philosophy: Toward a New Paradigm of Contemporary Thought.* New York: Gordon and Breach. Related works include Laszlo's *The Systems View of the World: The Natural Philosophy of the New Developments in the Sciences,* New York: G. Braziller, 1972; *The Relevance of General Systems Theory,* New York: G. Braziller, 1972; and *A Strategy for the Future: The Systems Approach to World Order,* New York: G. Braziller, 1974. Work which attempts to carry on with the general systems movement of Ludwig von Bertalanffy.

Lehman, Hugh

1966 "R. K. Merton's Concepts of Function and Functionalism." *Inquiry* IX (Autumn), 274–283. Summary and critique of Merton's conceptualization.

Lenin, V. I.

1932 *State and Revolution.* New York: International Publishers. Lenin's synthesis and analysis of the state, based on Marx and Engels, with a critique of Kautsky.

Leslie, Peter
1972 "General Theory in Political Science: A Critique of Easton's Systems Analysis." *British Journal of Political Science* II (April), 155–172. Critically examines Easton's concepts of persistence and allocation and suggests some new theoretical formulations.

Levy, Marion J., Jr.
1952 *The Structure of Society.* Princeton: Princeton University Press. Attempts a synthesis of Parsons and Merton.

1958 "Some Aspects of 'Structural-Functional' Analysis and Political Science." In Roland Young (ed.), *Approaches to the Study of Politics*, pp. 52–65. Evanston: Northwestern University Press. The author, a sociologist, applies his concepts and understanding of structural functionalism to the study of politics.

Lewis, Thomas J.
1974 "Parsons' and David Easton's Analyses of the Support System." *Canadian Journal of Political Science* VII (December), 672–686. The author discusses the concepts of equality and consent as used in classical liberalism and relates them to Parsons's and Easton's concepts of the support system. He concludes that Easton's concepts are nonliberal, whereas Parsons's concepts are liberal.

Lijphart, Arend
1968 "Typologies of Democratic Systems." *Comparative Political Studies* I (April), 3–44. Reviews comparative typologies of political systems from which are extracted two typologies of democratic systems: the traditional two-party versus multiparty system typology and the Anglo-American versus continental European systems typology.

Lilienfeld, Robert
1975 "Systems Theory as an Ideology." *Social Research* XLII (Winter), 637–660. Identifies the origins of systems theory in biology, cybernetics, economics, communication and information theory, and operations research. Systems theory is examined as a social movement and a social philosophy. The author concludes that systems theory cannot be described as empirical science, that it has no relation to concrete human history, and that it can only be understood as an ideology.

Ludz, Peter C.
1975 "Marxism and Systems Theory in a Bureaucratic Society." *Social Research* XLII (Winter), 661–674. Critical examination of systems analysis in the light of the experience of Marxist East Germany.

Mackenzie, W. J. M.
1967 *Politics and Social Science.* Baltimore, Maryland: Penguin Books. A critical look at political science with attention to a critique of contemporary theory in Part 3. Here overarching theory, with emphasis on the work of Parsons and Easton, is stressed along with partial theories.

McLeod, John
1974 "System Simulation, Behavioral Science, System Theory—and Simulation." *Behavioral Science* XIX (January), 57–69. Compelled to solve the problems facing present and future society, McLeod proposes to combine systems theory with techniques of simulation.

Macridis, Roy C.

1961 "Interest Groups in Comparative Analysis." *Journal of Politics* XXIII (February), 25–45. Critique of the revival of interest group inquiry, which warns of its theoretical limitations.

Malinowski, Bronislaw

1945 *The Dynamics of Cultural Change: An Inquiry into Race Relations in Africa*. New Haven: Yale University Press. The first part of this book is especially useful; it delineates the "new tasks" for modern anthropology, and it sets forth the author's functional theory of culture change.

Mannheim, Karl

1957 *Systematic Sociology: An Introduction to the Study of Society*. Editorial preface by J. S. Eros and W.A.C. Steward. New York: Grove Press. Based on lectures given at the London School of Economics, Mannheim focuses on "man and his psychic equipment," elementary social processes, social integration, and social stability and social change.

Martindale, Don (ed.)

1965 *Functionalism in the Social Sciences: The Strength and Limits of Functionalism in Anthropology, Economics, Political Science, and Sociology*. Monograph 5. Philadelphia: American Academy of Political and Social Science. Collection of critical essays on functionalism in anthropology, economics, sociology, and political science. Reviews by I. C. Jarvie, Sherman Roy Krupp, Robert T. Holt, William Flanigan and Edwin Fogelman, Don Martindale, and others. Martindale's concluding essay is an excellent analysis of the origins and influences of structural theory upon the social sciences.

Marx, Karl

1975 *Early Writings*. Introduction by Lucio Colletti. New York: Vintage Books. Includes *Critique of Hegel's Doctrine of the State* and *Economic and Philosophical Manuscripts*, along with other early writings of 1843 and 1844.

Marx, Karl, and Frederick Engels

1970 *The German Ideology*. Edited with introduction by C. J. Arthur. New York: International Publishers. A very useful synthesis of Marxist thought. Especially appropriate for understanding forces and modes of production, division of labor, and class struggle.

Masters, Roger D.

1964 "World Politics as a Primitive Political System." *World Politics* XVI (July), 595–619. Compares the international system to primitive tribal systems and concludes that the structures and functions of the two are similar.

Meehan, Eugene J.

1968 *Explanation in Social Science: A System Paradigm*. Homewood, Illinois: Dorsey Press. Attacks prevailing interpretations and uses of social science theory as "the deductive paradigm of explanation," but Meehan sets forth his own systems theory as the basis of explanation.

Melanson, Philip H., and Lauriston R. King

1971 "Theory in Comparative Politics: A Critical Appraisal." *Comparative Political Studies* IV (July), 205–231. Criticism of contemporary comparative theory with attention to problems in Almond and Powell. In particular, examines ambiguity of terms, the resurgence of hyperfactualism, and the implicit assumptions that shape inquiry.

Merriam, Charles E.

1966 *Systematic Politics*. Chicago: University of Chicago Press. The author sets out "to analyze political behavior in the light of the factors that surround institutional forms, ideologies, political patterns, or clusters of patterns in particular political societies," and he uses "both the naturalistic and the rationalistic approach. . . . they are inseparable in the understanding of politics."

Merton, Robert K.

1949 *Social Theory and Social Structure*. Glencoe, Illinois: Free Press of Glencoe. Revised and enlarged, 1957. Clear exposition of structural functionalism as the author seeks a middle range of analysis.

Miliband, Ralph

1969 *The State in Capitalist Society: An Analysis of the Western System of Power*. New York: Basic Books. The author's line of thinking follows an instrumentalist view of the capitalist state, that is, the ruling class uses the state to ensure its dominance over society.

Miller, Eugene F.

1971 "David Easton's Political Theory." *Political Science Reviewer* I (Fall), 184–235. A detailed and in-depth critical review of Easton's major work on systems through three stages: preparation, construction, and reappraisal. Identification of difficulties in Easton's methodology and an assessment of his theoretical position.

Miller, James G.

1969 "Living Systems: Basic Concepts." In William Gray, D. F. Duhl, and N. Rizzo (eds.), *General Systems Theory and Psychiatry*, pp. 51–134. Boston: Little, Brown and Co. The author, who initiated interdisciplinary efforts that involved Easton in the search for systems theory, sets forth concepts that run parallel to those of Easton.

Mills, C. Wright

1959 *The Sociological Imagination*. New York: Grove Press. Chapter 2 presents a devastating indictment of Parsons's "grand theory."

Mitchell, William C.

1958 "The Polity and Society: A Structural-Functional Analysis." *Midwest Journal of Political Science* II (November), 403–420. Sets forth "a conceptual scheme for the analysis of political action," which draws from Easton and Lasswell but relies on Parsons, with illustrations limited to the U.S. polity.

1961 "Politics as the Allocation of Values: A Critique." *Ethics* LXXI (January), 79–89. Critical examination of the "allocative approach to politics." Identifies the major postulates of the approach, indicates some reservations, and suggests consequences for the future of political science. Discussion particularly relates to the work of Easton and Parsons.

1967 *Sociological Analysis and Politics: The Theories of Talcott Parsons*. Englewood Cliffs, New Jersey: Prentice-Hall. Contemporary Political Theory Series, David Easton, editor. Summary synthesis and critique of the work of Talcott Parsons in an effort to convince other political scientists of the usefulness of that work. This is a coherent statement of what Parsons has to say about polity.

1969 "The Shape of Political Theory to Come: From Political Sociology to Political Economy." In Seymour Martin Lipset (ed.), *Politics and the Social Sciences,* Chapter 5, pp. 101–136. New York: Oxford University Press. Identifies the paradigm of "new political economy" based on exchange models of politics.

Moore, Barrington, Jr.

1955 "The New Scholasticism and the Study of Politics." *World Politics* VI (October), 122–138. Parsons is castigated as the New Scholastic.

Nicholson, M. B., and P. A. Reynolds

1967 "General Systems, the International System, and the Eastonian Analysis." *Political Studies* 15 (February), 12–31. The authors find little basis for Easton's claim that his systems formulation has an applicability to international systems.

O'Connor, James

1973 *The Fiscal Crisis of the State.* New York: St. Martin's Press. Attempts to relate state structures and policies to class struggle.

Offe, Claus

1972 "Advanced Capitalism and the Welfare State." *Politics and Society* II (Summer), 479–488. Examines the class character of the capitalist state and looks at mechanisms within the state that reflect its class relationships. Critical of the instrumentalist and structuralist perspectives of the capitalist state.

Parsons, Talcott

1937 *The Structure of Social Action.* New York: McGraw-Hill. Reprinted by Free Press of Glencoe, 1949. Parsons's initial effort to set forth a theory of action, focused on the actor; considered to be the first of two stages in the formulation of this theory.

1951 *The Social System.* Glencoe, Illinois: Free Press. Systematic and general outline of a conceptual scheme for the analysis of structure and processes or functions of social systems.

1966 "The Political Aspect of Social Structure and Process." In David Easton (ed.), *Varieties of Political Theory,* pp. 71–112. Englewood Cliffs, New Jersey: Prentice-Hall. Parsons attempts to apply his concept of system and structural functionalism to the study of politics.

Parsons, Talcott, and Edward A. Shils (eds.)

1951 *Toward a General Theory of Action.* Cambridge: Harvard University Press. Sets forth an elaboration of earlier Parsonian ideas, now in a somewhat positivist fashion. Herein is the second-stage theory of action and the revision of Parsons's earlier notions.

Parsons, Talcott, Robert F. Bales, and Edward A. Shils

1953 *Working Papers in the Theory of Action.* Glencoe, Illinois: Free Press. This work gives more attention to politics as a subsystem and provides conceptual detail on the internal structure and function of systems in general.

Poulantzas, Nicos

1973 *Political Power and Social Classes.* London: New Left Books and Sheed and Ward. The author develops a structuralist perspective on the capitalist state.

Powell, Charles A.
1971 "Structural-Functionalism and the Study of Comparative Communist Systems: Some Caveats." *Studies in Comparative Communism* IV (July-October), 58–67. Critical of culture-bound "theory" of structural-functionalism and its misapplications to cases of socialist society.

Radcliffe-Brown, A. R.
1935 "On the Concept of Function in Social Science." *American Anthropologist* XXXVII (July-September), 394–402. Demonstrates explicitly the analogy between social life and organic life in formulating a conceptualization of function.

1952 *Structure and Function in Primitive Society.* New York: Free Press. Collection of essays on structural functionalism as drawn from the author's field and other work.

1957 *A Natural Science of Society.* Glencoe, Illinois: Free Press. Posthumously published work, which makes clear the organicist influences upon the author's conception of the social system.

Reading, Reid R.
1972 "Is Easton's Systems-Persistence Framework Useful?: A Research Note." *Journal of Politics* XXXIV (February), 258–267. A critique of Easton's framework and its stress on persistence by examining the socialization work of Easton and Dennis.

Sanford, Jonathan A.
1971 "Political Development and Economic Change: A Radical Interpretation of Almond and Powell's Developmental Approach." *Journal of International and Comparative Studies* IV (Summer), 1–36. Critical comments of the liberal structural functionalism of Almond and Powell. Offers a radical revision of this theory and attempts to operationalize it.

Scott, Roger
1972 "Systems Analysis Without Tears: Easton and Almond." *Politics* VII (May), 74–81. An attempt to simplify the writings of systems theorists Easton and Almond.

Singer, J. David
1971 *A General Systems Taxonomy for Political Science.* New York: General Learning Press. The systems literature is viewed as systems analysis, which the author criticizes and rejects; and as general systems, which he accepts as a taxonomy, not a theory.

Sorzano, J. S.
1975 "David Easton and the Invisible Hand." *American Political Science Review* LXIX (March), 91–106. Analysis of the similarities between the Eastonian framework and that of traditional economics. The concepts and assumptions of Easton are recognized in the characteristics of the classical economic model of Adam Smith.

Spiro, Herbert J.
1962 "Comparative Politics: A Comprehensive Approach." *American Political Science Review* LVI (September), 577–595. Obviously influenced by Easton's

search for a systemic approach to politics, the author sets forth his own scheme for comparative politics. At the heart of this scheme is his flow-of-policy process, involving formulation of an issue, deliberation, resolution, and solution.

1966 "The Primacy of Political Development." In Spiro, *Africa: The Primacy of Politics*, pp. 150–169. New York: Random House. Attacks the Almond formulation of political system as ethnocentric.

Stephens, Jerone

1969 "The Logic of Functional and Systems Analyses in Political Science." *Midwest Journal of Political Science* XIII (August), 367–394. Examination of the similarities between functional and systems analyses in political science and a discussion of their respective problems in the use of small as well as large systems.

1972 "An Appraisal of Some System Approaches in the Study of International Systems." *International Studies Quarterly* XVI (September), 321–349. A critical look at the major writers who have focused on systems theory in the study of international politics. Traces their work to general systems theory and to functionalism.

Sweezy, Paul

1942 *The Theory of Captialist Development: Principles of Marxian Political Economy.* New York: Monthly Review Press. An examination of value and surplus value, the accumulation process, crises and depressions, and imperialism using an instrumentalist perspective.

Szymanski, Al

1972 "Malinowski, Marx, and Functionalism." *Insurgent Sociologist* II (Summer), 35–43. Argues that functionalism has been and still is conservative, but if interpreted dialectically, "is a fundamental part of Marxist methodology, and a very powerful tool for the advance of social science."

Teune, Henry, and Krzysztof Ostrowski

1973 "Political Systems as Residual Variables: Explaining Differences Within Systems." *Comparative Political Studies* VI (April), 3–21. Conflict and collective performance are measured and analyzed to two different national systems, Poland and the United States.

Thorson, Thomas Landon

1970 *Biopolitics.* New York: Holt, Rinehart and Winston. A critical examination of "the Newtonian universal-generalization paradigm of understanding," "the Darwinian evolutionary-developmental paradigm of understanding," and the utility and nonutility of these paradigms in contemporary political science.

Tierney, Byron, Jr.

1972 "The Use of Systems Theories in International Political Analysis." *World Affairs* CXXXIV (Spring), 306–324. A critical look at the use of systems theory in international politics. Kaplan (1957) is recognized as having introduced systems to the field of international politics, but the origins of systems theory are traced to the physical sciences, to biology in the work of Bertalanffy, to epistemology and positivist philosophy as rooted in Hume and Comte, and to the writings and thought of David Easton.

Truman, David B.

1951 *The Governmental Process.* New York: Alfred A. Knopf. Seminal work on pluralism in U.S. politics, which revives the tradition of Bentley and others.

Wallerstein, Immanuel

1974 *The Modern World-System: Capitalist Agriculture and the Origins of the European World-Economy in the Sixteenth Century.* New York: Academic Press. An ambitious "unidisciplinary" overview, which places system into a framework of international capitalism.

Weltman, John

1972 "The Processes of a Systemicist." *Journal of Politics* XXXIV (February), 592–611. Attention to Kaplan (1957) and to identification of the origins and development of systems theory in international politics. In particular, looks at "sociological functionalism" and "general systems theory," which originated outside the study of politics.

Whitaker, Ian

1965 "The Nature and Value of Functionalism in Sociology." In Don Martindale (ed.), *Functionalism in the Social Sciences: The Strength and Limits of Functionalism in Anthropology, Economics, Political Science, and Sociology,* pp. 127–143. Monograph 5. Philadelphia: American Academy of Political and Social Science. Elaborates on Martindale's formulation of macro- and micro-functionalism to provide a critical overview of the major theories at both levels.

Wiener, Norbert

1954 *The Human Use of Human Beings.* Garden City, New York: Doubleday Anchor Books. Systems theory viewed in terms of cybernetics and communications as related to machines and people.

1961 *Cybernetics.* New York: John Wiley. Mathematics and cybernetics are combined to demonstrate that communications patterns relate to both machines and man.

Wilson, Richard B.

1961 "System and Process: Polar Concepts for Political Research." *Western Political Quarterly* XIV (September), 748–763. An overview of contemporary efforts to seek a systematic ordering of political data. In particular, examines characteristics common to the work of thinkers who stress unity rather than diversity: they reject traditional concepts, they postulate concepts that attempt to explain the totality of political knowledge, and they seek interdisciplinary cooperation.

Wiseman, H. V.

1966 *Political Systems: Some Sociological Approaches.* New York: Frederick A. Praeger. Attempts to synthesize approaches to the study of political systems. The typologies of Almond, Parsons, and others are discussed in a sympathetic and uncritical manner.

Wolfe, Alan

1974 "New Directions in the Marxist Theory of Politics." *Politics and Society* IV

(Winter), 131–160. An overview of recent writings concerned with a Marxist theory of the state.

Wuthnow, Robert

1979 "The Emergence of Modern Science and World System Theory." *Theory and Society* VIII (September), 159–214.

Theories of
Political Culture:
Collectivity and
the New Person

Contemporary orthodox and radical theories of political culture are the concern of this chapter. First, these theories are related to some basic assumptions about culture in the works of Marx and Weber. Then a variety of views emanating from anthropology, sociology, and psychology are examined in seeking the origin of the term political culture. Major interpretations of political culture, as conceived on a general or macro level as well as interpretations on a more particular or micro level, are identified while assessing current research on socialization and communication. Finally, a critique of orthodox interpretations and evolving radical theories of political culture and socialization are dealt with.

On a general level, Marx conceived of the beliefs and symbols of culture in capitalist society as part of a superstructure of ideology and false consciousness. The superstructure, representing the interests of the bourgeoisie, assimilates the ideology inherent in the dominant mode of production and social class relations. Culture therefore becomes static, because it protects the interests of the ruling bourgeoisie. Only through historical changes in the material base, through a transformation in the mode of production and in class relations, are changes in the generally persistent culture possible. Culture thus derives from the material practices of society and, more particularly, from the consequences of the relationship of the workers to their production. Although the capitalists are free to exploit labor, the workers are forced to sell their labor and thus are alienated from the product of their work and from themselves.

Weber as well as Marx dealt with general and particular levels of culture.

On the general level, he viewed culture as being composed of the beliefs and symbols of ideal types of authority: traditional, charismatic, and rational. Those ideal types of authority are legitimized by the actions of individuals who shape the collective society. Individual actions are conditioned by custom and tend to become increasingly rational. Consequently, individual actions are oriented to beliefs that support and maintain the collective society at large. A rationalization of authority accompanies a secularization of this society: rules of procedure become routine, and administrative activities are specified. In sum, Weber explained the political, social, and economic setting by referring to a somewhat autonomous culture shaped by individual orientations of rational self-interest, whereas Marx explained culture in terms of its dependence on the political, social, and economic setting of the society at large.

THE ORTHODOX CONCEPTUALIZATION OF CULTURE AND POLITICAL CULTURE

Political culture theory originated with conceptualizations and studies of culture itself. Therefore, this section begins with a discussion of culture, then political culture. A plethora of meanings has emanated from the anthropological use of the term culture. In 1871 E. B. Taylor introduced the concept of culture to anthropology as "that complex whole which includes knowledge, belief, art, morals, law, custom, and any other capabilities and habits acquired by man as a member of society" (quoted in Kluckhohn 1964: 165–168).

Among the hundreds of definitions that were introduced thereafter, Kroeber and Kluckhohn (1952: 43–55) reviewed some 160 meanings offered by social scientists. Anthropologist Franz Boas's descriptive definition is similar to that of Taylor: "Culture embraces all the manifestations of social habits of a community, the reactions of the individual as affected by the habits of the group in which he lives, and the products of human activities as determined by these habits." Boas viewed culture in its totality with an emphasis on cultural content. In contrast, Ralph Linton stressed a historical feature of culture, such as social inheritance or social tradition. O. Klineberg emphasized a normative connotation; culture is "that whole 'way of life' which is determined by the social environment." C. S. Ford presented culture in terms of its psychological implications, as a means of satisfying needs and solving problems: "Culture consists of learned problem-solutions."

In a widely accepted definition, Clyde Kluckhohn gave an abstract meaning to culture.

> Culture consists of patterns, explicit and implicit, of and for behavior acquired and transmitted by symbols, constituting the distinctive achievement of human groups, including their embodiments in artifacts; the essential core of culture consists of traditional (i.e., historically derived and selected) ideas and especially their attached values; culture systems may, on the one hand, be considered as products of action, on the other as conditioning influences upon further action. [Kluckhohn 1962: 73]

Such varied definitions have guided the prevalent social science thinking on culture. These and other definitions and interpretations of culture are found in Malinowski (1930), Moore (1952), and Kroeber (1952).

Other definitions are noteworthy. Sociologist Edward Shils (1961), for example, directed attention to a new order of society, mass society, which has appeared in the United States and much of Western Europe since the end of the First World War. His observation that the new order tends to aggregate large numbers of people into uncoerced association and to promote individual attachment to society as a whole has been reiterated by Gabriel Almond and other political scientists who emphasize democratic traditions. This growth of mass society Shils interpreted as having been accompanied by a decline in superior or refined culture (in great works of poetry, novels, philosophy, scientific theory, paintings, musical compositions, history, and the like). Mass society tends to embrace more of the mediocre (less original, more reproductive) and brutal (elementary) culture. It has been argued (Van Den Haag 1962) that such interpretations of culture are timeless, ahistorical, descriptive, and imbued with an ethnocentric value judgment.

Shils's conception of culture might be called humanistic in that it selects human activities and designates them as cultural, whereas the anthropologist tends to be nonselective and views culture as the entire social heritage. The humanist argues that some people are more cultured than others just as some societies are culturally richer than others. This normative and evaluative view is countered by the anthropologist's criticism that such assertions are ethnocentric.

Sociologists Jaeger and Selznick (1964) sought to bridge the gap between the anthropological and the humanist conceptions of culture by arguing that there is a tendency for many anthropologists to reflect a concern for cultural ideals, no matter how bland and noncommittal the character of their definitions might be. Jaeger and Selznick illustrate this position with reference to an authoritative statement by anthropologist Alfred Kroeber and sociologist Talcott Parsons who indicated their agreement that the concepts of culture and society are distinguishable. Acknowledging that in the past anthropologists used "culture" and sociologists used "society" as roughly equivalent terms to distinguish social heredity from biological heredity,

Kroeber and Parsons offered a selective view of culture and society.

> It is useful to define the concept *culture* for most usages more narrowly than has been generally the case in the anthropological tradition, restricting its reference to transmitted and created content and patterns of values, ideas, and other symbolic-meaningful systems as factors in the shaping of human behavior and the artifacts produced through behavior. On the other hand, we suggest that the term *society*—or more generally, *social system*—be used to designate the specifically relational system of interaction among individuals and collectivities. [1958: 582–583]

Such a selective view stresses the ideal, the symbolic, and the meaningful aspects of culture and is not much different from the distinction between culture and society made by Pitirim A. Sorokin (1947) or by R. M. MacIver, who viewed civilization as accumulative and irreversible while culture was seen as unique and variable (Kluckhohn 1964: 167).

Since the middle 1930s many British social anthropologists have emphasized the term social structure rather than culture. Many other social scientists have simply avoided the use of a concept of culture. Jaeger and Selznick recognized a variety of human settings within which socialization takes place. Consequently, sociologists have sought to improve inadequate socialization processes, and there appears to be a convergence between the humanist ideal and the prescriptive social scientist. "Culture is intimately associated with the realization of values. An understanding of the nature of the values at stake, and the conditions of their realization, must form a part of the theory of culture. It is in this sense a normative theory, one that does not shrink from identifying some cultures as attenuated, some symbols as emptied out, some experiences as truncated or distorted" (1964: 666).

Talcott Parsons devoted his early research to the study and interpretation of the writings and thought of Max Weber. Although Parsons has not written a volume on culture to supplement his work on society or social system, he has devoted a great deal of attention to culture. In *Toward a General Theory of Action*, he designated culture as a system, and in *The Social System* (1951), he devoted two chapters to culture. Briefly, his ideas on culture, as drawn from the latter work, are sketched.

At the outset, Parsons (1951: 15) identified three commonalities in the anthropological theory of culture. First, culture is transmitted, it constitutes a heritage or social tradition; second, culture is learned, it is not a manifestation of human beings; third, culture is shared, it is a product of human interaction. Parsons offered a definition of culture as "patterned or ordered systems of symbols which are objects of the orientation of action, internalized components of the personalities of individual actors and institutionalized patterns of social systems" (1951: 327). He delineated culture in terms of three basic "functional" categories or systems: cognitive or belief systems, cathectic or systems of expressive symbols, and evaluative or systems of value orientation. Parsons thereby acknowledged that beliefs, expressive symbols, and values are relevant in an analysis of a society. Parsons's categories have attracted political scientists, whose discipline traditionally has studied beliefs and ideas, symbols, and values.

> What makes Parsons' work attractive is that it honors the intellectual historian's endeavors by both emphasizing ideal factors and attempting to incorporate them into a scientific theory of action. It . . . appeals to modern behavioralists who study attitudes, beliefs, values, and norms. Thus, a behavioralist—Almond—uses Parsons' notions of culture, and a more traditionally oriented student—Beer, for example—also finds him useful. [Mitchell 1967: 119]

Parsons conceived of culture as consisting of systems with their own internal organization. Therefore cultural systems enjoy some measure of autonomy, yet Parsons also stressed the interconnections between cultural and social as well as psychological phenomena. He summarized his theory of culture:

> As part of the theory of action, then, the theory of culture must be the theory concerned not only with the properties of culture as such but with the interdependence of patterns of culture with the other components of systems of action. It is, of course, concerned with the structure of systems of culture patterns, with the different types of such systems and their classification. But it is also concerned with their involvement in social systems and personalities. . . . The focus, however, is always on the culture pattern system as such, and neither on the social system in which it is involved nor on the personalities as systems. [Parsons 1951: 553]

Parsons as a sociologist incorporated anthropological and psychological orientations into his theory of culture. Like Weber before him he emphasized individual action and orientations treating personality much the same as social systems. Whereas aspects of personality such as learning, rationalization, repression, and so on are studied by the psychologist at the individual level, the sociologist studies them at the level of the social system. Personalities are likely to encounter problems similar to those of social systems. Personalities utilize beliefs, symbols, and values—all elements of the culture system. Culture thus is relevant to the individual or personality level as well as to the collective or societal level. Cultures carry on from generation to generation and are shaped by persons through learning and socialization.

Harold Lasswell (1939) elaborated the systematic relationships of personality and culture, and his work influenced the past generation's study of national character or national culture; see, for example, Alex Inkeles and Daniel Levinson (1954), Margaret Mead (1951), Inkeles (1961), and Walter Metzger (1963). In his study of nationalism Leonard Doob (1964) projected personality characteristics and orientations to the level of the nation-state. Lucian Pye (1962) contributed a theory of national culture by examining the personality and political attitudes among elites in Burma.

In political science, and especially in comparative politics, there has been a substantial effort to view culture in a political context, and a dissatisfaction with national-character studies prompted a reformulation of concepts. Thus political culture became a "version of that old and rather imprecise concept *national character* that can be traced back to the writings of Montesquieu" (Mayer 1972: 163). Gabriel Almond and Sidney Verba preferred political culture rather than national character because that term allowed them to use the conceptual frameworks of anthropology, sociology, and psychology. "Our thinking is enriched when we employ, for example, such categories of anthropology and psychology as socialization, culture conflict, and acculturation" (Almond and Verba 1963: 13). Lucian Pye saw political culture as a means "to discover a method for working back from the complex subtleties of individual psychology to the level of the social aggregate which is the traditional plateau of political science" (Pye 1965: 9).

The accepted conceptual premises of political culture were clearly identified by Almond and Verba (1963).

1. *Civic virtue and responsibility.* Political culture theory assimilates a traditional concern of political science with classical themes, in particular what the Greeks called civic virtue, "the kind of community life, social organizations, and upbringing of children that fosters civic virtue" (Almond and Verba 1963: vii). In the contemporary world this civic culture would reflect democratic personality characteristics, such as those identified by Harold Lasswell: a warm attitude toward people, a sharing of values with others, trust and confidence in one's fellow being, and freedom from anxiety (11).

2. *Participatory and pluralistic democracy.* The civic culture is democratic and premised on the toleration of individual freedoms and government through a consensus of the governed (in this sense inspired by James Madison's *Federalist Papers*). The prospects are bright in the contemporary world. "Large groups of people who have been outside of politics are demanding entrance into the political system. And the elites are rare who do not profess commitment to this goal" (1963: 4).

3. *Order through rational bureaucracy.* In the spirit of Weberian thought, "the doctrine and practice of a rational bureaucracy as an instrument of the democratic political power" (1963: 5) can be conveyed to the elites of new nations. These nations can emulate the Western "technocratic image of . . . a

polity in which authoritarian bureaucracy predominates and political organization becomes a device for human and social engineering" (6).

4. *Stability through modernization*. Stable economic and social conditions are related to such indexes of modernization as the degree of industrialization and urbanization, rate of literacy, and level of education. The diffusion of such modernizing tendencies from the advanced nations enhances the probability of development and stability in the backward world. The problem with this premise "is that the cultural and psychological consequences of 'modern' technologies and processes are left to inference" (1963): 11).

These premises led Almond and Verba to political culture. Drawing from the cultural contributions of Kroeber, Parsons, Weber, Lasswell, and others, they emphasized "psychological orientations" and the "cognitions, feelings, and evaluations" of people in relation to their political system (1963: 14). In the light of their theory the general definition or the meaning of political culture on a macro level is examined, and then the more specific or micro aspects are looked at (in particular the socialization and communication processes that shape political culture). This dichotomy manifests itself in political culture studies, even though the theorists of political culture insist that their conceptualization was in response "to the need to bridge a growing gap in the behavioral approach in political science between the level of microanalysis based on psychological interpretations of the individual's political behavior and the level of macroanalysis based on the variables common to political sociology" (Pye 1965: 8; see also Rosenbaum 1975).

Interpretations of Political Culture at a General Level

Gabriel Almond first introduced the concept of political culture in 1956, in his early attempt to offer a classification for comparing political systems. "Every political system is embedded in a particular pattern of orientations to political action. I have found it useful to refer to this as the political culture" (Almond 1956: 396). Almond suggested that the political culture had a certain autonomy and yet was related to the general culture; it did not "coincide" with the political system since patterns of orientation to politics transcend the boundaries of political systems. Yet he related political culture to his classification of political systems. The political culture of the Anglo-American system, for example, is homogeneous and secular, that of continental Europe is fragmented, that of the preindustrial system is mixed, and that of the totalitarian system is synthetic. Almond intended that his concept should replace less useful terminology such as national character and cultural ethos.

In *The Civic Culture* (1963) Almond and Verba refined this conception of political culture and used it in an empirical study and survey of attitudes in five nations. They defined political culture in terms of political orientations and attitudes held by individuals in relation to their political system. "When we speak of the political culture of a society, we refer to the political system as internalized in the cognitions, feelings, and evaluations of its population. People are induced into it just as they are socialized into nonpolitical roles and social systems" (Almond and Verba 1963: 14). *Cognitive orientations* include knowledge and beliefs about the political system, its leaders, and operation. *Affective orientations* involve feelings about the system such as attachment or alienation. *Evaluative orientations* comprise judgments and opinions about the system and might, for example, include the application of values such as democratic norms. These orientations become the basis for types of political culture. Three types are postulated: *parochial*, implying that individuals have low expectations and awareness of government and generally are not involved; *subject*, in which individuals are aware of the outcomes of government but do not participate in the processes that result in policy decisions; and *participant*, in which individuals are active and involved in the system as a whole, that is, in both the input and output processes.

In a collaborative effort with G. Bingham Powell, Jr., Almond elaborated further his conception of political culture, tying it both to the political system and to political development (Almond and Powell 1966: 50–72). "Political culture is the pattern of individual attitudes and orientations toward politics among the members of a political system. It is the subjective realm which underlies and gives meaning to political actions" (50). Political culture is explained in terms of its relationship to the capabilities of the political system. Development is a reflection of the degree of secularization of the political culture. Cultural secularization implies bargaining and give-and-take interactions, a kind of "marketplace attitude which permeates the conduct of politics" (57). Additionally, cultural secularization is seen in the movement from diffuseness to a specificity of orientations and a differentiation of roles in the polity; diffuseness characterizes parochial cultures in which there is little or no awareness of the political system as a separate entity, whereas specificity and differentiation characterize subject and participant political cultures. In newer nations a "cultural dualism" is evident, in which a small elite is modernized or "socialized in the specific, universalistic, and pragmatic orientations which typify 'modern' culture—while the vast majority remains tied to the rigid, diffuse, and ascriptive patterns of tradition" (72).

At this point Almond defended the explanatory potential of political culture. He argued that his categories were not merely descriptive; they could be measured through public opinion surveys, interviews, and other techniques. Further, political culture is a conceptual tool that bridges the gap between studies of the individual and studies of the political system as a whole.

Other writers have reiterated Almond's formulation of political culture. Pye, for example, viewed political culture as providing "an ordered subjective realm of politics," which is found on two levels. "For the individual the political culture provides controlling guidelines for effective political behavior, and for the collectivity it gives a systematic structure of values and rational considerations which ensures coherence in the performance of institutions and organizations" (Pye 1965: 7). Political culture thus is the product both of collective histories and of individual life histories of the political system. It evolves from conscious learnings about politics. Analytically, it gives a behavior form of analysis to such terms as ideology, national spirit, and values of people.

Sidney Verba concurred that political culture "consists of the system of empirical beliefs, expressive symbols, and values which defines the situation in which political action takes place" (Verba 1965: 513). Political culture is a system of control, related to the beliefs held by individuals. In focusing on beliefs, Verba suggested a number of dimensions of political culture, including beliefs identifying with politics, especially with the nation-state; with one's fellow citizens; with governmental output and operation; and with the process of making decisions—the political input.

Many interpretations of political culture diverge somewhat from the Almond-Pye-Verba formulation. Samuel Beer, for example, described political culture as a pattern of ideas and traditions about authority, yet he, too, returned to Parsons's classification of culture along the lines of cognition, expressive symbols, and value orientations. Primarily Beer conceived of political culture at the national level. Roy Macridis has written that political culture is made up of shared goals and commonly accepted rules of individual and group interaction. (For a review and critique of Beer and Macridis the reader might benefit from articles by Young C. Kim [1964] and Carole Pateman [1971].)

Interpretations of Political Culture at a Specific Level

Orthodox social scientists tend to apply their culture theory to empirical studies of communication and socialization. Briefly, we examine some of these studies and assess their contributions to theories of political culture.

COMMUNICATION STUDIES

Communication is a somewhat peripheral and not fully elaborated aspect of comparative politics. The study of communication is essential and facilitates an understanding of culture and development, however. It is frequently suggested, for example, that the pressure of communication has precipitated the downfall of traditional societies and that new channels of communication can be decisive in the process of nation building. Given this significance, the following discussion draws from the literature a definition of communication and examines models and patterns of communication as well as possible directions for inquiry. An attempt is also made to identify some of the relevant theories and empirical studies produced by social scientists interested in communication.

Lucian Pye believed that all social processes may be analyzed in terms of structure, content, and flow of communication.

> Communication is the web of human society. The structure of a communications system with its more or less well-defined channels is in a sense the skeleton of the social body which envelops it. The content of communication is of course the very substance of human intercourse. The flow of communications determines the direction and the pace of dynamic social development. [Pye 1963: 4]

Beyond this definition, characteristics of communication that relate to politics and culture might be identified. First, as implied above, communication permeates human relations with intended and unintended messages. Second, communication applies to mass media institutions: press, radio, television, popular arts, and the like. Pye suggested that communication provides a framework for an orderly establishment in society of power relationships and rationality and consensus in mass politics.

With these basic characteristics in mind, Pye posited a "world culture" as an ideal type of what we think of as "modern life."

> It is based on a scientific and rational outlook and the application in all phases of life of ever higher levels of technology. It is a reflection of urban and industrial society in which human relations are premised on secular rather than sacred considerations. It embraces the spirit of enlightenment, at least a formal acknowledgement of humane values, and acceptance of rational-legal norms for governmental behavior. Also within the realm of government, it implies a strong need to pay deference to democratic values and practices. [Pye 1963: 19]

Pye's world culture incorporates the rational bureaucracy of Weber and the civic culture of Almond into a formulation that transcends the nation-state. Communication, he believed, serves to diffuse this world culture throughout different societies, therefore ensuring the political development of nations everywhere.

In projecting this world culture, Pye (1963: 24–29) wrote of communication models: traditional, transitional, and modern. Development through communication is evident in the evolution of societies from a traditional or transitional stage to a modern stage. This "stage theory" classifies and describes societies at particular points in time. Following is a brief summary of each.

Stage 1 — *Traditional*: The communication process is not sharply differentiated from other social processes. The social hierarchy determines the flow and content of information, thereby reinforcing its own interests. Professional communicators are lacking.

Stage 2 — *Transitional*: The communication is bifurcated and fragmented; oriented, on the one hand, toward a system of modern technology in urbanized and Westernized centers of population, and, on the other hand, toward a traditional system of face-to-face relations and communal life. Each system tends to maintain an autonomous pattern of communications. Domestic control over communications tends to be lacking, and there is a reliance on foreign and international means of communication.

Stage 3 — *Modern*: Mass media communications are professionalized and relatively independent of government; they are guided by universalistic standards of objective and unbiased reporting. This level of highly organized media complements another level of informal-opinion leaders who communicate in positions of influence in the networks of personal and face-to-face communication channels. Interactions and feedback characterize the flow of information between the two levels.

Finally, this synthesis reviews comparative communications theory in relation to some essential political activities: interest articulation and aggregation, recruitment, mobilization, participation, and influence. Most of these processes were utilized by Almond as input functions in his model of a political system, which was discussed in Chapter 5. Since the reader may wish to examine these processes in more detail, a description of each is sketched, and literature that may be helpful to comparative inquiry is identified.

The basic character of a political culture is determined in part by the relationship between communications and the processes through which political interests are expressed. *Articulation* and *aggregation* constitute two such processes of interest expression. Almond, Pye, and other orthodox comparativists have insisted that every political system articulates interests, claims, and demands for political action. Usually this articulation is expressed through pressure and interest groups. Articulation can instill in people new values and new outlooks, and an articulation of interests is understood as a means for strengthening the possibilities for a rationally based system of interest aggregation. Aggregation is a process in which demands or interests are combined, for instance, in the formulation of a policy. Such interest aggregation may be accompanied by a recruitment of people. Integration is another term implying aggregation (Blau 1960). Articulation, aggregation, and recruitment were concepts employed by Almond and Coleman in their pioneer study of developing areas.

Communication relates to other processes such as mobilization, participation, and influence. Mobilization is "the process in which major clusters of old social, economic, and psychological commitments are eroded or broken and people become available for new patterns of socialization and behavior" (Deutsch 1961: 493). Mobilization thus is a process of change that can have political consequences, such as expanding a politically aware and relevant population or enhancing the quality of politics or even generating pressures for reform. Mobilization also facilitates communication between government and the governed. Additionally, with an increase in the numbers of mobilized people and a greater awareness of their needs, *participation* is likely to increase.

Participation involves the process of how and why people get involved in politics. Lester Milbrath has classified political involvement along the lines of the typology of political culture set forth by Almond and Verba. In Milbrath's terms (1965: 18), parochials are "apathetics" and not involved; subjects are "spectators," involved in such activities as voting and political discussion; and participants are "gladiators," who hold public office or are active in campaigns and party affairs. Lippitt and Sprecher (1960), Nie, Powell, and Prewitt (1969), and Kievit (1964) have contributed theoretical perspectives on political participation, and Inkeles (1969), Rokkan (1960), and Verba (1962) have combined theory with data in comparative study.

Finally, political influence is involved in communication. Influence is the "ability to get others to act, think, or feel as one intends" (Banfield 1961: 3). The mobilization of people and the aggregation of interests may influence some political action. The use of symbols may influence political consequences (Edelman 1967). Public opinion may be decisively influential (Bowman and Boynton 1974).

This discussion of communication concludes with a review of the major directions of thought and inquiry on the subject. Those interested in comparative study may benefit from a cursory look at some of the early writings on communication, for example, Park (1939), Lasswell (1948), and Lazarsfeld and Merton (1957). Those studies set forth general theory and are focused on mass media. Eisenstadt (1955) and Wright (1960) have contributed more recent articles. In the tradition of these studies, Fagen (1964 and 1966) has introduced the student to communications and comparative politics. He identified ideas about systems and cybernetics as influential on communication study, especially as formulated by David Easton but more specifically as directed to comparative politics by Karl Deutsch in his *Nerves of Government* (1963) and *Nationalism and Social Communication* (1965).

Deutsch's classical studies are complemented by Lucian Pye's work in the comparative study of communications (1956, 1962, 1963, and 1964).

SOCIALIZATION STUDIES

Clearly communication, especially within the mass media, contributes to political socialization, a subject of intense interest to specialists of comparative politics. In capitalist countries like the United States the political scientist examines political socialization as a means of verifying his assumptions about the democratic polity. Studies of socialist countries like China, Cuba, and the Soviet Union focus on patterns of thought that socialize the populations so that they adopt the beliefs and values about revolutionary society. In the less developed Third World, the U.S. social scientist views the mass media as the instrument for socializing backward peoples into the modern world. This view of the socializing mass media is expressed by Herbert Hyman: "They are a major hope. As instruments of socialization, they are efficient and their sweep is vast enough to cover the huge populations requiring modernization" (Hyman, in Pye 1963: 142).

The following discussion reviews the evolution of the concepts of socialization and political socialization, then turns to various definitions of political socialization, and finally examines such aspects as the roles, content, and agents of political socialization. In addition, theoretical directions in the literature are identified, and the principal comparative research on political socialization is summarized.

Although social scientists have long been interested in the ways in which members of a society learn about politics, there has been no consensus on what should be studied or how research should be carried out. Historically two approaches, each with different emphases and different disciplinary roots, have prevailed in the study of socialization. One might be called the sociopsychological approach; the other, the political approach.

The sociopsychological approach emanates from the tradition of work in sociology and psychology as well as anthropology, and this discussion draws from the excellent review by John Clausen (Clausen et al. 1968). The term *socialization* apparently was in vogue before its use by social scientists. The *Oxford Dictionary of the English Language* dates the term to 1828, giving socialization the connotation of "to render social, to make fit for living in society" (Clausen et al. 1968: 21). Other early uses emphasized a moral thrust, with socialization understood as the process of perfecting the individual for society. The early conceptual usage of socialization was identified in the United States about 1895 in a paper by G. Simmel, which influenced F. P. Giddings and E. W. Burgess to elaborate the term in sociological textbooks.

Although socialization received attention in the major sociological writings thereafter, its application was relegated to studies of culture and personality in the late 1920s, and during the 1930s it was the concern of many interdisciplinary studies. With the publication of two articles that focused on socialization in the July 1939 issue of the *American Journal of Sociology*, the term came to be widely used in sociology. In psychology, socialization was not widely utilized until the 1930s, when it was incorporated into theories of learning and personality. In recent decades anthropologists have shown an interest in socialization. Their concern with combining culture and personality was initially evident in the late 1920s. The relevance to political science of the sociopsychological approach to socialization is found in its attention on why and how individuals acquire beliefs about politics. Research in this area tends to be meticulous and narrowly focused.

The general political approach, in contrast, assesses the consequences of socialization for the whole political system. It is less concerned with individual beliefs about politics and instead directs attention to those institutions that shape the patterns of authority and legitimacy. Research in this area is broad or macro in orientation. The political approach emanates from the traditional concerns of political science with ideology, stability, and civic training. In the United States interest in civic training was reflected in the educational literature at the turn of the century, when the assimilation of large immigrant populations was an issue. Even today formal civic education remains a concern of schools, in which attention to patriotism, for example, is a common theme. Greenstein (1968) has neatly summarized the main lines of thought that run through political studies of socialization in the present century. The first dates to the late 1920s and early 1930s when political scientists directed attention to formal aspects of civic training (Merriam 1931, for example). A second line revolves around the studies of personality and politics and national character (Inkeles and Levinson 1954) made during the Second World War and the decade thereafter. A third orientation developed in the late 1950s when behavioral studies of the political socialization of children and adolescents were conducted. Herbert Hyman (1959), for instance, stimulated considerable interest in political socialization.

Given these two approaches, what definitions guide the study of political socialization? A general study of socialization by social psychologists, sociologists, and some anthropologists would focus on the learning process whereby new members of society, such as infants, interact and acquire a social behavior. In that kind of study, individual socialization equates with all social learning, although some social scientists would narrow the process to individual learning based on behavior that a group approves, and others would identify socialization as the process whereby a child internalizes parental norms. Although the concept generally is used in relation to children, it also is applicable to adults. Thus socialization might be simply the inculcation of skills, motives, attitudes for the performance of roles in society.

Prominent social scientists have taken turns at defining the politics of socialization. Somewhat in the light of the above social science usage, Dennis referred "to a process by which persons new to a society, or who grow up in it, acquire characteristic patterns of political orientation and behavior" (1975: 5–6). Hess and Torney expanded upon this conception and emphasized childhood experience in their characterization of "the process whereby a junior or new member of a group or institution is taught its values, attitudes, and other behavior. Socialization may be regarded as a life-long process although much of the basic teaching is apparently accomplished in the early years" (Hess and Torney 1967: 6). Greenstein offered both a narrow and a broad conception of the term. "Narrowly conceived, political socialization is the deliberate inculcation of political information, values, and practices by instructional agents who have been formally charged with this responsibility." Broadly conceived, political socialization encompasses "*all* political learning, formal or informal, deliberate and unplanned, at every stage of the life cycle, including not only explicitly political learning but also nominally non-political learning" (Greenstein 1968: 551).

Langton pursued a narrow conception by defining political socialization as "the process, mediated through various agencies of society, by which an individual learns politically relevant attitudinal dispositions and behavior patterns. These agencies include such environmental categories as the family, peer group, school, adult organizations, and the mass media . . . class, sex, and age sub-cultures might also be included" (Langton 1969: 5). Easton and Dennis gave a restricted definition, political socialization being "those developmental processes through which persons acquire political orientations and patterns of behavior" (1969: 7). Finally, Coleman delineated a broad interpretation. "It refers to that process by which individuals acquire attitudes and feelings toward the political system and toward their role in it, including *cognition* (what one knows or believes about the system, its existence as well as its *modus operandi*), *feeling* (how one feels toward the system, including loyalty and sense of civic obligation), and one's *sense of political competence* (what one's role is or can be in the system)" (Coleman 1965: 18). This definition approximates Almond's view that political socialization is a process of induction into the political culture.

Generalizing from the definitions, political socialization involves individual roles, content, and agents in the process of learning about politics. As to who participates, Greenstein (1965a) suggested that research tells us that male children, beginning with their preschool play activity, orient themselves to politics more readily than female children, who are encouraged by their social environment to turn to domestic concerns. Such assumptions about sex roles are misrepresented, according to Morgan (1974). Greenstein (1965a) also argued that class differences relate to political socialization, since parents in the upper social strata are politically more active and likely to provide their children with a model of civic involvement, whereas children in the lower strata may be less likely to acquire the skills and resources for high levels of civic activity. Although these class assumptions may rest upon the results of current research, the assumptions, too, may be suspect. In any event, it is clear that political socialization, in varying degrees, affects all individuals at all stages of life and that the focus of most studies has been upon childhood political learning.

What is learned relates to the *content* of political socialization. Content may include knowledge, that is, certain dispositions and beliefs about politics. Content also involves attitudes learned through political activity such as partisan attachment, ideology, voting, and the like. Additionally, content may relate to orientations toward authority.

Studies have tended to concentrate on the agents of political socialization. Agents may be formal or informal. The school serves as one agent of formal learning, for the school is involved in the formation of culture and political culture through such activities as the inculcation of a national identity. The content of textbooks and the information imparted by teachers usually contribute to an awareness of politics among students. The mass media also transmit political information. The family, peer group, neighborhood, and work place exemplify informal settings in which face-to-face communication may take place. The family is significant in socialization, especially in the acquisition of beliefs. Dawson and Prewitt (1968) suggested a different formulation of political socialization agents, which may prove useful to the reader. Their classification falls roughly into three categories: (1) agents that have authority over the child, for example, teachers and parents; (2) agents that are equal to the learner, for example, age peers in school, friendship cliques, and work associates; and (3) agents that are political, such as contact with political authorities and voting.

The literature on political socialization is extensive, and it would not serve much purpose to review all the major sources. That task has been fulfilled elsewhere, for example, in the scholarly literature assessments in Clausen et al. (1968) and in the bibliographies by Dennis (1973a) and Kenneth I. Rothman (in Coleman 1965: 585–609). In addition, useful collections of essays are incorporated in Coleman (1965), Dennis (1973b), Havighurst (1968), Dennis and Jennings (1970), Sigel (1970), and Wright and Turk (1967).

It may help to identify theoretical directions as well as some representative examples of the literature on political socialization, however. The general theoretical works have already been referred to: Dawson and Prewitt (1968), Hess and Torney (1967), Easton and Dennis (1969), Hyman (1959), and Langton (1969) as well as the collections cited above. In addition, varying assumptions, conceptions, and assessments of what constitutes orthodox theory of political socialization today are evident in Aberle (1961), Bender (1967), Argyle and Delin (1965), Hess and Bear (1968), Jaros (1973), Merelman (1966 and 1969), and Sigel (1965). Efforts to tie personality theory to political socialization are represented by Froman (1961) and Greenstein (1965b, 1967a, and 1967b). Sources that deal specifically with the agents of political socialization include Jones (1971) on teachers; Prewitt (1965) and Jaros, Hirsch, and Fleron (1968) on leaders; Jennings and Niemi (1968) and Lane (1959a) on parents; Davies (1965) on the family; and Chaffee, Ward, and Tipton (1970) on mass media.

Research on political socialization has produced numerous studies, some of which have been received enthusiastically but others have not met expectations. A critical review of this literature is made in the next section but first it may be instructive to identify some of the contributions that are relevant to comparative politics. This literature is classified into works on the United States, configurative studies on other countries, and cross-national studies that compare data for two or more nations.

Empirical work on political socialization in the United States includes Czudnowski (1968), Dodge and Uyeki (1962), Easton and Dennis (1965, 1967, and 1969), Easton and Hess (1962), Greenstein (1965a), Hess and Torney (1967), Jennings (1967), Langton (1967), Langton and Jennings (1968), Langton and Karns (1969), Prewitt, Eulau, and Zisk (1966–1967), Searing, Schwartz, and Lind (1973), Schubert (1977), and Sigel (1968). Some examples of research that is focused on a single country other than the United States include Cornelius (1973) on low-income communities in Mexico, Hardgrave (1969) on South India, LaPalombara and Walters (1961) on Italy, Kuroda (1965) on Japan, and Stern and Palmer (1971) on Colombian university students.

Finally, there have been some ambitious attempts to examine political socialization through data comparisons of two or more countries. Agger and others (1970) examined education and personality in the United States, Czechoslovakia, and two republics of Yugoslavia. Dennis and others (1968) studied democratic orientations in four Western systems, and Eisenstadt (1964) synthesized research of age groups among different types of societies. Greenstein (1975 and Greenstein and Tarrow 1970) utilized semiprojective interviews with children in Britain, France, and the United States; Hess (1963) attempted some cross-national comparisons; and Jahoda (1963) compared children's ideas about nationality in the United States and Western Europe. Langton (1969) compared national samples of high school students in Jamaica and the United States, then later joined with Karns (Langston and Karns 1974) to utilize the five-nation survey data of Almond and Verba to study political socialization. Koplin (1968), Mishler et al. (1974), and Moskos and Bell (1964) reported on their research, respectively, on students, parties, and democracy. Putnam (1971) looked at ideology and elite political culture in Britain and Italy, and Searing (1969) attempted a secondary analysis of the civic culture survey to examine elite socialization. Sharkansky (1969) applied theory to data in three cultures, and Stern et al. (1973) presented factor analysis of forty-eight variables in Almond and Verba's five-nation study. Schubert (1977) linked judicial activity to political culture in South Africa and Switzerland.

A Critique of Culture Theory

Anthropologist Anthony Wallace has applied Kuhn's formulation of paradigmatic processes to the experience, study, and theory of culture. Rather systematically he identified stages in the evolution of a paradigm of culture and the pervasive influence that paradigm has exerted upon social science (Wallace 1972). In the present work the political culture basis of the orthodox paradigm, which has come to dominate comparative politics, has been outlined, but a critique of culture theory has not yet been offered. Thus, I now raise some questions and illustrate the concern about culture theory with some comments from students. These questions and comments serve as a basis for assessing both the general theory of political culture and political socialization studies.

Exposing students in my classes to the political culture literature has elicited the following sort of questions. Does the theory not tend to be purely descriptive or classificatory? Are not the classificatory schemes of political culture far too simplistic and static? What about the relationship of political culture to systems analysis? Does the literature offer any analytical possibilities for dealing with political culture, especially given that political scientists working with such theory have failed to apply it as such?

The comments below are representative of criticisms by my graduate students over the past decade. They reflect a range of views along orthodox as well as radical lines of thinking.

In most theoretical essays dealing with political culture we are told that the concept has analytical promise. Pye and Verba suggest that the concept will reveal the character of political development and an understanding of why a political system is stable or unstable, as well as identify the socializing agents that will produce the desired changes and policies in a nation's politics. Almond and Verba suggest that political culture tells us about the prospects for democracy, stability, effectiveness, and cohesiveness of politics. The concept purports to be a tool of analysis, an independent variable that relates significantly to the operation of political systems, but the concept is rarely utilized as a tool of analysis. Few political scientists have applied political culture so as to realize its theoretical promise as an explanatory variable.

Studies of political culture tend not to focus on how political culture is related to or affects the political system, but rather on such topics as what the elements of political culture are, how a political culture develops or changes, and the classification of different kinds of political cultures. Analytically political culture must bridge the gap between statements of what a particular political system is to statements about how that culture might affect the political system.

The major attempts at relating political culture to political system result in typologies, classifications, comparisons. Writers such as Almond, Verba, Pye, and others do no more than democratize the concept of development into an ideal of capitalist-technological political secularization, which even to the most naive reader will spell out a parochial, incomplete, and probably meaningless approach.

There is the inadequacy in explaining the dynamics. The authors never really attempt to deal with dialectical forces of change. Their concept of change is wedded to a gradual, incremental process, which carries the political system to its natural end, to the ideal civic culture. Once the allegiant culture is created and change is no longer necessary, the relationship between system and culture will be characterized by reinforcement and maintenance. These advocates of political culture are looking to the ideal system and adjusting accordingly, resulting in the reverse of what was intended: political culture does not exist independently of the system but instead is dependent on the system.

A major reason for the shortcomings of the political culture approach, in providing a one-time relationship between political cultures and political system, is that the underlying assumptions of political culture are either inadequate, ambiguous, unproven, or false. The assumption of many writers is that based on the political culture we can determine the nature of the political system, but such an assumption is invalid. It can be shown that in assuming a one-way, direct, and perfect relationship between psychological orientation and political systems, the political culture theorists have engaged in a series of psychological reductionisms. It can be argued that the political culture theorists have failed to focus on the links that need to be considered in examining the chain of causation that runs, or fails to run, from underlying childhood political socialization to the nature of political system. The first link that should be examined is the relationship between childhood political socialization and adulthood political beliefs.

An examination of the literature of political culture shows that such criticisms are justified. In his presidential address to the American Political Science Association, Robert Ward (1974) raised questions about the past work in political culture. William Bostock exclaimed that the majority of the political scientists tend to fall upon weak and naive generalizations about political culture, that their understanding rests upon such consciously or unconsciously held assumptions as "Politics exists in isolation from society, and the political behavior of individuals can be understood without reference to society," "Culture does not exist or is not important," "Culture can be studied in a naturalistic fashion, " "Culture exists within individuals but not societies" (Bostock 1973: 37). Such observations lead us to a look at four major criticisms of political culture theory, relating to reductionism, bias, explanatory value, and autonomy.

Studies of political culture "reduce cultural factors either to social system characteristics" or "treat them as merely the statistical aggregation of the intrapsychic orientations of the individual members of society" (Lehman 1972: 362). Lehman suggested that there is a need for two sets of categories, for example, cultural and structural—shifting from cultural to structural aspects raises questions about research methodologies. Further, the utilization of survey method may explain some aspects of culture, but there is the problem of "allowing one's methodological preference to define one's theoretical formulations" (362).

In his early work on political systems, David Easton warned that most social science is culture-bound and that we should be aware that most generalizations are valid only within the limits of a particular cultural situation. Hitchner (1968: 552) and Tucker (1973: 175) referred to political culture as reflecting cultural bias, namely, the preconceptions of Western notions of modernity. Lehman (1972: 362) expressed concern about the "normative bias" of political culture, toward consensus, for example, as a primary basis of social order.

Still another concern relates to the explanatory value of political culture. Tucker queried, "Might not the central importance of a concept like that of political culture be that it assists us to take our bearings in the study of the political life of society, to focus on what is happening or not happening, to describe and analyze and order many significant data, and to raise fruitful questions for thought and research—*without explaining anything?*" (1973: 179). Hughes and Pinney (1966) offered a similar position, and Bostock, emphasizing this theme, indicted political scientists for asserting weak and naive assumptions in their explanations of political culture. He argued that the typology of political culture suggested by Almond and Verba is based on descriptive rather than analytic criteria and that since no theoretical construct is employed, this use of political culture is nonexplanatory and nonpredictive. Bostock also argued that political culture analyzed in terms of the individual is "incorrect and grossly misleading."

> It is thus quite wrong to seek the explanation of culture within individuals. . . . the culture of any group of people is a truly collective phenomenon over which they have very little power of choice or control. Any view of culture which

> denies its collective and largely autonomous nature is bound to have serious
> consequences for those who would seek to employ it. [Bostock 1973: 47]

Finally, critics have questioned the issue of autonomy. Hitchner (1968: 553) advocated paying closer attention to the political culture of the national political systems we study. Almond has emphasized the autonomy of political culture, arguing that a society's political system is embedded in a political culture. Given that the approach to political culture is "rather deeply embedded in the culture of American political science," Tucker wondered "whether we should think of political culture as comprising an autonomous realm within the total culture of a society" (1973: 175–176). Further, he suggested that the notion of an autonomous political culture may "reflect a cultural bias" (179). This problem of bias is seen in Pye's attempt to relate political culture to political development. Pye looked for a democratic environment, a rational bureaucratic development, the extent to which modern patterns prevail over traditional ones, and development "in the sense of liberty, popular sovereignty, and free institutions" – all aspects that Pye identified in the U.S. political culture (Pye 1965: 11–12). Bostock countered that political scientists should not generalize from one political culture to another, because each political culture is unique.

> Political scientists who fail to perceive the uniqueness of individual political
> culture are in danger of overlooking its most important characteristics, whilst
> those who overlook political culture itself in their explanations will not have
> succeeded at all; they will have no conception of the tensions, reinforcements
> and contradictions within and between individuals, social systems, and
> cultures, at various levels and across these levels. [Bostock 1973: 48]

A critique of culture theory necessarily should incorporate a focus on the theory and methods of socialization research. Such research has served as the empirical basis of orthodox paradigmatic perspectives of culture and political culture. As an illustration of one such orthodox perspective, Dawson and Prewitt (1968) affirmed that they engaged in an ideal type of analysis: "As such, we suggest something other than an empirically accurate description of political socialization for a specific set of individuals or for a given society" (1968: 202). They acknowledged that there are many aspects of socialization that they did not know or understand. For example, they admitted that they imposed homogeneity and order on processes that were essentially heterogeneous. They spoke of socialization as a universal phenomenon yet acknowledged that their discussion was based on knowledge of the U.S. and Western experience; at the same time they recognized differences from culture to culture. On another level they implied that political socialization agencies operate in roughly a similar direction when in fact they do not necessarily do so. There may be discontinuities among agencies during the different periods of an individual's life, a fact overlooked by the socialization literature. Then too, major political events, many of them unanticipated such as a war or a depression, affect individual socialization. Finally, it is clear that the political socialization process is conservative since parents and other socializing agents tend to teach what they in turn have learned; such a focus may ignore major changes in society and culture. These and other criticisms by orthodox researchers are reflected in the writings of Cook and Scioli (1972), Dennis (1968), Greenstein (1967b and 1970), and Pye (1972).

In his appraisal of contemporary political socialization research, Schonfeld (1971: 551–555) suggested four areas of concern. First, the thrust of investigation concerns childhood and adolescent rather than adult learning. Essential is the relationship between what a child learns and his or her future adult political behavior and attitudes, yet studies of political socialization do not analyze such a relationship. Instead they concentrate on the effect that social institutions such as the family and school have upon the formation of children's political attitudes, not on the differences between those institutions. Second, researchers are interested in how individuals learn to relate to politics, generally in early life but also in adulthood. This type of work tends to be tentative and suggestive. Third, there is an interest in identifying adult normative images about politics, on the assumption that adults transmit their "idealized" conceptions of political life to their children, but the primary direction of political socialization research skirts this theme. Fourth, the world of childhood might be examined heuristically as a means of more fully understanding complex political phenomena; however, researchers have not explored this possibility.

Any theory of political socialization appears to be speculative and tentative. Schonfeld referred to the fourfold typology of Hess and Torney as "an important theoretical contribution," yet he concluded that their "arguments are not empirically supported; they are simple speculation" (Schonfeld 1971: 554–555). Although Easton and Dennis argued for the need to formulate a political theory of socialization, their study tended to move in a "vague and imprecise fashion" (Schonfeld 1971: 567). Roberta Sigel saw Hess and Torney as emphasizing orientations toward participation as "a cornerstone of democratic theory," and Easton and Dennis as stressing "a sense of personal efficacy," but she concluded that a theory of political socialization has yet to emerge (Siegel 1966: 11). She complained that existing attempts at theory tended to deal with aspects of rather than the whole system. Further, she argued that we should pay attention to cultural as well as political norms and values. Additionally, we should search for a model of political socialization that transcends the present static and homogeneous formulations in order to examine political conflict, cleavage, or rapid change so that we can assess processes of desocialization and resocialization. The present model, she asserted, "is simply too static and too culture bound" (1966: 15).

Although a theory of political socialization may not yet have established itself, the paradigmatic and methodological thrust of liberal democratic theory has implanted itself upon contemporary research. A particularistic rather than a holistic approach to theory, as suggested by Sigel, exemplifies this tendency. The mainstream of research focuses almost exclusively on the development of children's political attitudes in stable, democratic societies. As a consequence, the literature deals primarily with the experience of the United States and Western Europe, and it treats adult experiences as only marginally significant. Such a research tradition clearly is inadequate for studying the less developed nations. Some critics have suggested that this tradition has distorted our understanding of the developed nations as well.

The weaknesses in political socialization methodology are evident in the apparent bias that pervades the interpretations of political scientists who work in the orthodox tradition. For one thing, these interpretations imply some possible political consequence. Linking patterns of childhood with features of the political system might reveal liberal or conservative positions, as was emphasized in the work of Dawson and Prewitt, Greenstein, and Easton and Dennis. Further, there is a tendency to assume that children are passive and that their political socialization is based on a consensual understanding of politics and society. Their view of the world is necessarily conservative, and if socialization has not prepared them to deal with new situations, then it is assumed that a breakdown in the polity and society may ensue. Thus socialization studies generally overlook the uniqueness of the individual. Children are treated as incomplete adults whose socialization leads them in a linear fashion toward adulthood. Another bias is evident in the ahistorical character of most political socialization studies, for writers assume but do not adequately demonstrate the direct relationship between early and later socialization and political beliefs. Baker (1971), for example, noted the tendency of many political scientists to apply "objective reality" to an individual's subjective perceptions of the world. From this reality are derived generalizations, which become laws, relevant to present and past behavior so that the present is read into the past and processes identifiable in the present are related to earlier periods.

The methods or techniques of political socialization research are suspect. Sigel questioned the preferential use of survey questionnaires and suggested that a researcher might benefit from face-to-face interviews as well as from direct observation of learning in socialization settings such as the classroom. She worried about a child's reaction to structured questionnaires, for answers do not reveal why a child thinks well or ill of a government; for example, "Our failure to know the reasons has often led us unwittingly to misconstrue the meaning of children's responses" (Sigel 1966: 7). Sigel also regretted the inability of the researcher to imagine the significance to a child of certain words and personalities—an especially crucial consideration in the wording of questions. Connell and Goot (1972–1973) were especially critical of researchers who assume that an adult researcher and a child reach a common understanding about the meaning of their questions and answers. "Theorists almost always fall back on tacit assumptions of consensus and indeed of some kind of consensual control" (Connell and Goot 1972–1973: 179). Connell and Goot despaired the avoidance of political questions and issues. "The investigators rarely ask hard political questions about who benfits, who controls, and who attempts to control, the processes they study. That children have a 'benevolent' image of the political world is mostly a myth. But it is dead certain that political socialization theorists do" (1972–1973: 181).

TOWARD A RADICAL CHALLENGE

A radical challenge to the mainstream theories of political culture and political socialization initially might characterize orthodox conceptions by summarizing the above criticisms. Accordingly, such theories are

- Idealized as capitalist-technological political secularization
- Inadequate, ambiguous, unproven or false in assumption
- Reductionist, culture-bound, nonexplanatory, and descriptive
- Particularistic rather than holistic, speculative
- Static, limited in method, and oriented to passive and conditioned rather than active and spontaneous behavior

Beyond these characterizations, the radical observer might probe into the ideological implications of culture and socialization. Education in particular might be understood to be crucial to state-sponsored socialization. Socialization might be simply some ideological induction into the political system. In the United States, for instance, values and norms of liberal democratic pluralism might be induced into the system so that culture and socialization become not independent of but dependent on the state or system itself. This pervasive diffusion of ideology could contribute to the passivity and false consciousness of the world in which individuals live. Individuals, for example, might be socialized to view needs or problems as unimportant. For an elaboration of these themes, see Bell (1976), Kanth (1978), and Mattelart (1979).

Such problems prompt an exploration of the alternatives to the orthodox conception. A look at the tentative directions suggested by a few writers leads to the conclusion that Marxist theory usefully contributes to a radical view of culture and socialization. The vulgar and humanist Marxist interpretations of culture are examined, and then Marxist theory is assessed in the light of experiences in three socialist countries.

In distinguishing culture from civilization's material and tangible manifestations, Bostock concluded that culture is "an abstract concept, consisting of ideas, and therefore incapable of material observation" (1973: 44). Political culture is made up of central values that give meaning to the individuals who are socialized for it and thus "unwittingly become its transmitters" (48). These observations imply serious consequences for researchers who may manipulate their findings to preserve a status quo society. Connell and Goot (1972–1973) indicted those academics whose world view may be shaped by their class position so that they see working-class children as "incompletely socialized," resulting in feelings of incompetence. Is it surprising, Connell and Goot asked, that such children feel unable to influence a capitalist state? They despaired of the academic effort to contain socialization that might disrupt stable conditions. They cited proposals by Langton (1969) to segregate classes on behalf of a modernizing elite and also cited an admonition by Hess and Torney (1967) that unpleasant aspects of political life should not be revealed too early to U.S. school children. These examples suggest that socialization research stifles the awareness problem by reference to distortions in studies by Easton and Dennis (1969) and by Lane (1959b), which "perpetuate the image that women are more conservative, more apathetic, and more concerned with persons and peripheral 'reform' issues than are men" (Morgan 1974: 54).

Connell and Goot sought an alternative approach to political socialization theory. They recognized that both capitalist and socialist orders may make use of political socialization. The formation of consciousness or false consciousness among the masses may affect both established and revolutionary societies. Rather than suppress the concreteness of the present, Connell and Goot advocated an approach that deals "with people acting in history." This emphasis on political consciousness is found in two strands of Marxist theory: one combines the thought of Marx with that of Georg Lukács and Antonio Gramsci and the other integrates Marxist and Freudian ideas in the thought of Karl Mannheim, Erich Fromm, Herbert Marcuse, and Jean-Paul Sartre. Connell and Goot opted for the latter but raised some questions about the acquisition of delusions or distortions about politics—or false consciousness and the extent to which consciousness is imposed upon a population in relation to patterns of domination and freedom that people have in determining their own choices (1972–1973: 182–187).

The relevance of politics to culture is more likely to be found in a Marxist

framework than in articles in the professional journals of political science, according to John Meisel (1974: 614). Legros (1977) argued that the cultural
evolutionism of U.S. anthropologists is quite inconsistent with Marxist
theory despite assertions to the contrary. Given this state of the disciplines,
we now turn to a discussion of Marxist theories of culture. Two levels, individual and societal, are of especial concern.

The Marxist view of the individual often is dichotomized along two lines.
Marx replaced Hegelian idealism with a concrete interpretation of material
society by rooting analysis in the mode of production and the process of
labor within it. Some Marxists would state that material forces determine
the extent of an individual's consciousness. Kovell (1976) argued that such a
conception is linear and deterministic, relegating people to a situation of
passivity and being unable to act alone. This view, he believed, reflects a
"vulgar" Marxism and is profoundly not Marxist, for the individual under
such conditions "is a robot as ripe for the domination of bureaucratic
socialism as for that of corporate capital" (Kovel 1976: 223). The alternative
view, Marxist humanism, suggests that the individual is shaped not only by
the material conditions of history but also by social activity in the present
and future. People do not exist in passivity, subject to their material relation,
but may become active in transforming their situation.

An extensive debate has evolved around the two views. Most notably
Freudian and Marxist theoreticians have differed in their interpretations,
probably because Freudians usually align themselves with bourgeois society.
Some Marxist scholars, however, have investigated the extent to which
Freudian psychoanalysis is compatible with the historical materialism of
Marx and whether psychoanalysis is compatible with proletarian revolution
and class struggle. Notable in this regard are an essay by Wilhelm Reich
(1966), an assessment of the differences by Kovel (1976), and an overview by
Brown (1973). A Marxist conception of individual and culture as drawn
from Marx's writings will now be outlined.

Marx first dealt with the individual by positing a theory of alienation in
the *Economic and Philosophic Manuscripts*, but in *Capital*, published more
than twenty years later, Marx did not focus on alienation. Thereafter a controversy ensued in which some writers argued that the mature Marx had
abandoned his earlier theory; others insisted that the vital theory was
rooted in the works of the young Marx. This dispute was resolved in part by
the publication of *Grundrisse*, a transitional work and the basis for the ideas
elaborated in *Capital*; therein a theory of alienation is evident (Marx 1973:
161–162, 172–173, 325, 487–488, 540–542). What seems apparent is that
there is both a continuity and an evolution of thought between Marx's
young and mature phases.

A theory of alienation rests upon economic, political, and social conditions, and such a theory may be found in all historical periods. Marx,

however, was interested in alienation in a capitalist society. In particular he examined the consequences for human labor of commodity production, economic scarcity, and social division of work. Essentially, alienation is a reflection of the relations between the classes of owners and workers.

> We have shown that the worker sinks to the level of a commodity, and to a most miserable commodity; that the misery of the worker increases with the power and volume of his production; that the necessary result of competition is the accumulation of capital in a few hands, and thus a restoration of monopoly in a more terrible form; and finally that the distinction between capitalist and landlord, and between agricultural laborer and industrial worker, must disappear and the whole of society divide into the two classes of property *owners* and propertyless *workers*. [Marx 1961: 93]

Implied in a theory of alienation is the possibility of the gradual disappearance of alienation brought about through the creation of conditions for a classless society and a world socialist revolution. It should be clear that such conditions do not exist in capitalist societies today, nor are they found in the Soviet Union and Eastern Europe or in China and Cuba where private property has been abolished for the most part but where society continues to have different social levels, division of labor, and commodity production—thereby permitting alienated labor to persist.

What are the prospects for the elimination of alienation? Bruce Brown (1973) referred to a "new praxis" of practice and theory that begins with an individual's experience with oppression, then turns to the discovery of alienation, and ends with the refusal of alienation through a process in which the self is politicized to attain "a truly social dimension, uniting the struggle for the creation of a new self with the struggle for the creation of a new society" (Brown 1973: 189). Frank Lindenfeld (1973) argued that in highly industrialized societies it is possible to eliminate alienation in work. He assumed that alienation is the consequence of job specialization and bureaucratization in industry under capitalism or socialism. Further, workers may not be conscious of their alienation because they receive high pay and fringe benefits. Lindenfeld believed, however, that work can be satisfying if large factories are decentralized into small units and if democratic self-management is established for the employees. Automated and decentralized production along with a free distribution of the basic necessities of life to all workers can liberate them from the need to work for income. Such an approach, he felt, might be implemented in the United States, where technological capacity could be combined with freely available necessities, voluntary work, and the workers' control of the productive process.

Although Brown alluded to a process in which the individual is politicized to reshape society and Lindenfeld suggested a means of contending directly with alienation, alienated labor and alienated people continue to characterize the contemporary world. Lindenfeld cited the cases of the Spanish Republic in 1936 and Yugoslavia today to illustrate his approach. Other observers might look to the practice of socialism in Europe or China as a solution to the problem. Yet alienation cannot be abolished in those societies without ending commodity production and social division of labor as well as eliminating differences between manual and intellectual labor and between producers and managers. Once these conditions are achieved, the prospects brighten for disalienation and a milieu in which people voluntarily work to provide not only for the needs of themselves and others in the society at large but also to express their talents in creative human activity.

Samir Amin (1977) identified three universal models of social organization and ideological formulation: the North American, the Soviet, and the Chinese. Departing from an analysis of the relations between the economic base and the ideological superstructure, Amin saw the first model as rooted in the capitalist formation and ideology of Europe and its philosophy of the Enlightenment based on a tradition of mechanistic materialism. This tradition assumes that science and technology will diffuse into every aspect of social life and transform social relations until a conscious, nonalienated and classless society emerges. But, argued Amin, "bourgeois 'science' has never transcended this primitive materialism because it conditions the reproduction of alienation, enabling capital to exploit labor" (1977: 27). The other two models are based on Marxism. The Soviet model shares with the first model the ideas that consumption, technology, and labor derive from the development of the productive forces and that capitalism distinguishes itself from socialism in relation to the private or public ownership of the means of production. The Chinese model, in contrast, does not anticipate that socialism can take over capitalism's patterns of consumption and labor.

Each of these models represents a different cultural sphere, according to Amin. In assessing each sphere, a Marxist approach combines materialism with dialectics and thus distinguishes itself from classical interpretations of materialism and from idealism. Marxism "demystifies" materialism and idealism by relating these terms to class struggle. This emphasis on class struggle is essential in a refutation of vulgar Marxism, which postulates, first, that the development of productive forces determines the changes in the relations of production and, second, that the superstructure reflects the demands of the economic base. Instead class struggle alters the relations of production, thus making possible the development of productive forces, and the relationship of base to superstructure must pertain to every mode of production. Amin also refuted the belief of some Marxists that society is governed by "laws": Such laws take us "back to bourgeois philosophy and religion" (1977: 28). Given this perspective, let us now examine culture theory in the experience of three socialist countries: the Soviet Union, China, and Cuba.

The Soviet Union

Marxist analysis concentrates on the mode of production, forces of production, and the social relations of production; thus the concept of culture is applicable to Marxism, not at the level of base but at the level of superstructure. Lenin understood culture as class culture, created in the image of the ruling class. In capitalism, the bourgeoisie uses culture to increase its wealth and to intensify the exploitation of those who work. In imperialism, bourgeois culture undergoes decay, and the cultural level of the population declines. In socialism, culture is directed toward the satisfaction of the needs of the popular masses. Thus Lenin saw culture as generated, on the one hand, in a democratic and socialist culture of the mass of working and exploited people and, on the other, in the ruling culture of the bourgeoisie.

Lenin criticized the use of culture by nationalists:

> The class-conscious workers know that the slogan of "national culture" is clerical or bourgeois bluff . . . when nations were not yet divided into bourgeoisie and proletariat, the slogan of national culture could be an unifying and total call to battle against feudalism and clericalism. But since then the class struggle of the bourgeoisie and the proletariat has broken out everywhere. The split of the "united" nation into exploiters and the exploited has become an accomplished fact. Only clericals or bourgeois can talk about national culture at all. The working masses can talk only about the international culture of the world movement of workers. [quoted in Meyer 1952: 214]

In this sense culture implies a struggle against bourgeois ideology, art, and philosophy. Culture involves socialization and resocialization. It also signifies leisure activities and enjoyment in the broadest context. International culture seeks to raise class consciousness and to make all people into proletarians.

Lenin developed his conception of class culture in the early years of the Russian revolution. Stalin modified that conception by giving attention to the national traditions and the many nationalities of the Soviet Union. His recognition of national culture transcended the use of culture by Lenin and Marx and juxtaposed his "national" position with the "international" stance of Lenin. Stalin developed a theory of nations in which he attacked reformist nationalism, for example, the tendency to substitute national for revolutionary aims. Stalin also set forth a theory of national minorities, calling an ethnic group a national minority if it did not possess the characteristics of a nation; the Jews of Russia, for example, constituted a national minority.

Stalin's theory of national minorities did not pertain to colonies, which Lenin incorporated into his theory of imperialism. Lenin associated bourgeois nationalism with oppressor nations in an age of imperialism, whereas nationalism in the oppressed nations took the form of a struggle for national liberation. Stalin's theory of national minorities has been described as incompatible with Lenin's theory of imperialism. The theory of national minorities, it is argued, was useful for describing an early period of rising capitalism in Europe; in contrast, a theory of imperialism includes all nations under contemporary capitalism and imperialism. These different theories have influenced the varying perspectives on national culture, from the melting-pot notion, in which immigrants lose their original nationalities and became ethnic minorities within the new nation, to the idea that the conditions of national assimilation are giving way to an increased imperialist exploitation and oppression of workers in a colony such as Puerto Rico (Blaut 1977).

The shaping of a socialist culture is dependent upon changes in education and ideology. Orthodox political scientists have failed to combine these considerations with the theoretical perspectives of Marx, Lenin, and Stalin on the questions of national and class culture. Kenneth Jowitt (1974), for example, differentiated three types of political culture: elite, regime, and community political culture—these types are described in jargonistic terms and are not effectively utilized in his analysis. However, he turned to tasks that shape the character of a regime and its relationship to socialist society. He identified attempts to transform or destroy values and behaviors as well as efforts to define problems and politics along procedural lines. He also examined the ideological commitment of Marxist-Leninist regimes to such principles as the dictatorship of the proletariat and democratic centralism. He concluded that most Marxist-Leninist regimes continue today to use the authoritative model shaped by Stalin.

If an authoritative model was shaped by Stalin, what then was the nature of political socialization in the Soviet Union? Robert W. Clawson (1973) examined the early childhood experiences of Russian children in family and preschool institutions. He was concerned with how one generation shapes the political standards and beliefs of successive generations, and he examined six historical periods. At the outset of the Russian revolution three groups with differing viewpoints prevailed: "radical-communalists," based in Petrograd (Leningrad), who favored the early separation of children from the conservative prerevolutionary milieu of the average family; "traditionalists," who supported the system of child rearing and education that prevailed prior to the revolution; and the "progressive-individualists," who favored freedom for the individual youth to develop according to personal motivations.

During 1917 to 1921 the Soviet leadership, including Lenin, hesitated to intervene in education, and the period was characterized by "decentralized experimentation" and "pedagogical anarchy." During 1921 to 1932 the progressive-individualists intervened, and the radical-communalists were virtually eliminated; emphasis centered on liberating the individual child and in eliminating competition between individuals. There followed, from 1932 to 1936, a period of transition to discipline under Stalin. Experimentalism was abolished as "collective-traditionalists" took command to advocate a traditional approach toward learning, including a formal curriculum, texts, exams, grades, and discipline as well as respect for traditional parental authority. From 1936 to 1953 there was official recognition of the significance of the family experience for the child. The collective-traditionalist pattern received broad exposure along with conservative family legislation, which placed constraints on divorce and abortion. This promotion of a stable family continued under Khrushchev, from 1953 to 1964, although there was an abandonment of the inculcation of a Stalinist image.

The end of that period reflected the rise and influence of a new group of data-oriented "empirical-progressives." Today, according to Clawson, Soviet education specialists recognize that deliberate political socialization during early childhood is ineffective, and they continue to stress the role of the family in the socializing experience. Clawson believed that changes in the family's role as political socializers will be more the consequence of the impact of urbanization (affecting housing, income distribution, and the like) than of official intervention into the affairs of the family.

> The likelihood of any substantial change in future specific Soviet policy toward the existence of the family is slight, if only because the radical communalist impulse seems to be rare in both the population as a whole and within the ruling elite. In addition, the ideological roots found in Marxist literature on the child-rearing family have been ignored by virtually everyone who has ever held top political power in the USSR. [Clawson 1973: 711]

Despite these trends, writers in the Soviet Union and Eastern Europe during the past decade have turned their attention to questions about the individual and the meaning of life. This renaissance of a Marxist humanism has centered around Marx's *Economic and Philosophical Manuscripts* and was a response to the constraining influences of the Stalin period.

One of those Marxists, Adam Schaff of Poland, wrote: "Marxism is humanism, a *radical* humanism" (Schaff 1970: 168). Schaff believed that Marxist humanism is autonomous in the sense that the individual creates his or her own development. The Marxist humanism is militant and committed and therefore rooted in practice. Marxist humanism thus is revolutionary in its struggle against the dehumanization of life. These characteristics suggest a theory of the new person. Such theory has been explicitly related to the experiences of China and Cuba.

China

After Mao and the Chinese revolutionaries came to power in 1949, they initially were influenced by the Stalinist orthodoxy and attempted to emulate the Soviet model of building heavy industry while deemphasizing light industry and the production of consumer goods. Application of this model in the Soviet Union had diverted attention from the peasantry, thus interfering with efforts to tie the peasant and working classes into an alliance. At the same time a repressive state emerged. The Chinese soon discovered that such a model was unrealistic in light of their concern with agriculture and the peasantry. Thus priorities were rearranged so that industry was related to agriculture, located in the countryside as well as in the cities, and employed surplus rural labor. Thus the capital or surplus needed to develop the Chinese economy was generated from increases in the productivity of all Chinese labor, agricultural and industrial alike. This made possible an alliance of worker and peasant. At the same time a repressive state was not necessary.

The Chinese revolution incorporated class struggle: first, in the overthrow of the old ruling and exploiting classes; second, in efforts to eradicate the counterrevolutionary ideas of the elites who took the place of the old ruling classes but continued to espouse their values and behavior; and, finally, in contending with the bureaucratic and vested interests of the administrators, managers, and technicians who run the postrevolutionary society. Thus it is a myth that the abolition of private property in the means of production will necessarily result in a classless society harmoniously evolving toward socialism.

Under Chinese socialism the ongoing class struggle aims not only to raise the material level of the population but also to promote the development of human beings on an equalitarian basis. According to John Gurley, a Maoist perspective places value on breaking down specialization, dismantling bureaucracies, and undermining centralizing and divisive tendencies.

> The proletarian world view, which Maoists believe must replace that of the bourgeoisie, stresses that only through struggle can progress be made; the selflessness and unity of purpose will release a huge reservoir of enthusiasm, energy, and creativeness; that active participation by "the masses" in decision-making will provide them with the knowledge to channel their energy most productively; and that elimination of specialization will not only increase workers' and peasants' willingness to work hard for the various goals of society

but will also increase their ability to do this by adding to their knowledge and awareness of the world around them. [Gurley 1971: 19]

Thus will emerge the new person, the making of the "Communist man," thereby eroding the alienation that besets human beings everywhere (Gurley 1970).

Cuba

With the triumph of the Cuban revolution in 1959, Ché Guevara placed emphasis on individual sacrifice in a collective society. "It is rather that the individual feels greater fulfillment, that he has greater inner wealth and many more responsibilities. In our country the individual knows that the glorious period in which it has fallen to him to live is one of sacrifice" (Guevara 1967: 42). Sacrifice implies overcoming feelings of individualism and placing emphasis, above all else, on a sense of solidarity among people. Political beings must be politically conscious and socially responsible, devoid of vestiges of selfishness and egotism. The new person must work for the benefit of the collectivity and must struggle against injustice and against the exploitation of person by person and the division of society into classes.

In Cuba, alienation was to disappear with the formation of the new person. Alienation did not disappear, however, with the break in Cuba's dependent relations with the capitalist world. Nor did it dissolve with the nationalization of the principal means of production and the shift from private to state ownership.

Alienation did diminish with the Cuban emphasis on changing patterns of consumption. All persons who so desired were given an opportunity to work. At the same time basic necessities for the population were provided to assure at least a minimally sufficient material standard of living. Income differences continued to exist, but luxury consumer goods were not available for purchase. Economic gains were not distributed to a few but to many through an increasing variety of goods and services, which were either free or made available without reference to income. Rather than being bombarded with media messages designed to create a desire for material goods, Cubans were encouraged to find satisfaction in contributing to their society.

Along with the changing consumption patterns was an emphasis on moral rather than material incentives. Workers would contribute to the development of the revolution rather than to their own personal gain. The new work ethic was the worker's desire to serve society, not the individual. Monetary incentives such as extra pay and bonuses would be reduced and eventually eliminated in favor of awards and special recognition. Although some material incentives were introduced during the early 1970s, Cuba persisted in its drive to reshape its political culture and the formation of the new person. Education encouraged workers to aspire to *conciencia*, a conscious commitment to the revolution (Fagen 1969). Education in the schools was mixed with work in the field. Further, the tasks of people were mixed so that rural people worked alongside urban people, the old with the young, bureaucrats with field laborers, and so on. In sum, Cuba strived to become one encompassing school, with individuals trained in the necessary skills and a conscious awareness relevant to becoming new persons.

PROSPECTS FOR A THEORY OF POLITICAL CULTURE

Orthodox theories of political culture continue to dominate and influence study and research in comparative politics today. We have examined the general theories of political culture that evolved during the late 1950s and have found that such underlying premises as civic virtue, pluralist democracy, rational bureaucracy, and stability tended to reflect ideal rather than real situations and were biased in terms of Anglo-American experience.

This chapter has looked at the specific applications of political culture, notably in communications and socialization studies. It has noted that communication studies tend to concentrate on the mass media as socializing agents and also that orthodox models of communication are based on developmental theory, which assumes an evolution of society from a traditional to a transitional and ultimately to a modern stage. In recent years comparativists have concentrated their studies on political socialization, and their work has focused on childhood and adolescent learning. Further, their formulations are static and culture-bound and emulate the liberal democratic theory of mainstream political science. For example, researchers uncover patterns of political attitudes that reflect socialization in stable and so-called democratic societies, then apply their findings to the less developed nations of the Third World.

In all these areas orthodox theory lacks explanatory promise. Studies are classificatory and descriptive rather than analytical. Political culture is conceived of in ideal form as a civic culture. Change is incremental and gradual. Rather than being independent of the political system, political culture instead depends on the system.

If orthodox theory remains limited in its contributions, what then are the prospects for a radical theory of political culture? Some of the radical alternatives to an orthodox conception of political culture and socialization have been assessed, and a distinction between vulgar and humanist Marxist conceptions has been made.

In general, a Marxist perspective perceives the orthodox understanding of political culture and socialization as one manifestation of the ideological superstructure of a bourgeois capitalist society. A Marxist perspective also identifies the bourgeois tendencies that may underlie the ongoing class struggle of societies in transition from capitalism to socialism. In this way alienation, consumption patterns, and work incentives may be assessed within a radical context. Ultimately, a Marxist orientation seeks the formation of the "new" person in a socialist or communist society. The new person implies a reshaping of the culture so as to eliminate specialization of work and sectarian bureaucracies and to ensure participatory democracy and unifying tendencies. Although some Marxists assume that the abolition of private property in the means of production will inevitably produce a classless society, the experiences of socialist nations demonstrate this not to be valid. What has emerged in countries such as China and Cuba is a theory that assumes the substitution of a bourgeois world view with a proletarian world view. Such a world view envisions the eradication of alienation and the promotion of selflessness, commitment, and creativeness on behalf of the society and culture at large.

References

Aberle, D. F.
    1961 "Culture and Socialization." In F.L.K. Hsu (ed.), *Psychological Anthropology*, pp. 381–399. Homewood, Illinois: Dorsey Press. Analysis of variations in agents, aims, techniques, and timing of socialization and the impact of culture upon these aspects

Agger, Robert E., Miroslav Disman, Zdravko Mlinar, and Vladimir Sultanovic
    1970 "Education, General Personal Orientations, and Community Involvement: A Cross-National Research Project." *Comparative Political Studies* III (April), 90–116. Description of research design and results of a comparative project that examined the personal orientation of adults in the United States, Czechoslovakia, and the two Yugoslav republics of Bosnia and Slovenia.

Almond, Gabriel A.
    1956 "Comparative Political Systems." *Journal of Politics* XVIII (August), 391–409. Almond first introduced the concept of political culture in this article.

Almond, Gabriel A., and G. Bingham Powell, Jr.
    1966 *Comparative Politics: A Developmental Approach*. Boston: Little, Brown and Co. Defines political culture as the "psychological dimension of the political system. . . . It consists of attitudes, beliefs, values, and skills which are current in an entire population, as well as those special propensities and patterns which may be found within separate parts of that population."

Almond, Gabriel A., and Sidney Verba
    1963 *The Civic Culture: Political Attitudes and Democracy in Five Nations.*

Princeton: Princeton University Press. A classic study of political culture, based on a survey of attitudes in Great Britain, Germany, Italy, Mexico, and the United States. Theory and method are set forth, and patterns, social relations, and profiles of political culture are analyzed.

Amin, Samir
1977 "Universality and Cultural Spheres." *Monthly Review* XXVIII (February), 25–38. A Marxist view and critique of models of social organization (North American, Soviet, Chinese) and the ideological formulations that sustain them.

Argyle, Michael, and Peter Delin
1965 "Non-Universal Laws of Socialization." *Human Relations* XVIII (February), 77–86. Socialization is examined in relation to variables of sex, personality traits, warmth of relationship with parents, strictness, and social class in order to determine if socialization is governed by laws. The authors conclude that laws of socialization are not universal but apply only to members of certain subpopulations.

Baker, Donald G.
1971 "Political Socialization: Parameters and Predispositions." *Polity* III (Summer), 586–600. A review of six recent books and two articles dealing with political socialization. Examines these studies for their "nomothetic," "ahistorical," and "spatiotemporal" biases.

Banfield, Edward C.
1961 *Political Influence.* New York: Free Press. The introductory chapter sets forth a conceptualization for a study of influence in Chicago.

Bell, Daniel
1976 *The Cultural Contradictions of Capitalism.* New York: Basic Books. A conservative perspective, critical of bourgeois and liberal capitalism, which finds contradictions within three segments of society: the techno-economic structure, the polity, and the culture.

Bender, Gerald J.
1967 "Political Socialization and Political Change." *Western Political Quarterly* XX (June), 390–407. Provides a summation of contemporary political socialization research, with attention to agencies of socialization, process of socialization, time span of process, and level of change.

Blau, Peter
1960 "A Theory of Social Integration." *American Journal of Sociology* LXV (May), 545–556. Presents a theory based on empirical study of competition and differentiation among groups that seek integrative ties. This use of social integration contributes to an understanding of the term political aggregation, used by Almond and others.

Blaut, James
1977 "Are Puerto Ricans a National Minority?" *Monthly Review* XXIX (May), 35–55. Clearly distinguishes between the theories of Stalin and Lenin on national minority and culture. Turns to Lenin in an interpretation of the Puerto Rican situation.

Bostock, William
1973 "The Cultural Explanation of Politics." *Political Science* XXV (July), 37–48. Questions assumptions about political culture. Among conclusions is the observa-

tion that Almond and Verba have applied descriptive rather than analytic criteria—they employ no theoretical construct.

Bowman, Lewis, and G. R. Boynton
1974 *Political Behavior and Public Opinion: Comparative Analyses.* Englewood Cliffs, New Jersey: Prentice-Hall. Previously published essays are combined in a reader on political culture and socialization (essays by Hess, Dennis, Zeitlin, and others), political participation, and voting decision.

Brown, Bruce
1973 *Marx, Freud, and the Critique of Everyday Life.* New York: Monthly Review Press. Explores the subjective and psychological dimensions of the revolutionary process. Reviews literature and ideas that attempt to assimilate Freudianism into a broader framework of historical materialism.

Chaffee, Steven H., L. Scott Ward, and Leonard P. Tipton
1970 "Mass Communication and Political Socialization." *Journalism Quarterly* (Winter), 647–659, 666. A focus on the mass media as agents of political socialization, with attention to a sample of 1,291 students in five Wisconsin cities.

Clausen, John A. et al.
1968 *Socialization and Society.* Boston: Little, Brown and Co. A collection of essays emanating from the work of the Social Science Research Council's Committee on Socialization and Social Structure. The authors, drawn from the fields of sociology and psychology, include Clausen (in introduction) dealing with concept and field as well as a historical and comparative view of socialization theory and research; Alex Inkeles on child socialization; Orville Brim on adult socialization; and Ronald Lippitt on improving the socialization process.

Clawson, Robert W.
1973 "Political Socialization of Children in the USSR." *Political Science Quarterly* LXXXVIII (December), 684–712. A review of sparse and recent political socialization studies of children in the Soviet Union as well as a chronological discussion and summary of Soviet socialization policies, in family and in education, since 1917. One conclusion suggests that "Soviet political behavior . . . is more likely to be influenced by the indirect effects of urbanization than by regime-sponsored, deliberate political socialization."

Coleman, James S. (ed.)
1965 *Education and Political Development.* Princeton: Princeton University Press. Collection of essays sponsored by the Committee on Comparative Politics of the Social Science Research Council. The authors attempt to analyze the relationship between education and political development. This volume includes an excellent overview by Coleman as well as an extensive bibliographic guide to education and political socialization.

Connell, R. W., and Murray Goot
1972–1973 "Science and Ideology in American 'Political Socialization' Research." *Berkeley Journal of Sociology* XVII, 165–193. A critique of the aims, methods, and conclusions of political socialization research. Sketch of a different approach, a radical one, to deal with similar problems.

Cook, Thomas, and Frank Scioli, Jr.
1972 "A Critique of the Learning Concept in Political Socialization Research." *Social Science Quarterly* LII (March), 946–962. Examines a central but neglected

segment of political socialization research, the learning concept. Sets forth a research strategy for use of that concept in studies of political socialization.

Cornelius, Wayne A.

1973 *Political Learning Among the Migrant Poor: The Impact of Residential Context.* Beverly Hills, California: Sage Publications. Sage Papers in Comparative Politics (01-037). Focus on low-income urban communities as agents of political socialization, based on a sample of 747 male heads of family residing in six low-income communities within the periphery of Mexico City.

Czudnowski, Moshe M.

1968 "A Salience Dimension of Politics for the Study of Political Culture." *American Political Science Review* LXII (September), 878-888. Presents an "operational" conception of the salience of politics within the framework of comparative cultural analysis. Discussion focuses on the application of concept to the studies of others rather than to the author's own empirical study.

Davies, James C.

1965 "The Family's Role in Political Socialization." *Annals* CCCLXI (September), 10-19. Focuses on the role of the family in socializing the child to identify with patterns of the larger society.

Dawson, Richard E., and Kenneth Prewitt

1968 *Political Socialization.* Boston: Little, Brown and Co. Foreword by Almond, James S. Coleman, and Lucian W. Pye. Influenced by the early formulations of Almond and Coleman on political culture and system, the authors offer an examination of the political self, political culture, methods of political learning, and agents of political learning.

Dennis, Jack

1968 "Major Problems of Political Socialization Research." *Midwest Journal of Political Science* XII (January), 85-114. Identifies and discusses ten problems: the system relevance of political socialization, its content, life-cycle patterns, generational differences, cross-cultural comparisons, subgroup and subcultural variations, the political learning process, the agencies of political socialization, the extent of its impact upon individuals, and specialized political socialization.

1973a *Political Socialization Research: A Bibliography.* Beverly Hills, California: Sage Publications. Professional Papers in American Politics (04-002). A useful and comprehensive bibliography of the literature on political socialization.

1973b *Socialization to Politics.* New York: Wiley and Sons. An anthology of previously published material by the major writers on political socialization. Includes three cross-national studies and useful introductory and concluding essays by the editor.

1975 "Political Socialization." *DEN News* 7 (Fall), s-6-9. Proposes that political socialization be offered as the first course in a political science curriculum; gives an outline and bibliography for such a course.

Dennis, Jack, and M. Kent Jennings (eds.)

1970 "Political Socialization." *Comparative Political Studies* III (July), 135-263. Entire issue devoted to political socialization, including comparative attention to Japan by Akira Kubota and Robert E. Ward; Chile and Peru by Daniel Goldrich;

Tanzania by Kenneth Prewitt et al.; Britain, Germany, and the United States by Judith Gallatin and Joseph Adelson; and Western democracies by Jack Dennis and Donald J. McCrone.

Dennis, Jack, Leon Lindberg, Donald McCrone, and Rodney Stiefbold
1968 "Political Socialization to Democratic Orientations in Four Western Systems." *Comparative Political Studies* I (April), 71–101. Empirical study of pre-adult political socialization in the United States, Britain, Italy, and Germany; in particular looks at commitment to or disenchantment with democratic norms and institutions in the four countries.

Deutsch, Karl W.
1961 "Social Mobilization and Political Development." *American Political Science Review* LV (September), 493–514. Relates mobilization to processes of change and identifies indicators and political effects of social mobilization.

1963 *The Nerves of Government: Models of Political Communication and Control.* New York: Free Press of Glencoe. A survey of communications theory, influenced by Wiener's theory of cybernetics.

1965 *Nationalism and Social Communication: An Inquiry into the Foundations of Nationality.* Cambridge, Massachusetts: M.I.T. Press. A classic study of nationalism and its implications for the contemporary world as related to communication theory. First published in 1953.

Dodge, Richard W., and Eugene S. Uyeki
1962 "Political Affiliation and Imagery Across Two Related Generations: Socialization and Children's Attitudes." *Midwest Journal of Political Science* VI (August), 266–276. Analysis of 175 interviews of students and one or the other of their parents, with a particular look at their partisan positions.

Doob, Leonard W.
1964 *Patriotism and Nationalism: Their Psychological Foundations.* New Haven: Yale University Press. Personality characteristics are projected to patriotism and nationalism in nation-states.

Easton, David, and Jack Dennis
1965 "The Child's Image of Government." *Annals* CCCLXI (September), 40–57. Based on a massive survey of children in the United States, the data presented suggests that "a supportive image of government is being widely and regularly reproduced for young new members."

1967 "The Child's Acquisition of Regime Norms: Political Efficacy." *American Political Science Review* LXI (March), 25–38. Empirical study of political efficacy as a norm in the U.S. political system. Argues for comparative research on primary political socialization.

1969 *Children in the Political System: Origins of Political Legitimacy.* New York: McGraw-Hill Book Company. An examination of the political socialization of children, based on a survey and data collected jointly with Robert Hess (Hess and Torney 1967). The authors are particularly concerned with the relationship of political socialization and the political system, and they focus on the structure of authority as well.

Easton, David, and Robert D. Hess
1962 "The Child's Political World." *Midwest Journal of Political Science* VI (August), 229–246. Sets forth some theoretical formulations and analysis on pretesting data for a national study in areas of political socialization of 12,000 elementary school children.

Edelman, Murray
1967 *Symbolic Uses of Politics*. Urbana: University of Illinois Press. This incisive study of symbols and politics contributes to an understanding of communication and political culture.

Eisenstadt, S. N.
1955 "Communication Systems and Social Structure: An Exploratory Comparative Study." *Public Opinion Quarterly* XIX (Summer), 153–167. Compares four immigrant communities in Israel, including three rural or semirural communities of Algerians, Tunisians, and Moroccans; Yemenites; and Yugoslavs. In addition one urban quarter was studied. "Technical," "cognitive," and "normative" communications are examined.

1964 *From Generation to Generation: Age Groups and Social Structure*. New York: Free Press of Glencoe, Collier-Macmillan. Influenced by Parsons, the author synthesizes studies and research of age groups in different types of societies. He is interested in biological as well as cultural processes in the transition through age stages and from generation to generation.

Fagen, Richard R.
1964 "Relation of Communication Growth to National Political Systems in the Less Developed Countries." *Journalism Quarterly* XXXI (Winter), 87–94. Empirical study of communication data in fifty countries, which are classified into four political types.

1966 *Politics and Communication*. Boston: Little, Brown and Co. An introduction to communications and comparative politics. Examines components of communication networks, determinants of communication patterns and uses, political images, and other aspects.

1969 *The Transformation of Political Culture in Cuba*. Stanford: Stanford University Press. An examination of the changing political culture in Cuba through an analysis of the literacy campaign, the committees for defense of the revolution, and the schools of revolutionary instruction.

Froman, L. A., Jr.
1961 "Personality and Political Socialization." *Journal of Politics* XXIII (May), 341–352. Offers prior conceptualization in an effort to develop a theory of socialization. Adopts Hyman's definition of political socialization, then relates that definition to the concepts of environment, personality, and behavior.

Greenstein, Fred I.
1965a *Children and Politics*. New Haven: Yale University Press. Empirical study of early childhood political socialization in New Haven.

1965b "Personality and Political Socialization: The Theories of Authoritarian and Democratic Character." *Annals* CCCLXI (September), 81–95. Examines non-political personal development, which culminates in adult citizenship. Reviews the theory and research on "democratic " and "authoritarian" character types, exposes flaws in this "old" socialization literature, and suggests care in conceptualization.

1967a "Impact of Personality on Politics: An Attempt to Clear Away Under-brush." *American Political Science Review* LXI (September), 629–641. Examination of five "intellectually challenging assertions about the lack of relevance of 'personality' to the endeavors of the student of politics." Shows that two of the assertions are based on misconception, and the others can be rephrased so as to advance propositions about how personality affects political behavior.

1967b "Personality and Politics: Problems of Evidence, Inference, and Conceptualization." *American Behavioral Scientist* XI (November-December), 38–53. A look at politics and personality through examining the literature and noting conceptual distinctions and observations about research strategy. Groups personality and politics literature into three categories: psychological case histories of single political actors, psychological studies of types of political actors, and aggregative accounts of the collective effects of the distribution of individual political actors on the functioning of political institutions.

1968 "Political Socialization." In *International Encyclopedia of Social Sciences* XV, pp. 551–555. New York: Macmillan and Free Press Publishing Company. Excellent summary of conceptualization of political socialization.

1970 "Research Notes: A Note on the Ambiguity of 'Political Socialization': Definitions, Criticisms, and Strategies of Inquiry." *Journal of Politics* XXXII (November), 969–978. Identifies four usages of political socialization to demonstrate ambiguity. Suggests three criticisms of the concept, including conservative bias, the inability to predict behavior, and the failure to relate the study of political socialization to general theories of human development.

1975 "The Benevolent Leader Revisited: Children's Images of Political Leaders in Three Democracies." *American Political Science Review* LXIX (December), 1371–1398. Follow-up study to that of Greenstein and Tarrow (1970), utilizing semiprojective interviews with children in Britain, France, and the United States.

Greenstein, Fred I., and Sidney Tarrow

    1970 *Political Orientations of Children: The Use of a Semi-Projective Technique in Three Nations.* Beverly Hills, California: Sage Publications. Sage Comparative Politics Series (01-009). Study of political socialization of children in Britain, France, and the United States. Reviews semiprojective interview technique and presents preliminary data.

Guevara, Ernesto Ché

    1967 *Man and Socialism in Cuba.* Havana: Book Institute. Originally in the form of a letter, Guevara refers to the difficult task of creating a new human being in harmony with the new society.

Gurley, John

    1970 "The New Man in the New China: Maoist Economic Development." *Center Magazine* III (May), 25–33. Affirms that capitalist development, even when successful, is trickle-down development. Then he elaborates on the Maoist differences with capitalist development and distinguishes between their proletarian world view and that of the bourgeois in the Western world.

1971 "Capitalist and Maoist Economic Development." *Monthly Review* XXII (February), 15–35. Outlines clearly the distinctions between capitalist and Maoist development, including a section on the making of Communist man.

Hardgrave, Robert L., Jr.

1969 "Political Culture and Projective Techniques." *Comparative Political Studies* II (July), 249–255. A look at various approaches to political culture as well as at projective techniques that explore unconscious or latent aspects of personality. The author then reviews his study of twelve individuals of the Nadar caste in South India, modeled after an interview schedule used by Robert Lane.

Havighurst, Robert J. (ed.)

1968 *Comparative Perspectives on Education.* Boston: Little, Brown and Co. Comparative essays on education in a variety of societies: a preliterate society of the Hopi Indians; modern societies such as in France, the Soviet Union, Japan, and Brazil; transitional societies such as in China and Ghana; and religious societies. Twenty-two essays by different authors.

Hess, Robert D.

1963 "The Socialization of Attitudes Toward Political Authority: Some Cross-National Comparisons." *International Social Science Journal* XV (4), 542–559. Suggests a connection between the child's view of the family and the child's views of nonfamily authority figures. Extends his discussion from his own study of children's views of the president in the United States to findings of other studies of children's views of authority figures in Chile, Puerto Rico, Australia, and Japan.

Hess, Robert D., and Roberta Meyer Bear (eds.)

1968 *Early Education: Current Theory, Research, and Practice.* Chicago: Aldine Publishing Co. Papers presented to a conference in 1966, sponsored by the Committee on Learning and the Educational Process of the Social Science Research Council. Emphasis on specific aspects of preschool education.

Hess, Robert D., and Judith V. Torney

1967 *The Development of Political Attitudes in Children.* Chicago: Aldine Publishing Co. The results of a massive survey of children in eight cities in the four regions of the United States are analyzed in an attempt to examine "the ways that individuals learn to interact with these large segments of the social system."

Hitchner, Dell Gillette

1968 "Political Science and Political Culture." *Western Political Quarterly* XXI (December), 551–559. Presidential address to the Pacific Northwest Political Science Association. An appeal to study the cultural aspects of politics in a comparative perspective.

Hughes, Delos D., and Edward L. Pinney

1966 "Political Culture and the Idioms of Political Development." In Edward L. Pinney (ed.), *Comparative Politics and Political Theory*, pp. 67–96. Chapel Hill: University of North Carolina Press. Affirms that the results of studies that use political culture as a concept do not measure up to their promise, primarily because they concern themselves with conceptualization rather than with operationalization. Examines the links of political culture to political development.

Hyman, Herbert H.
1959 *Political Socialization: A Study in the Psychology of Political Behavior.* New York: Free Press of Glencoe. A pioneering synthesis of political socialization literature, which stimulated a plethora of studies. Focuses on psychological aspects of politics. Examines subgroup differentiations in pre-adult life, processes underlying particular socialization patterns, agencies of socialization into politics, political stability, and change in socialization.

Inkeles, Alex
1961 "National Character and Modern Political Systems." In Francis L. K. Hsu (ed.), *Psychological Anthropology*, pp. 172–208. Homewood, Illinois: Dorsey Press. A review of definitions (national character as institutional pattern, as culture theme, and as action) and empirical studies of national character. Concerned with the relationship of national character to modern political systems, specifically to the establishment and maintenance of democracy.

1969 "Participant Citizenship in Six Developing Countries." *American Political Science Review* LXIII (December), 1120–1141. Tests assumptions and concepts of participant citizenship (which are known in advanced countries) in Argentina, Chile, India, Israel, Nigeria, and East Pakistan (Bangladesh).

Inkeles, Alex, and Daniel Levinson
1954 "National Character: The Study of Model Personality and Socio-Cultural Systems." In Gardner Lindzey (ed.), *Handbook of Social Psychology*, vol. 2, pp. 977–1020. Cambridge, Massachusetts: Addison-Wesley. Representative of the culture-personality or psychocultural approach to the study of politics, which Almond and Verba's concept of political culture attempts to supplant. Here the authors systematically review the literature of "national character," "personality structure," and "social character."

Jaeger, Gertrude, and Philip Selznick
1964 "A Normative Theory of Culture." *American Sociological Review* XXIX (October), 653–669. Searches for a theoretical synthesis of humanism and social science concepts of culture. Argues for a view of culture as expressive symbolism.

Jahoda, Gustav
1963 "The Development of Children's Ideas About Country and Nationality." *British Journal of Educational Psychology* XXXIII (June), 143–153. Compares political socialization of children in the United States and Western Europe.

Jaros, Dean
1973 *Socialization to Politics.* New York: Praeger Publishers. A sympathetic review of the literature of political socialization, with attention to concept, objects, limits of political socialization; family, school, and peer group; theory; and prospects.

Jaros, Dean, Herbert Hirsch, and Frederic J. Fleron, Jr.
1968 "The Malevolent Leader: Political Socialization in an American Sub-Culture." *American Political Science Review* LXII (June), 654–675. Empirical study of 2,432 children in the Appalachian region of eastern Kentucky.

Jennings, M. Kent
1967 "Pre-Adult Orientations to Multiple Systems of Government." *Midwest Jour-*

nal of Political Science XI (August), 291–317. Analysis and results of a national survey of high school students in the United States.

Jennings, M. Kent, and Richard G. Niemi
1968 "The Transmission of Political Values from Parent to Child." *American Political Science Review* LXII (March), 169–184. Based on a sample of 1,669 high school seniors, the authors examine the transmission of values from parent to child and offer a qualified conclusion that parents exert less influence than other socializing agents, such as mass media.

Jones, Ruth S.
1971 "Teachers as Agents of Political Socialization." *Education and Urban Society* IV (November), 100–114. Based on a questionnaire administered to teachers in the school district of a community of 50,000 population, the author concludes that schools and teachers have a tremendous potential for political socialization.

Jowitt, Kenneth
1974 "An Organizational Approach to the Study of Political Culture in Marxist-Leninist Systems." *American Political Science Review* LXVIII (September), 1171–1191. Reviews orientations and definitions of political culture, then outlines an analytic framework to study political culture in Marxist-Leninist regimes.

Kanth, Rajani
1978 "Political Culture Revisited: Notes on a Coercive Ideology." *Indian Journal of Political Studies* XXXIX (January–March), 89–98. Attacks the concept of political culture and political culture studies as a reflection of imperialist intervention in the internal affairs of the Third World.

Kievit, M. B.
1964 "Social Participation and Some Demographic Variables." *Journal of Social Psychology* LXIV (December), 355–368. Details of a study of 377 respondents in an effort to analyze their social participation in organizations.

Kim, Young C.
1964 "The Concept of Political Culture in Comparative Politics." *Journal of Politics* XXVI (May), 313–336. A review of definition and meaning in the literature of political culture, with particular attention to Almond, Beer, and Macridis.

Kluckhohn, Clyde
1962 *Culture and Behavior: The Collected Papers of Clyde Kluckhohn.* Edited by Richard Kluckhohn. New York: Free Press of Glencoe. Collection of essays representing the contributions of Kluckhohn to the anthropological theory of culture.

1964 "Culture." In Julius Gould and William Kolb (eds.), *Dictionary of the Social Sciences*, pp. 165–168. New York: Free Press of Glencoe. Synthesis of past conceptions and trends related to culture and its analysis.

Koplin, Roberta E.
1968 "A Model of Student Politicization in the Developing Nations." *Comparative Political Studies* I (October), 373–390. Offers definitions and a model for the study of the politicization of students in developing nations.

Kovel, Joel
1976 "The Marxist View of Man and Psychoanalysis." *Social Research* XLIII (Sum-

mer), 220–245. Examines the Marxist view of man, the limits of Marxist psychology, and the compatibility of Marxism and Freudianism.

Kroeber, Alfred L.
1952 *The Nature of Culture.* Chicago: University of Chicago Press. A major anthropological conception of the term culture, based on an anthology of fifty of the author's previous writings. Eighteen essays in the first part focus on a theory of culture.

Kroeber, Alfred L., and Clyde Kluckhohn
1952 *Culture: A Critical Review of Concepts and Definitions.* Cambridge, Massachusetts: Peabody Museum. A review of nearly a century of definitions and conceptions of the term culture. Begins with an historical overview of the term, then identifies definitions according to six categories: descriptive, historical, normative, psychological, structural, genetic.

Kroeber, Alfred L., and Talcott Parsons
1958 "The Concepts of Culture and of Social System." *American Sociological Review* XXIII (October), 582–583. Announcement of their agreement to distinguish between culture and society in an effort to give direction to the content of social science theory. See Ogles, Levy, and Parsons (1959) for communications on this subject.

Kuroda, Yasumasa
1965 "Agencies of Political Socialization and Political Change." *Human Organization* XXIV (Winter), 328–331. Findings of an empirical study that tests the hypothesis that there is a weak correlation between the political preference of Japanese law students and that of their parents.

Lane, Robert E.
1959a "Fathers and Sons: Foundations of Political Belief." *American Sociological Review* XXIV (August), 502–511. Analysis of depth interviews with fifteen men, which concludes that U.S. culture discourages youthful rebellion against the father as well as the society at large. The relationship of fathers and sons in the United States contributes to several features of U.S. politics: high consensus, great interest and information combined with low emotional commitment, and strong idealism in foreign affairs.

1959b *Political Life: Why People Get Involved in Politics.* New York: Free Press of Glencoe. A classic study of political participation, based on the U.S. experience. Chapter 19 deals with mass media and mass politics.

Langton, Kenneth P.
1967 "Peer Group and School and the Political Socialization Process." *American Political Science Review* LXI (September), 751–758. Examination of the peer group and school as agents in the political socialization process.

1969 *Political Socialization: Studies in Behavioral Political Science.* New York: Oxford University Press. Focuses on the influence of different social agencies in the political socialization process. Cross-cultural in orientation, with an emphasis on national samples of high school students in Jamaica and the United States. Langton argues that the manipulation of children is justified and works out ideas designed to further the aims of elites and segregate social classes—Connell and

Goot (1972–1973) call them "fascistic."

Langton, Kenneth P., and M. Kent Jennings

1968 "Political Socialization and the High School Civics Curriculum in the United States." *American Political Science Review* LXII (September), 852–867. Explores the relationship of the civics curriculum to political attitudes and behavior in U.S. high schools, based on a sample of 1,669 high school seniors in ninety-seven secondary schools.

Langton, Kenneth P., and David A. Karns

1969 "The Relative Influence of the Family, Peer Group, and School in the Development of Political Efficacy." *Political Science Quarterly* XXII (December), 813–826. Empirical study of family, peer group, and school as socializing agents.

1974 "Political Socialization and National Development: Some Hypotheses and Data." *Western Political Quarterly* XXVII (June), 217–238. Using the data collected by Almond and Verba in their five-nation civic culture survey, the authors apply multivariate analysis to postulate that "cross-cultural difference in the relative influence of socialization agents is a function of differences in national socioeconomic development" (217).

LaPalombara, Joseph, and Jeremy B. Walters

1961 "Values, Expectations, and Political Predispositions of Italian Youth." *Midwest Journal of Political Science* II (February), 39–58. Secondary analysis of data gathered in a 1958 national survey of three thousand Italian respondents, ranging in age from eighteen to twenty-five years. Finds that the youths are rather confused as to the values they consider important.

Lasswell, Harold D.

1939 "Person, Personality, Group, Culture." *Psychiatry* II (November), 533–561. A search for method through examination of the four terms and various definitions about culture and personality.

1948 "The Structure and Function of Communication in Society." In Lyman Bryson (ed.), *The Communication of Ideas*, pp. 37–51. New York: Harper and Row. Communication patterns are related to power and influence among individuals in society. The communication process is seen as involving three functions: surveillance of the environment, correlation of societal elements, and transmission of the social inheritance.

Lazarsfeld, Paul F., and Robert F. Merton

1957 "Mass Communication, Popular Taste, and Organized Social Action." In Bernard Rosenberg and David Manning White (eds.), *Mass Culture*, pp. 457–473. Glencoe, Illinois: Free Press. Examines the power of mass media and concludes that "the mass media of communication operate toward the maintenance of the going social and cultural structure rather than toward its change."

Legros, Dominique

1977 "Chance, Necessity, and Mode of Production: A Marxist Critique of Cultural Evolutionism." *American Anthropologist* LXXIX (March), 26–41. Attempts to demonstrate that Marxism radically differs from cultural evolutionism: first, in definition of concepts such as society and mode of production; second, in interpretation of superstructure and base; and third, in perspectives of materialism.

Lehman, Edward W.
1972 "On the Concept of Political Culture: A Theoretical Reassessment." *Social Forces* L (March), 361–370. Critiques the pitfalls of reductionism and normative bias found in current usage of political culture; examines dimensions of political culture—participational and institutional, power and legitimation, general culture; assesses generalizations between general culture and political culture and between symbols of political institutions and political legitimizations.

Lindenfeld, Frank
1973 "Work, Automation, and Alienation." In Lindenfeld (ed.), *Radical Perspectives on Social Problems*, pp. 238–249. 2d ed. New York: Macmillan Company. An examination of Marxist and other theories of alienation and an argument for workers' control of what and how they shall produce.

Lippitt, Gordon L., and Drexel A. Sprecher
1960 "Factors Motivating Citizens to Become Active in Politics as Seen by Practical Politicians." *Journal of Social Issues* XVI (1), 11–17. Based on an informal survey of eighty-six practical politicians. Analysis of questions about why people become or do not become involved in politics, the authors conclude that people become active as a result of interest and involvement in issues and candidates, not because of the self-images that politics confer upon people.

Malinowski, Bronislaw
1930 "Culture." In *The Encyclopedia of Social Sciences*, pp. 621–645. New York: Macmillan Company. A full discussion of culture and the definitions and interpretations of culture that prevail in the social sciences.

Marx, Karl
1961 "*Economic and Philosophical Manuscripts.*" Translated by T. B. Bottomore and included in Erich Fromm, *Marx's Concept of Man*. New York: Frederick Ungar Publishing. A Marxist humanist stance and review of the manuscripts is presented by Fromm in a lengthy introduction.

1973 *Grundrisse: Foundations of the Critique of Political Economy.* Translated with a foreword by Martin Nicolaus. New York: Vintage Books. Originally seven notebooks drafted as an outline of Marx's attempt to elaborate fully a conception of political economy.

Mattelart, Armand
1979 *Multinational Corporations and the Control of Culture: The Ideological Apparatuses of Imperialism.* Atlantic Highlands, New Jersey: Humanities Press. Comprehensive analysis of the impact of multinational corporations on culture and ideology.

Mayer, Lawrence C.
1972 *Comparative Political Inquiry: A Methodological Survey.* Homewood, Illinois: Dorsey Press. Chapter 9 summarizes and critiques approaches to political culture.

Mead, Margaret
1951 "The Study of National Character." In Daniel Lerner and Harold D. Lasswell (eds.), *The Policy Sciences*, pp. 70–85. Stanford: Stanford University Press. A review of the approaches to the study of national culture that evolved with the Second World War.

Meisel, John
1974 "Political Culture and the Politics of Culture." *Canadian Journal of Political Science* VII (December), 601–615. Presidential address to the Canadian Political Science Association. Describes four meanings of culture: anthropological, aesthetic, political, and leisure culture. Discusses implications of culture for political science by examining the reciprocal interaction between culture and politics; cultural policy and class; culture and the international context; cultural policies and values. Concludes that a Marxist framework is likely to focus more on cultural concerns than is U.S. political science.

Merelman, Richard M.
1966 "Learning and Legitimacy." *American Political Science Review* LX (September), 548–561. Examination of the theory of political legitimacy through a framework of psychological learning theory and the theory of cognitive dissonance.

1969 "The Development of Political Ideology: A Framework for the Analysis of Political Socialization." *American Political Science Review* LXIII (September), 750–767. Outlines four theories of ideology, sets forth a model of ideology formation, then relates political socialization to the development of ideology.

Merriam, Charles (ed.)
1931 *The Making of Citizens: A Comparative Study of Methods of Civic Training.* Chicago: University of Chicago Press. Descriptive summary and comparison of systems of civic education in eight countries: France, Germany, England, Italy, Russia, Austria-Hungary, Switzerland, and the United States.

Metzger, Walter P.
1963 "Generalizations About National Character: An Analytical Essay." In Louis Gottschalk (ed.), *Generalization in the Writing of History*, pp. 77–102. Chicago: University of Chicago Press. An examination in the literature of definitions of national character and a look at the problems of classifying the term.

Meyer, Alfred G.
1952 "The Use of the Term Culture in the Soviet Union." In Alfred Kroeber and Clyde Kluckhohn, *Culture: A Critical Review of Concepts and Definitions*, pp. 213–217. Cambridge, Massachusetts: Peabody Museum.

Milbrath, Lester W.
1965 *Political Participation: How and Why Do People Get Involved in Politics?* Chicago: Rand McNally and Co. Synthesis of the literature and conceptualization of political participation.

Mishler, William et al.
1974 "Patterns of Political Socialization: Stimulating the Development of Party Identification in Two Political Elites." *Comparative Political Studies* VI (January), 399–430. Examination of political socialization in four metropolitan areas in the United States and Canada. Focused on socializing agents in the formation of partisan identification and on identification of party leaders.

Mitchell, William C.
1967 *Sociological Analysis and Politics: The Theories of Talcott Parsons.* Englewood Cliffs, New Jersey: Prentice-Hall. Contemporary Political Theory Series, David Easton, editor. The last sections of Chapter 19 offer an assessment of Parsons's

contributions to theories of political culture.

Moore, Omar Khayyam
1952 "Nominal Definitions of 'Culture.'" *Philosophy of Science* XIX (October), 245–256. A technical review of definitions of culture and a conclusion that much work must be spent in clarifying a definition.

Morgan, Jan
1974 "Women and Political Socialization: Fact and Fantasy in Easton and Dennis, and in Lane." *Politics* IX (May), 50–55. Argues that the authors misrepresent women's sex roles, a consequence of prejudice, misrepresentation of data, and use of inadequate and meaningless questions.

Moskos, Charles C., Jr., and Wendell Bell
1964 "Attitudes Towards Democracy Among Leaders in Four Emergent Nations." *British Journal of Sociology* XV (December), 317–337. An examination of four emergent nations in the British Caribbean (Jamaica, Trinidad and Tobago, British Guyana, and the "little eight" islands). Analysis of interviews with 111 top leaders and their attitudes toward democracy.

Nie, Norman H., G. Bingham Powell, Jr., and Kenneth Prewitt
1969 "Social Structure and Political Participation: Developmental Relationships, Part I." *American Political Science Review* LXIII (June), 361–378. Secondary analysis of the Almond-Verba civic culture data drawn from a survey in Britain, Germany, Italy, Mexico, and the United States.

Ogles, R., M. Levy, and T. Parsons
1959 "Culture and Social System: An Exchange." *American Sociological Review* XXIV (April), 246–250. Three communications that criticize Kroeber and Parsons (1958).

Park, Robert E.
1939 "Reflections on Communication and Culture." *American Journal of Sociology* XLIV (September), 191–205. Understands communications as a "web of custom and mutual expectation which binds together diverse social units." Reviews the literature on communication and its function in the cultural process.

Parsons, Talcott
1951 *The Social System.* Glencoe, Illinois: Free Press. Chapters 8 on belief systems and the social system and 9 on expressive symbols and the social system are especially relevant for an examination of Parsons's contributions to political culture theory.

Pateman, Carole
1971 "Political Culture, Political Structure, and Political Change." *British Journal of Political Science* I, part 3 (July), 291–305. A review of the literature on political culture, including attention to its problem of definition and use.

Prewitt, Kenneth
1965 "Political Socialization and Leadership Selection." *Annals* CCCLXI (September), 96–111. Discounts some traditional variables such as status and personality in an explanation of leadership recruitment, and emphasizes a hypothesis centering around a self-selection process where socialization experiences leading to political activism account for leadership selection patterns.

Prewitt, Kenneth, Heinz Eulau, and Betty H. Zisk
1966–1967 "Political Socialization and Political Roles." *Public Opinion Quarterly*

XXX (Winter), 569–582. Empirical study of 421 state legislators in four states and 129 city councilmen from twenty-three cities. Challenges the theory that adult political behavior is simply an elaboration of patterns found in childhood.

Putnam, Robert D.

1971l "Studying Elite Political Culture: The Case of 'Ideology.'" *American Political Science Review* LXV (September), 651–681. Based on interviews with deputies in Great Britain and Italy, this analysis examines ideological aspects of political culture.

Pye, Lucian W.

1956 "Communication Patterns and the Problems of Representative Government in Non-Western Societies." *Public Opinion Quarterly* XX (Spring), 249–256. The culture of Third World society is characterized by traditional patterns of communication and special problems of political communication affected by Westernization and urbanization.

1962 *Politics, Personality, and Nation Building: Burma's Search for Identity.* New Haven: Yale University Press. Attempts to develop a general theory of personality and political attitudes through the study of Burmese national life.

1963 *Communications and Political Development.* Princeton: Princeton University Press. Contains an introductory overview as well as description of models of traditional, transitional, and modern communication systems by Pye. In addition there are articles by Wilbur Schramm on communication development; by Herbert Hyman on mass media and political socialization; and by Daniel Lerner on a communication theory of modernization. A selected bibliography is appended.

1964 "The Non-Western Political Process." In Harry Eckstein and David E. Apter (eds.), *Comparative Politics*, pp. 657–665. New York: Free Press of Glencoe. Originally published in *Journal of Politics* XX (August 1958), 468–486. Presents a series of propositions that attempt to distinguish between politics in the Western and non-Western worlds.

1965 "Introduction: Political Culture and Political Development." In Pye and Sidney Verba (eds.), *Political Culture and Political Development*, pp. 3–26. Princeton: Princeton University Press. Offers definitions of political culture and political development, then synthesizes patterns of political culture that emanate from ten country essays, which follow.

1972 "Culture and Political Science: Problems in the Evaluation of the Concept of Political Culture." *Social Science Quarterly* LIII (September), 285–296. An assessment of political culture theory. Reviews its origins from Almond's introduction of the concept in 1956 to the present. Acknowledges its advantages over national character but focuses on the problems of linking micro with macro study and the "misplaced precision" of attitudinal and opinion surveys.

Pye, Lucian W., and Sidney Verba (eds.)

1965 *Political Culture and Political Development.* Princeton: Princeton University Press. Studies in Political Development (5).

Reich, Wilhelm

1966 "Dialectical Materialism and Psychoanalysis." *Studies on the Left* VI (July-August), 5-46. Publication of a paper originally issued in German in 1929. Searches for compatibility of Freudian psychoanalysis and Marxist historical materialism.

Rokkan, Stein (ed.)

1960 "Citizen Participation in Political Life." *International Social Science Journal* XII (1), entire issue. An introduction (pages 7-14) to a series of country studies dealing with citizen participation. Concerned with the threatening decline in participation and increasing public apathy about public affairs.

Rosenbaum, Walter A.

1975 *Political Culture.* New York: Praeger Publishers. Examines definition, patterns, and issues of political culture, with attention to case studies: Great Britain, the United States, Italy, and the Congo (Zaire). Also offers distinctions between political culture and public opinion.

Schaff, Adam

1970 *Marxism and the Human Individual.* Introduction by Erich Fromm; edited by Robert S. Cohen. New York: McGraw-Hill Book Co. An important statement by a Polish philosopher.

Schonfeld, William R.

1971 "The Focus of Political Socialization Research: An Evaluation." *World Politics* XXIII (April), 544-578. A critical review of recent literature and research on political socialization. Concludes that "during the past decade we have not come much closer to gathering the type of information that political socialization research ostensibly sought."

Schubert, Glendon

1977 "Political Culture and Judicial Ideology: Some Cross and Subcultural Comparisons." *Comparative Political Studies* IX (January), 363-408. Preliminary report on field research on judicial behavior in Switzerland and South Africa. Drawing upon earlier studies Schubert attempts to link judicial behavior to the political culture at large.

Searing, Donald D.

1969 "The Comparative Study of Elite Socialization." *Comparative Political Studies* I (January), 471-500. Secondary analysis of data from five separate studies. Elite data analyzed for France, West Germany, United States, Israel, and Venezuela.

Searing, Donald D., Joel J. Schwartz, and E. Lind

1973 "The Structuring Principle: Political Socialization and Belief Systems." *American Political Science Review* LXVII (June), 415-432. Examines the assumption that basic orientations acquired during childhood tend to structure the later learning of specific issue beliefs. Sets forth concept and theory and tests the structuring principle with two national cross-section samples.

Sharkansky, Ira

1969 "The Utility of Elazar's Political Culture: A Research Note." *Polity* II (Fall), 66-83. A critical review of Daniel J. Elazar's attempt to identify varying political cultures in the United States. Using observation and solid as well as impressionistic data, Elazar describes three principal cultures: moralist, individualist, and traditionalist. Sharkansky demonstrates the usefulness of as well as the limitations of Elazar's theory.

Shils, Edward
1961 "Mass Society and Its Culture." In Norman Jacobs (ed.), *Culture for the Millions*, pp. 1–27. New York: D. Van Nostrand. Suggests that a growing individual attachment to society has resulted in a new order, a mass society of consensus and civility.

Sigel, Roberta S.
1965 "Assumptions About the Learning of Political Values." *Annals* CCCLXI (September), 1–9. Discussion of the intergenerational transmission of political values, norms, and processes in a society in which people must deal simultaneously with status quo and change. Concludes that the overall effect of political socialization is in the direction of supporting the status quo.

1966 "Political Socialization: Some Reactions on Current Approaches and Conceptualizations." New York: Paper presented to the Annual Meetings, American Political Science Association. A review of the shortcomings in the methods and theory of political socialization research. Criticizes the reliance on written questionnaires and calls for a use of a variety of techniques. Attacks the current model of political socialization as static and homogeneous.

1968 "Image of a President: Some Insights into the Political Views of School Children." *American Political Science Review* LXII (March), 216–226. Examines the political content of the affective orientations children show toward the U.S. president. Based on a questionnaire administered to 1,349 children in primary and secondary schools in Detroit.

Sigel, Roberta S. (ed.)
1970 *Learning About Politics: A Reader in Political Socialization*. New York: Random House. An anthology of previously published materials on political socialization.

Sorokin, Pitirim A.
1947 *Society, Culture, and Personality*. New York: Harper. Sharply distinguishes between culture and society as concepts useful in sociology.

Stern, Larry, and Monte Palmer
1971 "Political Socialization, Student Attitudes, and Political Participation: A Sample of Colombian University Students." *Journal of Developing Areas* VI (October), 63–76. Analysis and data results of a survey of university students in Colombia.

Stern, Larry N. et al.
1973 "On the Dimensions of Political Culture: A New Perspective." *Comparative Political Studies* V (January), 493–511. A review of recent literature on political culture, especially Almond (1956), Almond and Verba (1963), and Verba in Pye and Verba (1965). Based on a factor analysis of forty-eight variables in Almond and Verba, a number of dimensions of political culture are examined.

Tucker, Robert C.
1973 "Culture, Political Culture, and Communist Society." *Political Science*

Quarterly LXXXVIII (June), 173–190. Discusses various definitions of culture and political culture that emanate from anthropology and political science. Reviews the use of political culture as a concept in studying communist society.

Van Den Haag, Ernest

1962 "A Dissent from the Consensual Society." In Norman Jacobs (ed.), *Culture for the Millions*, pp. 53–62. New York: D. Van Nostrand. A critique of Shils's (1961) discussion of mass society and culture. Shils's categories of superior, mediocre, and brutal culture are viewed as descriptive and ahistorical.

Verba, Sidney

1962 "Political Participation and Strategies of Influence: A Comparative Study." *Acta Sociologica* VI, 22–42. An examination and analysis of the perceptions and behavior of the ordinary citizen in five countries—the United States, Britain, Germany, Italy, and Mexico; in particular looks at the extent to which citizens in a nation perceive themselves as "competent" to influence government and the strategies they would employ.

1965 "Comparative Political Culture." In Lucian Pye and Sidney Verba (eds.), *Political Culture and Political Development*, pp. 512–560. Princeton: Princeton University Press. Detailed examination of political culture: approach, dimensions, political beliefs, political style, origins, and political crises.

Wallace, Anthony F. C.

1972 "Paradigmatic Processes in Culture Change." *American Anthropologist* LXXIV (June), 467–478. Synthesizes generalizations into a paradigm of cultural change and outlines some applications, with reference to England and the United States.

Ward, Robert E.

1974 "Culture and the Comparative Study of Politics, or the Constipated Dialectic." *American Political Science Review* LXVIII (March), 190–201. Examines the tensions between area specialists and behavioralists as well as the former's sensitivity to questions of culture in the study of comparative politics. Recommends a synthesis of the two approaches.

Wright, Charles R.

1960 "Functional Analysis and Mass Communication." *Public Opinion Quarterly* XXIV (Winter), 605–620. Discusses problems in functional analysis and in setting forth hypotheses about mass communication.

Wright, Charles R., and Herman Turk

1967 "Introductory Comments on the Socialization of Adults." *Socialization Inquiry* XXXVII (Winter), 3–10. Introduction to a special issue of studies in adult socialization.

Theories of Development and Underdevelopment

A prolific amount of literature by both orthodox and radical theorists exists on the subject of development and underdevelopment. Marxist theorists, in particular, have contributed to a critique of both bourgeois and radical thought, and significant debate has ensued. Some of the issues they confront stem from the dichotomous thinking set forth by Marx and Weber. Other issues, however, have surfaced in the attempt to refine the early thought of Marx and Weber. The complexity of these issues becomes awesome for the student recently initiated to the literature on development. In an attempt to clarify the issues, this chapter sets forth a synthesis and an assessment of six general themes that run through the literature.

- Political Development
- Development and Nationalism
- Modernization
- Underdevelopment
- Dependency
- Imperialism

Orthodox comparativists favor the first three of these topics, radical comparativists prefer the last three, although differences are obscured by overlapping theory as well as by contradictions and imprecisions of terminology. As noted above and in Chapter 4, the orthodox and radical perspectives of development are demarcated by the varying interpretations of Marx and Weber. Marx concerned himself with development premised on the interaction of people with the material world of productive forces and modes of production. Weber identified distinctive rational characteristics of the bureaucratic order of industrial states. Both thinkers focused on bourgeois capitalism but Marx looked for transformations in the structural base and attempted to ground his theory on facts of historical reality, and Weber dealt with the requisites of development–emphasizing routinization, efficiency, professionalization, secularity, differentiation, and specalization–and related his theory to ideal conceptions. Some critics would characterize Marx's perspective as revolutionary and realist, his conception of development as dynamic, his method as dialectical; and Weber's understanding would be seen as static, his conception of development as evolutionary and idealist, and his method as rooted in ideal typologies. The influence of these different approaches is evident in the contemporary literature on development.

POLITICAL DEVELOPMENT

The literature on political development emphasizes the political ramifications of development and tends to distinguish political from economic development. This literature clusters into at least three types: one associating with notions of democracy; another focusing on aspects of political development and change; and a third examining the crises and sequences of political development.

Traditionally political scientists have addressed questions of democracy. James Bryce's *Modern Democracies* (1921) and Carl J. Friedrich's *Constitutional Government and Democracy* (1937) are representative of this trend. Attention to democracy incorporates issues of elections and constitutional legitimacy into political analysis. Lucian Pye (1965 and 1966) emphasized development as strengthening the values and practices of Western capitalist democracy. He argued for pluralistic participation, multiparty systems, and competitive politics, as well as political stability and an avoidance of excessive tension. Democratic development, however, must balance with strong government and ordered authority. Along these lines Russell Fitzgibbon (1956) sought the opinions of Latin American specialists on a number of criteria that measure political democracy. His questions concerned the degree of press freedom, the nature of the party system, voting regularity, the standard of living, and the like. A somewhat similar exercise, based on aggregate data rather than on attitudinal responses, was attempted by Arthur K. Smith, Jr. (1969). Seymour Martin Lipset (1959) outlined the requisites of democracy in the context of economic development and political legitimacy. His conditions of democracy included an open class system, economic wealth, and a capitalist economy; the higher the level of industrialization, wealth, and education, the greater the prospects for democracy.

These premises about democracy continue to pervade conceptions of political development. The effort of Almond (1965) to tie orthodox systems and culture theory to political development exemplifies this unchanged view of reality. In his *Aspects of Political Development*, Pye (1966, especially chap. 4) revealed his biases toward Western democracy while acknowledging a diversity of definitions, generally associated with change. For example, he referred to political development as institution building and citizen development; mass mobilization and participation are essential to democracy and order. Inherent in the references to democracy are value-laden and Western-oriented assumptions, and, thus, attention to political development rather than to democracy implies a more value-neutral basis. This view is found in Packenham (1964), Spengler (1960), and Tanter (1967), and Cnudde (1972) related developmental theory to quantitative applications.

Many writers find efforts to identify neutral explanations of development to be static, and this places attention on change. C. S. Whitaker, Jr. (1967) referred to the "dysrhythmic process" of political change. Fred W. Riggs (1968) examined the "dialectics of developmental change," and Lewis A. Coser (1957) stressed "social conflict" in a theory of change. Robert A. Nisbet (1969) provided a synthesis of theories of change and development in the nineteenth and twentieth centuries. Dudley Seers (1977) defined development in terms of basic human needs. What is clear from these and other studies of change is that no single orthodox theory of change prevails in comparative politics. This lack of theory was recognized by the Committee on Comparative Politics of the Social Science Research Council, which turned to the study of crisis and sequences of development.

The product of the committee's deliberations comprised contributions by Leonard Binder, James S. Coleman, Joseph LaPalombara, Lucian Pye, Sidney Verba, and Myron Weiner (Binder et al. 1971). Their studies were published in the last in a series of seven volumes on political development. While attempting to transcend "the formal and institutional bias" of comparative studies, these specialists searched for a theoretical basis. Their conception centered on a "development syndrome" or the three dimensions of a political system—differentiation, equality, and capacity. Differentiation refers to "the process of progressive separation and specialization of roles, institutional spheres, and associations in societies undergoing modernization." Equality relates to "national citizenship, a universalistic legal order, and achievement norms" (1971: 77–80). Capacity involves how the polity manages tensions and stimulates new change. As the polity develops through increases in differentiation, equality, and capacity crises may occur: crises of identity, legitimacy, participation, penetration, and distribution.

Each of these crises is described separately. An identity crisis relates to mass and elite culture in terms of nationalist feelings about territory, cleavages that undermine national unity, and conflict between ethnic loyalty and national commitments. A legitimacy crisis arises because of differences over authority, for example, when a ruling group is forced to compete for power with other groups or a ruler's claim to authority is rejected as illegitimate by the masses. A crisis of participation is "a conflict that occurs when the governing elite views the demands or behavior of individuals and groups seeking to participate in the political system as illegitimate" (Binder et al. 1971: 187). A crisis of penetration is characterized by "pressures on the governing elite to make institutional adaptation or innovations of a particular variety" (205–206). A crisis of distribution is analyzed in terms of such problems as ideology, physical and human resources, and the institutional environment.

Holt and Turner offered a critique of this conceptual framework: "There is little emphasis during the early stages on rigorous concept formation, systematic analysis, or the development of interrelated propositions. . . . The process by which one moves from the raw material to the theory is never made explicit. Rules of inference are not spelled out" (Holt and Turner 1975: 987). Binder and his colleagues raised questions about the sequential or evolutionary theory that underlies the attention to a development syndrome. As to the conceptualization of the five crises, Holt and Turner "detect the rudiments of a classification structure which has five different categories. The problem is that the categories are not defined with sufficient sharpness, and there is considerable overlap" (1975: 992).

Two decades of study and hundreds of thousands of dollars worth of research funds did not result in a new theory of development. Only the broad outline of an orthodox conception was revealed. Kesselman argued that although Binder and his colleagues were able to transcend prevailing assumptions that pluralism, political stability, and the end of ideology would inevitably characterize development, they emphasized change and crises yet gave "no satisfactory explanation . . . for the dynamics of change. . . . In the absence of a theory of structural change, change appears to occur in a random, inexplicable, and ahistorical fashion" (Kesselman 1973: 148–149). Moreover, Kesselman argued, those comparativists were ideological in their desire "to freeze alternatives and reduce irregularity" (1973: 153). They placed priority on "an implicit belief in the superiority of American political values, institutions, and processes," an ethnocentric premise that "originated during the cold war, a war the United States was never in danger of losing" (153–154). Dodd alluded to political development in the context of capitalist development and the rise of Third World states.

For American scholars this challenge, like all challenges to American enterprise and effort, has been irresistible; inspired by the writings, principally, of

Max Weber, Durkheim, and Talcott Parsons, with Herbert Spencer hovering in the background, and sidestepping Marxism-Leninism and the claims of political anthropology, American political scientists have responded enthusiastically to the challenge set by the third world. [Dodd 1973: 367]

This approach draws on "Weberian ideal types" and elaborates "differences between the traditional and modern worlds each considered as a self-contained model, with political modernization or development defined as movement from ancient to modern" (1973: 367). Dodd concluded that "the enterprise has not achieved its early promise."

A substantial, well-sustained theory of political development can hardly be said to have emerged, as the authors would themselves no doubt agree. Where the theorizing is based on empirical evidence it is open to serious question because the use of evidence is selective, not exhaustive. Where the theorizing, as so often, lifts itself high off the ground it loses force through its abstractness. [1973: 373]

DEVELOPMENT AND NATIONALISM

Development often is associated with nationalism, and recently this relationship has been emphasized in reference to the emerging national states in Africa, Asia, and Latin America. In these states a "new nationalism" is evident; it seeks a common political loyalty for groups divided by major linguistic, ethnic, and religious differences through a struggle for independence and nationhood. The "classical" origins of nationalism, however, are European and are based on common cultural traditions such as a single language or closely related dialects; a heritage of customs and interests common to people; symbols of national experience, including the flag, anthem, parades, processions, pilgrimages; institutional solidarity, including a single government; sovereignty of the "state" or nation; a territorial unit; and a creed of loyalty and a common feeling or will associated with the consciousness of the nation in the minds of the people. Such characteristics are identified by major writers on nationalism, including Hayes (1960), Kohn (1968), and Shafer (1955).

Most historians date nationalism to the French Revolution, although nationalism sometimes is associated with primitive peoples or was submerged in the city-state, local villages, or region (Snyder 1964). Some writers root nationalism in mid-seventeenth-century England where new institutions emerged such as Parliament, civic interests, and new national symbols. Classical nationalism, however, was spurred on by the French Revolution as well as by Napoleon's expansion into Europe, which brought together opposing states into bonds of national unity and a shared community interest. According to Carlton J. H. Hayes and Louis L. Snyder, nationalism evolved through four historical periods thereafter: 1815 to 1871, when nationalism and an emerging capitalism unified states formerly subject to feudal division; 1871 to 1900, when nationalism forged unity in Germany and Italy and prompted other nationalities to call for independence based on unity of geography, language, and culture; 1900 to 1918, a period of international rivalry in which imperialism was disguised in the form of supranationalism; and 1918 to date, when the new nationalism challenged colonialism and imperialism with the formation of new states.

Historians and social scientists have suggested a classification of nationalisms, and at least nine types of nationalisms are identifiable in the general literature. *Indigenous nationalism* is associated with primitive and tribal organizations, which are small but homogeneous and held together through a system of beliefs and practices that shape the loyalty and devotion of individual members to their "nation." *Traditional nationalism* favors the preservation of an aristocracy, upholds God as the supreme arbiter of a nation, and encourages the "civilizing" of backward peoples. *Religious or symbolic nationalism* is characterized by emotion-laden symbols and, in secular form, is like a religion whose god is the national state. *Humanitarian nationalism* arose from eighteenth-century thought and is similar to traditional forms of nationalism; it promises an escape from present evils to a future millenium, substitutes the natural for the supernatural and science for theology, and exalts human reason and promises for the perfection of the human race.

Liberal nationalism also originated with eighteenth-century thought, and it stresses political democracy, humanitarian values, and individual liberties as well as patriotism and sovereignty as the bases for the nation-state. *Integral nationalism* rejects liberalism, insists on patriotic allegiance, is hostile to foreign influences, and exalts the nation as a stepping stone to a new order, which will evolve through physical force, militarism, and imperialism. *Bourgeois nationalism* is expressed through old and new forms. The old variant is supported by the commercial and professional middle classes who profess national unification and political and economic liberalism; they profess national unification while believing that the nation can be strengthened through foreign investment, enterprise, and culture. The newer form of bourgeois nationalism is manifested by the "national bourgeoisie" whose interests are rooted in private capital tied to the nation rather than to foreign influences. *Technological nationalism* is evident in industrializing countries where progress is promoted through centralized planning and development; this nationalism believes that heavy industry will provide a panacea to developmental problems and that an infrastructure of transportation and power should be established as the base of all development. Finally, *Jacobin or radical nationalism* is identified with contemporary liberation movements;

it advocates disciplined political and economic centralization, popular sovereignty, liberty, and equality as well as a reliance on force to attain its ends. (For elaboration of these nine types of nationalism, see the synthesis in Chilcote 1969.)

The "new nationalism" caught the attention of comparative politics specialists. Karl Deutsch wrote, "Nation-preserving, nation-building, and nationalism. . . . these still remain a major and even a still growing force in politics which statesmen of good will would ignore at their peril" (1953: 4). This theme runs through Deutsch's witings (1953 and 1969) as well as through a collection of essays on nation building (Deutsch and Foltz 1963). Other contributions include Reinhard Bendix's (1969) study on nation building; Leonard Binder's (1964) article on national integration and political development, Leonard Doob's (1964) treatment of the psychological basis of patriotism and nationalism, and Rupert Emerson's (1960b) attention to nationalism and political development. Applications of theory to the real world include works by Emerson (1960a) on Africa, Pye (1962) on Burma, and Whitaker and Jordan (1966) on Latin America. A collection of essays organized by Silvert (1963) focuses on countries throughout the developing areas of the world.

The literature on nationalism usually interprets development as an incremental or asynchronous process of change and growth. Incremental development implies a linear progression from traditional to modern stages, and asynchronous development involves a complex series of changes in the rates of growth from sector to sector in society; the establishment of a manufacturing plant, for example, may lead to pressures for the training of a new type of labor force.

Comparative political scientists tend to emphasize political development in relation to nationalism. They stress socialization as the means through which nationalism provides the ideological impetus and motivation for development. They also give attention to patterns of inculcating behavior so that people not only will recognize their nation with pride but also will render respect and obedience to authority and governmental legitimacy. The literature, however, also examines the impact of nationalism on economic development (through demands for higher levels and varied styles of production and consumption, equalitarian distribution, and degrees of specialization); on social development (through an awareness of the gaps between classes and the potential for mobilization and aggregation); and on cultural and psychological development (through learning and the common patterns of life and thought shaped by the day-to-day and generation-to-generation experiences).

Thus nationalism provides an ideological impetus for all development—political, economic, social, cultural, and psychological. Although some nationalisms may be more effective than others in stimulating national development, a basic assumption runs through the literature: the stronger the nationalism the greater the probability that new demands and actions will arise for involvement in national life; these demands and actions may lead to change and development.

The pervasive nature of nationalism has given relevance to the study of nationalism in emerging socialist societies. Horace Davis (1967) has analyzed the connections between nationalism and socialism by initially distinguishing destructive tendencies from constructive ones. "While nationalism has been used as a cloak to cover up some of history's greatest crimes, it has also inspired constructive movements. The problem of the Marxist is to distinguish between these two aspects of nationalism — to learn to harness nationalist movements where possible to serve the interests of progress while condemning and curbing them when they are used for anti-social ends" (1967: xi). Nationalism therefore may be progressive. Citing Marx and Engels, Davis described how nationalism becomes the necessary condition for the emergence of an internationalism with the harmonious cooperation of people under the rule of the proletariat. The nation is the basis for the building of the international society of the future. Although the internationalism of the advanced industrial nations accompanies ruthless imperialist expansion and capitalist development in the undeveloped nations, the contradictions inherent in this process may eventually permit the rise of socialism (213).

The question of nationalism as a force leading to socialist development is much debated in the literature. Lenin, Stalin, and Mao held divergent views on the question. Marx and Engels generally viewed nationalism in relation to the development of Western European nations, but the revolutions in Russia and China brought new conditions and necessitated new theoretical perspectives. The breakup of the European empires and the emergence of many new nations provoked more interpretations and theories. Consequently, considerable confusion continues to characterize the literature on nationalism and development today, and a clear theory has yet to establish itself in comparative study.

MODERNIZATION

The experience of Western Europe has suggested a linear path toward modern development. Nineteenth-century theories of evolution asserted that the Western world had pursued a path through successive stages of development. Implied in this view of "progress" was the belief that the Western world could civilize other less developed areas, and conquest and expansion combined with the spread of European values to these areas. In social science Max Weber contrasted traditional and modern societies, and Talcott Parsons offered dichotomous variables so that ascriptive statuses, diffuse roles, and particularistic values of traditional society were juxtaposed with achievement statuses, specific roles, and universalistic values of modern society. This ideal typing of traditional and modern societies influenced the orthodox approaches to the study of development as modernization. For example, S. N. Eisenstadt (1964) identified the major structural characteristics of modernization somewhat along the lines suggested by Weber and Parsons. He associated modernization with a highly differentiated political structure and the diffusion of political power and authority into all spheres of society. Marion J. Levy, Jr. (1966), known for his neo-Parsonian structural-functional framework in *The Structure of Society* (1952), assimilated his basic categories in a two-volume work that presents a comprehensive outline of propositions for the analysis of societies undergoing modernization.

Although the literature on modernization is extensive and varied, three examples will reflect the contrasting approaches.

STAGE THEORY AND MODERNIZATION

After the Second World War the interest of the Western capitalist nations in the poorer nations focused not only on profits, extraction of raw materials, and new markets, but on the assumption that massive financial and technical assistance would transform the agricultural subsistence societies into modern industrial societies. Western scholars have described this transformation in terms of developmental stages. Inherent in this theory are some premises: through change higher levels of order may be achieved, change continuously and necessarily occurs through a sequence of stages and toward certain qualities characteristic of Western Europe, and change emanates from uniform causes (Nisbet 1969).

The most influential proponent of this theory was the U.S. economic historian, Walt W. Rostow, who in his *Stages of Economic Growth: A Non-Communist Manifesto* outlined five stages: (1) traditional society, (2) preconditions for takeoff, (3) takeoff, (4) drive toward maturity, and (5) age of high mass consumption. The takeoff stage is especially relevant to new nations, for it appears when "resistances to steady growth are finally overcome" (1960: 7). A decade later Rostow added "the search for quality" as a sixth stage in his treatise on *Politics and the Stages of Growth*. Rostow's stage theory has been adopted by many political scientists. A.F.K. Organski examined the role of government through four stages in his *Stages of Political Development* (1965): (1) primitive national unification, (2) industrialization, (3) national welfare, and (4) abundance. Organski defined political development in terms of increasing government efficiency in the mobilizing of human and material resources toward national ends. His notion of development assumes, as was the case for the new advanced nations, that the Third World will grow from a stage of underdevelopment to one of capitalist democracy, abundance, and mass consumption. C. E. Black (1966) described phases of modernization in an effort to avoid the unilinear and evolutionary implications of the simplistic stage theory. He referred to criteria that facilitate the assessment of such phases as (1) the challenge of modernity to traditional society, (2) the consolidation of modernizing leadership as traditional leaders decline in significance, (3) the transformation of economy and society from rural and agrarian to urban and industrial, and (4) the integration of society.

Modernization and Decay of Society

Samuel P. Huntington (1965 and 1968) placed emphasis on stability in the face of the rapid social and economic changes that accompany modernization. Modernization implies industrialization, economic growth, increasing social mobility, and political participation. He advocated a control and regulation of the process of modernization by constraining new groups from entering into politics, limiting exposure to mass media and access to higher education, and suppressing the mobilization of the masses. Preferring the status quo to the uncertainty of instability and revolution, Huntington focused on the issue of political decay. Political decay is a reflection of instability, corruption, authoritarianism, and violence and is the result of the failure of development, which is defined as the enhancing of the capacity to sustain the continuous transformation necessitated by the challenge of modernization and the demands of expanding participation. An imbalance toward institutionalization and order, thereby enhancing capacity, may result in repression, whereas an excessive increase in demands leading to greater participation may lead to decay and instability.

Huntington's complex model attempts to avoid the pitfalls of writers who understand political change as the outcome of social and economic conditions or of those who emphasize unilinear growth. Yet in *Political Order in Changing Societies* (1968) Huntington revealed an emphasis on containing change. His fundamental understanding of development was essentially conservative, resting upon values of stability, order, balance, and harmony. Notwithstanding claims that his approach to development was dialectical, fluctuating between demand and capacity, Huntington ultimately leaned toward institutional stability rather than toward the potentially disruptive demands of a participating and mobilizing society. Curiously he repeatedly referred to Leninism and the ability of Communist societies to govern, provide effective authority, and legitimize a mobilizing party organization. In fact, he emphasized (especially military) order and institutionalization as essential to all political systems and as such he slighted modernization in the form of mobilization and participation. According to Rustow, "of the two possible strategies for keeping political development in balance, he now emphasizes the creation of institutions rather than the delaying of modernization" (Rustow 1969: 131).

In a later work Huntington and Nelson (1976) examined participation in relation to five models of development. The *liberal* model, evident in U.S. society, assumes that modernization and development will enhance the material conditions of society and correct the inequality, violence, and lack of democratic participation found in backward societies. Such a model, however, "has been shown to be methodologically weak, empirically questionable, and historically irrelevant" (Huntington and Nelson 1976: 20). The *bourgeois* model of development accounts for the political needs of an emerging middle class whose demands center on urban economic growth and the development of electoral and legislative institutions. In the *autocratic* model, government authority may use the power of the state to suppress middle-class participation and to secure the support of the lower classes. The *technocratic* model of development is characterized by low political participation and high foreign investment; participation is restrained in favor of economic development and increases in income inequality. In contrast, the *populist* model emphasizes high political participation as well as economic equality along with low economic growth. Huntington and Nelson applied these models to two phases of development, one in which economic development begins and economic inequalities appear and the other in which social classes begin to demand access to political participation and power. All models were cast as ideal types, but the authors attempted to distinguish the positivist and determinist liberal type from the other four, thus trying to explain how the expansion or contraction of political participation affects the degree of socioeconomic equality.

The Politics of Modernization

David Apter (1965) presented a typology of government and some theories about change. His approach moved "toward a more applied form of structural-functional requisite analysis, suitable for political analysis, which follows in the tradition associated first with Talcott Parsons, and, more immediately for me, with Marion J. Levy, Jr." (Apter 1965: viii). Apter distinguished between development and modernization.

> Development, the most general, results from the proliferation and integration of functional roles in a community. Modernization is a particular case of development. Modernization implies three conditions—a social system that can constantly innovate without falling apart . . . ; differentiated, flexible social

structures; and a social framework to provide the skills and knowledge necessary for living in a technologically advanced world. Industrialization, a special aspect of modernization, may be defined as the period in a society in which the strategic functional roles are related to manufacturing. [1965: 67]

Apter identified two models: "secular-libertarian" or pluralistic systems and "sacred-collectivity" or mobilizing systems. These models are formulated as a dichotomy of ideal types along a continuum of authority. The secular-libertarian model is represented by the modern reconciliation system, characterized by diversified power and leadership, bargaining, and compromise as exemplified by a liberal democracy such as the United States. The sacred-collectivity model is represented by the modern mobilization system, characterized by personalized and charismatic leadership, political religiosity, and the organization of a mass party. China under Mao, Ghana under Nkrumah, and Egypt under Nasser are examples of mobilization systems. Apter conceded that reconciliation systems do not seem to work in the new nations; many parties, for example, tend to fragment and disunify a political order. The mobilization system tends to involve people in rallies and demonstrations; involvement in a single-party system enables the voter to engage in tangible, albeit largely symbolic, participation.

Apter remained optimistic about the future of democracy and the reconciliation system, however. On the one hand, he believed that the reconciliation system will lead to new "consummatory values" and to a search for humanness in ending the alienation of the individual. "Having lost its religious basis, our society is in danger of becoming a system of organized plunder in which meaning derives only from personal gain, orderliness becomes mere containment of anarchy, and the concept of humanness has no wider dimension than an individual's functional value" (Apter 1965: 426). On the other hand, he assumed that the reconciliation system will benefit from science and that science will regenerate democracy. "The scientific ethic is based on the need for free exchange of knowledge and information. This is particularly necessary in modernizing societies, where, although their numbers are small, scientists, social scientists, and technicians are modernizers" (1965: 436). Apter described this scientific ethic in terms of rationality and empirical research. "The scientific spirit is the basis of an ideology that provokes a measure of identity for those who subscribe to it and a measure of solidarity for the members of a society in the midst of change" (437). In this notion of science Apter appeared to be affirming the prevailing scientific paradigm of orthodox comparative politics.

In his appraisal of Apter's *Politics of Modernization*, Gianfranco Pasquino (1970) linked Apter's political system types to Rostow's stages of economic growth. Rostow's preconditions for the takeoff stage are created by Apter's reconciliation system or, alternately, by a modernizing autocracy or a military oligarchy. The takeoff stage is achieved by a mobilization system that draws on national resources, disrupts social stratification, and destroys the agrarian sector. Apter's reconciliation and mobilization systems are in effect during Rostow's stage of the drive to maturity. Both systems may be replaced by the final stage of development, that of the age of high mass communication (Pasquino 1970: 308–313). Pasquino offered a fourfold critique of Apter's concept of mobilization. First, Apter's concept is too broad and not operational in research. Second, Apter focused exclusively on the capability of the system rather than on its demands. Third, Apter imprecisely and loosely formulated three stages—traditional, transitional, and modern. Fourth, Apter resorted to the use of ideal types, which sometimes are mistaken for accurate descriptions (1970: 314–318).

Critical Views of Orthodox Theories

The orthodox theories of development were uncritically and nearly universally accepted during the early 1960s, when they experienced their greatest reception by the specialists of comparative politics. A very useful synthesis of these theories, including some case studies, is found in Szymon Chodak's *Societal Development* (1973), which presents five approaches to development. One deals with the evolutionary theories of development, including the formulations of Lewis H. Morgan, Marx, Comte, Spencer, and others. Another approach concerns the macrosociological theories of industrialization found in the writings of Durkheim, Bendix, and Neil Smelser. A third approach looks at the mechanisms of development, relying especially on the psychological explanations found in Max Weber's study of capitalism and the Protestant ethic or David McClellan's theory of achievement motivation. A fourth approach emphasizes political and economic development, in particular in planning and goal-oriented actions. A last approach emphasizes theories of modernization as found in the writings of Levy, Bendix, Apter, and Eisenstadt. Although Chodak succeeded in placing these theories in a critical perspective, he nevertheless remained largely sympathetic.

Since the late 1960s an abundant criticism of the orthodox theories of development has somewhat obscured their influence in comparative politics. Although these theories pervade the policy areas of government and the classrooms of the mainstream political scientists, a search for a new and more vital theory is discernible among questioning scholars and students. In U.S. academic circles attention has focused on a critique of the old theories, and the search for a new and radical perspective has not yet produced a unified and coherent theory of development. Before turning to radical theory, however, a brief review of some of the criticism of orthodox theory is presented.

In a devastating attack on social science theory of development, André Gunder Frank (1967b) scrutinized several approaches. One was the ideal typical approach conceived by Weber, systematized by Parsons, and elaborated by Bert Hoselitz and others. Frank faulted these writers on theoretical as well as on empirical grounds and demonstrated that their attempts to apply theory to underdeveloped countries proved to be totally ineffective. Frank also attacked the stage theory of Rostow for its assumption that underdevelopment is an original stage of traditional society when in fact underdevelopment in the underdeveloped countries is the consequence of the economic and political expansion of Europe since the fifteenth century. Stage theory ignores both historical conditions as well as the relations of the underdeveloped countries with the now developed countries. Frank went on to expose the fallacies of a second approach — the diffusionist view that development can evolve through the spread of knowledge, skills, organization, values, technology, and capital from the advanced to the backward areas of the world. Finally, he showed the weaknesses of psychological approaches to a theory of development. By utilizing the jargon and terminology of the very theory he sought to demolish, Frank penetrated and revealed the weaknesses of orthodox theories of development. His solution rests with the underdeveloped countries themselves.

> If the developed countries cannot diffuse development, development theory, or development policy to the underdeveloped countries, then the people of these countries will have to develop them by themselves. These three modes of approach are the emperor's clothes, which have served to hide his naked imperialism. Rather than fashion the emperor a new suit, these people will have to dethrone him and clothe themselves. [Frank 1967b: 73]

A. R. Dennon and Susanne Bodenheimer directly criticized political scientists for their failure to build a theory of development. Dennon (1969) indicted political scientists for dealing with trivia, abstractions, and obscure terminology: "The literature is not only ahistorical and apolitical, but, behind all the analytical techniques, it is consciously or unconsciously prostituted to the goals of American foreign policy" (Dennon 1969: 285). Apter, for example, relied on static categorization, with catastrophic results. "On the particular level, a country once placed in the appropriate box is frozen in time and cannot be discussed as a living entity with a past and a future — it has only an eternal present; on the general level, once a model has been raised to such a level of abstraction that its historical significance is obliterated, it makes just as much sense for it to occur at one time as at another, and a multitude of useless generalizations can be deduced from speculation on its occurrence at any given time" (1969: 288). Black's criteria of development became irrelevant to his concept of modernity. Further, he imposed ideas upon his data, uncritically fit countries to his typologies, and projected a utopian conception of modernization that restricts attention to political conflict. As to Pye, "his preoccupation with the surface characteristics and formal institutions . . . developed to the point where he believed the government capable of acting independently of society" (291).

Bodenheimer (1970) examined the "ideology of developmentalism," in particular criticizing the "notion that knowledge is built up through patient, piecemeal accumulation of new observations, which has reached its triumphant culmination in the modern data bank" (Bodenheimer 1970: 100). Theorizing and the premises upon which it is based are tied to cumulative empirical research and a "cult of data-gathering" in comparative politics. Such practice, she argued, lends credence to theory that stresses continuous and linear progression from traditional to modern stages through an irreversible process. Bodenheimer also attacked the emphasis on stability found in structural-functional theory and exposed the ideological nature of U.S. pluralism and social science. The idea that development can be diffused from developed to underdeveloped nations also was debunked.

Some of these criticisms are echoed in other writings. Chalmers (1972) and Schmitter (1972) reached for a middle ground between the proponents of "developmentalism," or those who argue that progress can be diffused to backward areas, and the radical scholars who call those old ideas into question. Chalmers saw the leftist critics as accepting most of the goals and analysis of the orthodox perspective of how development occurs. At the same time he acknowledged the exploitative relationship of developed to underdeveloped nations. Likewise, he noted the failure of developmentalism to deal with the special conditions and cultural backgrounds of the underdeveloped nations. He questioned the assumptions and values of developmentalism, in particular the emphasis on stability. The search for a theory of development remains a worthy enterprise, he believed, although the advocacy of developmentalism by the United States and other developed nations in the underdeveloped parts of the world should be avoided. Schmitter discussed varying types of modern politics, ranging from pluralist democratic to corporatist authoritarian to collectivist monocratic. He favored the corporatist-authoritarian explanation for Latin America and suggested that Latin Americans need not continue, as in the past, to employ alien conceptions and theories but now can utilize their own models.

A further review of the critical literature on development reveals other perspectives. Willner (1964) wrote that the work on development tends to be too vague, redundant, and concentrates on modernization without adequate attention to an understanding of tradition. She was especially critical of Edward Shils's *Political Development in the New States* because of its emphasis on egalitarian democracy modeled after the United States and Western Europe. Tipps (1973) found no consensus as to the meaning of modernization and summarized the criticisms that modernization theory is a product of an ethnocentric world view, a reflection of an idea developed by U.S. social scientists after the Second World War and representative of the expansion of U.S. interests throughout the world. Beyond these ideological considerations, Tipps offered an empirical critique of the erroneous or misleading assertions that have crept into conceptual frameworks and of the phenomena that have been overlooked during investigation. He concluded, "The results of almost two decades of modernization theory do not justify a third. The time has come to begin working toward an alternative paradigm" (Tipps 1973: 224). Sachs attacked "the crude and cramping simplicity of the theories of development current after the Second World War . . . proceeding from an interpretation of history based on a grossly simplified mechanistic materialism" (Sachs 1972: 37). Milne (1973) found no satisfactory definition of development. The study of development is "overdeveloped": "The notion of political development is therefore useless, even misleading, both as an analytical tool and as a guide to policymaking" (Milne 1972: 560). Nieuwenhuijze (1971) was similarly disillusioned, and Pratt (1973) noted the "underdevelopment" of political science work on development.

Jackson (1972) critically assessed the approach and methodology of writings by Eisenstadt, Almond, Shils, Kautsky, Riggs, and Huntington. Coulter (1972) also focused on methodological and technical problems, observing that "too much research in this field has involved a reckless sort of data collection, variable definition, operationalization, and statistical manipulation without benefit of theory" (1972: 233–234). He noted an "insensitivity to the forms, substances, and processes of political development itself" (234) as well as a tendency toward reductionism. Havens (1972) outlined assumptions for three equilibrium models (behavioral, psychodynamic, and diffusionist) and two conflict models (structuralist non-Marxist and Marxist) of development. Donald Cruise O'Brien (1972) observed a trend toward theories that lean toward authoritarian solutions and find merit in the achievements of totalitarian regimes, which maintain stable institutions.

The search for an alternative understanding is evident in the literature. Goulet (1968) attempted to define development "as a crucial means for obtaining the good life": sustenance of life (involving the basic requirements of food, shelter, health, and survival); esteem or recognition (involving one's identity, self-respect, and dignity); and freedom from oppression (1968: 299–301). Goulet claimed that as presently conceived, development, in terms of industrialization, urbanization, and modernization or growth, is largely dehumanized. This theme was emphasized by Berger (1976), who argued persuasively that both capitalist and socialist models of development are based on "mythical undercurrents." Western capitalism's "anemic" formulations are weak and of little use, and Marxism's synthesis of science and socialism often becomes relegated to bureaucratic formulas as revolutionary leaders fail when they turn to the practical concerns of administration and planning (Berger 1976: 28–29). Although Hamid (1974) described the negative impacts of the development strategy based on aid, which was employed by the United States in the underdeveloped world, he argued that foreign aid may be necessary for underdeveloped countries to achieve higher rates of growth. The problem is to avoid the concentration of income in a few hands and to implement a policy leading to self-sustained growth as well as to equity and social justice within a capitalist framework. A reliance on foreign aid, however, involves many contradictions, so an alternative strategy emphasizes the mobilization of domestic resources, both urban and rural, to achieve such an objective.

Three distinct paths to development and modernization were traced by Barrington Moore, Jr., in *Social Origins of Dictatorship and Democracy: Lord and Peasant in the Making of the Modern World* (1966). Each path leads to a political outcome: Western democracy, fascism, and communism. Moore examined the paths and outcomes through a historical analysis of particular national experiences. According to Theda Skocpol (1973), Moore's work "is virtually the only well-elaborated Marxist work on the politics of modernization to which one can point. *Social Origins* does not postulate one route to the modern world which must be taken by all countries. Nor does it assign the strategic political roles in modernizing revolutions to the bourgeoisie or the proletariat" (Skocpol 1973: 1).

This synthesis and assessment of the orthodox theories of political development, development and nationalism, and modernization leave the student with the choice of revising or rejecting most of these contributions to comparative politics. A major problem has been the attempt to apply theories and ideas drawn from the experience of the advanced nations to an understanding of the rapid and perplexing events in the underdeveloped nations. The results have been unsatisfactory, prompting scholars and political leaders to turn to alternative theories and interpretations of underdevelopment, dependency, and imperialism. Radical perspectives have proliferated, but the issues and debates that have ensued have stimulated a new generation of thought and intellectual and practical activity that deserve serious consideration in the field of comparative politics. Thus, we now turn to a critical overview of underdevelopment, dependency, and imperialism.

UNDERDEVELOPMENT

Theories of development generally relate to the experience of the advanced nations. Thus traditional perspectives of development in the less developed nations usually assume the possibility of development everywhere; capital and technology might filter down from the advanced to the less developed nations. Diffusion of capitalism, it is believed, will resolve the problems of poverty, hunger, health, and the like. After the Second World War, however, it was clear that this diffusionist approach was not resolving the problems of the less developed nations. The intellectual reaction that followed (principally from the less developed nations) included differing perspectives, both non-Marxist and Marxist.

The non-Marxist reaction sprang from the economists associated with the United Nations Economic Commission for Latin America (ECLA), under the aegis of Raúl Prebisch of Argentina. Essentially ECLA accepted the proposition that a new bourgeoisie, commercial and industrial in character, would emerge as a supporter of national interests in the face of foreign penetration into the domestic economies of the less developed nations. ECLA thus assumed a nationalist yet an anti-imperialist stance. ECLA, figuratively speaking, divided the world into an industrial center and a periphery producing raw materials and assumed that both could benefit from the maximizing of production, income, and consumption. This bifurcation of the world kindled an interest in underdevelopment as well as in development. The writing of Celso Furtado, a Brazilian economist once active in ECLA, is representative of this approach.

Furtado criticized bourgeois neoclassical as well as Marxist theories in his work, *Development and Underdevelopment* (1964). Furtado examined various trends in the development of the European industrial economy and noted that expansionism led to dualism—some structures characterize the capitalist system and others perpetuate the features of the previous precapitalist system. European industrial development manifested itself in various stages so that underdevelopment was not necessarily a stage in the formation of the modern capitalist economies. Furtado then went on to analyze the structural causes of the external disequilibrium in the underdeveloped economies. Elaborating a contrasting perspective to traditional bourgeois theory, Furtado essentially favored autonomy as a solution to national development. He opposed imperialism and foreign penetration into the domestic economy, but his approach did not embrace a Marxist framework.

It has been argued that the idea of development is firmly rooted in Marxist origins but that underdevelopment is essentially non-Marxist in its original conception, and thus, recent Marxist attention to underdevelopment should be viewed as critically as bourgeois theory. Aiden Foster-Carter (1974: 69) noted Marx's aversion to dealing with forms of underdevelopment, yet acknowledged that Marx was aware of the tendency of capitalism to generate both wealth and poverty. Foster-Carter argued that Marx saw such a dichotomy as occurring within national societies, not in the international sphere. Further, Marx saw capitalism as inherently progressive and not as a process in which the relationship between unequal partners would allow one to develop at the expense of the other—as in the less developed nations of Africa, Asia, and Latin America, areas that are not the major concern of Marx's writings. In the case of Ireland, however, Marx referred to the notion of "stunting": Ireland "has been stunted in its development by the English invasion and thrown back. . . . By consistent oppression (the Irish) have been artificially converted into an utterly impoverished nation" (Marx and Engels, *On Ireland*, quoted in Foster-Carter 1974: 71).

Samir Amin stressed Marx's "brilliant insight" about non-European societies, given the dearth of knowledge at the time Marx wrote. Amin argued that Marx foresaw that no colonial power would be able to preclude for long the local development of capitalism. With the rise of monopolies, however, the "development of capitalism in the periphery was to remain extraverted, based on the external market, and could therefore not lead to a full flowering of the capitalist mode of production in the periphery (Amin 1976: 199).

Marxism, as interpreted by Lenin, was concerned with precapitalist societies, and the Soviet Union, in spite of its long European tradition, was viewed as a backward nation at the time of the 1917 revolution. David Lane (1974) has synthesized Lenin's views on social change in backward areas. First, despite his condemnation of the evils of capitalism, Lenin recognized the benefits of advanced forms of industrial organization, even under capitalism, which he opposed. Second, Lenin's theory of imperialism condemned capitalism as it affected the less developed countries. Third, his theory embraced centralized decision making. Fourth, his theory envisioned mass participation. These views led to the belief that industrialization on a large scale and modern technology constitute elements of a model for development that has been implemented by the Soviet Union, but the model does not conform to all of Lenin's original concerns. State ownership and control, the facilitation of rapid economic growth, and direct forms of political participation for social equality must be combined in the less developed areas. The consequence may be a policy of industrialization without capitalism in combination with greater participation and equality than has been evidenced in the Soviet Union.

Stephen Clarkson (1972) evaluated Soviet Marxist-Leninist writings on underdevelopment and found them normative, value-laden, and superficial.

He did find Marxism-Leninism useful for comparative analysis, however, because it uses uniformly applied concepts, norms, and hypotheses. It offers a total view of the system, coherence, and broad intelligibility, and Clarkson expected that such analysis would improve in quality.

Several theories of underdevelopment have become influential. Three overlapping theoretical tendencies will now be looked at: capitalist development in the center and underdevelopment in the periphery, unequal development, and uneven development.

Capitalist Development in the Center and Underdevelopment in the Periphery

While Celso Furtado and other ECLA economists critiqued, then modified, bourgeois theories of development, André Gunder Frank and a handful of others attempted to formulate a theory of underdevelopment within a Marxist context. Frank (1966) distinguished center and periphery by referring to metropole and satellite. He argued that an adequate theory of development could not be formulated without attention to the past economic and social history of underdevelopment suffered by the majority of the world's population. He was concerned that most theory fails to account for the relationship between metropolis and colony in times of mercantilist and capitalist expansion.

Frank set forth a number of premises. First, underdevelopment is not original or traditional. The now developed countries may once have been undeveloped, but they were never underdeveloped. Contemporary underdevelopment is a consequence of the relationships between the now developed metropolitan countries and the underdeveloped satellite countries, a reflection of the development of the capitalist system on a world scale. Second, the view of dual societies — one modern, capitalist, and developed and the other isolated, feudal or precapitalist, and underdeveloped — is false because the underdevelopment of backward areas is a product of the same historical process of capitalist development that shaped the development of the progressive areas. Third, metropole-satellite relations thus are found at the international level as well as in the economic, political, and social lives of the colonies and neocolonial countries. A chain of metropoles and satellites connects all parts of the world system from the metropolitan center in Europe or the United States to the hinterland of the backward countries. Fourth, times of war and depression allowed for some autonomous capitalist development in the satellites, but within the present capitalist system such development is destined to result in underdevelopment. Fifth, the most underdeveloped regions are those that in the past had the closest ties to the metropole. They were the greatest exporters of primary products and a major source for capital, but they were abandoned once business declined.

The theory of a capitalist development of underdevelopment stimulated writing about underdevelopment in Africa, Asia, and Latin America. Frank (1967a) used Brazil and Chile as case studies to back up his theory. Keith Griffin (1969) offered an analysis of Latin America along similar lines, and Kenneth Grundy (1966) explored African underdevelopment by examining explanations of African leaders. While Walter Rodney (1972) amassed historical detail in support of his thesis that Europe underdeveloped Africa, he perceived underdevelopment to be related to exploitation. The under-developed countries are products of capitalist, imperialist, and colonialist ex-ploitation; they are underdeveloped, not developing, because they are not escaping from their backward conditions. Like Frank, Rodney examined metropoles and satellites and the dependent relationship between them. Among the case studies illustrating a theory of underdevelopment in Africa is a work by McHenry (1976), who concluded that propositions linking foreign investment, commercial bourgeoisie, and imperialism to underdevelopment do not hold up in his study of British exploitation of the fishing industry in Tanzania. Another work is by Samoff and Samoff (1976), who studied underdevelopment and local power in Tanzania and found that changes in the local leadership can lead to new productive and redistributive policies to form a strategy of self-reliant development. Such a change will be generated by the contradiction between the petty bourgeoisie and the increasing agricultural proletariat.

Victor Lippit (1976) looked at the development of underdevelopment in the century preceding China's socialist revolution in 1949. He analyzed the process by which China declined from one of the world's most advanced countries in 1270 to one of its most underdeveloped countries in 1949. Szentes (1976) examined imperialism and the underdeveloped world in general, relating data to a Marxist analysis.

Beyond these studies, there have been attempts to rework the theory of underdevelopment. Geoffrey Kay (1975) offered a contribution that analyzes both mercantile and industrial capital in the process of underdevelopment. He identified contradictions in radical theory and clarified the place of Marxism in a theory of development and underdevelopment. He attacked most economists who use the concept of dependency because they do not "recognize the law of value" and employ "an eclectic combination of or-thodox economic theory and revolutionary phraseology, seasoned with self-explanatory facts" (1975: 103–104). Kay felt that their historical accounts of underdevelopment are elaborated through such empirical categories as metropole and satellite, "which collapse into hopeless contradiction in the face of close investigation" (104).

Such criticism echoes other appraisals of the theories of Frank and his supporters. Frank has neatly rebutted his critics (1972 and 1974) for insisting that he analyze underdevelopment in terms of classes and that his theory transcends a structural-functional position and thus gives a dynamic rather than a static character to his argument. Frank has identified critics on the Right, the traditional Marxist Left, and the new Left who have contended with his theory.

Unequal Development

Utilizing somewhat similar arguments as the theorists of underdevelopment, several writers have focused on questions of unequal exchange. Arghiri Emmanuel (1972), for example, stated that relations between the center and the periphery are unequal and therefore necessitate an analysis of the problem of class struggle. According to Amin (1974 and 1976) such a sweeping generalization has provoked misguided criticism. With transfers of value from the periphery to the center, might not the world be analyzed in terms of bourgeois and proletarian nations? If the transfer of value from the periphery to the center improves the reward of labor at the center, might not the proletariat align itself with its bourgeoisie to ensure the status quo? Amin answered in the negative, arguing that we cannot think of class struggle as occurring within separate national contexts but most think of it as occurring within the context of the world system. We turn now to a summary of Amin's views as elaborated in his *Unequal Development* (1976), then to an assessment of his approach.

The theory of unequal development acknowledges the different patterns of transition to peripheral capitalism and to central capitalism as the consequence of the impact of the capitalist mode of production and its mechanism of trade upon precapitalist formations, resulting, for instance, in the destruction of crafts without their being replaced by local industrial production. Unequal international specialization is manifested by distortions in the export activities, bureaucracy, and light industries of the periphery. Given the periphery's integration within the world market, the periphery is without adequate economic means to challenge foreign monopolies. The underdeveloped countries should not be confused with the advanced countries at an earlier stage of their development, for the underdeveloped countries are characterized by an extreme unevenness in the distribution of production, which primarily serves the needs of the dominant center. Underdevelopment is accentuated and growth is blocked in the periphery, making autonomous development impossible. The capitalist mode of production tends to become exclusive at the center, but not in the periphery where other modes may be evident. In the periphery national capitalism may be limited to activities of the state.

Whatever their differences of origin, the peripheral formations all tend to converge upon a typical model, characterized by the dominance of agrarian capital and ancillary (comprador) commercial capital. The domination by central capital over the system as a whole, and the vital mechanisms of primitive accumulation for its benefit which express this domination, subject the development of peripheral national capitalism to strict limitations, which are ultimately dependent upon political relations. The mutilated nature of the national community in the periphery confers an apparent relative weight and special functions upon the local bureaucracy that are not the same as those of the bureaucratic and technocratic social groups at the center. The contradictions typical of the development of underdevelopment, and the rise of petty-bourgeois strata reflecting these contradictions, explain the present tendency to state capitalism. This new path of development for capitalism in the periphery does not constitute a mode of transition to socialism but rather expresses the future form in which new relations will be organized between center and periphery. [Amin 1976: 202–203]

Two issues are apparent in theoretical discussions of inequality. One is the question of national and international development to which I have already alluded. Amin leans to an interpretation that sees capitalism as a world system upon which national entities may be dependent. Class, production, struggle, and transition all must be analyzed in a world context. Thus, the transition from capitalism to socialism must be on an international order, and it must begin in the periphery. "Under the present conditions of inequality between the nations, a development that is not merely development of underdevelopment will therefore be both national, popular-democractic, and socialist, by virtue of the world project of which it forms part" (Amin 1976: 383).

The other issue is the debate as to whether analysis should concern exchange or production. Writers such as Emmanuel and Frank stressed exchange and market inequalities, whereas Amin seemed to use concepts such as the mode of production to move beyond market categories while focusing on the world system, center, and periphery. Amin followed in the tradition of Marx who noted the crises generated by financial and trade cycles in the capitalist system, but who also focused on the development of productive capacity by capitalism (including technology and resource accumulation), which would create the conditions, probably spurred on by these exchange crises, that would lead to change. These distinctions between production and exchange have fueled debates about the origins of capitalism and the transition from feudalism to capitalism. These concerns are dealt with in the next chapter.

Ira Gerstein provided one of the few critiques of Amin's work. He argued that Amin's treatment of the class struggle and possible transition to socialism is "somewhat ambiguous, perhaps reflecting . . . his commitment to the national bourgeoisie of the peripheral countries" (Gerstein 1977: 15). Although Amin correctly negated Emmanuel's thesis that the dichotomy of center and periphery relates to a division and therefore potential class struggle between bourgeois and proletarian nations, "his emphasis on the market with resulting tendency toward dualism, masking the class struggle, and ignoring the relations of production, lead him to a questionable world class analysis" (1977: 15). Amin's rebuttal to these charges emphasized that the world capitalist system is heterogeneous, composed of central dominant formations and peripheral dominated ones. Within this framework, class conflicts canot be considered within the narrow scope of national entities but only on a world scale. Thus attention to national bourgeoisie is suspect, for they are the main allies of contemporary imperialism.

Uneven Development

Barry Bluestone (1972) described the dynamics of the U.S. economy in terms of the law of uneven development. Simply stated, those in control of capital resources invest in products, machinery, regions, and workers where the highest return can be anticipated. The result is continuous growth and prosperity in such sectors in contrast to stagnation and impoverishment in sectors where investment declines or does not occur. A gap between rich and poor increases, whether the difference be between nations or within nations. Bluestone went on to demonstrate that the advanced capitalist state becomes involved in regulating the economy so as to offset inequalities, but that a realignment of state priorities to offset uneven development and fiscal crises is unrealistic. Uneven development will persist as long as private investment decisions dominate economic planning, and efforts of the capitalist state to expand its role in the economy may lead to political instability. The wealthy will have to bear the cost of expanding welfare services or face political discontent. In the short run, the wealthy may be able to buy off the rest of society. In the long run, however, "the inevitability of uneven development between classes in society will lead to the downfall of the capitalist form" (Bluestone 1972: 82).

Notions of uneven development were partially a response to nineteenth-century ideas of evolution and gradualism, which became associated with the advocates of capitalist progress who maintained that all activist peoples would emerge from their precapitalist state to a world of bourgeois capitalism and free competition. Events of the twentieth century have demonstrated the accumulating effects of world capitalist development and have manifested extreme irregularities, because capitalist commerce, banking, and industry have concentrated in Western Europe and the United

States while the majority of mankind have been relegated to backward conditions. Marx, Engels, as well as Lenin, and Trotsky all noted uneven development. But Trotsky went so far as to formulate his understanding into the law of uneven and combined development.

The uneven and combined features of development have been succinctly described by George Novack. For uneven development,

> The mainspring of human progress is man's command over the forces of production. As history advances, there occurs a faster or slower growth of productive forces in this or that segment of society, owing to the differences in natural conditions and historical connections. These disparities give either an expanded or a compressed character to entire historical epochs and impart varying rates and extents of growth to different peoples, different branches of economy, different classes, different social institutions and fields of culture. This is the essence of uneven development. [Novack 1966: 5]

For combined development,

> These variations amongst the multiple factors in history provide the basis for the emergence of exceptional phenomena in which features of a lower stage are merged with those of a superior stage of social development. These combined formations have a highly contradictory character and exhibit marked peculiarities. They may deviate so much from the rule and effect such an upheaval as to produce a qualitative leap in social evolution and enable a formerly backward people to outdistance, for a certain time, a more advanced. This is the gist of the law of combined development. [Novack 1966: 6]

In an analysis of the early phase of the Russian revolution, Lenin attributed the success of the revolutionary events to "an unusual historical conjuncture where there combined, in a strikingly 'favorable' manner, absolutely dissimilar movements, absolutely different class interests, absolutely opposed political and social tendencies" (quoted in Novack 1966: 7). In his *History of the Russian Revolution*, Trotsky related those laws to his theory of permanent revolution, which was applicable to the period of transition from capitalism to socialism.

The criticisms of uneven and combined development are similar to those of other theories of underdevelopment. It is claimed, for example, that the law focuses not on the historical development of different modes of production, but on the emergence of "social formations." Further, there is emphasis on external forces of exchange rather than on historical materialism, which examines the mode of production and relates exchange and commerce to any mode of production (see Romagnolo 1974 for this and other criticism).

DEPENDENCY

Dependency is a concept popularly used in comparative analysis of the Third World countries in Asia, Africa, and Latin America. It evolved in Latin America during the 1960s and later it found favor in some writings about Africa and Asia. Both orthodox as well as radical writers have assimilated dependency into their interpretations of development and underdevelopment, resulting in considerable confusion. This effort concentrates on distinguishing among various usages of dependency. Briefly I trace its origins and attempt to differentiate between a bourgeois and a Marxist view of dependency; I look at some applications and finally conclude with some criticial observations and affirm that there is no unified body of thought called dependency theory.

Definitions of Dependency

In his elaboration of a theory of imperialism Lenin referred to the concept of dependency. He understood capitalist imperialism to be a manifestation of the struggle among the colonial powers for the economic and political division of the world. Although the colonial powers were sharply distinguishable from the colonies, formally independent yet dependent countries also were evident. "Not only are there two main groups of countries, those owning colonies, and the colonies themselves, but also the diverse forms of dependent countries which, politically, are formally independent, but in fact, are enmeshed in the net of financial and diplomatic dependency" (Lenin 1967: 1:742–743).

Contemporary perspectives of dependency reveal the contrasting forms of dominance and dependence among the nations of the capitalist world. Capitalism may be either progressive or regressive. Dependent nations may develop as a reflection of the expansion of dominant nations or underdevelop as a consequence of their subjective relationship. The Brazilian social scientist, Dos Santos, has affirmed that

> By dependence we mean a situation in which the economy of certain countries is conditioned by the development and expansion of another economy to which the former is subjected. The relation of inter-dependence between two or more economies, and between these and world trade, assumes the form of dependence when some countries (the dominant ones) can do this only as a reflection of that expansion, which can have either a positive or a negative effect on their immediate development. [Dos Santos 1970: 231]

Those who employ dependency in the analysis of development and underdevelopment often focus on the problem of foreign penetration into the political economies of the Third World. Outside economic and political influences affect local development and reinforce ruling classes at the expense of the marginal classes. The Chilean economist, Osvaldo Sunkel, elaborated on this interpretation.

> Foreign factors are seen not as external but as intrinsic to the system, with manifold and sometimes hidden or subtle political, financial, economic, technical and cultural effects inside the underdeveloped country. . . . Thus the concept of "dependencia" links the postwar evolution of capitalism internationally to the discriminatory nature of the local process of development, as we know it. Access to the means and benefits of development is selective; rather than spreading them, the process tends to ensure a self-reinforcing accumulation of privilege for special groups as well as the continued existence of a marginal class. [Sunkel 1972: 519]

Orthodox and radical comparativists might agree on these definitions. Marxists as well as anti-Marxists might find that these definitions depict the world today. At the same time, it is clear that there is no consensus about a theory of dependency. Indeed no common theory exists; the literature on dependency moves in many directions, and critics set forth a multitude of positions. Some critics attack the nationalist inclinations of some advocates of dependency who oppose outside influence. Many argue that attention to external considerations of dependency avoids considerations of the internal class struggle, and others believe that dependency obscures the analysis of imperialism.

Classifications of Dependency Theory

Table 7.1 outlines various classifications of dependency theory. Each represents an attempt to synthesize the many positions and directions that are to be found in the literature. A brief discussion of the classifications as elaborated by Fernando Henrique Cardoso (1973b), Claire Savit Bacha (1971), Philip J. O'Brien (1975), and Ronald H. Chilcote (1974) follows.

Cardoso examined three tendencies in the literature on dependency. One, autonomous national development, established itself in Brazil and elsewhere as a response to the prevailing belief that development would occur through the export of commodities or foreign investment. Three alternatives faced the underdeveloped nations: dependency, autonomy, revolution. In the struggle to eliminate obstacles to national development, dependency can be overcome through autonomy and incremental change. Such a view is held by Helio Jaguaribe (Jaguaribe et al. 1970), a Brazilian social scientist. A second tendency incorporates an analysis of international capitalism in its

TABLE 7.1
Four Classifications of Dependency Theory

Cardoso	Bacha	O'Brien	Chilcote
Autonomous national development (Jaguaribe)	Center-peripheral dependency (Vasconi)	ECLA structuralist (Sunkel and Furtado)	Development of underdevelopment (Frank, Rodney)
International monopoly capitalism (Baran and Sweezy)	Dependency and imperialism (Lenin)	Marxist dependency (Marini, Dos Santos, Frank)	New dependency (Dos Santos)
Structural dependency and dependent capitalism (Cardoso)	Capitalist development of underdevelopment (Frank)	Marxist-structuralist synthesis (Quijano, Cardoso, and Ianni)	Dependency and development (Cardoso)
	New dependency (Dos Santos)		Dependency and imperialism (Baran and Sweezy, and Quijano)
	Internal dependency (Cardoso and Faletto)		

monopolistic phase and is represented by the early ideas of Paul Baran and Paul Sweezy (1966) and Harry Magdoff (1969), all independent Marxist thinkers. Cardoso claimed to represent the third tendency, which he believed examined a structural process of dependency, historically in terms of class relations, in an effort to analyze internal contradictions in the light of international politics and economics.

Bacha set forth five conceptions of dependency. The first emanated from Tomás Vasconi's (1969) effort to distinguish development from underdevelopment by analyzing center and periphery as interdependent parts of a worldwide capitalist system. A second conception dates to Lenin's works on imperialism. It is in this conception that *dependentistas* find the underpinnings of their theory, for, according to Bacha, Lenin was able to combine internal and external forces in an interpretation of the experience of a dependent nation. A third view sprang from the work of André Gunder Frank (1967a) who analyzed the metropolis-satellite structure and the internal contradictions of the capitalist system. A fourth perspective relates to Dos Santos (1968) and the "new dependency," also known as technological-industrial dependence. In contrast to colonial dependency, based on trade export, and financial-industrial dependency, characterized by the domination of big capital in the hegemonic centers at the end of the nineteenth century, the new dependency is a recent phenomenon, based on multinational corporations, which after the Second World War invested in industries geared to the internal markets of underdeveloped countries. Bacha identified a fifth conception in the early work of Cardoso and Faletto (1969), who stressed internal structure and looked at class relations in dependent nations. They emphasized politics and internal forces as being more decisive than economics and external forces in determining forms of dependency.

Philip O'Brien suggested three different traditions in the theories of dependency. One evolved from the structuralist perspective of the Economic Commission for Latin America (ECLA), under the aegis of the Argentine economist Raúl Prebisch, who argued that Latin America should set high tariff barriers and establish national industries to substitute for the increasing demand for products from abroad. It was believed that import-substitution policies would bring about a more locally controlled economy, undermine the traditional ruling classes, and stimulate national development and the emergence of a modern state. Sunkel (1972) and the Brazilian economist Celso Furtado (1963) elaborated a deeper understanding of dependency in this anti-imperialist, non-Marxist tradition. Another tradition of dependency stemmed from a Marxist framework. Led by Dos Santos and fellow Brazilian Ruy Mauro Marini (1969), these dependentistas rebelled against the orthodoxy and dogmatism of Stalinism. They attempted to assimilate dependency into their Marxist theory of capitalism and their Leninist theory of imperialism. O'Brien identified sociologists Cardoso, his Brazilian contemporary Octávio Ianni, and Peruvian Aníbal Quijano (1971) as combining both the Marxist and structural perspectives, thereby forming a third tradition in dependency theory.

My own synthesis of theories of dependency distinguished a model of dependency from a model of diffusion. The ECLA school, as well as theories of internal colonialism (which stress internal conditions of colonialism but deemphasize external conditions), associates with the diffusion model, which sees development as the consequence of the spreading of capitalism and technology from modern to backward areas. Under the dependency model, I outlined four formulations: the development of underdevelopment, following Frank's thinking; the new dependency, in the light of Dos Santos's argument; dependency and development, drawing from Cardoso's assumption that dependent capitalist development has become a new form of monopolistic expansion in the Third World (Cardoso 1973a); and dependency and imperialism, following in the thought of Baran and Sweezy as elaborated by Quijano (1974), Cardoso (1972), and others. The effort to tie external and internal aspects of dependency together represented an attempt to extend traditional Leninist and other theories of imperialism to an analysis of underdevelopment in the Third World. Cardoso, as well as many

Marxists who advocate dependency, believed that modern capitalism and imperialism differ from Lenin's earlier conceptions.

Approaches to Dependency Theory

Table 7.2 outlines the major approaches to a theory of dependency. All these approaches assume an anti-imperialist stance, yet they are distinguishable through non-Marxist and Marxist categories. These categories are suggested because many of the diffusionist theories of development are incorporated into a theory of dependency. The consequence has been a great deal of confusion and contradiction in the writing on dependency. For example, Marxists seeking to influence radical bourgeois reformers frequently have utilized bourgeois social science concepts. Marxists who have opposed such an approach have associated *dependentistas* with non-Marxist perspectives of imperialism. At the same time social scientists unfamiliar with Marxist thought often have assumed that *dependentistas* were Marxist because of a common opposition to foreign penetration. We turn now to the non-Marxist anti-imperialist approaches to dependency, then look at the Marxist anti-imperialist approaches.

DESARROLLISTA, STRUCTURALIST, NATIONAL AUTONOMOUS DEVELOPMENT

For centuries dominant nations have intervened in the internal affairs of other nations. In the case of the United States during the nineteenth and twentieth centuries intervention occurred with the advances of U.S. manifest destiny. The establishment of international financial institutions

TABLE 7.2
Approaches to Dependency

Non-Marxist Anti-Imperialist	Marxist Anti-Imperialist
Desarrollista, Structuralist, and Nationalist autonomous development (Prebisch, Furtado, and Sunkel)	Monopoly capitalism (Baran and Sweezy)
Internal colonialism (González Casanova)	Subimperialism (Marini)
Poles of development (Andrade)	Capitalist development of under-development (Frank, Rodney)
	New dependency (Dos Santos)
Dependent capitalist development (Cardoso)	

helped ensure the hegemony of dominant nations over dependent ones, and the establishment of aid programs such as the Alliance for Progress served as a facade for old strategies to serve U.S. capitalism. The United States was to serve as benefactor to rid the backward world of underdevelopment and to diffuse civilization everywhere.

Since colonial times Latin America has depended on exports of raw materials and agricultural commodities in its pursuit of development, but this strategy of outward *desarrollo* or development was undermined by a decline in export earnings during the depression of the 1930s. Under ECLA, strategy turned to inward *desarrollo*. The new strategy was premised on the achievement of national autonomy through state control and planning of the political economy under the petty bourgeois intelligentsia and the industrial bourgeoisie. Under the modernizing state the bourgeoisie would become progressive and a supporter of national interests as capitalist development diffused itself into rural areas and as economic and political policies restricted the influence of foreign interests.

The ECLA approach was based on two essential propositions. One held that the developing nations are structured into dual societies, one advanced and modern and the other backward and feudal. Under the capitalist state and the growing autonomy of national interests, an infrastructure of roads, power, and other essentials could be established to ensure the path toward industrialization. The other proposition divided the world into an industrial center and a periphery. Under unrestrained competition the center tends to appropriate most of the increment in world income to the disadvantage of the periphery.

The ECLA approach was anti-imperialist in that it linked Latin American underdevelopment to the international economic system. Its preference for autonomous capitalist development was echoed by the democratic leftist or social democratic politicians of the times, such as Haya de la Torre of Peru, Rómulo Betancourt of Venezuela, and Arturo Frondizi of Argentina. Although Haya was prevented from coming to power by the military, Betancourt and Frondizi were elected to the presidency of their respective countries. All three believed that the capitalist stage must be promoted and that a dynamic bourgeoisie would emerge under the leadership of the anti-imperialist state.

Osvaldo Sunkel and Celso Furtado elaborated upon the ECLA position. Furtado examined the inequalities in Brazil throughout historical periods, tracing the shift of major economic activity and production from the Northeast to the Center-South region where São Paulo is situated. Before the 1964 military intervention and Furtado's exile, an attempt to rectify the economic imbalance was made by Furtado as head of SUDENE, a regional agency in the Northeast whose principal task was to mediate on behalf of the state the future course of capitalist development. In this way the state was to serve the masses by preventing a concentration of income in the privileged sectors, by widening the market to all segments of the population, and by influencing technological change (Furtado 1970).

Sunkel agreed that this transformation of the existing structures was necessary for autonomous growth; he believed that participation of the masses, including the marginal population, was essential. Underdevelopment, he argued, is not a stage in the evolution of an autonomous society.

> We postulate that development and underdevelopment are the two faces of the same universal process . . . and that its geographic expression is translated into two great polarizations: on the one hand the polarization of the world between industrial, advanced, developed and metropolitan countries and underdeveloped, backward, poor, peripheral and dependent countries; and on the other hand, a polarization within countries in terms of space, backward, primitive, marginal and dependent groups and activities. [Sunkel, quoted in P. O'Brien 1975: 14]

Sunkel seemed to assume that underdevelopment is a part of the process of world capitalist development, that the manifestations of underdevelopment are normal. He saw a complex of structures, held together by laws and composing a system that is affected by change. Change in a structure is identifiable once one relates the parts to the whole system. Thus, planning and control can result in structural transformations and make development possible.

INTERNAL COLONIALISM

Sunkel alluded to polarization within countries, reminiscent of the theory of internal colonialism proposed by the Mexican sociologist Pablo González Casanova (1970). The same conditions of traditional colonialism, he argued, are found internally in nations today. These conditions include monopoly and dependence (the metropolis dominates the isolated communities, creating a deformation of the native economy and decapitalization); relations of production and social control (exploitation plunders the land and discriminates everywhere); and culture and living standards (subsistence economies accentuate poverty, backward techniques, low productivity, lack of services). These are the conditions of marginal peoples who suffer from low levels of education, unemployment and underemployment, and lack of nourishment. Such people experience a sense of resignation and fatalism similar to that of colonized peoples. González Casanova believed that external conditions no longer have a great impact in Mexico, so that a national solution is possible. This will occur as the marginal peoples are assimilated into a collective society through the formation of a national bourgeoisie. Thusly, resistance can be mounted against monopoly capitalism turned inward and capitalist exploitation.

POLES OF DEVELOPMENT

A derivation of internal colonialism is the theory of poles of development, first set forth by the French economist François Perroux (1968) and elaborated by the Brazilian geographer Manuel Correia de Andrade (1967). Andrade was concerned especially with unequal development, which, he believed, was evident between nations as well as between regions within a single country. The experience in capitalist nations of a concentrated growth of people and markets in areas of natural resources and in socialist nations of planned industrial centers served as the basis of a poles-of-development theory.

This theory assumes that underdeveloped economies are characterized by a lack of infrastructure in transportation and communication; by a dual economy, with advanced areas existing alongside subsistence ones; and by dependence upon external decisions that pertain to the production of primary products. These conditions may be overcome by diffusing capital and technology to undeveloped centers that promise potential for industrialization. Through careful planning a balance in the economy can be achieved, resulting in autonomous development.

DEPENDENT CAPITALIST DEVELOPMENT

Fernando Henrique Cardoso contended with the idea that capitalism promotes underdevelopment. To the contrary, he argued that capitalist development can occur in dependent situations. He believed that dependent capitalist development has become a new form of monopolistic expansion in the Third World. Development thus takes place within the new dependency. This development benefits all classes associated with international capital, including the local agrarian, commercial, financial, and industrial bourgeoisie and even the working class employed in the international sector, but it undermines national interests that are not linked to the multinational corporations, such as local entrepreneurs. The consequence is a fragmentation of interests into a structural dualism between those associated with the multinationals and those marginalized by them. Under such conditions the bourgeoisie often becomes unstable, prompting military intervention and rule.

Cardoso defended his approach by suggesting that modern capitalism and imperialism differ from Lenin's earlier conceptions. Capital accumulation is largely the consequence of the activities of multinational corporations rather than of financial control, and investment has moved away from raw materials and agriculture to industry. Further, new trends in international capitalism have resulted in an increased interdependence in production activities at the international level and in a modification in the patterns of dependence that limit developmental policy in the peripheral countries of the international capitalist system. He agreed that international capitalism has obtained a disproportionate influence in industry in the peripheral areas, but he found misleading the assumption that there is a lack of growth in dependent economies because of imperialism (Cardoso 1972: 94).

Clearly Cardoso's approach is anti-imperialist, but is it Marxist? Cardoso probably would respond in the affirmative, arguing that his ideas constitute an updating of a foundation of theory established by Marx and Lenin. Certainly he attempted to transcend the writings of Celso Furtado and Helio Jaguaribe, who Cardoso felt "contributed to conceptual confusion" with "overly static, mechanistic views of the relationship between the economy and the polity" (Cardoso 1973a: 143). He considered unrealistic the possibility that the state, supported by the bourgeoisie, might confront the excesses of international capitalism and promote development along national autonomous lines. And he considered his approach to be flexible in the face of orthodox and dogmatic Marxist conceptions. He was critical of many of the dependency writers, including Frank, and unlike many *dependentistas*, he attempted to combine his theory with empirical analysis (Cardoso 1971). The test of his theory, then, may rest with its revolutionary potential. One critic, for example, has suggested that Cardoso's theory is simply a "non-revolutionary response" (Myer 1975: 47).

MONOPOLY CAPITALISM

Although Cardoso's thought might be marginally Marxist, the writings on monopoly capitalism of several independent socialists fall more clearly into a Marxist framework, even though some critics have found fault with them for not following a "pure" Marxist or Leninist line. Lenin of course developed a theory of imperialism. Imperialism, in his view, was simply the monopoly stage of capitalism; this stage combined bank capital with capital of monopolist industrialists. Lenin called this a merger of finance capital under a financial oligarchy. Today such a merger would be represented by the multinational corporations, which are referred to later in this chapter. Some writers on the Left argue that corporate capital today has replaced finance capital as the dominant form of capital, a view that has not been without dissent from economists who write from a classical Leninist position. Perhaps the major contemporary line of thinking on the subject was set forth by Paul Baran and Paul Sweezy (1966) as they attempted to update and refine Lenin's earlier thought.

Baran and Sweezy revitalized what they called the stagnation of Marxian social science. They credited Lenin with advancing Marxist theory from an analysis of capitalism based on an assumption of a competitive economy, generally of small firms, to the proposition that imperialism constitutes a monopoly stage of capitalism composed of large-scale enterprises. Marx acknowledged that monopolies are remnants of the feudal and mercantile past, not intrinsic segments of capitalism. Engels commented on monopolies in the late nineteenth century, but he did not integrate them into Marxist theory. Baran and Sweezy turned to the generation and absorption of surplus under monopoly capitalism. Surplus is "the difference between what a society produces and the costs of producing it" (1966: 9). Attention to surplus, they believed, allows for an analysis that links the economic base of society with the ideological superstructure.

Baran and Sweezy examined the United States in the light of this approach, but their work also serves as a foundation for understanding the external impact monopoly capitalism of the center exerts upon the peripheral nations of the world. Harry Magdoff (1969) traced imperialism from its beginnings to the modern period and attempted to relate the behavior of private enterprise to U.S. foreign policy. Each line of thinking arises from a separate concern, but they converge in their analysis of the large multinational corporations of modern capitalism and their domestic governments. Cardoso related this concern with multinational corporations to a theory of dependency and also attempted to update Lenin. Samir Amin (1974) provided even greater depth in an analysis of monopolies and dependency in an accumulating capitalist world of center and periphery.

SUBIMPERIALISM

Theories of imperialism in the literature on development and underdevelopment are discussed later in this chapter, but this discussion of the approaches to dependency must not overlook Ruy Mauro Marini's notion of subimperialism as it pertains to Brazilian capitalist development. He characterized Brazilian capitalism as superexploitative, with a rapid accumulation of capital benefiting the owners of the means of production and an absolute poverty accruing to the masses. With the diminution of the internal consumer market and a related decline in surplus, the Brazilian economy reached an impasse in 1964. At that time the military regime initiated its subimperialist scheme on two fronts: first, to further exploit mass consumption and, second, to penetrate foreign markets. Compromised by the interests of the multinationals and the exploitation of the proletariat, Brazilian expansion depended on the ability of the bourgeoisie to compete in foreign markets (Marini 1969: 122–129).

Whatever the successes and failures of this model, subimperialism implies a means for military rulers and bourgeoisie to promote national and semiautonomous development. Marini analyzed the difficulties of an escape from dependency and underdevelopment in the face of ties to international capitalism and imperialism. His approach combined a dependency perspective with a Marxist anti-imperialist framework.

Capitalist Development of Underdevelopment

The early writing of André Gunder Frank (1966) provided another foundation for dependency theory. Frank emphasized commercial monopoly rather than feudalism and precapitalist forms as the economic means whereby national and regional metropolises exploit and appropriate surplus from the economic satellites. Thus capitalism on a world scale promotes developing metropolises at the expense of underdeveloping and dependent satellites.

Frank (1975) certainly was influenced by the ECLA structuralist approach and reaction to the orthodox perspectives of development, as demonstrated by David Booth (1975). Frank's dichotomy of metropolis and satellite paralleled the ECLA formula of center and periphery. Frank, however, was a critic of ECLA, which led him to an anticapitalist and a Marxist position. He rejected the stage theory of Rostow and others and also indicted orthodox Marxist theory as placing the history of capitalism into deterministic formulas. Frank's Marxism was influenced by Paul Baran's early work (1957) and by the efforts of Baran, Sweezy, and others to set forth original and imaginative ideas within a Marxist tradition. In this spirit, Frank took exception to the notion of a dual society. He also outlined the major contradictions of capitalism that led to underdevelopment.

New Dependency

Theotonio Dos Santos took exception to Frank's emphasis on surplus extraction as the principal cause of underdevelopment: "The process under consideration, rather than being one of satellization as Frank believes, is a case of the formation of a certain type of internal structure conditioned by international relationships of dependence" (Dos Santos, quoted in P. O'Brien 1975: 71). Dos Santos outlined several types of dependency. Colonial dependency characterized relations between Europeans and the colonies whereby a monopoly of trade complemented a monopoly of land, mines, and manpower in the colonized countries. Financial-industrial dependency consolidated itself at the end of the nineteenth century with, on the one hand, a domination of capital by the hegemonic centers and, on the other, the investment of capital in the peripheral colonies for raw materials and agricultural products, which in turn would be consumed by the centers. The new dependency, which emerged after the Second World War, was based on investments by multinational corporations. The theory of the new dependency is elaborated in Dos Santos's writings.

This theory understands industrial development to be dependent on exports, which generate foreign currency to buy imported capital goods. Exports are usually tied to the traditional sectors of an economy, which are controlled by the landed bourgeoisie and which, in turn, are tied to foreign capital. Since that bourgeoisie remits its capital abroad, it is not surprising that foreign capital controls the marketing of exported products, even though the dependent countries have attempted to impose policies of exchange restrictions and taxes on foreign exports and have leaned toward the nationalization of production. Industrial development is conditioned by fluctuations in the balance of payments, which in dependent countries often leads to deficits caused by trading in a highly monopolized international market, the repatriation of foreign profits, and the need to rely on foreign capital aid. Industrial development also is conditioned by the technological monopoly of the imperialist centers.

The theory of new dependency attempts to demonstrate that the relationship of dependent countries to dominant countries cannot be altered without a change in internal structure and external relations. Further, the structure of the dependency deepens, leads dependent countries to underdevelopment, and aggravates the problems of the people as those countries conform to an international and internal structure strongly influenced by the role of multinational corporations as well as by the international commodity and capital markets. In particular, the dependent structure affects productivity, according to Dos Santos.

> In the first place, the need to conserve the agrarian or mining export structure generates a combination between more advanced economic centers that extract surplus value from the more backward sectors, and also between internal "metropolitan" centers and internal interdependent "colonial" centers. The unequal and combined character of capitalist development at the international level is reproduced internally in an acute form. In the second place, the industrial and technological structure responds more closely to the interests of the multinational corporations than to internal developmental needs. . . . In the third place, the same technological and economic-financial concentration of the hegemonic economies is transferred without substantial alteration to very different economies and societies, giving rise to a highly unequal productive structure, a high concentration of incomes, underutilization of installed capacity, intensive exploitation of existing markets concentrated in large cities, etc. [Dos Santos 1970: 234–235]

The Lack of a Unified Dependency Theory:
A Critical Assessment

This discussion reveals no unified theory of dependency, a reflection of the various approaches introduced above. We turn now to a critique of those approaches.

In setting forth its center-periphery thesis, ECLA correctly linked underdevelopment to the international system and thus affirmed an underlying assumption of dependency theory. Yet the thesis neglects a close examination of the policies and specific needs of the nations of the center, and it mistakenly attributes backwardness to traditional or feudal oligarchies, assumes that development would be promoted by a progressive national bourgeoisie, and advocates import substitution as a solution to consumptive dependence on the outside world. The early work of Prebisch and others argued against specialization in primary products and advocated government intervention in the internal economy in support of the private industrialization effort, for industrialization would provide the basis for the establishment of a genuinely national economy.

Sunkel elaborated on the need for national development but departed from the mainstream of ECLA thinking by advocating (1) regional economic integration and national investment in heavy industry, such as steel and petrochemicals; (2) a redistribution of income and land to the agricultural population; (3) state intervention and even nationalization in traditional export sectors; (4) joint national-multinational arrangements for the introduction of foreign technology and the development of national technology; and (5) the formation of large, specialized units under joint national and multinational control. Sunkel referred to mechanisms of dependency (agricultural stagnation, commodity concentration of exports, foreign ownership of industry, and foreign public debt) and incorporated them into a global view of an economic process characterized by external dependence. His policy suggestions focused on changes in the structure of internal production so as to eliminate the mechanisms of dependency and in the structure of institutions, namely the multinationals, which reinforce the mechanisms of dependency. Furtado also was concerned with the structural and institutional context of dependency, particularly external dependency.

Although these writers rejected old developmental formulas, they also set into motion a new orthodoxy, which soon outlived the reality it sought to depict. Others sometimes cast these views into a conception of interdependence, implying a connection between a capitalist center and the developing periphery whereby mutual cooperation presumably would benefit both sides, although it actually would serve the multinational corporations by keeping intact the foundations of capitalist dominance and exploitation. The search for a national and autonomous development was offset by the challenge of other theorists who believed that independent capitalist development was not feasible and that, instead, socialism must be introduced along with a planned political economy and an intensive utilization of natural resources.

Other non-Marxist but anti-imperialist approaches to dependency also suffer from weak conceptualization. The internal colonial model of González Casanova stresses national rather than external conditions. It appropriately focuses on monopoly and relations of dependency, on relations of production and social control. However, the emphasis on internal forms or conditions of colonialism may be misleading. The assimilation of marginal peoples into a collective society through the formation of a national bourgeoisie remains an unrealistic proposition. The belief that autonomous development under capitalism may resolve the contradictions of dependency in backward nations overlooks the force of international capital, technology, and markets. Likewise, Andrade's poles-of-development theory envisages a rational allocation and use of resources around geographical centers in the dependent country, thereby implying that international capitalism need not be a great concern.

Cardoso's theory of dependent development was partially in response to the inadequacies of the assumptions that depend on the emergence of a national bourgeoisie. With the view that capitalist development can indeed occur within dependency, Cardoso attempted to avoid deterministic interpretations. He desired not to fit Latin America into an inflexible mold. His theory has been the subject of criticism, however. Rather than utilize class as a central concept, he focused on the structural relations of various groups, and he overlooked the role of class struggle.

> While Cardoso's analysis strongly indicates the futility of a classic "bourgeois revolution," as well as the unlikelihood of a straightforward "proletarian revolution" of the sort predicted by Marx in the advanced countries, his analysis does nothing to indicate either the inapplicability, much less the futility of a revolutionary struggle of the type referred to by Lenin as struggle for national liberation. [Myer 1975: 47]

The Marxist, anti-imperialist approaches to dependency attempt to throw fresh light on the relations between center and periphery. The principal concerns are imperialism and the hegemonic impact of capital in the form of monopolies whose global strategy is oriented toward global expansion. Contradictions in the center may be mitigated by expansion in the periphery through exploitation and a dominance of the workers and peasants; the contradictions shift to the periphery where the corporation increasingly has become decisive in monopoly capitalism. Baran and Sweezy argued thusly. Their attention to the corporation led them to the proposition that corporate capital has replaced bank capital as the principal means of controlling industry. The views of Baran and Sweezy promoted a split among the Marxists over which form of capital remains prominent today. James O'Connor (1968) backed the position of Baran and Sweezy and attributed the Marxist split to the absence of a systematic theory of corporate capital.

Although the subimperialism of Marini has received scant attention, the development of underdevelopment thesis of Frank has influenced many theorists (for example, Griffin 1969), yet it has suffered from substantial criticism as well. Among the arguments is that underdevelopment must be analyzed in terms of classes, and that the descriptions of class structure offered in dependency theory are overly schematic. Another criticism sees dependency as an external phenomenon imposed upon the periphery rather than as an integral element. Another view holds that the theory statically describes forms of dependency and fails to show changes. It is also believed that the term lacks specific content, is indefinable, and therefore cannot be operational in research. Ernesto Laclau (1971) demonstrated that Frank's theory departs from the rigor of Marxism. For example, Frank defined feudalism and capitalism as social systems rather than as modes of production; thus it is difficult to discern various forms of transition between feudalism and capitalism. Foster-Carter (1976), Leaver (1977), and Leys (1977) also have offered useful critiques of Frank.

Still other criticisms of dependency theory abound. Orthodox critics include Ray (1973) who attempted to compare capitalist dependency to socialist dependency, a view countered by Gilbert (1974). Bath and James (1976) sought a synthesis of radical and traditional approaches to dependency and concluded by suggesting that dependency as a term be replaced by "linkage politics." Horowitz and Trimberger (1976) argued that dependency theories tend to see internal class and political relations as structured primarily by external capital; at the same time these theories do not provide for national differences. Lall (1975) concluded that "the concept of dependence as applied to less developed countries is impossible to define and cannot be shown to be causally related to a continuance of underdevelopment" (1975: 808).

Agustín Cueva (1976) offered a Marxist overview of dependency. He believed that Frank failed to root his discussion of capitalism in an analysis of the prevailing modes of production and thus his insistence that capitalism has prevailed throughout Latin America since the sixteenth century departed from Marx's own understanding of capitalism. In reference to the theories of internal colonialism, Cueva argued that González Casanova replaced questions of class conflict and exploitation with a concern for regional and national differences, thus conferring a nationalist character on dependency. Further, although acknowledging the usefulness of a dependency critique of orthodox political economy, dependency theory tends to become entrapped by traditional developmental thinking; thus questions of class conflict and exploitation are replaced by a search for balanced development and assumptions that development occurs under capitalism rather than socialism. Cueva went on to accuse Dos Santos of confusing the worldwide expansion of capitalism with economic growth in the periphery. At the same time he indicted Cardoso and Falleto for ambiguously mixing Marxist and *desarrollista* concepts.

The criticism of the dependency theories reflects the lack of conceptual clarity in the interpretations of orthodox and radical writers alike. Distinctions between these types of writers are clear, however. An orthodox or bourgeois view of dependency usually concerns itself with the building of national capitalism within the context of international imperialism. Reform of capitalism through an understanding of and a struggle with dependency, it is believed, can lead to independent national development and the emergence of autonomous social classes. A national bourgeoisie, with the support of the state, will promote the interests of the nation on the path toward development. The radical or Marxist view relates the elimination of dependency to the struggle of workers to supplant the capitalist owners of the means of production and to establish socialism.

Given these distinctions, what then are the tasks for a radical theory that incorporates a view of dependency? The tasks for a Marxist theory have been elaborated elsewhere (Chilcote 1978), but they can be briefly identified here. First there is the need to set forth revolutionary theory within such conceptualization as historical materialism, class struggle, and imperialism. Marx perceived materialism as the basis of all history and as the means and modes whereby people continue their existence through reproduction. Marx used such terminology as modes of production, relations of production, and forces of production to examine the underlying circumstances that permitted change. Change for Marx was a reflection of dialectical contradiction in diverse social forces emerging from conflict. Marx did not fully elaborate a conception of class, although class analysis is a central concern of his work. Imperialism too is a concern for those attempting to relate Marxist theory to dependency. *Dependentistas* can turn to Lenin for the theoretical underpinnings of their argument, for Lenin made clear the external impact of imperialism upon many nations, and he combined internal and external forces in an interpretation of the reality faced by dependent nations.

Marxists interested in dependency must turn to a second task. They must relate both Marxist theory and a view of dependency to actual experience. Marx utilized a flexible dialectical method that emphasized the continuous revision of theory according to new facts as well as the interpretation of new facts according to new theory. Marx stressed the grounding of theory on the facts of historical reality. He separated the material base of successive genera- tions of history from all idealistic views of history. He believed that human consciousness is conditioned by the dialectical interplay of human beings with the material world.

In this light there are only a handful of studies that attempt to apply assumptions of dependency to real situations (see the summary of empirical research on dependency in Jackson, Russett, Snidal, and Sylvan 1979). Frank (1967a) offered a historical analysis of Brazil and Chile, and Rodney (1972) presented an overview of Africa. Country studies of Latin America are in Chilcote and Edelstein (1974), and Norman Girvan (1970) examined dependent underdevelopment in satellite economies structured around mineral-export industries run by large multinational firms in the Caribbean. Norman Long (1975) used the case of Peru to analyze the mechanism by which the expropriation and utilization of economic surplus occur at the local and regional levels; he examined patterns of dependency and dominance as well as inequalities in the national economy and society.

Tyler and Wogart (1973) tested some of Sunkel's assumptions and con- cluded that "there is not sufficient evidence to reject the dependency hypothesis" (1973: 43). Kaufman, Chernotsky, and Geller (1975) reported on a preliminary test of dependency based on a comparison of seventeen Latin American nations, and they found it necessary to reassess "the extravagant claims sometimes made for dependency theory as a framework of understand- ing all of the problems of Latin American development" (1975: 330). Szymanski (1976) analyzed data for Latin American nations and concluded that a synthesis of contemporary and classical Marxist positions was in order. He affirmed the thesis of Baran, Frank, and other dependency theorists that the less developed peripheral nations are exploited and kept relatively backward by their dependence on advanced capitalist nations. At the same time, he noted that within the dependent countries, the greater the dependence, the more rapid the economic growth, a situation that confirms the classical Marxist position (1976: 63).

There remains the task of applying aspects of dependency to particular situations in the less developed world. Marxist and dependency theory have been loosely applied to that area, usually in abstract and generalized terms. Likewise, the verification of many assumptions of dependency remains to be demonstrated in terms of the area's historical experience.

IMPERIALISM

A variety of interpretations cloud a definitive theory of imperialism. Jonah Raskin (1971) contrasted the highlights of liberal and radical perspectives of imperialism as they are reflected in the contemporary novel: The world of imperialism "came crashing through the walls of the nineteenth century novel." For example, although Kipling hid the "truth of imperialism," Joseph Conrad examined the expansion of international capitalism, the extraction and expropriation of wealth by foreigners, and the conflict between imperial and colonial lands. Both writers reflected "the broad and deep tensions within the culture of British imperialism."

> Both were dedicated to the British Empire, but Conrad saw beyond its limits to imperialism, exploitation, racism. . . . Kipling wanted order and a hierarchical society which negated conflicts. . . . they both saw the extremes, the contrasts, but Conrad immersed himself in them, squeezing his art from the clash of opposites. Kipling retreated from the extremes, from the conflicts. He ensured that they were frozen, separated, they would never rebound against one another. [Raskin 1971: 36]

Theories of imperialism generally relate to the activities of some dominant nations in the world. Along this line imperialism might be defined as a "relationship of effective domination or control, political or economic, direct or indirect, of one nation over another" (Cohen 1973: 15). The relationship could be that of dominance and dependence, of big and small, of industry and agriculture, or of rich and poor.

George Lichtheim described empire or imperialism as "the relationship of a ruling or controlling power to those under its domination" (1970: 1:42). He traced imperialism from its classic roots in the Greek and Roman empires. He believed that domination and subjection constitute the elements of imperialism. The loss of sovereignty or autonomy implies that a nation is under imperial domination, which may come about through direct and overt intervention by one nation into the affairs of another, by diplomatic advantage or treaty, or by economic means. Lichtheim insisted that most theories of imperialism are fragile. He argued, for example, that the liberal view has been proved theoretically inadequate and that the fusion of social imperialism with social Darwinism in the theory and practice of European fascism during the 1930s and 1940s was discredited. He also argued that the Marxist-Leninist analysis of capitalist imperialism has become suspect, now that the Soviet Union has manifested its imperial pretensions in the less developed areas of the world. In contrast, he saw some hope for the ultra-imperialism of Kautsky, who envisioned a unified ruling elite of managers who leave their national loyalties behind and form a global cartel of the industrial centers of the world.

That conception of imperialism, as a relationship of domination and subjection, derives not only from the traditional understandings of imperialism dating from the Greek and Roman empires but also is associated with the influence of mercantile interests, along with the rise of the nation-state and the spread of European power overseas to Africa, Asia, and Latin America. Indeed the terms empire and imperialism cannot be limited "to one particular form of domination over conquered peoples, let alone to overseas colonization prompted by mercantile interests" (Lichtheim 1970: 1:55). Once mercantilism faded away, one might ask why imperialism survived into the nineteenth and twentieth centuries. The answer rests with the forms and manifestations of capitalism that took root.

The principal forms of imperialism are identifiable in history. First, during the sixteenth and seventeenth centuries European mercantilism was characteristic of the old or classical imperialism. Portugal, as one of the first mercantile states, briefly established commercial dominance in the first half of the sixteenth century. In an early phase Portugal implemented an imperialism of "exchange," especially in Africa and in the Far East where major trading points along the coasts were seized and controlled. In a later phase exchange imperialism evolved into an imperialism of "extraction," whereby the Portuguese penetrated inland areas to assure their hegemony over the source of raw materials—gold, ivory, and later slaves.

Second, a period of new or "transformer" imperialism emerged in 1870 and thereafter with the European empire building, and it represented a shift from informal to formal mechanisms of control and influence in the colonies. The new imperialism focused on economic considerations, and two theories were evident. One, Marxist in conception, argued that imperialism was a reflection of an expanding capitalism, necessitated by the contradictions in the capitalist mode of production. The other, liberal in thrust, played down the consequences of the Marxist interpretation and argued that the inequalities of the capitalist system could be readily adjusted.

Writers also speak of modern imperialism in reference to the breakup of empires and the rise of neocolonialism. A theory of modern imperialism emphasizes two views. The view from the center or metropolis stresses that imperialism is necessary for the advanced capitalist economies, and the view from the periphery focuses on the negative consequences of capitalism in the poorer economies of the world. Notions of dependency generally have been assimilated or subsumed under the latter view.

The liberal and Marxist theories of imperialism emerge in the writing of a number of important thinkers. Liberal theory is found in J. A. Hobson's work at the turn of the century. Karl Kautsky drew his ideas from Marx and others who followed in a Marxist tradition, but his belief in a peaceful reconciliation of international capital interests has tended to influence the liberal conception of imperialism. Joseph Schumpeter used Marxist terminology but assumed an anti-Marxist stance in his polemic against Otto Bauer and Rudolf Hilferding on the Left and Hobson and others on the Right. Johan Galtung built on those theories by empirically examining imperialist relationships between the center and the periphery. In contrast to liberal theory, Marxist theory was consolidated by Lenin who combined the contributions of Marx with those of Hobson and Hilferding. Rosa Luxemburg and Nikolai Bukharin also contributed to the Marxist theory of imperialism, and later contributions by Paul Baran, Paul Sweezy, and Harry Magdoff carried on that tradition. These theories are outlined in Table 7.3, and a review of them follows.

Hobson: Domestic Underconsumption as a Cause of Imperialism

In 1902 J. A. Hobson offered an interpretation of imperialism that shaped ensuing non-Marxist conceptions and influenced some Marxist conceptions as well. Prior to Hobson, two "neutral" connotations of imperialism existed: one was used by those who desired to keep British settlements under imperial control rather than allowing them to become independent states, and the other was associated with expansionism and the control of the "uncivilized" parts of the world (Fieldhouse 1961: 187–188). Although these con-

TABLE 7.3
Theories of Imperialism

Liberal Non-Marxist	Radical Marxist
Domestic underconsumption (Hobson)	Continuous capital accumulation and penetration in primitive societies (Luxemburg)
Peaceful resolution by the capitalist class (Kautsky)	Finance capital (Hilferding)
Withering away of imperialism under progressive capitalism (Schumpeter)	Monopolies of banks and corporations in advanced stage of capitalism (Bukharin, Lenin)
Structural view of collectivities in center and periphery (Galtung)	Monopoly and oligopoly and impact of capital surplus (Baran and Sweezy)
	Multinationals and U.S. expanding trade and aid (Magdoff)

notations continue to shape some thinking on imperialism, the more contemporary and common understanding dates from Hobson who emphasized
that the drive to invest capital abroad was dependent on underconsumption
at home.

> As one nation after another enters the machine economy and adopts advanced
> industrial methods, it becomes more difficult for its manufacturers, merchants,
> and financiers to dispose profitably of their economic resources, and they are
> tempted more and more to use their Governments in order to secure for their
> particular use some distant undeveloped country by annexation and protec-
> tion. [Hobson 1965: 80]

Hobson believed that if an increase in domestic consumption were to occur, then there would be no excess of goods or capital. There would be no
expansion into foreign markets, savings would be used at home to ensure
full employment among the working class, and imperialism would fade
away. Thus, Hobson's understanding of underconsumption became an
alternative to the Marxist concept of surplus value.

Even critics sympathetic to Hobson's work do not hesitate to attack his
theory. Fieldhouse labeled Hobson's doctrine of imperialism "a dogmatic interpretation," and one that cannot be explained in terms of economic theory
and capitalism; yet he also acknowledged that Hobson's non-Marxist theory
became generally accepted (Fieldhouse 1961: 188). Lichtheim considered the
Leninist theory of imperialism as more firmly grounded because it avoids
Hobson's "theoretical mistake of making capital investment abroad dependent on underconsumption at home" (Lichtheim 1970: 39). Tarbuck valued
Hobson's "material explanation for imperialism, rather than a vulgar,
jingoistic or militaristic one" (Tarbuck in Luxemburg and Bukharin 1972:
34). However, one major defect is this theory's emphasis on policy and the
assumption that changes in policy rather than in the class relationships in
English society can be used to eliminate imperialism.

Kautsky: Peaceful Resolution of Imperialism

Karl Kautsky, born of Czech parents, spent most of his life in Germany
where he was associated with the German Social Democrat party. After the
death of Marx and Engels, he was a leading advocate of many of their
theories. Until 1914 Lenin associated himself with many of Kautsky's views,
but thereafter the two thinkers engaged in written polemical debates. Kautsky attacked Lenin and the Bolsheviks for undermining the democratic
essentials of Marxism. He believed that the rise of the Bolsheviks to power in
Russia was followed by a dictatorship, not of all the proletariat as Marx had

envisaged but of only a segment of the proletariat represented by the party. This dictatorship was unacceptable because it lacked universal suffrage and popular participation in politics. In this regard Kautsky assumed an orthodox Marxist position, arguing that a democratic revolution could not occur until certain conditions of advanced capitalism were evident, namely large-scale industry and a majority of the proletariat interested in socialism. Kautsky believed that the class conflicts of capitalism and capitalism itself would diminish through peaceful processes.

> This so-called peaceful method of the class struggle, which is confined to non-militant methods, Parliamentarism, strikes, demonstrations, the Press, and similar means of pressure, will retain its importance in every country according to the effectiveness of the democratic institutions which prevail there, the degree of political and economic enlightenment and the self-mastery of the people. On these grounds, I anticipate that the social revolution of the proletariat will assume quite other forms than that of the middle class, and that it will be possible to carry it out by peaceful economic, legal and moral means, instead of by physical force, in all places where democracy has been established. [Kautsky 1964: 37–38]

Kautsky's pacificism was clearly evident in his view of imperialism. His explanation of imperialism in 1914–1915 was more complex and sophisticated than that of Hobson, for it was couched in Marxist rather than in liberal terminology. Kautsky utilized some of Hobson's lines of thinking, however, especially the emphasis on imperialism as a manifestation of protectionism and militarism. Kautsky envisioned an imperialism in which there might be collective exploitation of the world by international finance. The interests of the capitalist class as a whole conflicted with those of capital—a minority of powerful capitalists who relied on military means to support their expansionist efforts. An internationally united finance capital thus might lead to a peaceful resolution of real and potential conflict generated by the rivalry of national finance capitals. Lenin attacked this position, arguing that the struggle among the leading powers would inevitably lead to a collapse of capitalism. Although Lenin's assumption has not yet become a reality, Kautsky's hopes for a benevolent and peaceful alliance of international finance capital have been undermined by the events of the past half century.

Although devastated by events of the present century, Kautsky's view continues to carry weight among some non-Marxists today. S. M. Miller, Roy Bennett, and Cyril Alapatt (1970) questioned the necessity of imperialism in their criticism of Harry Magdoff's *The Age of Imperialism* (1969). They examined economic penetration only in underdeveloped countries and limited their discussion to exports and direct private investment. Their theoretical position is illustrated by a reference to Kautsky's belief that the majority of capitalists will eventually oppose and prevent military imperialist expansion. They distinguished between a minority of capitalists who need expansion and a majority who do not need expansion. Thus capitalism should be able to exist without imperialism. Magdoff (1970) rebutted their "limited and crude" economic interpretation of imperialism and argued that capitalism prospers by molding the world to the needs of the advanced capitalist countries, that the less developed countries become dependencies of the industrial and financial centers, and that imperialism is characterized by the rise of an intensive competitive struggle among advanced capitalist nations. Thus the prospects of an anti-imperialist coalition of capitalists are diminished by recent developments.

Schumpeter: Withering Away of Imperialism

Joseph Schumpeter acknowledged the significance of Marxist theory, which "views imperialism simply as the reflex of the interests of the capitalist upper structure, at a given stage of capitalist development" (1955: 7). However, he disassociated this view from an economic interpretation of history. His line of thinking is traced as follows. First, he examined types of imperialism, ranging from the empires of antiquity to modern experiences that are rooted in precapitalist economics. Turning to the England of the mid–nineteenth century, Schumpeter established the basis of his thesis. "Even in England imperialism will remain a play-thing of politics for a long time to come. But in terms of *practical* politics, there is no room left for it there – except possibly as a means for defense – nor any support among the real powers behind the policies of the day" (1955: 22). Historically, imperialism has been irrational, a reflection of the needs of people who want to survive, and a response to the social and economic interests of ruling classes and individuals. Imperialism stems from conditions of the past, not the present. It is precapitalist and thus will disappear in a rational and progressive era of capitalism.

> Since the vital needs that created it have passed away for good, it too must gradually disappear, even though every warlike involvement, no matter how non-imperialist in character, tends to revive it. It tends to disappear as a structural element because the structure that brought it to the fore goes into a decline, giving way, in the course of social development, to other structures that have no room for it and eliminate the power factors that supported it. . . . If our theory is correct, cases of imperialism should decline in intensity the later they occur in the history of a people and of a culture. [Schumpeter 1955: 65]

Schumpeter developed his argument by contrasting eras of absolute autocracy and industrial revolution. With capitalism and the industrial revolution, the working masses emerged to transform the earlier milieu of guild and aristocracy. The production of commodities and the market of consumers that developed in the second half of the nineteenth century brought about a specialized, mechanized world. The people of that world were democratized, individualized, and rationalized.

> They were democratized because the picture of time-honored power and privilege gave way to one of continual change, set in motion by industrial life. They were individualized, because subjective opportunities to shape their lives took the place of immutable objective factors. They were rationalized, because the instability of economic position made their survival hinge on continual, deliberately rationalist decisions. [1955: 68]

Thus the world of capitalism represses imperialist impulses, although there may be interests that advocate imperialist expansion. Schumpeter cited evidence for this assumption. Opposition to war, expansion, armaments, and professional armies arise under modern capitalism. Strong peace parties and vigorously anti-imperialist workers characterize the politics of the modern epoch. No class desires expansion if free trade prevails. Even the alliance of "high finance and the cartel magnates" is untenable and will disappear either peacefully or by revolution. Monopolies, wars, and imperialisms will eventually "wither and die." The modern capitalist world will destroy all these irrational "precapitalist elements" and endure (98).

Although he was critical of Schumpeter, Henry Pachter nevertheless also rested his case with progressive capitalism. He examined imperialism as "a deliberate, well-profiled policy, executed with powerful means and accompanied by an ideology that justifies the striving for empire and domination" (Pachter 1970: 461). His focus on policy negates, on the one hand, the optimistic interpretations that he attributed to reformist liberals and pacifists, including those on the democratic Left as well as isolationists and others on the Right, and, on the other hand, the "pessimist" and "determinist" view of militants on the Left who adhere to Lenin's perspective of imperialism as the last stage of capitalism.

What then is the crux of Pachter's position? He argued that the underdevelopment of nations is not a consequence of imperialism but of the population explosion. The less developed nations, therefore, "must telescope the three industrial revolutions through which the West has passed into the lifetime of one generation" (1970: 485). Among the reforms that might enhance this process are common-market arangements that would allow the less developed nations to protect their markets, agreements to stabilize prices and allocate the production of raw materials and foodstuffs, the transfer of military budgets to development projects, the establishment of each nation's

control over its national resources, and a shift from foreign to state ownership of industry in those nations. These reforms will not necessarily
eliminate rivalries among the advanced nations, nor will they immediately
close the economic gaps among nations. Imperialism thus is not necessarily a
consequence of economic activity but reflects polemics that "are nothing but
exaggerated, perverted, unleashed functions of the legitimate security interests of national states" (487).

Galtung: Structural Theory of Imperialism

Johan Galtung (1971) offered a structural theory of imperialism that has
had wide acceptance among non-Marxists. He argued against the "reductionist" thrust of the Leninist view of imperialism as an expanding economic
force under capitalism; instead, he understood imperialism as a structural
relationship between collectivities. "Imperialism is a system that splits up collectivities and relates some of the parts to each other in relations of *harmony
of interest*, and other parts in relations of *disharmony of interest*, or *conflict of
interest*" (Galtung 1971: 81). Collectivities may be nations of the center and
the periphery, and each nation in turn may have its own center and
periphery. Imperialism is defined in terms of a number of relationships between the center and the periphery. For example, a harmony of interests is
evident in the centers of both center and periphery nations. Disharmony exists between the periphery of the center nation and the periphery of the
periphery nation (1971: 83). The relationship of a peripheral nation to a
center nation is characterized by dependency.

Galtung outlined some dimensions and effects of that relationship and
related them to five types of imperialism: (1) *economic*, in which new means
of production develop in the center and nothing develops in the periphery;
(2) *political*, where there is a reinforcement of position, respectively, in the
center and the periphery; (3) *military*, signified by a production of the means
of destruction in the center, with no production in the periphery; (4) *communication*, easily developed in the center and undeveloped in the periphery;
and (5) *cultural*, reflected in education and training so that a feeling of self-
reliance and autonomy pervades the center while a feeling of dependence
runs through the periphery. Galtung went on to identify phases of imperialism. His concepts are applied to two nations, then to three nations and
three classes (including the middle class). Variables are examined
qualitatively and quantitatively, and a number of strategies for change and
development are offered.

Galtung's approach defines terms, identifies relationships between center
and periphery, then examines data to test some generalizations and
hypotheses. As such the approach is static in its reliance on descriptive

categories. The fragmentation of a single notion of imperialism into a variety of types tends to neutralize the term, deprive it of theoretical significance, and deemphasize its economic thrust. Nevertheless, the approach follows in the tradition of orthodox political science, with its reliance on mystifying abstractions and description that offers little analytical potential. Its influence, however, is clearly apparent in the writing of Klaus Jürgen Gantzel (1973), who viewed relations of dominance and dependency between centers and peripheries of capitalist and socialist societies. An appendix to Gantzel's article identifies some forty studies undertaken by German social scientists, many of whom seem to follow the structural approach of Galtung and Gantzel.

Luxemburg and Bukharin: Accumulation of Capital and Imperialism

As early as 1913 Rosa Luxemburg, a Polish Marxist whose late years were devoted to German socialism, began to elaborate a theory of imperialism in order to explain continuous capital accumulation. Her central concern was the examination of capital penetration into primitive economies. She distinguished three phases of capital accumulation. The first involves the struggle of capital with natural economy in areas where there are primitive peasant communities and a common ownership of land or a feudal system or an economic organization oriented to internal demand and where there is little surplus production or demand for foreign goods. In a second phase capital struggles with a commodity economy. Finally, there is the imperialist phase of capitalist accumulation.

> For capital, the standstill of accumulation means that the development of the productive forces is arrested, and the collapse of capitalism follows inevitably, as an objective historical necessity. This is the reason for the contradictory behaviour of capitalism in the final stage of its historical career: imperialism. [Luxemburg 1951: 417]

Luxemburg saw imperialism as the conversion of surplus into capital, which finds itself everywhere in the world economy and does not limit its accumulation to an isolated capitalist society. The drive of capital to expand is the outstanding feature of modern development, and in its final phase capitalism "has adopted such an unbridled character that it puts the whole civilization of mankind in question. Indeed, this untamable drive of capital to expand has gradually constructed a world market, connected the modern world economy and so laid the basis for socialism" (Luxemburg and Bukharin 1972: 143).

Luxemburg offered a wealth of detail and description, but what is the significance of the theory? One critic has concluded that "Luxemburg's works offer very little theory to explain the specific capitalist forms of imperialism" (Tarbuck in Luxemburg and Bukharin 1972: 33). Nikolai Bukharin, a leading Bolshevik theoretician, argued that Luxemburg's theory of imperialism led her to the position of those who believe in the harmonious development of capitalism and that her theory is "voluntaristic" and similar to that of Hobson.

Bukharin's work on imperialism (1929) was written in 1915 and included a preface by Lenin, a year before Lenin prepared his own treatise on the subject. Bukharin related the world economy to imperialism, which was seen as an advanced stage of capitalism. His argument follows. The world economy consists of a system of production relations and exchange relations on a world scale. Exchange relations constitute the most primitive form and trusts and cartels represent the highest form of capitalist organization at the international level. Uneven development reflects differences in the productive forces of various countries, yet a rapid development of the productive forces of world capitalism has accounted for the expansion of the world economy since the end of the nineteenth century. This expansion is the consequence of new economic formations, namely, capitalist monopoly organizations such as cartels and trusts and the banks that finance them—banking capital transforms into industrial capital to become finance capital. This formation of capitalist monopolies transcends national boundaries and results in a consolidation of developed powers at the center and undeveloped countries in the periphery: "a few consolidated, organised economic bodies ("the great civilized powers") on the one hand, and periphery of underdeveloped countries with semi-agrarian or agrarian system on the other" (Bukharin 1929: 74). National capitalism seeks expansion, extending itself into three spheres of the world economy: markets for the sale of commodities, markets for raw materials, and capital investment. The inevitable result is conflict, capitalist expansion, and imperialism.

> It follows that the recent phase of capitalism sharpens the conflicts also in this sphere. The faster the tempo of capitalist development, the stronger the process of industrialization of the economic life and urbanisation of the country, the more disturbed is the equilibrium between industry and agriculture, the stronger is the competition between industrially developed countries for the possession of backward countries, the more unavoidable becomes an open conflict between them. [Bukharin 1929: 95]

Bukharin criticized two "vulgar" interpretations of imperialism, relating to race and conquest. Then he demonstrated how a Marxist should approach the analysis of imperialism, and he defined imperialism as a policy of finance capital. "It upholds the structure of finance capital; it subjugates the world to the domination of finance capital; in place of the old pre-capitalist, or the old capitalist, production relations, it put the production relations of finance capital" (1929: 114).

Lenin: Imperialism, the Highest Stage of Capitalism

In his work on imperialism Lenin acknowledged his debt to Hobson's description of imperialism: "This author, whose point of view is that of bourgeois social-reformism and pacifism which, in essence, is identical with the present point of view of the ex-Marxist, Karl Kautsky, gives a very good and comprehensive description of the principal specific economic and political features of imperialism" (Lenin 1967: 1:684). At the same time Lenin also recognized Hilferding's suggestion that imperialism in the form of finance capital is a stage of capitalism in its latest and most highly developed form. "In spite of a certain inclination on his part to reconcile Marxism with opportunism, this work gives a very valuable theoretical analysis of 'the latest phase of capitalist development'" (684). Hilferding argued that finance capital struggles against any "harmony of interests." "As an ideal there now appears the conquest of world mastery for one's own nation, a striving as unlimited as capital's striving for profit from which it springs. Capital becomes the conqueror of the world, and with every new land conquered sets a new border which must be overstepped" (Hilferding 1910: 376).

Lenin's theory of imperialism as the highest stage of capitalism is based on a close analysis of several principal economic features. One is the rapid concentration of production in large industrial monopolies. Another feature is the role of the banks, which concentrate into powerful monopolies with control over money, raw materials, and a means of production. The capital of industrial and bank monopolies combines into finance capital, a term Lenin attributed to Hilferding who wrote, "Finance capital is capital controlled by banks and employed by industrialists" (Hilferding, in Lenin 1967: 1:711).

In his explanation of finance capital, Lenin defined capitalism as "commodity production at its highest stage of development, when labour-power itself becomes a commmodity" (1967: 1:723). Characteristic of old capitalism, in an era of free competition, is the export of goods. Under the new capitalism, characterized by monopolies, capital is exported. This export of capital is another major feature of imperialism (723–724); it is associated with uneven development and the accumulation of a surplus of capital in the advanced nations under the control of a financial oligarchy of bankers who increasingly invest their money in industry and transform themselves into industrial capitalists (710–711). Thus, finance capital and the financial oligarchy reign supreme over all other forms of capital (721). Under monopoly capitalism, cartels, syndicates, and trusts divide the domestic market and take control of industry in their own countries, but capitalism also creates a world market. Domestic markets are tied to foreign markets, and the export of capital increases, resulting in the economic division of the world among the international capitalist associations.

For Lenin "imperialism is monopoly capitalism. This in itself determines its place in history, for monopoly that grows out of the soil of free competition, is the transition from the capitalist system to a higher socio-economic order" (1967: 1:773). He identified four manifestations of this monopoly capitalism: first, the formation of the capitalist associations, cartels, syndicates, and trusts as monopoly arises out of the concentration of production; second, the monopoly control of the most important raw materials; third, the emergence of banks as the monopolists of finance capital, resulting in "a financial oligarchy, which throws a close network of dependence relationships over all the economic and political institutions of present-day bourgeois society without exception" (773); fourth, the division of the colonial world into spheres of influence, a reflection of the struggle of finance capital for raw materials and of the export of capital.

Baran and Sweezy and Magdoff:
Monopoly Capital and the Multinationals

Paul Baran and Paul Sweezy (1966) referred to Hilferding, Luxemburg, and Lenin as major contributors to a Marxist theory of imperialism. In their work, *Monopoly Capital*, they suggested that such a theory explains international relations in the capitalist world, clarifies the development of social and economic conditions in capitalist countries, and analyzes the unequal relations between advanced and underdeveloped nations. Their own contribution to a theory of imperialism concerns what happens to economic surplus, defined as "the difference between what a society produces and the costs of producing it" (Baran and Sweeezy 1966: 9). They focused not only on the generation of surplus capital but on its disposal. In particular, they examined monopolies. Lenin, they acknowledged, based his theory of imperialism on the prevalence of monopoly in the advanced capitalist nations, but "neither he nor his followers pursued the matter into the fundamentals of Marxian economic theory" (1966: 5). Baran and Sweezy insisted that contemporary analysis turn from the competitive model, which absorbed Marx's attention, to monopoly and oligopoly.

In their own analysis, they almost exclusively examined the giant corporations and their managers, neglecting the role of the working class (Tarbuck, in Luxemburg and Bukharin 1972: 40). Other criticisms of their work have addressed the meaning of such terms as economic surplus, firm, and industry, as well as the relation between base and superstructure under conditions of monopoly capitalism (O'Connor 1966). Even the definition of monopoly capitalism as a system of giant corporations has been attacked for imprecision and ambiguity (Nathan 1966).

This emphasis on monopoly capital influenced many writers to study corporate life in the United States and abroad. Harry Magdoff in *The Age of Imperialism* (1969) traced the patterns of U.S. foreign policy and examined its impact upon the internationalist expansion of U.S. business. He distinguished between the old and the new imperialisms. The new imperialism marks a new period in world capitalism and is distinguished by, first, the rise of such industrial powers as the United States, Germany, France, and Japan to challenge England and, second, power shifts to a small number of large integrated industrial and financial firms—the multinationals, which have become especially predominant since the Second World War. Magdoff aggregated data and information to show a coincidence of the military and political presence of the United States overseas, the dominant position of U.S. capital in the multinationals, and the dominance of multinational banking. He also examined patterns of U.S. aid and trade and looked at the foundations of the ever-expanding U.S. empire.

A focus on giant corporations or multinationals pervades a massive amount of the literature. Representative of that literature is Barnet and Muller's *Global Reach* (1974). Although the literature tends to focus on corporate capital, it should be acknowledged that Marxists are divided over the question of whether corporate or bank capital is more important in the world today. Baran and Sweezy subscribed to the view that large corporations have increasingly succeeded in breaking the hold of the bankers and stockholders. Their view departs from the classical Leninist position, which continues to influence many Marxists who stress the significance of bank control and industry (O'Connor 1968).

THE PROSPECTS FOR A THEORY OF DEVELOPMENT

In this review of six prominent themes in the literature on development and underdevelopment, contradictions and imprecisions in terminology and disparities in theory have been noted. The views of both orthodox and radical theorists are influential in the literature on each theme, but I believe that both views help to clarify direction in the struggle to formulate a successful theory of development. Given this optimism, the works of three important contributors and social scientists from the less developed world are now discussed: Samir Amin of Egypt, Clive Thomas of Guyana, and

Francisco López Segrera of Cuba.

Amin identified and contended with the major issues of development and underdevelopment while (1) critiquing orthodox thinking on capitalist accumulation, (2) refining Marxist and Leninist interpretations of capitalism in the center or advanced nations, and (3) setting forth a new theory of precapitalist and capitalist social formations and modes of production in the periphery or less developed nations. He attempted to apply a Marxist methodology to underdevelopment, dependency, and imperialism, and he clarified conceptualization and tried to resolve theoretical issues on the Left while illustrating his theory with historical experiences of the contemporary world.

Amin's discussion is worked out in *Accumulation on a World Scale* (1974) and refined in *Unequal Development* (1976). The thrust of his major arguments is that all the nations of the world, socialist and capitalist alike, are integrated in varying degrees into an international commercial and financial network. Only one world market—the capitalist world market—prevails, and the Soviet Union and Eastern Europe relate to this market even though they are not yet part of the world capitalist system. This system depends on accumulation or expanded reproduction, essential to the capitalist mode of production and probably to the socialist mode of production as well, but not necessarily to precapitalist modes of production. However, relations between the developed world or center and the underdeveloped world or periphery are affected by transfers of value. When, for instance, the precapitalist modes of production are subject to the capitalist modes, then values are transferred to the center—a result of the mechanisms of "primitive accumulation."

This dynamic is overlooked in such contemporary orthodox theories of underdevelopment as the stage theory of Rostow, in which the underdeveloped countries are seen as being similar to the developed countries but at an earlier stage of their development. A radical theory of underdevelopment, in contrast, examines three structural features: unevenness of productivity, disarticulation of the economic system, and domination from outside. Unevenness of productivity is less conspicuous in the developed countries where some benefits of progress tend to be diffused throughout the economy, but it is apparent in the underdeveloped countries where segments of the economy may be dependent on large international enterprises, the governing centers of which are outside the underdeveloped economy. Lacking basic industries, for example, a consumer industry may be dependent on the outside world for equipment and semifinished goods. Agriculture may be characterized as a subsistence and export activity, but the commercialization of a rural economy depends principally on foreign demand.

Amin drew the conclusion that at the center growth has an integrating effect and, therefore, is development; at the periphery, however, growth produces the development of underdevelopment.

> It is on the basis of this history that a theory of the international division of labor can be constructed that will enable us to understand how underdevelopment originated, and the place of the underdeveloped countries in this mechanism of capitalist accumulation on a world scale. The theory of underdevelopment and development can only be the theory of the accumulation of capital on a world scale. [Amin 1974: 20]

Although Amin accepted Marx's fundamental concepts in a theory of accumulation on a world scale, Lenin's analysis of transformations of the system at the center, and Baran and Sweezy's updating of Lenin's analysis, he attempted to extend his analysis to the study of transformations in the periphery, where he understood underdevelopment to be the consequence of primitive accumulation for the benefit of the center.

Although the focus on precapitalist and capitalist modes of production allows distinctions between center and periphery, Amin reminded us that capitalism has become a world system, not a system of national capitalisms. Thus the distinctive social formations, the bourgeoisie and the proletariat, must not be distinguished in isolation within nations but on an international level. The world bourgeoisie then is found at the center, and the bourgeoisie of the periphery is influenced and shaped by the forces of the world market but dependent upon and dominated by the center. During Marx's time, the world proletariat was located at the center, but today it is found in the periphery, composed of the wage workers of large enterprise and the masses of peasants who are integrated into world exchanges. The reason for this realignment is the need to counter the tendency for the rate of profit to decline in the center by increasing the rate of surplus value extracted from the periphery.

Given the hegemony of the world capitalist system, Amin argued that socialism cannot exist until it transcends capitalism in every way. It must eliminate inequality. It must not be based on the market, either on a national or an international scale, for the market accentuates inequalities in the division of labor and the distribution of wealth.

Francisco López Segrera combined theories of underdevelopment, dependency, and imperialism in formulating a historical analysis of the Cuban political economy. In his book (1972) he stated that socialism is possible in a country dominated by imperialism no matter what the force of its dependent ties, but the essential task of his study was to examine the conditions of dependency and the consequences of imperialism that capitalism brought to Cuba. Inspired by the proliferation of revolutionary Marxist social science literature, his approach counters the "independent" developmental policy of ECLA. His basic thesis affirms that from the arrival of the Spaniards during the sixteenth century until 1959 Cuba was part of the international capitalist system. Cuban underdevelopment was a consequence of international capitalism and constituted a particular form—that of dependent capitalism. Dependency is the essential concept in his understanding of underdevelopment. Historical periods of Cuban dependency are identifiable in relation to international capitalism: mercantile capitalism (commercial capital), 1510–1762; free exchange (industrial capital), 1762–1880; imperialism (finance capital), 1880–1934; and neoimperialism (heavy industrial capital), 1934–1959.

López Segrera examined the characteristics of Cuban capitalist dependency in terms of diverse historical periods, such as the *encomienda*, hacienda, and plantation; in terms of function, for example, the furnishing of metals, raw materials, or agricultural commodities; of autonomy (Cuba was allowed some autonomous development during the period 1550–1700 because of Spain's conflict with other European countries and economic depression); of foreign control (sugar was under Cuban control from 1762 to 1860, at which time it passed into the hands of Spanish capital); and in terms of the political ties between Cuba and the metropolitan center. Finally, López Segrera examined the political and ideological alliance between the ruling classes of the colonial power and the colony. Among the basic propositions emanating from this study of Cuba are, first, historical analysis reveals that underdeveloped countries do not necessarily pass through the stages experienced by the developed countries; second, the colonization process in Latin America was promoted by Europe during a stage of expanding mercantile capitalism and the economy that emerged complemented the world economy; third, imperialism and neoimperialism served not to develop but to underdevelop the area. Fourth, the dialectical interdependence between the developed and the underdeveloped countries reflects the structural character of dependence: on the one hand, the historical development of and the system of relations between dependent and metropolitan countries and, on the other, the specific mode of production of each one of the dominant and dependent countries. Fifth, underdevelopment is not the result of a lack of entrepreneurial spirit but the consequence of objective historical conditions and, in particular, of centuries of capitalist exploitation.

López Segrera set forth his principal hypotheses to clarify the nature of Cuban capitalist underdevelopment. First, since the arrival of the Spaniards, Cuba has been characterized by dependent capitalism. Second, Cuban capitalist underdevelopment began early in the sixteenth century. Third, once a country such as Cuba has initiated capitalist underdevelopment it can advance toward development only by isolating itself from the world capitalist structure. Fourth, from the beginnings of capital accumulation until 1959 metropolitan capital (through the foreign bourgeoisie) associated itself with indigenous capital (the dependent bourgeoisie), first exploiting the colony (under Spanish mercantile capitalism) and later the neocolony (under North American imperialism). Fifth, dependency related almost exclusively to a single foreign market (first Spanish, then North American) and to a single commodity (first gold, then livestock and sugar). Sixth, as the metropolis developed through Cuban underdevelopment, so too did some regions, cities, classes, groups, and individuals benefit from the underdevelopment of others. Seventh, underdevelopment does not precede capitalism but, on the contrary, is a consequence of capitalism. Eighth, production in the colony is subordinate to the needs of the foreign market.

López Segrera's case study is addressed principally to dependency and capitalism and analyzes the consequences of historical relationships between metropolis and colony or neocolony. It does not attempt to analyze developments after the Cuban revolutionaries under Fidel Castro came to power and confronted the realities of a transition from capitalism to socialism. That task is the concern of Clive Thomas in his *Dependence and Transformation: The Economics of the Transition to Socialism* (1974).

Thomas was not concerned with the debates over the transition to socialism in industrial societies in Eastern Europe and to a lesser extent in China. Instead he focused on the problems of underdeveloped societies. Unlike many other dependency theorists, Thomas analyzed the productive forces and relations of production in the periphery of the capitalist system. He attempted to assimilate dependency theory and a Marxist framework and to link his Marxist dependency synthesis to social practice. His effort represents a considerable contribution to the discussion of the nature of the transition to socialism in the less developed nations.

The thrust of Thomas's work is prescriptive. He wanted to avoid a developmental strategy that might be influenced by the ECLA import-substituting industrialization solution, the Soviet model of heavy industry, or neoclassical economic notions of comparative advantage. Specifically, he wanted to deal "exclusively with the problems of developing the productive forces that would confront what would contemporaneously be described as an underdeveloped economy during the 'transition to socialism'" (1974: 27). He limited himself to countries like Cuba and Tanzania in which "a political revolution has been initiated and has succeeded in transferring state power to a worker/peasant alliance, thereby fundamentally altering production relations so that the struggle to bring the productive forces under their control and direction, to disengage from international capitalism, and to raise the material levels of welfare of the population are central economic issues at that stage in constructing socialism" (29).

The three works above represent serious efforts to construct a theory of development in the contemporary world. They assess the relevance of both orthodox and radical theories of dependency and underdevelopment. They suggest the possibility of an analysis that combines theory with practice in the examination of case studies. Finally, they move us toward a critical examination of the issues and problems of revolutionary societies that attempt to escape capitalism and mold their future in a socialist direction.

References

Almond, Gabriel A.
1965 "A Developmental Approach to Political Systems." *World Politics* XVII (January), 183–214. An effort to deal with criticisms suggesting that systems theory is static. Almond ties systems to development by dressing his old framework and terminology in a "new" conception of development and change.

Amin, Samir
1974 *Accumulation on a World Scale: A Critique of the Theory of Underdevelopment.* New York: Monthly Review Press. An ambitious critique of bourgeois economic theory and a serious synthesis and assessment of contemporary issues and theories of underdevelopment in the periphery of the less developed world.

1976 *Unequal Development: An Essay on the Social Transformations of Peripheral Capitalism.* New York: Monthly Review Press. Amin argues that the confrontation with imperialism must start from the periphery rather than from the center. His book is a theoretical exploration into precapitalist formations, laws of the capitalist mode, dependency, the development of underdevelopment, and social formations in the periphery.

Andrade, Manuel Correia de
1967 *Espaço, polarização e desenvolvimento: a teoria dos polos de desenvolvimento e a realidade nordestina.* Recife: Centro Regional de Administração Municipal. Sets forth a description of Northeast Brazil, identifying potential poles of development and following in the thought of François Perroux.

Apter, David E.
1965 *The Politics of Modernization.* Chicago: University of Chicago Press. Emphasizes two models of modernization—the Western democratic and the sacred collectivity models. Examines characteristics of modernization and tradition within a structural-functional framework.

Bacha, Claire Savit
1971 "A dependência nas relações internacionais: uma introdução a experência brasileira." Rio de Janeiro: Instituto Universitário de Pesquisas do Rio de Janeiro. A review and classification of the literature and ideas of dependency.

Baran, Paul
1957 *The Political Economy of Growth.* New York: Monthly Review Press. A

pioneering effort to depict relations between dominant and dependent areas of the world with emphasis on the extraction of surplus.

Baran, Paul, and Paul Sweezy
1966 *Monopoly Capital: An Essay on the American Economic and Social Order*. New York: Monthly Review Press. An influential and popular treatment of the thesis that corporate capital has become dominant in the capitalist world.

Barnet, Richard J., and Ronald E. Muller
1974 *Global Reach: The Power of the Multinational Corporations*. New York: Simon and Schuster. An overview and analysis of the role of the multinational corporations.

Bath, C. Richard, and Dilmus D. James
1976 "Dependency Analysis of Latin America." *Latin American Research Review* XI (3), 3–54. A review of the literature on dependency. Classifies the *dependentistas* as conservative, moderate, and radical. Offers nine suggestions for combining the dependency view with bourgeois social science concepts and methods.

Bendix, Reinhard
1969 *Nation-Building and Citizenship: Studies of Our Changing Social Order*. New York: Doubleday, Anchor Books. Theoretical essays and case studies of nation building.

Berger, Peter L.
1976 *Pyramids of Sacrifice: Political Ethics and Social Change*. Garden City, New York: Anchor Books. A look at Third World development as well as at political ethics as applied to social change. Argues against capitalist ideology as based on the myth of growth and against socialist ideology as based on the myth of revolution in a search for morally acceptable developmental policy.

Binder, Leonard
1964 "National Integration and Political Development." *American Political Science Review* LVIII (September), 622–631. A major article that synthesizes conceptualizations of integration and development in the process of nation building.

Binder, Leonard et al.
1971 *Crises and Sequences in Political Development*. Princeton: Princeton University Press. The last in a series on political development under the auspices of the Social Science Research Council. The authors reaffirm an emphasis on the concepts of equality, capacity, and differentiation, which compose the "development syndrome."

Black, C. E.
1966 *The Dynamics of Modernization*. New York: Harper and Row. Elaborates on four phases of modernization and focuses on critical problems.

Bluestone, Barry
1972 "Economic Crises and the Law of Uneven Development." *Politics and Society* III (Fall), 65–82. Examines uneven development in the case of the United States and concludes that uneven development will bring about the fall of capitalism.

Bodenheimer, Susanne J.
1970 "The Ideology of Developmentalism: American Political Science's Paradigm-Surrogate for Latin American Studies." *Berkeley Journal of Sociology* XV, 95–137. Prevailing values and methodology of U.S. political science have established both

ideology and paradigm to obscure an understanding of development.

Booth, David
1975 "André Gunder Frank: An Introduction and Appreciation." In Ivar Oxaal, Tony Barnett, and David Booth (eds.), *Beyond the Sociology of Development*, pp. 50–85. London: Routledge and Kegan Paul. A detailed review and assessment of the work and thought of André Gunder Frank, showing the origins of his thinking and some criticisms.

Bukharin, Nikolai
1929 *Imperialism and World Economy*. Introduction by V. I. Lenin. New York: Monthly Review Press. Originally published by International Publishers in 1929 and republished in this edition at a later date, this is a major theoretical synthesis of imperialism.

Cardoso, Fernando Henrique
1971 *Política e desenvolvimento em sociedades dependentes*. Rio de Janeiro: Biblioteca de Ciências Sociais, Zahar Editores. The author introduces a theory of dependency and underdevelopment and draws upon his research focused on the ideologies of the Argentine and Brazilian industrial entrepreneur.

1972 "Dependency and Development in Latin America." *New Left Review* 74 (July-August), 83–95. Elaboration of his ideas of dependency, here suggesting an update of Lenin's theory of imperialism.

1973a "Associated-Dependent Development: Theoretical and Practical Implications." In Alfred Stepan (ed.), *Authoritarian Brazil: Origins, Policies, and Future*, pp. 142–176. New Haven: Yale University Press. Outlines his theory of associated dependent development, arguing that dependency and capitalist development can be compatible.

1973b "Notas sobre estado e dependência." São Paulo: Centro Brasileiro de Análise e Planejamento (Caderno II). Review and classification of theories of dependency.

Cardoso, Fernando Henrique, and Enzo Faletto
1969 *Dependencia y desarrollo en América Latina*. Mexico City: Siglo Veintiuno Editores. A pioneering effort to examine the internal aspects of dependency.

Chalmers, Douglas A.
1972 "The Demystification of Development." In Douglas A. Chalmers (ed.), *Changing Latin America: New Interpretations of Its Politics and Society*, pp. 109–122. New York: Proceedings of the Academy of Political Science, Columbia University. Concludes that developmentalism, the notion that development can be diffused from advanced to backward areas, is no longer of utility but that there is a need to search for a theory of development.

Chilcote, Ronald H.
1969 "Development and Nationalism in Brazil and Portuguese Africa." *Comparative Political Studies* I (January), 501–525. Examines nine types of nationalism and five dimensions of development, using Brazil and Portuguese Africa as examples.

1974 "Dependency: A Critical Synthesis of the Literature." *Latin American*

Perspectives I (Fall), 4–29. A detailed overview and assessment of the literature on dependency.

1978 "A Question of Dependency." *Latin American Research Review* XII (2), 55–68. A restatement of earlier views and a synthesis of theories of dependency. Identifies criteria and terminology necessary for Marxist theory, which incorporates a view of dependency.

Chilcote, Ronald H., and Joel C. Edelstein (eds.)
1974 *Latin America: The Struggle with Dependency and Beyond.* Cambridge, Massachusetts: Schenkman Publishing. An introduction on underdevelopment and development is followed by country essays on Guatemala, Mexico, Argentina, Brazil, Chile, and Cuba.

Chodak, Szymon
1973 *Societal Development: Five Approaches with Conclusions from Comparative Analysis.* New York: Oxford University Press. A useful overview of approaches to development, critical but sympathetic to orthodox theory.

Clarkson, Stephen
1972 "Marxism-Leninism as a System for Comparative Analysis of Under-Development." *Political Science Review* XI (April), 124–137. Examines Marxist-Leninist writings on underdevelopment. Very critical of these writings but concludes that they are useful for their total view of the political system, coherence, high degree of conceptual stability, and broad intelligibility. Anticipates improvement in quality, both individually and comparatively.

Cnudde, Charles
1972 "Theories of Political Development and the Assumptions of Statistical Models: An Evaluation of Two Models." *Comparative Political Studies* V (July), 131–150. Using two models of cross-national literature on political development, the author tests them with aggregate data.

Cohen, Benjamin
1973 *The Question of Imperialism: The Political Economy of Dominance and Dependence.* New York: Basic Books. A synthesis of definitions and interpretations of imperialism, from the nineteenth century until today.

Coser, Lewis A.
1957 "Social Conflict and the Theory of Social Change." *British Journal of Sociology* VIII (September), 197–207. A review of the theories of conflict and change, including those of class struggle.

Coulter, Phillip
1972 "Political Development and Political Theory: Methodological and Technological Problems in the Comparative Study of Political Development." *Polity* V (Winter), 233–242. Examines the methodological problems in comparative studies of development that are now ahistorical, multidisciplinary, cross-culturally comparative, macro, and quantitative.

Cueva, Agustín
1976 "A Summary of 'Problems and Perspectives of Dependency Theory.'" *Latin American Perspectives* III (Fall), 12–16. A critical assessment of the theories of dependency from a Marxist point of view. Argues that a theory of dependency has

not established itself but that dependency will continue to be a major feature of Latin American societies.

Davis, Horace B.
1967 *Nationalism and Socialism: Marxist and Labor Theories of Nationalism to 1917.* New York: Monthly Review Press. An exhaustive synthesis and assessment of Marxist perspectives of nationalism, with attention to Marx, Engels, and Lenin.

Dennon, A. R.
1969 "Political Science and Political Development." *Science and Society* XXXIII (Summer-Fall), 285–298. Finds political science theories of development trivial, ahistorical, static, and superficial.

Deutsch, Karl W.
1953 *Nationalism and Social Communication: An Inquiry into the Foundation of Nationality.* New York: Technology Press of the Massachusetts Institute of Technology and John Wiley & Sons. A classic study of nationalism and its developmental implications.

1969 *Nationalism and Its Alternatives.* New York: Alfred A. Knopf. Further elaboration and synthesis of the author's earlier work on nationalism.

Deutsch, Karl W., and William J. Foltz (eds.)
1963 *Nation-Building.* New York: Atherton Press. Essays relating nation-building to various parts of the world.

Deutsch, Karl W., and Richard L. Merritt (eds.)
1970 *Nationalism and National Development: An Interdisciplinary Bibliography.* Cambridge, Massachusetts: M.I.T. Press. A bibliographical essay on the literature of nationalism and development.

Dodd, Clement H.
1973 "Political Development: The End of an Era?" *Government and Opposition* VIII (Summer), 367–374. A critical yet sympathetic review of Binder et al. (1971).

Doob, Leonard W.
1964 *Patriotism and Nationalism: Their Psychological Foundations.* New Haven: Yale University Press. Explores the content and expression of patriotism and nationalism.

Dos Santos, Theotonio
1968 *El nuevo caracter de la dependencia.* Santiago: Centro de Estudios Socio-Económicos (CESO), Universidad de Chile. Cuadernos de Estudios Socio-Económicos (10). Elaborates on his theory of the new dependency.

1970 "The Structure of Dependency." *American Economic Review* LX (May), 231–236. A synthesis and conceptualization of the new dependency theory. Offers a definition and identifies historical forms of dependence.

Eisenstadt, S. N.
1964 "Modernization and Conditions of Sustained Growth." *World Politics* XVI (July), 576–594. Theoretical observations of modernization and growth.

Emerson, Rupert
1960a *From Empire to Nation.* Cambridge: Harvard University Press. A major study of nationalism and its emergence in Africa.

1960b "Nationalism and Political Development." *Journal of Politics* XXII (February), 137–149. An early effort to relate the concepts of nationalism and development.

Emmanuel, Arghiri
1972 *Unequal Exchange: A Study of the Imperialism of Trade.* New York: Monthly Review Press. Discusses various cases of exchange through trade of products in light of current theory. Demonstrates that unequal exchange is a reflection of relations of developed to underdeveloped nations. Includes critical views of Charles Bettelheim and rejoinders by Emmanuel.

Fieldhouse, D. K.
1961 "'Imperialism': An Historiographical Revision." *Economic History Review* 2d ser. XIV (2), 187–209. A critical examination of the pros and cons of Hobson's theory of imperialism. Concludes that his theory was "defective" and that it is unacceptable as a historical interpretation of the expansion of European empires between 1870 and 1914.

Fitzgibbon, Russell
1956 "A Statistical Evaluation of Latin American Democracy." *Western Political Quarterly* IX (September), 607–619. Opinions from Latin American experts based on their perceptions of the degree of democracy in the nations of Latin America. This is one of several surveys conducted by the author at five-year intervals.

Foster-Carter, Aiden
1974 "Neo-Marxist Approaches to Development and Underdevelopment." In Emanuel De Kadt and Gavin Williams (eds.), *Sociology and Development*, pp. 67–105. London: Tavistock Publications. A detailed examination of neo-Marxist thought, namely, that thought that has reassessed Marxism's practical successes and failures since 1945.

1976 "From Rostow to Gunder Frank: Conflicting Paradigms in the Analysis of Underdevelopment." *World Development* IV (March), 167–180. Within the Kuhnian concept of scientific revolution the author examines the paradigmatic conflict between the theories of Rostow and André Gunder Frank.

Frank, André Gunder
1966 "The Development of Underdevelopment.'" *Monthly Review* XVIII (September), 17–31. Here Frank first sets forth his influential and controversial theory of capitalist development of underdevelopment.

1967a *Capitalism and Underdevelopment in Latin America: Historical Studies of Chile and Brazil.* New York: Monthly Review Press. The author's pioneer effort to set forth a theory of capitalist underdevelopment, with case studies of Brazil and Chile.

1967b "Sociology of Development and Underdevelopment of Sociology." *Catalyst* III (Summer), 20–73. An exhaustive critique of prevailing orthodox conceptions of development in the social sciences.

1972 *Lumpenbourgeoisie: Lumpendevelopment — Dependence, Class, and Politics in Latin America.* New York: Monthly Review Press. Frank answers critics in a "mea culpa" introduction.

1974 "Dependence Is Dead, Long Live Dependence and the Class Struggle: An Answer to Critics." *Latin American Perspectives* I (Spring), 87–106. A rebuttal to critics of the Right, traditional Marxist Left, and new Left.

1975 "Development and Underdevelopment in the New World: Smith and Marx vs. the Weberians." *Theory and Society* II (Spring), 431–466. Reviews contrasting interpretations of development and underdevelopment.

Furtado, Celso

1963 *Economic Growth of Brazil: A Survey from Colonial to Modern Times*. Berkeley: University of California Press. Historical analysis of economic growth and decline in Brazil, a case study of dependency and underdevelopment within a non-Marxist context.

1964 *Development and Underdevelopment*. Translated by Ricardo W. de Aguiar and Eric Charles Drysdale. Berkeley: University of California Press. Theoretical essays on classical and Marxist interpretations of underdevelopment.

1970 *Economic Development of Latin America: A Survey from Colonial Times to the Cuban Revolution*. Cambridge: Cambridge University Press. An overview of development and underdevelopment in Latin America.

Galtung, Johan

1971 "A Structural Theory of Imperialism." *Journal of Peace Research* VIII (2), 81–117. Non-Marxist but detailed theory of imperialism based on the definition that "imperialism is a system that splits up collectivities and relates some of the parts to each other in relations of *harmony of interest*, and other parts in relations of *disharmony of interest*, or *conflict of interest*."

Gantzel, Klaus Jürgen

1973 "Dependency Structures as the Dominant Pattern in World Society." *Journal of Peace Research* X (3), 203–215. Examines dependency and imperialism in terms of center and periphery with attention to four perspectives: relations between capitalist center nations; relations between capitalist center nations and the periphery; relations between capitalist and socialist centers; relations between socialist societies.

Gerstein, Ira

1977 "Theories of the World Economy and Imperialism." *Insurgent Sociologist* VII (Spring), 9–22 with responses from Amin and others following. A critical review of works by Wallerstein, Amin, Palloix, and Poulantzas.

Gilbert, Guy J.

1974 "Socialism and Dependency." *Latin American Perspectives* I (Spring), 107–123. Refutation of the criticism of Ray (1973), who argues that socialist dependency must be studied alongside capitalist dependency.

Girvan, Norman

1970 "Multinational Corporations and Dependent Underdevelopment in Mineral-Export Economies." *Social and Economic Studies* XIX (December), 490–526. Analyzes the anatomy of dependent underdevelopment for economies structured around mineral export industries operated by large multinational firms in Venezuela, Chile, Surinam, Guyana, Jamaica, Trinidad and Tobago, and the Netherlands Antilles.

González Casanova, Pablo
  1970 *Sociología de la explotación*. 2d ed. Mexico City: Siglo Veintiuno Editores. Sets forth the theory of internal colonialism.
Goulet, Denis A.
  1968 "Development for What?" *Comparative Political Studies* I (July), 295–312. Searches for a definition of development based on values and goals that affect individual survival, esteem, and freedom.
Griffin, Keith
  1969 *Underdevelopment in Spanish America: An Interpretation*. Cambridge: M.I.T. Press. Historical overview with economic emphasis of underdevelopment in Latin America.
Grundy, Kenneth W.
  1966 "African Explanations of Underdevelopment: The Theoretical Basis for Political Action." *Review of Politics* XXVIII (January), 62–75. A review of the views of African leaders, concluding with a comparative analysis of these views on underdevelopment.
Hamid, Naved
  1974 "Alternative Development Strategies." *Monthly Review* XXVI (October), 31–52. Demonstrates the contradictions in attempting to balance foreign investment with domestic control over economy and welfare and concludes that an underdeveloped country must first mobilize its domestic resources.
Havens, A. Eugene
  1972 "Methodological Issues in the Study of Development."*Sociologia Ruralis* XII (3/4), 252–272. A useful inventory of major issues that emanate from equilibrium and conflict models and approaches to development.
Hayes, Carlton
  1960 *Nationalism: A Religion*. New York: Macmillan Company. A major treatment of nationalism that examines its European origins and evolution.
Hilferding, Rudolf
  1910 *Das Finanzkapital*. Pages 426–429 translated into English in Paul Sweezy, *The Theory of Capitalist Development: Principles of Marxian Political Economy*, pp. 375–378. New York: Monthly Review Press, 1942. The notion of finance capital influenced Lenin in his study of imperialism.
Hobson, J. A.
  1965 *Imperialism: A Study*. Ann Arbor: Ann Arbor Paperbacks, University of Michigan Press. Reprinting of Hobson's classic study, first published in 1902, with an introduction by Philip Siegelman. A Liberal interpretation that was to influence Lenin in his own study of imperialism.
Holt, Robert T., and John E. Turner
  1975 "Crises and Sequences in Collective Theory Development." *American Political Science Review* LXIX (September), 979–994. A critical review of the work on development by the Social Science Research Council.
Horowitz, Irving Louis, and Ellen Kay Trimberger
  1976 "State Power and Military Nationalism in Latin America." *Comparative Politics* VIII (January), 223–244. Sees in dependency theory a failing in the emphasis on forces of external capital and not analyzing national differences. Looks

at an autonomous military bureaucracy and successful development, which follows three patterns: state-initiated national capitalist development; state-initiated dependent development; and state-directed socialist development.

Huntington, Samuel P.

1965 "Political Development and Political Decay." *World Politics* XVII (April), 386–430. Examines the relationship between institutionalization and stability, on the one hand, and mobilization and participation, on the other. Where mobilization and participation outpace institutionalization, political decay sets in.

1968 *Political Order in Changing Societies.* New Haven: Yale University Press. Elaboration of his thesis (1965), in which he notes political decay appears with an imbalance toward mobilization and participation. Argues for stability and order.

Huntington, Samuel P., and Joan M. Nelson

1976 *No Easy Choice: Political Participation in Developing Countries.* Cambridge: Harvard University Press. Attempts to depart from Huntington's earlier analysis of political instability (1968) by turning to political participation in countries of the Third World.

Jackson, Gary

1972 "Some Approaches to the Study of Modernization and Development." *Journal of International and Comparative Studies* V (Winter), 54–77. With attention to approach and methodology, the author provides a critical assessment of writings by Eisenstadt, Almond, Shils, and others.

Jackson, Steven, Bruce Russett, Duncan Snidal, and David Sylvan

1979 "An Assessment of Empirical Research on *Dependencia.*" *Latin American Research Review* XIV (3), 7–28. Reviews the origins of dependency theory through the work of Frank, Cardoso, Amin, and the Economic Commission for Latin America; examines case studies by Quijano on Peru, Leys on Kenya, and Biersteker on Nigeria; and assesses U.S. empirical applications of dependency theory. Describes the Yale project that has applied statistics and mathematics to dependency analysis.

Jaguaribe, Helio et al.

1970 *La dependencia politico-económica de América Latina.* 2d ed. Mexico City: Siglo Veintiuno Editores. Jaguaribe in this collection of essays argues for autonomous national development as a solution for eliminating dependency.

Kaufman, Robert R., Harry I. Chernotsky, and Daniel S. Geller

1975 "A Preliminary Test of the Theory of Dependency." *Comparative Politics* VI (April), 303–330. Attempts to operationalize and test bivariate propositions of dependency theory by looking at data for seventeen Latin American nations. Concludes that the concept of dependency requires refinement and redefinition, that attention should be directed to political, social, and cultural variables that may intervene between economic dependency and its alleged consequences, and that new techniques should be devised for a systematic exploration of dependency hypotheses.

Kautsky, Karl

1964 *The Dictatorship of the Proletariat.* Ann Arbor: University of Michigan. This was the initial polemic in the debates between Kautsky and Lenin and their interpretations of Marxism. Attacks the undemocratic regime of the Bolsheviks in Russia.

Kay, Geoffrey
1975 *Development and Underdevelopment: A Marxist Analysis.* London: Macmillan Press. Systematically analyzes both merchant and industrial capital in the process of underdevelopment, unequal exchange, and other aspects of classical and contemporary Marxist theory.

Kesselman, Mark
1973 "Order or Movement: The Literature of Political Development as Ideology." *World Politics* XXVI (October), 139–154. A critical review of Binder et al. (1971) and Huntington (1968).

Kohn, Hans
1968 *The Age of Nationalism: The First Era of Global History.* New York: Harper and Row. A classic study of nationalism in historical perspective.

Laclau, Ernesto
1971 "Feudalism and Capitalism in Latin America." *New Left Review* 67 (May-June), 19–38. Critical of Frank's theory of underdevelopment.

Lall, Sanjaya
1975 "Is 'Dependence' a Useful Concept in Analyzing Underdevelopment?" *World Development* III (November-December), 799–810. A sympathetic but critical assessment of dependency. Argues that many conclusions about the impact of dependence on development apply to particular cases but cannot be generalized.

Lane, David
1974 "Leninism as an Ideology of Soviet Development." In Emanuel de Kadt and Gavin Williams (eds.), *Sociology and Development*, pp. 23–37. London: Tavistock Publications. Identifies the major aspects of Lenin's views about social change in backward areas, then examines the ways in which Soviet policies of social change deviated from Lenin's intentions.

Leaver, Richard
1977 "The Debate on Underdevelopment: On Situating André Gunder Frank." *Journal of Contemporary Asia* VII (1), 108–115. Reassesses Laclau's criticism of André Gunder Frank and examines Frank's theory of underdevelopment and dependency.

Lenin, V. I.
1967 *Selected Works in Three Volumes.* Moscow: Progress Publishers.

Levy, Marion J., Jr.
1966 *Modernization and the Structure of Societies.* Princeton: Princeton University Press. A structural-functional framework is used to generate two volumes of propositions on modernization.

Leys, Colin
1977 "Underdevelopment and Dependency: Critical Notes." *Journal of Contemporary Asia* VII (1), 92–107. Critical assessment of theories of underdevelopment and dependency. Argues that these theories must be transcended.

Lichtheim, George
1970 "Imperialism." *Commentary* XLIX, Part 1 (April), 42–75; Part 2 (May), 33–58. The first part outlines the background relevant to a general understanding of im-

perialism in the contemporary world; the second part deals with the ideas and theories of imperialism since the late nineteenth century. These essays were included in the author's *Imperialism.* New York: Praeger Publishers, 1971.

Lippit, Victor D.
1976 " The Development of Underdevelopment in China." Working Paper Series, no. 8 (May). Department of Economics, University of California, Riverside. Applies the thesis of capitalist development of underdevelopment in a historical analysis of prerevolutionary China.

Lipset, Seymour Martin
1959 "Some Social Requisites of Democracy: Economic Development and Political Legitimacy." *American Political Science Review* LIII (March), 69–105. Presents some requisites for democracy. This paper represents a major synthesis of criteria relating to democracy and development.

Long, Norman
1975 "Structural Dependency, Modes of Production, and Economic Brokerage in Rural Peru." In Ivar Oxaal, Tony Barnett, and David Booth (eds.), *Beyond the Sociology of Development*, pp. 253–282. London: Routledge and Kegan Paul. Using Peru as a case example, the author criticizes various approaches to the interpretation of problems of underdevelopment and structural dependency.

López Segrera, Francisco
1972 *Cuba: capitalismo dependiente y subdesarrollo (1510–1959)*, Havana: Casa de las Américas. A case study of Cuba under dependent capitalism, as early as the sixteenth century. Examines each historical period systematically for the impact of dependency, underdevelopment, and imperialism.

Luxemburg, Rosa
1951 *The Accumulation of Capital.* Translated by Agnes Schwarzschild. New Haven: Yale University Press. Reprinted by Monthly Review Press, 1964. A useful introduction by Joan Robinson summarizes and criticizes the theories of Luxemburg. The central thesis of this book is set forth in chapter 26 on the reproduction of capital, in which Rosa Luxemburg argues that capitalism subsists on its penetration of primitive economies and their subsequent underdevelopment.

Luxemburg, Rosa, and Nicolai I. Bukharin
1972 *The Accumulation of Capital – An Anti-critique* and *Imperialism and the Accumulation of Capital.* Edited with an introduction by Kenneth J. Tarbuck. New York: Monthly Review Press. Two volumes dealing with Marx's theory of accumulation.

McHenry, Dean E., Jr.
1976 "The Underdevelopment Theory: A Case-Study from Tanzania." *Journal of African Studies* XIV (December), 621–636. Locates the conditions for underdevelopment within a colonial or neocolonial country, then examines Tanzania as a subject country of Great Britain and concludes that colonialism and imperialism do not link to underdevelopment.

Magdoff, Harry
1969 *The Age of Imperialism: The Economics of U.S. Foreign Policy.* New York: Monthly Review Press. A contemporary Marxist statement of imperialism.

1970 "Is Imperialism Really Necessary?" *Monthly Review* XXII (October), 1–14. Reply to an article by S. M. Miller, Roy Bennett, and Cyril Alapatt (1970), who take a liberal stance and deemphasize the economic implications of imperialism. This article was originally published in *Social Policy* I (September-October 1970), 19–29.

Marini, Ruy Mauro
1969 *Subdesarrollo y revolución*. Mexico City: Siglo Veintiuno Editores. Examines underdevelopment and revolution, the dialectic of capitalist development in Brazil, and the impact of subimperialism on the working masses.

Miller, S. M., Roy Bennett, and Cyril Alapatt
1970 "Does the U.S. Economy Require Imperialism?" *Social Policy* I (September-October), 13–19. A Liberal critique of Magdoff (1969); argues that capitalism will transcend world conflict generated by imperialism. Magdoff offers a rebuttal in the same issue, pages 19–29.

Milne, R. S.
1972 "The Overdeveloped Study of Political Development." *Canadian Journal of Political Science* V (December), 560–568. The study of political development has been overdeveloped so that the term tends to confuse and obscure understanding.

Moore, Stanley W.
1957 *The Critique of Capitalist Democracy: An Introduction to the Theory of the State in Marx, Engels, and Lenin*. New York: Paine-Whitman Publishers. A tight synthesis of the theory of the state with attention to dictatorship, capitalist exploitation, capitalism and democracy, and ideology and alienation.

Myer, John
1975 "A Crown of Thorns: Cardoso and Counter-Revolution." *Latin American Perspectives* II (Spring), 33–48. A review and critique of the works and thoughts of Cardoso. Exposes the alleged non-Marxist tendencies in his theory.

Nathan, Otto
1966 "Marxism and Monopoly Capital." *Science and Society* XXX (Fall), 487–496. A critical review of Baran and Sweezy's treatise on monopoly capitalism (1966).

Nieuwenhuijze, C.A.O. van
1971 "The Sociology of Development: *per aspera ad astra?*" *Civilizations* XXI (1) 67–82. Examines some of the conceptual and methodological problems affecting economics and sociology in the study of development.

Nisbet, Robert A.
1969 *Social Change and History*. New York: Oxford University Press. An overview of past and present conceptions of development and change.

Novack, George
1966 *Uneven and Combined Development in History*. New York: Merit Publishers. Full discussions of these laws as elaborated by Trotsky and others.

O'Brien, Donald Cruise
1972 "Modernization, Order, and the Erosion of a Democratic Ideal." *Journal of Development Studies* VIII (July), 351–378. Notes a shift from the study of democracy to a normative emphasis on authoritarianism as the explanation of U.S. politics for an ideology of authoritarianism and institutional order.

O'Brien, Philip J.
1975 "A Critique of Latin American Theories of Dependency." In Ivar Oxaal, Tony Barnett, and David Booth (eds.), *Beyond the Sociology of Development*, pp. 7–85. London: Routledge and Kegan Paul. A review of the dependency literature from ECLA to the present. Classifies the literature into theories around ECLA structuralism, Marxist dependency, and the Marxist-structuralist synthesis.

O'Connor, James
1966 "Monopoly Capital." *New Left Review* 40 (November-December), 38–50. A critique of the work of Baran and Sweezy on monopoly capital (1966).

1968 "Finance Capital or Corporate Capital?" *Monthly Review* XX (December), 30–35. Identifies and contrasts two Marxist approaches, one that looks to corporate capital and the other that sees bank capital as the dominant form of capital in the world. O'Connor favors the position of Baran and Sweezy, which focuses on corporate capital, but argues that there is a need to develop a systematic theory of corporate capital.

Organski, A.F.K.
1965 *The Stages of Political Development*. New York: Alfred A. Knopf. An application of stage theory to politics, influenced by Rostow's theory of economic stages (1960).

Pachter, Henry
1970 "The Problem of Imperialism." *Dissent* XVII (September-October), 461–488. Argues that Lenin has misled an entire generation of anti-imperialists by insisting that the root was always economic and looks for non-Marxist explanations to describe different types of imperialism.

Packenham, Robert A.
1964 "Approaches to the Study of Political Development." *World Politics* XVII (October), 108–120. A research note on the primary determinants of political development: legal-formal, economic, administrative, social system, and political culture.

Pasquino, Gianfranco
1970 "The Politics of Modernization: An Appraisal of David Apter's Contributions." *Comparative Political Studies* III (October), 297–322. Rejoinder by Apter, in the same issue, pages 323–332. A critical review of Apter's work, from his field studies in Africa to his attempt to evolve a theory of modernization.

Perroux, François
1968 "Multinational Investment and the Analysis of Development and Integration Poles." In Inter-American Development Bank, *Multinational Investment, Public and Private, in the Economic Development and Integration of Latin America*, pp. 95–125. Bogotá: Inter-American Development Bank. Synthesizes Perroux's work on development poles and integration poles, setting forth theory and methods of application.

Pratt, Raymond B.
1973 "The Underdeveloped Political Science of Development." *Studies in Comparative International Development* VIII (Spring), 88–112. Identifies weaknesses in political science conceptions of development: they show little concern with the

human dimension; they suffer from misplaced emphases, for example, ignoring wealth and power as key ingredients in the politics of development; and they skirt questions of political economy.

Pye, Lucian W.

1958 "The Non-Western Political Process." *Journal of Politics* XX (August), 468–486. Outlines seventeen dominant characteristics of the non-Western political process, which in fact tend to reflect Western orientations toward politics.

1962 *Politics, Personality, and Nation Building: Burma's Search for Identity.* New Haven: Yale University Press. An examination and analysis of attitudes toward nationalism in Burma, based on field research.

1965 "The Concept of Political Development." *Annals of the American Academy of Political and Social Science* CCCLVIII (March), 3–13. Reviews ten definitions of political development.

1966 *Aspects of Political Development.* Boston: Little, Brown and Co. An overview of theories of development imbued with the author's bias toward Western democracy.

Quijano, Aníbal

1971 *Nationalism and Colonialism in Peru: A Study in Neo-Imperialism.* New York: Monthly Review Press. A case study of the military effort to restructure Peru so as to allow for autonomous national development. The author is critical of this approach and offers a class analysis of Peruvian problems.

1974 "Imperialism and International Relations in Latin America." In Julio Cotler and Richard R. Fagen (eds.), *Latin America and the United States*, pp. 67–91. Stanford: Stanford University Press. Explicit treatment of imperialism and its impact.

Raskin, Jonah

1971 *The Mythology of Imperialism.* New York: Random House. Critical essays on radical thought in the works of famous novelists such as Kipling, Conrad, Forster, Lawrence, and Cary.

Ray, David

1973 "The Dependency Model of Latin American Underdevelopment: Three Basic Fallacies." *Journal of Interamerican Studies and World Affairs* XV (February), 4–20. Attempts to demonstrate weaknesses in dependency theory. Argues that socialist dependency as well as capitalist dependency should be examined.

Riggs, Fred W.

1968 "The Dialectics of Developmental Conflict." *Comparative Political Studies* I (July), 197–226. From an orthodox perspective the author questions assumptions of writers who assume processes of change are unidirectional, irreversible, and conflict-free.

Rodney, Walter

1972 *How Europe Underdeveloped Africa.* London and Dar es Salaam: Bogle-l'Ouverture and Tanzania Publishing House. Published in the United States by Howard University Press. A sequel to Frank's (1967b) study of Latin America.

Romagnolo, David J.
   1974 "The So-Called 'Law' of Uneven and Combined Development." *Latin American Perspectives* II (Spring), 7–31. Detailed critique of the law of uneven and combined development.
Rostow, Walt W.
   1960 *The Stages of Economic Growth: A Non-Communist Manifesto.* Cambridge: Cambridge University Press. An effort to set forth five stages of capitalist development.
Rustow, Dankwart A.
   1969 "The Organization Triumphs over Its Function: Huntington on Modernization." *Journal of International Affairs* XXIII (1), 119–132. Sympathetic yet critical review of Huntington (1968). Especially useful for contradictions identified in Huntington's argument.
Sachs, Ignacy
   1972 "The Logic of Development." *International Social Science Journal* XXIV (1), 37–43. Critical of simplistic and mechanistic theories of development.
Samoff, Joel, and Rachel Samoff
   1976 "The Local Politics of Underdevelopment." *American Review* VI (1), 69–97. Accepts the proposition that Europe underdeveloped Africa and examines this process of underdevelopment in a local community in Tanzania.
Schmitter, Phillippe C.
   1972 "Paths to Political Development in Latin America." In Douglas A. Chalmers (ed.), *Changing Latin America: New Interpretations of Its Politics and Society,* pp. 83–105. New York: Proceedings of the Academy of Political Science, Columbia University. Assesses paradigm shifts in the literature on development and evaluates the implications for Latin America of a variety of development models.
Schumpeter, Joseph
   1955 *Imperialism: Social Classes.* Cleveland and New York: Meridian Books and World Publishing Company. Argues that imperialism is not a significant force in an era of advanced capitalism.
Seers, Dudley
   1977 "The Meaning of Development." *International Development Review* XIX (2) 2–7. Attempts to define development in terms of needs such as food, jobs, and equality and examines these criteria in terms of the Third World.
Shafer, Boyd C.
   1955 *Nationalism, Myth and Reality.* New York: Harcourt Brace and Co. Conceptualization and definition of nationalism are explored in synthesis form.
Silvert, Kalman H.
   1963 *Expectant Peoples: Nationalism and Development.* New York: Random House. Case studies on nationalism and development in countries of the Third World.
Skocpol, Theda
   1973 "A Critical Review of Barrington Moore's Social Origins of Dictatorship and Democracy." *Politics and Society* IV (Fall), 1–34. Praise for Moore's work as the only useful Marxist study of politics and modernization.
Smith, Arthur K., Jr.
   1969 "Socio-Economic Development and Political Democracy: A Causal

Analysis." *Midwest Journal of Political Science* XIII (February), 95–125. Looks at the problems of defining and measuring political democracy on a cross-national level.

Snyder, Louis L. (ed.)
1964 *The Dynamics of Nationalism: Readings in Its Meaning and Development.* University Series in History. Princeton, New Jersey: D. Van Nostrand Co. A collection of readings about nationalism in theory as well as in practice in many countries.

Spengler, J. J.
1960 "Economic Development: Political Pre-Conditions and Political Consequences." *Journal of Politics* XXII (August), 387–416. Examines conditions of the underdeveloped world, then looks at the functions of government affecting economic development.

Sunkel, Osvaldo
1972 "Big Business and 'Dependencia.'" *Foreign Affairs* L (April), 517–531. A general statement of the author's theory of dependency.

Szentes, Tamás
1976 *The Political Economy of Underdevelopment.* 3d ed. Budapest: Akadémiai Kiadó. A critical overview of literature and theories of underdevelopment. Argues that Marxism has always offered a historical explanation for the causes of underdevelopment and attempts to combine method and terminology into an effective Marxist-Leninist conception of underdevelopment.

Szymanski, Albert
1976 "Dependence, Exploitation, and Economic Growth." *Journal of Political and Military Sociology* IV (Spring), 53–65. Using empirical evidence, the author assesses classical Marxist and dependency arguments about development and underdevelopment. His findings lean toward the dependency arguments of Baran and Frank but also support the traditional argument that the more dependent, the more rapid is a country's economic growth.

Tanter, Raymond
1967 "Toward a Theory of Political Development." *Midwest Journal of Political Science* XI (May), 145–172. Review of cross-national studies of political development and an assessment of "the quantitative techniques and the mathematics of causal inference for revision of such theories."

Thomas, Clive Y.
1974 *Dependence and Transformation: The Economics of the Transition to Socialism.* New York: Monthly Review Press. Theoretical treatment of dependency and underdevelopment, with concern for the problem of transition from capitalism to socialism in countries where a political revolution has been initiated.

Tipps, Dean C.
1973 "Modernization Theory and the Comparative Study of Societies: A Critical Perspective." *Comparative Studies in Society and History* XV (March), 199–226. A very detailed, critical review of orthodox modernization theory.

Tyler, William G. and J. Peter Wogart
1973 "Economic Dependence and Marginalization: Some Empirical Evidence." *Journal of Interamerican Studies and World Affairs* XV (February), 36–45. Tests assumptions of dependency suggested by Sunkel and concludes that there is not

sufficient evidence to reject the dependency thesis.

Vasconi, Tomás

1969 "De la dependencia como una categoria básica para el análisis de desarrollo latinoamericano." In Carlos Lessa and Tomás Vasconi, *Hacia una crítica de las interpretaciones del desarrollo latinoamericano*, pp. 34–51. Caracas: Universidad Central de Venezuela. An early elaboration of the center-periphery framework as a basis for analyzing dependency.

Whitaker, Arthur P., and David C. Jordan

1966 *Nationalism in Contemporary Latin America*. New York: Free Press. Overview of nationalism in historical and contemporary forms throughout Latin America.

Whitaker, C. S., Jr.

1967 "A Dysrhythmic Process of Political Change." *World Politics* XIX (January), 190–217. The introductory sections of this paper challenge the assumptions of a traditional-modern dichotomy in contemporary societies.

Willner, Ann Ruth

1964 "The Underdeveloped Study of Political Development." *World Politics* XVI (April), 468–482. An early critique of literature on political development with attention to the writings of Edward Shils, John H. Kautsky, and John J. Johnson.

Theories of Class:
From Pluralist Elite
to Ruling Class and Mass

Terminology such as pluralist elite, power elite, power structure, circulating elite, ruling elite, governing class, and ruling class pervades the literature on social class. Each of these terms emanates from past thought. Marx and Weber, for example, offered different perspectives.

Although Marx did not fully develop a theory of class, he used class to describe and analyze the relations of production associated with various historical epochs and modes of production. In general, he referred to the three big classes of landowners, industrial capitalists, and workers. On the one side was the bourgeoisie of modern capitalists and owners of the means of production, and on the other side there were the modern wage workers who sell their labor to live and have no means of production. Marx examined the conflict between these opposing forces. At the same time Marx acknowledged the existence of smaller classes—bureaucrats and professionals, for example—and he used such class terms as the finance aristocracy, industrial bourgeoisie, peasantry, lumpenproletariat, industrial proletariat, and so on. At the heart of his analysis is a focus not on ruling classes alone, but on ruling classes and ruled masses in conflict and the struggle generated by one class's dominant rule materially over production and intellectually over ideas, resulting in an exploitation of a repressed class.

Weber argued that status groups as well as classes affect the control over a community. Status groups are found within economic classes, stratified and hierarchically ranked according to the demands of the market and reflecting a diversity of interests and preferences. With changes in market, status groups are rearranged within a class so that a lower group might be elevated to a higher one, and others might drop in ranking. The status groups as well as the individuals within them are mobile and in flux; individual talent and initiative may bring about changes in individual and group position in society. Weber thus saw class as an ideal type, not a consequence of the productive forces and relations. Weber anticipated unlimited class and group situations in contrast to Marx who emphasized two or three large classes. Weber also argued that class fragmentation would result from nationalism and ethnic loyalties, whereas Marx believed that class consciousness would solidify the proletariat into a revolutionary force.

A recognition of these divergent lines of thought helps in understanding at least five schools of scholarship that today are attempting to formulate a theory of class.

- Pluralism
- Instrumentalism
- Structuralism
- Criticalism
- Statism and Class Struggle

This chapter reviews the origins, epistemological strains, and theory of each of these schools and attempts to distinguish orthodox and radical ideas that have influenced them. As an introduction to a discussion of these schools, several observations are offered.

First, it should be clear that the concern with class and class struggle inevitably becomes entangled with the effort to understand the nature of the state. Various approaches to the study of the state are identified at the end of Chapter 5, and the present chapter assesses these perspectives of the state in the light of various conceptions and theories of class. Although Marx never fully elaborated a theory of state and class, his work focused directly on those vital themes. His early thought is in *Critique of the Doctrine of State in Hegel's Philosophy of Right,* and a clearer statement, revealing the theoretical underpinnings of his position, appears in his joint effort with Engels, *The German Ideology.* Certainly *The Eighteenth Brumaire* and *Class Struggles in France, 1848–1850* are representative works on state and class that reveal an ingenious linking of theory to historical experience. In those and later writings, including *Capital,* reference to state becomes a backdrop for discussion of class. The concept of state allowed Marx to focus on bourgeois or capitalist politics, and the concept of class served as the foundation of Marx's understanding of political economy. A class commonly is identified as a group of people sharing common characteristics, although in a Marxist context a class of people constitutes a component of society. Marx differentiated between a class of producers or a working class and a class that controls the means of production or the ruling class. As the working class produces beyond its needs, the ruling class appropriates the surplus. Inevitably, according to Marx, conflict and struggle will characterize the relationship between these two classes. Engels, in *Origin of the Family, Private Property, and the State,* and Lenin, in *The State and Revolution,* synthesized and popularized Marx's theory on state and class.

Inadequate attention to state and class perhaps accounts for the dearth of serious Marxist literature on these themes since Lenin. Stanley Moore's *Critique of Capitalist Democracy: An Introduction to the Theory of the State in Marx, Engels, and Lenin* (1957) offers a synthesis of past theory and paves the way toward a reassessment. Hal Draper's *Karl Marx's Theory of Revolution* (1977) is an outstanding restatement of Marx's theories of state and class. Perry Anderson's *Lineages of the Absolutist State* (1974) analyzes the emergence of the absolute state and the centralized monarchies in western Europe during the sixteenth century; those regimes constituted a form of state power to rule over the class struggle between the old feudal nobility and the new urban bourgeoisie. In *Late Capitalism* (1975), Ernest Mandel traced the role of society from mercantilist times to the present.

Those contributions entice the student of politics to delve into the theories and issues of state and class. Political science and comparative politics now confront the task of incorporating an understanding of state and class into the study of politics. Several publications emphasize that the discipline should recognize those concerns. Jean-Claude Girardin (1974) and Alan Wolfe (1974) offered overviews in the radical journal, *Politics and Society.* Girardin assessed humanist and structuralist perspectives of a Marxist theory of state, and Wolfe reviewed the new directions in a Marxist theory of politics by synthesizing critical and scientific perspectives. They affirmed that state and class, generally ignored in contemporary political science, in reality are core concepts. "The return of interest in a Marxist theory of the state is a development filled with significance for contemporary political scientists with a critical perspective. Instead of spending our time continuously criticizing models which most people know to be intellectually bankrupt, we have a chance to develop our own theory and use it to change for the better the society in which we live" (Wolfe 1974: 159). Ralph Miliband, in *Marxism and Politics* (1977), advocated the construction of a Marxist politics based on a systematic but flexible analysis of the fragmented material that forms Marxism as set forth in writings of Marx and Engels and their successors. At the core of Marxist politics, he argued, are the state, class, and class conflict. Albert Szymanski emphasized those themes in his lucid text, *The Capitalist State and the Politics of Class* (1978).

The search for a theory of the state has been advanced considerably by the theoretical journal, *Kapitalistate,* which publishes for six groups in the

United States and many individuals in England, the Federal Republic of Germany, and other countries. The most useful syntheses of current work on the state and class are in Gold, Lo, and Wright (1975) and Esping-Andersen, Friedland, and Wright (1976), and Jessop (1977) has provided an overview of Marxist theories of capitialist state.

Finally, each of the emerging theoretical schools roots itself in a particular intellectual tradition. For example, pluralism is a distinctly U.S. phenomenon; instrumentalism has its origins in studies of community power structures in the United States, but also has been advanced in England; structuralism stems from influential social science circles in France; criticalism owes its debt to a number of German thinkers, and the school of statism and class struggle represents an attempt to synthesize and transcend the other schools.

PLURALISM

Political scientists generally allude to the pluralist character of Anglo-American politics. Pluralism holds that democracy is premised on diverse interests and the dispersion of power. Theories of pluralism stem from liberal economic and political thought. On the one hand, John Locke and Jeremy Bentham stressed individual property rights and private initiative. On the other, James Madison envisioned competing interests in the struggle for power. Those thinkers provided a basis for group and interest theory, enhanced by the contributions of Arthur Bentley and David Truman to contemporary political science in the United States. Several positions are evident among pluralists. One, often called an elitist theory of democracy, distinguishes between rulers and ruled but emphasizes changes in elite membership over time; Vilfredo Pareto called this a theory of circulating elites, and Gaetano Mosca's theory of ruling classes was similar. Another position examines pluralism as a fundamental practice in Western plutocratic society and is represented in the work of Robert Dahl and other prominent U.S. political scientists and sociologists. Lastly, pluralism sometimes relates to certain lines of socialist thought, and in this position theories of conflict and consensus may be applicable as well as tendencies to tie pluralism to a Marxist perspective and the ideal of a classless society.

Pluralism and the Elitist Theory of Democracy

A central premise of the classical elitist theory of democracy is that in every society a minority makes the major decisions. The origins of this theory are in Plato, but its elaboration is in the thought of two Italian political sociologists, Vilfredo Pareto and Gaetano Mosca.

Pareto (1966) emphasized distinctions between elites and nonelites and downgraded Marx's emphasis on economic forces as well as Mosca's concern with organizational ability. Pareto referred to the idea of a circulation of elites, which seems to have two basic meanings. On the one hand, one elite may be replaced by another elite, as, for example, when aristocracies decay or regenerate. On the other, individuals circulate between two levels—a high stratum of elite and a low stratum of nonelite. Pareto divided the high stratum into a governing class or elite (those who directly or indirectly govern) and a nongoverning elite (the rest of the elite who are not in government). Pareto clearly did not imply that the governing class or elite is a particular socioeconomic class, as in a Marxist context. At one point in his writings he argued that in the mass democratic state the governing class consists of a tacit alliance of entrepreneurs and their workers against fixed-income groups; the objective of the governing class or elite is to satisfy all clienteles.

S. E. Finer and T. B. Bottomore acknowledged the great influence of Pareto's theory of elites, but they had reservations as well. First, Finer (in Pareto 1966: 77–81) asserted that Pareto did not relate his elite to social and economic classes. Apparently this reflects Pareto's concern with the ideas of Marx, which he "denatured" rather than contradicted; in his retort to Marx he transcended Marxist categories so that elite rule takes the place of class rule, and so on. Second, Pareto's concept of the governing class or elite is all inclusive and is used to reveal a typology of regimes that are scarcely described. Nor are any criteria offered to explain the differences between the regimes. Bottomore (1964: 48–54) found the circulation-of-elites thesis unsatisfactory in the sense that Pareto provided historical examples of the rise and decline of elites drawn exclusively from the Italian experience, when instead he might have synthesized a large number of cases in order to demonstrate regularity in the elite circulation of individuals and groups. Propositions are asserted, not supported, and generalizations appear to be readily invalidated by historical example. Sally Cook Lopreato (1973) attempted to clarify some of this confusion with a formal reconstruction of Pareto's theory of circulating elites, which she presented in outline form in order to establish the beginning of genuine theory. Alan Zuckerman (1977) alluded to the confusion in the writings of political theorists who have distorted the ideas of Pareto and Mosca and urged a closer look at their original writings in order to escape "the conceptual swamp."

Mosca differed slightly in his conceptions. The term elite is not emphasized in his writings. Instead he preferred such terms as political class, ruling class, and governing class. His conception of rule was similar to that of

Pareto, however: "In all societies—from societies that are very meagerly developed and have barely attained the dawnings of civilization, down to the most advanced and powerful societies—two classes of people appear—a class that rules and a class that is ruled" (Mosca 1939: 50).

Mosca offered a number of propositions that relate to that conception of rule. First, the ruling class is less numerous, monopolizes power, and benefits materially from its position, whereas the class that is ruled is more numerous and dominated. Second, if and when the masses are discontented, they can influence the policies of the ruling class. Third, the person at the head of the state cannot govern without the support of the masses, which are capable of deposing a ruling class. In the event that a ruling class is deposed, another organized minority within the masses has to assume the functions of the ruling class.

Mosca essentially recognized a circulation of classes or elites. An old class may be replaced by a new one. New groups may gain access to the ruling class whose ranks are open. Position in the ruling class is not necessarily determined by individual intellectual or moral qualities, as stressed by Pareto. More important is the rise of new interests and groups, for instance, in the development of a new source of wealth in a society, which may cause dislocations in the ruling class itself. Bottomore (1964: 56–57) noted that this interpretation approximates Marxist thinking but that Mosca attempted to distinguish his theory from that of Marx by limiting an economic interpretation of history; in this regard Mosca was close to Weber's position. Although Mosca opposed Marxism and socialism, he also opposed democratic theory, which promised rule by the masses. He agreed with Montesquieu's revision of Aristotle's classification of government (monarchies, aristocracies, and democracies were replaced by absolute monarchies, limited monarchies, and republics). He argued that Aristotle's democracy was in fact an aristocracy with a broad base of members. Mosca's principal concern was that although a minority class rules in every society, upward mobility through various social strata leaves open the ranks of the ruling class. Thus circulation occurs through assimilation, cooptation, and other moderate changes; if these are denied, then circulation may occur through rebellion, revolution, and other forms of violence.

Having outlined these conceptions of a circulating elite, what criticism might be considered? Idealistic pluralists would argue that the elitist theory of democracy overlooks the power of electoral politics and citizen participation. At the same time, the doctrine of elitism strengthens the tendency to place power with a centralized bureaucracy while rationalizing the economic power of the privileged classes. Such criticism moved Dahl and other pluralists to adopt a conception of power devoid of any notion of a ruling elite or ruling class.

Pluralism and Polyarchy

Robert Dahl (1971) devoted attention to the study of polyarchies in which barriers to political opposition are not substantial. Political scientists characterize polyarchies as marked by subsystem autonomy and organizational pluralism. In *A Preface to Democratic Theory* (1956) Dahl acknowledged his intellectual debt to James Madison. From Madison's writings, Dahl extrapolated the basis of theoretical argument on pluralism. This is traced in Dahl's *Pluralist Democracy in the United States* (1967). Dahl and other pluralists have described the United States as a democratic order with a wide dispersion of power and authority among government officials and private individuals and groups alike. The structure of power is segmented, not organized into a clear hierarchical pattern. Characteristic of this democratic order are opportunities for freedom of thought, consensus and dissension, and participation in politics; the peaceful management of conflict and constraints on violence; and a widespread confidence and loyalty to a constitutional and democratic polity.

Three basic concepts of this theory—interest group, power, and conflict—are clearly evident in the work of such established pluralists as Seymour Martin Lipset, Arnold Rose, and David Truman. The concept of an interest group, especially found in the work of Bentley and Truman, is fundamental. References to the individual must focus on group relationships, on shared attitudes and interests, although this emphasis breaks down as pluralists distinguish between leaders and followers. For example, Dahl in his New Haven study, *Who Governs?* (1961), identified leaders, subleaders, and followers, and Arnold Rose (1967) dealt with elites, publics, groups, and masses. The concept of power also is basic but inadequately defined in the pluralist literature. Power is understood in relation to interest and interest groups. In *Community Power and Political Theory* (1963) Nelson Polsby defined power as "the capacity of one actor to do something affecting another actor, which changes the probable pattern of specified future events" (1963: 3). Pluralists tend to narrow and qualify their definitions of power, however, prompting one critic to comment, "One thesis of the present critique of the pluralists is that they *do not have* a rich theory, and continually push the burden of their methodological problems from one part of their theory to another" (Cunningham 1975-1976: 401). The problems of power and pluralism are discussed by Michael Parenti (1970: especially 501-507). Finally, the concept of conflict is utilized by pluralists in the sense that all societies are believed to constrain groups in conflict. In *Political Man* (1960) Lipset assumed that conflict is both inevitable and desirable, but his theory remains vague. "The effect is to promote either piecemeal explanation or explanations based on some presupposed but unstated theory"

(Cunningham 1975–1976: 405).

In his criticism of these three concepts Cunningham identified three tendencies in pluralism. One is to take a piecemeal approach and look for interrelationships among types of conflict and explanations of beliefs. Another is to use game theory in which simplistic models incorporate only certain conflict. The third tendency, a dominant one in the literature of pluralism, is to move toward a functionalist equilibrium theory: The challenge to politics by a class or group leads to the search for a new equilibrium while politics functions to maintain peace among the conflicting interests.

All of these tendencies are stressed in the pluralistic studies of power in the United States, where it is assumed that there is a wide diversity of equally powerful groups. However, critics have noted that even in a group-oriented society like the United States only half of the people are in voluntary associations and such associations are only peripherally involved in politics. It is also assumed by pluralists that state policies reflect accurately the demands of diverse interest groups. However, critics have commented that only certain policies can be implemented under capitalism and a class society. For example, policies to reduce inflation or unemployment might be acceptable, but other policies could be perceived as socially and economically disruptive. Thus policy reflects economic and political conditions rather than conscious decision making (Szymanski 1978: 5).

Pluralism and Socialism

Dahl has argued that pluralism "is no longer limited to Western bourgeois thought" (1978: 192), and he distinguished between organizational pluralism and conflictive pluralism. Organizational pluralism implies an increase in autonomy relative to the increase in the number of organizations. Conflictive pluralism refers "to the number and pattern of relatively enduring cleavages that must be taken into account in order to characterize conflicts among a given collection of persons" (192). Dahl suggested that organizational pluralism need not be exclusively a product of capitalism, as is so often assumed. He believed that socialist economies can be highly decentralized and pluralistic and that a decentralized socialist order might create as much or more organizational pluralism as a nonsocialist order. In taking this position he deemphasized the significance of class in conflictive pluralism. "Orthodox class interpretations have tended vastly to underestimate the extent to which ideological diversity among elites leads to fragmentation rather than solidarity. . . . 'class' in its various manifestations is only an element, albeit nearly always a significant one, in a fragmented pattern of cleavages and conflicts that is persistently pluralistic" (193). He concluded that a shift from capitalism to socialism does not necessarily result in less organizational pluralism in a country. Organizational pluralism is not dependent on whether a country is capitalist or socialist in terms of private or social ownership of the means of production, but it is dependent on the extent to which decisions are decentralized and autonomy is permitted to enterprises. He cited Yugoslavia after 1950, Czechoslovakia in early 1968, Chile during the Allende period, and Portugal after 1974 as examples of this tendency.

Evident in this position are several interrelated issues. One concerns the usefulness to pluralism of theories of conflict and consensus. There is also the question of whether pluralism can assimilate a Marxist perspective. Finally, the ideal of a classless society sometimes is implied in the pluralist stance.

Theories of conflict and consensus assume that all societies are in a state of flux or mix between the incidence of conflict and the incidence of consensus. Conflict implies a disagreement about basic values in a society, and consensus refers to an agreement about basic values. The degree of conflict and consensus may determine the stability or instability of a society. Pluralists generally argue that in the United States consensus greatly outweighs conflict over basic values—for example, see Lane (1965) and McClosky (1964). Many other societies may experience considerable conflict as a consequence of basic historical differences such as social and economic class, religious and ethnic, geographical, and racial and ideological cleavages—Bailey (1968) offered an interesting and useful synthesis of conflict theories.

Given the propensity of most U.S. social scientists to favor pluralistic consensus, discussions of conflict rarely, if ever seriously, relate to class. An emphasis on resolution and bargaining moves analysis away from contradictions inherent in class society and renders suspect any endeavor that attempts to combine pluralism with a Marxist perspective. Ralf Dahrendorf in his *Class and Class Conflict in Industrial Society* (1959) attempted to construct Marx's theory of class society, then examined recent theories of class and class conflict, and concluded with a critique of Marx. Dahrendorf's synthesis of Marxist class theory remains invaluable, yet his analysis confirms the difficulty of incorporating a Marxist view in a theory of pluralism. This point is emphasized in his sketch of classes in a "postcapitalist society" in which ideal types are described in order to distinguish totalitarian from free societies. According to Dahrendorf, in contrast to the monistic structure of conflict and monopoly of authority found in totalitarian, especially communist, societies, political conflict is reduced to a minimum in a free society.

> The scales of stratification are largely separate; possession of authority does not
> necessarily imply wealth, prestige, security. There are competing elites at the

top of the various scales. Conflicts in different associations are dissociated. . . .
Class conflict and other clashes between groups are dissociated too. . . .
Pluralism of institutions, conflict patterns, groupings, and interests makes for a
lively, colorful, and creative conflict which provides an opportunity for success
for every interest that is voiced. [Dahrendorf 1959: 317]

Marxism focuses on a class society in which some people privately own the
means of production and appropriate the surplus of others, thus
necessitating a fundamental division of labor between owners and workers.
The interests and groupings of people are determined by their relations to
the process of production. A theory of class struggle is dialectical. Class
elements struggle against one another so that, in the Marxist view, the proletariat might be more powerful than the capitalists because it is crucial to
the production process and it produces the surplus; at the same time the
capitalists might be more powerful because they own the means of production and control the coercive mechanisms of the state. In contrast, pluralists
would state simply that the capitalists as an interest group might hold certain power relative to the proletariat as another interest group—a view that
lacks analysis and explanation. Pluralism thus envisions power as a
characteristic of groups in society, whereas Marxism seeks an overview of an
entire society in which power is related to the development of a mode of production, ideology, class, and class struggle.

Marx believed that the struggle of the proletariat against the bourgeoisie
would ultimately result in the replacement of the old bourgeois society by a
new society that would exclude classes and their struggle. This proposition
leads some observers to the position that socialist societies are classless. That
position is both supported and defended by Marxists and pluralists alike
(Parkin 1971: 137–159). In the case of the Soviet Union, for example, Russian Marxists and their supporters argue that since private property has
been abolished, there can be no classes. Although material and social differences may exist between groups, antagonistic relationships based on production are not evident. Thus there may be differences between industrial
workers and intellectuals, but those differences bear no inherent antagonisms of a class character; further such differences are narrowed as
socialist society drives toward full communism. This idea of classlessness, of
course, is vigorously contested by Maoists and others who believe that the
Soviet Union reflects many traits of the capitalist state even though ownership of production does not remain in private hands. Milovan Djilas argued
in *The New Class* (1957) that a bureaucratic class had emerged to power in
his native Yugoslavia and in neighboring socialist countries. Western writers
like Raymond Aron and William Kornhauser have noted that the sharp
cleavage between the members of the party and the people transcends all

other divisions; the coercive activities of the party and secret police are so pervasive as to mitigate differences in social background, income, occupation, and other characteristics of a class nature. Furthermore, sharp differences in values and outlook are lacking—evidence of the classlessness notion. Those writers, however, have distinguished between the monopolistic and totalitarian distribution of power in the Soviet Union and the pluralist distribution of power in most Western societies. Alex Inkeles and other critics of the Soviet Union have contested this view of classlessness, suggesting that contemporary industrialism necessitates class distinctions under either capitalism or socialism.

INSTRUMENTALISM

Instrumentalism assumes that the state is controlled by and serves the interests of the capitalist class. Instrumentalists argue that an elitist or minority class rules in most societies, a position not dissimilar to the views of Pareto and Mosca. This assumption also is found in a generation of studies of power structure in U.S. communities. It is a central premise of the work of C. Wright Mills and of the work of G. William Domhoff, both of whom have elaborated on power structure theory. Much of instrumentalist theory skirts Marxist premises, but the work of Ralph Miliband takes an explicit Marxist stance. According to Miliband, the capitalist ruling class exercises the power to use the state as its instrument for a domination of society. His view is drawn from the *Communist Manifesto* in which Marx and Engels asserted that "the modern state is but a committee for managing the common affairs of the whole bourgeoisie."

The Legacy of Power Structure in the Community

Traditionally community studies have addressed the question of who rules, and generally these studies employ stratification theory. Nelson Polsby (1963: 8–11) alluded to some important assertions of stratification studies of power in the United States. A ladder of strata usually is envisaged with an upper class at the top that rules the local community. This class is identifiable by such criteria as income, occupation, housing, and consumption pattern. As a consequence of its economic position the upper class has greater power than do the political and civic leaders. Sometimes this upper class is thought of as a power elite that stands at the apex of a pyramid of power. This upper class rules in its own interests, and its dominance and position ensure its separation from the lower classes of a community; this separation leads to social conflict.

Among the community studies that employ stratification theory, that of

Middletown or Muncie, Indiana, remains a classic. Conducted by Robert and Helen Lynd, first in the middle 1920s and again a decade later, the study of Middletown identified the "business class," which in turn was controlled by one family, as dominant in every sphere of community activity. William Lloyd Warner and associates published during the 1940s and 1950s five studies of Yankee City or Newburyport, Massachusetts, in which attention is directed to position and social status. These studies demonstrate a dominance of the upper classes, even though conflict between the upper and lower classes sometimes is evident. Warner also studied the small town of Morris, in northern Illinois, during the late 1930s and early 1940s. He called it Elmtown. Hollingshead confirmed that the upper classes controlled community life. Digby Baltzell observed that Philadelphia businessmen constitute a ruling class of families with high status and old wealth. He identified them through *Who's Who in America* and the *Social Register*. During the early 1950s Floyd Hunter utilized panels of persons knowledgeable about community life to identify decision makers in Regional City or Atlanta, Georgia. This reputational approach served to describe community power structure.

These studies tend to view power as being in the hands of a ruling class or elite, and thus these studies have established the orientation of most community research in the United States. The existence of a single center of power or a tight coalition of groups that wield power in U.S. communities is, of course, a proposition that has been challenged by many pluralists. Arnold Rose (1967: 483–492) asserted that a power structure is found at every level of U.S. life — national, regional, state, and local. Although small numbers of persons hold the greatest amount of power within this variety of power structures, their power depends on the extent to which they interact in order to influence public opinion. Rose believed that power structure in the United States is highly complex and diversified rather than unitary and monolithic. In their studies of New Haven, Robert Dahl, Nelson Polsby, and Raymond Wolfinger offered an alternative perspective, noting multiple centers of influence and limits on the power of leaders. Dahl solidified a consensus around pluralist theory with his attack on the ruling elite model (1958: 463–469). Dahl's emphasis on pluralistic patterns of decision making was challenged by Peter Bachrach and Morton Baratz (1962), who argued that "two faces of power" characterize decision making. One is manifested overtly in the decision-making process, and the other is evident in the capacity of powerful individuals and groups to prevent issues that threaten their interests from arising. Using power structure methodology William Domhoff (1978) replicated Dahl's study of New Haven (1961) and concluded that evidence of pluralism does not contradict a ruling class view that suggests that a ruling class often struggles to implement its policies.

Power Structure and Instrumentalism:
Mills and Domhoff

The attention of many community studies on power structure has provided an initial impetus for an instrumentalist theory of state and class. The state becomes an instrument in the hands of the ruling class and allows that class to dominate in its own interests. Power structure studies tend to show that such a class exists, especially in a capitalist society. Direct personal links between the ruling class and the state apparatus are identified. Sometimes the actions and nature of the ruling class are studied. Mechanisms that tie this class to the state are described, and class interests are related to state policies. C. Wright Mills and Floyd Hunter focused on some of these concerns, and G. William Domhoff elaborated their work in greater sophistication. Their work concentrated on showing the social connections among the individuals who occupy positions of power.

Mills's *The Power Elite* (1956) offered a general analysis of elites in the United States. Hunter in *Top Leadership USA* (1959) extended his research on community power structure to the entire United States and utilized empirical research with few theoretical underpinnings to demonstrate his thesis of dominance by a ruling elite. Thomas R. Dye, in *Who's Running America?* (1976), followed this approach, hesitated to confirm or deny the tenets of either pluralist or elitist models of national power, and in fact skirted theoretical implications altogether. Mills, however, provided a more sophisticated study and theoretical framework. Miliband has summarized Mills's central thesis: "that in America some men have enormous power denied to everyone else; that these men are, increasingly, a self-perpetuating elite; that their power is, increasingly, unchecked and irresponsible; and that their decision-making, based on an increasingly 'military definition of reality' and on 'crackpot realism,' is oriented to immoral ends" (Miliband, in Domhoff and Ballard 1968: 5). Mills examined vertical and horizontal dimensions of the power structure in the United States. The structure of vertical power comprises an elite at the top, a middle level of special interest groups, and a mass society. The structure of horizontal power embraces three groups at the top—an interlocking power elite consisting of a political directorate of politicians and bureaucrats, high corporate executives, and prominent military figures. These groups are bound together by common interests, for example, corporate interest in military armaments.

Criticism of Mills's power structure theory includes liberal and radical perspectives (see especially essays in Domhoff and Ballard 1968; and Prewitt and Stone 1973: chap. 4, 83–113). Dahl (1958) launched an attack on Mills's methods by suggesting a number of tests of Mills's thesis. Pluralists like Rose (1967) also claimed that Mills exaggerated the influence of the corporate elite. Although liberal critics such as William Kornhauser, Talcott Parsons, and A. A. Berle, Jr., all joined in this criticism, radical critics of the power elite manifested a critical stance as well. Robert Lynd (in Domhoff and Ballard 1968: 103–115) addressed unanswered questions and vagueness about class. Paul Sweezy expressed concern that although Mills appeared to hold the military in contempt, his theory of the military is similar to that of Cold War liberals: "Semi-elitists like Mills—people who think they can adopt the terminology without any of the basic ideas of elitist theory—tend to get bogged down in confusion from which the only escape is to borrow the most banal ideas of their opponents" (Sweezy, in Domhoff and Ballard 1968: 127). He also indicted Mills for blurring his analysis of class and class relations.

Domhoff (in Domhoff and Ballard 1968: 251–278) departed from this criticism and affirmed that in fact Mills's own position ranged between the positions of his liberal and radical critics. The liberals challenged Mills to focus on an analysis of decisions—decisions by the power elite would be based on the input of a variety of interest groups, they argued. Radicals argued that Mills should relate institutions and leaders to socioeconomic classes—Mills did not carry his analysis far enough, they believed. Although both liberals and radicals rejected Mills's theory, Domhoff in *Who Rules America* (1967) attempted to build upon some of Mills's premises. Empirically he linked members of the upper class to control of the corporate economy, thus affirming the idea that U.S. life is dominated by a relatively unified corporate elite rather than by a "managerial revolution." He also demonstrated the existence of an interacting national power structure through interviews in which the respondents acknowledged they personally knew each other. He showed unity among the various institutions of the power elite. Persons who run the corporate world are involved in foundations, political parties, and civic associations. Domhoff believed that the concept of the power elite is a bridge between pluralist and radical positions. He saw the power elite as an extension of the concept of the ruling class.

In his early study Domhoff utilized the concept of governing class. In a later work he appeared to equate ruling class and governing class and turn to what he described as a Marxist position. In addition to *Who Rules America*, Domhoff's *The Higher Circles: The Governing Class in America* (1970) exemplifies his early emphasis on the governing class. The work looks at the social institutions of the upper class and identifies the members of such a class through contingency, reputational, and positional analysis. Contingency analysis examines the association of people listed in various biographies and social registers with schools and clubs. Reputational analysis is personal and subjective and involves asking knowledgeable persons whom they believe to be important. Positional analysis identifies influential people on the basis of their position in a corporation, bank, foundation, or the like. Domhoff not only identified the upper class through these techniques, but he also demonstrated that the upper class is a cohesive governing class or power elite, by which he meant "a social upper class which owns a disproportionate amount of the country's yearly income, contributes a disproportionate number of its members to governmental bodies and decision-making groups, and dominates the policy-forming process" (Domhoff 1970: 109). In contrast to this early emphasis on the governing class, Domhoff later turned to the ruling class, which he claimed is a term "roughly interchangeable" with power elite (Domhoff 1975: 173). One of his concerns was to show the cohesiveness of the ruling class by studying small-group settings such as summer resort residential patterns, private school attendance, overlapping club memberships, and interlocking directorships in major charitable, educational, and cultural organizations. Domhoff focused on "networks" of clubs and policy groups that are tightly interlocked with corporate directorships.

Domhoff's work has been popularly received, yet assessment of it has been critical. Gold, Lo, and Wright (1975) labeled his work as instrumentalist and limited to showing ties among persons who occupy important positions. Esping-Andersen, Friedland, and Wright (1976) referred to it as a sophisticated version of instrumentalism that incorporates a theory of corporate liberalism. "This theory stresses the ability of progressive fractions of capital to preemptively determine the limits of reform through corporate financed, controlled, and staffed policy research and policy formation groups which originate model legislation and set the ideological boundaries within which partisan battles will be contained" (1976: 187).

Domhoff replied to some of these criticisms (1976: 221–224), arguing that his notion of ruling class should be understood in a Marxist context: the ruling class is based on the national corporate economy and its institutions, and the ruling class manifests itself through what Mills called the power elite, a term Domhoff redefined as "the leadership group" of the upper or governing class. Domhoff objected to the characterization of his work as corporate liberal instrumentalist, arguing that his perspective incorporates an analysis of class struggle that is not incompatible with power structure research conceptualized in terms of networks. Further, Domhoff took exception to leftist critics who allege that his work is "personalistic" and "voluntaristic," and although he proclaimed that he is not an instrumentalist, he acknowledged that his approach allowed readers to view class in static, one-dimensional terms rather than as a dynamic dialectical relationship involving more than a single class.

Marxist Instrumentalism: Miliband

Ralph Miliband's *The State in Capitalist Society* (1969) is firmly rooted in instrumentalism. The work attacks pluralistic theory and contributes to a Marxist theory of the state and class under capitalism. The state is understood in terms of the instrumental use of power by people in important positions. In citing the famous passage in the *Communist Manifesto*, Miliband sided with Marx and Engels: "They never departed from the view that in capitalist society the state was above all the coercive instrument of a ruling class, itself defined in terms of its ownership and control of the means of production" (Miliband 1969: 5). The ruling class of a capitalist society thus holds the reins of economic power and uses the state as its instrument for the domination of society. Miliband wrote about two classes under capitalism—the class that owns and controls and the class that works. Between these "polar" classes one finds two elements of a "middle class," one consisting of professional people and the other made up of businessmen and farmers of small and medium enterprises. In addition, there is a mass of professional people who run the state.

Critics of Miliband have noted the sophistication with which he moved his analysis away from a mere positioning of people into an economic power structure. His analysis centers on personal and social ties among people in different segments of the ruling class, yet, according to Gold, Lo, and Wright, he "attempted to situate the analysis of personal connections in a more structural context. . . . even if these personal ties were weak or absent . . . the policies of the state would still be severely constrained by the economic structure in which it operates" (1975: 33). Miliband did not deny the position of Marxist instrumentalism that critics attributed to him, yet he probably would object to this characterization. In fact his debate with Nicos Poulantzas, a well-known structuralist, cast Miliband in an instrumentalist position. Until recently the instrumentalist interpretation of the executive committee idea in Marx and Engels dominated Marxist thinking on the relationship of class to state. However, Miliband reminded us that Marx and Engels referred to the executive of the state as a committee for managing the affairs of the *whole* bourgeoisie, that the idea of a whole bourgeoisie implies the existence of separate parts as well as a degree of autonomy so that the state may act in the interests of capitalists but not necessarily at their command (1973: 85). This interpretation differs from a central instrumentalist premise, that the ruling class manipulates the state in its own interests.

A Critical Overview of Instrumentalist Theory

Power structure researchers and instrumentalists have encountered conceptual difficulty with the loose categories that they indiscriminately employ. The terms ruling elite, circulating elite, power elite, upper class, governing class, and ruling class are not always distinguishable in studies of community power and structure. Futhermore, those terms are used abstractly in isolation from other levels of socioeconomic class. This one-dimensional focus on class results in static and sometimes insignificant perspectives.

At the heart of Marxist theory is class dynamism. Marx referred to class in a popular and a formal sense. On the one hand, a social class shares certain characteristics, for example, related to income, so that Marx frequently wrote of the moneyed or industrial class; sometimes he mentioned ideological classes, unproductive classes, uneducated classes, and so on. On the other hand, Marx showed that historically the differentiation of classses occurs with the development of the forces of production and the creation of a surplus product beyond the needs of the direct producers or workers. In this light two basic classes appear—the ruling class and the class of workers—and these classes are described in terms of relations of production. A mode of production is socially structured around such a relationship. It should be clear, however, that one cannot determine a mode of production by the structure of classes in a particular society. Classes are understood in terms of a society's mode of production. Thus, an abstract consideration of certain criteria in order to identify a particular class of a society may be misleading, as is the problem found in the instrumentalist interpretation. Marx offered no formal definition of class, avoiding definitions for categories and abstract ideas.

This emphasis on class and production differs from the emphasis of Max Weber and a host of followers who locate class in the market and relations of circulation. A focus on market implies bargaining power so that classes may compete on common ground, which of course leads to pluralist premises and to a fundamental argument against power structure theory as well as Marxist instrumentalist theory. This problem is discussed by Therborn (1976). Curiously, scholars in some socialist countries have attempted to combine pluralist and Marxist theory in their attention to the ruling class. Consequently, the contrasting paradigms of bourgeois and Marxist thought have been blurred by this attempt to fuse opposing theory. J. W. Freiberg offered an explanation: "The Russian and Eastern Europe ruling class has, among other interests in common with the American and Western European ruling class, a desire for maintenance of the respective internal situations of domination" (1973: 17–18).

STRUCTURALISM

Theories of structuralism and power structure differ substantially. Rather than be subject to the manipulation of the ruling bourgeoisie under capitalism, the state may operate in a way determined by the development of capitalism itself. Nicos Poulantzas (1969), for instance, argued that the direct participation of members in the ruling class does not necessarily account for the actions of the state. In fact, he affirmed that "the capitalist state best serves the interests of the capitalist class only when the members of this class do not participate in the state apparatus" (1969: 74).

The origins of structuralism have been traced to Marx and the French anthropologist, Claude Lévi-Strauss. Within the structuralist school political and economic currents are evident. Political structuralists like Althusser and Poulantzas focus on state mechanisms of repression and ideology and the way they provide an ordered structure for capitalism. This political structuralism contrasts with the economic structuralist approach, examples of which are found in the writings of Baran and Sweezy and O'Connor. In addition there is the effort to develop a class analysis of world economy introduced by Wallerstein. All of these aspects of structuralism are described below, along with the assessments of them by critical observers.

Structuralism in Marx and Lévi-Strauss

In an essay on structure and the contradictions of capitalism analyzed in Marx, Maurice Godelier (1973) outlined the proximity of structuralism and Marxism. Marx, he claimed, described social life in terms of structure by reference to infrastructure and superstructure. Marx also offered a scientific understanding of the capitalist system by discovering "the internal structures hidden behind its visible functioning" (1973: 336). Godelier suggested that Marx and Lévi-Strauss find common ground.

> For Marx, as for Claude Lévi-Strauss, "structures" should not be confused with visible "social relations" but constitute a level of *reality* invisible but present behind the visible social relations. The logic of the latter, and the laws of social practice more generally, depend on the functioning of these hidden structures and the discovery of these should allow us to "account for all the facts observed." [1973: 336]

Godelier believed that Marx initiated the modern structuralist condition. Godelier carefully distinguished this tradition from the U.S. and British belief in empirical social science in which a structure must be directly visible. The early texts of Claude Lévi-Strauss clearly reveal the contradictory effects of his work. On the one hand, Lévi-Strauss's attention to structuralism at a time when functionalism was in decline within anthropology "served to shore up the discipline's crumbling edifice." On the other hand, in France "it was appropriated by a left-wing intelligentsia still hesitant in its ideological and political commitment" (Keleman 1976: 859). The thought of Louis Althusser and Nicos Poulantzas is representative of this latter trend and is examined below.

Lévi-Strauss's work represents a significant theoretical contribution to contemporary anthropology, and although it is not Marxist, it has been incorporated into a Marxist model. Jonathan Friedman (1974) analyzed similarities in the thought of Marx and Lévi-Strauss and concluded that although works such as Lévi-Strauss's *Les Structures élémentaires de la parenté* (1967) and Marx's *Capital* are different, "they both attempt to explain reality in terms of what are conceived of as fundamental underlying relations" (1974: 453).

Political Structuralism:
Gramsci, Althusser, and Poulantzas

Antonio Gramsci was a founder of the Italian Communist Party in 1921, a parliamentary deputy in 1925, and a prisoner under Mussolini's fascist government throughout the late 1920s until near the time of his death in 1937. During his imprisonment under difficult conditions he wrote a series of political tracts that have been translated and published in English as *Selections from the Prison Notebooks* (1971) and *Selections from Political Writings 1910–1920* (1977). Giuseppe Fiori's *Antonio Gramsci: Life of a Revolutionary* (1970) provides us with a sympathetic and revealing biography of Gramsci's life.

Gramsci's notes on the state provide one basis for structuralist thought and have influenced Althusser and Poulantzas. Gramsci directed us toward a Marxist theory of politics. His emphasis on hegemony or dominance of some social group or class in power has prompted some critics to suggest he was advocating reformist interpretations or undialectically separating politics from economics. Gramsci tended to utilize categories of analysis, for example, in distinguishing between state and civil society, as did Hegel and Marx, in his early work. Gramsci's conception of state is varied, however. Crises occur in the hegemony of the ruling class because it fails in some political undertaking and the masses become discontented and actively resistant. Such a crisis of hegemony is a crisis of authority or crisis of the state. Under such conditions a ruling class may seize control and retain power by crushing its adversaries. Gramsci examined this activity in terms of the experiences of Italy and other nations in Europe. He seemed to be agreeing with the structuralist position that the activities of the state are determined by the structures of society rather than by persons in positions of state power.

> The fact that the State/government, conceived as an autonomous force, should reflect back its prestige upon the class upon which it is based, is of the greatest practical and theoretical importance, and deserves to be analyzed fully if one wants a more realistic concept of the State itself. . . . It can, it seems, be incorporated into the function of elites or vanguards, i.e. of parties, in relation to the class which they represent. This class, often, as a economic fact . . . might not enjoy any intellectual or moral prestige, i.e. might be incapable of establishing its hegemony, hence of founding a state. [Gramsci 1971: 269]

There are scattered references to Gramsci in the work of French structuralist Louis Althusser. For example, in *For Marx* (1970), Althusser commented, "The jottings and developments in his *Prison Notebooks* touch on all the basic problems of Italian and European history: economic, social, political and cultural. There are also some completely original and in some cases general insights into the problem, basic today, of the superstructure. Also, as always with true discoveries, there are *new concepts*, for example, hegemony: a remarkable example of a theoretical solution in outline to the problem of the interpenetration of the economic and the political" (1970: 114). Althusser's major works in English, in addition to *For Marx*, include *Reading Capital* (with Étiènne Balibar, 1970), *Lenin and Philosophy and Other Essays* (1971), and *Politics and History: Montesquieu, Rousseau, Hegel, and Marx* (1972). Althusser's thought was shaped by an attack on Marxist humanists and by an effort to sharply distinguish the humanist ideas in Marx's early writings from the structuralist formulations found in the later writings. Mark Poster (1974) has provided an excellent summary of Althusser's ideas. He characterized Althusser's structuralism as "an escape from ideology into science," and "a theoretically more sophisticated Marxism that could analyze various segments of society without reducing them all to the economy" (1974: 397).

Althusser's thought is difficult to comprehend, subject to changing conceptualization, and burdened with jargon and philosophical terminology. One essay (1971) on the state and ideology, outlines the structuralist approach to state and class and reveals some differences with Marx. Whereas Marx understood ideologies as illusions, Althusser saw them as systematic elements of every society. This perspective and Althusser's elaboration of structuralism are evident in the following summary.

In his essay on ideology and the state Althusser sketched Marx's representation of the structure of every society in terms of levels: infrastructure or economic base composed of productive forces and relations of production, on the one hand, and superstructure composed of politico-legal and ideological aspects, on the other hand. Althusser referred to this representation as a spatial metaphor, that is, it remains descriptive, and he set forth a different formulation. Following Marx he conceived of the state as a repressive apparatus that permits the ruling classes to dominate over and exploit the working class. This apparatus includes the bureaucracy, police, courts, prisons, and the army, which intervenes in times of crisis. The state then is a force of repression and intervention that shields the bourgeoisie and its allies in the class struggle against the proletariat. Indeed the whole of the political class struggle revolves around the state. The objective of the class struggle concerns state power, for the proletariat must seize state power, destroy the bourgeois state apparatus, replace it with a proletarian state apparatus, and then in the end destroy the state itself.

Althusser thus distinguished between state power and repressive state apparatus, and he identified the structural elements of this state apparatus. In conjunction with the repressive state apparatus he alluded to a plurality of ideological state apparatuses, which appear to the observer in the form of distinct and specialized institutions, including the religious system of churches, schools, family, political parties, trade unions, communications, and cultural enterprises. These ideological state apparatuses operate generally in the private domain in contrast to the repressive state apparatuses, which are public. The former functions predominantly by ideology; the latter, by violence. Such diversity should not disguise the real unity of the ruling class, which holds state power and may utilize both the repressive and ideological state apparatuses. These conditions ensure the reproduction of relations of production through historical periods.

> The role of the repressive State apparatus, insofar as it is a repressive apparatus, consists essentially in securing by force (physical or otherwise) the political conditions of the reproduction of relations of production which are in the last resort relations of exploitation . . . , but also and above all, the State apparatus secures by repression . . . the political conditions for the action of the Ideological State Apparatus. [Althusser 1971: 142]

In a late or mature capitalist society the ruling bourgeoisie has installed the educational ideological apparatus in the dominant position. The schools of an advanced capitalist society have assumed the role of the church in a precapitalist society. Althusser noted the paradoxical nature of this thesis, in view of the common belief that parliamentary democracy with its universal suffrage and party struggle represents the dominant ideological apparatus or force under contemporary capitalism. Lurking behind this democratic facade is the powerful and pervasive educational apparatus.

Althusser's emphasis on structure has evoked among critics the charge that he is a positivist. He isolated social phenomena so that they appear to be static, and critics have alleged that he elevated the scientific method as an absolute means for knowledge. Poster defended Althusser on these matters. "Althusser avoids positivism, I would argue, because he does not leave the choice of historical subject either to the accident of facts not previously uncovered or to a fetish of available methodology. . . . In any case, Althusser's investigations seem to avoid both mechanical, economic determinism and the moralism of many Marxist humanists" (Poster 1974: 406).

Not all French Marxists are structuralists, as in the case of Girardin (1974) who looked to Jean-Paul Sartre's *Critique de la raison dialectique* (1960) as a basis for a humanistic approach to Marx. Girardin assessed a Marxist theory of the state and the role of dominant classes. In particular he contended with Althusser on a number of grounds. First, Althusser distinguished his conception of state from the class struggle. His methodology "cannot rediscover the real world of class struggle . . . in the congealed world of superstructures systematized by Althusser, no contradictions can arise since the indeterminations which emerge are always in the last instance controlled from a distance by the ultimately dominant economic structure" (1974: 198). Second, Althusser's "bureaucratic conception of social relationships . . . is more Weberian than Marxist." Violence is obscured by the state apparatus, which regulates social relations. The state must be taken over by the working class through legal electoral means, a position Girardin called "reformism" and "a bourgeois view of working class politics" (196–197). "The radical anti-humanism of Althusser, aiming at a scientific reconstruction of historical materialism, has placed him in the reassuring world of objectivity" (198).

Nicos Poulantzas elaborated an Althusserian structuralist model of the state and class. In line with the French structuralist perspective, Poulantzas believed that the structures of society rather than influential people generally determine the functions of the state. He examined the structure of class in society in order to identify the contradictions in the economy and to analyze how the state attempts to mitigate or eliminate those contradictions. Poulantzas's theory of the capitalist state was introduced in his *Political Power and Social Classes* (1973). Other contributions include his *Fascism and Dictatorship* (1974) and *Classes in Contemporary Capitalism* (1975). Although Poulantzas's writings have been received with interest if not acclaim, it is clear that English and U.S. critics recognize their contribution to a Marxist theory of politics, especially in conceptualizations of state, class, and power. His work, however, suffers from an abundance of formal terminology, abstraction, and a failure to elucidate and explicate many terms. The writing is obscure and often redundant (Barbalet 1974). Despite these limitations, some essential aspects of his thought are summarized below.

In *Political Power and Social Classes*, Poulantzas offered a theory that relates to the functions of the capitalist state and to the impact of the state on the capitalist and working classes. The state functions in several ways to reproduce the capitalist society as a whole. The state maintains cohesion and equilibrium on behalf of the political interests of the dominant class. The state characterizes all social relations as competitive so that workers and capitalist owners appear to be free and equal, thereby isolating them as individuals and obscuring their division into classes. Second, the state attempts to represent itself on behalf of the "unity" of the mass of isolated individuals as if a class struggle could not exist. Third, the state functions to allow classes to organize their own parties, which left to themselves promote internal contradiction and fractionalization, resulting in struggles within the working class and disunity within the bourgeoisie so that it is unable to rise to hegemonic domination as a united class. Thus the structure of the state permits the working class to organize and place demands on the state in ways that may conflict with the economic interests (but not the political interests) of the dominant classes. This demonstrates that the state is not simply the instrument of the dominating classes. Instead the state through its relative autonomy is able to ensure the stability of the interests of the dominating capitalist classes. The state structure stands above the special interests of individual capitalists and capitalist class fractions.

In his *Classes in Contemporary Capitalism*, Poulantzas systematically examined classes in capitalist society. This work has been digested by Erik Olin Wright (1976), who identified three basic premises. First, classes are defined in terms of class practices as reflected in antagonistic social relations, division of labor, and class struggle. Second, classes hold positions in the division of labor, these positions representing the structured determination of class. Third, classes are structured at economic, political, and ideological levels. Poulantzas argued that a new petty bourgeoisie of white-collar employees, technicians, and civil servants has arisen as the traditional petty bourgeoisie of artisans and small shopkeepers has declined. He analyzed the relationship of this new petty bourgeoisie to the working class, distinguishing between productive and unproductive labor. He also looked at the economic ownership and control that the bourgeoisie has over the means of production. Wright attacked this distinction between productive and unproductive labor and argued further that Poulantzas's use of political and ideological criteria undermines the primacy of economic relations in determining class position. He also questioned Poulantzas's insistence that the traditional and new petty bourgeoisie are of the same class.

Other criticisms of Poulantzas abound. Although acknowledging that Althusser and Poulantzas seek to rescue Marxism from empiricist, idealist, and historicist tendencies, Dale Johnson (1978) concluded that structuralism "is seriously deficient in terms of historical grounding and dialectical conception" (41). He expressed interest in the "Weberian-sounding conception of the three-dimensional determination of social class," whereby the new petty bourgeoisie appears as a sort of new middle class. Finally, he indicted structuralism for its static formalism or functionalism in which the "Marxist concept of reproduction becomes transformed into an almost Parsonian preoccupation with 'system maintenance'" (43). Gold, Lo, and Wright (1975) were concerned with the failure of Poulantzas to explain the social mechanisms that guarantee that the state will function autonomously to protect the interests of the dominant class (1975: 38). Amy Bridges (1974) argued that Poulantzas was antimaterialist, antihumanist, ahistorical, and descriptive in his view of the state as a dual structure that is both cohesive and transforming (178–181). Ernesto Laclau (1975) indicted Poulantzas for theoreticism and formalism, which result in a neglect of concrete analysis. In admitting the validity of some of these criticisms, Poulantzas (1976) retorted with his own criticism and self-criticism. In this process he rebutted Miliband's (1973) charges and argued that the debate between them was based on false and misleading premises.

Economic Structuralism:
Sweezy and Baran and O'Connor

In *The Theory of Capitalist Development* (1942) Paul Sweezy distinguished between a theory of class mediation and a theory of class domination. Liberal theorists advocate a class-mediation conception of the state, which assumes the existence of a certain class structure and recognizes the state as the mediator of conflicting interests of various classes. Marxist theorists employ a class-domination conception of the state. As the instrument of the ruling classes the state maintains and guarantees a given set of property relations and enforces and ensures the stability of the state itself. In this view the state is an *economic* instrument within capitalism. Specifically the state may act to solve particular crises of capitalism, it may be used on behalf of the interests of the bourgeoisie, and it may serve to blunt class antagonisms and revolution by providing concessions to the working class. Sweezy, whose criticism of power structure research has already been mentioned, thus alluded to Marxist theory, which had largely been ignored. His perspective of the state as an economic instrument of the ruling classes also accounted for the constraints of bourgeois democracy. Democracy, he argued, brings the contradictions and conflicts of capitalist society into the open so that capitalists may not freely use the state in their own interests.

This perception of state response to economic contradictions also reflects a view of economic structuralism. In this view political influences on economic policy are considered to be of secondary importance. In *Monopoly Capital* (1966) Sweezy and Baran combined instrumentalist and structuralist analysis.

> The particular actions of capitalist groups are seen as being in conflict with the need for the state to act for the class as a whole, so that the actual ways in which the state attempts to absorb the rising surplus are a result of an interaction between the structural needs and the particular interests. But the economic contradictions dominate the analysis and the instrumentalist evidence is interpreted within that framework. Other contradictions, such as those arising from ideology or class conflicts, play a minor role. The thrust of the work, then, is basically that of economic structuralism. [Gold, Lo, and Wright 1975: 39–40]

Baran and Sweezy focused on how the state facilitates the process of surplus absorption. The state acts to avert crises of monopoly capitalism, thereby guaranteeing absorption of surplus.

James O'Connor in *The Fiscal Crisis of the State* (1973) expanded on this view by arguing that the state is a complex structure of authority relations and itself possesses some autonomy. O'Connor did not see the state as merely an instrument for the ruling class or even specific segments of that class. O'Connor argued that the state does not produce but instead appropriates surplus to enhance the conditions requisite for capital accumulation. The state shapes the conditions for monopoly and competitive capitalism. Although the monopoly sector constantly reproduces the conditions for the competitive sector, competitive capitalism occupies a subordinate role to monopoly capitalism, which is the driving force in the productive process.

Class Analysis of the Modern World System: Wallerstein

Somewhat related to economic structuralism is the work of Immanuel Wallerstein (1975) on class in the capitalist world economy. His argument runs as follows. Class is a concept historically linked to the capitalist world economy or the modern world system. This world system consists of three basic elements: a single market, a series of state structures or nations that affect the workings of the market, and three levels (core, semiperiphery, and periphery) in an exploitative process involving the appropriation of surplus labor. Class struggle emanates from the relationship among these levels.

"Those on top always seek to ensure the existence of three tiers in order the better to preserve their privilege, whereas those on the bottom conversely seek to reduce the three to two, the better to destroy this same privilege. This fight over the existence of the middle tier goes on continually, both in political terms and in terms of basic ideological constructs" (Wallerstein 1975: 368). In this struggle classes are formed, consolidated, disintegrated, and reformulated as capitalism evolves and develops. This changing struggle is located in the capitalist world economy.

> The capitalist world economy as a totality—its structure, its historical evolution, its contradictions—is the arena of social action. The fundamental political reality of that world economy is a class struggle which however takes constantly changing forms: overt class consciousness versus ethno-national consciousness, classes within nations versus classes across nations. [1975: 375]

Wallerstein has expanded a conception of center and periphery that originated with the Argentine economist Raúl Prebisch and the UN Economic Commission for Latin America. He came close to the formulations of unequal development thesis of Samir Amin who, however, attempted to give weight to the productive process of capitalism as well as the market. Wallerstein also attempted to move beyond a conception of class within nations, thereby escaping some of the problems in a class analysis of internal colonialism, such as advocated by the Mexican political sociologist Pablo González Casanova, or the attention to national bourgeoisie found in writings by Marxists and non-Marxists alike.

Terence K. Hopkins (1977) clarified and elaborated on this formulation of class in the capitalist world economy. He argued that Wallerstein provided a theory of the global capitalist economy as a world system, not a theory of the development of national economies or of an international economy. Hopkins believed that with the evolution of this world system there has been the establishment of an organized world capitalist class in contrast to alliances among national bourgeoisie. A parallel development has been the formation of an international movement of labor through the organization of a worldwide labor market. The multinational corporations have proved effective in organizing this world system along such class lines.

This imaginative yet somewhat eclectic theory of Wallerstein has been widely criticized for its attention to market rather than to production as a basis for analyzing class relations in the contemporary capitalist world. Wallerstein cited Marx for support of his theory and attempted to disassociate his thought from the ideas of Max Weber. His concern with structure transcended national state boundaries and attempted to explore the roots of the world capitalist economy. Wallerstein elaborated and recast dimensions of the dependency theory and thus has influenced many or-thodox social scientists to alter their perspectives of development, state, and class. The reader, however, will discover significant differences, theoretically and methodologically, between Wallerstein and other structuralists such as Althusser and Poulantzas.

Critical Views of Structuralist Theory

A major problem of structuralist theory is that it does little to explain class action arising from class consciousness, a concern of Marx, especially in his early works, and of the critical school, which is examined later in this chapter. Esping-Andersen, Friedland, and Wright (1976) deplored a lack of theory that ties political inputs and constraints to outputs of state activity; neither structuralist nor instrumentalist theory solves this problem (1976: 189). John Mollenkopf believed that structuralists have offered useful cri-tiques of instrumentalism, which studies of power structure exemplify. At the same time both economic and political structuralism remain inadequate. First, economic structuralism limits the state to a superficial conception, to a kind of systemic checklist. "It assigns solely economic, rather than political motives to the state in the face of substantial evidence to the contrary. It also projects an economistic 'inevitability' for crises which politics should not be able to allay, but somehow does." Second, political instrumentalists such as Poulantzas focus on the ideological and repressive institutions that sustain capitalism. This emphasis on the political aspects of structuralism leads to what Miliband called structuralist "abstractionism" or "superdetermination." "The state becomes an all pervasive political/ideological realm shorn of institutional location, visible boundaries, or even political struggle" (Mollenkopf 1975: 256). The structuralist work tends to be highly abstract and oriented to conceptual schemes rather than theory. It permits an understanding of the workings of the capitalist state and its agencies and policies. It also allows for distinctions between class and group interests, although Mollenkopf advocated work on a theory of class political action that would explain the aims and actions of late capitalism. Finally, Amy Beth Bridges (1974) summed up the reservations of many U.S. critics.

> A sterile functionalism—marxist or not—cannot inform either social understanding or revolutionary politics. In fact, the structuralist framework, presenting the social formation as self-reinforcing, can lead only to anarchist politics or to the worst kinds of reformism. Those who struggled against this kind of analytic perspective in mainstream sociology . . . will find its anti-humanism no more acceptable when couched in marxist terms than when it was unabashedly bourgeois. [1974: 180]

CRITICALISM: IDEOLOGY AND CONSCIOUSNESS

Although some structuralists like Althusser and Poulantzas dwelt on political questions of state and class, in particular relating to ideology, they attacked the loose conceptions that characterized Marx's early writings as well as a host of successors, most of whom are associated with the Frankfurt school. The brief discussion below returns to the "critical" studies of the early Marx and his followers who concentrated attention on the nature of the superstructure, the activities of the state, ideology, and class consciousness.

The critical school draws from the early Marx who contended with Hegel. Marx's critique of Hegel's notions of state gives the school its "critical" orientation. Hegel distinguished between the institutions of civil or private society (family, for example) and the state but showed that the split between them could be overcome, a proposition Marx argued was false. Marx believed that the state is separate from civil society and is the organization the bourgeoisie adopts for the protection of its property and interests. Despite Marx's criticism, he was indebted to Hegel for attention to a political theory of the state, for elaboration of dialectical method, and, finally, for seeking meaning in the concept of freedom and the unfolding of human consciousness. For this reason critical thought is often referred to as emanating from a Hegelian-Marxist tradition.

What then are the major lines of thought within this Hegelian-Marxist tradition? In the sense that Marx desired to expose the false consciousness or ideology that accompanies the capitalist era, the objective of contemporary Marxism becomes the creation of a genuine consciousness (Cornforth 1963). Marx uncovered the meaning of consciousness in the *Economic and Philosophical Manuscripts of 1844* in his analysis of the alienation of labor. Work is external to the worker who thus cannot satisfy himself and feels miserable, physically exhausted and mentally depressed. The alien nature of work is shown by the fact that the worker produces for someone else, not himself. Eric Fromm in *Marx's Concept of Man* (1961) analyzed this phenomenon, but Georg Lukács in *History and Class Consciousness*, first published in 1923, offered a seminal work on class consciousness. Later contributions include István Mezáros's *Marx's Theory of Alienation* (1970) and Bertell Ollman's *Alienation* (1970).

In the preface to the 1967 edition of his study, Lukács offered a self-assessment. His theoretical formulation emerged through his experiences as a student in Heidelberg and Vienna and as a revolutionary in his native Hungary. The influence of Hegel, together with idealism and utopianism, characterized his early thinking, and although he was steadfastly opposed to the social democratic and opportunistic currents of the early 1920s, Lukács acknowledged that his work tended to view Marxism exclusively as a theory of society and not as a theory of nature. For this reason he overlooked labor as an interacting concept between society and nature. "What I failed to realize, however, was that in the absence of a basis in real praxis, in labour as its original form and model, the over-extension of the concept of praxis would lead to its opposite: a relapse into idealistic contemplation" (Lukács 1971: xviii). Lukács lamented that his work placed the concept of totality at the center, thereby diminishing the significance of economics. This was a Hegelian "distortion" but nevertheless helped to counter revisionist efforts to cast Marxism as science. The revival of the Hegelian tradition also provoked interest within bourgeois philosophy. These considerations exemplify the confusion not only in Lukács's thought but in the writings of others attracted to the Hegelian-Marxist theory.

Lucien Goldmann (1977) in his comparison of the thought of Lukács and Martin Heidegger established Lukács as the representative figure of the break with positivism and the Kantian influence that had prevailed during the second half of the nineteenth century and until 1910. In Heidelberg, Kantian philosophers came into contact with social scientists such as Weber, and at the neighboring university in Freiburg there emerged a new philosophical current of phenomenology under Edmund Husserl. Lukács, of course, became a prominent name in these developments.

> It was at the beginning of this century, around two German universities, Heidelberg and Freiburg, and within what is usually called "the south-west German philosophical school," that a change was effected which was to prove the source of the principal European philosophical currents of the first half of the twentieth century. This change was to take two directions: on the one hand, the birth of phenomenology and, from it, existentialism, and, on the other hand, via phenomenology and existentialism, the birth of dialectical Marxism, with Lukács and the Lukácsian school. [Goldmann 1977: 1–2]

The thought of Lukács influenced the Frankfurt school of philosophers (Slater 1977), which in turn generated an impact on some of the early leaders of Austro-Marxism (Bottomore 1978).

From Lukács many lines of thought appear. The Frankfurt school carried on in the struggle against positivism. Michael Harrington in *The Twilight of Capitalism* (1976) identified during the Second World War two tendencies opposed to the "scientific" ideals of nazism under Hitler. Theodor Adorno, Max Horkheimer, and Herbert Marcuse represented one tendency. Adorno and Horkheimer in *Dialectic of the Enlightenment* (1944) argued that the Nazi regime, in its arbitrary engineering of the destiny of individuals, reflected practices of the Enlightenment. Marcuse in *Reason and Revolution* (1941) argued that fascism is a totalitarian form of capitalism. Franz Neumann represented a second tendency. In *Behemoth* (1958) he argued that Nazi Germany was under the control of capitalists and run according to their interests and priorities.

The concern of the critical theorists with positivism set in motion a debate since 1961 with German social scientific and philosophical circles. A detailed exposition of this debate, together with essays representing divergent perspectives, was organized by Adorno (1976). One of the participants in the ongoing dispute is Jürgen Habermas who is one of Germany's most outstanding political theorists (McCarthy 1978). His major works are available in English, including *Toward a Rational Society: Student Protest, Science, and Politics* (1971), *Knowledge and Human Interests* (1972), *Theory and Practice* (1974), and *Legitimation Crisis* (1975).

Habermas represents the younger generation of the Frankfurt philosophers. According to Anthony Giddens, Habermas pursued two lines of thought developed by the older generation of Frankfurt scholars: the relation between theory and critique and the developments of Western capitalism. His attention to Marx incorporated the Hegelian influences, critiqued orthodox Marxism, and offered perspectives distinguishable from the positions of Adorno, Horkheimer, and Marcuse. Habermas offered a reappraisal of Marx's understanding of capitalist development, prompting Giddens to comment,

> His reappraisal of Marx, in respect of the latter's analysis of liberal capitalism at least, seems to me to be both too revisionist and not revisionist enough. Not revisionist enough, because he accepts too readily that Marx's account was valid in the 19th century; Habermas' portrayal of competitive capitalism is a rather orthodox one in this regard. Too revisionist, because he writes off too completely the relevance of some central Marxian ideas today." [Giddens 1977: 212]

Tony Flood (1977–1978) referred to the claim of Habermas that Marx showed that the class struggle takes the form of ideological delusion, a novel notion that suggests that class struggle is not recognizable by capitalists and workers alike. Habermas also called for a reconstruction of the manifestations of the consciousness of classes as well as for a revision of theory so as to avoid a mechanistic treatment of the relationship of base to superstructure. These reviews emphasize the significant contributions of Habermas to critical theory.

Critical theory has influenced other perspectives of state and class. Alan Wolfe (1974) tied the Hegelian-Marxist tradition to some aspects of structuralism and focused on alienated politics in an attempt to set forth a new theory. Claus Offe, a student of the critical school under Habermas, rejected both instrumentalism and structuralism as theories that fail to deal with the mechanisms within the state that shape its class character. Offe focused on specific mechanisms such as ideology and repression. Julian Hochfeld (1967), a Polish sociologist, examined consciousness in relation to class interests. His conceptualization parallels the ideal typing in Max Weber rather than the notion of consciousness in Lukács, a position one critic has described as dogmatic (Rich 1976).

STATISM AND CLASS STRUGGLE

Esping-Andersen, Friedland, and Wright (1976) elaborated on the interconnections among class struggle, state structures, and state policies. They examined ways in which the class struggle shapes the structure of the state and the ways in which the structure of the state shapes the class struggle. They also looked at how the policies of the state shape and are shaped by demands raised in the class struggle. Specifically, they drew upon theory implicit in the work of Claus Offe and James O'Connor.

Offe examined the structure of authority in liberal capitalist societies and argued that political institutions should be analyzed in class terms. First, the bourgeoisie uses its ideology to align state policy with its own interests in foreign affairs, finance, and social areas. Second, action of the state is limited to maintaining public order through the military, courts, and police, thus creating conditions for private capital accumulation. In the advanced or late capitalist society, however, "an all-pervasive system of mechanisms for state intervention has been established" (Offe 1972b: 80). In contrast to liberal capitalist societies in which the bourgeois state limits authority, late capitalist societies are regulated and sustained by permanent political intervention. Thus the state may assume responsibility for managing crises in the economy. Offe contended that the establishment of a "welfare" state implies support of the lower classes, but in fact it allows corporate business to derive far greater benefits (1972a). At the same time the state remains independent of direct class controls. Esping-Andersen et al. believed that Offe's conception of autonomy and state intervention into crisis situations "leads him to ignore the extent to which classes are differentially able to shape the state machinery and voice specific demands for state action" (1976: 191).

James O'Connor's *The Fiscal Crisis of the State* (1973) deals with the relation of the internal structure of the state to contradictions in the accumulation process. He also analyzed the relationship between the class struggle and the internal structure. In particular, he looked at how the class struggle limits the state's ability to rationalize capitalism and how state structures serve as barriers to the challenge of the working class.

The theory implicit in Offe and O'Connor led Esping-Andersen et al. to four propositions as to how state structures are shaped by class struggle. First, they saw state structures as the outcome of class struggle, not simply as mechanisms conceived and maintained for the reproduction of capital and the repression of the working class. Second, these structures mediate, on the one hand, demands to the state from the ruling class and, on the other, state policies that constrain the class struggle. Third, the capitalist class shapes these structures with the objective of limiting the state to intervention compatible with the needs of capital accumulation and of politically neutralizing the demands of the working class. Fourth, these structures are inevitably contradictory and never totally neutralize the class struggle and incorporate the working class into an apolitical state.

Esping-Andersen et al. also examined how the forms and direction of the class struggle are shaped by the state. They began with a typology of the political class struggle, which incorporates aspects of the production process and circulation between commodities. They also considered the "class content," "transformations," and "contradictions" of the political class struggle.

In a critical response to Esping-Andersen et al., the Capitol Kapitalistate Group (1977) reaffirmed the significance of according the class struggle a central place in the historical process that shapes the state. However, they found fault with the methodology, especially the typology, used by Esping-Andersen et al.: "While thought provoking, their typology appears to be static and undialectical, reproducing some of the methodological shortcomings of bourgeois social science." Despite this reservation Esping-Andersen et al. "pioneered the integration of class struggle into the analysis of the state" (1977: 209). Clearly effort in this direction is needed in an attempt to transcend the various schools of theory on state and class and to find both a useful theory and a useful analysis.

THE ISSUES OF A CLASS ANALYSIS

Pluralism continues to influence comparative study. Western specialists of comparative politics ignore approaches shaped by Marxist theory and methodology, and the field stagnates in the face of the exciting and innovative contributions of rival disciplines. Fortunately, we can turn to Miliband, Wolfe, and a handful of other political scientists who are interested in questions of state and class. We find various lines of thought, debate, and a plethora of unresolved issues. As a way of summarizing some of the divergent trends that run through the present chapter, issues of class analysis are identified and discussed: (1) the role of the state and the ruling class, (2) the class categories of analysis, (3) the levels of conceptualization of class, (4) the relationship of base and superstructure, (5) the implications of precapitalist and capitalist social formations.

The Role of State and Ruling Class

Primitive forms of state were organized along lines of kinship rather than of class. Prior to such primitive forms, societies were organized communally and collectively to deal with order and conflict. Modern forms of the state developed in response to the social division of labor into classes, those who produce goods and services and those who manage and profit from the production. The prevalent contemporary form of the state evolved from a period of usury and primitive accumulation of merchant capital to an era of expanding money capital in which the state increasingly serves progressive capital accumulation and the capitalist mode of production. The absolutist state replaced the feudal state as the monarchies of Europe consolidated their rule over the nobles. The bourgeois state evolved from the absolutist state as the emerging bourgeois class seized power and the state institutions.

What then are the principal activities of the bourgeois state? Mandel classified these activities into three categories: provision of conditions of production not guaranteed by the ruling class; repression of any threat to the prevailing mode of production through the use of army, police, judiciary system, and prison; and cohesion of the exploited classes to ensure their acceptance of the ruling ideology. Szymanski (1978) identified ways in which the state stimulates the process of capital accumulation: providing a labor force for corporations, facilitating commerce, stimulating consumption, repressing cyclical tendencies in the economy, subsidizing individual corporations, allowing corporations to regulate their own activities, and providing economic and military assistance to enhance corporate foreign activities.

Given this description of the bourgeois state, the central theoretical issue then revolves around the relationship of the state to the ruling class. In the Communist Manifesto Marx and Engels referred to the "executive" of the state as a committee that manages the affairs of the bourgeoisie. Lenin wrote of the army and the police as "instruments" of the state. Perry Anderson essentially analyzed the absolutist state in an instrumentalist context. Ernest Mandel argued that the hierarchical organization as well as its total structure determines the state's role as an instrument of bourgeois rule. He agreed with Ralph Miliband that in Great Britain advancement to state executive positions is determined not so much by professional competence as by conformity to the norms of bourgeois conduct. Domhoff, of course, believed a similar pattern exists in the United States. These views have been questioned by structuralists such as Althusser and Poulantzas, who suggested that the state functions independently of class forces in order to protect the interests of the bourgeois capitalist class.

These contrasting perspectives reflect the experience of advanced industrial societies, but what of underdeveloped societies that display precapitalist forms? The question is complex and deserving of elaboration elsewhere, but it may suffice to note the findings of some observers.

Horowitz and Trimberger (1976), for example, examined the state in Latin America as a means for transcending the dependency model, which overlooks national differences. They examined the relationship of the state apparatus to the class structure of Latin American societies and concluded that capitalism, and ultimately socialism, can advance only when the state breaks down class barriers to industrialization or creates an independent entrepreneurial class. In the face of constraints upon external expansion, the state must turn inward to mobilize capital; the state must become centralized, efficient, and autonomous. State autonomy requires that bureaucrats not be from the ruling classes nor be controlled by a parliamentary or party apparatus; the military bureaucracy fulfills such a role in a state, which necessarily will be authoritarian. Horowitz and Trimberger distinguished their model from the structuralist position of Poulantzas, then they outlined three patterns: state-initiated national capitalist development, organized by military and civil bureaucrats who gain power through revolution from above; state-initiated dependent capitalist development, under the control of a coalition of military and civil bureaucrats who have broken the power of the landed bourgeoisie; and state-directed socialist development, led by military bureaucrats who seize power through mass revolution, destroy the landed bourgeoisie and national bourgeoisie, and seize foreign investments.

The role of the state in Africa and Asia apparently differs from that in Latin America. Colin Leys (1976) assessed the work of Hamza Alavi on Pakistan and Bangladesh and of John Saul on Tanzania. Both analyzed postcolonial society. Alavi believed that the postcolonial state inherits a strong military and administrative base whose origins are rooted in the metropole. During colonial times the task of this state is to control all internal classes. After independence, the state wins the support of at least one of those classes, and thus it becomes "overdeveloped" in relation to its previous status. This overdeveloped state appropriates a large share of the economic surplus and allocates it to bureaucratically directed developmental activity. In relating Alavi's propositions to Africa, Saul noted the absence of strong internal classes. He argued that the state's independence is due to a balance between internal and external class forces, so the state is likely to be dependent on strong external classes. If the state is strong, the absence of internal classes may make it more powerful. Saul believed that the state bureaucracy is likely to be a new type of class, which appropriates and controls productive resources by regulating them or acquiring private capital. Alternatively, the state bureaucracy may be exposed to contradictory forces as national, working-class, and peasant-class interests confront domestic and foreign capital. Saul used this latter position in his analysis of Tanzania. Leys criticized this stance, arguing that the notion of a "bureaucratic bourgeoisie" as a ruling class is nebulous: "the contradictions of the situation are obscured by this lumping together of different elements in the state apparatus" (1976: 48).

Class Categories of Analysis

The unique conditions of each society largely determine which classes can be analyzed. Social scientists who employ stratification analysis refer to a classification of upper, middle, and lower classes. The identification of such classes usually relates to such criteria as income, status, and education, and the categories of class are used in isolation one from another. Thus stratification analysis tends to be static, focused at any particular time on position within a system of hierarchical levels rather than on a theory of change. An analysis of ruling elites or power elites looks to a small, cohesive, and relatively closed elite that controls decisions of importance and defends its interests in maintaining the status quo. Both elite and stratification analysis are differentiated from the Marxist analysis of class, which assumes that at least two classes stand in dialectical opposition to each other, that conflict is likely to be the outcome between contradictory interests. Marx offered no explicit definition of class but analyzed the structure of classes in terms of each society's mode of production. Marx analyzed society in terms of a dominant or ruling class and a subordinate class. Thus, the feudal lords and serfs were the two major classes in feudal Europe; slave owners and slaves, in the United States prior to the Civil War; and capitalists and workers, in contemporary capitalist society. Class analysis, however, also refers to related classes as well as to elements within classes. At issue is a recognition of Marx's methodology as a basis for class analysis. Otherwise the student may be misguided by pointless endeavors to formulate new theories of class. To facilitate an understanding of contrasting situations, we now turn to various attempts to identify classes within a Marxist methodology.

In the *Communist Manifesto* Marx and Engels emphasized two principal classes under capitalism — one that lives by owning; the other, by working. In the last chapter of volume three of *Capital*, Marx alluded to the three great classes of landowners, capitalists, and wage laborers, but in the *Eighteenth Brumaire*, he analyzed French politics of the mid–nineteenth century in terms of shifting class alignments, the monarchy being divided by the Legitimists, bolstered by large landed property, and the Orleanists, supported by high finance, large-scale industry, and commerce. Ultimately a bourgeois republic came to power, supported by an aristocracy of finance, industrial bourgeoisie, middle class, petty bourgeoisie, army, and lumpenproletariat. Repressed were the proletariat and their opposing interests. Marx's multiple use of classes reflected the emerging class struggles of an era in which feudalism and absolute monarchical rule were succumbing to bourgeois class forces, which emerged in the mercantile and industrial forms of capitalism.

The consolidation of capitalism during the twentieth century makes the task of a class analysis exceedingly complex. Although in the industrial nations like the United States classes are more clearly delineated in a mode of advanced monopoly capitalism and multinational enterprise, in the underdeveloped nations foreign capital and technology intrude upon conditions usually characterized as precapitalist. Thus, Szymanski focused on four classes in the United States: the capitalist class, which owns the means of production; the petty bourgeoisie of professionals, small merchants, independent farmers, and artisans; the working class of industrial, rural, and white-collar laborers; and the lumpenproletariat of people who live by means of welfare or crime (1978: 26).

In an analysis of classes in Latin America, however, it is not unusual to find reference to old oligarchies and new groups of petty bourgeoisie and white-collar workers, the urban industrial proletariat. Often an imperialist or international bourgeoisie, tied to foreign interests, is contrasted to a dependent or national bourgeoisie. Such is the case of Aníbal Quijano's *Nationalism and Capitalism in Peru* (1971). Quijano concentrated on a dominant class of landholding bourgeoisie and industrial bourgeoisie, and he referred to upper and middle levels within each segment.

In Africa and areas recently liberated from colonial rule, a capitalist mode of production may be scarcely evident, as was the case in Guinea-Bissau, once a Portuguese possession. Although Portuguese monopolists operated in the colony, no industrialization implanted itself. A small indigenous colonial bureaucracy and a small class of foreign merchants, along with a minuscule urban labor force, constituted the major classes when the nation achieved independence in 1975. Relatively undeveloped, independent Guinea-Bissau was led by petty bourgeois revolutionaries and supported by a mass of subsistence-farming peasants. The basis of their revolutionary organization stemmed from the horizontal and communalistic structures of the Balantu tribe. The Balantus traditionally had resisted Portuguese colonialism and had quarreled with the rival Fula tribes. The Fulas were traders who carried their enterprise over a long distance and in protection of their interests tended to ally with the Portuguese during colonial times. Basil Davidson, in *Let Freedom Come: Africa in Modern History* (1978), labeled such activity a "lineage mode," comprising elements of a capitalist mode yet lacking the force to build fully capitalist formations. Gail Omvedt (1973) also contributed to class theory in colonial situations with her classification and assessment of such classes as an industrial bourgeoisie (small, often nonexistent because of the dominance of foreign monopoly capital); commercial bourgeoisie (a dominant force in urban areas and merged with the rural class of rentier landlords); intelligentsia (Western-educated and often in positions of the colonial bureaucracy); petty bourgeoisie (a subelite of clerks, lower-level teachers, and traders who often became leaders of the national liberation movements); traditional aristocracy (nobles, rulers, and chieftains who cooperated with colonial administrators); rentier landlords (the ruling class on the land); peasantry; and industrial working class.

The present discussion is intended only to guide the student toward establishing categories for class analysis and at the same time to reveal some misconceptions that may arise in such a task. Among some sources on Marx's use of class, in Chapter 4 we referred to Friedman (1974), Ollman (1968), and Bendix and Lipset (1966). In addition to those sources the following may also be useful. Anthony Giddens (1973) reviewed the problems of class theory and suggested that levels of "class structuration" be used in an analysis of advanced societies. Other perspectives on a conceptualization of class are in Dos Santos (1970), Ossowski (1963), Hodges (1959), and Stolzman and Gamberg (1973–1974), and Hazelrigg (1972) and Zeitlin (1974) moved toward a Marxist view in rebutting bourgeois conceptions of class.

Levels of Conceptualization of Class

Dos Santos (1970) argued that Marx intended to analyze the concept of class on several interdependent levels and that this approach is consistent with the dialectical method. Marx situated the first of these levels in an analysis of the mode of production. When this mode and its relations of production are based on private property, then social classes engage in struggle as a result of their antagonistic and contradictory relations. Although this level of analysis tends toward abstraction in its emphasis on theoretical categories, Dos Santos believed that it arises from "practice" and "the concrete relations in which men live in the reality of history" (1970: 176). A second level emphasized an analysis of social structure in which the analysis will be descriptive and concrete, examining specific forms of relations among the components of the mode of production; for example, social forms that are antagonistic to the ruling formation so that there is a struggle between ruling and ruled classes in opposing modes of production such as feudalism and capitalism. A third level relates to social situations, in particular, social stratification or hierarchization of individuals in society; according to class as well as to differences in income, profession, politics, and so on. "On this level important problems arise concerning contradictions between *class* interests of a class and its immediate interests; contradictions between its class interests and its historical origins; between its mentality as conditioned by the existing structure, the values of social stratification, race relations, etc., and the class interests that are the condition of its possibilities for class action" (Dos Santos 1970: 179). A fourth level looks at the crises and deep changes that occur in the cycles of capitalism. Dos Santos observed that the prolonged capitalist development leads to tendencies to deny capitalist crises. Mass consumption also obscures class relations since "empiricists substitute mass society for class society" (180). In identifying these different perceptions, Marx, according to Dos Santos, established "a structured system of planes of abstraction ranging from the most concrete to the most abstract and from the most abstract to the most concrete" (180). In dealing with the concrete, Marxism must define general laws in complex terms; the abstract must relate to social reality but not as formal theory, which stresses empirical observation and allows for absolutes, codification, and ideal types.

Relationship of Base and Superstructure

The emphasis that Marxists give the economic base in the analysis of class must not overshadow a concern with ideological implications of class as related to the superstructure. Bourgeois conceptions of state, bureaucracy, and party, for example, may result in some of the misplaced emphasis on elite position that runs through the instrumentalist school, or they may result in the rigid categories of structure and institution that reveal the shortcomings of the structuralist school. Likewise, attention to ideology and consciousness, central concerns of the critical school, must not outweigh analysis of mode of production, forces of production, and the like. A dialectical assessment is demanded.

The elements of class consciousness and ideology are of crucial importance in Marxist politics. Class consciousness refers to the consciousness that members of a class have of their own interests. Under capitalism, these interests would be defined by the possession or lack of possession of property and privilege. It may be that a class manifests a false consciousness, believing that its interests are of universal and classless character. Thus, ideology implies the attempt by a class to give ideal form to a class interest, and this, according to Marx, is a false representation of reality. Deliberate deception also might be employed in defense of a class interest. Recognition and understanding of deception or false consciousness by an exploited class, for instance, the urban workers, may lead to a revolutionary struggle for the exploited class's liberation, the overthrow of capitalism. But revolutionary consciousness may be a highly subjective phenomenon and cannot be described simply by given formulas and categories. At issue, then, is a need to recognize the subtle implications of class analysis and to combine and synthesize the various approaches, thereby avoiding some of the pitfalls of past investigation.

Implications of Precapitalist and Capitalist Social Formations

In the previous chapter, I alluded to the debate over the various interpretations of dual society in Latin America. The widely accepted view assumes that the area is feudal, a remnant of times in Spain and Portugal when the conquest and settlement of Latin America took place and the Iberian monarchies imposed a feudal aristocracy and system. The development of capitalism in the countryside was impeded, but commercial contact in urban areas allowed for development in the cities. Consequently, there emerged two societies, one rural, feudal, and backward, and the other urban, capitalist, and advanced. This view has been defended on the Left by critics who have contended that Latin American societies have always been feudal in character and continue today as closed, traditional, resistant to change, and unintegrated into a market economy; that is, those societies remain clearly precapitalist in mode. But, it is argued, a bourgeois-democratic revolution is imminent, which will usher in capitalism and break down the feudal stagnation. That position has been challenged by those on the Left who claim that the area has been capitalist from its conception when it was incorporated into the world market of the colonial period. Capitalism, however, has promoted the present backwardness and underdevelopment of the area, and only a struggle by the masses against the bourgeoisie and imperialism will lead to socialism and a break with dependent capitalism. At issue is an emphasis on production, on the one hand, and on market or exchange, on the other.

Such diverse interpretations challenge theoretical understandings of the role of classes in the transition of feudalism to capitalism and of capitalism to socialism. Proponents of the view that precapitalist economic formations prevail in a given society may emphasize the role of the feudal class elements while looking to an emerging national bourgeoisie in the promotion of progressive capitalism in a backward society. Opponents of this view would argue that rural and urban industrial interests determine the class character of the ruling class and that a national bourgeoisie cannot assume a progressive role in the face of imperialist capital.

This discussion has concerned economies other than those of industrial capitalist countries, but the debate over the transition from feudalism to capitalism has its origins in diverse understandings of the European experience. Marx elaborated on precapitalist economic formations, and Eric Hobsbawm (1965), the English historian, brought this material together with his own introduction. The English economic historian Maurice Dobb presented an overview in *Studies in the Development of Capitalism* (1946), and Paul Sweezy, Dobb, and others debated questions about the transition in the ensuing decade (edited by Rodney Hilton, 1976). Perry Anderson's *Passages from Antiquity to Feudalism* (1974) attempts to move from a theoretical stance to a historical interpretation of the various social formations that characterized the feudal mode of production in the medieval epoch of Western Europe. His sequel, *Lineages of the Absolutist State* (1974), deals with the transition of feudalism to capitalism. Immanuel Wallerstein's *The Modern World-System* (1974) also sheds light on this controversial topic, as does Barry Hindess and Paul Q. Hirst's *Pre-Capitalist Modes of Production* (1975).

At least three debates emanate from this literature, according to Matthew Edel. The first deals with the origins of capitalism, whether they date to the expansion of trade as early as the twelfth century or to the production activities and wage labor of the sixteenth to nineteenth centuries. Edel sided with the latter view; "For Marx, and most Marxists, the origin of capitalism as a system is placed when merchant capital was formed, for the first time, by the availability of propertyless free labor available for wage-work. This allowed the development of a new form of production, and the properties of capitalism" (Edel 1972: 10). A second debate centers on contemporary Europe and the various perspectives on socialism and communism in questions about the transition to socialism. A third debate concerns whether the now underdeveloped countries are capitalist even though they are dominated by imperialism and foreign capitalist powers.

References

Adorno, Theodor W. (ed.)
    1976 *Positivist Dispute in German Ideology.* Translated by Glyn Adey and David Frisby. London: Heinemann. Collection of essays that deal with issues relating to positivism and critical theory that have divided German philosophers during the twentieth century. Includes an introduction by David Frisby and essays by Adorno, Jürgen Habermas, and Karl Popper.
Althusser, Louis
    1970 *For Marx.* Translated by Ben Brewster. New York: Vintage Books. One of the more popular of the author's works in English. Essays deal with the criticism of Marxist humanism.

1971 "Ideology and Ideological State Apparatuses (Notes Towards an Investigation)." In Althusser, *Lenin and Philosophy and Other Essays*, pp. 121–173. London: New Left Books. Outlines the structure of state in terms of repressive and ideological apparatuses that serve the interests of the ruling class.

Bachrach, Peter, and Morton Baratz
1962 "The Two Faces of Power." *American Political Science Review* LVII (December), 947–952. Argues for a look at the "nondecision" and attacks pluralist and decision-making studies of power.

Bailey, Norman A.
1968 "Toward a Praxeological Theory of Conflict." *Orbis* XI (Winter), 1081–1112. An exhaustive review of the literature on conflict with attention to Polish thought on praxeology.

Barbalet, J. M.
1974 "Political Science, the State, and Marx." *Politics* IX (May), 69–73. A review of Poulantzas (1973).

Bottomore, T. B.
1964 *Elites and Society*. Middlesex, England: Penguin Books. A useful synthesis of various conceptions of elite within Marxist and non-Marxist theories.

Bottomore, T. B. (ed.)
1978 *Austro-Marxism*. Texts translated and edited by T. B. Bottomore and Patrick Goode with an introduction by Bottomore. Oxford: Clarendon Press. Essays by Otto Bauer, Max Adler, Rudolf Hilferding, Karl Renner, and Wilhelm Hausenstein who were the leading Austro-Marxists. Although there were connections with the Frankfurt school, the Austro-Marxists moved in a different direction, away from critical questions and metaphysical orientations toward the development of Marxism as an empirical social science.

Bridges, Amy Beth
1974 "Nicos Poulantzas and the Marxist Theory of the State." *Politics and Society* IV (Winter), 161–190. A detailed and devastating review of Poulantzas (1973).

Capitol Kapitalistate Group
1977 "Typology and Class Struggle: Critical Notes on 'Modes of Class Struggle and the Capitalist State." *Kapitalistate* VI (Fall), 209–215. Critical review of Esping-Andersen and others (1976).

Cornforth, Maurice
1963 *The Theory of Knowledge*. New York: International Publishers. A Marxist synthesis of the nature of mind and body in relation to thinking, language, and logic; of the development of ideas from abstractions to ideological illusions and science; of truth and freedom. Especially important for understanding ideology and consciousness and false consciousness and their impact on bourgeois society.

Cunningham, Frank
1975–1976 "Pluralism and Class Struggle." *Science and Society* XXXIX (Winter), 385–416. Contrasts pluralist analysis to Marxist analysis, with a preference for the latter.

Dahl, Robert A.
1958 "A Critique of the Ruling Elite Model." *American Political Science Review* LII (June), 463–469. Attacks ruling elite methodology and defends pluralism.

1961 *Who Governs? Democracy and Power in an American City.* New Haven: Yale University Press. A community study of New Haven, which emphasizes the pluralist basis of power politics.

1971 *Polyarchy, Participation, and Opposition.* New Haven: Yale University Press. A focus on polyarchies, generally Western states in which autonomy and pluralism are evident.

1978 "Pluralism Revisited." *Comparative Politics* X (January), 191–203. A restatement of earlier perspectives on pluralism. Here Dahl attempts to combine liberal and Marxist views of imperialism.

Dahrendorf, Ralf
1959 *Class and Class Conflict in Industrial Society.* Stanford: Stanford University Press. Synthesizes Marx's theory of class and criticizes it in relation to later theory and experience.

Domhoff, G. William
1970 *The Higher Circles: The Governing Class in America.* New York: Vintage Books. Utilizing his power structure methods, Domhoff analyzes the results of his research on the governing class of the United States.

1976 "I Am Not an 'Instrumentalist': A Reply to 'Modes of Class Struggle and the Capitalist State' and Other *Kapitalistate* Critics." *Kapitalistate* 4–5 (Summer), 221–224. Argues that his work does not follow instrumentalist thought, that it is Marxist in conception.

1978 *Who Really Rules? New Haven and Community Power Reexamined.* New Brunswick, New Jersey: Transaction Books. Using a methodology different than that of Dahl (1961), Domhoff presents a new analysis and understanding of that city's power structure.

Domhoff, G. William (ed.)
1975 "New Directions in Power Structure Research." *Insurgent Sociologist* V (Spring), 1–264. Full issue. Includes studies of various state agencies, socioeconomic connections of government decision makers, mapping power structures, and critiques of power structure research. Domhoff edited a follow-up issue, "Power Structure Research II," *Insurgent Sociologist* IX (Winter 1980), 1–142.

Domhoff, G. William, and Hoyt B. Ballard (eds.)
1968 *C. Wright Mills and the Power Elite.* Boston: Beacon Press. A collection of essays critical of Mills's thought, including liberal, radical, and highbrow critics and a response by Mills himself.

Dos Santos, Theotonio
1970 "The Concept of Social Classes." *Science and Society* XXXIV (Summer), 166–193. Demonstrates that the concept of social class was not initially formulated by Marx. Shows that Marx did not give systematic treatment to class and reviews criticisms by Georges Gurvitch and Stanislaw Ossowski. Finally, identifies five levels that Marx used to deal with class analysis: mode of production, social structure, social situation, cycles, and class consciousness.

Dye, Thomas R.
1976 *Who's Running America? Institutional Leadership in the United States.*

Englewood Cliffs, New Jersey: Prentice-Hall. A recent example of power structure research in the tradition of Hunter and Mills, which is based on biographical data for over 5,000 elite members.

Edel, Matthew

1972 "Exchange and Production: A Controversy in Anthropology and Political Economy." Toronto: Paper presented at the Meetings of the American Anthropological Association. Critically reviews the debate in economic anthropology on emphasis on production rather than on exchange and finds arguments in Marx to support the former position.

Esping-Andersen, Gosta, Rodger Friedland, and Erik Olin Wright

1976 "Modes of Class Struggle and the Capitalist State." *Kapitalistate* 4–5 (Summer), 186–220. Review of current approaches to a theory of the capitalist state. Critically reviewed by the Capitol Kapitalistate Group (1977).

Flood, Tony

1977–1978 "Jürgen Habermas's Critique of Marxism." *Science and Society* XLI (Winter), 448–464. A sympathetic review of Habermas's efforts to place Marx within critical theory.

Freiburg, J. W.

1973 "Sociology and the Ruling Class." *Insurgent Sociologist* III (Summer), 12–26. Examines Western bourgeois thought and Eastern European socialist thought on the question of ruling class and notes common interests.

Friedman, Jonathan

1974 "Marxism, Structuralism, and Vulgar Materialism." *Man* IX (September), 444–469. Besides its attack on vulgar and mechanical materialism, this article examines the structuralist Marxist model.

Giddens, Anthony

1973 *The Class Structure of the Advanced Societies.* London: Hutchinson University Library. A detailed analysis of past and current uses of class. Examines Marxian and Weberian interpretations as well as theories by Ralf Dahrendorf, Raymond Aron, and others. Reassesses a theory of class and discusses the prospects for a class society.

1977 "Review Essay: Habermas's Social and Political Theory." *American Journal of Sociology* LXXXIII (July), 198–212. Useful review of Habermas's major works in English.

Girardin, Jean-Claude

1974 "On the Marxist Theory of the State." *Politics and Society* IV (Winter), 193–223. Critical assessment of the French structuralist approach to a theory of the state along with other perspectives.

Godelier, Maurice

1973 "Structure and Contradiction in Capital." In Robin Blackburn (ed.), *Ideology in Social Science*, Chapter 15, pp. 334–368. New York: Vintage Books. Identifies elements of structuralism that appear in Marx and Lévi-Strauss.

Gold, David A., Clarence Y. H. Lo, and Erik Olin Wright

1975 "Recent Developments in Marxist Theories of the Capitalist State." *Monthly Review* XXVII (October), 29–43 and (November), 36–51. Comprehensive review of various approaches to the study of the capitalist state.

Goldmann, Lucien
   1977 *Lukács and Heidegger: Towards a New Philosophy*. Translated by William Q.
   Boelhower. London: Routledge and Kegan Paul. Attempts to portray similarities
   and differences between Heidegger's existentialism and Lukács's Marxism. Includes a glossary of terms and concepts related to their critical perspectives.
Gramsci, Antonio
   1971 *Selections from the Prison Notebooks of Antonio Gramsci*. Edited and translated
   by Quintin Hoare and Geoffrey Nowell Smith. London: Lawrence and Wishart.
   Especially useful are the selections on state and civil society.
Hazelrigg, Lawrence E.
   1972 "Class, Property, and Authority: Dahrendorf's Critique of Marx's Theory of
   Class." *Social Forces* L (June), 473–487. Exposes Dahrendorf's critique of Marx's
   class theory and concludes with support for Marx.
Hilton, Rodney (ed.)
   1976 *The Transition from Feudalism to Capitalism*. London: New Left Books. Collection of articles published during the 1950s and 1960s that reflect a debate
   among Sweezy, Dobb, and others concerning the transition from feudalism to
   capitalism.
Hobsbawm, Eric J.
   1965 "Introduction." In Karl Marx, *Pre-Capitalist Economic Formations*. Translated
   by Jack Cohen. New York: International Publishers. A useful overview of Marx's
   treatment of precapitalist formations, which introduces a segment from the
   Grundrisse.
Hochfeld, Julian
   1967 "The Concept of Class Interest." *Polish Sociological Bulletin* XVI (2), 5–14. An
   orthodox Marxist perspective of class and class interest as related to consciousness.
Hodges, Donald Clark
   1959 "The Role of Classes in Historical Materialism." *Science and Society* XXIII
   (Winter), 16–26. Explores Marx's basic proposition that "the division into classes
   lies at the root of historical modes of production and at the heart of historical
   materialism."
Hopkins, Terence K.
   1977 "Notes on Class Analysis and the World-System." *Review* I (Summer),
   67–72. Elaboration of how class analysis may be used in Wallerstein's conception
   of world system.
Horowitz, Irving Louis, and Ellen Kay Trimberger
   1976 "State Power and Military Nationalism in Latin America." *Comparative
   Politics* VIII (January), 223–244. Assessment of the role of the state in Latin
   America in light of approaches toward achieving autonomous development.
Jessop, Bob
   1977 "Recent Theories of the Capitalist State." *Cambridge Journal of Economics* I,
   353–373. A critical review of Marxist theories of the capitalist state.
Johnson, Dale
   1978 "Strategic Implications of Recent Social Class Theory." *Insurgent Sociologist*
   VIII (Winter), 40–44. Acknowledges advances in structuralist theory of state and
   class but remains critical of its static implications.

Keleman, Paul
1976 "Towards a Marxist Critique of Structuralist Anthropology." *Sociological Review* XXIV (November), 869–875. A critique of some of the ideas in the early writings of structuralist Lévi-Strauss.

Laclau, Ernesto
1975 "The Specificity of the Political: Around the Poulantzas-Miliband Debate." *Economy and Society* V (February), 87–110. Reprinted in Laclau, *Politics and Ideology in Marxist Theory*. London: New Left Books. A critique of Poulantzas (1973) and an assessment of Miliband (1973).

Lane, Robert E.
1965 "The Politics of Consensus in An Age of Affluence." *American Political Science Review* LIX (December), 974–996. In defense of consensus as a prevailing norm in U.S. political life.

Leys, Colin
1976 "The 'Overdeveloped' Post-Colonial State: A Re-evaluation." *Review of African Political Economy* V (January-April), 39–48. Critique of writings on the postcolonial state in Africa, including the work of Hamza Alavi and John Saul.

Lopreato, Sally Cook
1973 "Toward a Formal Restatement of Vilfredo Pareto's Theory of the Circulation of Elites." *Social Science Quarterly* LIV (December), 491–507. A formal reconstruction of Pareto's theory in outline form.

Lukács, Georg
1971 *History and Class Consciousness: Studies in Marxist Dialectics*. Translated by Rodney Livingstone. London: Merlin Press. A seminal work that establishes, along with Marx's early writings, a basis for critical theory of class and class consciousness.

McCarthy, Thomas
1978 *The Critical Theory of Jürgen Habermas*. Cambridge, Massachusetts: M.I.T. Press. Detailed analysis of Habermas divided into five sections: on theory and practice in our scientific civilization; knowledge and human interests; toward a methodology of critical theory; foundations—a theory of communication; and legitimation problems in advanced capitalism. A biobibliographic study.

McClosky, Herbert
1964 "Consensus and Ideology in American Politics." *American Political Science Review* LVIII (June), 361–382. Defense of the thesis that U.S. politics is characterized by consensus.

Miliband, Ralph
1969 *The State in Capitalist Society: An Analysis of the Western System of Power*. New York: Basic Books. An "instrumentalist" approach to the state and class by a leading British Marxist.
1973 "Poulantzas and the Capitalist State." *New Left Review* 82 (November-December), 83–92. A review of Poulantzas's structuralist theory.

Mollenkopf, John
1975 "Theories of the State and Power Structure Research." *Insurgent Sociologist* III (Summer), 245–264. Critique of the instrumentalist and structuralist schools. Attempts to transcend those schools by proposing a research agenda for future study.

Mosca, Gaetano
1939 *The Ruling Class: Elementi di Scienza Politica.* Edited and revised with an introduction by Arthur Livingston, translated by Hannah D. Kahn. New York: McGraw-Hill Book Co.
Offe, Claus
1972a "Advanced Capitalism and the Welfare State." *Politics and Society* II, no. 4 (Summer), 479–488. Examines the contradictions of the welfare state under advanced capitalism.

1972b "Political Authority and Class Structures—An Analysis of Late Capitalist Societies." *International Journal of Sociology* II (Spring), 73–108. Looks at the tendency of states to intervene in late capitalist societies and emphasizes analysis in terms of class.
Omvedt, Gail
1973 "Towards a Theory of Colonialism." *Insurgent Sociologist* III (Spring), 1–24. An analysis of various classes in colonial society.
Ossowski, Stanislaw
1963 *Class Structure in the Social Consciousness.* Translated by Sheila Patterson. London: Routledge and Kegan Paul. A critical overview of historical and contemporary conceptions of class by a Polish scholar.
Parenti, Michael
1970 "Power and Pluralism: A View from the Bottom." *Journal of Politics* XXXII (August), 501–530. Examines pluralist and antipluralist views to questions of power.
Pareto, Vilfredo
1966 *Sociological Writings.* Selected and introduced by S. E. Finer, translated by Derick Mirfin. New York: Frederick A. Praeger. Selections from Pareto, *Treatise on General Sociology* with a useful introduction to the thought of Pareto.
Parkin, Frank
1971 *Class Inequality and Political Order: Social Stratification in Capitalist and Communist Societies.* New York: Praeger Publishers. Critique of neo-Weberian approaches to stratification and an examination of ideas relating to the nature of social class in capitalist and communist societies.
Polsby, Nelson W.
1963 *Community Power and Political Theory.* New Haven: Yale University Press. A critical and systematic look at previous community studies and a plea for the pluralist alternative.
Poster, Mark
1974 "Althusser on History Without Man." *Political Theory* II (November), 393–409. A useful overview of the central ideas in Althusser's thought.
Poulantzas, Nicos
1969 "The Problem of the Capitalist State." *New Left Review* 58 (November-December), 67–78. A review of Miliband (1969).

1973 *Political Power and Social Classes.* London: New Left Books and Sheed and Ward. The author introduces his structuralist theory on state and classes.

1976 "The Capitalist State: A Reply to Miliband and Laclau." *New Left Review* 95 (January-February), 63–83. Criticism and self-criticism, taking into account the concerns of Miliband and Laclau in earlier reviews of Poulantzas's work.

Prewitt, Kenneth, and Alan Stone
1973 *The Ruling Elite: Elite Theory, Power, and American Democracy.* New York: Harper and Row. A systematic review of perspectives on elite theory, with attention to the debate between those advocating the power elite thesis and those in favor of the pluralist thesis.

Rich, Harvey
1976 "Marxism as Dogma, Ideology, and Theory in Contemporary Political Sociology." *Canadian Journal of Political Science* IX (December), 654–667. Examination of three contemporary applications of Marxism to political sociology: the dogmatic application by Julian Hochfeld of Marxist categories to contemporary class structures; the extension of Marxist theory of the state to contemporary bourgeois democracies by Ralph Miliband; and the empirical assessment of working class polarization in advanced countries by Michael Mann.

Rose, Arnold M.
1967 *The Power Structure: Political Process in American Society.* London: Oxford University Press. Critical of previous definitions of power. The author argues for a pluralistic conception of power in his examination of U.S. politics.

Slater, Phil
1977 *Origin and Significance of the Frankfurt School: A Marxist Perspective.* London: Routledge and Kegan Paul. A detailed study of the origins and evolution of the Frankfurt school and its major participants.

Stolzman, James, and Herbert Gamberg
1973–1974 "Marxist Analysis Versus Stratification Analysis as General Approaches to Social Inequality." *Berkeley Journal of Sociology* XVIII, 105–125. Argues that a comprehension of Marx's approach to class must include an understanding of the theory of surplus value and of the processes of capital accumulation.

Szymanski, Albert
1978 *The Capitalist State and the Politics of Class.* Cambridge, Massachusetts: Winthrop Publishers. A useful text on the state and class, with emphasis on a Marxist approach and the experience of the United States.

Therborn, Göran
1976 "What Does the Ruling Class Do When It Rules? Some Different Approaches to the Study of Power in Society." *Insurgent Sociologist* VI (Spring), 1–16. Critical appraisal of major approaches to the study of class and power. Affirms that Marx conceptualizes classes in terms of relations of production, not market and the relations of circulation.

Wallerstein, Immanuel
1975 "Class-Formation in the Capitalist World-Economy." *Politics and Society* V (3), 367–375. Within a triad of world system (core, semiperiphery, and periphery), assesses the significance of classes and ethnonations.

Wolfe, Alan
1974 "New Directions in the Marxist Theory of Politics." *Politics and Society* IV

(Winter), 131–160. A review of recent efforts to formulate a theory of the state. Especially significant is the emphasis on the role of the state as a theme in contemporary political science.

Wright, Erik Olin
    1976 "Class Boundaries in Advanced Capitalist Societies." *New Left Review* 98 (July-August), 3–44. A detailed and critical appraisal of Poulantzas's *Classes in Contemporary Capitalism.*

Zeitlin, Maurice
    1974 "Corporate Ownership and Control: The Large Corporation and the Capitalist Class." *American Journal of Sociology* LXXIX (March), 1073–1119. Critique of various theories on ownership and control of large corporations in an attempt to suggest an approach for research on the dominant class in the United States.

Zuckerman, Alan
    1977 "The Concept 'Political Elite': Lessons from Mosca and Pareto." *Journal of Politics* XXXIX (May), 324–344. Returns to Mosca and Pareto in order to bring clarity to the concept of a political elite in an attempt to clarify the confusion in the contemporary literature.

PART 4
Conclusion

Political Economy
and a Reconstitution
of Comparative Politics
and Political Science

This book initially argues that comparative politics embraces all questions of politics and that the study of politics cannot be isolated from social and economic questions. The orthodox literature of comparative politics, however, tends to ignore these propositions, yet it enhances and perpetuates the ethnocentric and static orthodox paradigm that originated in nineteenth-century positivism and now pervades contemporary Western social science. I have summarized the content of this literature by reference to theories of system, development and underdevelopment, culture, and class and have synthesized the major criticisms of these theories. This critique exposes the weaknesses and contradictions of the orthodox literature and paradigm and identifies the attempts of scholars to move comparative politics toward a radical paradigm. In their search for a radical paradigm these scholars inevitably have turned to Marx and to questions of political economy. Marx's critique of political economy drew on methodology alien to bourgeois social science but in turn established a counter paradigm that promises to influence generations of future scholarship.

In this concluding chapter I focus on political economy and summarize the discussion of the earlier chapters by reference to major thinkers and ideas. First, I review some definitions of political economy and identify a problem central to it, and then I explore several possibilities for transcending that problem. Second, I examine the epistemological origins and strains that have shaped the intellectual traditions of political economy from classical to modern times, in particular, with a focus on Marx's assessment of those efforts. Last, I call for a new synthesis of political economy, suggesting lines of inquiry that may be pursued in the study of comparative and international political economy and identifying the major thinkers who shape our focus on political economic themes today. An attempt is made to distinguish between non-Marxist and Marxist thought so that academics and their students clearly perceive the methodologies and values upon which their investigations are based.

TOWARD A MARXIST UNDERSTANDING OF POLITICAL ECONOMY

Webster's Third New International Dictionary defines political economy as a "social science dealing with the interrelationship of political and economic processes." Economists usually stress the economic ramifications of political economy. Mandel dated political economy to "the development of a society based on petty commodity production" (1968: 2:692). Marx's major work, *Capital*, is subtitled "A Critique of Political Economy" and emphasizes commodities, money, surplus value, and accumulation of capital. In his preface to *A Contribution to the Critique of Political Economy*, Marx began with such terms as capital, landed property, and wage labor (1904: 9). In his introduction, Marx focused on "all material production by individuals as determined by society" (265), and he indicted his predecessors, Adam Smith and Pierre Joseph Proudhon, among others, for basing their conceptions of political economy upon illusions of an eighteeenth-century society of free competition in which the individual appears liberated from the constraints of nature. Marx reminded us that this notion of individual freedom evolved with the breakup of feudal forms of society and, since the sixteenth century, with the creation of new forces of production. By the eighteenth century, bourgeois society had implanted itself. It was a period in which the view of the isolated individual prevailed, yet was one in which the interrelationships of individual and society had reached such a high level that the individual could develop only in society, not in isolation from it. Against this illusion of individualism, personified in Daniel Defoe's *Robinson Crusoe*, Marx set his critique of the early bourgeois conceptions of political economy. The work of Adam Smith tended to perpetuate this bourgeois conception, influencing David Ricardo whose theory of value served the utopian socialists such as Robert Owen in England and Pierre Joseph Proudhon in France. Marx's discovery of Ricardo's thought led him to a reassessment, critique, and a new understanding of political economy.

If economics has dominated the theories of political economy, what about politics? Webster's dictionary identifies political economy in the eighteenth century as a field of government concerned with directing policies toward the enhancement of government and community wealth. The dictionary adds that in the nineteenth century political economy was a social science related to economics but primarily concerned with government rather than commercial or personal economics. Curiously, no great tradition of political economy seems to have established itself in the discipline of government or political science. During the early decades of the present century, the work of political scientists tended to be more descriptive than theoretical and focused on formal legal and governmental institutions. The work of the middle decades of this century followed in this tradition but also turned attention to informal institutions and processes and to problems often limited in scope and significance. The contemporary revival of interest in political economy is more the consequence of efforts by radical economists and sociologists than of efforts by political scientists.

Only a decade ago the *International Encyclopedia of the Social Sciences* conspicuously neglected to include an article on political economy, and David Easton, writing on political science, failed to mention political economy. Easton described political science as a discipline in search of an identity, and he acknowledged the discipline's debt to Marx for differentiating between state and society. "In part, political science could emerge as a discipline separate from the other social sciences because of the impetus Marx had given to the idea of the difference between state and society, an idea virtually unheard of before his time" (Easton 1968: 295). In his critique of Hegel, Marx examined the emergence of the state in modern times. The separation between civil society and the state, he argued, was a modern phenomenon reinforced by capitalism. Although Easton credited Marx with this insight, Easton himself influenced and set in motion the movement in political science to discard the state as a concept, replacing it with political system. The Marxist understanding of state had also been denuded of its significance by the attention of German positivist political scientists who emphasized the legal and constitutional aspects of the state and influenced the early U.S. political scientists.

In his political and economic studies, Marx discovered this conception of the state. Early in the 1840s, embarrassed by his ignorance on economic questions, Marx shifted his attention from jurisprudence to material interests. "I was led by my studies to the conclusion that legal relations as well as forms of state could neither be understood by themselves, nor explained by the so-called general progress of the human mind, but that they are rooted in the material conditions of life" (Marx 1904: 11). In 1845 and 1846 Marx and Engels related their conception of the state to the productive base of society through successive periods of history. They examined the interests of the individual, the individual family, and the communal interests of all individuals. Division of labor and private property tend to promote contradictions between individual and community interests so that the latter takes on an independent form as the state separates from the real interests of individual and community. In showing this separation of state from society, Marx and Engels argued that we should not look for categories in every period of history; that would be idealistic. Instead we must be able to explain the formation of ideas from material practice; we should examine the whole or the totality of interrelationships between material production and the state along with its forms of consciousness, religion, and the like.

> This conception of history depends on our ability to expound the real process of production, starting out from the material production of life itself, and to comprehend the form of intercourse connected with this and created by this mode of production . . . , as the basis of all history; and to show it in its action as State, to explain all the different theoretical products and forms of consciousness, religion, philosophy, ethics, etc, etc. and trace their origins and growth from that basis; by which means, of course, the whole thing can be depicted in its totality. [Marx and Engels 1970: 58]

Marx and Engels are quoted to show that in this early period they had worked out a conception of base and superstructure that Marx later delineated in 1859 (Marx 1904: 11–13). Accordingly, the base or economic structure of society becomes the real foundation on which people enter into essential relations over which they exercise little control. In contrast, the legal and political superstructure is a reflection of that base, and changes in the economic foundation bring about transformations in the superstructure. The famous passage in the preface to *A Contribution to the Critique of Political Economy*, in which this conception of base and superstructure is depicted, has been attacked as determinist, dogmatic, and static. Admittedly Marx's synthesis of his own perspective appears to reduce societal relationships to a dichotomy of categories and to simplistic formulations. Yet one also finds in this passage the essential concepts of Marxism as well as a departure point for comprehending the relationship of politics and economics. We turn to these concepts below, but the dubious academic and student should also read Marx's writings extensively in order to capture the depth and insight that his orientation to political economy has provided us.

Although a focus on political economy may help to bridge the gap that today divides politics from economics, the problem of the separation of politics into comparative and international fields should be addressed. Traditionally, comparative politics looked at the role of government and the state, but in the late 1950s specialists in the field determined that the concept of political system should replace that of state. Influenced by Easton, Gabriel Almond and others believed that the concept of state was limited by legal and institutional meanings. As a more neutral term, the use of system diverted attention from class society, from the relationship of different classes to the means of production and productive forces. Today the use of system usually pertains to a nation, and comparative politics tends toward configurative country studies. System also has been employed in the study of international politics, notably by Richard Snyder and Morton Kaplan. Alongside the systems approach, the conventional historic, geopolitical, behavioral, and balanced-power or equilibrium approaches are evident in the field of international politics. These approaches generally emphasize politics and conspicuously overlook economic considerations. When international politics addresses questions of imperialism or dependency, however, perspectives on political economy become possible.

Once we turn to imperialism and dependency, however, still another problem confronts us. The First and Second Worlds are separated from a Third World and, sometimes, even a Fourth World. Developed or advanced nations are contrasted with developing, underdeveloped, or less developed nations. A look at capitalism on a world scale often leads to an examination of activity in nations of the industrial or modern center as well as in the backward nations of the periphery. External considerations are distinguished from internal ones, or metropolises from satellites. Rarely does synthesis adequately integrate these apparently dichotomous areas or phenomena as we succumb to segmented rather than holistic perspectives. Clearly there is a need to transcend these problems. A solution is possible with pedagogy, theory, method, and concept, and we briefly turn to each of these concerns.

PEDAGOGY

Following in the tradition of Thomas Kuhn, awareness of paradigmatic differences may lead to new directions in teaching and learning (Deol 1976). Kuhn suggested that scientific practice is guided by paradigms. A paradigm is the perspective of the world generated by the scientific community and includes beliefs and commitments to theory, methodology, method, and concept.

I have characterized the dominant orthodox paradigm of political science today. The origins of this paradigm are found in the positivist traditions that influenced many thinkers of the late nineteenth century and the behavioralists of the twentieth century. Their thought contributed to the separation of fact from value in the contemporary study of politics. The orthodox paradigm also assimilates the liberal premise that every person is entitled to hold and profess an opinion. Liberty of conscience and secularism are ideals of the paradigm and buttress the prevailing U.S. view that pluralism and consensus pervade politics. The thought of Max Weber has been influential for this view. In contrast, the effort to formulate a radical paradigm may be traced to its historicist origins and the antipositivistic reactions to the present century. Radical thought draws its assumptions primarily from Marxist thought.

THEORY

Marxist thought is holistic, broadly ranged, unified, and interdisciplinary in contrast to the ahistorical, compartmentalized, and often narrow parameters of the orthodox paradigm. A recognition of these differences allows us to make some distinctions between the Marxist and bourgeois influences that have shaped the epistemological strains of political economy over the past century as well as distinctions among the major lines of inquiry that can be suggested for our proposal to combine comparative with international political economy. My use of Marxism is intended to be open and flexible since I believe that Marx himself considered Marxism to be unfinished and in a state of flux, subject to change and adjustment in accordance with reality and practical experience.

METHOD

Dialectics may be employed as a method in our search for a theory of Marxism. I reject the vulgar Marxist assumption promoted by Stalinists and others that dialectics inevitably leads to scientific truth; likewise, I do not accept the view of materialist Marxists who cast aside dialectics as unscientific. I believe, as did Marx, that dialectics should be combined with a materialist, not an idealist, view of history.

Hegel's dialectic was idealist and mystical and was set forth rigidly as a system. Marx's dialectic was intended to be a flexible method of analysis, not a dogma or a complete and closed system. Dialectics allows for the building of theory upon new facts as well as for the interpreting of facts in relation to new theory. Dialectics does not need to be intended as a set of universal laws that solve all problems and relate to all knowledge of past and present history. There is no precise formula for dialectical inquiry, but some guidelines might be employed. For example, always look for the interconnections of problems to all of society, but avoid dealing with problems in isolation. Always approach problems in a dynamic, not a static, way by examining their origin and evolution. Always identify opposing forces, their relationship and conflict. Always explain the relation of quantitative to qualitative changes and vice versa. Always ask if one aspect may be eliminated when it has eliminated or negated an opposing aspect or if a new aspect may supersede or include an old aspect. Such guidelines, even in abstract form, may lead to questions that can be asked about everyday problems. Such guidelines serve as the foundation for a scientifically viable method, in the sense indicated by Marx, who emphasized that the study of political economy necessitates concreteness, unity of many elements, and synthesis. A category or a concept treated in isolation leads to abstraction, but the method of political economy must combine abstract definition with concrete synthesis.

> The concrete is concrete, because it is a combination of many objects with different destination, i.e. a unity of diverse elements. In our thought, it therefore appears as a process of synthesis, as a result, and not as a starting point, although it is the real starting point and, therefore, also the starting point of observation and conception . . . the abstract definitions lead to the reproduction of the concrete subject in the course of reasoning. [Marx 1904: 293]

CONCEPT

If theory is Marxist, and the method is dialectical, then what concepts are useful to comparative and international political economy? Some of the essential concepts are defined in Table 9.1; these concepts, of course, should be utilized in relations to each other. Marxist methodology includes a plethora of concepts. Necessary production, for example, satisfies the basic

TABLE 9.1
Concepts of Political Economy

Economic Base	Political Superstructure
"The sum total of these relations of production constitutes the economic structure of society—the real foundation, on which rise legal and political superstructures and to which correspond definite forms of social consciousness." (Marx 1904:11)	
Mode of Production: the mix of productive forces and relations of production among people in society at a given time in history. Examples include primitive communism, feudalism, capitalism, and socialism.	*State:* the legal forms and instruments, such as police and standing army, that maintain class rule.
Forces of Production: the productive capacity, including plant and machinery, technology, and labor skill.	*Class:* large groups of people distinguishable from one another by relations to means of production, division of labor, share of wealth, and position. Marx identified three large classes: wage laborers, capitalists, and landowners.
Relations of Production: the division of labor that puts productive forces in motion and whose activity is related to property and ownership of means of production.	*Ideology:* (or false consciousness) related to legal, political, religious, and philosophical forms.
Means of Production: the tools, land, buildings, and machinery with which workers produce material goods for themselves and society.	

human needs for food, drink, and so on. Surplus production evolved with inventions and new knowledge that made possible increases in the productivity of labor. Surplus production led to the division and specialization of labor. Changes in the forces of production affected relations of production so that revolution and class struggle became possible at certain junctures of history. As Marx described this process,

> At a certain stage of their development, the material forces of production in society come in conflict with the existing relations of production, or—what is but a legal expression for the same thing—with the property relations within which they had been at work before. From forms of development of the forces of production these relations turn into their fetters. Then comes the period of social revolution. With the change of the economic foundation the entire immense superstructure is more or less rapidly transformed. In considering such transformations the distinction should always be made between the material transformation of the economic conditions of production which can be determined with the precision of natural science, and the legal, political, religious, aesthetic or philosophic—in short ideological forms in which men become conscious of this conflict and fight it out. . . . No social order ever disappears before all the productive forces for which there is room in it, have been developed and new higher relations of production never appeared before the material conditions of their existence have matured in the womb of the old society. [Marx 1904: 12]

Let me summarize my thinking to this point. First, I have advocated that inquiry be holistically and historically oriented rather than limited to segments and current affairs. I seek synthesis and overview in the search for an understanding and explanation of the problems and issues of society. Second, I believe that the study of politics should be combined with economics. Distinctions between politics and economics as well as between the fields of comparative and international politics in political science often lead to confusion and a distortion of reality. Theoretical and conceptual difficulties also arise with such dichotomous terms as center and periphery, metropolis and satellite. I suggest the use of dialectics as a method in the hope that dynamic and integrated analysis will ensue. Third, contrasting methodologies are identifiable in the study of political economy—orthodox and radical methodologies, which generate sharply different questions and explanations. I argue for a distinction between Marxist and non-Marxist criteria in order to perceive the differences between those methodologies. I eschew dogmatic and inflexible interpretations and acknowledge the failure of much of the scholarly work to clarify concepts and theory. I note a tendency to rely on fuzzy notions of politics and economics as well as on impressionistic observations and descriptions. Thus, I see Marxism as a methodology rather than an ideology and as such hope to diffuse some of the polarization that the term evokes. At the same time, I believe that academics and students can legitimately pursue inquiry along Marxist as well as non-Marxist lines. Thus I now turn to a discussion of the epistemological origins and strains of political economy in an effort to show the differences between those two lines of inquiry.

ORIGINS AND EVOLUTION OF POLITICAL ECONOMY

The origins and evolution of political economy are identifiable in historical phases as portrayed in Table 9.2, and this discussion draws from various sources. E. K. Hunt (1972) offered a very general but comprehensive overview, which is especially useful to beginning students. Paresh Chattopadhyay (1974) reviewed varying interpretations of political economy from its earliest usage to the present. Daniel R. Fusfeld (1966) traced the evolution of economic thought in a similar fashion, but in more depth and detail. Although Robert L. Heilbroner (1961) examined the lives, times, and ideas of specific economic thinkers, including Smith, Ricardo, Marx, Veblen, and Keynes, Ronald L. Meek (1956) focused on studies on the labor theory of value as the foundation for understanding political economy. He began with Aquinas, briefly reviewed the contributions of mercantilist writers, and then emphasized the thought of Smith, Ricardo, and Marx. Meek also examined the critics of Marxist political economy, a concern that pervades Nikolai Bukharin's (1927) treatment of the theory of value. Among all these writers, Ernest Mandel (1968: 2, chap. 18:690–730) has provided the most recent interpretation and summary of developments in political economy from ancient times until today. All these works emphasize the theoretical, conceptual, and methodological differences between bourgeois and Marxist political economy. A recognition of these differences may assist us in turning to past thought in an effort to constitute a contemporary understanding of political economy.

TABLE 9.2
Phases in the Theory of Political Economy

Petty commodityism
Mercantilism
Classical liberalism
Utopian socialism
Marxism
Marginalism and neoclassicalism
Keynesianism
Neo-Marxism

The following outline is necessarily sketchy, but it is intended to be a general overview of the major thinkers, trends, and influences that have shaped the conceptions of political economy. In short, the following remarks serve as a guide to the past in order to facilitate those seeking a contemporary understanding of political economy. Mandel (1968: 2:692) dated the origin of political economy to petty commodity production. Once commodity production responds to market and money appears, then fluctuations in prices occur, some producers fall into debt, and primitive communal relations begin to dissolve. Below the major thinkers and ideas that shaped a theory of political economy from ancient to modern times are identified.

Theorists of the Ancient and Middle Ages

Petty commodity production seems to have first emerged in ancient China and Greece. Mang-Tsze in China and Plato and Aristotle in Greece attempted to analyze the instability that accompanied petty commodity production and to find ways to overcome it on behalf of the communal society. They recognized the impact of the division of labor on commodity production and were able to distinguish between use value and exchange value. Aristotle in particular identified this dual concept of commodity. Mang-Tsze believed that agricultural labor was the source of value, and Plato came close to offering "a real theory of labor value" (Mandel 1968: 2:694). The expansion of petty commodity production in the Middle Ages stimulated the scholastic theologians Albert Magnus and Thomas Aquinas to set forth the "canonist approach to the value problem" (Meek 1956: 12). Aquinas sought to find a "just" price, thereby justifying the merchant's profit and defending the established order. In the face of international trade and money, this medieval concept of just price lost its significance. Duns Scotus, another scholastic thinker, worked with a theory of exchange value based on labor, and Abd-al-Rahman-Ibn-Khaldun, an Islamic philosopher, elaborated a historical-materialist view of history (Mandel 1968: 2:697).

The Mercantilists

Between the fourteenth and seventeenth centuries, great advances in political economy were not evident. The principal concern was the nature of wealth in an impersonal system of markets. The transformation of Europe from feudalism to a profit-oriented market economy of buyers and sellers was marked by a period that witnessed the discovery and conquest of new geographical areas, new flows of capital to and from the New World, and the rise of monarchs and merchants who promoted nationalism, undermined local barriers to commerce, and benefited from foreign trade and the erosion of the power of the old order of church and nobility.

Mercantilist writings of the period pragmatically analyzed how nations produce wealth. They assumed that regulation and control were necessary in order to constrain the selfish individualism that would lead to less wealth. Their attention was to a credit balance of payments, a favorable trade balance, manufacturing, and fertile soil. The early mercantilists described economic life in terms of a circulation of commodities, and writers in the late seventeenth and eighteenth centuries addressed questions about the social surplus product that became evident with the growth in manufacturing and technology in agriculture. Two strains of political economy appeared, according to Mandel. One, the British school, was represented by William Petty (*Political Arithmetic*, 1631), who concentrated his analysis on the agricultural origins of surplus value. Petty wrote about rent, not profit, while the mercantilists in general encountered difficulty in reconciling the relationship of labor and land. The French Physiocratic school, represented by Pierre Boisguillebert (*Détail de la France*, 1695), constituted the other strain. Boisguillebert emphasized agricultural labor as the only source of value. François Quesnay (*Economic Table*, 1758), a leading Physiocrat, argued against the mercantilist assumption that wealth springs from trade and industry and placed emphasis on the surplus produced in agriculture. He advocated that taxes be paid by the landowners, not the small farmers, merchants, and manufacturers who were considered to be productive. Although he did not consider industrial capital as significant and instead emphasized communal profit, Nicholas Barbon (*A Discourse of Trade*, 1690) related the value of a commodity to the cost of making goods. Meek believed Barbon represents a transition from mercantilism to the classical approach of Adam Smith and others.

The Classical Liberals

Fusfeld (1966) began with the English thinkers, Dudley North (*Discourses Upon Trade*, 1691) and John Locke, who contributed to the economic liberalism of the classical theory developed by Smith. North criticized the nationalistic policies of mercantilism and advocated free trade. Locke tied labor to private property and wealth, arguing that production is the consequence of individual effort to satisfy human needs and that the worker should be able to use or consume his or her own product. Liberals believed that private property should be protected and that the production of wealth was based on the incentive to work that the right to property instilled in the individual. They agreed that individual initiative must be free of mercantilist constraints.

Adam Smith consolidated these ideas into classical political economy. In his *Inquiry into the Nature and Causes of the Wealth of Nations* (1776), he

brought together the major themes of commodity, capital and value, simple
and complex labor. He was the first to formulate a labor theory of value
"which reduces the value of commodities to the amounts of labour contained in them" (Mandel 1968: 2:701–702). Smith identified laws of the
market that explain the drive of individual self-interest in a competitive
milieu and how this results in goods desired by society according to demand
and the price it is willing to pay. Individualism signified order, not chaos, in
the market economy as Smith envisaged a competitive market equilibrium.

David Ricardo in *Principles of Political Economy and Taxation* (1817) was
both a disciple and critic of Smith, and he offered refinements to political
economy. Ricardo advocated the accumulation of capital as the basis for
economic expansion. He believed that restrictions on private investment
should be eliminated and that governments should not intervene in the
economy. He applied these principles to the international political economy,
arguing that a division of labor and free trade policies would benefit all nations. Thus, he related Smith's ideas of orderly growth and market
equilibrium to the international economic system. He also noted the conflict
between the interests of landlords and capitalists—the interests of the
landlord were opposed to the community, the interests of the capitalist were
favorable to it. Engels reflected on the importance of Ricardo's work, especially its influence on socialist interpretations of political economy.

> In so far as modern socialism, no matter of what tendency, starts out from
> bourgeois political economy, it almost exclusively links itself to the Ricardian
> theory of value. The two propositions which Ricardo proclaimed in 1817 right
> at the beginning of his *Principles*, (1) that the value of any commodity is purely
> and solely determined by the quantity of labour required for its production,
> and (2) that the product of the entire social labour is divided among the three
> classes: landowners (rent), capitalists (profit) and workers (wages), had ever
> since 1821 been utilized in England for socialist conclusions, and in part with
> such sharpness and decisiveness that this literature, which has now almost
> disappeared, and which to a large extent was first rediscovered by Marx, re-
> mained unsurpassed until the appearance of *Capital*. [Preface to Marx 1955: 6]

Among other classical liberals were Thomas R. Malthus (*Principles of
Political Economy*, 1820) and Jeremy Bentham (*Introduction to the Principles of
Morals and Legislation*, 1789). Malthus contributed a theory of population to
political economy, arguing that population reproduces faster than food production so that unless population growth were checked, the masses would
face starvation and death. Thus government should not aid the poor, for
such action drains wealth and income from the higher echelons of society.
Bentham viewed man's selfishness as natural and desirable but believed that
individual and public interests should coincide. Government action was ac-

ceptable if not in response to the narrow interests of special groups, and individuals should be allowed freedom within a framework of moral and legal constraint.

The Utopian Socialists

Through the insights of Ricardo into labor and production and the gloomy prognosis of Malthus, there evolved a group of utopian socialists—romantic nineteenth-century protesters of capitalism in its most devastating form. Robert Owen struggled for labor reforms, including a shorter working day and the ending of child labor. He believed that with a change in conditions a paradise could be established, and he promoted village cooperatives as his utopian scheme, then turned to the organization of the English working classes. Count Claude Henri de Rouvroy de Saint-Simon, an aristocrat later relegated to conditions of poverty, believed that the workers deserved the highest rewards of society; the idlers, the least. He argued for the reorganization of society. Heilbroner included John Stuart Mill among the utopians. Mill manifested socialist leanings in his *Principles of Political Economy* (1848) in which he retraced the path of Smith and Ricardo but placed emphasis on production rather than on distribution. Proudhon, another utopian socialist, was a critic of the orthodox economics of his time.

Marx

Marx transcended the theory of the utopian socialists as well as the classical liberal thinkers. He worked out a theory of surplus value as well as a synthesis that allowed for an explanation of class struggle. He developed theories on the prices of production and the tendency of the rate of profit to fall. He set forth basic laws of development: "Through his working out of a theory of the reproduction of capital and of national income, and through his adumbration of a theory of crises, he simultaneously achieved a first practical synthesis of micro-economic and macro-economic ideas" (Mandel 1968: 2:705). Marx's early work attacked the utopian socialists (Marx 1955), and his later work concentrated on all his predecessors, but in particular on the classical liberal economists Ricardo and Smith (Marx 1904, 1967, and 1973). For example, in *The Poverty of Philosophy* Marx exposed the "metaphysics" of Proudhon's political economy, and he argued against the use of "fixed, immutable eternal categories." Instead, one should examine "the historical movement of production relations," not their theoretical expression as categories nor as spontaneous or abstract ideas. In addition, he insisted that the production relations of every society form a whole; the parts cannot be separated from the whole so that one can explain society in terms of all relations simultaneously coexisting and supporting one another (Marx 1955: 91–110).

The Marginalist Neoclassicists

The threat of socialism led to the formation of the marginalist theory of value and neoclassical political economy. The popularization of Ricardo's thought, the impact of the utopian socialists, and the influence of Marx as well as Engels led not only to a bourgeois onslaught on Marxism but to efforts to bring about the demise of the labor theory of value, which had evolved through Smith, Ricardo, and the classical thinkers. The neoclassicists attempted to be rigorous, detailed, and abstract in the tradition of microeconomics. Various neoclassical schools opposed Marxism, including the historicist school in Germany, represented by Wilhelm Roscher, Eduard Hildebrandt, Gustav Schmoller, Karl Bücher, and others; the Austrian school of Karl Menger, Eugen von Böhm-Bawerk, and Friedrich von Wieser; the British school of William Stanley Jevons; and the Swiss school of Léon Walras. Bukharin systematically examined the ideas and thought of these schools, in particular focusing on Böhm-Bawerk. The neoclassicists emphasize equilibrium and so are often criticized for not accounting for the disturbances that affect equilibrium; their framework is static, not dynamic, it does not deal with structural crises, nor does it relate capitalism to imperialism.

The Keynesians

These problems led some economists, including Schumpeter, to study periodical crises. After the great depression, John Maynard Keynes in his *General Theory of Employment, Interest, and Money* (1936) moved political economy from an apologetic stance on capitalism to a pragmatic one. Rather than justify capitalism in theory, it was now essential to preserve it in practice by mitigating the extent of periodical fluctuations. One of Keynes's followers, Paul Samuelson, and others have followed in this macroeconomic tradition to the present period.

The Neo-Marxists

Although bourgeois economics remained dominant in the United States and much of Europe, followers of Marx carried on in a Marxist tradition. Engels edited and published the second and third volumes of Marx's *Capital*, followed by Kautsky's editing of Marx's *History of Economic Doctrines*.

Thereafter, Kautsky's treatment of capitalism in agriculture, Rudolf Hilferding's *Das Finanzkapital* (1910), Rosa Luxemburg's *Accumulation of Capital* (1913), and Lenin's *Imperialism: The Last Phase of Capitalism* (1917) were efforts to expand upon Marx's earlier work.

The Stalinist period dampened interest in Marxist theories of political economy, but since about 1960 there has been a revival of interest, promoted by the work of Paul Baran, Leo Huberman, and Paul Sweezy along with the writings and teachings of hundreds of other Marxists throughout the United States and other parts of the world.

Mandel has given us a provocative and controversial observation. He stated that "for Marx, political economy was essentially an ideology" and that Marx's work went beyond ideology. "Political economy withers away together with the economic categories it tries to explain." A new science will evolve.

> What is certain is that, by virtue of the questions it will seek to answer, it will have little in common with past and present economic theory, with bourgeois political economy, or with the Marxist criticism of it. Marxist economists can claim the honour of being the first category of men of learning to work consciously towards the abolition of their own profession. [Mandel 1968: 2:730]

GUIDELINES FOR THE STUDY OF POLITICAL ECONOMY

The examination of epistemology, theory, method, and concept suggests a dichotomy between bourgeois and Marxist political economy. As long as contrasting values are recognized and premises are set forth explicitly, both bourgeois and Marxist approaches may be useful to the study of comparative and international political economy. Figure 9.1 identifies some lines of inquiry. Attention to capitalist accumulation allows for an examination of political as well as economic issues. The study of capitalist accumulation with emphasis on precapitalist and capitalist formations and modes of production makes possible an integration of inquiry that heretofore has led economists to investigate questions relating to the material base of society and political scientists to be concerned with issues of the idealized political superstructure. Some might argue that economists should deal primarily with theories of imperialism and dependency and political scientists, with theories of the state and class, but I believe that all these concerns need to be assimilated by the political economist. The solution would seem to be the reconstitution of economics and political science into political economy. With this thought in mind, some guidelines are sketched that may be helpful for the study of accumulation, material base, and ideological superstructure.

FIGURE 9.1
Lines of Inquiry for Comparative and International Political Economy

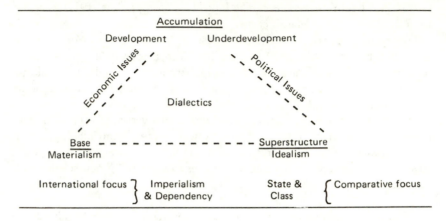

Accumulation: Theories of Development and Underdevelopment

A focus on accumulation begins with the process of capitalism and the general theories of the motion of capital uncovered by Marx. Marx examined commodities and money, noting differences in use and exchange values. He looked at the circulation of commodities and capital, the transformation of money into capital, labor power and surplus value, and the process of capitalist production as a whole. The last sections of the first volume of *Capital* concern primitive accumulation and the accumulation of capital. Marx described the process by which money and commodities transform into capital and in which the owners of money and the means of production confront workers.

The capitalist system pre-supposes the complete separation of the labourers from all property in the means by which they can realise their labour. As soon as capitalist production is once on its own legs, it not only maintains this separation, but reproduces it on a continually extending scale. The process, therefore, that clears the way for the capitalist system, can be none other than the process which takes away from the labourer the possession of his means of production; a process that transforms, on the one hand, the social means of susbsistence and of production into capital, on the other, the immediate producers into wage-labourers. The so-called primitive accumulation, therefore, is nothing else than the historical process of divorcing the producer from the means of production. It appears as primitive, because it forms the prehistoric stage of capital and of the mode of production corresponding with it [Marx 1967: 1:714–715]

Primitive communal production, in which labor collectively participates in and owns the means of production and in which there is no exploitation of classes, had disappeared long before. Slavery, in which the owner of the means of production owns the worker and in which accumulation of wealth falls into the hands of a few, also had been largely overcome. However, competitive capitalism grew out of feudalism, in which the feudal lord owns the means of production but does not fully own the worker. Alongside feudal ownership there was some private property in the hands of peasants and artisans whose ownership was based on personal labor. Marx described how capitalist accumulation disrupted those relations of production as large mills and factories replaced handicraft shops and large farms with machinery took the place of the old feudal estates and peasant farms.

Thus, political economy fundamentally addresses this broad historical sweep of capitalism, especially over the past hundred years. In the *Grundrisse* and *Capital* Marx gave us the foundations for such study. Paul Sweezy in *The Theory of Capitalist Development* (1942) and Ernest Mandel in *Marxist Economic Theory* (1968) summarized and interpreted Marx's findings, emphasizing the economic implications in particular, whereas the synthesis by Stanley W. Moore in *The Critique of Capitalist Democracy* (1957) focused on the political ramifications.

Mandel asked how the history of the past hundred years relates to "the unfolding development of internal conditions" in the capitalist mode of production, to "its combinations of expanding capital and pre-capitalist spheres" (1975: 22). He distinguished competitive (1780–1880) and imperialist (1880–1940) capitalism from "late" capitalism, which has evolved since the Second World War. Mandel's *Late Capitalism* (1975) attempts to integrate theory and history in the tradition of Marx, dialectically moving from abstract to concrete and concrete to abstract, from the parts to the whole and from the whole to the parts, from essence to appearance and from appearance to essence, from totality to contradiction and contradiction to totality, from object to subject and subject to object. Although Mandel failed to give us a modern version of *Capital*, his work is a serious holistic effort to fill a gap in political economy. "Why is it that the integration of theory and history which Marx applied with such mastery . . . has never since been repeated successfully to explain the successive stages of the capitalist mode of production?" (Mandel 1975: 23). He attributed this failure to Stalinism's distortions of Marxism and to efforts by some Marxists to concentrate on single themes like the state or monopoly power.

Samir Amin in *Accumulation on a World Scale* (1974) combined theory with history on a holistic level. He argued that accumulation or expanded reproduction is essential to the capitalist mode of production as well as to the socialist mode of production, but not to precapitalist modes of production. He insisted that analysis incorporate capitalist modes in combination with precapitalist modes. In fact, all modes and formations of the contemporary world reflect accumulation on a world scale. Primitive accumulation does not belong to the prehistory of capitalism but is contemporary as well. Capitalist and socialist world markets are not distinguishable, for there is only one, the world capitalist market, in which socialist countries marginally participate. Furthermore, capitalism is a world system, not a mixture of national capitalisms.

Other ambitious attempts to provide a holistic overview of political economy include Perry Anderson's *Passages from Antiquity to Feudalism* (1974) and *Lineages of the Absolute State* (1974); in them Anderson delved into questions relevant to feudalism and capitalism as Europe emerged from the Middle Ages. Immanuel Wallerstein in *The Modern World-System* (1974) dated the modern world system from the sixteenth century but saw four periods in its evolution: origins (1450–1640), mercantile consolidation (1640–1815), industrial expansion (1815–1917), and the contemporary capitalist world (1917–present). Wallerstein elaborated and refined André Gunder Frank's theory of capitalist development of underdevelopment and emphasized market relations. Robert Brenner (1977) took both thinkers to task for locating their analysis of the origins of capitalism in market processes identified in the work of Adam Smith.

Four thinkers—Mandel, Amin, Anderson, and Wallerstein—among others have rekindled an interest in the history of political economy. However imperfect their work may be, it orients us toward old and new questions neglected by much of the contemporary work in economics and political science. All four drew heavily on a foundation of Marxist thought. Their work also helps to transcend some of the problems found in many theories of development and underdevelopment. Underdevelopment cannot be understood in isolation from development. Both development and underdevelopment are unified and integrated into the world capitalist system of accumulation. Mandel explained this relationship.

> The entire capitalist system thus appears as a hierarchical structure of different levels of productivity, and as the outcome of the uneven and combined development of states, religions, branches of industry and firms, unleashed by the quest for surplus-profit. It forms an integrated unity but it is an integrated unity of non-homogeneous parts, and it is precisely the unity that here determines the lack of homogeneity. In this whole system development and underdevelopment reciprocally determine each other, for while the quest for surplus-profits constitutes the prime motive power behind the mechanisms of growth, surplus-profit can only be achieved at the expense of less productive

countries, regions and branches of production. Hence development takes place only in juxtaposition with underdevelopment; it perpetuates the latter and itself develops thanks to this perpetuation. [Mandel 1975: 102]

Such an understanding of development and underdevelopment allows for a critical overview of recent theory. In Chapter 7 three theoretical tendencies are identified. One tendency is to examine capitalist development in the center and underdevelopment in the periphery, and this tendency was first associated with the bourgeois economists of the Economic Commission for Latin America (ECLA). They favored autonomy as a national solution and opposed imperialism and foreign penetration in the economy. In opposition to this view Frank formulated his theory of the capitalist development of underdevelopment. A second tendency is to accept many of the premises of the above writers and to look at unequal development. The works of Arghiri Emmanuel and Amin are representative of this theory. A third tendency is to address the question of uneven development, which was noted by Marx, Engels, Lenin, and Trotsky, although Trotsky developed the theory of uneven and combined development. According to this theory, the growth of productive forces varies from segment to segment of society and may be affected by differences in natural conditions and historical connections from epoch to epoch. Given these variations, features of lower stages may combine with those of upper stages to produce a formation of contradictory character and allow a qualitative leap in the social evolution of a backward people. Criticisms of these three theories by Brenner (1977) and others center around whether the market has been stressed to the neglect of relations of production and class struggle or whether a national solution will prevail over the problems of worldwide accumulation.

International Political Economy and Theories of Imperialism and Dependency

Beyond the historical studies that are concerned with accumulation and theories of development and underdevelopment, it would seem reasonable to concentrate inquiry on international political economy around theories of imperialism and dependency. The following discussion, drawn from Chapter 7, summarizes the major lines of thought on imperialism and dependency.

Imperialism can be traced from the Greek and Roman empires to its mercantile "old" form in the sixteenth and seventeenth centuries to its monopolistic "new" form in the nineteenth and twentieth centuries. Two views of the new imperialism prevailed. One, the radical or Marxist view, argued that imperialism was a reflection of an expanding capitalism, necessitated by the contradictions of the capitalist mode of production; the other, the liberal or non-Marxist view, argued that the inequities of the capitalist system could be readily adjusted.

The thought of Hobson, Kautsky, Schumpeter, and Galtung contributed to a liberal view of imperialism. J. A. Hobson believed that underconsumption is the cause of imperialism and that with an increase in domestic consumption in his home country, Great Britain, there would be no drive to expand into foreign markets. Karl Kautsky, a leading Marxist of his time whose view tended toward liberalism, felt that the class conflicts of capitalism would diminish through peaceful processes, that the interests of the capitalist class as a whole would conflict with a minority of powerful capitalists who relied on military means to support their expansionist efforts. Joseph Schumpeter emphasized that imperialism is a precapitalist phenomenon and will disappear in a rational and progressive era of capitalism. Johan Galtung set forth a structural view of imperialism, which has wide acceptance today among non-Marxists.

Representative of the Marxist view of imperialism would be the thought of Luxemburg, Bukharin, Lenin, Baran and Sweezy, and Magdoff. Rosa Luxemburg elaborated a theory of imperialism that explained continuous capital accumulation and, in particular, examined the penetration of capital into primitive economies. Nikolai Bukharin, a leading Bolshevik theoretician at the time of the Russian revolution, attacked Luxemburg's theory as "voluntaristic" and modeled after Hobson. Bukharin drew his theory from Rudolf Hilferding's notion of finance capital and offered a clear and detailed exposition of imperialism as an advanced stage of capitalism, while criticizing interpretations related to race and conquest. V. I. Lenin acknowledged the influence of Hobson and Hilferding upon the theory of imperialism. He understood imperialism to be the highest stage of capitalism, and he studied the rapid concentration of production in large industrial monopolies as well as the growing influence of large banks in the powerful monopolies. Paul Baran and Paul Sweezy referred specifically to Hilferding, Luxemburg, and Lenin in their formulation of a Marxist theory of imperialism. They suggested that such a theory explains relations within the capitalist world, clarifies the development of social and economic conditions in capitalist countries, and analyzes the unequal relations between advanced and underdeveloped nations. In particular they focused on the generation of capital surplus and its disposal. They turned analysis from competitive capitalism to monopoly and oligopoly and assessed the role of the giant corporations and their managers. Harry Magdoff traced the patterns of U.S. foreign policy and its impact on the international expansion of U.S. business. He aggregated data and information to show the coincidence of the military and political presence of the United States overseas, the dominant position of U.S. capital in the multinationals, and the dominance of multinational banking; he examined patterns of U.S. aid and trade as well as the ever-expanding U.S. "empire."

Efforts to promote a theory of dependency have emanated from both non-Marxist and Marxist understandings of imperialism. Raúl Prebisch and the ECLA school of economists argued that Latin America should set high tariff barriers and establish national industries to substitute for the increasing demand for foreign products; import substitution policies would bring local control over the economy and stimulate national development. Osvaldo Sunkel and Celso Furtado elaborated a deeper understanding of dependency in this anti-imperialist, non-Marxist tradition. Pablo González Casanova's notion of internal colonialism followed a somewhat similar line, and the poles-of-development conceptions of François Perroux should also be considered. Another tradition of dependency stems from Marxism. Lenin wrote of dependency in his work on imperialism. Trotsky influenced Silvio Frondizi and other Latin Americans to write about dependency after the Second World War. Rebelling against the orthodoxy and dogmatism of Stalinism, Theotonio Dos Santos and fellow Brazilian Ruy Mauro Marini attempted to assimilate dependency into their Marxist theory of capitalism and Leninist theory of imperialism. In this way an analysis of imperialism could be combined with a class analysis of international conditions in the underdeveloped world. At the same time, Fernando Henrique Cardoso and some Marxists advocating dependency believed that modern capitalism and imperialism differ from Lenin's earlier conception.

All of these theories assume an anti-imperialist stance, yet they are distinguishable along Marxist and non-Marxist lines. This distinction is important because many social scientists incorporate dependency into their view that the diffusion of capital and technology from the industrial to the backward nations will inevitably bring about development. Consequently, confusion and contradiction pervade much of the writing on dependency. Let us now turn to a brief discussion of the non-Marxist and Marxist theories of dependency.

The non-Marxist theories are based on several positions. One position advocates turning inward to development or *desarrollo* by promoting national autonomy through state control and planning of the political economy under the direction of the petty-bourgeois intelligentsia and the industrial bourgeoisie. Under the modernizing state the bourgeoisie will become a progressive influence and support national interests as capitalist development diffuses itself into rural areas and as economic and political policies restrict the influence of foreign interests. A dual society, one advanced and modern and the other backward and feudal, characterizes the developing nations, which in turn represent a primary producing periphery whose resources tend to be appropriated by the industrial center. Furtado developed this position by examining inequalities in Brazil throughout historical periods and tracing the shift of major economic activity and production from the Northeast to the

Center-South region where São Paulo is located. He believed that the state should intervene to rectify this imbalance and to move capitalist development along its future course. Sunkel has argued that the transformation of existing structures is necesssary for autonomous growth and that planning and control can bring about structural changes to eliminate underdevelopment and make capitalist development possible. Following another non-Marxist position, González Casanova alluded to internal colonialism, in which the center-peripheral conditions of colonialism are found internally within nations. Monopoly and dependency create deformation and decapitalization of the national economy and promote backwardness. He believed that a national solution is possible as marginal peoples are assimilated into society through the formation of a national bourgeoisie, which itself can resist the intrusions of monopoly capitalism and capitalist exploitation.

A third position, somewhat similar to internal colonialism and promoted by Perroux, identifies centers of natural resources where concentrated growth and markets can develop. Thus, capital and technology can be diffused to undeveloped centers that have a potential for industrialization. Cardoso contended with the idea that capitalism promotes underdevelopment, arguing that development can occur within dependent societies. He believed that dependent capitalist development becomes a new form of monopolistic expansion in the peripheral nations. New trends in international capitalism result in increased interdependence in production activities at the international level and in a modification in the patterns of dependence that limit developmental policy in the peripheral countries. He agreed that international capitalism has gained a disproportionate influence over industry in the peripheral areas, but he found misleading the assumption that there is a lack of growth in dependent economies because of imperialism. Cardoso believed that his approach updates theory established by Marx and Lenin, and he considered his understanding of dependency to be flexible in the face of orthodox and dogmatic Marxist conceptions.

Other writings on dependency fall more clearly into a Marxist framework. Baran and Sweezy are representative of independent Marxist thinkers whose ideas have influenced some *dependentistas*, but they have attempted to update Lenin and are sometimes criticized for not following a "pure" line. Marini's notion of subimperialism considers Brazilian capitalism as superexploitative, with a rapid accumulation of capital benefiting the owners of the means of production. Brazilian expansion and penetration into foreign markets have been based on the ability of the bourgeoisie to compete abroad. André Gunder Frank provided another facet of dependency theory with his emphasis on commercial monopoly as the means whereby national and regional metropolises exploit and appropriate surplus from the economic satellites. Thus capitalism on a world scale is viewed as promoting developing metropolises at the expense of underdeveloping and dependent satellites. Dos Santos took exception to Frank's emphasis on surplus extraction as the principal cause of underdevelopment and instead was concerned with the formation of internal structure conditioned by the international relationships of dependency. He stressed that the cause for the new dependency that emerged after the Second World War was massive investments by multinationals.

Criticisms of dependency theory abound. The non-Marxist theories are attacked for the emphasis on interdependence, implying that mutual cooperation between capitalist center and developing periphery might benefit both sides. Internal colonialism emphasizes internal forms and the role of a national bourgeoisie without taking into account the force of international capital and markets. Other theories overlook the role of class struggle — a criticism that applies to most of the Marxist theories as well. Critics accuse Frank of failing to relate analysis of capitalism to modes of production; González Casanova is attacked for conferring on dependency a "nationalist" character; Dos Santos is charged with confusing worldwide expansion of capitalism with economic growth in the periphery; and Cardoso is indicted for mixing Marxist and bourgeois concepts.

One must conclude that to date no unified theory of dependency exists, and it may be that dependency can be utilized only to enhance a theory of imperialism. Indeed critics doubt that dependency is compatible with Marxist theory. Yet, even though the search for a unified theory of dependency may prove unproductive, it is clear that such a theory must be grounded in historical reality and should address such conceptualization as historical materialism and class struggle. *Dependentistas* will have to turn to Lenin and others for the theoretical underpinnings of their argument.

Comparative Political Economy and Theories of State and Class

Although recognizing that the central concerns of international political economy are imperialism and dependency, I also briefly review the complementary concerns of comparative political economy, namely state and class. As with theories of imperialism and dependency, distinctions can be made between bourgeois and Marxist theories of state and class.

Bourgeois theory might return to the formal-legal studies of James Bryce and Woodrow Wilson, among others of the early twentieth century. Or perhaps it might turn to the structural-functional categories of Gabriel Almond. The prevailing bourgeois conception, however, sees the state as a political marketplace through which filter the demands and interests of competing groups and individuals. Two views prevail. On the one hand, neutral state agencies mediate conflict that emanates from party and group competition. On the other, agencies of the state function as bases of political power; competition among these agencies for funding determines their relationship to parties and interest groups. These views reflect the liberal, non-Marxist tradition of U.S. social science. They may also be applicable to some socialist states, for example the workers' control practiced in Yugoslavia or the proliferation of organizational life that emerged in Czechoslovakia during the spring of 1968. Eurocommunism in France and Italy exhibits strains of pluralism, and "socialist pluralism" was a manifestation of leftist groups in the aftermath of the Portuguese coup of 1974. Robert Dahl, once the leading liberal proponent of pluralism, has drawn attention to these bourgeois and socialist perspectives of the pluralist state and incorporated social class trends, cleavages, and conflict into a theory of organizational pluralism.

Marx never fully developed a theory of state and class, nor did he elaborate a systematic theory of politics. Raph Miliband noted that "a Marxist politics has to be constructed or reconstructed from the mass of variegated and fragmented material which forms the corpus of Marxism" (1977: 2). Miliband referred to A. Gramsci during his years in an Italian prison and Leon Trotsky during his years in exile as two writers who sustained a Marxist commentary on the role of the state through a period of Stalinism and fascism. Searching for a Marxist politics, Miliband reminded us that (1) textual priority should be given to Marx and Engels, then to others who followed in their tradition; (2) review will reveal different and sometimes contradictory Marxist interpretations; (3) the separation of politics from economics is an ideological distortion—politics is an integral part of political economy; and (4) the emphasis of many Marxists on the economic base has led to economic determinism and to the neglect of the superstructure, but Marx and Engels rejected mechanistic and deterministic explanations. As to the primacy of economics,

> the notion of "primacy" constitutes an important and illuminating guideline, not an analytical straitjacket. The ways in which that "primacy" determines and conditions political and other forms remain to be discovered, and must be treated in each case as specific, circumstantial, and contingent; and this also leaves open for assessment the ways in which political forms and processes in turn affect, determine, condition, and shape the economic realm, as of course they do and as they are acknowledged to do by Marxists, beginning with Marx. [Miliband 1977: 8–9]

The construction of a Marxist politics and theory of state and class necessitates initially an examination of the thought of Hegel, Marx, Engels, and Lenin. Marx critiqued Hegel's doctrine of the state, accepting that a fundamental contradiction exists between the state and the civil society of citizens but insisting that forms of the state be separated from an ideal or abstract conception and instead be rooted in the material conditions of life. Whereas in ancient Greece and during medieval times there was a sense of unity between the people and the state and between private and public interests, under capitalism, Marx argued, there is a separation of state from civil society, and an estrangement develops between public and private life. In addition, the civil society fragments into private interests competing against one another as the state legitimizes the pursuit of particular interests through private property. Private property promotes inequality and disunity among the people. One solution to this would be a return to a people's democracy, not a bourgeois democracy. In *The Origin of the Family, Private Property, and the State*, Engels summed up Marx's early writing on the state and class and also showed the significance of economic considerations. In *State and Revolution* (1932), Lenin drew on the theory of state elaborated by Marx and Engels. He insisted that the state does not reconcile class conflict but ensures the oppression of one class by another. Furthermore, he argued that state power must be destroyed through violent revolution, that compromise and reformist solutions do not resolve class antagonisms. He saw the police and standing army as "instruments" of state power. The proletariat struggles against the state until bourgeois democracy becomes proletarian democracy, the existence of classes is no longer necessary, and the state disappears altogether.

Marx, Engels, and Lenin emphasized a theory of state premised on the impact of capitalism. This focus stimulated recent work in the journal, *Kapitalistate: Working Papers on the Capitalist State*. Three traditions seem to have caught the attention of contemporary scholars who are concerned with state and class. One tradition, known as instrumentalism and prevalent in the United States, emanated from community studies that identified power along the lines of position and reputation. This perspective is enhanced by Lenin's reference to instruments of state power and by Marx and Engels's concern expressed in the *Communist Manifesto* that the executive of the state "is but a committee for managing the affairs of the whole bourgeoisie" (Marx 1974: 69). Thus the state is the instrument of the ruling or dominant class. Instrumentalism focuses on the class that rules and the ties and mechanisms that link ruling class instruments and state policies. Instrumentalism has been criticized for its failure to transcend the pluralist emphasis on social and political groupings rather than on classes tied to the means of production. The instrumentalist perspective of state has been advanced by G. William Domhoff and Ralph Miliband.

A second tradition revolves around the structuralist view of the state and is found in the writings of French Marxists. Nicos Poulantzas elaborated a political side of this structuralism by arguing that the bourgeoisie is unable as a class to dominate the state, that the state itself organizes and unifies the interest of that class. An economic side of structuralism is exemplified by Baran and Sweezy who stressed the activity of the state in resolving economic contradictions and averting crises related to monopoly capitalism. Critics of structuralism argue that it cannot explain class action arising from class consciousness, that analysis tends to be static and tied to inputs and outputs rather than to class activity.

A third tradition, rooted in the critical perspectives of Hegel and Marx and carried on by Herbert Marcuse and others of the Frankfurt school, attempts to expose the mystification of the state and its ideology and false consciousness. This "critical" perspective sometimes is seen as abstract and unrelated to concrete politics and state activity. Beyond these three perspectives, Claus Offe and Esping-Andersen, Friedland, and Wright have suggested a focus on political class struggle—on the internal structures of the state and how these structures shape the class struggle. They examined the relationship of class struggle and state policies.

Marx and Engels distinguished state from society in order to clarify the interrelationship of political and economic life. They defined politics in terms of the power of the state, the superstructure that represents bourgeois society and reflects the economic needs of the class controlling production. Has a Marxist paradigm established itself? In *The Twilight of Capitalism* Michael Harrington responded in the affirmative.

> Even though it shares insights with, and has influenced, the various social sciences, it is distinctive and cohesive both as a method and in the results it facilitates. . . . It poses the right questions about the contemporary world; it suggests some profound ways of seeking out the answers; and it is therefore relevant to the theory and practice of the twenty-first century. [1976: 184]

Harrington traced the crusade against Marxism that has been waged by U.S. academic disciplines during the past half century. The Marxist paradigm, he argued, integrates the separate analyses of the social science disciplines. He made clear, however, that the Marxist paradigm does not consist of some preconceived Marxist model of society. To the contrary, it offers important methodological themes. It is critical, even of its own concepts and terminology. It is rigorously scientific, yet it makes no pretense of being free of values but is aware of biases and ideologies that permeate social science; the values of Marxism link to politics favoring the working class rather than the ruling bourgeoisie. The Marxist paradigm also does not prescribe any particular solution for the ills of capitalist society—whether that society be democratic planning by the majority or bureaucratic and exploitative collectivism. Further, the Marxist paradigm looks for contradictions in society; it offers a complex theory of social classes, and it distinguishes possibilities, symptoms, and causes in an analysis of crisis and changing technology.

The present generation of political scientists wrestles with the question of what is political and what is political science. Although a few acknowledge the contributions of Marx to this question, most tend to steer clear of the onus of Marxism, preferring instead to distinguish politics from economics and to avoid issues of state, power, class, and class struggle. It is to be hoped that such issues will be meaningfully addressed through attention to comparative and international political economy.

References

Brenner, Robert
1977 "The Origins of Capitalist Development: A Critique of Neo-Smithian Marxism." *New Left Review* 104 (July-August), 25–92. A detailed critique of André Gunder Frank, Paul Sweezy, and Immanuel Wallerstein, which traces the roots of their theory to Adam Smith.

Bukharin, Nikolai I.
1927 *The Economic Theory of the Leisure Class.* London: Martin Lawrence Limited. Originally written in 1914, this work contains a useful introduction that reviews bourgeois political economy since Marx, as well as a first chapter that distinguishes methodological foundations of bourgeois and Marxist theory.

Chattopadhyay, Paresh
1974 "Political Economy: What's in a Name?" *Monthly Review* XXV (April), 23–33. A historical overview of various interpretations and understandings of political economy, from its origins to the present.

Deol, D.
1976 *Liberalism and Marxism: An Introduction to the Study of Contemporary Politics.* Delhi: Sterling Publishers. Elementary but useful synthesis of contrasting methodologies in political science.

Easton, David
1968 "Political Science." In *International Encyclopedia of the Social Sciences,* 12: 282–297. Edited by David L. Sills. New York: Macmillan Company and Free Press. Review of the struggle to establish political science as a discipline. Demonstrates the importance of Marx's conception of the state, yet argues that current inquiry has transcended concepts such as state, with recent attention to the political system.

Fusfeld, Daniel R.
1966 *The Age of the Economist: The Development of Modern Economic Thought.* Glenview, Illinois: Scott, Foresman and Co. Overview that sharply distinguishes positions of Marxists from bourgeois economists. Looks at various periods of political economic thought from the rise of market economy to central economic planning. Includes chapters on Smith, Ricardo, Marx.

Harrington, Michael
  1976 *The Twilight of Capitalism.* New York: Simon & Schuster. Chapter 7 outlines eight methodological themes that constitute the Marxist paradigm that the author favors.
Heilbroner, Robert L.
  1961 *The Worldly Philosophers: The Lives, Times, and Ideas of the Great Economic Thinkers.* New York: Simon and Schuster. An overview of economic thinking with attention to the work and thought of Smith, Malthus and Ricardo, the utopian socialists, and Marx, Veblen, and Keynes.
Hunt, E. K.
  1972 *Property and Prophets: The Evolution of Economic Institutions and Ideologies.* New York: Harper and Row. A general statement and overview, from a Marxist perspective, of economic developments from precapitalist Europe to contemporary corporate and liberal capitalism.
Mandel, Ernest
  1968 *Marxist Economic Theory.* Translated by Brian Pearce. New York: Monthly Review Press. 2 vols. Chapter 18 synthesizes trends of political economy and provides an excellent critical overview.

  1975 *Late Capitalism.* Translated by Joris De Bres. London: New Left Books. An overview of capitalism during the past hundred years with attention to late capitalism, evident since the Second World War.
Marx, Karl
  1904 *A Contribution to the Critique of Political Economy.* Translated from the second German edition by N. I. Stoke. Calcutta: Bharati Libaray. Translation of an edition published in 1897 by Karl Kautsky. Includes the famous preface and two chapters on capital, which deal with commodities and money, as well as an appendix consisting of the introduction to the *Critique of Political Economy.*

  1955 *The Poverty of Philosophy: Answer to the "Philosophy of Poverty" by M. Proudhon.* Moscow: Progress Publishers. An early Marxist critique of utopian socialist and idealist metaphysical interpretations of political economy.

  1967 *Capital: A Critique of Political Economy.* Ed. Frederick Engels. New York: International Publishers. 3 vols.

  1973 *Grundrisse: Foundations of the Critique of Political Economy.* Translated with a foreword by Martin Nicolaus. New York: Vintage Books.

  1974 *The Revolutions of 1848.* Edited with an introduction by David Fernbach. New York: Vintage Books.
Marx, Karl, and Frederick Engels
  1970 *The German Ideology.* Edited with introduction by C. J. Arthur. New York: International Publishers. The authors show the relationship between material base and ideology as a manifestation of the state in its separation from the whole society.
Meek, Ronald L.
  1956 *The Labour Theory of Value.* London: Lawrence and Wishart. An excellent critical overview of labor theory, which examines theories prior to Adam Smith,

the theories of Smith, Ricardo, and Marx, and critiques of Marxian theory.

Miliband, Ralph

1977 *Marxism and Politics.* Oxford: Oxford University Press. An attempt to summarize the politics of Marxism or the Marxist approach to politics through a synthesis of the ideas in Marx, Engels, and Lenin.

A Survey of the General Literature of Comparative Politics

The literature of comparative politics is both prolific and disparate. Therefore, this section reviews the basic texts, readers, and other works, including the major journal articles, that deal with comparative politics. This literature, of course, is indicative of what has been done in the field. My synthesis attempts to render some tentative order and to provide the beginning and advanced student alike with a broad sweep of materials. At the same time, it is hoped that the reader will be stimulated to use the appropriate general references to investigate particular aspects of the field.

Evolution of the Comparative Literature

A survey of the comparative politics literature usually begins with Aristotle and others who classified types or forms of the state from which were drawn generalizations about political life. Until the nineteenth century the prevailing typology classified politics into monarchies, aristocracies, and democracies. In the middle of the nineteenth century, Karl Marx, Saint-Simon, and others formulated a division of society into types of classes; for Marx the principal classes were feudal, bourgeois, and proletarian. Later Max Weber classified politics according to types of authority: traditional, charismatic, and legal-rational.

Since the Second World War and the emergence of new states out of crumbling colonial empires, political scientists have tended to distinguish between Western and non-Western systems (Pye 1958; Kahin, Pauker, and Pye 1955; and Rustow 1964). They also have tended to cast their comparisons into a continuum of stages, from totalitarian to constitutional and democratic, from traditional to transitional to modern. A pioneering effort to type politics was Gabriel Almond's classification into Anglo-American, continental European, totalitarian, and preindustrial systems (Almond 1956). A later, more ambitious, attempt at typing democratic systems was that of Lijphart (1968). Such typologies have served to tie together the disparate directions in the comparative politics literature. Let us now identify these directions by identifying the major developments in the field since the end of the Second World War.

There have been few efforts to provide students with an overview of the field of comparative politics. A brief synthesis by Harry Eckstein (1963) is one major exception, for it critically assesses trends in the field since the time of the Greek political philosophers, and it notes dominant tendencies that have influenced the field during the late nineteenth and the twentieth centuries. A half-century appraisal of the field by Sigmund Neumann (1957) is also helpful. There have been at least three major assessments of the field during the past generation, however.

The first of these appeared in 1944 in a committee report of the American Political Science Association. This report referred to the "tedious and stagnating routine" in the study of comparative government and called for some methodological reorientation and attention to substantive comparative studies through the use of a variety of approaches, ranging from institutional to behavioral (Loewenstein 1944).

The second assessment, at a 1952 seminar at Northwestern University, was contained in another report to the association. Prepared by the Social Science Research Council's Interuniversity Research Seminar on Comparative Politics, the report criticized the traditional reports and urged the elaboration of tentative classificatory schemes, conceptualization, hypothesizing, and the testing of hypotheses by empirical data (Macridis and Cox 1953). Roy Macridis (1955) elaborated on these concerns and called for a change in the field. He also joined with Gabriel Almond and Taylor Cole (Almond, Cole, and Macridis 1955) in setting forth some research strategies for the study of European government and politics. Further examination of these and other themes occurred at the 1954 conference on comparative government, held in Florence, Italy, under the auspices of the International Political Science Association (reported in Heckscher 1958).

The third assessment of the field occurred at a May 1968 conference on the comparative method, held at New York University. The conference papers appeared in the inaugural issue of the quarterly journal *Comparative Politics*. Earlier, Apter (1958) had proposed the clustering of variables to generate a theory for comparative political study. Deutsch (1960) attempted to combine quantitative and experimental methods with humanistic and historical orientations, and Merritt and Rokkan (1966) assessed problems in methods of comparison. The 1968 papers served to direct renewed attention to the comparative method. Macridis (1968a) updated his earlier critique by attacking the attempt of behavioralists to build grand theory or systems theory, on the one hand, and for their attention to trivia, on the other. He called for a return to the study of ideology. LaPalombara (1968) lent support to the criticism of Macridis with an attack on systems theory and on structural functionalism, upon which the theory generally is premised. He suggested instead the application of rigorous methodologies to important problems at a middle-range level or to emphasis on partial systems in the hope of correcting deficiencies in whole-systems analysis.

The basis upon which *Comparative Politics* was founded was offset partially by the attention to systematic data and empirical research of a rival quarterly journal, *Comparative Political Studies*, which also was established in 1968. These are the major journals of comparative politics. Although the latter journal published annotated bibliographies of the comparative politics literature and the former included book reviews (for example, see Gregor 1971), neither journal has published a comprehensive, critical synthesis of the literature since 1968. Nor have there been many serious appraisals of the field in other journals, one exception being a review by Holt and Turner (1975) of the comparative series on political development published by Princeton University Press (Social Science Research Council 1963–1975). I should add that *World Politics* and *Government and Opposition* publish a considerable amount of material relevant to comparative politics. There are also articles pertaining to the subject in the *American Political Science Review* and other major journals of the profession.

Classifying the Comparative Politics Literature

Familiarity with the existing literature of comparative politics may assist the reader in reaching an understanding of the strengths and weaknesses of the field. Thus I now turn to a critical review of the basic literature, and the review will classify the literature into general overviews of the field, including introductory texts and theoretical works; cross-national studies; comparative series of monographs and anthologies; area and configurative studies of Europe and the Third World; and institutional studies.

Several previous efforts provide a basis for a critical systhesis of the literature of the field. The first, a collection of basic courses in comparative politics edited by Ted Robert Gurr and Francisco José Moreno (1970), allowed students of comparative politics to examine the syllabi of the various course offerings by specialists teaching in many universities. It was an effort that deserves of updating, although it did not include a critical assessment or an interpretation of the literature used in teaching. The collection of twenty syllabi was drawn from fifty-eight that were submitted. More than half of them offered a general survey of comparative politics or of the developing areas. Some 150 books were required or assigned in the fifty-eight syllabi, but only 11 titles were listed in four or more of the syllabi. The most frequently adopted texts were Almond and Powell's *Comparative Politics: A Developmental Approach* (1974) and Almond and Verba's *Civic Culture* (1963). Norman Furniss (1974) provided the second effort to synthesize the general literature of comparative politics. A summary of his findings reaffirms my earlier stance that definitions of what is comparative are far-ranging and varied. His judgment of the literature is based on three criteria: provision of an adequate data base; fostering of critical thought; and stimulating students to think imaginatively. He faults the comparative politics literature on all three criteria, and he attributes these deficiencies to a paucity of comparative government theory. He suggests five possible remedies: (1) abandon the search for theory and return to a country-by-country approach; (2) focus on a topic or institution and study governments across national boundaries; (3) employ a macro cross-national approach utilizing descriptive information about all countries; (4) focus on middle-range concepts with attention to what is relevant to politics; and (5) emphasize cross-national historical trends and forces that shape political life. In some form or another all of these remedies are evident in the literature discussed below. The current state of the field precludes the predominance, indeed the widespread acceptance by the profession, of any single remedy. Finally, Angelo Codevilla (1974) offered a less comprehensive, yet critical overview of some of the introductory texts in comparative politics.

General Overviews

The general comparative works can be divided into several categories. My particular concerns relate to introductory texts, to readers, and to works that attempt to integrate theory with substance.

Since the middle 1960s a number of political analysts have prepared texts that focus comparatively on institutional life rather than on specific countries. The early examples of such texts were those by Fried (1966), Curtis (1968), and Hitchner and Levine (1968). The first two works dwell on formal governmental life, including constitutions, executives, legislatures, judiciaries, administrative systems, political parties, and electorates, and they describe those institutions in considerable detail. The last work does likewise but with some reference to the country examples. Eisenstadt's (1965) essays on comparative institutions may be useful. Some recent examples of texts that carry on the tradition of examining institutional structure are Blondel

(1972), Carter and Herz (1973), Finer (1970), Kousoulas (1968), Merkl (1970), LaPalombara (1974), Bertsch, Clark, and Wood (1978), Cattell and Sisson (1978), Palmer and Thompson (1978), and Hagopian (1978).

Other introductory texts such as Samuel Johnson (1964), Roth and Wilson (1976), Andrain (1979), and Spiro (1959) focus on institutional life but also draw very concretely upon the experiences of a variety of countries. Almond and Powell (1974) simplified some of their earlier structural-functional conceptualization and then drew upon an interesting variety of country examples in attempts to relate theory to real situations. McLennan (1975) adapted Almond's structural-functional approach to nine countries in advanced and backward parts of the world. Gordon (1972) applied a model of conflict management to comparative analysis and illustrated that analysis with reference to a variety of countries. Deutsch offered a similarly ambitious effort (1970) in an attempt to set forth the major concepts of comparative politics as they relate to six countries. Finally, Sherman and Wood (1979) introduced both traditional and radical perspectives in an analysis of social issues applicable to nations everywhere.

Eckstein and Apter (1963) and Macridis and Brown (1964) remain the best, although dated, readers or anthologies on the mainstream, established concerns of comparative politics. Essays therein combine institutional and theoretical concerns. Noteworthy among other readers and collections of essays are Bendix et al. (1968), Dahl (1966), Jackson and Stein (1971), Lewis, Potter, and Castles (1973), Munger (1967), Smock (1973), and Young (1958). The last one was an early effort to focus theoretically on a variety of concepts useful to comparative study. Bendix's sophisticated collection examines the state and society in a number of countries since the eighteenth century, and Dahl brought together an interesting set of essays on political opposition in the countries of Western Europe. The Jackson and Stein reader topically focuses on such important issues as political development, integration, stability, protest, and revolution. Smock united a variety of essays on mobilization in four geographic areas, and Munger combined significant segments of five important comparative works by Almond, Duverger, and others.

Noteworthy are a number of texts written as introductions but oriented toward theory and concepts. In this regard Almond and Powell's (1966) attempt to apply structural functionalism to a theory of development certainly is one of the more widely used texts. Less coherent but comprehensive in its attempt to review the terminology of the Western political tradition is Peter Merkl (1967). Bill and Hardgrave (1973) offered the best of the comparative works, in this writer's judgment. They covered the major concerns of comparative political analysis, in a way similar to the present book, and they placed their discussion into a theoretical context. Maurice Duverger's (1974) interesting examination of the theoretical roots of the Western political system involves a provocative interpretation of the political experiences of Great Britain and the United States. Irving Louis Horowitz (1972) ambitiously divided the world into three parts and offered theoretical perspectives on development. Finally, Fred Riggs (1964), in his most prominent work, demonstrated the need for a theoretical understanding of the administrative structures in the developing countries, and he set forth some provocative, sometimes obscure, propositions. Mayer and Burnett (1977) examined mature industrial society.

Cross-National Studies

Attempts to promote cross-national research generally have been limited to the selection of variables common to a large number of countries and then to reporting data related to those variables. Arthur Banks and Robert Textor (1963) examined demographic, social, political, and economic data for 115 nations, and Bruce Russett and others (1964) assembled data for seventy-five variables and 133 countries into a handbook of information. Richard Merritt and Stein Rokkan (1966) edited papers from a 1963 Yale conference, which studied the uses of quantitative data in international research; the introductory essay by Rokkan is an especially useful assessment of past and ongoing work in this area. Michael Haas (1970) and Alexander Szalai et al. (1966) delved into the ramifications of quantitative cross-national analysis. Robert Agger and others (1970) presented the preliminary findings of a study on education and community involvement in Czechoslovakia, Yugoslavia, and the United States, and Alex Inkeles (1969) offered findings on individual participation in six developing countries. The last study combines the gathering of quantitative data with a need "to help cope with the dehumanizing, destructive conditions of modern man." Hadley Cantril (1966) moved his analysis in the same direction as he examined patterns of human concern in fourteen nations. Verba, Nie, and Kim (1978) analyzed types of participation with data from a seven-nation survey.

Less dependent on quantification, but sensitive to common problems of nations throughout the world, are a study by Barrington Moore (1966) on the origins and evolution of capitalism in England, France, and the United States as well as patterns of disintegration and development in several nations of Asia, and another study by William McCord (1965) who analyzed the impact of industrialization on the experience of both advanced and backward nations. Roland Pennock (1964) brought together contributions from five comparative analysts who concerned themselves with nation building and self-government in the nations of the Third World. Heidenheimer, Heclo, and Adams (1975) focused on public policy in a cross-national analysis of Europe and the United States, Andrews and Ra'anan (1969) brought together four case studies on the political implications of the coup d'etat, and Mostafa Rejai (1977) examined revolutionary strategy in Bolivia, France, and North Vietnam. Reinhard Bendix (1979) looked at power and rule through kings and people with attention to Japan, Russia, Prussia, England, France, Germany, and other nations.

Comparative Series

Since 1960, many publishers have committed themselves to series of volumes specifically oriented toward college class use. The most renowned has been the Little, Brown series edited by Gabriel Almond, James S. Coleman, and Lucian Pye for which Almond and Powell (1966) wrote the core volume. The series combines analytical studies on topics such as communication and development with studies on nations in various parts of the world. These country studies generally follow a pattern set forth by the editors who cast Almond's well-known structural-functional classification into a national framework. Less rigid in framework and more concerned with the formal workings of government are the volumes of four series. One of the series, edited by Dayton D. McKean (1960 to present) for Houghton Mifflin has produced interesting studies on Italy, Great Britain, Switzerland, Israel, Japan, India, Germany, and South Vietnam. Another, edited by Arnold Rogow (1960 to present) for Thomas Y. Crowell has volumes on Japan, France, Germany, Italy, Great Britain, the Soviet Union, and Eastern Europe. Michael Curtis (1968) edited the Harper and Row Comparative Government Series, which includes volumes on Great Britain and Eastern Europe. Peter Merkl (1970) wrote the core volume for a series of country studies, but the publishers—first Holt, Rinehart and Winston and later Dryden Press—have produced only a handful of the promised studies. Relevant to the study of politics is the Modern Nations in Historical Perspective Series, edited by Robin Winks (1960 to present). The series envisaged the publication of more than fifty volumes, most of which have indeed appeared in print.

Other comparative series are institutionally or topically oriented. Joseph LaPalombara (1974) has edited a Prentice-Hall series of volumes, which delve into the problems of comparing politics and governments; comparative studies of legislatures, legal cultures, revolutionary movements, corruption, and violence are among the studies that have appeared. Martin Heisler (1970s) has edited a series of comparative studies, ranging from pollution and ecology to legislatures. Reference has already been made to the Studies in Political Development Series, sponsored by the Social Science Research Council's Committee on Comparative Politics (1963–1975) and published by Princeton University Press. The eight volumes in this series aggregate essays by comparative specialists on communications, bureaucracy, modernization, education, political culture, political parties, development, and the formation of national states. Harry Eckstein and Ted Robert Gurr (1970–1977) edited the *Sage Professional Papers in Comparative Politics*. Twelve papers, focused on comparative politics topics, were published annually; usually they are longer than journal articles but briefer than monographs, and they reflect recent research and study in the field. This series was modeled after *Studies in Comparative International Development*, edited originally as a series of papers by Irving Louis Horowitz (1965 to present) at Washington University in St. Louis and later incorporated in a journal of the same title, published three times yearly. Sociologists Alex Inkeles (1968–1969) edited the Comparative Perspectives Series for Little, Brown and Company, and the collections of essays on stratification, social change, social problems, industrial society, and formal organizations contribute to comparative politics. Myron Weiner (1964 to present) edited the Rand McNally Studies in Political Change Series, which examines specific problems of the developing nations. K. C. Wheare has written a series of works (1963, 1964, 1966), published by Oxford University Press, that focus comparatively on legislatures, federal government, and constitutions.

Area and Configurative Studies

Traditionally the field of comparative politics oriented itself to the study of major European countries. First, I examine that literature on Europe, differentiating texts from collections of case studies and documents, and then I turn to some of the literature on the Third World.

An early example of a text on Europe is that of William Bennett Munro (1931) who focused major attention on constitutional history, the executive, the legislature, the courts, political parties, and local government in Great Britain, France, Germany, and Italy. Munro also briefly looked at Switzerland, Russia, Austria, and Hungary. Munro's individual and comprehensive achievements were not indicative of later efforts to compile texts on Europe: generally, country specialists were to collaborate, although several exceptions can be noted. Robert Neumann (1960) gave attention to Great Britain, France, Germany, and the Soviet Union, which comparative specialists in the United States clearly recognized as the major foreign powers. Like his contemporaries Neumann chose to divide his text into separate country sections, to stress history and detail, and to ignore direct comparisons, although in early editions he also included a section on comparative institutions. Essentially this approach was followed by Alex Dragnich (1961) and S. Rothman (1970). Herbert Spiro (1959) clearly offered an imaginative and interesting comparative text; he analyzed traditional institutions and processes, and he included all the major democratic systems, including those of Europe, Canada, and the United States. Robert A. Isaak (1980), examined questions of political economy and policymaking in West Germany, France, Great Britain, and Italy.

Beyond these individual efforts, the comparative texts on European politics combine the essays of various specialists. The most readable, interesting, and incisive is Beer and Ulam's *Patterns of Government* (1962). Also popular are the texts by Macridis and Ward (1963) and Carter and Herz (1967), the latter being a favorite exposition of European history and politics. Another, less popular, text that followed in this tradition was edited by Clifford Rich (1962), and Groth, Lieber, and Lieber (1976) included sections on Spain, Portugal, Greece, and Yugoslavia as well as on the traditional European systems. Jacobs and Zink (1966) focused on the traditional systems along with Scandinavia, the Americas, and Asia, and William Andrews (1966) edited five interpretative essays on the major European countries. Two other works on European government and politics moved in different directions. One, by Gunnar Heckscher (1958) deals with methodological issues of comparative politics, with explicit reference to Europe. The other, by Martin Heisler (1970s) sets forth some conceptual and theoretical foundations for the study of politics, followed by illustrative cases on European countries and policymaking. Edward Feit (1978) edited essays that combine biographies of major leaders with descriptions of their countries.

Among the volumes that contain specific case studies, three are especially significant. Carter and Westin (1965) edited five studies on European government; Roy Macridis (1968b) brought together eight cases on issues of politics in the major European nations; and James Christoph (1965) included case studies of India along with others on Great Britain, France, West Germany, and the Soviet Union.

Collections of documents and readings have been utilized in courses on European comparative politics. Among these collections are Albinski and Pettit's (1974) original essays, integrated with selected readings from the writings of twenty European specialists; Andrews's (1962) documents on the executives, legislatures, and political parties of the four major European systems; Dogan and Rose's (1971) edited selections on European nations; Muller's (1963) documents on constitutions, political parties, and electoral procedures; and Vig and Stiefbold's (1974) reader on developmental theory, which focuses primarily on Europe.

Most of the comparative politics materials on Europe include the Soviet Union but do not treat other socialist states in Europe. There is, however, some literature that compares the nations of socialist Europe. John Kautsky (1973) discussed the issues of comparison, which was of concern also to Paul Shoup (1968), although Kautsky argued against the separation of Communist from non-Communist systems. Works by Benes, Gyorgy, and Stambuk (1966) and H. Gordon Skilling (1966) are examples of attempts to draw comparisons between socialist systems.

Once a number of area specialists had turned their attention to the nations of the Third World, to which they applied Almond's structural-functional categories (Almond and Coleman 1960), other texts for classroom use appeared. John Kautsky (1962) introduced a volume of essays on the underdeveloped areas, with a lengthy analysis of underdevelopment and industrialization. Other collections of essays were organized by Barringer, Blanksten, and Mack (1965) who attempted to apply a theory of evolutionary change to developing nations; Lewis P. Pickett, Jr. (1966) who mixed selected readings with his own case studies of six countries; Harvey Kebschull (1968) who combined theoretical and substantive essays on many topics and on Africa, Asia, and Latin America; and Frank Tachau (1972) who coordinated twenty-three essays on modernization and change in parts of the Third World. Individual treatments of issues and problems of the Third World include Fred von der Mehden's (1964) examination of national identity, political parties, elites, military, and ideology; F. La Mond Tullis's (1973) attention to social change in Brazil, Libya, and Peru; and Robert F. Gamer's (1976) stimulating essays on disruptive forces, patrons and clients, alienation, and reform. Influenced by comparative analysis of the Third World, Ira Sharkansky (1975) drew upon that analysis in a critical treatment of the United States, which he considered to be a developing country.

A multitude of introductory texts exists on specific areas of the Third World. Generally instructors select edited collections of essays by many country specialists, often ignoring ambitious individual efforts on the assumption that no single scholar can effectively assimilate and analyze the information on politics in many countries. A few of the more popular collections can be cited. For Asia, Robert Ward and Roy Macridis edited a companion volume to their text on Europe, *Modern Political Systems: Asia* (1963), with contributions on Japan, China, India, Southeast Asia, and Southwest Asia. For the Middle East, Benjamin Rivlin and Joseph Szyliowicz brought together more than fifty essays on such topics as modernism and nationalism in their *Contemporary Middle East: Tradition and Innovation* (1965). For Africa, Gwendolen Carter's once popular *African One-Party States* (1962), with contributions from six specialists, was organized like the traditional texts on European politics, and James S. Coleman and Carl G.

Rosberg edited sixteen essays in *Political Parties and National Integration in Tropical Africa* (1964). The popular texts on Latin America include brief, often superficial, essays on the politics of each of the area's countries, examples being Martin Needler's *Political Systems of Latin America* (1964 and 1970) and Ben Burnett and Kenneth Johnson's *Political Forces in Latin America* (1968). A radical interpretation and an in-depth presentation on six countries composes Ronald Chilcote and Joel Edelstein's *Latin America: The Struggle with Dependency and Beyond* (1974). In regard to all of the above materials, the relationship of area studies to comparative politics long has been in dispute (see Kling 1964 and Ward 1974 for fuller discussion).

Institutional Studies

Considerable attention in recent years has been devoted to comparative studies of institutions that affect political life. I do not attempt here or elsewhere in the present work to focus specifically on the prolific literature of comparative administration, but the curious reader may wish to consult two useful, although now dated, essays by Alfred Diamant (1960) and Ferrel Heady (1960). Additionally useful among journal articles might be the essays on comparative policy analysis by Pierce (1963), Smith (1969), and Anderson (1971). McLennan (1979) compared public policy among various nations, and Groth (1971) looked at various issues of policy. I also make no effort to delve systematically into the literature of comparative urban politics except as it relates to elite studies. Comparison of political parties has captured the most attention, although there is a small but growing literature on interest groups such as the military, labor, church, business, and the like. Although political parties and interest groups also are not a principal concern of the present work, I feel compelled to identify some of the literature on these institutions.

Robert Michels (1962) and Maurice Duverger (1963) have contributed the classical comparative studies of political parties, and they examined the experiences of European parties. In the recent literature on parties, Duverger, in particular, has been the focus of discussion and criticism (May 1969; Crotty 1970). Kay Lawson (1976) attempted a comparative analysis of parties in France, Guinea, and the United States. Beyond these singular contributions, the major comparative literature on political parties is found in anthologies of readings and original essays. Among the more prominent works are Allardt and Littunen (1964) on consensus and cleavage in party organization; Allardt and Rokkan (1969) on cleavage and mass voting behavior in Great Britain, Spain, Poland, and Italy; David Butler (1959) on electoral analysis during 1957 and 1958 in France, Poland, Ireland, and South Africa; Arnold Heidenheimer (1970) on the financing of political parties in Europe, the United States, Canada, and the Third World; Lipset and Rokkan (1967) on party systems and voter alignments in several nations; Munger and Price (1964) on Anglo-American party and pressure-group traditions and processes; Sigmund Neumann (1956) on case studies of party politics in Europe and the United States; Giuseppe di Palma (1972) on mass politics in industrial societies; William Wright (1971) on party organization based on the British and North American experiences; and Belloni and Beller (1978) on parties and factionalism.

The results of empirical research on political parties constitute a central thrust of the *Sage Professional Papers in Comparative Politics* (Eckstein and Gurr 1970–1977). Especially noteworthy are papers by J. Zvi Namenwirth and Harold D. Lasswell (Paper 1) on language values and party platforms; Kenneth Janda (Paper 2) on the outline of his comparative political parties project; Kenneth Thompson (Paper 3) on cross-national voting behavior and multivariate analysis in Britain and the United States; Ergun Ozbudun (Paper 6) on party cohesion in Western democracies; Richard A. Pride (Paper 12) on a cross-national study on mobilization, party systems, and democratic stability; Sidney Verba, Norman H. Nie, and Jae-on Kim (Paper 13) on a cross-national comparison of modes of democratic participation; and Harry Eckstein (Paper 17) and Ted Robert Gurr and Muriel McClelland (Paper 18) on a twelve-nation study of political performance.

Students of comparative party politics might desire to examine Neumann's (1956: Introduction) exploratory synthesis on the subject. Then too the surveys of writings on political parties by Neil A. McDonald and Frederick Engelmann (in Eckstein and Apter 1963: 332–350 and 378–386) may be instructive. An essay by Colin Leys (Eckstein and Apter 1963: 305–315) looks at models and theories of political parties. Other journal articles of significance to the comparative study of political parties include Baum (1967), Palma (1969), and Tucker (1961). Rokkan's (1962) contribution on the comparative study of political participation also might be helpful.

Many years ago Gabriel Almond attempted to outline some assumptions about comparisons of interest groups. In recent years some effort has been directed toward comparing group interests other than political parties. For example, Janowitz (1964) set forth some propositions about the role of the military in newly established nations, and John Johnson (1962) edited diverse essays on the same subject. Other comparative studies of particular institutional forces include Alderfer (1964) on local government and Millen (1963) on the political role of labor—both works focus on the developing nations. Even the multinational corporation has received attention in the literature (see, for example, Stauffer 1973).

In summary, this survey has classified the literature into general works, including the basic texts, readers, case studies, and documents. Some of the major cross-national studies have been identified, and the major series of comparative studies, organized around countries and topics, also have been noted. Complementing these series are the area and configurative studies as well as the institutional studies. Citations to this literature should aid the reader, student and instructor alike. Critical judgments as to the utility of the literature depend on each reader's awareness of the fundamental issues that frequently divide the political scientists into sometimes competing, sometimes opposing camps. In addition, the reader must assess the intellectual tendencies that have shaped political thinking over the past century and have exerted a profound impact on the field of comparative politics.

Selected Bibliography

All of the following materials have been discussed in "A Survey of the General Literature." The listing is somewhat comprehensive in its inclusion of books and monographs. Only a very small number of selected journal articles are cited, however. Foreign language sources have not been included.

Agger, Robert E., Miroslav Disman, Zdravko Mlinar, and Vladimir Sultanovic
1970 "Education, General Personal Orientations, and Community Involvement; A Cross-National Research Project." *Comparative Political Studies* III (April), 90–116. Preliminary results and analysis of survey research in several countries. The research assessed the role of education, particularly adult education, in shaping the attitudes of citizens toward community institutions and processes.
Albinski, Henry S., and Lawrence K. Pettit (eds.)
1974 *European Political Processes: Essays and Readings.* Boston: Allyn and Bacon. Original essays on the four major European nations with attention to value systems, group interests and electorates, parties and their elites, policy process, and administration.
Alderfer, Harold F.
1964 *Local Government in Developing Countries.* New York: McGraw-Hill. Examines general patterns of local government in developing nations.
Allardt, Erik, and Yrjo Littunen (eds.)
1964 *Cleavages, Ideologies, and Party Systems: Contributions to Comparative Political Sociology.* Turku, Finland: Transaction of the Westermark Society. Comparative essays by various authors on consensus and cleavage, party systems and organizations, and party organizations and patterns of political recruitment.

Allardt, Erik, and Stein Rokkan (eds.)
1969 *Mass Politics: Studies in Political Sociology.* Introduction by S. M. Lipset. New York: Free Press and Macmillan. Essays by Ulf Himmelstrand, Ulf Torgersen, James Cornford, Kevin Cox, T. J. Nossiter, Juan J. Linz, Warren E. Miller, Jerzy J. Wiatr, Giovanni Sartori, and others on cleavage systems and mass politics, voting behavior, and political parties. Focuses on Norway, Great Britain, Spain, Poland, and Italy.

Almond, Gabriel A.
1956 "Comparative Political Systems." *Journal of Politics* XVIII (August), 391–409. Drawing upon the work of Max Weber and Talcott Parsons, Almond proposes a conception and a typology of political systems: Anglo-American, preindustrial, totalitarian, and continental European political systems.

Almond, Gabriel A. and James S. Coleman (eds.)
1960 *The Politics of the Developing Areas.* Princeton: Princeton University Press. Structural-functional approach proposed in the introduction is applied to studies of geographic areas of the "developing" world.

Almond, Gabriel A., and G. Bingham Powell, Jr.
1966 *Comparative Politics: A Developmental Approach.* Boston: Little, Brown and Co. 2d ed., 1978. The core volume for an analytical and a country series. Uses a structural-functional approach and attempts to move toward a theory of development. Among the analytical studies are those on development by Lucian Pye and on communication by Richard Fagen. Among the country studies are those on the Soviet Union by Frederick Barghoorn, Germany by Lewis Edinger, France by Henry Ehrmann, England by Richard Rose, Israel by Leonard Fein, the Philippines by Jean Grossholtz, Japan by Frank Langdon, South Africa by Leonard Thompson.

Almond, Gabriel A., and G. Bingham Powell, Jr. (eds.)
1974 *Comparative Politics Today: A World View.* Boston: Little, Brown and Co. 2d ed., 1980. An introductory text focused topically on political socialization and culture, political participation and recruitment, interest groups, political parties, and policymaking in government institutions and agencies. Country studies include England, France, Soviet Union, China, Mexico, and Tanzania.

Almond, Gabriel A., Taylor Cole, and Roy C. Macridis
1955 "A Suggested Research Strategy in Western European Government and Politics." *American Political Science Review* XLIX (December), 1042–1049. Notes divergent tendencies in research on U.S. politics and European politics in contrast to the period prior to the First World War when the leading Americanists had their training in European centers. Calls for the reunification of the European-U.S. tradition in the face of threats to "parliamentary and democratic institutions on the European continent."

Anderson, Charles
1971 "Comparative Policy Analysis." *Comparative Politics* IV (October), 117–132. Focusing on the problem of public choice, policy analysis is related to the role of comparative politics.

Andrain, Charles F.
1979 *Politics and Economic Policy in Western Democracies.* Belmont, California:

Duxbury Press. With attention to the United States, Canada, Great Britain, West Germany, Sweden, France, and Italy, this text examines the impact of public policies on the economy; analyzes interaction among government institutions, corporations, and labor unions, and explores international influences on inflation and unemployment.

Andrews, William G.
1962 *European Political Institutions: A Comparative Government Reader.* Princeton, New Jersey: D. Van Nostrand Co. Documents on the four major European systems with attention to political parties, legislatures, and executives.

Andrews, William G. (ed.)
1966 *European Politics I: The Restless Search.* Princeton, New Jersey: D. Van Nostrand Co. Contributions by Carl J. Friedrich on the search for a model political order, Anthony King on Britain, William G. Andrews and Stanley Hoffmann on France, Elmer Plischke on West Germany, and Samuel Hendel on the Soviet Union.

Andrews, William G., and Uri Ra'anan (eds.)
1969 *The Politics of the Coup d'Etat: Five Case Studies.* New York: Van Nostrand Reinhold Co. Contributions by Martin C. Needler on Ecuador, Uri Ra'anan on Indonesia, Majid Khadduri on Iraq, and Robert Conquest on Bulgaria.

Apter, David E.
1958 "A Comparative Method for the Study of Politics." *American Journal of Sociology* LXIV (November), 221–237. Attributes the weakness in comparative politics theory to the limited utility of variables and inadequate core concepts. Suggests a three-dimensional model—social stratification, political groups, and government—to generate a clustering of variables to provide the basis for the development of theory.

Banks, Arthur, and Robert Textor
1963 *A Cross-Polity Survey.* Cambridge, Massachusetts: M.I.T. Press. Reference work on 115 nations and fifty-seven variables useful for cross-national investigation of demographic, social, political, and economic relationships.

Barringer, Herbert R., George I. Blanksten, and Raymond W. Mack (eds.)
1965 *Social Change in Developing Areas: A Reinterpretation of Evolutionary Theory.* Cambridge, Massachusetts: Schenkman Publishing Co. Original essays on evolutionary theory and change with attention to developing nations.

Baum, Richard D.
1967 "Apples, Oranges, and the Comparative Study of Political Parties." *Western Political Quarterly* XX (March), 132–148. Perspectives for the comparative inquiry of political parties.

Beer, Samuel H., and Adam B. Ulam (eds.)
1962 *Patterns of Government: The Major Political Systems of Europe.* New York: Random House. Interesting synthesis and analysis of the four major European nations: Great Britain, France, Germany, and the Soviet Union. 3d ed. in 1973 includes two new authors.

Belloni, Frank P., and Dennis C. Beller (eds.)
1978 *Faction Politics: Political Parties and Factionalism in Comparative Perspective.* Santa Barbara, California: American Bibliographical Center-Clio Press. Seventeen essays by specialists on various countries.

Bendix, Reinhard
1979 *Kings or People: Power and the Mandate to Rule.* Berkeley: University of California Press. A focus on power and the mandate to rule with a look at a variety of countries through history. A first part addresses the authority of kings, with attention to Japan, Russia, imperial Germany and Prussia, and England. A second part examines the mandate of the people, with attention to England, France, Germany, Japan, and Russia.

Bendix, Reinhard et al. (eds.)
1968 *State and Society: A Reader in Comparative Political Sociology.* Boston: Little, Brown and Co. Examines premodern structures and transformations of Western European societies since the eighteenth century, looks at private and public authority in Western Europe and Russia, compares preconditions of development in Japan and Germany, and presents a case study of public authority in India.

Benes, Vaclav, Andrew Gyorgy, and George Stambuk
1966 *Eastern European Government and Politics.* New York: Harper and Row. Introductory essays on Eastern Europe in historical perspective, followed by essays on the past and present politics of Poland, Czechoslovakia, East Germany, Hungary, Yugoslavia, and Rumania.

Bertsch, Gary K., Robert P. Clark, and David M. Wood
1978 *Comparing Political Systems: Power and Policy in Three Worlds.* New York: John Wiley and Sons. An introductory text, also published in three books as Gary K. Bertsch, *Power and Policy in Communist Systems*; Robert P. Clark, *Power and Policy in the Third World*; and David M. Wood, *Power and Policy in Western European Democracies.*

Bill, James A., and Robert L. Hardgrave, Jr.
1973 *Comparative Politics: The Quest for Theory.* Columbus, Ohio: Charles E. Merrill Publishing Co. An introduction to various theoretical approaches to the study of comparative politics, which focuses on systems, modernization and development, political culture and socialization, group politics, elites, class analysis, and functionalism.

Blondel, Jean
1972 *Comparative Political Systems.* New York: Praeger Publishers. Examines the structure and functions of political systems, norms, and legitimacy; the structure of government, including groups and parties, bureaucracy, and military; and types of political systems in the contemporary world: traditional conservative, liberal democratic, communist, populist, authoritarian conservative.

Butler, David E. (ed.)
1959 *Elections Abroad.* New York: Macmillan. Comparative study of electoral results during 1957 and 1958 in France, Poland, Ireland, and South Africa.

Cantril, Hadley
1966 *The Pattern of Human Concerns.* New Brunswick, New Jersey: Rutgers University Press. Survey of fourteen nations—Brazil, Egypt, Israel, Cuba, the Philippines, Japan, Dominican Republic, United States, India, Panama, Poland, Yugoslavia, West Germany, and Nigeria.

Carter, Gwendolen M., and John H. Herz
1967 *Major Foreign Powers.* New York: Harcourt, Brace and World. 5th ed. A

detailed examination of the history and politics of four major European nations: Great Britain, France, Germany, and the Soviet Union.

1973 *Government and Politics in the Twentieth Century*. New York: Praeger Publishers. 3d ed. Topical overview of comparative politics. Examines patterns of government, elections and political parties, administration, belief systems, change, and other aspects of politics.

Carter, Gwendolen M., and Alan F. Westin (eds.)

1965 *Politics in Europe: 5 Cases in European Government*. New York: Harcourt, Brace and World. Case studies by H. H. Wilson on Great Britain, Stanley Hoffmann on France, Otto Kirchheimer and Constantine Menges on Germany, Michael Duerr on the Common Market, and Harold Berman on the Soviet Union.

Cattell, David T., and Richard Sisson

1978 *Comparative Politics: Institutions, Behavior, and Development*. Palo Alto, California: Mayfield Publishing Co. An introduction to politics, which examines Great Britain, France, Soviet Union, and India along topical lines: public authority and political power, political culture and socialization, political parties and interest groups, the policy process, and military regimes and revolutionary change.

Chase, Harold W., Robert T. Holt, and John E. Turner

1979 *American Government in Comparative Perspective*. New York: New Viewpoints. A textbook that examines topics of U.S. government such as parties and interest groups, the electoral process, separation of powers, the criminal justice system, and intervention by government in the economy and analyzes the ways in which other nations (Canada, Great Britain, France, Germany, Sweden, and Japan) have handled those problems.

Christoph, James B. (ed.)

1965 *Cases in Comparative Politics*. Boston: Little, Brown and Co. Case studies by Christoph on the National Health Service of Great Britain, Bernard Brown on France, Gerard Braunthal on West Germany, John E. Turner on the Soviet Union, and Gene D. Overstreet on India. Additional case studies were included in a later edition with Bernard Brown; 3d ed., 1976.

Codevilla, Angelo

1974 "On Comparing Governments." *Political Science Reviewer* IV (Fall), 265–308. A critical look at some of the major texts of comparative government, including works by Beer and Ulam, Macridis and Ward, Dragnich, Blondel, and Neumann. Suggests that these works offer frameworks for understanding politics but do not offer much comparison of the countries they cover.

Crotty, William J.

1970 "A Perspective for the Comparative Analysis of Political Parties." *Comparative Political Studies* III (October), 267–296. Argues that investigation of political parties within a theoretical framework across cultural lines has not yet progressed far and attempts to deal with a number of questions in an effort to make such research feasible.

Curtis, Michael

1968 *Comparative Government and Politics: An Introductory Essay in Political Science*.

New York: Harper and Row. Core volume in a series of country studies. Topically focused on constitutions, representation and voting, interests and parties, party systems, assemblies and rule making, political executives, and administrative systems. The series includes volumes by Curtis on Western European integration, Douglas Verney on British politics, and Benes, Gyorgy, and Stambuk on Eastern European government and politics.

Dahl, Robert A.

1966 *Political Oppositions in Western Democracies.* New Haven: Yale University Press. Essays on the United States and nine European nations by various contributors with three concluding chapters by the editor.

Deutsch, Karl W.

1960 "Toward an Inventory of Basic Trends and Patterns in Comparative and International Politics." *American Political Science Review* LIV (March), 34–57. An effort to combine quantitative and experimental methods with humanistic literary and historical traditions of scholarship by demonstrating the applicability of country profile variables to comparative analysis.

1970 *Politics and Government.* New York: Houghton Mifflin. Sets forth concepts of comparative politics, then relates the concepts to the study of the United States, Soviet Union, United Kingdom, France, German Federal Republic, and the Chinese People's Republic.

Diamant, Alfred

1960 "The Relevance of Comparative Politics to the Study of Comparative Administration." *Administrative Science Quarterly* V (June), 87–112. Focuses on two major approaches to comparative politics, the "general systems" and "culture" approaches. Relates these and other approaches to empirical research in comparative administration.

Dogan, Mattei, and Richard Rose

1971 *European Politics: A Reader.* Boston: Little, Brown and Co. Essays on European nations, reprinted from books and journal articles and focused on political culture, political socialization, voting alignments, political parties, pressure groups, political leaders, and power.

Dragnich, Alex N.

1961 *Major European Governments.* Homewood, Illinois: Dorsey Press. 3d ed., 1970; 4th ed., 1974, with Jorgen Rasmussen. A basic text focused on Great Britain, France, Germany, and the Soviet Union with a brief concluding section on the study of comparative government.

Duverger, Maurice

1963 *Political Parties: Their Organization and Activity in the Modern State.* Translated by Barbara and Robert North with a foreword by D. W. Brogan. New York: John Wiley and Sons. Classic comparative study of party systems and organizations by a French political scientist.

1974 *Modern Democracies: Economic Power Versus Political Power.* Hinsdale, Illinois: Dryden Press. A provocative examination of the Western "system," with analysis of its British and North American origins, the rise of liberal ideology, the crisis of liberal democracy, and challenges to the system.

Eckstein, Harry

1963 "A Perspective on Comparative Politics, Past and Present." In Harry Eckstein and David E. Apter (eds.), *Comparative Politics*, pp. 3–32. New York: Free Press of Glencoe. An historical overview of the field of comparative politics, with critical synthesis and identification of major trends.

Eckstein, Harry, and David E. Apter (eds.)

1963 *Comparative Politics: A Reader.* New York: Free Press of Glencoe. One of the major readers of the field, incorporating major articles published in political science journals. Includes selections on theory and methods, classical and other studies of constitutional government, electoral systems, political parties, interest groups, totalitarianism and autocracy, political change, and non-Western government and politics.

Eckstein, Harry, and Ted Robert Gurr (eds.)

1970–1977 *Sage Professional Papers in Comparative Politics.* Beverly Hills, California: Sage Publications. Twelve papers published annually with a focus on comparative politics topics.

Eisenstadt, S. N.

1965 *Essays on Comparative Institutions.* New York: John Wiley and Sons. The author has gathered together his previously published essays on age groups and youth culture, bureaucratic structures and processes, problems of social mobility, and processes of communication and reference-group behavior. The central focus is on an analysis of the processes of institutions and the comparative study of institutions.

Feit, Edward (ed.)

1978 *Governments and Leaders: An Approach to Comparative Politics.* Boston: Houghton Mifflin. Combines biographical sketches of major leaders with a description of their countries. Introductory text examines Macmillan and British politics, Giscard d'Estaing and French government, Willy Brandt and West Germany, Khrushchev and Soviet politics, Castro and the Cuban revolution.

Finer, S. E.

1970 *Comparative Government.* Middlesex, England: Allen Lane, Penguin Press. Also New York: Basic Books, 1971. Text divides the world into categories and then discusses them by referring to specific countries. Topics are liberal democracy, totalitarianism, and autocracy and oligarchy; countries generally are European.

Fried, Robert C.

1966 *Comparative Political Institutions.* New York: Macmillan Company. Types of institutional power are examined in the study of executives, legislatures, courts, bureaucracies, military, political parties, and electorates.

Furniss, Norman

1974 "Comparative Government Texts, Problems and Performance." *International Studies Quarterly* XVIII (March), 105–127. A review and critique of the major texts in comparative government.

Gamer, Robert E.

1976 *The Developing Nations: A Comparative Perspective.* Boston: Allyn and Bacon. A look at the Third World through a variety of provocative perspectives:

political systems of past ages, disruptive forces, patrons and clients, alienation, and reform.

Gordon, Morton
1972 *Comparative Political Systems: Managing Conflict.* New York: Macmillan Company. An effort to apply a model of conflict management to comparative analysis. Aspects of the model as well as chapters of the book focus on goals, rules of exposure, spokesmen, organizations for action, bargaining, and implementation. The experience of a variety of countries is related to the model.

Gregg, Phillip M., and Arthur S. Banks
1965 "Dimensions of Political Systems: Factor Analysis of a Cross-Polity Survey." *American Political Science Review* LIX (September), 602–614. Factor analysis of survey data provides evidence for inferring seven basic political dimensions useful for comparing political systems and typology construction in cross-national study.

Gregor, A. James
1971 "Theory, Metatheory, and Comparative Politics." *Comparative Politics* III (July), 575–586. Critical review of works on comparative politics by Almond and Powell, Holt and Turner, Merkl, and others.

Groth, Alexander J.
1971 *Comparative Politics: A Distributive Approach.* New York: Macmillan Company. A comparative examination of the benefits and burdens of public policy, including an overview of democratic and authoritarian states in terms of their output differences. Policy is examined in relation to taxation and the budget; economy, education and culture; justice and police power, and public service.

Groth, Alexander J., Robert J. Lieber, and Nancy I. Lieber
1976 *Contemporary Politics: Europe.* Cambridge, Massachusetts: Winthrop Publishers. Text covers the major European systems—Britain, France, Germany, and the Soviet Union—as well as alternative European politics—Spain, Portugal, Greece, and Yugoslavia.

Gurr, Ted Robert, and Francisco José Moreno
1970 *Basic Courses in Comparative Politics: An Anthology of Syllabi.* Sage Publications for the International Studies Association. Beverly Hills, California: Sage Publications. Comprises syllabi from general comparative courses, as well as courses on democratic and communist systems, developing areas, and special topics.

Haas, Michael
1970 "Dimensional Analysis in Cross-National Research." *Comparative Political Studies* III (April), 3–35. Critical assessment of the search for a universal set of dimensions useful to cross-national research and a discussion of the quantitative techniques that might be utilized.

Hagopian, Mark N.
1978 *Regimes, Movements, and Ideologies: A Comparative Introduction to Political Science.* London: Longman. An introductory text in comparative politics. Examines types of regimes, movements, and ideologies.

Heady, Ferrel
1960 "Recent Literature on Comparative Public Administration." *Administrative Science Quarterly* V (June), 134–154. Classifies and discusses the comparative administration literature into four categories: materials on theory, approach,

methodology, and model building; comparative studies of Western societies; comparative studies of non-Western societies; and materials on individual countries of interest for comparative purposes.

Heckscher, Gunnar
1958 *The Study of Comparative Government and Politics.* New York: Macmillan. Focuses on the methodological issues of comparative politics with reference to countries in Western Europe. Divided into two sections: methods (classification, typology, terminology, interdisciplinary studies); and application of methods (configurative approach, institutional comparisons, functional comparisons, etc.).

Heidenheimer, Arnold J. (ed.)
1970 *Comparative Political Finance: The Financing of Party Organizations and Election Campaigns.* Lexington, Massachusetts: D. C. Heath and Company. Comparative study by various authors on the financing of political parties in Europe, the United States and Canada, and the Third World.

Heidenheimer, Arnold J., Hugh Helco, and Carolyn Teich Adams
1975 *Comparative Public Policy: The Politics of Social Choice in Europe and America.* New York: St. Martin's Press. Cross-national analysis of social service reforms, local-national interaction in policy implementation, coordination in income distribution policies, and public programs.

Heisler, Martin O. (ed.)
1970s Comparative Studies of Political Life. New York: David McKay Company. Series of comparative studies including Carl Beck et al., *Comparative Communist Political Leadership*; Roger W. Benjamin et al., *Patterns of Political Development: Japan, India, Isarel*; Cynthia H. Enlow, *The Politics of Pollution in a Comparative Perspective: Ecology and Power in Four Nations*; Wolfram F. Hanrieder (ed.), *Comparative Foreign Policy: Theoretical Essays*; Martin O. Heisler (ed.), *Politics in Europe: Structures and Processes in Some Postindustrial Democracies*; Gregory Henderson, Richard Ned Lebow, and John G. Stoessinger (eds.), *Divided Nations in a Divided World*; Allan Kornberg (ed.), *Legislatures in Comparative Perspective*; Stein Rokkan (with Angus Campbell et al.), *Citizens, Elections, Parties: Approaches to the Comparative Study of the Processes of Development*; Jonathan Wilkenfeld (ed.), *Conflict Behavior and Linkage Politics*; Mostafa Rejai, *The Comparative Study of Revolutionary Strategy*.

Hitchner, Dell Gillette, and Carol Levine
1968 *Comparative Government and Politics.* New York: Dodd, Mead and Co. Emphasis on government institutions with example reference to nations everywhere. Chapter topics include constitutions, interest groups, political parties, the executive, legislature, judiciary, and administration.

Holt, Robert T., and John E. Turner
1975 "Crises and Sequences in Collective Theory Development." *American Political Science Review* LXIX (September), 979–994. A critical overview and review of the first seven volumes in the series Studies in Political Development sponsored by the Social Science Research Council's Committee on Comparative Politics.

Horowitz, Irving Louis
1965 to present *Studies in Comparative International Development.* New Brunswick: Rutgers University. Originally published at Washington University as a

series of brief monographs; later distributed by Sage Publications; and finally incorporated into a journal with the same series title, published three times yearly. The papers in the early volumes are especially significant and relevant in comparative politics.

1972 *Three Worlds of Development: The Theory and Practice of International Stratification.* New York: Oxford University Press. 2d ed. Comparative perspectives within a triadic relationship: the First World led by the United States, the Second World led by the Soviet Union, and the Third World comprising the Afro-Asian bloc and portions of Latin America.

Inkeles, Alex
1969 "Participant Citizenship in Six Developing Countries." *American Political Science Review* LXIII (December), 1120–1141. An analysis of individual orientations to politics in Argentina, Chile, India, Israel, Nigeria, and East Pakistan (Bangladesh). Based on data from the Harvard Project on the Social and Cultural Aspects of Economic Development.

Inkeles, Alex (ed.)
Comparative Perspectives Series. Boston: Little, Brown and Co.

1968 *Comparative Perspectives on Social Change.* Edited by S. N. Eisenstadt.

1968 *Comparative Perspectives on Stratification: Mexico, Great Britain, Japan.* Edited by Joseph A. Kahl.

1969 *Comparative Perspectives on Formal Organizations.* Edited by Henry A. Landsberger.

1969 *Comparative Perspectives on Industrial Society.* Edited by William A. Faunce and William H. Form.

1969 *Comparative Perspectives on Social Problems.* Edited by Vytautas Kavolis.

Isaak, Robert A.
1980 *European Politics: Political Economy and Policy Making in Western Democracies.* New York: St. Martin's Press. Emphasis on political economy and bargaining power in a comparison of West Germany, France, Great Britain, and Italy.

Jackson, Robert J., and Michael B. Stein (eds.)
1971 *Issues in Comparative Politics: A Text with Readings.* New York: St. Martin's Press. An effort to move away from country and institutional aproaches and to focus on issues of comparative politics: political development, political integration, political stability, political protest, and political revolution.

Jacobs, Walter Darnell, and Harold Zink
1966 *Modern Governments.* Princeton, New Jersey: D. Van Nostrand Co. 3d ed. Text examines the governments of Great Britain, France, Germany, Scandinavia, the Soviet Union, the Americas, and Asia.

Janowitz, Morris
1964 *The Military in the Political Development of New Nations: An Essay in Comparative Analysis.* Chicago: University of Chicago Press. Comparison of military institutions and military elites with emphasis on common characteristics and national differences in order to reflect on patterns of civil-military relations in the new nations.

Johnson, John J. (ed.)

1962 *The Role of the Military in Underdeveloped Countries.* Princeton: Princeton University Press. Essays by various specialists on the military in Asia, Africa, and Latin America.

Johnson, Samuel A.

1964 *Essentials of Comparative Government.* Woodbury, New York: Barron's Educational Series. Focuses on political institutions, including constitutions, legislatures, political parties, executives, judiciaries, and local governments. Each of the branches of government is compared for the United States and several major European countries.

Kahin, George M., Guy J. Pauker, and Lucian W. Pye

1955 "Comparative Politics of Non-Western Countries." *American Political Science Review* XLIX (December), 1022–1039. An early effort to characterize the political process of non-Western or Third World countries and to encourage comparative political analysts to study those countries.

Kautsky, John H.

1973 "Communism and Modernization, Comparative Communism Versus Comparative Politics." *Comparative Communism* I /II (Spring/Summer), 136–170. Based on a review of Chalmers Johnson's *Change in Communist Systems*, Kautsky argues forcefully for the comparison of communist with noncommunist systems; artificial separation of the two phenomena does not result in a useful theory.

Kautsky, John H. (ed.)

1962 *Political Change in Underdeveloped Areas: Nationalism and Communism.* New York: John Wiley and Sons. Introductory essay by Kautsky on underdevelopment and industrialization, nationalism, communism, and totalitarianism. Followed by essays on the underdeveloped areas.

Kebschull, Harvey G. (ed.)

1968 *Politics in Transitional Societies: The Challenge of Change in Asia, Africa, and Latin America.* New York: Appleton-Century-Crofts. Theoretical and substantive essays on Africa, Asia, and Latin America. Topics include approaches to the study of political systems, ideologies, political system leadership, groups, and policymaking; political and social problems; economic development; and international relations.

Kling, Merle

1964 "Area Studies and Comparative Politics." *American Behavioral Scientist* VIII (September), 7–10. Elaborates issues that separate area study from discipline study and, in particular, demonstrates the usefulness of comparative politics.

Kousoulas, D. George

1968 *On Government: A Comparative Introduction.* Belmont, California: Wadsworth. Studies essential features and functions of government by drawing illustrations from a wide variety of countries rather than centering the study on three or four countries.

LaPalombara, Joseph

1968 "Macrotheories and Microapplications in Comparative Politics: A Widening Chasm." *Comparative Politics* I (October), 52–78. Argues for use of rigorous methodologies at a middle level of politics in the hope that an emphasis on partial systems may correct deficiencies in whole-systems analysis.

1974 *Politics Within Nations.* Englewood Cliffs, New Jersey: Prentice-Hall. "Empirically-based, genuinely comparative book about national politics" that delves into problems of comparing politics and governments, examines political institutions and their functions, and looks at political participation and the politics of inequality. An introductory text. Core volume for a series of studies, Contemporary Comparative Politics Series, that includes J. Blondel, *Comparative Legislatures*; Henry W. Ehrmann, *Comparative Legal Cultures*; Carl J. Friedrich, *Limited Government: A Comparison*; Thomas H. Greene, *Comparative Revolutionary Movements*; James C. Scott, *Comparative Political Corruption*; Fred R. von der Mehden, *Comparative Political Violence*; and others.

Lawson, Kay
1976 *The Comparative Study of Political Parties.* New York: St. Martin's Press. Comparative analysis of parties in France, Guinea, and the United States, with attention to party origins, organization, members, leaders, formulation of issues, and role in government.

Lewis, Paul G., David C. Potter, and Francis G. Castles
1973 *The Practice of Comparative Politics: A Reader.* London: Longman and Open University Press. General readings on the field, including case examples, problems of research, and theory.

Lijphart, Arend
1968 "Typologies of Democratic Systems." *Comparative Political Studies* I (April), 3–44. Detailed examination of typologies of systems in the literature.

Lipset, Seymour M., and Stein Rokkan (eds.)
1967 *Party Systems and Voter Alignments: Cross-National Perspectives.* Preface by Heinz Eulau. New York: Free Press. Collection of essays on party politics in a variety of nations.

Loewenstein, Karl
1944 "Report on the Research Panel on Comparative Government." *American Political Science Review* XXXVIII (June), 540–548. Critical report to the American Political Science Association on the status of comparative politics.

McCord, William
1965 *The Springtime of Freedom: The Evolution of Developing Societies.* New York: Oxford University Press. A comparative analysis of issues, including industrialization, education, and freedom, in relation to the experiences of Europe and the Third World.

McKean, Dayton D. (ed.)
1960 to present Country Series. Boston: Houghton Mifflin Co. Series includes works by John Clarke Adams and Paolo Barile, *The Government of Republican Italy*; Sydney D. Bailey, *British Parliamentary Democracy*; George A. Codding, Jr., *The Federal Government of Switzerland*; Oscar Kraines, *Government and Politics in Israel*; Theodore McNelly, *Contemporary Government of Japan*; Norman D. Palmer, *The Indian Political System*; Elmer Plischke, *Comtemporary Government of Germany*; and Robert Sciglioano, *South Vietnam*.

McLennan, Barbara
1975 *Comparative Political Systems: Political Processes in Developed and Developing States.* North Scituate, Massachusetts: Duxbury Press. Attempts to adapt concepts

of Almond's structural-functional approach to nine countries. Focuses on Great Britain, India, Chile, France, Indonesia, Zaire, the Soviet Union, Egypt, and China in an examination of political culture and socialization, political processes and public policy. Serves as an introductory text.

1979 *Comparative Politics and Public Policy.* Belmont, California: Duxbury Press. A comparative examination of public policy in competitive (Great Britain, France, India), fragmented (Indonesia, Zaire, Chile), and noncompetitive (Egypt, China) political systems.

Macridis, Roy C.

1955 *The Study of Comparative Government.* Studies in Political Science (21). New York: Random House. Classic critique of the traditional approach in comparative political analysis. Insists on new classifications, conceptualizations, and hypotheses.

1968a "Comparative Politics and the Study of Government: The Search for Focus." *Comparative Politics* I (October), 79–90. Update of the author's 1953 critique of comparative politics. Calls for the study of the state and rejects behavioralists for their attempts to build grand theory and for their attention to trivia.

Macridis, Roy C. (ed.)

1968b *Modern European Governments: Cases in Comparative Policy Making.* Englewood Cliffs, New Jersey: Prentice-Hall. Case studies on issues of politics in the major European nations by Kenneth N. Waltz, Eric A. Nordlinger, William G. Andrews, Roy Macridis, Wolfram F. Hanrieder, Richard L. Merritt, Adam Ulam, and Vernon V. Aspaturian.

Macridis, Roy C., and Bernard E. Brown

1964 *Comparative Politics: Notes and Readings.* Homewood, Illinois: Dorsey Press. Rev. ed. Introductory reader incorporating major journal articles and other selections. Topically organized around problems of comparative analysis; political dynamics (group theory and group action, party systems, party organization, electoral systems); political institutions (constitutions, representative government, administration); and political change (patterns of legitimacy, revolution, modernization, democracy).

Macridis, Roy C., and Richard Cox

1953 "Research in Comparative Politics." *American Political Science Review* XLVII (September), 641–675. Critical assessment of comparative politics by the Interuniversity Research Seminar on Comparative Politics. Participants included Samuel Beer, Harry Eckstein, George Blanksten, Karl Deutsch, Kenneth Thompson, and Robert Ward, along with Macridis and Cox. The findings of these men and their later work were to shape the field in the ensuing two decades.

Macridis, Roy C., and Robert E. Ward (eds.)

1963 *Modern Political Systems: Europe.* Englewood Cliffs, New Jersey: Prentice-Hall. 3d ed., 1972. Basic text that deals with the history and politics of the four major European systems: Great Britain, France, Germany, and the Soviet Union.

May, John D.

1969 "Democracy, Party 'Evolution,' Duverger." *Comparative Political Studies* II

(July), 216–248. Examines criticism of Duverger's study of political parties and attempts to clarify confusions in the writings of Duverger and his critics.

Mayer, Lawrence C., and John H. Burnett
1977 *Politics in Industrial Societies: A Comparative Perspective.* New York: John Wiley and Sons. An examination of mature industrial society with attention to nation building and politics and social stratification, then to the policy process and outcomes.

Mehden, Fred R. von der
1964 *Politics of the Developing Nations.* Englewood Cliffs, New Jersey: Prentice-Hall. An early effort to develop comparative perspectives on the Third World. Examines national identity, political parties, elites, military, and ideology.

Merkl, Peter H.
1967 *Political Continuity and Change.* New York: Harper and Row. Ambitious and comprehensive text that attempts to combine theory and analysis. Examines the Western political tradition by looking at thought and practices; describes the processes of Western political institutions; and assesses the impacts of modernization and change, communism, fascism, and nationalism and imperialism.

1970 *Modern Comparative Politics.* New York: Holt, Rinehart and Winston. Core volume in a series of country studies (later volumes published by Dryden Press). Topically focused on political development, socialization, participation, recruitment, political culture, local-national relationship, political parties, policymaking institutions and processes, constitutions, and courts. Rev. ed., *Comparative Politics,* 1977.

Merritt, Richard L., and Stein Rokkan (eds.)
1966 *Comparing Nations: The Use of Quantitative Data in Cross-National Research.* New Haven: Yale University Press. Papers from a Yale conference in 1963 that assessed uses of quantitative data in international social science research.

Michels, Robert
1962 *Political Parties.* Translated by Eden and Cedar Paul, introduction by Seymour Martin Lipset. New York: Collier Books. Classic study of political parties by a European political sociologist with particular attention to Germany and France.

Millen, Bruce H.
1963 *The Political Role of Labor in Developing Countries.* Washington, D.C.: Brookings Institution. A look at unions in advanced and in developing countries, their political setting, and their role in nationalism and national development.

Moore, Barrington, Jr.
1966 *Social Origins of Dictatorship and Democracy: Lord and Peasant in the Making of the Modern World.* Boston: Beacon Press. Examination of the revolutionary origins of capitalist democracy in England, France, and the United States; the experience of Asia, in China, Japan, and India; and some theoretical implications and projections.

Muller, Steven (ed.)
1963 *Documents on European Government.* New York: Macmillan. Documents include the constitutions, programs and statutes of the major political parties, and electoral legislation in Great Britain, France, Germany, and the Soviet Union.

Munger, Frank (ed.)
1967 *Studies in Comparative Politics.* New York: Thomas Y. Crowell. Selections from major comparative studies on civic culture (Almond and Verba), party and society (Alford), political parties (Duverger), political man (Lipset), and cross-polity survey (Banks and Textor).

Munger, Frank, and Douglas Price (eds.)
1964 *Readings in Political Parties and Pressure Groups.* New York: Thomas Y. Crowell. Essays on party politics, reprinted from books and journals, which focus on the Anglo-American traditions and processes.

Munro, William Bennett
1931 *The Governments of Europe.* New York: Macmillan Company. An early text that examines institutions and processes of government in Great Britain, France, Germany, and Italy; also briefly reviews the governments of Switzerland, Russia, Austria, and Hungary.

Neumann, Robert G.
1960 *European and Comparative Government.* New York: McGraw Hill. 3d ed. 4th ed., 1968. A basic text that examines government institutions in Great Britain, France, Germany, and the Soviet Union.

Neumann, Sigmund
1957 "Comparative Politics: A Half-Century Appraisal." *Journal of Politics* XIX (August), 369–390. Appraisal that critically examines developments during three phases: idealistic, positivistic, and realistic.

Neumann, Sigmund (ed.)
1956 *Modern Political Parties: Approaches to Comparative Politics.* Chicago: University of Chicago Press. Case studies of party politics in Great Britain by Samuel Beer, the Commonwealth by G. Carter, France by Charles Micaud, Belgium by Felix E. Oppenheim, Scandinavia by Dankwart Rustow, the United States by E. E. Schattschneider, the USSR by Frederick Barghoorn, Eastern Europe by Andrew Gyorgy, Japan by Robert Scalapino, Germany by Neumann.

Palma, Giuseppe di
1969 "Disaffection and Participation in Western Democracies: The Role of Political Oppositions." *Journal of Politics* XXXI (November), 984–1010. An early examination of participation and opposition, complementing the collective effort of Dahl (1966).

Palma, Giuseppe di (ed.)
1972 *Mass Politics in Industrial Societies: A Reader in Comparative Politics.* Chicago: Markham Publishing Co. Essays by various authors focused on political party recruitment, participation, organization, and ideology.

Palmer, Monte, and William Thompson
1978 *Comparative Analysis of Politics.* Itasca, Illinois: F. E. Peacock Publishers. Introductory text that examines democracy, modernization, political institutions, elites, political parties, and violence.

Palombara
See LaPalombara.

Pennock, Roland J. (ed.)
1964 *Self-government in Modernizing Nations.* Englewood Cliffs, New Jersey: Prentice-Hall. Essays by Lucian Pye, Francis Sutton, Thomas Hodgkin, Zibgniew

Brzezinski, and W. Howard Wriggins with attention to nation building and self-government in the nations of the Third World and the Western and Communist influences that affect those nations.

Pickett, Lewis P., Jr., (ed.)
1966 *Problems of the Developing Nations: Readings and Case Studies.* New York: Thomas Y. Crowell. Undergraduate text of readings on the problems of the developing nations. Theoretical essays are combined with case studies of Algeria, Tunisia, India, Pakistan, Indonesia, and Thailand.

Pierce, Roy
1963 "Comparative Politics: Liberty and Policy as Variables." *American Political Science Review* LVII (September), 655–660. An early effort to analyze policy in a comparative context.

Pye, Lucian W.
1958 "The Non-Western Political Process." *Journal of Politics* XX (August), 468–486. Presents a series of propositions that attempt to distinguish between politics in the Western and non-Western worlds.

Rejai, Mostafa
1977 *The Comparative Study of Revolutionary Strategy.* New York: David McKay Co. Examination of definitions, typologies, and strategies of revolution along with case studies on Bolivia, North Vietnam, and France.

Rich, Clifford A. L. (ed.)
1962 *European Politics and Government: A Comparative Approach.* New York: Ronald Press. A college text that focuses on government institutions and processes in Great Britain, France, Italy, Germany, and the Soviet Union.

Riggs, Fred W.
1964 *Administration in Developing Countries: The Theory of Prismatic Society.* Boston: Houghton Mifflin Co. Theoretical formulations for the comparative study of administration, with the Philippines used as a case study.

Roberts, Geoffrey
1972 "Comparative Politics Today." *Government and Opposition* VII (Winter), 38–55. First, this article distinguishes among four terms: comparative government, comparative politics, comparative analysis, and comparative method. Then it turns to a critique of conceptualization in the field.

Rogow, Arnold A. (ed.)
1960 to present. *Comparative Government Series.* New York: Thomas Y. Crowell. Series of country studies, including Ardath W. Burks, *The Government of Japan;* Jean Blondel and E. Drexel Godfrey, Jr., *The Government of France;* Arnold J. Heidenheimer, *The Governments of Germany;* Norman Kogan, *The Government of Italy;* Graeme C. Moodie, *The Government of Great Britain;* Frederick L. Schuman, *Government of the Soviet Union;* Gordon Skilling, *The Governments of Communist East Europe.*

Rokkan, Stein
1962 "The Comparative Study of Political Participation: Notes Toward a Perspective on Current Research." In Austin Ranney (ed.), *Essays on the Behavioral Study of Politics,* pp. 47–90. Urbana: University of Illinois Press. Critical overview of work on comparative study of participation, especially through political parties.

Roth, David F., and Frank L. Wilson
1976 *The Comparative Study of Politics.* Boston: Houghton Mifflin Co. Introductory text that topically examines history, society, and politics; participation, interest groups, and political parties; political leadership and bureaucracy; the military; public policy, stability, and change. Three types of systems are examined along with country examples: Liberal-Democratic (Britain and France), Communist (Soviet Union and China), and Third World (Mexico and Nigeria).

Rothman, S.
1970 *European Society and Politics.* Indianapolis: Bobbs-Merrill. Text examines Britain, France, Germany, and the Soviet Union. Focuses on historical background, political culture, parties, structures of government, policy implementation, and manipulation of aggregate data.

Russett, Bruce M., Hayward R. Alker, Jr., Karl W. Deutsch, and Harold D. Lasswell
1964 *World Handbook of Political and Social Indicators.* New Haven: Yale University Press. Presents data on seventy-five variables for 133 states and colonies; data serves as a basis for the investigation of a variety of social, political, and economic questions.

Rustow, Dankwart A.
1964 "New Horizons for Comparative Politics." *World Politics* IX (July), 530–549. Reprinted in Eckstein and Apter (1963, pp. 57–66). Argues that the study of non-Western politics is complex and confused and that differences between Western and non-Western countries pose sharply the question of comparability.

Sharkansky, Ira
1975 *The United States: A Study of a Developing Country.* New York: David McKay Co. Influenced by comparative analysis of Third World problems the author attempts to relate those problems to the United States.

Sherman, Howard J., and James L. Wood
1979 *Sociology, Traditional and Radical Perspectives.* New York: Harper and Row. An economist and a sociologist join together in presenting traditional and radical approaches to issues and topics of sociology and social science. This is intended to be an introductory text.

Shoup, Paul
1968 "Comparing Communist Nations: Prospects for an Empirical Approach." *American Political Science Review* LXII (March), 185–204. Comprehensive review of the literature on comparative communist systems. Examines problems and suggests directions for developing an empirically oriented comparative analysis.

Skilling, H. Gordon
1966 *The Governments of Communist East Europe.* New York: Thomas Y. Crowell. Comprehensive and topical analysis of Eastern Europe with a look at the historical rise of communism, the pattern of contemporary power, the holders of power, the process of governing, the implementation of decisions, and totalitarianism in transition.

Smith, T. Alexander
1969 "Toward a Comparative Theory of the Policy-Process." *Comparative Politics* I (July), 498–515. Sets forth a number of hypotheses as a basis for comparative

theory of the policy process, especially as related to political parties and interest groups.

Smock, Audrey C.
1973 *Comparative Politics: A Reader in Institutionalization and Mobilization.* Boston: Allyn and Bacon. Divided into four areas (Soviet Union, China, Great Britain and the United States, and Africa), this reader includes three journal articles on each area.

Social Science Research Council, Committee on Comparative Politics, Studies in Political Development Series. Princeton University Press.
1963 *Communications and Political Development.* Edited by Lucian W. Pye. Volume 1.

1963 *Bureaucracy and Political Development.* Edited by Joseph LaPalombara. Volume 2.

1964 *Political Modernization in Japan and Turkey.* Edited by Robert E. Ward and Dankwart A. Rustow. Volume 3.

1965 *Education and Political Development.* Edited by James S. Coleman. Volume 4.

1965 *Political Culture and Political Development.* Edited by Lucian W. Pye and Sidney Verba. Volume 5.

1966 *Political Parties and Political Development.* Edited by Joseph LaPalombara and Myron Weiner. Volume 6.

1971 *Crises and Sequences in Political Development.* Edited by Leonard Binder et al. Volume 7.

1975 *The Formation of National States in Western Europe.* Edited by Charles Tilly. Volume 8.

Spiro, Herbert J.
1959 *Government by Constitution: The Political Systems of Democracy.* New York: Random House. Examines political style, institutions and procedures, representation, and conditions of constitutional success in the United States, Canada, Great Britain, France, Germany, Italy, Switzerland, and Sweden. One of the first texts to attempt comparative analysis of many nations.

Stauffer, Robert B.
1973 *Nation-Building in a Global Economy: The Role of the Multinational Corporation.* Sage Professional Papers in Comparative Politics (Paper 39). Beverly Hills, California: Sage Publications. Contrasting perspectives on national and multinational forces in the world economy.

Szalai, Alexander et al.
1966 "Multinational Comparative Social Research." *American Behavioral Scientist* X (December), 1–31. Reflects the relevance and importance of comparative research on a multinational level.

Tachau, Frank (ed.)
1972 *The Developing Nations: What Path to Modernization?* New York: Dodd, Mead and Co. Twenty-three essays by various authors on modernization and change, with theoretical and substantive attention to countries of the Third World.

Tucker, Robert C.
1961 "A Comparative Politics of Movement-Regimes." *American Political Science Review* LV (June), 281–289. Also in Macridis and Brown (1964, pp. 543–557). An attempt to expand theory on communist mass movements by examining fascist, nationalist, and other movements as well.

Tullis, F. La Mond
1973 *Politics and Social Change in Third World Countries.* New York: John Wiley and Sons. Theoretical and empirical approach with case studies on Brazil, Libya, and Peru.

Verba, Sidney, Norman H. Nie, and Jae-on Kim
1978 *Participation and Political Equality: A Seven-Nation Comparison.* New York: Cambridge University Press. Political participation is examined according to four common types: campaign activity, voting activity, communal activity, and particularized contact. Data and analysis are drawn from a survey of seven nations: Nigeria, Austria, Japan, India, the Netherlands, Yugoslavia, and the United States.

Vig, Norman J., and Rodney P. Stiefbold (eds.)
1974 *Politics in Advanced Nations: Modernization, Development, and Contemporary Change.* Englewood Cliffs, New Jersey: Prentice-Hall. A reader comprising essays on development theory; crises in political modernization; emergence of mass politics; social cleavages, party competition, and group interests in the welfare state; and mass participation, representation, and support. Europe is the area focus.

Ward, Robert E.
1974 "Culture and the Comparative Study of Politics, or the Constipated Dialectic." *American Political Science Review* LXVIII (March), 190–201. APSA presidential address; explores the antagonism between area approach specialists and behavioralists in the study of comparative politics. Argues that both orientations have demonstrated their utility and should be integrated.

Weiner, Myron (ed.)
1964 to present Studies in Political Change Series. New York: Rand McNally. A comparative framework applied to specific problems in political change in the developing countries. Series includes works by David H. Bayley on public liberties; Leo Despres on race, culture, and nationalist politics; Aristide Zolberg on one-party democracies in Africa; Gene Overstreet on Communist strategies in developing areas; and Robert Meagher on the impact of U.S. foreign policy on the domestic politics of new states.

Wheare, K. C.
1963 *Legislatures.* New York: Oxford University Press.

1964 *Federal Government.* New York: Oxford University Press. 4th ed.

1966 *Modern Constitutions.* New York: Oxford University Press.

Each book focuses on the composition, structure, and working of political institutions so as to establish a foundation for comparative study.

Winks, Robin W. (ed.)
1960 to present Modern Nations in Historical Perspective Series. Englewood Cliffs, New Jersey: Prentice-Hall. Series of country studies or studies of closely

related nations throughout the world. Among these studies are John C. Cairns, *France*; Henry Ashby Turner, Jr., *Germany*; Massimo Salvadori, *Italy*; Richard Herr, *Spain*; Robert V. Daniels, *Russia*; Robert O. Collins and Robert L. Tignor, *Egypt and the Sudan*; John E. Flint, *Nigeria and Ghana*; Ronald H. Chilcote, *Portuguese Africa*; John D. Hargreaves, *West Africa: The Former French States*; Arthur P. Whitaker, *Argentina*; Harry Bernstein, *Venezuela and Colombia*; Robert E. Quirk, *Mexico*; Kenneth Scott Latourette, *China*.

Wright, William E. (ed.)
1971 *A Comparative Study of Party Organization*. Columbus, Ohio: Charles E. Merrill Publishing. Essays on party theory, recruitment, ideology, activities and roles, leaders and followers, and effectiveness; generally drawn from the British and North American experiences.

Young, Roland (ed.)
1958 *Approaches to the Study of Politics*. Evanston, Illinois: Northwestern University Press. Theoretically oriented essays focused on political concepts (power, group theory, decision making, structural functionalism); political theory; analytic systems; and community (power structure, individual participation, decision making, etc.).

Index

Aberle, D. F., 233, 251
Abrahamson, Mark, 181, 202
Abramson, Paul R., 153, 202
Accumulation, 85, 118, 303, 321, 323, 327, 377, 378, 379, 398, 408, 411, 412–415: imperialism and, 416; on a world scale, 413–415. *See also* Capitalism; Imperialism
Adorno, Theodor W., 62, 75, 375, 376, 386
Africa, 289, 291, 296, 312, 314, 380, 383
Agger, Robert E., 233, 251, 432, 441
Alavi, Hamza, 380
Alienation, 87–88, 251: in capitalism, 244; culture as, 111; and disalienation, 244; Hegel on, 87; Marx on, 84, 242–243. *See also* Labor; Ideology
Almond, Gabriel A., 8, 11, 60, 68, 75, 103–104, 111, 139, 140, 144, 159, 177, 182, 187, 188, 200, 201, 202, 251–252, 272, 330, 400, 419, 428, 430, 431, 433, 436, 438, 442: contrasts with Easton, 170; and culture, 219, 211; and political

culture, 222–223, 227–228, 231, 234, 236, 237; and structural functional approach, 162–186
Althusser, Louis, 87, 88, 126, 364, 365, 366–368, 370, 373, 374, 379–380, 386–387; and ideology, 366; and science, 366, 368
American Political Science Association, 36–37, 41, 44, 48, 56, 428
Amin, Samir, 199, 203, 244–245, 252, 289, 291–294, 305, 325, 326–337, 330, 373, 413–414, 415
Anderson, Perry, 349, 379, 386, 414
Andrade, Manuel Correia de, 303, 309
Andrain, Charles, 19–21, 24, 431, 442
Andrew, Edward, 124, 126
Anthropology, and comparative politics, 4, 68; divisions within, 38–39. *See also* Culture; Systems theory
Apter, David, 9, 19–21, 24, 33, 48, 115, 140, 179, 203, 281, 283, 284, 330, 428, 431, 443, 447
Aptheker, Herbert, 35, 48
Aquinas, Thomas, 405, 406